LA GUAIRA
CARACAS
BARRANQUILLA
VENEZUELA
GUIAN
BOGOTA
COLUMBIA
QUITO
ECUADOR
Amazon River
B R A Z I L
P E R U
CALLAO
LIMA
BOLIVIA
LA PAZ
Pacific Ocean
PARAGUAY
ASUNCION
RIO DE JANEIRO
C H I L E
A R G E N T I N A
URUGUAY
VALPARAISO
SANTIAGO
BUENOS AIRES
MONTEVIDEO
ANDEAN ZONE 1527-
RIVER PLATE ZONE 1536-
CHILEAN ZONE 1541-
SCALE
0 100 200 300 400 500 MILES

AMERICAN-SPANISH SYNTAX

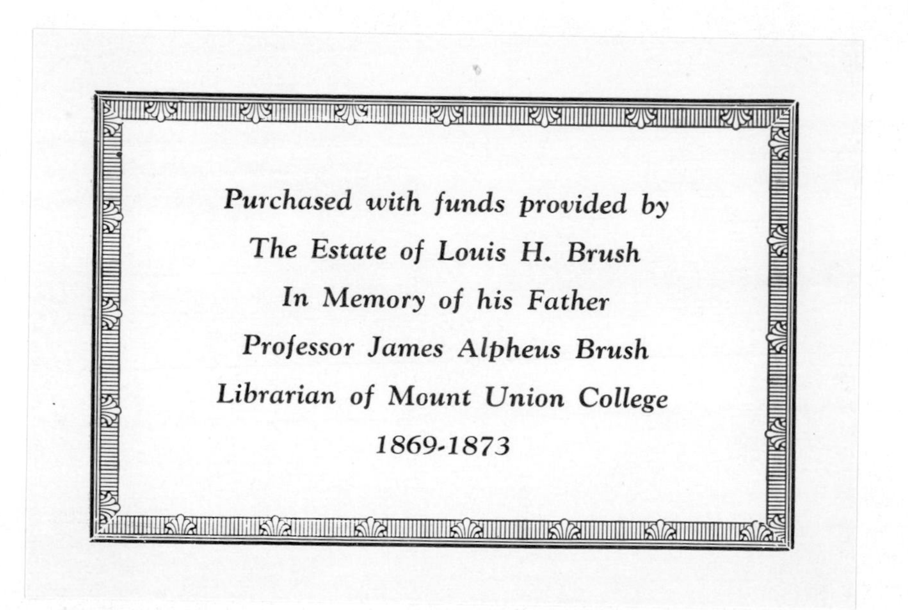

AMERICAN-SPANISH SYNTAX

By

Charles E. Kany

SECOND EDITION

THE UNIVERSITY OF CHICAGO PRESS

THE UNIVERSITY OF CHICAGO PRESS, CHICAGO 37
Cambridge University Press, London, N.W. 1, England
W. J. Gage & Co., Limited, Toronto 2B, Canada

 Published 1945. Second Edition 1951. Composed and printed by THE UNIVERSITY OF CHICAGO PRESS, *Chicago, Illinois, U.S.A.*

INTRODUCTION

THE purpose of this book is to bring together under one cover the most important tendencies of American-Spanish syntax with special reference to popular expression; that is, to offer a compendium of the chief syntactical phenomena or peculiarities that diverge from the recognized standard usage of contemporary Spain (where, to be sure, many of them are not unknown locally or in popular speech). The first comprehensive work of its kind ever to appear, it should provide for students and young teachers drilled only in Castilian usage and suddenly confronted with the rich new varieties of American-Spanish phraseology a reference or textbook for their guidance in perplexities generally unexplained elsewhere, problems of syntactic variation having hitherto suffered much neglect.

Such a work has long been a desideratum and is now a necessity, owing particularly to the definite trend which Spanish-American letters have taken in the last three or four decades. While nationalism (*criollismo* or *nativismo*) cropped forth sporadically as early as the middle of the nineteenth century, it was only at the beginning of the twentieth that novelists and playwrights wholeheartedly abandoned scholastic preoccupation with language and directed their observation realistically to their local milieu. They emancipated themselves in outlook and idiom from the earlier slavish adherence to foreign models: French in conception, Spanish in language. World War I engendered a new collective consciousness having positive national values. This feeling flowered exuberantly from the twenties on. Novelists gave literary form to the vernacular expression in an effort to reproduce faithfully all their regional differences, social problems, and ideals, even at the expense of apparent crudity and unaesthetic values. It was at this period that the important representative novels appeared, bearing such names as Güiraldes, Gallegos, Rivera, Lynch, Azuela, Icaza, etc. While today still another movement is attempting to discard the less agreeable aspects of a severe realism in favor of a higher conception of reality with a more elevated and universal approach, the fact remains that a large portion of significant Spanish-American literature now placed before our students contains such local language as baffles the average student of Spanish whose knowledge embraces only the standard speech (which, to be sure, is limited even in Spain to cultured groups). The editorial comments of many recent school editions of Spanish-American novels and short stories published in this country provide eloquent evidence of this restricted and therefore defective knowledge.

Needless to say, no complete scientific exposition can as yet be presented of Spanish-American linguistic usage. Something has been accomplished in the most modern method, but much more is to be done. The final result must await, possibly for decades to come, a painstaking survey of geographic linguistics throughout the nineteen countries involved. This means local exploration of every town and village with well-organized questionnaires on all minutiae (such as Navarro Tomás' *Cuestionario lingüístico hispanoamericano* [Buenos Aires, 1945]) and, based on this study, the making of thousands of maps or charts, each one of which will limit the geographical area of a single phenomenon—phonetic, morphological, or syntactical, as the case may be. This is an extremely slow, troublesome, and expensive procedure. But with patience, determination, and enthusiasm it can be accomplished. It was done in France, for example, by Gilliéron and Edmont (*Atlas linguistique de la France* [1902–10]) after fifteen years of unrelenting toil. That comprehensive monument, involving 639 localities and comprising 35 folio-fascicles and 1,920 maps, introduced the geographical method of approach. In its wake have followed a number of regional studies in France, Belgium, Switzerland, Italy (notably Jaberg and Jud), and Spain.[1] At the present time isolated studies are being carried on for certain regions of Spanish America,[2] which offers an excellent field of exploration in language in the making, in the historical processes of substratum activity, and in the migration of loan words from one tongue to another. Together with a complete geographical survey, we shall need a thorough study of the Spanish language in the fourteenth and fifteenth centuries, that is of the preclassic language, as well as a complete account of all Spanish dialects.

Until such a task can be brought to a felicitous conclusion, it is hoped that the present work will serve its purpose. Results here pre-

[1] After many years of labor Professor Navarro Tomás and colleagues have now completed the linguistic atlas of Spain (begun as early as 1925, with field trips in 1931–36). It will not be published until Portugal can be included.

[2] We now have Professor Navarro's *El español en Puerto Rico: Contribución a la geografía lingüística hispanoamericana* (1948). Areas being studied include Guatemala, El Salvador, and Colombia.

sented are based on materials gathered during the author's frequent sojourns in the countries involved, on available printed treatises, monographs and local dictionaries, all of this enlarged with illustrative examples from the modern regional novel and short story published in the main since 1920, and with occasional examples from important works of an earlier period. Geographical and social limits for each phenomenon have been indicated in so far as they have been discovered. In this regard especial attention has been given to cases of apparently restricted usage. However, for cases appearing to be quite general, it has not seemed necessary to indicate subdivisions within a larger zone. It will be remembered that reference to any country does not mean that the locution under discussion is current throughout the country or in all social classes. Furthermore, forms current near the frontier of any country are likely to be identical with those on the bordering frontier of a contiguous country, while such forms may be quite different from those current in the interior of either country. For instance, the speech of Mendoza (Argentina) resembles that of Chile more than that of Buenos Aires; similarly, identical forms may be found, for example, in southern Peru and northern Bolivia, southern Colombia and Ecuador, eastern Colombia and Venezuela, northern Panama and Costa Rica. At our present stage of knowledge it is often exceedingly hazardous to call a given expression an Argentinism, for instance, because it is found in a given Argentine novel. It may be restricted to a single area and unknown elsewhere. To avoid this pitfall, when the locution seems dubious, the particular region involved will be indicated. However, if the locution is current in Buenos Aires (or, similarly, the capital of any country under discussion), or at least not unknown there, such a locution may for our purposes be termed an Argentinism, though it may actually be in very limited use.

The source of cited examples is indicated as briefly as is consistent with clarity, complete titles being listed in the Bibliography. An author represented by a single work is generally referred to merely by his name followed by the page number (if a play, sometimes by act and scene) of that work. In the case of two or more works by the same author, complete titles, unless extremely short, are not repeated but only enough of the title is given to identify the work (Arguedas, *Raza*, etc.). If clarity permits, single family names only are used (Benvenutto, Batres, etc.); otherwise the double family name appears (Herrera García, Núñez Guzmán, etc.) or, if an author has only one family name, this appears with his given name (Flavio Herrera, Ciro Alegría, Fernando Alegría, etc.). Examples labeled "(C)" I have heard in conversation with Spanish Americans; those labeled "(L)" I have taken from letters addressed to me by Spanish-American correspondents. Any work referred to but once, and whose title is given in complete form on that occasion, is not included in the Bibliography, nor are certain well-known classics.

Arrangement of examples is by countries beginning with the southernmost (Argentina) and advancing northward in geographical sequence, an arrangement that shows at a glance the status of the form in contiguous countries. Some will ask "Why begin at the south rather than at the north?" My decision was reached only after mature deliberation. Under a possible alphabetical arrangement Argentina would have headed the list, but such a sequence was out of the question. Yet for a number of reasons other than her notable progress and importance among Spanish republics, Argentina seemed to cling to first place. The spoken language there (and in other southern republics) deviates more than elsewhere from standard Castilian, and therefore offers a richer basis of study, and demands lengthier treatment. Furthermore, it appears rather likely that Argentina will influence the future aspect of general Spanish more than the majority of her sister-republics because Buenos Aires has today become perhaps the leading editorial center for Spanish. Amado Alonso (*La Nación*, August 4, 11, 18, 1940) believes that writers seeking publication of their works in Buenos Aires will accommodate their language as far as feasible to what is general in Argentina.

To be sure, beginning at the north would have followed more strictly a certain historical and chronological pattern and would have fitted more conveniently into the linguistic zone system expounded by Henríquez Ureña (*RFE*, VIII [1921], 358–61; *BDH*, IV [1938], 334–35; V, 29). As is well known, this scholar divides Spanish America into five linguistic zones according to substrata, historical and political influence, geographical environment, nuclei of Spanish culture, and characteristics of conquistadores and settlers.[3]

[3] Briefly and partially outlined by Juan Ignacio de Armas (*Orijenes del lenguaje criollo* [2d ed.; Havana, 1882], pp. 5–6), the zones are carefully studied and elaborated by Henríquez Ureña (the numerous subdivisions are here omitted): (1) the Caribbean zone (from 1492 on) includes the Antilles, a large part of Venezuela and the Atlantic coast of Colombia, with a substratum of Arawak and Carib; (2) the Mexican zone (from 1519 on) comprises southwestern United States, Mexico, and Central America, with a substratum of Náhuatl and Maya-Quiché; (3) the Andean zone (from 1527 on) includes a part of Venezuela, most of Colombia, all of Ecuador, Peru, Bolivia, and northwestern Argentina,

At first I made an attempt to group syntactical phenomena under the five zones but later decided against such an arrangement because it would have entailed too many disconcerting subdivisions. Furthermore, the exact limitations of the zones themselves have not been definitely established or universally accepted.[4] Navarro Tomás suggests a somewhat modified division, subject to further change according to future findings, since he considers Henríquez Ureña's proposal "rather an intelligently conceived hypothesis than a definite and proven reality."[5] Then, too, the five zones are differentiated principally in vocabulary, in borrowings from the substratum languages. Henríquez Ureña admits (*RFE*, VIII, 360) that in its phonetic aspect none of the zones is completely uniform. This statement could be extended to include morphology and, in a much greater measure, syntax.

It must not be forgotten that the general literary language is relatively uniform throughout the Spanish-speaking world; but the spoken standard speech of Spain differs in a number of respects from the spoken language of America—not that any uniformity exists in spoken American Spanish. Furthermore, standard Spanish is limited even in Spain to cultured groups. Elsewhere are found practices current also in American Spanish, though some expressions considered popular or vulgar in the peninsula have often found acceptance in socially higher circles in America. Be that as it may, the fact remains that the gap between the spoken tongue and the literary language is considerably wider in America. When taking pen in hand the Spanish-American author withdraws more completely from linguistic reality than does the Spaniard.

Emancipation of the Spanish-American literary language from the peninsular prototype has taken place to some extent, and in many instances the literary language has been approximated to the spoken language. Whether this will continue in the future is unpredictable. Desire for a larger reading public and greater universality of appeal will possibly lead the writer into more general channels. Even among the regionalists, we find some hesitancy in choice of expression. Formerly, for instance, a good stylist adapted his literary pattern strictly

---

with a substratum of Quechua and Aimará; (4) the River Plate zone (from 1536 on) includes Argentina, Uruguay, and Paraguay, with a substratum of Tupí-Guaraní and Mapuche; and (5) the Chilean zone (from 1541 on) with a substratum of Mapuche.

[4] Cf. Malaret, "Geografía lingüística," *BAAL*, V, 213–25.

[5] "The linguistic atlas of Spain and the Spanish of America," in *Bulletin of the American Council of Learned Societies*, No. 34 (1942), pp. 68–74.

to the Castilian mode, which naturally would completely violate many of his daily speech habits. If Chilean or Argentinian, for instance, he would say *vereda* 'path' in his conversation to designate a 'sidewalk' (a survival from the days when there were more paths than sidewalks); but when he sat down to write he would transform *vereda* to standard *acera*. If he were a Mexican, he would say *banqueta*, but only *acera* would appear in his manuscript. The well-known Chilean stylist, Pedro Prado, for instance, not concerned with local atmosphere but rather with a more universal outlook, uses *acera* throughout *Un juez rural*, and not once the Chilean equivalent *vereda*. His compatriot, Luis Durand, on the other hand, avoids *acera* in his *Mercedes Urízar*, remaining faithful to *vereda*, the form current in Chilean conversation. The literary background and culture which supplies words like *acera* to the author's pen is undoubtedly weaker or entirely lacking in second-, third-, or fourth-rate writers who are more concerned with their local milieu and local expression. For this reason, such writers are generally more valuable in the study of popular idiom than writers of the first water. Again, though most Spanish Americans use *lo* for 'him' in their daily speech, many still write *le*, the Castilian preference, because, being less common, *le* appears more elegant and literary. Others tend to use the standard in their narrative passages and use the local form in their dialogue. The novelist, Pedro Joaquín Chamorro, uses the American Spanish *el vuelto* 'change' in dialogue but prefers the peninsular Spanish *la vuelta* in the narrative passages of *Entre dos filos:*

> Don Robustiano sacó de la cartera un billete de veinte córdobas.
> —¿Tiene *vuelto* para veinte córdobas?
> Pasaron horas, pasaron días, pasaron años y Riverita no volvía con *la vuelta* ni menos con el pago [p. 190].

Cases of such dual forms are very numerous in Spanish-American literature. Utmost caution is therefore required in determining local usage.

Speculation as to future linguistic unity or chaos in Spanish America may be, to some extent, idle. There have been two opposing schools of thought: first, the puristic unitarians, often adhering stubbornly to outmoded or conservative Academic precept deriving from Spain; second, the separatists, who desire to sever all bonds with a peninsular minority—extremists in one case have unsuccessfully attempted to establish a local national language (Argentina). The majority of scholars today, as one would expect, take a middle ground.

While they abhor anarchy and loss of norms, they do not reject any necessary new forms, for language is constantly being renovated, new terms enrich it rather than adulterate it, and unity must not be confused with an exaggerated, lifeless purity. While the literary language may act as a unifying tie that will preserve the basic linguistic ideal, there will and must be abundant room for inevitable evolution.

It is logical that many local differences should have developed from the beginning, particularly in the spoken tongue, where they still thrive vigorously. When America was discovered, the Spanish language was still in a state of turmoil, its fluctuating forms were still aggressively combating one another for survival and preferment. Partial stability was attained only a century or a century and a half later. That early confusion was America's immediate heritage. Furthermore, the provenance and character of the colonists and early settlers differed from region to region. Mexico and Peru, for instance, represented an aristocratic nonprogressive regime, an extension of peninsular feudalism, in which adventurers could live in luxury and indolence. In Argentina and Chile, on the other hand, no ready wealth was available other than the hard-earned products of a soil that had to be wrested, inch by inch, from roving bands of savage Indians. The hegemony of Madrid over Mexico City and Lima, centers of colonial culture, was naturally much greater than over regions like Argentina and Chile, which lay beyond the pale of such cultural influence. These countries, lacking vice-royal courts, experienced a more rapid break in language tradition. The balance of social and linguistic values that was gradually being established in Spain failed to emerge where the impervious social fabric of the Old World was not maintained by vice-royal courts. Since social conventions and discipline were here relaxed, rural linguistic forms became urban, and traits considered vulgar or dialectal in Spain were here often raised to the dignity of an approved norm. The greater the culture of any group, the closer the adhesion to peninsular standards; but as the oral tradition of cultured speech crumbled, drift set in toward lower and impoverished expression, everyone spoke as he pleased, and measuring rods were lost. The speech habits of the original settlers, then, generally laid the foundation of a local mode, which may well have been altered in some degree by substratum and later by immigrants (such as Italians in Argentina, Negroes in the Antilles, Basques and Catalans in Venezuela, northern Spaniards in Chile, Cuba, etc.).

Local differences, however, are not nearly so great as many lexicographers have heretofore inclined us to believe. Ignorance of peninsular Spanish dialects and of the language of neighboring republics has often led Spanish-American investigators and compilers into great blunders. It happens again and again that such a compiler claims as strictly local a word or expression current not only in parts of Spain but also in most of Spanish America. Juan de Arona, for instance, confesses in his *Diccionario de peruanismos* (one of the earliest of such collections) that at first he considered the locution *donde fulano* (= standard *a casa de fulano*) as strictly Peruvian, was surprised to discover it to be an Americanism, and still later astonished to find it could be heard even in Castile.

The present work points toward unity in that it proves that many such locutions, formerly considered limited to one or two regions, enjoy a much greater geographical range and often are part of a general heritage from Spain. Further study will undoubtedly support the contention that linguistic usage in the different countries is tending toward unity rather than toward chaos. And unification of linguistic conscience may eventually obliterate local peculiarities.[6]

SECOND EDITION

The first edition (1945) has now been revised and brought up to date. Some repetitious and less pertinent matter has been deleted to make room for many scattered additions and emendations. The original pagination has, in the main, been kept intact. For new material we are indebted not only to recent publications but also to many new correspondents, among them: Luis Cifuentes García (Chile), Antonio Díaz Villamil (Bolivia), Marcos A. Morínigo (Paraguay), Alfredo F. Padrón (Cuba), and Ángel Rosenblat (Argentina and Venezuela). To these and to many others, including our original consultants too numerous to mention, we wish to express our gratitude.

May we again insist that phenomena here discussed are not *ipso facto* to be considered local standard usage. In many cases they are alternates, or merely the least common of such alternates; but, as divergencies from standard Castilian, they find a haven here.

1950

[6] To Professor Robert K. Spaulding a special word of thanks is due for his assistance in reading the proofs of this book and in offering valuable suggestions.

TABLE OF CONTENTS

I

NOUNS AND ARTICLES

DIRECT AND INDIRECT OBJECTS

THE omission of the preposition *a* before a direct or an indirect noun object when preceding a verb is fairly frequent in careless speech both in Spain and in Spanish America. It is a survival of older usage (Hanssen, § 500). Keniston (p. 31) treats of substantives placed often at the beginning of a sentence in sixteenth-century prose without indication of their relationship to the rest of the sentence: "The construction is logically similar to the modern use of *en cuanto a* or *lo que es* before a stressed substantive." Such an "independent subject" placed at the beginning of a sentence for emotional stress may be the direct or the indirect object of the main verb, and its function is generally indicated by a personal pronoun immediately before the verb. In Spain the construction is still current in popular and rustic speech: "—Este mendigo [= a este mendigo] nadien le conoce" (Aurelio Espinosa, *Cuentos*, III, 394 [León]); "Juan Tonto [= a Juan Tonto] le dijo su madre que buscaría novia pa casarse" (III, 408 [Burgos]). In some regions of Spanish America the construction appears to have a higher social status and has found its way into realistic literature more freely than in Spain, where popular elements of speech are and have been less readily accepted.

ARGENTINA: *El corrector* [= al corrector] de pruebas de alguna edición se le antojó rectificarla (L). *El* [= al] muy burro se le dió por jugar al foot-ball (Petit de Murat, p. 83).

CHILE: —Voy por el licor. Lo traeré yo mismo, porque *el animal* [= al animal] de Parra, mi sirviente, le di permiso el mes pasado y todavía no llega (Rojas and Fernández, *La hoja de Parra*, p. 13).

VENEZUELA: —Simangal dice que *el negro* [= al negro] José Kalasán no le hace nada la culebra (Díaz-Solís, p. 24: the same sentence, on the same page, with *al negro*); *Ese negro* [= a ese negro] no lo mata nada (p. 30).

MEXICO: De pie ... Lulú permaneció en espera de que *el señor* [= al señor] cajero se le diera la gana de levantar sus ojos de los papeles de su pupitre (Azuela, *Las tribulaciones*, p. 18). Ahora mismo, si *la señorita* [= a la señorita] le parece (Robles, *La virgen*, p. 48).

Contrary to older usage, the preposition *a* is also omitted today before geographical proper names: *he visto Roma; visitaré también Buenos Aires.* This is common with many Spanish as well as Spanish-American writers. Though stigmatized as a Gallicism by conservative grammarians, the practice is gaining ground and may eventually prevail. Inversely—and this is more noteworthy—the so-called personal *a* is frequently used in some regions before an unpersonified common noun where the standard language would reject it. Argentine preceptists, in particular, list it among the chief syntactical errors found in local writers, of whom Costa Álvarez (p. 254) grotesquely remarks: "la *a* inútil pulula en sus escritos tan profusamente que les da el aspecto papilar de la piel de gallina desplumada." It is heard in the spoken language as well.

ARGENTINA:—Saqué *a* la bolilla que sabía; vi *a* la película nacional (Herrero Mayor, p. 87). Trae *al* libro, cosecharon *al* maíz, ya me la sé *a* la lección (*BAAL*, XVI, 268); Esos cambios mejoran *al* habla (XII, 19); *a* la investigación no la realizan los laboratorios (p. 144). *A* su talle, delgado y flexible, lo cubría una blusa de tul (Candioti, p. 309).

PARAGUAY: Benítez estaba afilando *al* machete (Casaccia, p. 132).

PUERTO RICO: Tocando *a* la medalla ... divisaron *a* la isla (María Cadilla, *Hitos de la raza*, p. 29); dejar *a* la montaña (p. 35); entorpecían *a* la verdad (p. 59); vió *a* las sierras (p. 113).

The expression *dar vuelta(s) a* 'to revolve, turn over, turn around, twirl' has, at least in the River Plate region, in Chile and Bolivia, come to be used without the preposition *a;* that is, it takes a direct object rather than the standard indirect. This phrase is then analogous to standard verbal locutions consisting of a verb + a noun that, through constant use, have come to be felt as a single verbal concept capable of governing a direct object: *hacer pedazos una cosa* 'to break a thing to bits.' The rustic form of *vuelta* is *güelta*.

ARGENTINA: El mozo ... miraba apampao, *dando güelta* el sombrero entre las manos (Lynch, *Romance*, p. 14). *Dar vuelta la pisada* = Procedimiento que usa la gente de campo como remedio para diversos fines. ... Consiste en recortar con el cuchillo el trozo de tierra sobre el cual descansa uno de los vasos ['hoofs'] del caballo;

dicho trozo se da vuelta, poniendo la parte abajo para arriba ... (Saubidet, p. 128). Hay quien *da vuelta* el asado y deja que se tueste bien el pelo (Inchauspe, *Voces,* p. 86; cf. also Vidal, p. 400).

URUGUAY: De un tirón de las riendas *dió vuelta* su pingo (Montiel, *Luz mala,* p. 87).

CHILE: *Dieron güelta* la mesa (Juan del Campo, p. 12). Tomó por la orilla del río ... *dando vuelta* los matorrales (Manuel Rojas, in *LCC,* p. 463).

BOLIVIA: El esbirro galoneado ... *da toda una vuelta* la plazoleta con el prisionero (Augusto Guzmán, p. 183).

However, the observer may rightly contend that the foregoing examples are not conclusive evidence, since the preposition *a* in pronunciation is generally absorbed into an immediately preceding -*a* or a following *a*-, and this pronunciation is occasionally still reflected in writing. Examples like the following, therefore, will dispel any misgiving.

ARGENTINA: Nuestros conceptos *serán dados vuelta* (Candioti, p. 26). —*Lo di vuelta* tan ligero como pude (Güiraldes, *Don Segundo,* p. 191). Pues apenas atinó/a *dar güelta* como un trompo/su caballo y disparó ... apenas *lo* hizo dar *güelta* (Ascasubi, p. 168).

URUGUAY: *Dió vueltas* el sombrero en la mano (Montiel, *Cuentos,* p. 16); cuando *daba vuelta* en el magín la idea de pedirle relaciones a Candelaria (p. 29). Agárrenlos de los cuernos y la cola y *denlos vuelta* (Reyles, *El gaucho,* p. 34).

CHILE: *Dando vueltas* la chupalla [= sombrero] entre las temblorosas manos (Guerrero, p. 128). A cada instante [el gallo] se detiene, levanta una pata, *da vueltas* la cabeza (Díaz Garcés, in *Hispanoamericanos,* p. 121). El vendedor le trae uno [barómetro]. El guasito lo *da vuelta* por un lado (*Tallas chilenas,* p. 128).

In Chile, and sporadically elsewhere, *de* (or *con*) is often omitted after *hacer* before a noun or pronoun in questions: *¿qué lo hizo?* for standard *¿qué hizo de* (or *con*) *él?* This omission may well involve an original absorption of *e*, after the disappearance of the *d* (*de* > *e*), into the preceding vowel. Cf. also standard *lo hizo pedazos.*

CHILE: —¿Qué *hizo* la cuchilla, cabro? —La tiré al río (Alberto Romero, *Perucho González,* p. 72). —¿Qué *hiciste* tu sueldo que no me lo has entregado? (Juan Castro, p. 400). ¿Esta señora te dió cincuenta pesos ... ? ¿Qué los *hiciste?* (Prado, *Un juez rural*, p. 55).

COLOMBIA (ANTIOQUIA): ¿Qué *hiciste* aquellos brazos gordos? (Restrepo Jaramillo, p. 35). (BOGOTÁ): ¿Qué lo *hizo?* (Flórez, p. 374).

In some regions *de* is omitted after the verb *murmurar* 'to gossip about' (*BDH*, V, 233). This was done in the older language: examples abound in Lope de Vega, Góngora, Alarcón, etc. Both constructions stand side by side in *La estrella de Sevilla* (I, 6): "Aquél murmura hoy de aquél/Que el otro ayer murmuró." By analogy with *murmurar*, the verb *chismear* may be found similarly construed.

ARGENTINA (SAN LUIS): *Me chismean*, etc. (Vidal, p. 391).

PERU: *Chismearon a la vieja* (Benvenutto, p. 153).

COLOMBIA (ANTIOQUIA): Señores los que me oyeren,/No me *murmuren la voz*,/Que me ha dado el romadizo/Y me quiere dar la tos (Antonio Restrepo, p. 127).

VENEZUELA: —Pero como Ramón Piña ya venía siendo amo, no faltó el adulante que *los* fuera a *chismear* (Briceño, p. 61).

SANTO DOMINGO: —Don Marcial *lo había murmurado* con Abelardo (Moscoso, p. 18); —Yo sé que *me chismean* los envidiosos (p. 106).

En in some regions is omitted after *pensar* where standard usage demands it: *te pienso mucho* for standard *pienso mucho en ti* 'I think of you often.' This is particularly common in Colombia but is also found in other adjacent countries, through Central America, and occasionally elsewhere. It arose possibly by confusion with other meanings of *pensar* with which no preposition is used (*pensarlo* 'to think it over') and influenced by such semantically related words as *recordar* 'to remember' and *soñar* 'to dream of' (*soñé contigo, soñé en ti*, and then *te soñé*). Occasionally *reparar* and *fijarse* 'to pay attention to, note,' are found without *en*, which generally accompanies these verbs in standard usage, and *tirar* 'to shoot at' without *a*.

ARGENTINA: *Te pensé* en todas mis noches y muchas veces te lloré (Martínez Cuitiño, p. 36). *¿Te fijás* la cábula? (Filloy, p. 429).

ECUADOR: *Te pensé* todo el día, y toda la noche. ... Estuve *pensándote* (García Muñoz, *Estampas*, p. 7); Te quiero, *te pienso* (p. 8).

COLOMBIA: *Te he pensado* mucho (C). *Piénseme* mucho; *¿me ha pensado* mucho? (Tascón, p. 220). *Te pienso* (Sundheim, p. 505). *Reparó* el sitio que indicaba su mujer (Buitrago, p. 172). Mucho *pensé* a Tomás Carrasquilla (Malaret, *Suplemento*, II, 284).

VENEZUELA: Ahora ... que *la pienso* (Briceño, p. 112). Usted que quería *tirar* caimanes (Gallegos, *Doña Bárbara*, p. 13); —No *lo tire* (p. 17).

PANAMA: *Pienso* mi novia; *pienso* mi hijo (Espino, p. 110). *¿Te fijas* lo enteco [=flaco] que ha quedado? (L. Aguilera, p. 259).

COSTA RICA: Anoche *te pensé* (Quesada, p. 309).

HONDURAS: —Y el sentirla a cada instante, y el *pensarla*, y el soñarla ... (Martínez Galindo, p. 125).

The verb *pelear(se)* 'to fight, quarrel' diverges variously from standard usage. Besides its general acceptance for standardly preferred *reñir* (*están peleados* = *están reñidos* 'they have quarreled, they have fallen out,' etc.), it is in some regions very often used transitively; that is, it takes a direct object rather than the standard prepositional *por* phrase: *pelear(se) una cosa* = standard *pelear(se)*, or *reñir*, *por una cosa* (or *con alguien*). The change is by analogy with transitive *pleitear* 'to litigate,' *disputar* 'to contest,' etc., and these meanings are sometimes assumed by *pelear*.

ARGENTINA (RURAL): De balde el rey ha mandado sus ejércitos a *peliarlo al tirano* (Draghi Lucero, p. 22). Cf. Vidal, p. 392.

CHILE: Los tres estudiantes *se peleaban el premio;* Las dos hermanas *se pelean el novio* (Román, IV, 188). Los perros *se peleaban un hueso* (C). *La pelean* los hombres (Acevedo H., *Árbol viejo*, p. 47).

ECUADOR (HIGHLANDS): Y no habla mucho y no *pelea los precios* (Jorge Fernández, p. 16).

GUATEMALA: —Dígame usted, señor licenciado, ¿querría usted *pelearme* [= pleitear] *ese asuntito?* (*ap.* Sandoval, II, 222).

SANTO DOMINGO: (Among fishermen): Tuvieron que *pelear* mucho *el jurel* [= luchar con él para sacarlo del agua]. (Patín Maceo, *Dom.*, p. 134).

CUBA: Fulano *me pelea* siempre por todo (Padrón).

In Colombia one hears *lo preguntan* instead of standard *preguntan por usted*, probably by analogy with *lo buscan*, etc. (Cuervo, § 426): "Te solicitan al teléfono. Eso me dijo el sirviente que anda *preguntándote*" (Tulio González, p. 160).

GENDER

The matter of gender falls mostly in the field of morphology. We need therefore not dwell on it here. It may be of interest, however, to note briefly that there seems to be a general tendency in American Spanish to differentiate natural gender of nouns, adjectives, and participles more carefully than in the standard language, which, here as elsewhere, lags behind popular usage. Forms like *la presidenta* (for *la presidente*), *la dependienta*, *la sirvienta*, *la taquígrafa*, *la ministra*, are current nearly everywhere, though not always recorded in dictionaries. This legitimate development appears to be carried further than in most of Spain. In Spanish America we find much more frequently than in Spain such popular feminine forms as *tigra*, *animala*, *criminala*, *diabla*, *federala*, *liberala*, *intelectuala*, *naturala*, *orientala*, *mayordoma*, *aborígena*, *individua*, *tipa*, *sujeta*, *yerna*, *negocianta*, *marchanta*, *atorranta*, etc. Nouns and adjectives standardly ending in *-ista* for both genders have assumed in some rural regions of America an unmistakable masculine ending in *-isto* beside *-ista* for the feminine: *campisto*, *modisto* (also in Spain; cf. Casares, *Crítica profana*, p. 57 n.), *bromisto*, *burlisto*, *cuentisto* 'gossip,' *pianisto*, *maquinisto*, *telegrafisto*, etc. Individual cases of gender divergence between standard Spanish and American Spanish cannot be recorded here, such as: *el vuelto* (general) for *la vuelta* 'change'; *la muelle* (Mexico) for *el muelle* 'spring'; *el bombillo* (Caribbean zone and Mexico) for *la bombilla* 'electric bulb'; etc.

Divergences of gender in syntactical expressions are not common: *la misma* (where probably *cosa* is understood) for standard *lo mismo* 'the same thing'; *a la mejor* in limited areas for *a lo mejor* 'at best, probably,' discussed under adverbial locutions (p. 281); *de seguido* for standard *de seguida* 'continuously'; etc.

CHILE: Otra vez con *la mesma* (Romanángel, p. 19).

COSTA RICA: —¿Cogemos misa en El Llano,/o bamos a l'otra iglesia?/—Como quedrás, Pelegrino;/si biene siendo *la mesma* (Agüero, p. 54). Yo digo *la misma* (C).

In some rural sections of Puerto Rico (Utuado, Lares, Moca) a gerund sometimes agrees with its attached object pronoun (*quemándolo*, *quemándala*): "La mujer está *muriéndase;* —¿Qué le hace la mujer a la niña? —Ta *peinándala*" (Navarro, p. 130). Apparently the same may be true elsewhere: "Es que la muy bandida s'está *hacienda* [*sic*] la tonta (Fallas, p. 26 [Costa Rica]).

NUMBER

In modern standard Spanish the singular is employed of nouns indicating parts of the body when the singular notion may be applied to each member of a group. From earliest times such nouns were often made plural by attraction. In the *Cid* we find: "de las sus *bocas* todas dezían una razón" (vs. 19), "ívanlas ferir de *fuertes corazones*" (vs. 718), "escudos a *los cuellos*" (vs. 1509), "páranlas en *cuerpos*" (vs. 2721), etc. Such plurals by attraction are today much less frequent in Spain than in Spanish America, where their widespread use may be seen from the geographical range of the following examples.

ARGENTINA: Ambos han torcido *las cabezas* al mismo tiempo (Sáenz, p. 54). En una mesa del extremo rincón hablaban dos hombres, *las cabezas* descubiertas (Mallea, *La ciudad*, p. 103). Las dos vaquitas ... lambiéndose con *sus lenguas* limpias y blancas *los hocicos* relumbrosos (Lynch, *Romance*, p. 100). Los miserandos se alejan en seguida por la picada, rebalsados *los corazones* de inmensa fe (*ACH*, p. 30).

URUGUAY: Los peones movieron *las cabezas* y se miraron (Acevedo Díaz, p. 115). Los indios se habían teñido *las caras* con tierras (Acevedo Díaz, *Cancha larga*, p. 215).

CHILE: Las sombras corrieron rápidamente detrás, y ellos, levantando *las obscuras cabezas*, dejaron que el aire helado de la carrera les refrescara *los rostros* (Manuel Rojas, *Travesía*, p. 8). Las muchachas se miran *las frentes* (Azócar, p. 152).

BOLIVIA: Máscaras idénticas de sombra les envolvían *las caras* (Céspedes, p. 127). Nos hemos mojado *las cabezas* (A. Guzmán, p. 37).

PERU: Y volvieron a beber hasta que se les hincharon *los vientres* (Ciro Alegría, *Los perros*, p. 97).

ECUADOR: Gozaban al ver que los tallos mozos caían sobre *sus caras y sus pechos* sudorosos (Mata, *Sanagüín*, p. 74); Menearon *sus frentes* en negativas silenciosas de ironías (p. 130). —Pero, se les embota *sus cerebros* ... y no pueden pensar (Mata, *Sumag Allpa*, p. 6); Enanchaban *sus bocazas* hediondas a tragazo (p. 11).

VENEZUELA: No caería en *los estómagos* de aquellos hombres (Gallegos, *Doña Bárbara*, p. 228).

COSTA RICA: Hay una alegría ... en *los rostros* de ambas (Fabián Dobles, p. 257).

HONDURAS: Eran cinco peones y todos traían *las caras* compungidas (Mejía Nieto, *El solterón*, p. 92).

GUATEMALA: Sin verse unos a otros *las caras*, principiaron a comer (Barnoya, p. 107).

MEXICO: Todos los soldados apenas se atrevían a asomar *sus cabezas* (Azuela, *Los de abajo*, p. 99). Los concurrentes volvieron *las caras* (Robles Castillo, p. 103).

With articles of clothing and personal attributes the plural is not infrequently used in peninsular Spanish, and even more frequently in American Spanish. We find the usage in Old Spanish (*Cid*, vs. 2721: "páranlas en cuerpos y en *camisas* y en *çiclatones*). In sixteenth-century prose the use of the plural "predominates slightly" over the singular when no adjective is used with the noun (Keniston, p. 37). Therefore American Spanish practice here again reflects the older Spanish usage as against the modern peninsular standard. A few examples will suffice.

ARGENTINA: Allí, descalzos, los hombres se quitan *los sombreros* (Mateo Booz, in *ACH*, p. 29).

URUGUAY: Los paisanos se quitaron *los sombreros* (Montiel, *Alma nuestra*, p. 87). —Muchachos, quitensén *los ponchos* (Reyles, *El gaucho*, p. 40).

BOLIVIA: Nos quitamos *las blusas* (Augusto Guzmán, p. 67).

MEXICO: Nos quitamos *los sombreros* (Urquizo, p. 51).

Perhaps by analogy with this usage the Old Spanish phrases like *ponerse de pies*[1] (which is generally *ponerse de pie* in present-day standard speech) have been retained in parts of Spanish America.

ECUADOR: María del Socorro se había quedado *de pies* muda de sorpresa (Pareja, *El muelle*, p. 129). Juan de la Cruz se puso *en pies* (Gil Gilbert, *Nuestro pan*, p. 40).

COLOMBIA: El estudiante tenía que ponerse *de pies* (Carrasquilla, *Hace tiempos*, III, 244). Se pusieron todos *de pies* (Bernardo Toro, p. 94). Se ponen *de pies* (Efe Gómez, p. 22); se puso *de pies* (p. 60).

VENEZUELA: Ibarra se pone *de pies* (Arráiz, p. 186); Se desprende y se pone *de pies* (p. 233). Poniéndose *de pies* se echó a la cara un rifle (Gallegos, *Doña Bárbara*, p. 13).

PANAMA: "Pararse" tiene en castellano la acepción perfectamente castiza de ponerse *de pies* (Garay, p. 106).

NICARAGUA: Los hombres ... duermen *de pies* (Robleto, p. 204). Mi esposa ... se quedó *de pies* (Orozco, p. 14). Los invitados ... se pusieron *de pies* (Chamorro, *Entre dos filos*, p. 144); [but also] Monjará se ponía *de pie* (p. 146).

HONDURAS: Todos los alumnos se pusieron *de pies* (Zúñiga, p. 153).

[1] *Calila e Dimna*, chap. xviii: "Et la raposa fué a buscarlo, et fallólo parado en *pies*"; *Don Quijote*, I, 43: "... Don Quijote se había *puesto de pies* sobre la silla de Rocinante ... estaba ... *de pies*"; Ramón de la Cruz, "Los segadores festivos," *Revue hispanique*, LXXVI, 404: "¿qué hacemos en *pies?* Sentaos."

Apparently there exists a more or less popular predilection for plural forms of certain nouns where standard speech prefers the singular.

ARGENTINA (CUYO): Cuanto más subía, más contenía *los resuellos* para no ser sentido (Draghi Lucero, p. 123).

ECUADOR: —Yo no puedo levantarme por *las reumas*—expresó mi Coronel (García Muñoz, *Estampas*, p. 284).

COSTA RICA: Luego la cogió en *los regazos* y se puso a hacerle cariño (Lyra, p. 82).

EL SALVADOR: Puso sobre *los regazos* de la vieja un corte para un traje obscuro (Torres Arjona, p. 31).

This rather unusual pluralization is particularly apparent with abstract nouns, where it serves for emphasis. As early as the *Cid* (1140), certain abstract nouns were pluralized when they referred to an act related to the abstraction, rather than to the abstraction itself: *amores* = *fineza* or *agasajo; vergüenças* = *afrenta*, etc. (Menéndez Pidal, *Cantar de mío Cid*, I, 120, 3). In Avellaneda's *Don Quijote* (1614) we read: "No hizo caso don Quijote de *los miedos* y conjuros de su escudero" (chap. xxvi). Villegas' *Oda sáfica* has: "temo sus *iras*," etc. This usage may be traced back to Latin (Meyer-Lübke, §27). While the correct standard language today rejects the majority of such plurals as in bad taste (Huidobro, p. 168), peninsular Spanish is not entirely free from them. American Spanish, however, is overrun with them, not only in popular speech but also in literary style.

ARGENTINA: Pondré en esta empresa *todos mis entusiasmos;* El señor ministro del ramo se propone en esta ocasión desplegar *sus energías* (Forgione, p. 111). Os halláis en *inteligencias* con los moriscos (Larreta, *La gloria*, p. 126).

URUGUAY: No me echés *las culpas* (Florencio Sánchez, p. 218); Tengo la certidumbre de haberla traído a *mis destinos* con el imán de *mis energías expansivas* (p. 610).

PERU: Tudela ... había encomendado a Peña ... que arrostrara *las iras* de las damas (Corrales, p. 121).

ECUADOR: —No me llames hijita porque he de tener *iras* y no he de poder tomar el chocolate (García Muñoz, *Estampas*, p. 32); —¿Estás con *iras?*—le pregunté a mi señora (p. 223); ¿Por qué son sus *cóleras*, Zoilita? (p. 263).

COLOMBIA: —Pueden seguir sin *miedos* (Buitrago, p. 158).

VENEZUELA: Tamara se acurrucó de *miedos* en el recodo de un playón ríspido (Briceño, p. 5); sabroso razonar sin *miedos* (p. 24).

COSTA RICA: Es como cuando a yo me agarraban *miedos* en la noche (Fabián Dobles, p. 323).

GUATEMALA: Barnoya Gálvez tiene las condiciones que para ser buen escritor se necesitan: *imaginaciones*, manera de ver y apreciar las cosas, soltura en la pluma y una fina sensibilidad (Máximo Soto Hall, "Prólogo" to Barnoya's *Han de estar*). Temerosos de despertar sus hasta entonces dormidas *iras* (Barnoya, p. 107).

MEXICO: ¿No te doy *ascos* a ti? (Gamboa, *Santa*, p. 315). Abandoné la casa ... con tanto miedo a *las iras* de aquel marido coronado de flores, que resolví dejar inmediatamente el pueblo (José Rubén Romero, p. 55).

In temporal expressions, likewise, the plural predominates in certain locutions in which the singular is usual in Spain. The expression *¿qué horas son?* is general in Spanish America for standard *¿qué hora es?* It arose by analogy with the replies, save one, to the question *¿qué hora es?*; that is, *son las dos* (*horas*), *son las tres* (*horas*), etc. Such a plural by attraction we see in the sentence *dieron las dos* 'it struck two,' which originally was (*el reloj*) *dió las dos*, etc. (*Lazarillo*, III: "*dió* las once ... antes que *el relox diesse* las cuatro ... hasta que *dió* las dos, etc.") Cf. Portuguese *que horas são?*

ARGENTINA: ¿Qué *horas son?* (Ascasubi, p. 165). ¿Qué *horas serán?* (Laferrère, *Locos de verano*, p. 14). ¡Vaya a saber uno *las horas* que *serían!* (Lynch, *Romance*, p. 498).

CHILE: ¿Qué *horas son?* (Edwards Bello, in *LCC*, p. 423). ¿A qué *horas* me recibirá el juez de agua? (Acevedo Hernández, *La canción rota*, p. 60). No veo *las horas* de hacerlo (C).

COLOMBIA: —¿Qué *horas son?* (Carrasquilla, *Hace tiempos*, III, 192). ¿A qué *horas* llegaría a Túquerres? (Álvarez Garzón, p. 170).

NICARAGUA: ¿A qué *horas* estaremos en San Juan? (Orozco, p. 133). *Son* la una (C).

GUATEMALA: ¿A qué *horas* llegó? (Flavio Herrera, p. 117).

MEXICO: ¿A qué *horas* llegó este nuevo pasajero? (Azuela, *Avanzada*, p. 144). Si alguno quiere saber/la hora con precisión,/no pregunta ¿qué hora es?/porque dice ¿qué *horas son?* (Sánchez Somoano, p. 55). (YUCATAN, POP.): *Son* la una (Víctor Suárez, p. 153).

CUBA: ¿Qué *hora es?* (CULT.); ¿qué *horas son?* (POP.) (Padrón).

EL SALVADOR: —*En horas buenas,* me alegro (Torres A., p. 89).

Occasionally we find an *-s* added to a numeral to make more patent its agreement with *horas* or *años,* etc. This usage is rustic and appears infrequently. Cf. English 'in his twenties,' etc.

COSTA RICA: A *las doces* llegó el Padre (Echeverría, p. 169). Estaba echada atisbando el tan tan de *las doces* (Luis Dobles, in *LCR,* p. 114). Ando en los *cuarentas,* en los *ochentas* ... allá por los años *ochentas* (Salesiano, p. 123).

Cuervo (§ 198) reports the use of *las onces* for *las once* (a light repast or drink taken originally at eleven o'clock, sometimes popularly believed to represent the eleven letters of *aguardiente* 'brandy'), and (§ 206) *hacer horas* for *hacer hora* 'to kill time.' In spite of protests from the grammarians, the plural *onces* is used also in Chile (Román, IV, 74), Venezuela, and elsewhere, as well as in Asturias (Corominas, p. 92). In parts of Colombia *las nueves* indicates a midmorning snack (Tobón, p. 131).

The expression *hace tiempo* frequently becomes *hace tiempos.* Cuervo, apparently unaware of the extent of this usage in Spanish America, suggests that *tiempos* is a contamination of *hace tiempo* + *hace días, años* ("Prólogo" to Gagini). But it may well be a preservation of the Latin neuter *tempus* or a formation analogical with other plural nouns used to indicate extent or abundance with the force of a singular, such as *amores, infiernos, mares, mientes, paces,* common in the sixteenth century (Keniston, p. 37). We read in Oviedo (*Historia general y natural de las Indias* [ed. 1851], II, 2): "esta tierra se supo *grandes tiempos* ha."

ARGENTINA: —Hombre, que sea pa *tiempos* y pa güeno (*Fray Mocho,* p. 43).

CHILE: Ahora *tiempos,* un oficial ... dejó olvidados unos fusiles (Barros Grez, I, 137).

PERU: Y velay que pasó *tiempos* (Ciro Alegría, *La serpiente,* p. 221).

ECUADOR (AZUAY): Las mujeres hace *tiempos* que están durmiendo (Mata, *Sanagüín,* p. 120). (COASTAL ZONE): Anda desde *tiempos* que nadie recuerda por todos los ríos buscando un niño (Gil Gilbert, *Nuestro pan,* p. 15).

COLOMBIA: Yo conozco *hace tiempos* a su taita (Carrasquilla, *Hace tiempos,* I, 66). Tengo *tiempos* de no salir (Obando, p. 190).

COSTA RICA: Hace *tiempos* o hace *tiempos de tiempos* = Ha tiempo o hace tiempo (Gagini, p. 156).

In some regions, particularly the River Plate and Caribbean zones, temporal expressions containing the words *día* and *noche* (occasionally *mañana*) are often employed in the plural: *los otros días* 'the other day,' *las otras noches* 'the other night,' *las otras mañanas* 'the other morning.' The plural seems to lend overtones of vagueness, as if the precise day or night could not be recalled. Cf. such temporal standard plurals as *a principios* (*mediados, fines*) *de*, etc.

ARGENTINA (RURAL): *Los otros días* tuve que estar dos horas contra el cerco (Martínez Payva, p. 11). Le hice una pregunta *las otras noches* (Candioti, p. 103). *Las otras mañanas* tuvimos un examen (C). Deberá cumplir su promesa de casamiento, que le diera *noches pasadas* en la estancia (Heredia, p. 234).

URUGUAY: Me la contaron las de Ibáñez *los otros días* (Sánchez, *M'hijo el dotor*, III, 2). Dice por qué no jué a la reunión de *los otros días* (Sánchez, *Barranca abajo*, II, 15). *Los otros días*, por compulsarla, le dejé entrever la posibilidad de que tú vinieras a la capital (Bellán, p. 16). *Los otros días* juí a verla (Pérez Petit, p. 62); —¿A que no sabe quién estuvo *los otros días* po aquí? (p. 63). *Las otras noches* fuí a pedirle una vela prestada y me la negó (Sánchez, *La pobre gente*, II, 3).

VENEZUELA: *Los otros días* vino a verme (C).

COSTA RICA: Son *los medios días* = es el medio día (Salesiano, p. 123).

PUERTO RICO: Me lo dió *los otros días* (C).

Conversely, we find the singular *buen día* for standard *buenos días* 'good day, etc.,' in many regions, generally colloquial or rustic. In Spain it is likewise rustic: (*Carretero*) "*—Güen día*" (Arniches, *La pena negra*, I, 3). Revollo (p. 105) thinks that "el singular revela mezquindad." Fidel Suárez (VIII, 102) feels the plural to be more cordial and friendly. Rarely *buena noche* (Sundheim, p. 237).

Interesting is *los julios* for *julio* 'July' in regions of Colombia, generally meaning 'the summer vacation period' (June to August), and *los inviernos* 'rainy weather.' Cf. *de los corrientes* for *del corriente* (*mes*).

(ANTIOQUIA): —Así es que cuando lleguen *los julios* del año entrante, podemos bajarnos al veraneo (Carrasquilla, *Hace tiempos*, I, 52); Evaristo dizque viene por mí en *los julios* (II, 285). A veces, por *los julios*, sabrosas lechoncillas (Arias Trujillo, p. 30).

Peculiarly American are the expressions *los altos* (standard *el piso alto* or *el primer piso*) and *los bajos* (standard *piso bajo*) of houses that are two-floor structures, corresponding to our 'second floor' and 'first' or 'ground floor,' respectively. Sometimes *altos* refers to all the floors above the ground floor, and in this sense it may be considered peninsular, since the Academy dictionary defines *alto* as "cada uno de los pisos o suelos." The use of *los altos* for our 'second floor' of two-story buildings is fairly general in America, being recorded for Argentina (Segovia), Chile (Román), Peru (Arona), Mexico (Icazbalceta), Cuba (Dihigo), Santo Domingo (Patín Maceo), and Puerto Rico (Malaret); and it is used elsewhere. In Paraguay one hears: "Vivo en una casa *de alto* [= de dos pisos]" (Morínigo).

PERU: ¿Cómo puede una saber lo que pasa en *los altos* si yo no vivo ahí? (López Albújar, *Matalaché*, p. 248). Vivir *en altos,* vivir *en bajos;* estar buscando *unos altos, unos bajos* para vivir (Arona, p. 19). En *los altos* vivía el Inca (Corrales, p. 135).

MEXICO: Fulano ocupa *los altos* de tal casa; Fulano tiene su tienda en *los bajos* de tal casa (Icazbalceta, p. 19). La vivienda de Hipólito formaba en *los altos,* y a ella subieron quietamente (Gamboa, *Santa,* p. 313).

This practice follows a peculiar Latin and Romance tendency to pluralize words denoting dwelling places, such as 'house,' 'court,' 'palace,' etc. (Meyer-Lübke, §32). So also the inside or interior of a house may become *los interiores:* "Un ciego feísimo ... llegando en coche al burdel, en cuyos *interiores* se precipitó auxiliado de un lazarillo" (Gamboa, *Santa*, p. 309).

The use of *las casas* seems to have been an alternative for *la casa* in the older language: "Fingiendo que por servicios,/ honró mis humildes *casas*/ de unos reposteros" (Lope de Vega, *Peribáñez*, IV, 27). It has survived in regions of America, though now restricted to country estates, farms, and the like. The plural, now fallen into desuetude in Spain, may have been retained in rural America (especially Argentina and Chile, occasionally elsewhere) because such country homes consisted generally of two dwellings (one for the owners, the other for the servants) or at least of a house and a barn or shed (*galpón*). *Las casas* has sometimes erroneously been considered a localism: a *chilenismo* (Zorobabel Rodríguez, p. 98), an *argentinismo* (Garzón, p. 100). Tiscornia (*Martín Fierro*, p. 80 n.) suggests that the plural *las casas* may possibly preserve "la idea principal primitiva de 'habitación rústica y pobre' " as indicated by Covarrubias (*Tesoro*, Part I, fol. 141[r]). Possibly so; but that *las casas* did not always have this depreciatory meaning in the colonies we may infer from examples like the following: "En la ciudad de Santiago ... lunes cinco días del mes de enero de 1545 años, en *las casas* del mui magnífico Pedro de Valdivia" (Zorobabel Rodríguez, p. 99). Furthermore, the plural *casas* (Latin *casa* 'a single-roomed hut') appears in early Spanish expressing "multiplicity with accompanying prestige" (Gillet, *HR*, XVIII, 179, who obviates Castro's Arabic 'injection': *casa* 'room,' *casas* 'house').

For present-day Argentina, Inchauspe (*Voces*, p. 54) explains: "En el campo, cuando se refieren a la vivienda, casi nunca se usa el singular. —Me voy para *las casas*— dicen, aun cuando se trate de una casa completamente aislada de toda otra vecindad."

ARGENTINA: La pobre, allá solita en *las casas*, estaría pensando en él (Lynch, *Romance*, p. 243).

CHILE: —Voy a ir a *las casas* (Acevedo H., *Por el atajo*, p. 35).

EL SALVADOR: Regresaban a *las casas* (González, *Don Benja*).

The plural of *palacio* 'palace' or 'inner room' in the older language, is still encountered both in popular or rustic speech in parts of Spain ("A *los palacios* del rey" [Pereda, *Obras*, VI, 410]) and in America:

ARGENTINA: "Al otro día ... se fué el mozo a *los palacios* del rey a pedirle un trabajito ... vió que más que palacio, aquello era una ruina (Draghi Lucero, p. 23).

The extension of these plurals to words like *campo* 'field,' *pago* (*pagos*, a preservation of Latin *pagus?*) 'town, village, district,' *lados* and *vecindades* 'neighborhood,' etc., was easily accomplished.

ARGENTINA: —Si no fuera por m'hijito ... no era yo la que seguía viviendo ni un día en *estos pagos* (Lynch, *Romance*, p. 388).

URUGUAY: Era domingo cuando llegó a *los pagos*, como él mismo amaba decir (Montiel, *Alma nuestra*, p. 42).

EL SALVADOR: A veces sale a *los campos* a hacer compras para su venta en el mercado (Torres Arjona, p. 85).

Perhaps we may mention here the Mexican custom of pluralizing *calle* in referring to a street of more than one block (*las calles de Bolívar*), since such streets are generally divided into *primera, segunda, tercera calle de*—: 1ª *Calle de Bolívar*, 2ª *Calle de Bolívar*, etc.

MEXICO: Septembrino ... caminaba melancólicamente por *la tercera calle de Bolívar* (Gómez Palacio, p. 31).

To morphology rather than to syntax belongs the consideration of other occasional plurals for standard singulars (such as *en ciernes* [also in Spain; cf. Casares, *Crítica efímera,* p. 186] for *en cierne* 'budding, beginning'; *quedar de nones* for *quedar de non* 'to remain alone, be an odd member of a party'; *a seguidas* for *de* or *en seguida* 'immediately' by analogy with expressions like *a sabiendas; sueltos* for *suelto* 'small change'; *vueltas* in Bogotá for *vuelta* 'change'; *perder de vistas* [Gallegos, *Doña Bárbara,* p. 67] for *perder de vista; a los lejos* for *a lo lejos; a tiros de* for *a tiro de; con sus permisos* and *voy en buscas de* [rural Colombia, Flórez, p. 375] for *con el permiso de Uds.* and *voy en busca de;* etc.) and of occasional singulars for standard plurals (such as *anda* for *andas* 'stretcher, litter'; *cortapluma* for *cortaplumas* 'penknife'; *paragua* for *paraguas* 'umbrella'; *pinza* for *pinzas* 'pincers, forceps'; *somos capaz de* [Revollo, p. 53] for *capaces de;* etc.).

VERBAL NOUNS IN '-ADA' AND '-IDA'

Peculiar to many regions of Spanish America is the excessive paraphrasing of simple verbs of action by means of an auxiliary verb + a feminine verbal noun in *-ada* (derived from the past participle of first conjugation verbs) or in *-ida* (derived from the past participle of second and third conjugation verbs): *me corté* > *me di una cortada, voy a nadar* > *voy a echar una nadada,* etc. Such locutions are congenial to the Spanish temper and language (cf. *dar* or *echar una mirada*), corresponding, as they do, to the desire to express action vivid and completed, or psychologically envisaged as completed.

As everyone knows, Spanish uses the imperfect tense (*miraba*) to express an uncompleted act in the past, and the preterite (*miré*) to express a completed act in the past. Future tenses (*miraré, voy a mirar,* etc.), however, do not distinguish between a continued act and a completed act. And yet the mind conceives of this difference for the future as easily as for the past. The locution of "auxiliary + verbal noun in *-ada* or *-ida*" (*voy a echar una mirada*) fulfils this need in future time.[2] For past time, in which its use is less essential because of the existing preterite, it nevertheless adds vividness and rapidity to the force of the action (*eché una mirada* as against *miré*).

[2] Keniston's statement (*Hispania,* XIX, 165) that "Spanish has not found it necessary to distinguish between the two [for the future]" needs modification, at least in regard to popular speech, of which the author did not take cognizance.

In other languages such aspects may be indicated by special verbs or verbal constructions. Compare English 'to look' and 'to take a look'; 'to swim' and 'to take a swim.' In Russian the imperfective form or "aspect" of a verb describes the action as lasting or going on in present, past, or future and stresses the action itself; the perfective form or "aspect," on the other hand, describes the action as completed with its beginning and its end in either past or future. The psychological attitude reflected in the perfective aspect of a Russian verb, then, is what in Spanish may be rendered (1) for the past: by the preterite (*miré*) or by auxiliary + noun (*eché una mirada*), and (2) for the future: by auxiliary + noun (*echaré una mirada, voy a echar una mirada*); that is, a single completed act, with beginning and end, indicated with the definiteness and sometimes the rapidity of a blow. It will be remembered that Spanish noun derivatives in *-ada* often express a blow or stroke (*puñal* 'dagger'—*puñalada* 'stab'; *cuchillo* 'knife'—*cuchillada* 'gash'); and further comparison may be made with French locutions containing *coup* 'blow': *jeter un coup d'œil sur* 'to have a look at, to glance over'; *donner un coup de fer à* 'to press, iron up,' and with Italian *fare una fumata* 'to have a smoke,' etc.

In Spain verbal-noun formations were more abundant in the older language than they are today, except such forms as *venida, ida, llegada*, etc., which are still very common. In the *Cid* (vs. 3043), for instance, we read: "*tornada da*" for *torna*. In the *Celestina* "—Queda abierta la puerta para mi *tornada*" (VI); "A esto fué aquí mi *venida*, a dar concierto en tu *despedida*" (XI); etc. In popular and rustic speech they may still be heard: "Me di una *pechá* [= pechada = hartada] de agua" (Rodríguez Marín, p. 81).

In the present-day familiar, popular, and rustic speech of many Spanish-American zones, the formation of such verbal nouns + an auxiliary (*dar, echar, pegar, hacer*, etc.) appears limitless. The spirit underlying their development and actuating their use reflects the alertness, physical and mental, that characterized the colonists and settlers facing new problems in need of quick solving. Dynamic awareness and reaction to the strange environment in the New World probably seized upon this tendency inherent in the language and carried it far beyond the peninsular standard.

ARGENTINA: Se presentó, y ai no más/*Hizo una arriada* ['rounding up'] en montón (*Martín Fierro*, p. 27). *Pegó* el güey *una tendida* [= una espantada] (Ascasubi, p. 238). Cf. nouns listed in Vidal, p. 220.

URUGUAY: Lo vide *pegar sinfinidá de rodadas* (Reyles, *El gaucho*, p. 28). Habría que *pegarse unas escapadas* de cuando en cuando (Montiel, *Luz mala*, p. 15).

CHILE: *Haciendo una encogida* de despecho de sus anchas espaldas (Acuña, *Huellas*, p. 138). Es inútil que yo puea seguir, si no *echo una escansaít'* aquí [= descansadita aquí] (Romanángel, p. 84). Voy a *echar una nadada;* me voy a *pegar una sudada* (C). Tenía ganas de *echarle una güena ormía* [= dormida] al cuerpo (Juan del Campo, p. 8).

PERU: Después de *darme una buena limpiada* de garganta, me puse a cantar (Corrales, p. 125); *pegó una reculada* rápida ... *le pego una arreada* de ganchos y uppers (p. 247).

ECUADOR: *Me pegué una magullada; Nos pegamos una atracada* (C).

COLOMBIA (ANTIOQUIA): *Péguese una asomaíta* a mi rancho (Carrasquilla, *Hace tiempos*, I, 216). Hija, *date una asomadita* por la despensa (Carrasquilla, *Novelas*, p. 19). *Échele una cargada al niño* [= tómelo en brazos] (Sundheim, p. 136); *Pegar una insultada* (p. 373). ¿Qué fué *la enamorada que te estabas dando* de una tal Nivia? (Buitrago, p. 53). *Me pegué una cortada* en un pie con el machete (Posada, p. 38). (BOGOTÁ): *dar una caminada, una almorzada, una volcada, una varada, una calentada* [= un disgusto], *una leída, una barrida, una quemada*, etc. (Flórez, p. 375).

VENEZUELA: —¿Ni de *echar una caminadita* conmigo? (Gallegos, *La trepadora*, p. 222). Tengo tantas ganas de *echar una conversada* larga contigo (Gallegos, *Doña Bárbara*, p. 306). En el hato de Antón Pérez/*hice la* primer *dormía* [= dormida] (Machado, p. 216). —Yo creo que no tengamos inconveniente en *darle una ayudaíta* (Briceño, p. 82). *Dió la callada* por respuesta (Gallegos, *Cantaclaro*, p. 72).

COSTA RICA: Después que *dió una* gran *almorzada*, se despidió y siguió su camino (Lyra, p. 11); Vengan mis muchachitos y *echen una bailadita* en esta tabla (p. 67). Ella encontraba ocasión de *dar una conversada* con él (Fabián Dobles, p. 66); esto de tener que *echar una* larga *conversada* (p. 75); —Sus güenas *platicaditas* que *se da* el hombre con ella (p. 238). *Ha echado sus lloradas* (Fallas, p. 113).

GUATEMALA: En *la acurrucada* que *me di*, se me rompieron los pantalones (Sandoval, I, 10); Una placera *dió una* gran *insultada* a mi patrona (I, 307); Sólo he podido *dar una leída* a la escritura (II, 17).

MEXICO: —Quédate tantito en mi caballo mientras *doy una registrada* en sus rincones (Inclán, I, 43); —¿Has visto ... qué *cambiada ha dado* ese pataratо? (II, 35). (NORTH ZONE): El juez se quedó allí ... *echando habladas* (Urquizo, p. 12); Buenas *hartadas me daba yo* con las sobras (p. 304); ¡qué *vacilada* [vacilar = divertirse, ir de juerga] *está usted dando!* ... Pásale pa dentro, mi alma, pa *darte una registradita* (p. 308). (NUEVO LEÓN): Aguardaban que Chabela *se diera una aliviadita* (García Roel, p. 55); —¿Por qué no le *dan una arreglada* [a la ermita]? (p. 97); *Dió* dos o tres *fumadas* largas (p. 98). (YUCATAN): *Me di la gran asoleada* en la playa; *una cambiada* de llanta, o de casa (Víctor Suárez, p. 69).

SANTO DOMINGO: ¡Qué *asustada se dió* cuando vino la noticia! (Patín Maceo, *Dom.*, p. 18); el sábado *dimos una gran bebida* (p. 23); *dimos una descansada* como de dos horas (p. 59); fué al tocador y *se dió una empolvada* (p. 68); ¡qué *engañada les dió* a sus amigos! (p. 70); *me di una escondida* de varios días (p. 73); etc.

Sometimes *tener* is used with the noun of action (cf. *tener una corazonada* 'to have a hunch'), or some other verb, or none at all, but the noun still has the force of a perfective aspect expressing completion and often rapidity:

ARGENTINA: Mientras ensillaba, tenía que cuidarme de *coceadas* (Güiraldes, *Don Segundo*, p. 264); venía a beber en el surco de agua nacido seguramente de las *baldeadas* [*baldear* 'to throw buckets (*balde* = standard *cubo*) of water'] (p. 268).

URUGUAY: Previa la consabida *escupida* para asegurar la puntería (Montiel, *Alma nuestra*, p. 185).

CHILE: So pretexto de ver *la amanecida* desde la cumbre (Acuña, *Huellas*, p. 66). *La colocada* de una inyección corriente es de tres pesos (C). En *una escuidá* [= descuidada] (Juan del Campo, p. 71).

COLOMBIA (ANTIOQUIA): Lo difícil que resulta *la conseguida* de tales guayabas agrias (Arango Villegas, p. 114). De una *leída* se aprendió los versos (Bueno, p. 27). Nuevo beso, nueva lágrima, nueva *enjugada* (Carrasquilla, *Hace tiempos*, II, 11). (SOUTH): Me voy ... a rogarle que venga a ayudarme a acabar la *arada* (Álvarez Garzón, p. 89). (BOGOTÁ): *la planchada, la lavada*, etc. (Flórez, p. 375).

EL SALVADOR: El chucho [se acercó] ... para olerle las rústicas sandalias. Eran unas *olidas* largas y profundas (Rivas Bonilla, p. 41). Bancos, sillas, taburetes ... estaban acondicionados en forma que no molestaran la *bailada* (González Montalvo, *Don Benja*). Meditó muy duro ... satisfecho de su *pensada*, dijo ... (Salarrué, *Cuentos*, p. 167).

COSTA RICA: La *amanecida* trajo alborozo de pájaros (Herrera García, p. 27). La *platicada* fué corta (Fabián Dobles, p. 66); con la *enviada* al hospital ... ya no pudo volver más a la finquilla (p. 71).

GUATEMALA: Las nueve es la hora de mi *acostada* (Sandoval, I, 8); según las *habladas* de la gente (I, 602).

MEXICO: Esperaba una eterna *regañada* porque no había hecho nada del encargo (Inclán, I, 282).

SANTO DOMINGO: Después de una *bailadita* la invité a tomar cerveza (Patín Maceo, *Dom.*, p. 20); después de la *bañada* se calmó el niño (p. 21).

THE DEFINITE ARTICLE

This is not the place to discuss the misuse of gender in the definite article. It may be worth noting, however, that Indians with little knowledge of Spanish occasionally use *la* with nouns of either gender, as in Paraguay (Morínigo, p. 51); or confuse the genders (*el mujer, la hombre*) as in Peru (Benvenutto, p. 135) and Mexico (Alcocer, p. 13; Gutiérrez Eskildsen, p. 60); but more often make the masculine article suffice for both genders, as especially in Guatemala (Bonilla Ruano, *Gramática*, III, 91), Chiloé, Chile (Cavada, p. 275), etc. Such confusion is largely due to the absence of grammatical gender in the substratum language or its noncorrespondence to Spanish gender.

The omission of the definite article with certain geographical names appears to be more widespread in the familiar speech of Spanish America than in Spain: *Estados Unidos* for *los Estados Unidos*, *Habana* for *la Habana*, *Argentina* for *la Argentina*, *Japón* for *el Japón*, etc. Curiously, the same speakers are likely to use the article when it is more generally omitted, as is the case with *(la) Rusia*, *(la) Francia*, *(la) Inglaterra*, etc. In very popular speech the article sometimes accompanies the name of a city with which it is never used in the standard language. In popular Chilean speech we find *el París* for *París:* "La otra hija acompañó a los patrones, ... en un viaje que hicieron para *el París*" (J. Modesto Castro, p. 96).

With a few nouns, like *casa, palacio*, etc., standard Spanish has from early times omitted the definite article, possibly because the "noun was originally felt as unique and in effect a proper noun" (Keniston, p. 237). The usage has in a few cases been extended in

American Spanish but, more generally, has fallen into disuse.

BOLIVIA: —No voy más a *colegio* (Ruiz, p. 29).

VENEZUELA: Eran las diez en *Catedral* (Rosenblat).

MEXICO: Las campanas de *Catedral* (Gómez Palacio, p. 113). (YUCATAN): Oí misa en *Catedral;* voy a *Tercera Orden;* lo compré frente a *Correos* (Víctor Suárez, p. 150).

CUBA: Anoche fuí a *Payret* [= al teatro Payret] (Padrón).

In Spanish America the article is general with *casa: voy a la casa* for standard *voy a casa* 'I am going home' (as also in Cuba).

ARGENTINA: ¿Te cres que las siet' y media son horas de venir a *la* casa? (*Fray Mocho*, p. 184).

URUGUAY: Púsose la escopeta al hombro y se fué a *la* casa (Acevedo Díaz, *Argentina*, p. 24).

VENEZUELA: La hermana y la novia volvieron a *la* casa (Julián Padrón, in *ACMV*, II, 117).

MEXICO: Pero lo peor fué cuando llegué a *la* casa (Galeana, p. 28).

In other locutions the article is found, occasionally also in Spain, where standardly it is omitted: *a la venta* for *de venta* 'on sale'; *a la pluma* for *a pluma* 'by pen'; *al propósito* for *a propósito* 'by the way'; *venir al pelo* for *venir a pelo* 'to come to the purpose'; *si alcaso* for *si acaso* 'if perchance'; *aldrede* for *adrede* 'purposely'; *al ojo* (Ecuador) for *a ojo* 'by guess'; *a los borbotones* (Argentina, rustic) for *a borbotones* 'violently, impetuously'; *a las malas* and *a las buenas* for *por malas* 'unwillingly, by foul means' and *por buenas* 'willingly, by fair means'; *a las patadas* for *a patadas; hacerse el cargo* for *hacerse cargo; a los gritos* for *a gritos;* etc. Much of this uncertainty of usage goes back to the older language (cf. Keniston, p. 637).

ARGENTINA: La pava ['teapot'] ... hirvía *a los borbotones* (Lynch, *Romance*, p. 433).

URUGUAY: —Mía ha de ser *a las güenas* o *las malas* (Reyles, *El gaucho*, p. 140); —El matungo, *a las patadas*, no me dejó cortar la estribera (p. 231).

PERU: A la voz de «aura» nos trenzamos *a los puñetes* (Corrales, p. 227); una mula ... se abrió [= huyó] *a los corcovos* (p. 243).

ECUADOR: No sé cuántos hay, los he comprado *al ojo* (Vázquez).

COLOMBIA: *A los brincos, a los gritos, a las patadas*, etc. (Flórez, p. 375). (ANTIOQUIA): Yo mise [= me hice] *de las nuevas* (Posada, p. 52).

VENEZUELA: Trataban de quitarle *a las malas* las chucherías que vendía (Briceño, p. 41). Me haré *el cargo* de que ha sido un sueño (Gallegos, *Doña Bárbara*, p. 295).

COSTA RICA: Si *al acaso* yo muero ayí (Echeverría, *Concherías*, p. 128).

GUATEMALA: Por si *alcaso* me busca ... digan que no estoy (Sandoval, II, 269).

MEXICO: Me ha apachurrado contra la pared *aldrede* (Gamboa, *Santa*, p. 137); ¿peleaban o te pegaron *a la mala?* (p. 163).

Inversely, the definite article is sometimes omitted, contrary to standard usage: *todo mundo* (Colombia, Venezuela, Mexican zone, etc.) for *todo el mundo* 'everybody,' perhaps by analogy with *todo hombre, toda persona*, and the like; *dichosos ojos* (Central America) for *dichosos los ojos* (*que lo ven*) 'delighted to see you'; *vez pasada* (River Plate area, Chile, etc.) 'the last time, once, sometime ago,' etc.; *primera vez* for *la primera vez; darle a uno gana* for *darle a uno la gana;* etc. Sundheim (p.456) reports for northern Colombia that some consider *todo mundo* "elegante" and "distinguido."

ARGENTINA: Se acordó, *vez pasada* en casa, que ... (Lynch, *Romance*, p. 56); no sé quién se acordó *la vez pasada*, en no sé qué reunión, de que ... (p. 57). —¿Todavía lo tenés trabajando al viejito? —Sí, *vez pasada* lo quise jubilar y pasarle una pensión pero no quiere (Llanderas and Malfatti, *Cuando las papas*, p. 13).

CHILE: Lo tenía en *vez pasada* (C).

BOLIVIA: No lo oyeron *segunda vez* (Arguedas, *Raza*, p. 115).

VENEZUELA: —Ya estoy hasta la coronilla de no hacer sino lo que *a ti te dé gana* (Gallegos, *Canaima*, p. 166). *Todo mundo* lo sabe (C).

COSTA RICA: *Todo mundo*, hasta las soldados ... volvieron a ver qué significaba aquel ruido (Lyra, p. 83); —*¡Dichosos ojos*, tío Conejo! (p. 12). —*¡Dichosos ojos*, hombre! (Fallas, p. 57).

EL SALVADOR: En lo general *todo mundo* está contento (Quijano Hernández, p. 7).

GUATEMALA: —*Dichosos ojos* que la ven; usté siempre tan hermosa (Quintana, p. 185). —Buenos días, señora comadre ... *dichosos ojos que la ven* (Guzmán Riore, p. 7).

MEXICO: *Todo mundo* estaba receloso (Ferretis, *Quijote*, p. 42). Para que fuera a contarlo a *todo mundo* (López y Fuentes, *¡Mi general!* p. 10). *Todo mundo* se pone en pie (García Roel, p. 221); *Todo mundo* listo para subirse a las carretas (p. 225); *Todo mundo* come cacahuates (p. 237), etc. Era *primera vez* que hablaba en público (Galeana, p. 115). *Todo mundo* está en pie (Urquizo, p. 47).

WITH PROPER NAMES

Standard Spanish normally does not use the definite article with names referring to persons: *Juan, Ana.* However, in familiar and rustic speech everywhere (including Spain), and occasionally in cultured speech (as in Chile), *la* may be heard before feminine names: *la María* 'Mary.' Of course *la* is ubiquitous even in cultured speech before a woman's family name, perhaps to identify the sex, especially with the names of well-known women: *la Pardo Bazán, la Xirgu, la Singerman, la Mistral,* etc. The use of *el* with masculine family names, on the other hand, implies contempt (*el López, el Hernández*) in present-day standard speech (Gili y Gaya, p. 217). With masculine given names, *el* is generally not used (*Juan, Carlos*), except in legal documents when the full name has already been mentioned: "careados Juan López y Pedro Pérez, dijo *el* Juan." Cervantes used the article with masculine names when repeating a name previously mentioned: at the beginning of "El curioso impertinente" (*Don Quijote,* I, 33) we read "*el* Anselmo" and "*el* Lotario." But today cultured speech in Spain restricts such usage to legal parlance. In certain rural areas, however, the article may be heard: *el Juan* (Aragon, Castile, etc.; cf. Borao, p. 95; *RFH,* III, 136, n. 1). Both these contemporary usages (standard legal *el Juan* and popular and rustic *el Juan*) probably go back to an older, more general practice. For sixteenth-century prose, however, Keniston (p. 225) reports that proper names "are not modified by the article" and that "the use of the article with the proper names of women is not widely developed." It must be remembered that these statements apply to the literary language. Colloquial speech undoubtedly employed the article frequently, as does Santa Teresa. There was a parallel practice with Arabic names (*el Cid*); with nouns in the vocative ("Digas tú, *el* marinero"); with nicknames, as today (*el Cojo, el Rubio*); before *don* in referring to a person just mentioned ("*el* don Diego" [Quevedo, p. 236]); and with its use in other languages: in Portuguese, as today (*o Manuel, o João*); in Italian, with famous names (*il Dante, il Carducci*).

The colonists must have carried the practice to America, where it has survived in the colloquial and rustic speech of many regions much more vigorously than in Spain. This appears to be especially true of regions in which the Indian population is greatest: Andean and Mexican zones. Its dominance in such areas may possibly reflect the rather widespread usage of preceding the name with some title or descriptive word which then requires the article: "ahí están *el taita* Mateas y *la mama* Melcha, *la china* Lucinda y *el caisha* Adán y también *el cholo* Lucas Vilca" (Ciro Alegría, *La serpiente*, p. 116). Often the article is used only before names of servants or peasants, thus indicating social class. Again it may carry emotion: affection, reproach, or scorn (as with family names).

ARGENTINA (NORTHWEST): Cuando *la* Eloísa terminó su cuento, *el* Ruperto se quedó en éxtasis (César Carrizo, p. 19; cf. Vidal, p. 384). (NORTHEAST): *el* Jacinto despertaba (Varela, p. 167).

CHILE: Don Audón dijo ... dueño del agua es *el* Audón. ... La pica [= el enojo] *del* Audón es por que *la* Mariana no se casó con él (Acevedo Hernández, *La canción rota*, p. 71).

BOLIVIA: *El* René (Díaz V., *La Rosita*, p. 80); lo ve entrar *al* René ... con *el* Gregorio ... *al* Gregorio (p. 82); *el* Gutiérrez (*El traje*, p. 94).

PERU: *el* Martín (Ciro Alegría, *La serpiente*, p. 13); *el* Arturo Romero, *el* Arturo (p. 17); *la* Lucinda mira *al* Arturo (p. 42).

ECUADOR: *La* Dolores sentía encontrar en *el* Francisco el abrigo de su tierra perdida (Icaza, *En las calles*, p. 130). *El* Julián (Icaza, *Cholos*, p. 39); *el* Adrián, *el* Juan (p. 138); *del* Chango (p. 218). Siguiendo *al* Carlos Quirós ... *el* Luis Mendieta (Gil G., *Yunga*, p. 61).

COLOMBIA: Decíle *al* Miguel (Rivera, p. 29); *el* Miguel y *el Jesús* (p. 34); *El* Jesús jué ... a yamá [= llamar] *al* Barrera [family name] (p. 37); *el* Tomás es indio (p. 227); Yo le di *al* Barrera (p. 249).

COSTA RICA: *El* Zacarías (Fallas, p. 47); *el* Juancito (p. 93).

EL SALVADOR: Los ojos *del* Ugenio (Ambrogi, p. 207).

GUATEMALA: ¿Qué le pasa *al* Pedro? (Barnoya, p. 25); *La* Josefa es casada ende hace un año con *el* Martín (p. 48).

MEXICO: —Porque no puedo ver al viejo ése ... *al* Demetrio (Azuela, *Los de abajo*, p. 84).

The use of the article before proper names of domestic animals varies considerably and, in any given region, does not necessarily follow the prevailing custom for the proper names of persons. For instance, in Ciro Alegría's *Los perros hambrientos* (Peruvian highlands), names of persons regularly take the article: *la Antuca* (p. 11), *el Pancho* (p. 13), *el Timoteo* (p. 15), *el Simón Robles* (p. 20), *la Vicenta* (p. 19), etc.; but names of dogs, in the majority of cases, do not:

Zambo, Güeso, Pellejo (p. 14), *Mañu* (p. 31), *el Mañu* (p. 32), etc.

In limited rural regions there seem to be stray survivals of the definite article with nouns or adjectival nouns in the vocative as in the older language ("Digas tú, *el* marinero"); or such third-person forms of address may be attempts to avoid the direct vocative.

PARAGUAY: —Buenos días, *el* señor (Fogelquist, p. 26).

COLOMBIA (ANTIOQUIA): —Vamos, ¿*el* joven? —dijo Romualdo (Osorio Lizarazo, *El hombre*, p. 36); —Pero éntrese, *el* negrito, para que lo vean (Carrasquilla, *Hace tiempos*, I, 34).

DÍA LUNES

The definite article is sometimes used and sometimes omitted before *día* with days of the week: (*el*) *día lunes*, etc. This construction is frequently found beside the standard *el lunes*. The usage may stem from the archaic and possibly dialectal *el día lunes* (<*dies lunae*) rather than from *el día del* (or *de*) *lunes*, found in the classics as an emphatic form of the commoner *el lunes* (Corominas, p. 97; Pietsch, *Homenaje a Menéndez Pidal*, I, 41). Cf. also (*el*) *día de mañana*.

ARGENTINA: *Día lunes*, por ser lunes, amaneció medio enfermo el artesano (Draghi Lucero, p. 242). —(Ésa) es más antipática que una cortada de pelo en *día sabado* (A. Vaccarezza, *Palomas y gavilanes*, p. 5). —¿Sabés que es pecao trabajar en *día domingo?* (Lynch, *Romance*, p. 68). No es *días domingo*, sino *días domingos* (Garrigós, p. 61). Cf. Vidal, p. 386.

CHILE: La audiencia de *los días martes* era característica (Prado, *Juez rural*, p. 121). "Hacer San Luis" significa no trabajar *el día lunes* (Román, III, 353). *Los días domingo* pasaba por la quinta (Durand, *Mercedes*, p. 31).

PERU: —Mal hecho que trabajes *día domingo;* Mañana que es *día domingo* descansarás (Benvenutto, p. 154).

COSTA RICA: —Yo iré *el día martes* (C).

MEXICO: *Día domingo:* sale sobrando el anteponer la palabra *día* a *domingo* y a cualquier otro de la semana (León, I, 34). *Día mañana* (C).

WITH THE INFINITIVE

The locution *hacerse del rogar* (less often *hacerse rogar*) for standard *hacerse de rogar* 'to like to be coaxed, let one's self be coaxed,' etc., while constantly censured as incorrect, is pretty general: Argentina

(Garzón, p. 238), Chile (Román, III, 98), Ecuador, Colombia (Cuervo, *Apuntaciones*, § 369), Central America (Salazar García, p. 149; Gagini, p. 156; Sandoval, I, 609), Mexico (Rubio, *Anarquía*, I, 294), Santo Domingo (*BDH*, V, 234), etc. In Chile *hacerse al rogar* is popular and rustic (cf. p. 339; also Cavada, p. 285). A few random examples will suffice.

CHILE: Se anda haciendo *'el* rogar (Acevedo H., *Cardo*, p. 34).

ECUADOR: No me he de hacer *del* rogar (Mera, p. 323).

COLOMBIA: —No se hagan *del* rogar (Buitrago, p. 88).

VENEZUELA: (ANDES) se hace *del* rogar; (LLANOS) se hace rogar, se hace *de* rogar (Rosenblat).

COSTA RICA: La otra no se hizo *del* rogar y se encaramó (Lyra, p. 95); —Sí, hombre, llevame, no te hagás *del* rogar (p. 103).

MEXICO: No iba a hacerme *del* rogar para aceptar la comisión (Gómez Palacio, p. 69). No se hicieron *del* rogar los otros (López y Fuentes, *Campamento*, p. 187). Y no se hacen *del* rogar, les dan gusto (García Roel, p. 215).

For examples of "*estar al* + inf." for standard "*estar para* or *a* + inf.," censured by Cuervo (*Apuntaciones*, § 361), see p. 344.

This leads us to the interesting use of *al* + the infinitive to express condition. In standard Spanish, *a* + *inf.* may replace a conditional clause with *si:* "*a saberlo* no hubiera ido" = "si lo hubiera sabido, no hubiera ido" 'if I had known it, I should not have gone.' In Old Spanish, however, this construction was very rare: Keniston (p. 532) reports that no example is found before 1550. Shortly after, nevertheless, the use was current and continued in vogue. Today it is rapidly being replaced by *de* + *inf.* both in Spain and in Spanish America.[3] Moreover, in some regions of America today the use of *al* + *inf.* rather than standard *a* + *inf.* is current in colloquial speech and occasionally finds its way into literary style. It is difficult to say at this time whether conditional *al* + *inf.* is an extension of the use of '*el* + *inf.* with substantive force' or whether it reflects some older dialectal or regional use. However, the evident decline of conditional *a* + *inf.* in favor of *de* + *inf.* makes plausible an assimilation of the rarer conditional *a* + *inf.* to the common temporal *al* + *inf.* More-

[3] Cf. C. E. Kany, "Conditions expressed by Spanish *de* plus infinitive," *Hispania*, XIX (1936), 211–16; "More about conditions expressed by Spanish *de* plus infinitive," *Hispania*, XXII (1939), 165–70.

over, the step from temporal to conditional is not difficult, especially in cases involving future time or negation (expressed or implied); for, in these, fact easily slips into the realm of hypothesis.

The use of conditional *al* + *inf.* has been censured for Bogotá by Cuervo (*Apuntaciones*, § 360); for Tabasco (Mexico) by Ramos Duarte (p. 28) and later by Santamaría (*El provincialismo*, I, 77), who is violent in his condemnation of a usage "propio de la gente indocta por completo ... a la cual no se puede corregir, porque antes hay que enseñarle la gramática y sus reglas más elementales." In Chile, Román (I, 38) is less vituperative when he remarks that a sentence like "*Al* tener yo dinero, me compraría una casa" is "mal dicho," since *al* + *inf.* expresses a temporal relation. Later Morales (I, 43) takes up the cudgels against conditional *al* + *inf.* since the use is so common not only among "la gente del pueblo sino entre otra gente que no se tiene por tal." This is an understatement for Chile, inasmuch as the expression is ubiquitous in conversation and examples may be found in their best-known writers, though in print *de* + *inf.* is preferred to *al* + *inf.* While some of the cases may seem explainable as temporal *al* + *inf.*, they are nevertheless to be considered conditional, since Chileans assert that they feel the relationship as conditional and not as temporal. (The use of the definite article *el* in *al*+*inf.* is closely related to another similar tendency in popular Chilean speech, namely, the use of the conjunctive phrase *del que* for *de que* or simply *que*, as discussed on p. 379.)

Argentina: *Al no obtener* respuesta, se procederá a suspenderle los envíos (Circular sent by the *Revista de educación y biblioteca* [La Plata], August 14, 1943).

Chile: Pensaba que *al venir* a solicitar su mano un príncipe y un jovencito estudiante, ella preferiría al jovencito (D'Halmar, *Lucero*, p. 49); *al provocar* un conflicto, ella ... sería de esas víctimas inevitables (p. 77). Créame que no le condeno; muy estúpida sería *al juzgar* lo que no entiendo (Edwards Bello, *Criollos*, p. 109). *Al haber sido* bufón de una corte, princesas habrían escuchado sus galanterías (Acuña, *Mingaco*, p. 186). *Al no tenerlo* la biblioteca, podría comprarlo aquí (C). Colo-Colo se dió cuenta de que, *al no intervenir*, la reunión corría el peligro de ser un fracaso (Fernando Alegría, *Lautaro*, p. 40).

Bolivia: Sirpa ve que destruiría su obra de transformación de aquella carne *al hacerla retroceder* a la existencia salvaje de los fortines (Céspedes, p. 69).

PERU: Saben que *al no dale,* la tierra se enojaría y ya no sería güena la cosecha (Ciro Alegría, *El mundo,* p. 49). *Al no vencer,* yo soy quien te va a poner ... bocado (López Albújar, *Matalaché,* p. 226); había estado segura de que José Manuel *al ser vencido* se habría matado (p. 230). Y perdóname, lector, que altere nombres y que no determine el lugar de la acción, pues *al hacerlo* te pondría los puntos sobre las íes (Ricardo Palma, in *ACP,* p. 24).

ECUADOR: Se hubiera quedado con el estómago a medio llenar *al no meterse* en los bolsillos abundante ración de tostado (Bustamante, p. 15). —*Al saber* esto, ti'ubiera asado unos cuicitos (Icaza, *En las calles,* p. 242). *Al ser* pulmonía no hubiera durado tres días (García Muñoz, *El médico,* p. 20). Comprendí que *al hacerlo,* ofendería a mi buena amiga Maruja (Salvador, *Noviembre,* p. 227). Su hijo ... se hubiese hecho señor General *al no haber nacido* idiota y baboso (Icaza, *Media vida,* p. 12); —*Al ser yo* ca no volviera nunca a esta porquería (p. 121). Tú has sido una mujer bonita, y *al no conocerme* te habrías casado mejor (Salvador, *Prometeo,* p. 109).

COLOMBIA: ... delante de mis ojos, que hubieran visto *al no haberse apagado* repentinamente la boquilla del gas; ... semejante expresión no hubiera salido de mis labios *al no saber* yo ... que mi cuenta estaba cancelada (Lozano).

VENEZUELA: Está claro que de no haber sido aquello una traición, tal cosa [una revolución] hubiera significado *al ser cierto* lo de nuestra incorporación (Briceño, p. 149).

PANAMA: Yerran, pues, los que dicen ... «*Al haberme saludado,* yo le habría correspondido» (Espino).

MEXICO: *Al no procederse* en esa forma, faltará el preciado flúido en el mes de marzo próximo (*El Universal de México,* December 25 (?), 1940). Mi razón era/que, *al no golver* por aquí,/quí sabe si no tuviera/ algo que sentir de mí (González Carrasco, p. 169). (TABASCO): *Al haber salido* temprano, lo habría encontrado (Santamaría, *El provincialismo,* I, 77).

Frequently *al* used with the infinitive has causal force rather than temporal or conditional:

ARGENTINA: Para ello comenzaremos por los instrumentos musicales, o sea aquellos materiales del canto que, *al ser* los más concretos y visibles, facilitan la solución del problema (Ricardo Rojas, *La literatura argentina*, I [2d ed.; Buenos Aires, 1924], p. 334).

PERU: El cura Silva se la da de generoso, *al no sacar* los cien soles que siempre cobró (Barrantes, p. 170).

CUBA: —¿Quiereh un trago? —Y *al ser* afirmativa la contestación, le llevó en un jarro un poco de aguardiente (Ciro Espinosa, p. 407). *Al no querer* nadie hablarnos, tampoco teníamos nada que decirnos entre nosotros (Montenegro, *Los héroes*, p. 135).

EL PASADO, LO PASADO

With *pasado*, *presente*, *porvenir*, and *futuro* we find the same hesitancy as in Spain between *el* (the word having the force of a noun) and *lo* (the word having the force of an adjective). While purists generally inveigh against the use of *el* with these words, calling it a Gallicism, such usage has gained much ground not only in colloquial speech but also in literature. Though *lo* was preferred by the Golden Age writers, it is now the rarer and therefore the more elegant in American Spanish. While there is thus a difference in usage, the difference in meaning is not always so clear as Cortejón (p. 36) implies when he remarks: "¿Quién sino la claridad ha enseñado no ser iguales *lo porvenir me tiene inquieto* y *el porvenir me tiene inquieto?*" Some grammarians (Barreto, I, 83–86; Fidel Suárez, I, 309) have advocated the acceptance of *el* in these expressions on the basis of its use by approved writers; others still insist on the older *lo* (Vázquez, p. 317; Fentanes, *Espulgos*, p. 22, etc.). Cf. *por el ordinario, por lo ordinario; el imposible, lo imposible*, etc.

THE INDEFINITE ARTICLE

The indefinite article offers fewer divergencies from the standard than does the definite article. However, we frequently find the singular *un(a)*, as occasionally in Spain, with the meaning of 'about, approximately,' by analogy with the standard plural *unos* (*-as*) of similar meaning.

CHILE: Hizo desfilar *una* media docena de personajes (Alberto Romero, *Perucho González*, p. 117).

COSTA RICA: —Que dice mamá si le puede prestar *una* media libra de frijoles (Fallas, p. 171); le servía *un* medio vaso de ron (p. 110).

MEXICO: Debió permanecer *una* media hora en ese estado (Rubín, p. 54).

We find interesting cases of superfluous *un* in the popular Chilean expressions *de un todo* and *de un cuanto hay*. *De un todo* means *de todo, todo, de cuanto se necesita; un cuanto hay* means *todo*. These expressions probably stem from peninsular usage. At least Borao (p. 95) mentions *de un todo* for Aragon: "tenían *de un todo* en casa;" and the Academy dictionary registers the expression *en un todo* as meaning *absoluta y generalmente*. Elsewhere we find *de un todo* in the sense of 'completely,' that is, with the meaning of standard *en un todo*: "—Es un crimen que dejemos sin esquilar, exponiéndolo a que se arruine *de un todo*, un borregaje tan lindo!" (Viana, *Tardes*, p. 62 [Uruguay]). "—Si querés tanto el río, olvidá *de un todo* a esa mujer" (Buitrago, p. 95 [Colombia]).

CHILE: Tengo *de un todo;* El marido provee *de un todo* la casa (Román, V, 486); Un vendedor dice que tiene *de un cuanto hay* en el género o negocio que trata; una dueña de casa, abastecida de todo, dice también que tiene *de un cuanto hay* (I, 471). Vivimos juntos, yo le doy *de un todo* (Juan Modesto Castro, p. 154); me proponía ... que no trabajaría, que tendría *de un todo* (p. 167). —Y na que haga, obligación que tenís de darme *de un too* que pa eso soy [= sois] mi marío (Malbrán, *En semana santa*). Otros dos días pasamos allí servíos *de un todo:* sus ricas comías, sus buenos tragos de mosto y gozando como recién casaos (Guzmán Maturana, p. 203). —Su mercé verá; a mi señora antes yo le manijaba *de un too*, y al presente apenas anda cubría (Durand, *Tierra*, p. 62).

II

ADJECTIVES

APOCOPATION

THE adjectives *primero*, *tercero*, and *postrero* (together with *bueno*, *malo*, *uno*, *alguno*, and *ninguno*) standardly drop their final *-o* when preceding a masculine singular noun (*el primer libro*) but do not drop the *-a* of the feminine singular (*la primera página*), except occasionally in literature. In early Spanish the apocopated forms were unknown before feminine nouns, but they were used frequently in the Golden Age, when practice fluctuated. Both forms were then used in both genders: *primer rey* and *primero rey*, *primer* *vez* and *primera vez.*[1] For the sixteenth century, Keniston (p. 301) remarks that the apocopated forms are "occasionally found before feminine nouns," and his frequency count is exceedingly small, being only [1–1] for feminine *primer* as against [16–38] for the full form, *primera.* However, a perusal of seventeenth-century literature appears to show a much higher frequency: *la primer vez, la primer fuente, la primer cosa* (Calderón, *Casa con dos puertas,* I); *la primer luz, la primer enamorada* (Rojas, *Del rey abajo ninguno,* I, II), etc. In any case, the apocopated feminine forms, though rare in standard speech today, are still found in rural sections of Spain: "—Y ¿pa qué más? No será la *primer* vez" (Pereda, *Obras,* XV, 358); "la *primer* cepillada" (Aurelio Espinosa, *Cuentos,* I, 95 [Zaragoza]); "la *primer* misa" (I, 131 [Avila]); "la *primer* mordida" (III, 441 [Valladolid]). But the apocopated feminine is certainly much commoner in American Spanish than in Spain and is used both in speech and in literature.

Argentina: —¿Qué viento te trae? —fué su *primer* pregunta (Güiraldes, *Don Segundo,* p. 36); en la *primer* parada (p. 74); la *primer* noche (p. 222); nuestra *tercer* jornada (p. 290); etc. Inició su *primer* campaña seguido de cuatro voluntarios (Yamandú Rodríguez, *Cimarrones,* p. 13); aquella *primer* "mano" (p. 30); la *primer* semana (p. 128); etc. Se pone a festejar a la *primer* mujer que le guste (Larreta, *Zogoibi,* p. 16). En Hamburgo tuvo la *primer* tribulación (Cuti Pereira, p. 89).

Uruguay: Su *primer* visita (Montiel, *La raza,* p. 188). La *postrer* tierna mirada (Montiel, *Cuentos,* p. 82). Es la *primer* vez que oigo su voz (Bellán, p. 89; also p. 176).

Chile: Pasó ... al camarín rojo, donde se refugiara Deusto en su *primer* visita (D'Halmar, *Pasión,* p. 210). Una *postrer* mirada (Lillo, p. 43).

Peru: En la *primer* ocasión (Gamarra, *Algo del Perú,* p. 164).

Colombia: Tomó la *primer* pareja que halló al entrar (Arias Trujillo, p. 56).

Venezuela: Dominando la *postrer* meseta de las serranías (Pocaterra, p. 201). —¿Bailamos esta *primer* vuelta, mi blanca? (Briceño, p. 119).

Costa Rica: No es *primer* bes que le hablo a un muerto (Agüero, p. 67). ¡No aguantó la *tercer* cucharada! (Echeverría, p. 125).

[1] See Keniston, p. 303; also M. A. Zeitlin, "La apócope en la -*a* final átona en español," *Hispanic Review,* VII (1939), 244.

El Salvador: La *primer* coquetería de nuestra Naturaleza (Miranda Ruano, p. 72). La *postrer* gota del café (Ambrogi, p. 32).

Mexico: —Cuéntame tu *primer* pelea (Benítez, p. 97); mi *primer* cobranza (p. 142). Volvería, empero, Payno a su *primer* manera (González Peña, *Historia de la lit. mexicana* [2d ed., 1940], p. 242). —Yo tuve a mi *primer* muchachita a los dieciséis años (García Roel, p. 257).

Cuba: Una *tercer* mañana (Loveira, p. 38). Recordaba cuando construyeron la *primer* bomba (Levi Marrero, in *CC*, p. 184).

In correct standard Spanish, *ciento* 'a hundred' is apocopated to *cien* only when preceding the noun it modifies: *cien hombres.* Both in Spain and in America, however, *cien* is today used in speech without a noun (*tengo cien*), although this form was called "un barbarismo" by Cuervo (§ 401), "viciosa" and "incorrecta" by Bello (Bello-Cuervo, § 193). Though not unknown even in writers of note (Pardo Bazán, Pereda, etc.), *cien* is much commoner today in America than in Spain. For instance, while Madrid says *cien por ciento* more frequently than *ciento por ciento,* Buenos Aires prefers *cien por cien* (*BDH*, IV, 28, n. 4), as do most other American cities. In fact, *ciento* is apparently so rare in some regions that it is readily misunderstood. In Mexico City I told a taxidriver to take me to Calle Monterrey 100, which I pronounced *ciento,* according to approved usage. He looked perplexed. "*¿Ciento?*" he queried. "Sí, *ciento,*" I repeated. "O será *cien,* o será *ciento uno* o *ciento dos,*" he insisted. For him there was no such number as *ciento* alone (cf. also *BDH*, II, 131).

Gagini (p. 91) remarks that no Costa Rican would say "Los concurrentes no llegaban a *ciento*" or "Tengo *ciento* o más pesos," but would use *cien* in all such cases. But certainly the reason for using *cien* instead of *ciento* can hardly be that adduced by Gagini: "sin duda para evitar el equívoco que resultaría con el verbo *siento,* a causa de la pronunciación americana de la *c.*" (!)

Argentina: —¿Por qué no vamos [= apostamos] *cien?* (Güiraldes, *Don Segundo,* p. 236); —Le doy desquite de los *cien* (p. 240).

Paraguay: *ciento por ciento* (preferred), *cien por ciento* (Morínigo).

Chile: De éstos hay que darte a ti *cien* (Malbrán, *El marido,* p. 8).

Colombia: Nada me ganaría con que me abonaran *cien* (Arango Villegas, p. 172).

GUATEMALA: En muchos negocios he ganado *cien* por *cien* y en otros he perdido el veinte por *cien* (Sandoval, I, 180).

MEXICO: Y tras él aparecieron otros, y otros diez, y otros *cien* (Azuela, *Los de abajo*, p. 8). Iban más de *cien* (Robles Castillo, p. 203). Se oye todavía *ciento por ciento* (*BDH*, IV, 28).

CUBA: Soy cubano *cien por cien* (C).

ADJECTIVES USED AS ADVERBS

It is well known that Spanish adjectives are frequently used as adverbs. Some of them (*alto, mucho*, etc.) may be considered as derived from the neuter of Latin adjectives and are definitely adverbs. Others are used as appositives, agreeing with a noun and having both adjective and adverbial force: *vivieron felices.*

In the older language the practice appears to be fairly common: "quiero hablar contigo más *largo*" (*Celestina*, II); "... habla *cortés*" (XI). Cuervo (§ 472) cites examples of *fácil* from Lope and Tirso.

By analogy with such real adverbs as *alto, mucho, bajo, recio, quedo, claro, cierto*, and *infinito*, etc., American Spanish has colloquially transformed other adjectives into adverbs, which, in many cases at least, would be considered incorrect in peninsular standard Spanish, though some of them may be heard there in popular speech. The commonest of these are *bonito* or *lindo* for *bien; rápido* for *rápidamente; suave* for *suavemente; ligero* for *ligeramente; fácil* for *fácilmente;* and many others which are to be considered local (*feo* for *mal, chulo* for *bien, galán* for *bien*, etc.). In colloquial American English the inflectional distinction between adverb and adjective has similarly broken down in such expressions as 'to talk *big*, run *slow*, sleep *good*, sing *pretty*,' etc.

ARGENTINA: [El maíz] germina *fácil* y en poco tiempo (Inchauspe, *Voces*, p. 90). Esperamos ... la noche ... como una cosa grande y mansa en la que nos íbamos a ir *suavecito* (Güiraldes, *Don Segundo*, p. 293). ¡Cha que se las ice *lindo* [= bien]! (Lynch, *Romance*, p. 278). Jineteó *lindo* (González Arrili, p. 115). Aixa ... púsose a girar *ligero*, muy *ligero* (Larreta, *La gloria*, p. 118). Un picao, de vigüela, medio poeta, que cantaba *fierísimo* [= feísimo] (*Fray Mocho*, p. 22). Equivocarse *feo* = equivocarse malamente, de cabo a rabo (Saubidet, p. 163). ¡Que le vaya *bonito* (o *lindo*)! (Morínigo).

URUGUAY: Toca *lindo* (Montiel, *Cuentos*, p. 29). El barberito cantaba también, y *lindo* (Montiel, *Luz mala*, p. 81). —Soñé *fiero* [= feo], me asusté (Montiel, *Alma nuestra*, p. 34).

Chile: —Que le vaya *bonito* [= bien] (Romanángel, p. 11). Voi a moverme *ligerito* (Barros Grez, I, 272). Mis veinte años ... no fueron *suficiente* fuertes para vencer las zozobras que me asaltaban (Durand, *Mi amigo*, p. 7).

Peru: Almorzar *fuerte* y *feo* (Gamarra, *Algo del Perú*, p. 85). —Pero toca muy *bonito* (Ciro Alegría, *El mundo*, p. 95); Unos acostumbran arreglar las cosas *bonito* (p. 235). ¡Ah, tan *lindo* que toca! (López Albújar, *Matalaché*, p. 144). (Zona del Marañón): —*Único* las peñas le respondía [*sic*] (Ciro Alegría, *La serpiente*, p. 21); Hay que maniobrar *rápido* (p. 89); *Único* él (p. 140).

Ecuador (Coast): Los brazos se alargaban y encogían *rápido* (Gil Gilbert, *Nuestro pan*, p. 78); apretaron *fuerte* y *largo* (p. 111); los hombres iban *lento* (p. 173). Y sollozaba tan *suave* que no molestaba su llanto (Gil Gilbert, *Yunga*, p. 86). Regresó María del Socorro. ... Iba *lento*, callada, con el silencio candoroso de siempre (Pareja, *El muelle*, p. 37). (Highlands): —Sírvete *breve* [= prontamente] este rico cognac (Icaza, *En las calles*, p. 121); —¿Por qué no saliste *breve?* (p. 128). Prendé [= prended] *breve* el alumbrado y *subí* [= subid] no más el chocolate (Icaza, *Cholos*, p. 8). —Claro pes, si canto *lindo* (García Muñoz, *Estampas*, p. 317). —¡Qué *lindo* habla usted, doctor! (Salvador, *Noviembre*, p. 175). Así hubiera podido hablar *claro* y *terminante* (Mata, *Sanagüín*, p. 94).

Colombia (Antioquia): Conversando tan *sabroso* (Carrasquilla, *Hace tiempos*, I, 45); ¡Qué *bonito* cose! (I, 188); a nosotras nos criaron tan *distinto* (II, 28); canta muy *bonito* (II, 68); cantaba muy *lindo* (II, 109); habla muy *corto* y muy *lindo* (III, 114); Si tiene cola se la jalamos bien *sabroso* (III, 149); oí y verés qué tan *feo* cantan los gallos criollos ... cantan muy *maluco* (III, 197). Si me ofrece mieles, las degusto *largo* (Arango Villegas, p. xi); Olía *maluco* (p. 24); diga *ligero*, ¿qué es? (p. 64); las medias sí nos las ponemos muy *fácil* (p. 188).

Venezuela: El que quiera beber *sabroso*, que le haga una visita a don Agustín (Gallegos, *La trepadora*, p. 17); Ya verá como aquí se alienta *ligero* (p. 37); tú lo cantas muy *sabroso* (p. 199). Yo no sé hablá *fino* (Pocaterra, p. 40). Respira *hondo* (Fabbiani Ruiz, p. 61). El líquido meloso pasa *suave* por la garganta (Díaz-Solís, p. 13); las palabras eran otras y sonaban *raro* (p. 25); suspirar *hondo* (p. 42).

Costa Rica (Rural): Tan *galán* [= bien] que muele esa máquina (Gagini, p. 144). Pensó que le podía ir *feo* (Lyra, p. 159). Había llovido *apretado* y *largo* (Fabián Dobles, in *CLC*, p. 113).

El Salvador: Seguía pringando [= lloviznando] *cernido* (Salarrué,

Cuentos, p. 58); Cuando vos naciste, taba lloviendo *tieso* [= fuertemente] (p. 82); sudaban *tieso* (p. 102); venía lloviendo *tieso* (p. 122). Nadie afirmaba *categórico* (Ambrogi, p. 83). *Fácil* lees tú (Salazar García, p. 134). Lucero corrió ... lo más *rápido, veloz* que pudo ... se lanzó de nuevo a correr tan *rápido*, tan *velozmente* como podía (Ramírez, p. 11).

GUATEMALA: *Fácil* se va hoy de la capital a Flores (Sandoval, I, 549); Ya iba yo tan *bonito* (I, 710); Esta comida ya huele *feo* (II, 169); *Perenne*, recibo cartas de mi hijo (II, 228). Íbamos ya tan *bonito* (Wyld Ospina, *La gringa*, p. 67). —¿Cómo han estado ustedes por acá? ... Tan *bonito* (Salomé Gil, *Cuadros*, p. 381).

MEXICO: La comida sabe *fea* [= mal], esa señora canta *bonito* [= bien], pinta *rechulo* [= muy bien], corre *macizo* [= aprisa], huele *feo* [= mal], etc. (A. Gutiérrez, p. 213, n. 1). Sentí tan *feo* que les volví la espalda (Azuela, *Las moscas*, p. 16). Si vieras qué *feo* siento que tú me digas eso (Azuela, *Los de abajo*, p. 84). ¡Me duele *feo!* ¡qué *feo* sabe! (Sánchez Somoano, p. 35). Se encuentra con un amigo para charlar *largo* y *sabroso* (López y Fuentes, *¡Mi general!* p. 37). ¡Qué *bonito* solloza! (Ferretis, *Quijote*, p. 267). Olía muy *bonito* (Anda, *Los bragados*, p. 102). Se la pasa *viejo* [= fácilmente] ... me lo llevo *viejo* (Rubio, *Refranes*, I, 282). —Sí ... vale más—dijo *sencillo* (García Roel, p. 38); platican *sabroso* (p. 170); Ni siquiera lograba disimular *discreto*. No, ya pensé *distinto* (Valle-Arizpe, p. 397).

CUBA: Hablaba tan *bonito* (Luis Felipe Rodríguez, p. 116). Pararse *bonito* [= asumir una actitud] (Padrón).

SANTO DOMINGO: ¡Qué *bonito* canta! (Requena, *Camino*, p. 14).

MEDIO

We find a general tendency to make the adverb *medio* (meaning *no del todo, no enteramente, casi enteramente*) 'not altogether, half, somewhat, rather, quite,' agree like an adjective by attraction with the word it modifies, whether this be an adjective, a past participle, or a noun used adjectivally: *media muerta* for *medio muerta, medios dormidos* for *medio dormidos.*

Bello carefully distinguishes between *medio* used as an adverb (*medio dormido, medio despierta*, § 371 n.) and *medio* used as a prefix ("puro afijo" or "partícula prepositiva": *la sirena era ... medio pez y medio mujer, se medio corrió el capellán*). In the latter usage, *medio* would naturally be invariable, equivalent to such adverbial prefixes as invariable *semi* and *cuasi*. Classical writers, nevertheless, occasionally made *medio* agree adjectivally with the noun modified (*media parienta*), though generally they used the invariable form (*medio parientas*). However, instead of making the somewhat artificial distinction between adverbial *medio* and prefix *medio*, it would seem as satisfactory, and simpler, to consider both as adverbs. The fact that the prefix form accompanies nouns is no objection, since such nouns may clearly be felt as adjectives. That the adjectival agreement of adverbial *medio* is ubiquitously common in popular speech cannot be denied. Its frequent appearance in modern Spanish-American realistic literature is noteworthy. It is not confined to any one country, as grammarians may often lead us to suppose (cf. Bello-Cuervo, § 371 n.), but is general throughout Spanish America, as well as in the popular speech of Spain ("Se levantó del suelo *media muerta*," Espinosa, *Cuentos*, III, 451 [Santander]). It is an old practice (Meyer-Lübke, § 130; Corominas, p. 94).

What has never been pointed out, as far as I know, is that *medio* when modifying an adverb or adverbial locution is sometimes made to agree adjectivally with the subject involved: *ella está media mal* for *ella está medio mal*. This occurs notably in rural Argentina.

Argentina (Rural): La señora repitió *media enojada* (Lynch, *Romance*, p. 115); me la halló a la señora *media mal* de salú (p. 247); —¡Y qué iba a hacer!—le retrucó la señora *media con rabea* (p. 248); los otros se quedaban *medios apampaos* de sorpresa (p. 253); La pobre e doña Cruz estaba *media mal* (p. 270); Y tan clarita le salió la voz a doña Cruz, dende la cama ande estaba estirada dandolé la espalda y *media boca abajo* (p. 370); Ella ... le contestó *media raindosé* (p. 426). Se rió contenta ... con los ojos *medios llorosos* (Payró, p. 26).

Uruguay: Están *medios flacos* (Trías du Pre, p. 12).

Paraguay: *Media enojada, medios dormidos* (Morínigo).

Chile: Los caballeros están *medios recelosos* (Poblete, in *LCC*, p. 274). Se casó con un tipo que canta y toca la guitarra, de estos *medios filóricos* (Juan Modesto Castro, p. 232). Los ñatos staban *medios emparafinaos* [= bebidos] (Rojas Gallardo, *Aventuras, 2a serie*, p. 37).

Peru: Estos cholos te están resultando *medios haraganes* (Benvenutto, p. 153). Yo creo que andas *media olvidada* del novio (López Albújar, *Matalaché*, p. 160).

Ecuador (Azuay): Tomaron hacia *media izquierda* para encaminarse hacia Patul (Mata, *Sanagüín*, p. 119). Mi mujer y mi'ja ... se pusieron *medias locas* (Icaza, *Media vida*, p. 152); —Asimismo salen todos ... *medios moraditos* (p. 181).

Guatemala: Manecían muertos, o *medios muertos* (Quintana, p. 156). Olimpia dice que está *media muerta* de cansada (Sandoval, II, 73); estuvieron *medias muertas* del susto (p. 74); los templos quedaron *medios arruinados* (p. 75).

Mexico: Van tres o cuatro muchachas *medias jinetes* en caballos regulares (Inclán, I, 322). Ella está *media mala*, ellas eran *medias molestas* ... ellos eran *medios hermanos*, ella llegó *media desilusionada* (A. Gutiérrez, p. 219).

Santo Domingo: Están *medias locas* (Henríquez Ureña, in *BDH*, V, 225).

Puerto Rico: —Está *media enferma* (Méndez Ballester, p. 85).

MERO, PURO

Modern visitors to Mexico, from Sánchez Somoano to J. B. Trend (*Mexico: a new Spain with old friends* [1940]), are struck by an unusual use of the adjectives *mero* and *puro*, a use not frequently found in correct peninsular Spanish. They believe such usage to be peculiarly Mexican. It is so only to a limited extent. Peculiarities of the so-called Mexican usage are found in varying degrees elsewhere: throughout Central America (Guatemala, El Salvador, Honduras, Nicaragua, Costa Rica), in Colombia, Venezuela, and Peru. This is particularly true of *mero*.

In standard Spanish *mero* means *puro* 'mere, sheer, pure, simple': *es la mera verdad.*

In Mexico *mero* (*merito*) as an adjective may mean:

1. *Mismo* 'itself, very,' etc. ¡Ése *mero* era el amo don Inacio! (Azuela, *Mala yerba*, p. 32). En la *mera* esquina (Ramos Duarte, p. 354). Está en la *merita* esquina (Sánchez Somoano, p. 85). —¿Quién es el jefe de las tropas acantonadas en este lugar? —¡Yo *mero!* (López y Fuentes, *Campamento*, p. 80). ¿Y por qué no le metiste el plomo mejor en la *mera* chapa ['right in the head']? (Azuela, *Los de abajo*, p. 33); A mí *mero* me lo dijo (p. 195).

2. *Principal* or *verdadero* 'main, real': Pedro es el *mero* malo. ... En la compañía X. Fulano es el *mero* amo. ... Después de esto viene lo *mero* bueno (Rubio, *Anarquía*, II, 39). —Se me olvidaba lo *mero* güeno (Madero, *Los alzados*, II, 6). El güero Margarito es mi *mero* amor (Azuela, *Los de abajo*, p. 189). Don Adolfo es de mis *meros* gallos: antes mueren en la raya que correr (Azuela, *Avanzada*, p. 278). Mañana es el *mero* día ['the big day'] (C). ¡Y todavía falta lo *mero* bueno! (Magdaleno, p. 120).

In referring to persons *el mero mero* is often used:

Después que desprendió la botella de sus labios la estrelló contra el suelo con ademán altanero. —Y güeno, ¿pos qué más has de servir, si ya bebieron en ti dos hombres de *los meros meros?* (Fernando Robles, p. 158). *El mero mero* di un regimiento/ ... llegó a su casa (García Jiménez, p. 121). (TABASCO): Ése es *el mero mero* (*Inv. ling.*, I, 297).

3. *Preciso, exacto:* A las *meras* once se acercaba el cuetero y le prendía fuego (Gómez Palacio, p. 108). Pedro llegó a la *mera* hora (Rubio, *Anarquía*, II, 39).

In Mexico *mero* (*merito*) as an adverb may mean:

4. *Mismo* 'right': *ya mero* = *ahora mismo, luego, en seguida* 'right now, very soon,' etc. —¿Cuándo nos casamos? —*Ya mero* (Galeana, p. 40). (NUEVO LEÓN): —Pepe vive en el jacal de *mero* enfrente (García Roel, p. 37); pasa por *merito* enfrente de la ermita (p. 96); *merito* debajo de la cabecera (p. 126). Ansina *mero* [= así mismo] hice yo (Fernando Robles, p. 135). ¿Dónde *mero* ['just where'] está el hospital? (Magdaleno, p. 255).

5. *Casi, por poco:* (*ya*) *mero* 'almost.' *Mero* [= casi] me deja el tren (Fentanes, *Tesoro*, p. 140). *Ya mero* [= por poco] me caigo (Ramos Duarte, p. 354). Pasaron dos años y *ya merito* se juntaba el dinero (Galeana, p. 93). *Mero* me caía (*Inv. ling.*, I, 297).

6. *Muy*, but this meaning is restricted to some southern regions, particularly Tabasco: Este niño es *mero* vivo. Pa el año que entra ya se casó este bruto, *mero* jovencito (Gutiérrez Eskildsen, p. 69).

The uses of *mero* (*merito*) mentioned above in 1, 4, and 5, that is, with the meaning of *mismo* as both adjective and adverb and of *casi* or *por poco*, are found not only in Mexico but also in most of Central America, in the rustic speech of Peru, Colombia, and possibly elsewhere.

PERU (CALEMAR–ZONA DEL MARAÑÓN): Sacó los cheques y se pusua secalos al *mero* solcito, dándoles viento con el sombrero (Ciro Alegría, *La serpiente*, p. 21); vive dentre las *meras* peñas (p. 22); jué a dar al *mero* pie e La Repisa (p. 24); [darse] cuenta con los *meros* ojos diuno (p. 141); Los cinco tiros en la *mera* nuca (p. 160).

COLOMBIA: Esto sí es muy peligroso, señora. Arriesga uno la *mera* hilacha [= la misma vida] (Carrasquilla, *Hace tiempos*, I, 70).

HONDURAS: —¡*Merito* ayer no más al mediodía que yo venía del rastrojo! (Martínez Galindo, p. 147).

El Salvador: *Ya merito* se cae (Salarrué, *Cuentos*, p. 176).

Guatemala: —No tenga pena, que *ya mero* va a estar (Quezada Silva, in *CLC*, p. 184). —El fuego arderá *ya merito* (Santa Cruz, in *CLC*, p. 235). Espérame tantito que *ya merito* vuelvo (Sandoval, II, 613).

The use of *mero* mentioned above in (2) with the meaning of *verdadero* is found not only in Mexico but also in Guatemala, where it is sometimes erroneously believed a local provincialism (Bonilla Ruano, III, 329: "provincialismo nuestro ... es *mero*"):

—Este diablo no era el *mero* sino una mujer llamada Lola (Quintana, p. 152). De monárquica me dicen/que ya no te queda nada,/ conduciéndote en un todo/por la *mera* democracia (Bonilla Ruano, III, 329).

The use of *mero* meaning *muy*, mentioned above in (6) as of restricted use in Mexico, is much commoner in the popular speech of Central America (especially Guatemala and El Salvador). While adverbial in function, it agrees like an adjective with the word modified. Sandoval (II, 81) calls this *mero* an adverb, and, as such, he makes it invariable in his examples: *mero orgullosa*, *mero mujer*, *mero hombres*, *mero bien*, etc. The following examples, however, prove that in popular speech *mero* often agrees in number and gender with the word modified.

El Salvador: —Don Rafáil es *mero nesio* (Ambrogi, p. 9); andan *meros tristones* los otros dos (p. 32); [la chicha] está *mera güena* (p. 100). Se conocía que pasaba hambres, pero aquí se reponía pronto, y pasaba *mero contento* (Mechín, *La muerte*, p. 106); Entre otras cosas me cuenta ruborosa que mis tíos eran «muy atrevidos.» Yo me escandalizo y le declaro que al contrario, son «*mero tímido*» [*sic*] (p. 41). La fragancia de la mañana venía *mera cargada* (Salarrué, *Cuentos*, p. 35).

Guatemala: —Viera un chivito cruzado *mero chulo* (Quintana, p. 19); dió un grito *mero feyo* (p. 214); tantas cosas *meras estrañas* que he visto (p. 216); una india *mera bonita* (p. 216).

And, finally, we discover still another meaning of *mero* (as an adjective), apparently restricted to rustic speech in Colombia and Venezuela: *solo* (adjective) and *sólo* or *solamente* 'only.'

Colombia: Cuélome por nuestra casa y la examino. Es *un mero* cuarto bastante grande (Carrasquilla, *Hace tiempos*, I, 63); Tan solamente truje seis platillos y *meras tres* tazas (I, 79); Pero tendrán otros niños. ... *Éste mero* (I, 157); —¿Y tienen mucha familia ... ? —*Cuatro meros* hijos (I, 323); *Una mera* vez (II, 100). No hubo sino un muerto y *diez meros* heridos (Arias Trujillo, p. 58).

Venezuela: ¿Cuántas cochas ['batches of raw sugar'] han sacado? —*Una mera* (Picón-Febres, p. 250).

For New Mexican *meramente* used as a verb, see p. 234.

The adjective *puro*, preceding its noun and meaning 'sheer,' was common in the older language: "deshaciéndose a *puras* uñadas" (Quevedo, *Buscón*, p. 202); "conservando la sangre a *pura* carne y pan" (p. 210); "con la cara rebozada a *puros* mojicones" (p. 218); "A *puro* correr, llegó a la hora" (Correas, p. 535). It is still found in modern regional Spain and to a limited degree in standard Spanish: "—Un *puro* peñasco ... *pura* música sin substancia (Pereda, *Obras*, XI, 186, 195); "le habían obligado a no ejercerla [su facultad] de *puro* no llamarle alma viviente" (Narciso Campillo, *Una docena de cuentos* [1878], p. 56); "de *puro* hacer el Quijote saldrá del Gobierno como Sancho Panza!" (Benavente, *La gobernadora* [1901], II, 1). In correct peninsular usage today it is considerably less frequent than it is in certain regions of America. In Mexico, for instance, its excessive use in colloquial speech in the sense of 'only' never fails to attract the amused attention of Spanish newcomers. One hears: "aquí se sirve la *pura* comida" meaning "solamente la comida"; that is, 'only dinner (and not supper or breakfast) is served here.'

In Chile, Román (IV, 507) speaks of "nuestra acepción" (that is, Chilean use) of *puro:* "Quien no tiene dineros tiene los *puros* bolsillos, la *pura* cartera, el *puro* portamonedas, porque todos ellos están vacíos de monedas." Guzmán Maturana in his popular Chilean novel, *Don Pancho Garuya*, reinforces the idea of *solamente* by adding *no más:* "trabajando enterraos en el barro ... en *puritos* cueros *no más*" (p. 256); "son *puros* planes *no más*" (p. 301); etc.

However, the use of *puro* in the sense of *solamente* is neither exclusively Mexican nor exclusively Chilean but is, to a lesser degree, rather general.

Argentina: Todo se les volvía a los dos mozos *puro* recortarle los vasos a los caballos preferidos; *puro* emparejarles el tuse; o *puro* ensebarse las botas (Lynch, *Romance*, p. 72); ¿De ánde mujeres? ¡Si estábamos *puros* varones! (p. 118).

URUGUAY: Lo que te prediqué fué *pura* paparrucha (Reyles, *El terruño*, p. 144).

CHILE: Con el *puro* té y el pan se mantenía (Juan Modesto Castro, p. 229). Pensamos en *puro* comer (C).

BOLIVIA: Era *pura* flor el guindal (Arguedas, *Vida criolla*, p. 11).

PERU: Lo hace de *puro* cantor, es decir 'por amor al arte' (Malaret, *BAAL*, IX, 198).

COLOMBIA: La despensa en las *puras* tablas (Carrasquilla, *Novelas*, p. 18).

VENEZUELA: Estuvimos en casa viviendo a *puro* maduro sancochado con leche hervida (Romero García, p. 57).

COSTA RICA (RURAL): Al *puro* «tan» de las doses [= doce] bolbió a manijar la lengua (Echeverría, *Concherías*, p. 171). —Sí, güena tierra ésta, muy negra. Lástima que esté en la *pura* calle (Fabián Dobles, p. 266).

GUATEMALA: Te van a ver a *puro* pie y te llevan flores de pascua (Barnoya, p. 53). Ir a *puritito* caite ['to hoof it,' *caite* being a kind of sandal used in those parts, whence the popular *caiteárselas* 'to run away'].

MEXICO: Pues si yo no comí nada: ya ves, la *pura* tortilla (C). No vendo nada ... el *puro* reló, y eso porque ya debo los doscientos pesos (Azuela, *Los de abajo*, p. 199); ¡Ah, las tropas de Villa! *Puros* hombres norteños (p. 123); doscientos por el *puro* reló (p. 198). No hay frijoles, no hay tortillas: *puro* chile picado y sal corriente (p. 249). Usted tiene un crédito tan bien cimentado ... que sobrará quien le facilite el dinero que pida, con su *pura* firma (Azuela, *Avanzada*, p. 46); no más son *puros* envidiosos (p. 89); no alojar en su casa sino *pura* gente decente (p. 241). Esta tierra mía, tan fea, donde *puros* sufrimientos he tenido (Galeana, p. 34). Haber manos puras donde había *puras* manos ['honest workers where once were thieves'] (Rubio, *Refranes*, I, 247).

Puro may also have the meaning of *mismo* (as in the case of *mero*).

CHILE: ¡Estamos en la *pura* boya! [= con toda felicidad] (Guzmán Maturana, p. 307); estar en la *pura* pega [= en su punto, en plena juventud] (p. 341).

COLOMBIA: Yo creí que era de *puro* Bogotá (C). Se quedó *puro afuera, puro adentro* (Flórez, p. 375).

COSTA RICA: Me puso la pata en la *pura* jeta (Agüero, p. 61); Y cayó en la *pura* puerta (p. 68).

EL SALVADOR: En algún rincón, en el *purisísimo* suelo ... han montado el garito (Ambrogi, p. 183).

GUATEMALA: El queso que fabricas tiene el *puro* sabor del suizo (Sandoval, II, 298).

MEXICO: ¡Toma! ¡En la *pura* calabaza! ['right in the head'] (Azuela, *Los de abajo,* p. 20). Yo soy de Limón ... del *puro* cañón de Juchipila (p. 74). —Soy de *puro* Guanajuato (Mendoza, *El romance,* p. 445). Encomenzó a darle golpes/¡nomás en la *pura* cara! (Rivas Larrauri, p. 122).

As an adverb, *puro* may mean *muy, sumamente,* etc.; and the adverbial phrase '*de puro* + an adjective' means *a fuerza de* 'by dint of': "María pasa por *puro honrada* ... pero *de puro tonta* perdió el empleo" (Sandoval, II, 298). In this usage it often incorrectly agrees like an adjective with the word it modifies, not only in popular speech but also in the familiar speech of cultured persons. Such mistaken agreements are occasionally found in the classics.

CHILE: Lo hice así *de pura tonta* (Román, IV, 507).

PERU: Ellos *de puros perversos* chismearon a la vieja (Benvenutto, p. 153).

ECUADOR: *De puras brutas* han venido a aviarles (Mata, *Sanagüín,* p. 49).

COLOMBIA: Lo hizo *de pura traviesa* (Cuervo, § 380).

In some regions, especially Venezuela, *puro* may mean 'single, only,' etc. (as is also the case with *mero*): "*Una pura* vaca ordeñó ahora; tan *puro tres* fanegas de maíz pude comprar; lo que tengo para vivir es *una pura* choza" (Picón-Febres, p. 291).

In Colombia (Cuervo, § 537), Venezuela (Alvarado), most of the Antilles (Malaret), Chile and Ecuador (personal observation), and probably elsewhere, including Spain, *puro* is used with still another meaning: that of *idéntico, muy parecido* 'identical, very similar,' as in the peninsular example cited by Cuervo: "*Purico, purico* a tu padre" (Hartzenbusch, *El niño desobediente,* II, 2).

VENEZUELA: Esta joven es *pura* a su hermana. ¡Tan *puro* que es a su padre! (Alvarado, p. 378).

POSSESSIVE ADJECTIVES

In modern standard Spanish the possessive adjective usually follows its noun in direct address and in exclamations (*hijo mío*). Occasionally it precedes the noun (*mi hijo*) as it standardly does with military titles (*mi capitán*) and often in prayer books (*¡Ay, mi Dios!*). Even in sixteenth-century Spain postposition was much the commoner usage and was considered much more courteous by Valdés (p. 46). The use of the unstressed form preceding its noun was more intimate, was the only form used in addressing inferiors (Keniston, p. 243), and is the form that has been retained in American Spanish (often after *pobre*), like so many others which in the older language were the more intimate or colloquial. It is not to be considered a Gallicism as some grammarians have dubbed it (Bonilla Ruano, II, 256).

ARGENTINA: —¡Pobre *mi* Almandos! (Greca, p. 167). *Mi* dotor, no se me asuste/que yo lo vengo a servir (*Fausto*, p. 269); —¡Pobre, *mi* caballito! (Lynch, *Los caranchos*, p. 141). Cf. also *RFH*, III, 126.

URUGUAY: —¡Pobre *mi* hermano! (Montiel, *La raza*, p. 247). —¿Cómo les va, *mis* hijos? (Florencio Sánchez, p. 443); —Está más desmejorada, *mi* vieja (p. 444); —Mire, *mi* tía (p. 259).

CHILE: —Una copa, *mis* amigos, viene bien para el frío (Durand, *Mercedes*, p. 40); —Pobre, *mi* hijita—suspiró doña Carmela (p. 262). ¡Pobrecita *mi* «guagüita»! (Pepe Rojas, *La banda*, p. 4). —¡Pobre *mi* Pascualita! (Brunet, in *ACH*, p. 254). —¿Regaron la chacra, *m'hija?* (Latorre, *Zurzulita*, p. 92); ¡No l'olvides, *m'hija!* (p. 93).

PERU: ¡Ay, *mi* madrecita! Cómpreme a mí, *mi* patrón (Benvenutto, p. 145).

COLOMBIA (ANTIOQUIA): —Sí, *mi* Niña (Carrasquilla, *Hace tiempos*, I, 174); —Prosigan, *mis* señoras (p. 187). —Hasta después, *mis* amigos (Buitrago, p. 67). —Pobrecita *mi* máma (Efe Gómez, p. 77).

ECUADOR: —¡Dios no lo quiera! ¡Pobre *mi* hija! (Gil Gilbert, *Nuestro pan*, p. 79). —Pobre *mi* Teresita (Mata, *Sumag Allpa*, p. 12).

VENEZUELA: —*Mi* doctor, ¿no hay esperanza? (Urbaneja, p. 197). —Desde hace un rato, *mi* negro (Díaz-Solís, p. 12); —Caray, *mi* hermano. ... —Qué hembra, *mi* hermano (pp. 12, 18).

EL SALVADOR: —¿No encontrastes nada, *mi* hija? (Torres A., p. 80).

GUATEMALA: —Te contemplaré, ¡oh *mi* amigo! (Bonilla Ruano, III, 256).

CUBA: *mi* socio, *mi* compadre, *mi* viejo, etc. (Padrón).

Very common in many Spanish-American countries are the familiar contracted forms: *mija, mijita, mijo, mijito,* for *mi hija, mi hijita, mi hijo, mi hijito.* These forms in standard Spanish would more regularly be: *hija mía* and *hijo mío.*

In Old Spanish and throughout the Golden Age the unstressed possessive adjective used with partitive force often stood after the indefinite article or demonstrative and indefinite adjectives and before the noun involved: *un mi amigo* 'a (certain) friend of mine,' *este mi amigo* 'this friend of mine,' etc. To be sure, the stressed form of the possessive adjective placed after the noun, as today, also expressed this same concept: *un amigo mío.* In present-day standard Spanish, postposition of the stressed form has almost entirely supplanted the use of the unstressed form, although the latter may still be found with a demonstrative pronoun (*este mi amigo*) and occasionally with the indefinite article (*un mi amigo*). Spanish America, however, has in many regions retained more vigorously the older Spanish usage. Because of its comparative rarity in peninsular Spanish and its archaic flavor, *un mi amigo* strikes most Spanish ears as more graceful, more poetic, and more suggestive than the common *un amigo mío.*

For popular New Mexican speech, Aurelio Espinosa (*Studies,* II, §§ 68, 69) reports new formations: the definite article or the possessive adjective + the demonstrative (*los ésos* 'those there'; *mi aquél* 'that one of mine'; *su ése* 'that one of his'). Such forms are sometimes used as adjectives (*mi aquel libro* = *aquel libro mío*).

ARGENTINA: Evocar *aquella mi vida* (*Fray Mocho,* p. 67).

URUGUAY: Hablaba como ... de *un su amigo* (Pérez Petit, p. 97).

PERU: Nos quedaremos hasta la media noche en esta choza de *unos mis compadres* (Barrantes, p. 143). Pero si yo, equivocando a S. E. con *algún mi pariente,* le dijera ... (Gamarra, *Algo del Perú,* p. 163).

COSTA RICA: Viniendo por la acera ella y *una su amiga* (González Rucavado, p. 10).

NICARAGUA: La hija ... pasaba lo más del día en casa de *unas sus tías* (Chamorro, *Entre dos filos,* p. 27). ¡Suficiente es lo que [he] sufrido ya con vos, con *esas tus cosas* y con *ese tu genio!* (Toruño, p. 90).

EL SALVADOR: Andáte a lavar *esa tu cara* (Torres Arjona, p. 142); Si vieras, tiene *un su marido* tan bueno como es feo (p. 154). Regresaba de rondar la casa de *una mi muchacha* (Martínez Galindo, p. 147). Va a venir *una mi hermana* (C).

GUATEMALA: Todos los días, echo *un mi sueñito* después de almorzar (Sandoval, II, 87). José teniya *un su amigo* mero traslapado [= amigo] (Quintana, p. 154). Se hizo pago de sus honorarios con *una mi vaquita* (Guzmán Riore, p. 8); se sacó ayer *una mi cajita* de plata (p. 84).

MEXICO: Me paso ... a recoger dizque una herencia de *un mi tío* que en paz descanse (Inclán, I, 240); Ahora vamos con *el otro mi tío* (I, 244).

NEW MEXICO: *Mi aquel* libro [= *aquel* libro *mío*], *tu ese* papel [= *ese* papel *tuyo*], *sus esos* caballos [= *esos* caballos *suyos*] (Espinosa, *Studies*, II, § 69).

We find a combination or fusion of both positions used by the populace in some regions, probably by way of reinforcement and by analogy with such double forms as *su casa de usted: mi casa mía* for *mi casa* or *la casa mía.*

CHILE: Hablo ... con *mi* lenguaje *mío* (Sepúlveda, *Hijuna,* p. 34).

GUATEMALA: *Mi* casa *mía* está muy lejos de aquí; *Mis* libros *míos* llevan el sello que tiene el nombre de mi papá (Sandoval, II, 87).

Such reinforcement in Chiloé, Chile, is popularly accomplished by the addition of the subject form denoting the possessor. Cavada (p. 283) attributes this construction to Mapuche, the language of the Araucanians: "Este es *mi* sombrero *yo;* ésta es *tu* camisa *tú;* ése es *su* caballo *él;* éste es *su* libro *el maestro.*" However, the loss of intervocalic *d* may be a contributing factor: *su caballo (d)e él* > *su caballo él.*

In the River Plate region particularly, and less frequently elsewhere, stressed postpositive possessive adjectives take the place of the standard prepositional phrase consisting of *de* + a personal pronoun after adverbs of place: *delante suyo* for *delante de él* (or *de sí*) 'in front of him.' The adverb thus becomes substantivized, probably by analogy with compound prepositions containing a noun with which the possessive adjective has objective force: *a causa tuya* (*a causa de ti*), *en busca suya* (*en busca de él*), *a pesar suyo, en derredor mío, en torno suyo, a la espera suya, a la siga mía* (Chile), etc.

Grammarians inveigh against constructions like *delante suyo.* Alonso and Henríquez Ureña (*Gramática,* I, § 78; II, § 221) exhort the Argentine student to use the standard *cerca de mí* rather than *cerca mío; detrás de ti* rather than *detrás* (or *atrás*) *tuyo; contra mí* rather than *contra mío; delante de ti* rather than *delante* (or *adelante*) *tuyo; lejos de nosotros* rather than *lejos nuestro;* etc. Apparently, however, the practice is so deeply intrenched in Argentina that the best writers have no scruples in using it. Nevertheless, it is not restricted to the River Plate region, as some may think, but is found, less profusely to be sure, in Chile, Bolivia, Peru, Ecuador, Venezuela, and sporadically in other countries as far north as Santo Domingo (*BDH*, V, 239). It is also found popularly in certain parts of Spain, whence it came, like Andalusia, Bilbao (Arriaga, p. 48: *atrás tuyo, atrás mío;* p. 308: *ensima nuestro*), and probably elsewhere.

It is interesting to observe the matter of occasional adjectival agreement in these locutions. In Andalusia, for instance, we find *mía* used with *encima:* "tendío yo der to y er toro tendío der to *ensima mía*" (Muñoz Seca, *El roble de la Jarosa*, p. 38). In Santo Domingo: *p'arriba mía* (cited in *BDH*, V, 239). The use of *mía* with *encima* and *arriba* (or with any other words having final *-a*) seems natural because the ending *-a* is generally feminine. Sometimes the feminine adjective appears (*delante suya*) when the person referred to is of feminine gender. This occurs likewise in Andalusia (*BDH*, V, 239). For Ecuador, Vázquez (p. 317) reports that some say *en pos suyo*, others *en pos suya*, with no particular reason for either. He suggests that, if the gender of the adjective is to change, it should agree with the gender of the person or thing referred to; but he prefers using *en pos de él* or *en su pos*.

In Bolivia, Peru, Ecuador, and southern Colombia we find *en* (*por*) *su delante* as a preferred variation to *delante suyo* (standard *delante de él*, etc.). In Peru this construction is reported as typical of the populace in the highlands and, to a less degree, in the coastal region; in Huánuco, however, it is reported current even among the cultured. Sometimes, particularly in Ecuador, both forms (*en su delante, delante suyo*) exist side by side and may be used alternately by the same speaker (*delante suyo* being the rarer); sometimes a fusion is heard: *en delante suyo*.

Argentina: El callejón, *delante mío*, se tendía obscuro (Güiraldes, *Don Segundo*, p. 21, also pp. 60, 78, etc.); *detrás mío* (pp. 16, 78), *detrás nuestro* (p. 138), *detrás suyo* (p. 69), *cerca mío* (p. 85), *cerca tuyo* (p. 204), *encima nuestro* (p. 89), *dentro mío* (p. 297), etc. Me invita a sentarme *frente suyo* (Güiraldes, *Xaimaca*, p. 17); *a la par nuestra* ... va tumbándose un río (p. 20); *atrás nuestro* (p. 189), etc. *Detrás suyo* quedaba la conmoción de los portazos (Mallea, *La ciudad*, p. 114). El cabo Gorosito está a *cinco pasos suyos* (Sáenz, p. 55); Viento *arriba mío* quedaban (p. 75).

URUGUAY: *Atrás suyo* debe andar un peón con la máquina de alambrar (Montiel, *Alma nuestra*, p. 137); si alguno se atreve a calumniar a Leonor *delante mío* (p. 144).

PARAGUAY: *Delante de él* alternates with *delante suyo; detrás de mí* and *detrás mío; en busca suyo*, etc. (Morínigo).

CHILE: Ya la peonada corría *detrás nuestro* (Manuel Rojas, *Hombres*, p. 35). Aquí me estoy, pues, *a la espera suya* (Barrios, *El hermano asno*, p. 214). Se cree que todos andan *a la siga mía* (Acevedo Hernández, *Árbol viejo*, p. 33).

BOLIVIA: No debo decir nada de él *en su delante* (Arguedas, *Vida criolla*, p. 97). Terneros, ovejas, gallos, patos y gansos pasaban orondamente *por su delante* (Arguedas, *Raza*, p. 76). Apartó al individuo *de su delante* (Pereyra, p. 72). —Sigan por acá, indios, *por mi detrás* (Augusto Guzmán, p. 170); se cuadran *en su delante* cuatro jovenzuelos sin zapatos (p. 179); corren *en pos mía* (p. 182).

PERU: *En mi delante* se atrevió a faltarla; es una ausenciera que *en su detrás* raja duro y *en su delante* lo adula; sólo saldré cuando tumben las paredes *en mi encima* (Benvenutto, p. 146). (PIURA): —¡Qué ponderación la tuya, José Manué! Y entoavía *en tu elante* (López Albújar, *Matalaché*, p. 100). (HUÁNUCO): *Por mi tras, en su tras, en tu encima*, etc. (Pulgar Vidal, p. 817).

ECUADOR (COAST): —Mi compadre Jaramillo va *en vez mío* (Gil Gilbert, *Nuestro pan*, p. 20); Oía golpes *a su detrás* (p. 73); un cajón que estaba *en su delante* (p. 75); Magdalena corrió un rato *en su detrás* (p. 114); iba *delante suyo* (p. 179), etc. (CUENCA): ¡Y eso *en mi delante*, cara a cara! (Mata, *Sanagüín*, p. 9); escondiendo *tras suyo* al pequeño (p. 123); *en su delante* (p. 173); Jaime oyó *tras suyo* un «aura es cuando» (p. 195); *en delante nuestro* (p. 196). *Delante nuestro* camina el muchacho de doce años (García Muñoz, *El médico*, p. 128). —No, si la llave está *cerca tuyo* (Pareja, *Don Balón*, p. 168). *En delante mío* no se dice esas cosas (Andrade, p. 127). —Reido estaba *delante mío* (Icaza, *Media vida*, p. 162).

COLOMBIA (SOUTH): —¿Cómo has de estar lloriquiando y despeinada *en su delante?* (Álvarez Garzón, p. 17); —De a buenas o de a malas les sacamos el papel del secreto y lo romperimos *en su delante* (p. 178).

VENEZUELA: *Junto suyo* había alguien que no quiso que le pegara a los caimanes (Gallegos, *Doña Bárbara*, p. 19); cuente que yo voy *detrás suyo* (p. 331). Aunque cuando el juicio está por encima del hombre y no por *debajo suyo*, que es como debe estar, el hombre está sin juicio (Gallegos, *Canaima*, p. 174).

POSSESSIVE ADJECTIVE REPLACED BY PERSONAL PRONOUN

Since the possessive adjective *su* has many possible meanings ('his, her, your, their') it is often necessary for the sake of clarity to use a phrase with *de* + a personal pronoun (*la casa de él, su casa de él, de ella, de usted,* etc.). In some Spanish-American countries *su* is commonly felt to be only second person polite form, to be used with *usted.* Consequently, it is avoided in popular speech when reference is to a third person, and in such cases the general practice is to use *de él, ella, ellos, ellas,* etc. The usage is found in sixteenth-century Spain but was apparently rare (Keniston, p. 245). Today *su* alone ordinarily refers to the third person in Spain (Gili y Gaya, § 181); but more commonly to the second person in Spanish America (notwithstanding Gili y Gaya, who misinterprets Tiscornia, *La lengua,* § 98).

CHILE: Mientras la muchacha hablaba, Lautaro advirtió que en los ojos *de ella* estaba la tristeza de su pueblo (Fernando Alegría, *Lautaro,* p. 60).

ECUADOR: Acaso vos sois taita ni mama *d'él* (Icaza, *Cholos,* p. 32). El señor Luis Díaz tuvo la culpa. Yo era huambra todavía y una vez que estuve en la casa *de él* ... (Bustamente, p. 61). En la vida *de ella* había una sarcástica contradicción (Salvador, *Noviembre,* p. 219). La hizo *de él* (Gil Gilbert, *Yunga,* p. 21). ¿No ve, patrón, que les gusta dar qué hacer a las mujeres *de ellos?* (Mata, *Sanagüín,* p. 160).

COLOMBIA (ANTIOQUIA): —Que se case. Está bien. No tengo derecho a oponerme, porque no soy el padre, ni la madre *de él* (Arango Villegas, p. 103).

VENEZUELA: No; ella volvería, a ser la amada, la compañera *de él* (Pocaterra, p. 200).

COSTA RICA: —¿Quieren que vayamos al cuarto *de él* a ver si está? (González Rucavado, p. 93).

This construction in the first person plural (*de nosotros* for *nuestro,* etc.), while very rare in sixteenth-century Spain, is popular in much of Spanish America. For Chile, Román (V, 708) remarks: "El pueblo nunca dice *nuestro* fuera del *pan nuestro* y del *padrenuestro.*" The loss of *vuestro* in favor of analytical *de ustedes* may have influenced the change of *nuestro* to popular *de nosotros* (*BDH,* II, 141).

ARGENTINA: Dice mama que te pide que no te olvidés de la notisia de la yegada *de nosotras* (*Fray Mocho,* p. 120); Eso es una invención *de nosotros* (p. 171). Es que ella está en la creencia de que es hija *de nojotro* (Larreta, *El linyera,* p. 157).

CHILE: El patrón, con el trabajo *e nosotros*, ha comprao otra hacienda (Acevedo Hernández, *Por el atajo*, p. 29). —Estos niños ... son nieto *e nosotro*, pué, señor (Romanángel, p. 70).

COLOMBIA (ANTIOQUIA): Los relojes *de nosotros* no van a ser de plata (Carrasquilla, *Hace tiempos*, II, 314). —Es un amigo de toda la confianza *de nosotros* (Buitrago, p. 157).

VENEZUELA: El papá *de nosotros* lo enseñó. ¿Tú no has oído hablar de Bocú? Ése era el papá *de nosotros* (Guillermo Meneses, in *ACMV*, II, 151). ¿No crees que sería bueno comprar un carro nuevo? Ya el *de nosotros* no está muy bien que digamos (Díaz-Solís, p. 65).

COSTA RICA: ¿Usted no ha encontrado un cintillo de terciopelo rojo? Tal vez en el cuarto *de nosotras*, barriendo (González Rucavado, p. 93).

HONDURAS: Recuerdo que fué un amigo *de nosotros* quien ... vino a llamar (Mejía Nieto, *El solterón*, p. 113).

EL SALVADOR: —Estas cosas son obra denantes, de los agüelos *de nosotros* (Salarrué, *Cuentos*, p. 10).

MEXICO: Las vecinas m'emprestaron sus gatos porque el *de nosotros* solo no 'biera resistío (García Roel, p. 49); ni sabe nada de las relaciones *de nosotros* (p. 137); dime el segundo verso de la canción *de nosotros* (p. 212). —¿De modo que tú eres orita de los *de nosotros?* (Rubín, p. 156). Éstos son de los *de nosotros* (Ángulo, p. 101).

CUBA: —Rafael, esto no es vida; estos hijos *de nosotros* tienen que vivir de otra manera (Ciro Espinosa, p. 17); dende que se murió la baca *e nosotroh* (p. 162); —Los padres *de nosotros* lo hicieron igual (p. 469).

INTERROGATIVE ADJECTIVES

In standard Spanish the interrogative adjective used attributively is normally *qué* 'what, which': "*¿qué* libro tiene usted?" Rarely is *cuál* used in such cases, though it may be found when indicating a choice from a very small group: "*¿cuál* libro tiene usted?" In sixteenth-century prose (Keniston, p. 281) the regular interrogative adjective was *qué;* the rare *cuál* was used "to stress the limitation within the class, as English 'which?' " Nevertheless *cuál* appears more frequently in the older language than today: "*¿Quál* consejo puede regir?" (*Celestina*, I), "*¿Quál* Dios te traxo por estos barrios?" (IV), "*¿Quál* muger jamás se vido en tan estrecha affrenta?" (VI); "*¿Quál* muger de mis años la passa con tantos sobresaltos y desdichas?" (Lope, *Dorotea*, I, 3). The comparative frequency of *cuál* in the older language is reflected in American Spanish, contrasting with its rarer use in present-day Spain.

ARGENTINA: Sin saber por qué, ni siguiendo *cuál* güella, se encontró de pronto en una pieza alumbrada por un candil mugriento (Güiraldes, *Don Segundo*, p. 126).

CHILE: No sé a *cuáles* asuntos se refiere (Luis Meléndez, p. 148); *cuáles* secretos posee (p. 180). ¿Por qué no consigue usted al chilenito de Pincheira? —*¿Cuál* chilenito? (Magdalena Petit, p. 132). —Me da la primera alegría de la semana. —*¿Cuál* alegría? (Acevedo Hernández, *De pura cepa*, p. 6).

PERU: —¿Y de *cuáles* caprichos me crees tú capaz? (López Albújar, *Matalaché*, p. 133).

ECUADOR: La madre ha simpatizado conmigo. —*¿Cuál* madre? (Salvador, *Noviembre*, p. 142). —¿Y *cuál* peón es el herido, patrón? (Mata, *Sanagüín*, p. 159).

COLOMBIA: Y si se demora un poco más, lo deja el tren. —*¿Cuál* tren? (Restrepo Jaramillo, p. 150).

VENEZUELA: ¿Con *cuáles* brazos defenderse, si la tenía enlazada en un abrazo salvaje? (Pocaterra, p. 191). ¿A *cuál* cabra quieres más? (Briceño, in *ACMV*, II, 122). Pregunto a mi mujer si hay desayuno. —*¿Cuál* desayuno? (Fabbiani Ruiz, in *ACMV*, II, 175).

HONDURAS: —¡Detenga a ese hombre! —*¿Cuál* hombre? (Martínez Galindo, p. 126).

MEXICO: Yo sé *cuál* pan es bueno, aunque no sea panadero (Robles Castillo, p. 21). —¡Ahora vamos a brindar por su conquista! —*¡Cuál* conquista! (Galeana, p. 89). —¿Pos *cuál* causa defendemos nosotros? (Azuela, *Los de abajo*, p. 35). —*¿Cuál* curandero? (M. A. Menéndez, p. 254).

SANTO DOMINGO: —Y yo, *¿cuál* rumbo tomo ahora? (Requena, *Los enemigos*, p. 174).

COMPARISON

Since all but four adjectives form their comparative and superlative degree by prefixing *más* (or *menos*) to the positive, the exceptions (*mejor*, *peor*, *mayor*, *menor*), derived directly from Latin comparatives, logically tend to accommodate themselves in popular speech to the vast majority. This practice goes back to Latin itself: *magis melior* (Meyer-Lübke, § 47). Spanish expressions like *más mejor* and *más peor* (pop. *pior*), while they may be found in the classics, are now relegated to the unlettered in popular and rustic usage everywhere, both in Spain and in America. On these linguistic levels the forms *mejor* and *peor* often come to be felt as positives and consequently need *más* to make them comparatives (cf. 'more better,' and 'nearer,' really a double comparison: *nigh, near*).

CHILE: No estoy *tan peor* [= tan malo *or* tan mal] como ayer; No lo hice *tan peor* [= tan mal]; No me salió *tan peor* [= tan malo] el discurso (Román, IV, 209). —Una vez había un hombre que tenía una mujer *tan pior* [= tan mala] como la Juana e Dios (Acevedo Hernández, *Árbol viejo,* p. 38). Es *más pior* (Juan del Campo, p. 39).

ARGENTINA: —¿Sabe cómo sigue el hombre? ¿Está *más pior?* ... El Toruno está ... muy mejor, cada vez *más mejor* (Lynch, *Romance,* p. 295). (SAN LUIS): *más peor, más mucho,* etc. (Vidal, p. 399).

PARAGUAY: Estoy *más mejor;* me siento *más peor* (Morínigo).

ECUADOR: —Y de más cerquísima ha de ser *más peor* (Pareja, *La Beldaca,* p. 60). —¡Ejtoy *maj pior* que antej! (Aguilera M., p. 60).

COLOMBIA: Otros enfermos *más piores* (Tulio González, p. 13).

VENEZUELA: O la [gente] del Siete Cueros, que es *más pior* (Gallegos, *Pobre negro,* p. 319).

MEXICO: *Más mejor* es mala pizca [= recolección] que buena cosecha en pie (Rubio, *Refranes,* I, 316). Los gachupines ... no eran tan *peores* [= tan malos] (Urquizo, p. 101).

For popular speech in Guatemala, Sandoval (II, 65) reports the variant *más a peor:* "El enfermo va *más a peor*" in which *más a peor* intensifies the force of *peor.* We find the same in rural Costa Rica ("Entre más lo cuido, *más a pior*" [Echeverría, *Concherías,* p. 155]), in rural Cuba ("Ha ido *a mejor, a mejor*" [Padrón]), and elsewhere. These popular forms are very dynamic, indicating, as they do, a progressive process.

In the foregoing examples *peor* and *mejor* are sometimes adjectives, sometimes adverbs. The superfluous *más* is frequently found also before other adverbs, as is often the case in rural Spain: *más antes* for *antes; más después* for *después;* etc. Such expressions may be heard in careless speech almost anywhere, even in the mouths of the educated. Occasionally they slip into literary style. Cf. the older language: "*más antes* no os vieron" (Torres Naharro, *Comedia Himenea* [1517], jornada II).

ARGENTINA: *Más después, más ahora, más luego* (Vidal, p. 395).

CHILE: —Ponga el disco de *más antes* (C). *Más luego* haré lo que me mandas (Chiloé: Cavada, p. 284).

BOLIVIA: Se oye distintamente el tableteo sonoro de las ametralladoras livianas ... y, *más después,* ... el bombo hiperbólico de la artillería que hace temblar la tierra mártir de los montes (Augusto Guzmán, p. 53).

PARAGUAY: *más antes, más luego* (Morínigo).

ECUADOR: —Quiero ir mucho *más antes* (C). —Pero [Sotero] jué mío *más* primero (La Cuadra, *Horno,* p. 181). Unos se van *más antes,* otros *más después* (Gil Gilbert, *Nuestro pan,* p. 14).

VENEZUELA: —De más lejos que *más nunca* (Gallegos, *Doña Bárbara,* p. 31); —Deje eso para *más después,* Capitán (p. 35). —Hasta *más luego,* como dicen ustedes. Hasta *más lueguito,* doña Bárbara (p. 161); *más después* fué visto por la sabana este caballo (p. 294).

COSTA RICA: Un poco *más luego* (Fabián Dobles, p. 260).

MEXICO (NORTH): Dicen que *más antes* no entraban las mujeres aquí (Urquizo, p. 303). —L'otro día me dió el mesmo vajido allá pa la sierra y *más dispués* en la casa (Rubín, p. 190).

We find, likewise, a popular *muy* or *más* with absolute superlatives both in parts of Spain and in parts of Spanish America: "Es *muy bonitísimo,* sí, señora, no se pué negá" (Muñoz Seca, *El roble de la Jarosa,* p. 34 [Andalusia]); —"Y de *más cerquísima* ha de ser más peor, ¿no?" (Pareja, *La Beldaca,* p. 60 [Ecuador]).

Perhaps because the force not only of the comparative but also of the superlative forms has thus occasionally been reduced to a mere positive, there arose the frequent use of the *-azo* ending for adjectives (and adverbs), especially in the popular and rustic language of the River Plate region and Chile, and sporadically elsewhere: *buenazo = buenísimo, feazo = feísimo,* often reinforced with *muy.*

ARGENTINA: —Si es *apuradazo* ... si es *ladinazo* pa'l retruque (Güiraldes, *Don Segundo,* p. 84); —Venía *cansadazo* (p. 293). La verdá del caso jué/Que me tuvo *apuradazo* (*Martín Fierro,* p. 43).

URUGUAY: —Debían arreglar los caminos. —¿Están feos? —*¡Feazos!* (Reyles, *El terruño,* p. 99). Ta [=está] *aquerenciadazo* con ustedes (Florencio Sánchez, p. 212).

CHILE: —Y el contenío estaba *muy aceitosazo* (Romanángel, p. 27); los [= nos] encontramos con una pelotera *muy grandaza* (p. 30); El méico estaba *ocupaaso* (p. 38); el coche iba *muy lejazo* (p. 43). Ella armó un boche *grandazo* (Romero, *La viuda,* p. 135). Vengo de *muy relejazo* (Guzmán Maturana, p. 22); lo recibió *cariñosazo* (p.

23). Hacía *tantazo* tiempo que no le veíamos (Brunet, *Montaña*, p. 91). —¿Murió hace mucho tiempo? —*Muchazo* (Latorre, *Zurzulita*, p. 76); esa gente tiene *malazo* genio (p. 106); le gustan *muchazo* (p. 118); Esta vuelta es *muy largaza* (p. 152); está *lindazo* (p. 135).

VENEZUELA: ¡Qué feliz fuera yo, con la *pocaza* riqueza que tenía y mi hombre en casa! (Urbaneja, p. 169).

GUATEMALA: Los padres de ella siempre fueron *abiertazos* [= muy espléndidos, generosos] (Sandoval, I, 3).

MEXICO: ¡Oh, los *buenazos* y rudos amigos de la arriería! (López y Fuentes, *¡Mi general!* p. 53).

For Teapa, Tabasco, the forms *peorsísimo* and *mejorsísimo* are recorded by Gutiérrez Eskildsen (p. 53). *Peor que peor* (meaning *tanto peor*) and *mejor que mejor* (meaning *tanto mejor*), though adverbial locutions, may be mentioned here as current everywhere in Spain and America: "pues casaos con rica, y si es feúcha *mejor que mejor* (Gamboa, *Santa*, p. 177 [Mexico]). In many regions one hears the colloquial *para peor* (rustic *pa pior*), which is equivalent to a forceful *peor que peor, tanto peor*, etc.

CHILE: —¿Pero quién se anima a decirle nada al hombre? Sería *pa pior*, usted lo conoce (Alberto Romero, *Perucho González*, p. 61; also p. 106); Pero fué *para peor*, porque se enfurecieron (p. 227).

URUGUAY: —No se meta con esas brujas, que es *pa pior* (Florencio Sánchez, p. 216).

PROPORTIONATE COMPARISON

Proportionate comparison, used with either adjectives or adverbs, is standardly expressed by the correlatives *cuanto más* (or *menos*) ... (*tanto*) *más* (or *menos*) = 'the more (*or* less) ... the more (*or* less).' The locution *mientras más* (or *menos*) ... *más* (or *menos*) is also found but it seems less usual than *cuanto más*, etc. In American Spanish the reverse is true: *mientras más* ... *más*, etc., is by far the commoner of the two ways of expressing proportionate comparison and seems to be preferred also in Andalusia. According to Keniston's count (p. 326), it was rare in sixteenth-century prose.

American writers on the subject, influenced by the frequency of *mientras más* in their own environment, give it primary consideration, erroneously believing it more current everywhere, and relegate *cuanto más* to a secondary place, if, indeed, they mention it at all.

Thus Cuervo (§ 450): "*mientras más*, etc. ... es la construcción castellana corriente. ... En vez de *mientras más*, *mientras menos*, se dice también *cuanto más*, *cuanto menos*." Santamaría (*Ensayos*, p. 291), representing Mexico, remarks: "La forma correcta debe ser ésta: *Mientras más* tiene, *más* quiere. Y así las demás. Siempre, con el adverbio *mientras*."

Of frequent use in many regions of Spanish America to express proportionate comparison is the locution *entre más ... más*, etc., both among the populace and among some cultured speakers. Cuervo (§ 450) mentions it for Colombia, Mexico, and Costa Rica; Román (II, 264) adds Chile. Now we know it is used throughout Central America, in Venezuela, Panama (*BAAL*, X, 649), the Antilles, and northwestern Argentina. It is not rare in rural Spain: "*entre más* quiero, *menos* me dan" (Garrote, § 64 [León]); "Y *entre más* se retiraba la vieja de él *más* iba aclarando el día" (Espinosa, *Cuentos*, II, 331 [Granada]); "*entre más* ricos, *más* animales" (Sánchez Sevilla, § 98 [Salamancan region]).

The origin of *entre más*, etc., has not been satisfactorily explained. Cuervo thinks it derives from the contamination of *entre tanto que* + *mientras más*, which is possible. Román (II, 264) thinks that this *entre* might be a corruption of *mientras*, "porque el vulgo es muy capaz de comerse la *m* inicial y la *s* final y, recortado así el vocablo por delante y por detrás, no le quedó más que metamorfosearse en *entre* o fundirse con éste en un solo ser." This explanation need be given no credence. Obviously, *entre* is a simple derivation from Latin *inter*. It must be remembered that *ínter* (besides *ínterin* or *interín*) was current in Spanish in the sense of *mientras* and has continued to live in a number of regions:

MEXICO: Saqué mi manojo de llaves *ínter* él amarró el caballo (Inclán, II, 179); *interín* unos publicaban ... el decreto, otros corrían a hacer lo mismo (II, 347); volteó su caballo y partió a escape por la cuesta arriba, *ínter* se reían de sus disparates y aturdimiento. *Ínter más* lo pienso, estoy más seguro (Rivas Larrauri, p. 149); *Ínter más* me cura, me pongo más malo (p. 164).

Furthermore, *entre* (< *inter*) is often interchanged with *mientras* (< *dum interim*), as in *entre tanto* = *mientras tanto*.

ARGENTINA (SAN LUIS): *Entre más* le pegan al muchacho, *pior* se pone (Vidal, p. 395).

CHILE: Las enfermedades *entre más* nos preocupan, *más* nos friegan (C).

COLOMBIA (BOGOTÁ): *Entre más* bebe, *más* sed le da. *Entre menos* tiene, *más* gasta (Cuervo, § 450). (VALLE DEL CAUCA): *Entre menos* coma, *menos* engorda (Tascón, p. 138). (ATLANTIC COAST): *Entre más* lo veo, *menos* me gusta; *Entre menos* le hable, *mejor* será (Sundheim, p. 274).

VENEZUELA: *Entre más* mira, *menos* ve (Alvarado, p. 181).

PANAMA: *Entre más* me regañan, *peor* es (L. Aguilera, p. 316).

COSTA RICA (RURAL): *Entre más* lo cuido, *más* a pior (Echeverría, *Concherías*, p. 155). *Entre más* plata, *mejor* (Fallas, p. 14).

EL SALVADOR: *Entre menos* personas haya en la Asamblea, *más* luego se entienden y armonizan (Quijano Hernández, p. 17).

GUATEMALA: *Entre más* dinero se gane, se pasa *mejor* la vida; *Entre menos* bulto, *más* claridad (Sandoval, I, 490). *Entre más* brazos, *más mejor* (Quintana, p. 61); *entre más* mal las tratan, *más* quieren a su hombre (p. 153).

MEXICO: *Entre más* sangre *más* abono (Taracena, p. 79). *Entre más* crítica sea la hora ... *más* importantes serán ... estos inesperados cambios (*Universal* [Mexico City], December 17, 1940). *Entre más* duro se den, *mejor* (*Informador* [Guadalajara], July 20, 1941). Y *entre más* médicos haya, ¡*más* enfermedades! (Ferretis, *San Automóvil*, p. 23). (YUCATAN): *Entre más* te doy, *más* quieres (V. Suárez, p. 62).

CUBA: *Entre más* dinero tiene, más quiere (Padrón).

In many rural regions of Spain we find the use of *contra* and *contri*: "*contra más* pobre, *más* generoso" (Borao, p. 198 [Aragon]); "*contra más* te digo, *menos* me oyes" (Garrote, § 64 [León]); "*contra más* pronto, mejor" (Lamano, p. 351 [Salamanca]); "*contri más* anda, *más* atrás estás" (Sánchez Sevilla, § 98 [Salamanca]); "*Contra más* me echo las cartas, *peores* cosas me dicen" (Álvarez Quintero, *Teatro*, X, 278 [Andalusia]). *Contra* is heard in Chile (Román, II, 264), Nicaragua ("*contra más* habla, *menos* se entiende" [A. Valle, p. 63]), and probably elsewhere. We find *contri* in rural Cuba ("*contrimás* piensa uno en eso, *peol* eh" [Ciro Espinosa, p. 157]). These forms may be merely a fusion of popular *contimás* (< *cuanto y más*) and of *contra*, reinforcing the antithesis.

III

THE 'VOSEO'

THE personal pronouns and corresponding verb forms offering the greatest divergencies between standard Castilian and American Spanish are those involving the second person familiar, both singular and plural. It must be stated, first of all, that the plural familiar form *vosotros* (and the second person plural verb form) has been lost in American Spanish, except for an occasional literary use, and in the mouths of fictional Spaniards. It has been replaced by *ustedes* (and the third person plural verb form). In Andalusia and elsewhere (Llorente, § 125) one may hear *ustedes* with the second person verb (*ustedes tenéis*).

River Plate Region: Si yo tengo que trabajar y *vos* y *tus* hermanas *pueden* estudiar en el pueblo, es porque el patrón es mano larga con *ustedes* (Acevedo Díaz, *Argentina*, p. 23).

Chile: Vaya uno de *ustedes: tú,* Pedro; *tú,* Nicolás; *tú,* Lorenzo (Lillo, p. 147). —Perros de ... ¡*salgan* pa fuera! (Marta Miranda, p. 115). A *vos* y a *tu* quiltro ['cur'] *los* voy a atravesar de un balazo (Latorre, *Hombres*, p. 203). *Tú* y *tu* pueblo *han* venido esta noche ... (Fernando Alegría, *Lautaro*, p. 26).

Ecuador: Me gusta que *vos* y *tu* mamacita, Fanny, *sean* de aguante para esto (Mata, *Sanagüín*, p. 117). He sabido que *tu* padre era casado, cuando *naciste tú* y una hermana *tuya*. Que *tu* madre *las* [= os] abandonó, que *fueron* [= fuisteis] recogidas las dos por esa señora que me *has* presentado como *tu* madre (Salvador, *Noviembre*, p. 149). *Tú* y *él cállense, vénganse* (Vázquez, p. 422).

Santo Domingo: Porque la tierra es buena y generosa, hijo mío. Me ha sostenido a mí, a *tu* madre, a *ustedes* y a muchos padres e hijos antes que nosotros (Requena, *Los enemigos*, p. 17).

Mexico: *Tú* ya sabes que a *ti* y a *tu* compadre *los* traen los españoles entre ojos (Urquizo, p. 11).

The double forms (the rare literary *vosotros* + a second person plural verb and the conversational *ustedes* + a third person plural verb) sometimes lead to confusion in the minds of the semicultured and grammatically untutored who, when on their best behavior, occasionally strive in vain to reproduce the correct Castilian familiar plural (*vosotros* + a second person plural verb), deeming it socially refined. Sooner or later they blunder into unorthodox mixtures, since the peninsular *vosotros* has become exceedingly rusty from lack of use. Such grammatical incongruities have been resorted to by some writers for humorous effect, to indicate the pedantry of the semicultured:

Ya sabíamos que *ustedes* no *faltaríais*. ... *Estáis* en *vuestra* casa. En seguidita *les* voy a dar cuenta del secreto. *Ustedes* no *sabían* a qué *veníais*, ¿verdad? (*Patoruzú* for November 11, 1940). *Tomen* nota de lo que *os* digo (Pereyra, p. 20); Tampoco hemos de olvidar el fijarnos en *vuestras* señales de regreso y aun entonces nos tocará asegurarnos que se trata de *ustedes* (p. 36); ¡me *responderán* con *vuestras* vidas! (p. 204); ¡*Digan* que *tenéis* suerte! (p. 304).

In the saying "Pies, ¿para qué *os* quiero?" the standard *os* is converted not only into the expected *los*, but also into the unexpected *te*. "Pies (*or* patitas), ¿pa qué *te* quiero?" is heard in Argentina (*BDH*, V, 174), Chile (Román), Bolivia, Cuba, and elsewhere.

Such incongruities are not limited to American Spanish, however. We now have sufficient proof of their use in Spain, principally in Andalusia but occasionally even in Madrid. At times the reflexive *os* is replaced in very vulgar speech by *se:* "*Les* voy a enseñá a *ustedes* una cosa que *se vais* a queá con la boca abierta (Muñoz Seca, *El roble de la Jarosa*, p. 63).[1] In Spain, however, these forms are popular, not pedantic.

Tuteo generally means the correct use of *tú* with the second person singular verb form, together with the pronouns *te*, *ti*, and the possessive adjectives *tu* and *tuyo*. *Voseo* means the use of the familiar singular *vos*, to replace *tú*, with oscillating second person singular and archaic second person plural verb forms, together with the pronouns *te*, *vos* (for *ti*), and the possessive adjectives *tu* and *tuyo*. *Vosear*, or *llamar de "vos,"* then, is in general opposed to *tutear* or *llamar de "tú."* Nevertheless, the verb *tutear* is frequently found referring to the use of *vos*, since both indicate familiar address.

ARGENTINA: *Vos mataste* a Machao. ... —¡Cómo es eso! ... Dígamé, /por más alcalde que sea:/¿por qué me gruñe y *tutea?* (Ascasubi, p. 172). —¿Y usté mesmo se doma los caballos? —*Tuteándome*, como a

[1] Quoted by R. K. Spaulding and F. Sánchez, "El uso de *ustedes* como sujeto de la segunda persona del plural," *Hispanic Review*, X (1942), 165–67. For Murcia, see García Soriano, § 66, 3.

veces se hace de primera intención entre muchachos, respondió burlón: —Hasta aura que *has venido vos* (Güiraldes, *Don Segundo*, p. 309). —*Decíme*. ... *Te* pueden ver ... no le hará bien a nadie, ni a *vos* ni a ella, excitarse así. ... Molesto se daba cuenta recién que habían comenzado a *tutearse* (Petit de Murat, p. 146).

Not only do we find *tutear* used to mean *vosear*, but we have found *tú* used in referring to *vos*, thus identifying completely *tú* and *vos*, in accordance with the phrase "hablarse de *tú* y de *vos*": "—Es linda ... pero no tan linda como *vos*. Era la primera ... vez que Lucio se atrevía a *tutearla*. ... Aquel *tú* que por primera vez volvía a resonar en sus oídos ..." (Viana, *Gaucha*, p. 79).

Vosear is sometimes jocosely referred to in Argentina as *chechear*, since the vocative particle *che*[2] often accompanies the second person verb forms with the force of a vocative *vos* or *tú* (occasionally also with *usted*, but almost exclusively by men), calling the attention of the person addressed, like the exclamatory *hombre*. Since the use of *che* in this sense is associated primarily with Argentina (though found also in Bolivia), it has become a stock device for indicating Argentine characters in the literature of other countries and, together with the expression *¡Qué esperanza!*, interlards the so-called Argentine dialogue in such writing. (In Chile *che* is substantivized as a derogatory epithet applied to Argentinians and Bolivians.) But the *voseo* itself is far from being a strictly Argentine practice, as is occasionally supposed by the uninitiated. Even Keniston (*Syntax list*, p. 47) misleads the student, when he states that "in Argentina and Uruguay *vos* is the common form of address in colloquial style," thus excluding all the other regions where it is almost equally colloquial. To be sure, the *voseo* may be said to have gained a greater foothold among all classes in Argentina and Uruguay than almost anywhere else. But its geographical diffusion includes two-thirds of Spanish America.[3] We know now that the *voseo* is general in Argentina, Uru-

[2] The origin of *che* has been much disputed. Probably it derives from the Old Spanish interjection *ce* (J. Martínez Orozco, "Origen del che," *Segundo congreso internacional de historia de América*, III [Buenos Aires, 1938], 678–86). Some have proposed a derivation from *mapuche*, language of the Araucanians (Lenz, *Dicc. etim.*, p. 270). See also Tiscornia, "La lengua de 'Martín Fierro,' " *BDH*, III, 126, n. 1. For a more detailed account of its present-day use see Frida Weber, "Fórmulas de tratamiento en la lengua de Buenos Aires," *RFH*, III (1941), 105–39. For rustic *chey*, cf. Vidal, p. 196.

[3] See Henríquez Ureña, "Observaciones sobre el español en América," *RFE*, VIII (1921), 379–90; Tiscornia, *La lengua*, § 97 and pp. 289–90, containing also a map called "Geografía del voseo"; Tiscornia's discussion is summarized in I. E. Chart, "The 'voseo' and 'tuteo' in America," *Modern Language Forum*, XXVIII (1943), 17–24.

guay, much of Paraguay, the Central American countries (Guatemala, El Salvador, Honduras, Nicaragua, most of Costa Rica) and the Mexican states of Chiapas and Tabasco. It exists in conflict with *tú* in Chile, southern Peru (bordering on Chile) and northern Peru (bordering on Ecuador), Bolivia, most of Ecuador, Colombia, and Venezuela, the interior of Panama, and a small eastern section of Cuba. On the other hand, *tú* is general in most of Mexico, Cuba, Peru, parts of Bolivia, northern Colombia and Venezuela (the Atlantic coast), western Ecuador, most of Panama (including Panama City and Colón), in Santo Domingo and Puerto Rico.

EARLY HISTORY OF 'VOS'

Before discussing the various types of *voseo* and their general diffusion, it might be well to review briefly the historical development of the second person pronoun and its use.

Vos was originally a plural form (surviving as such until the early sixteenth century). Soon *otros* was added to both *nos* and *vos*, and the amalgamated forms were then definitely plural and readily distinguishable from *nos* and *vos*, which from an early period had been used also as singular forms of respect, though always accompanied with the second person plural verb.

In the *Poema del Cid* (1140) *vos* is used as the respectful form of address between king and noble, between husband and wife, nobleman and nobleman (*vos tomades, tomedes, veedes, sodes, seredes, fincaredes, llegastes, fostes*, etc.); whereas *tú* is used in addressing persons of inferior rank: the Cid to his servant and vassal, Muño Gustioz; the Cid's champions to the Infantes de Carrión when challenging them to combat; the Cid to the Moorish King Búcar; Moors in speaking to Christians; and generally in prayer in addressing the Deity (*tú callas, dizes, eres, veerte as, dirás, fizist, mintist*, etc.). But even in this early monument both the singular form of *tú* and the plural form of *vos* are occasionally used in addressing the same person, though not in the same sentence: the King first addresses Muño Gustioz with *tú* (vss. 2954–67) and then uses the plural imperatives: *dizidle* (vs. 2968) and *saludádmelos* (vs. 2972), etc. In the fifteenth century this interchange of *vos* and *tú* was much more frequent; the *d* of the second person plural verb was falling (*vayaes* for *vayades, soes* for *sodes*, etc.), often with a fusion of the contiguous *e*'s in verbs of the second conjugation (*irés* < *irees* < *iredes; avés* < *avees* < *avedes; debés* < *debees* < *debedes*). Probably forms like *debés* gave rise to the analogical forms *sepás* (< *sepaes* < *sepades*), *sos* (< *soes* < *sodes*), *partís* (< *partíes* < *partides*), etc. On the other hand, the groups *ae* and *oe* readily diphthongized into *ai* and *oi* (*andais, sois*), and these diphthongs favored the development of *ei* from *ee* (*avees* > *aveis; debees* > *debeis*). By the middle of the fifteenth century all these forms are used promiscuously,[4] and many present-day American-Spanish *voseo* forms derive from this confusion.

In the fifteenth century, too, the polite form of address became *vuestra merced* with a third person singular verb, *vuessa merced,* and, in the seventeenth century, *usted.*

By the sixteenth century the most widely used forms were *vos tomáis, tomaréis, toméis, tomábades,*[5] *tomaríades, tomastes,*[5] etc.; *coméis* (at times *comés*), *comeréis, comáis, comíades, comeríades, comistes,* etc.; *decís, diréis, digáis, decíades, diríades, dixistes,* etc. The interchange of *vos* and *tú* continued to prevail, *vos* gradually losing most of its respectful status. As early as the first third of the sixteenth century, the use of *vos* often "implied, if not an insult, intimate familiarity or superior social rank on the part of the speaker." That this was the case has been amply proved with contemporary evidence.[6]

Literary usage in the sixteenth century, according to Keniston (pp. 42–44), is as follows: *Tú* was used to address "a humble person of inferior rank," to address "equals in a tone of familiar intimacy," "in lofty, literary style" such as epistles and prayers, as "a convention in the plays of the first half of the sixteenth century, all characters using *tú* as their regular form of address," and in "imagined speeches." *Vos,* with plural verb forms, on the other hand, was the customary manner of addressing "equals in formal discourse," of addressing "a superior respectfully," and "an inferior with respectful consideration"; or, if used in addressing a person ordinarily addressed with *tú,* it was "an evidence of irate seriousness."

I think we may safely assume that such usage did not exactly reflect conversational style in daily life, which by the end of the century had become more and more divorced from literary style. And the seventeenth-century literary practice became a much less reli-

[4] For examples see Cuervo "Las segundas personas de plural en la conjugación castellana," *Romania,* XXII (1893), 71–86, and in *Obras inéditas* (Bogotá, 1944).

[5] The *d* in forms like *tomábades, tomaríades, tomássedes, tomárades, tomáredes,* etc., was lost during the course of the seventeenth century, at the same time that perfect tenses, like *tomastes, comistes,* etc., became, by analogy with present tenses, *tomasteis, comisteis,* etc. Cf. also Y. Malkiel in *Hispanic Review,* XVII (1949), 159–65.

[6] Cuervo, § 332; J. Plá Cárceles, "La evolución del tratamiento de vuestra merced," *RFE,* X (1923), 245–80; Arturo Capdevila, pp. 77 ff.; etc.

able index of colloquial usage. Whereas *tú* was conventionally used (with sporadic exceptions) by all characters in plays of the first part of the sixteenth century (as it is used throughout the *Celestina*), in the seventeenth the *vos* has become preponderant and, to some degree, also conventionally so. But by now it alternates with *tú* to the point where it is sometimes used indiscriminately in the same scene or even in the same dialogue, sometimes denoting familiarity and again respectful consideration. This chaotic condition obtains in nearly every play of the time. In Lope de Vega's *Peribáñez*, for instance, the peasant Casilda addresses the Comendador sixteen times with *vos* and fourteen with *tú;* the Comendador addresses Casilda seventeen times with *vos* and eleven with *tú;* the Comendador addresses his servants, Luján and Leonardo, only with *tú*, and both servants reply to their master only with *tú*. The Condestable uses *tú* to his King, but the King uses *vos* to the Condestable. The painter uses *vos* to the peasant Peribáñez, but *tú* to the Comendador, etc.

This mixture was an advantage to the dramatic poet, who, while he might have recourse to either form conventionally, could thus select the form that more readily suited his syllabic line. Actual conversational usage is more clearly revealed from other contemporary testimony, such as that cited by Cuervo (§ 332): Covarrubias (in 1611) tells us that *vos* is not always well received; Ambrosio de Salazar (1622) says that *vos* is considered "afrenta muy grande"; Correas (1626) reveals that *merced* is used for respectful address; *él* lay between the loftier *merced* and the familiar *vos*. *Vos* was used to address servants and peasants or among intimate friends, and also in address to the King "con debido respeto y uso antiguo"; that is, it was a conventionalized usage as *tú* had been in sixteenth-century literature. The grammarian Juan de Luna remarks (1619): "El primero [título] y más bajo es *tú*, que se da a los niños o a las personas que queremos mostrar grande familiaridad o amor. *Vos* se dice a los criados y vasallos." In the *Buscón*, for instance, while the mother uses *tú* to her son and *vos* to her husband, the schoolmaster addresses the boy with *vos*. Lazarillo addresses the *escudero* as *vuestra merced;* but uses *vos* to the blind man, who in turn uses *tú* to Lazarillo. In *Don Quijote*, I, 51, we read: "Finalmente, con una no vista arrogancia llamaba de *vos* a sus iguales." Suárez de Figueroa (*El pasajero* [1617], Alivio II) confesses: "En breve se convirtió en tigre la que al principio pareció cordera. *Voséame* sin ocasión a cada paso, hace que la sirva de rodillas." Hurtado de Mendoza (in a letter to Cardinal Espinosa, dated

1579) wrote: "El secretario Antonio de Eraso llamó de *vos* a Gutierre López, estando en el Consejo, y por esto se acuchillaron."

During the course of the seventeenth century, *vos* was practically replaced by *tú* for familiar address, as was *vuessa merced* by *usted* for polite address.[7] But the *vos* has to this day survived vigorously in Spanish America, possibly, as Cuervo explains, because the *conquistadores* were to a large extent of lowly social rank and used *vos* among themselves; they addressed Indians and mestizos with *vos*, thus assuming an air of superiority. And *tú* was also used between equals among the common people, as well as confidentially between servants and masters except that, when a master became irate, he changed from *tú* to *vos*. And thus the several forms actually fused in colloquial speech: *tú* and *ti* were lost (being now distasteful to the populace) and were replaced by *vos; te* was kept as the objective case while *os* was lost; *vos* was generally used with the archaic second plural verb forms in the present and preterite, such as *amás* (= *amáis*), *tenés* (= *tenéis*), *amastes* (= *amasteis*), *tuvistes* (= *tuvisteis*); and the imperative was *amá* (= *amad*), *tené* (= *tened*), *vení* (= *venid*). Other tenses used the second singular verb form (by analogy with the archaic forms of *amás, amastes*, etc.): *vos amabas, tenías*, etc.

Whatever system of *voseo* forms is generally followed in vulgar and rustic speech in any particular country, the cultured and semicultured of the urban centers frequently try to avoid, or at least to meliorate, the lowly flavor of the *voseo* by substituting the correct second person singular verb form for the second person plural verb form accompanied by *vos* (the substitution also of *tú* would be stilted and pedantic): *vos tomas, comes, vives, tomaste, tomarás*, etc. Such usage is heard in some cities (Quito, La Paz, Bogotá, Tucumán, Salta, etc.), though never heard in the mouths of peasants. Thus for Quito, for instance, two types of usage in familiar conversation have been established (discussed later under Ecuador): the common or current type (*común*)—*vos tomas*, etc. —and the vulgar type—*vos tomás*, etc. Then again, in supersensitive and purist groups, *tú* and the corresponding correct verb forms are often used, with varying degrees of success. Habitual *voseo*-users generally employ the same familiar forms in improvised prayers, especially to the saints and to the Virgin

[7] There is some evidence of the continuance of *vos* in Spain even at the end of the eighteenth century: "del pronombre *vos* nos servimos hablando con inferiores y de ordinario con alguna suerte de enojo," says Gregorio Garcés in 1791 (*Fundamento del vigor y elegancia de la lengua castellana*), as quoted by Pla Cárceles, *RFE*, X, 247. Traces of it exist today in rural areas of Spain (Oviedo, Salamanca, etc.).

Mary, but usually recite memorized prayers according to the correct form of the text, whether it be *tú* or *vos*. All of which leads to a chaotic medley often bordering on anarchy. Local usage and variation will be mentioned below under each country.

This confusion was remedied in Spain (save for a few dialectal remnants still current; cf. Tiscornia, *La lengua*, p. 290) by the correct use of *tú* with second person singular verb forms, and *usted* with third person singular verb forms for polite address. But in two-thirds of Spanish America, regions that were free from certain social considerations of rank retained the *vos* of the masses. The other third was made up largely of the two vice-royalties of Peru and Mexico, centers of colonial culture, with their universities, poets, and literati, where the intellectual and cultured classes were able to exert great influence in matters of linguistic purity. These countries, on the whole, followed the usage of Spain in rejecting the offensive *vos* in favor of *tú*. The feeling for *tú* as the culturally superior form prevails today even in countries of most intense *voseo*, where the highest intellectual circles prefer it to the plebeian *vos*.

Purists in every country[8] where it is used have inveighed against the *voseo*, but none so violently as the Argentinian Arturo Capdevila, who in his *Babel y el castellano* (pp. 87 ff.) first pointed out that Peru and Mexico owe their present *tú* form to their superior cultural background. Capdevila becomes extremely caustic in his denunciation of the *voseo* in his native land. He calls it "sucio mal, negra cosa, horrendo voseo," and the like. However, it seems to be too deeply rooted ever to be exterminated in Argentina. Capdevila's diatribe is echoed in Central America by the Guatemalan grammarian, Bonilla Ruano (III, 11–13) in terms of "craso barbarismo," "repugnante vos," "el denigrante voseo," and the "infamante vos." The usage had been censured previously in Chile by Bello (*Advertencias* [1834]) and by Román (I, 397), who says that the popular system of conjugating verbs is "capaz por sí solo de desorientar a cualquier extranjero hasta creerlo un dialecto especial." In Colombia it was anathematized by Cuervo, who in the early editions of his *Apuntaciones* labeled it as "repugnante" and the mixture of pronouns as a "menjurge que encalabrina los sesos." In the later editions ([1914, 1939], § 332) he

[8] As will be seen farther along, Américo Castro is wrong in saying "... no existe[n] en Centro América ... críticas acerbas del voseo ... a nadie le calienta la pluma ni la cabeza el que hablen de vos en Honduras o Guatemala" (*La peculiaridad lingüística rioplatense*, p. 75). No one would make that statement who had ever heard the late Honduran writer, Froylán Turcios, launch into a tirade against the Central American *voseo*.

chastened his expression, limiting his denunciation to the words: "Inútil es decir que a quien esté acostumbrado al modo de expresarse culto y literario, todo esto le suena a barbarismo." In Ecuador, in addition to Lemos' *Barbarismos fonéticos*, we find a little-known article by Francisco Javier Salazar ("La pronunciación del castellano en el Ecuador," *Revista Ecuatoriana*, I [1889], 209–16), in which he contends that the irregular verb forms, together with other "provincialismos y barbarismos," will in time create "varios dialectos del castellano más o menos bárbaros, y tan diferentes entre sí como el árabe que se habla en Argel comparado con el de Egipto o de la Siria." In Costa Rica, Gagini (p. 244) remarks that such mixed forms "ponen los pelos de punta a los peninsulares que las oyen." He adds a commentary that is more curious than necessarily true, to the effect that the Spanish adventurers who came to America used the *voseo*, hoping thereby to conceal their humble birth and to pass as nobles in the eyes of the *criollos*.

Thus, condemnations are more or less severe, probably according to the degree in which the *voseo* has maintained its foothold in the local language. The more scientific commentators show greater serenity and, in the spirit of the later Cuervo, content themselves, as they should, with recording the forms rather than indulging in impassioned denunciation. Thus the Costa Rican grammarian, Quesada (p. 397), says, simply and appropriately: "En el tratamiento corriente, hasta entre las personas de distinción social, es desconocido el *tú;* se emplea el *vos* acordado con formas arcaicas o vulgares de la segunda persona del plural."

Perhaps the least complicated method of treating the *voseo* is by country and region.

THE RIVER PLATE REGION (ARGENTINA, URUGUAY, AND PARAGUAY)

In the River Plate region, the present indicative of *tomar* in colloquial speech would appear as follows beside the standard Castilian:

ARGENTINE	CASTILIAN
yo tomo	yo tomo
vos tomás	tú tomas
él toma	él toma
nosotros tomamos	nosotros tomamos
ustedes toman	vosotros tomáis
ellos toman	ellos toman

The two sets of forms are identical, save those of the second persons singular and plural. Since the second plural familiar is always *ustedes* + the third person plural verb, we may for convenience and brevity omit from further discussion of the *voseo* all forms except the second person singular.

PRESENT INDICATIVE

vos tomás	tú tomas
vos comés	tú comes
vos vivís	tú vives

PRESENT SUBJUNCTIVE

vos tomés	tú tomes
vos comás	tú comas
vos vivás	tú vivas

PRETERITE INDICATIVE

vos tomaste *or* tomastes[9]	tú tomaste
vos comiste *or* comistes	tú comiste
vos viviste *or* vivistes	tú viviste

IMPERATIVE

tomá	toma
comé	come
viví	vive

In all the other tenses the verb form is that of the second person singular, whose endings are in part similar to the archaic present endings *-ás* (for *-áis*), *-és* (for *-éis*), etc. Thus the imperfect indicative is

vos tomabas, comías, vivías, etc.

The future indicative is

vos tomarás, comerás, vivirás, etc.

The imperfect subjunctive is

vos tomaras, comieras, vivieras, etc.

The prepositional form *ti*, like the subject form *tú*, has yielded to

[9] *Tomastes*, *comistes*, etc., are also popular forms of the singular used with *tú: tú tomastes* for *tú tomaste*, etc. It seems logical to consider *tomastes* in *vos tomastes* as the archaic plural form; and the *tomastes* in *tú tomastes* as a popular singular form by analogy with other singular forms ending in *-s*. Its retention as a singular was strengthened when in the seventeenth century the correct second person plural became *tomasteis*, *comisteis*, etc.: *-eis* became definitely associated with the plural and *-es* with the singular. Sometimes we find *tomates*, *comites*, and *vivites* for *tomaste*(*s*), *comiste*(*s*), and *viviste*(*s*).

vos; the object form *os* has yielded to the object form *te;* the possessives are *tu* and *tuyo*. Thus one hears the following:

vos te acostás	*for*	tú te acuestas
acostáte	*for*	acuéstate
si vos te vas iré con vos	*for*	si tú te vas iré contigo
vos tenés tu libro, etc.	*for*	tú tienes tu libro, etc.

In the River Plate region the *voseo* not only is characteristic of rustic and vulgar speech, but it has also extended to the middle and upper classes. It is the wide *voseo* diffusion among all classes that is the outstanding characteristic in this region of Spanish America. Elsewhere it is considerably less employed, except in the lower classes, or is entirely rustic. In the River Plate region it is used in familiar address among equals and may be used by a superior to an inferior. In the latter case it serves to keep distance, but at the same time implies affection. It is used by parents to children, and in Buenos Aires by children to parents; but in the provinces and in rustic speech children address their parents with *usted.* Parents may alternate *vos* and *usted* in speaking to their children; *usted* being adopted either to express anger and reproach or, in the case of younger children, to express affection. *Vos* is, furthermore, used among brothers and sisters and relatives. Among boy friends, as well as among girl friends in Buenos Aires, *vos* is apparently becoming more widespread than before; whereas between men and women, though friends, *usted* is most frequently used.[10]

In the schools, teachers address their pupils with *tú*. The pupils use *tú* to each other in the classroom, but as soon as they reach the playground they resort to the less stilted *vos.* Occasionally, however, through the influence of the schoolroom, pupils continue the use of *tú* extra-murally. And the *tú* is heard elsewhere in Buenos Aires in Spanish and in some Argentine families. Tiscornia (*La lengua*, p. 127) reports that teachers in adult night schools invariably address their students with *vos.* Frida Weber reports (*RFH*, III, 107) that occasionally persons who habitually employ *vos* will, on making a new friendship, often resort to *tú* as a sort of intermediate or transitional form between the more ceremonious *usted* and the more intimate *vos.*

Strange as it may seem, some users of *vos* will avoid writing the form, even in the most intimate letter. They usually switch to the more literary *tú*, though, to be sure, they occasionally adhere to the incorrect verb form (*tú sos* for *tú eres*). For this reason caution

[10] See Frida Weber, "Fórmulas," *RFH*, III, 107.

must be exercised in judging the written language of certain authors, often in supposedly realistic dialogue, as indicative of actual spoken usage. (This applies also to the drama of the Golden Age.) In Argentine literature *vos* is used for special atmosphere in depicting local customs, as in the regional novel and drama. On the other hand, the *tú* form appears in translations and in novels that tend to idealize Argentine life, thus reproducing reality very inaccurately. Mixture of the habitual *vos* (*vos tomás*) and the occasional *tú* (*tú tomas*) in the spoken language of Buenos Aires often leads to such crosses as *tú tomás* and *vos tomas*, perhaps a meliorative tendency (cf. p. 61).

The use of *tú* in Montevideo has progressed further than in Buenos Aires. Américo Castro (pp. 74 ff.) is inclined to attribute this to a difference in "subtle collective psychology" between the inhabitants of the two cities: "La gente de Montevideo se muestra menos alardeante y desatada que la de Buenos Aires ... procura distinguirse espiritualmente, ya que no puede exceder en riquezas a su pujante rival." He is prone to ascribe the insistent and increasing use of *vos* in Argentina to a generally rebellious attitude toward cultural influences and a blustering aggressiveness against refinement in speech in the belief on the part of its users that "el plebeyo *vos* es el colmo de la argentinidad."

Paraguayan children address their parents with *usted* rather than with *vos*. Furthermore, the present subjunctives here are the purely singular forms: *vos tengas, dejes*, etc., instead of *vos tengás, dejés,* etc. Guaraní is usually preferred for greater intimacy and cordiality.

The foregoing Argentine paradigms are general in the larger portion of the country, particularly in the eastern and lowland areas, including Buenos Aires. It will be remembered that forms heard in northwestern Argentina are generally similar to those current in Chile and therefore will be mentioned in the discussion of the Chilean *voseo* (p. 69). The examples given below, then, are characteristic of almost all River Plate regions except northwestern Argentina.

Rural: —¿Quién *sos vos?* ... ¿Qué *tenés vos?* ¿Qué *te* pasa? ... ¿Qué *sentís?* (Lynch, *Palo verde*, p. 51); ¡*Mirá* que es preciso que *te curés!* (p. 52); ¡*Sacá* la lengua, *te* digo! ¡*Vos* no *tenés* nada! ¡*Estás* mintiendo! ¡No me *vengás* con compadradas! A *vos te* pasa alguna otra cosa ... ¿por qué *querés irte? ¿estás* loco? (p. 53); ¡*sos* un trompeta! (p. 54); ¿qué *te has* creído? ... *vos* lo *mataste* ... *fuiste* ... lo *escondiste* ... *merecerías* que *te* mataran ... Che, Troncoso (p. 59), etc. —*Andá decíle* algo (Güiraldes, *Don Segundo*, p. 15); —¿Cómo *te* va? ... tranca *tenés,* si ya no *sabés* quién soy. ... —No *ves* que soy Filumena, *tu* mujer, y que si *seguís* chupando ... cuantito *dentrés* a casa. ... —No *amagués* ... no vaya a ser que se *te* escape la mano y *rompás* algún vaso (p. 16); —¿Ande lo *has* visto? (p. 24); *Hacé* lo que *te* parezca (p. 37); —*Vos te has* juido 'el pueblo (p. 39); —*¿Sos* bien mandao? (p. 40); —Si *sos* gaucho ... no *has* de mudar ... *irás* (p. 303); —*¿Sabés* lo que *sos vos?* —*Vos dirás* (p. 310). ¿De qué *te reís vos?* ¡Ahí *tenés* lo que *has* conseguido! ... *¡ponéte* serio! *¡mirá* que *te* pego! ... *¡Calláte,* mujer! (Sánchez, *M'hijo el dotor,* I, 1); —No *seas* malo ... vos *sabés*. ... —¿Lo *oís?* ... *Vos* que *estabas* rezongando ... *vos* que *decías* ... ya lo *ves* (I, 2), etc.

URBAN: —¿Verdad que no *irás?* ¡No *podés* ir esta noche! (Petit de Murat, p. 154); —*Dejáte* de tragedias. Y *cuidáte*. ... *No empecés*. ... ¡Qué *vas* a saber, si *te quedás!* (p. 168). *¿Querés* ir? ... *¡Estás* loco! ... ¿me *viste?* ... *te vas* ... *hacéme* el favor ... *tomá* ... *tenés* (Laferrère, *Locos de verano,* p. 14); *¿has* estado *vos* en la casa? ... *¿has* visto? ... *decíme, ¿pensás* comprarles algo? ... *decís* ... *escucháme* ... no *te enojés* (p. 20, etc.).

As may be seen from the preceding examples, the Argentine present indicative *voseo* form of *haber* is generally *has*, rather than *habés;* and futures now usually end in *-ás* (*irás, dirás,* etc.). In highland and rural areas of Argentina one also finds *habés* (*habís* on the Chilean border).

CHILE

A century ago the *voseo,* with forms differing from those current in Argentina, was equally as widespread in Chile. However, with the help of grammarians (beginning with Bello in 1834) and strict vigil in the schools, the *voseo* has been to a large extent eradicated, having been lost completely among the cultured, who use *tú* and *usted* almost indifferently (Lenz, *La oración,* p. 156; *BDH,* VI, 261–68). But the *voseo* still holds its ground in vulgar and rustic speech, with variations from the previously discussed Argentine forms. While other forms are occasionally heard, the following indicate general usage:

PRESENT INDICATIVE

ARGENTINE	CHILEAN
vos tomás	vos tomái(s)
vos comés	vos comís[11]
vos vivís	vos vivís

[11] Oroz and Pino Saavedra consider these forms as very *vulgar,* nevertheless admitting their frequent use in the familiar language of certain people not lacking in culture. "Estas gentes emplean los giros *tú vis, tú comís,*" retaining the verb form corresponding

PRESENT SUBJUNCTIVE

vos tomés	vos tomís
vos comás	vos comái(s)
vos vivás	vos vivái(s)

FUTURE INDICATIVE

vos tomarás	vos tomarís
vos comerás	vos comerís
vos vivirás	vos vivirís

IMPERATIVE

tomá	toma or (less frequently) tomá
comé	come or (less frequently) comé[12]
viví	vive or (less frequently) viví

The *tomá*, *comé*, and *viví* forms are now used chiefly in zones bordering on Argentina.

IMPERFECT INDICATIVE

vos tomabas	vos tomábai(s)
vos comías	vos comíai(s)

IMPERFECT SUBJUNCTIVE

vos tomaras	vos tomárai(s)
vos comieras	vos comiérai(s)

It must be remembered that final *-s* in Chile is generally a mere aspiration or is not pronounced at all. In the ending *-ái(s)* it is practically silent; and therefore such forms are generally *-ai* or *-ay: estai, estay, tomai, tomay*, etc. In the *-ís* ending, however, because of the stressed high front vowel *í*, the aspiration is clearly heard; and such forms are generally written with an *s*, less frequently with an *h: venís* or *veníh; lleguís* or *lleguíh;* etc. Most writers attempting to reproduce popular speech are humanly inconsistent, and some have an individual method of recording actual pronunciation. Thus we find the following variations in spelling: *vos gozay, pongai, despreciáis, estaís, sepaih; vos comís, sentíh, valrí; vos soy, soís*, etc. Elsewhere this aspiration is recorded with *j: voj, soj*, etc.

From the foregoing paradigms we see that (1) the second person

to *vos*, even after the loss of *vos* (in a note to Bello's *Advertencias*, in "El español en Chile," *BDH*, VI [1940], 57). While it is true that forms like *tú comís* may be heard in the speech of persons possessed of a certain degree of culture, *veís* seems to be commoner than *vis* in such usage for the verb *ver* (*tú veís*); *vis* is the more vulgar form heard with *vos* rather than with *tú*.

[12] Henríquez Ureña (*RFE*, VIII, 384) remarks that the forms which should end in *-é* (*comé*) customarily end in *-í* (*comí*). The authorities he cites (Lenz and Bello) say nothing of an imperative *comí*, nor have we heard this form. Apparently he mistook Lenz's spelling *komí* as an imperative form rather than as the indicative (with aspirated *s*) which it represents.

plural ending in the present indicative of *-ar* verbs and in the present subjunctive of *-er* and *-ir* verbs is here *-ái(s)* rather than the archaic *-ás* form; (2) the *-és* ending in the present indicative of *-er* verbs and in the present subjunctive of *-ar* verbs becomes *-ís* (as occasionally in Aragonese and elsewhere in dialectal Spain: Salamancan region, Sánchez Sevilla, § 59) by analogy with the regular *-ís* ending of *-ir* verbs;[13] (3) the second person plural ending in the future of all verbs is here *-ís* rather than *-ás;*[14] and (4) the imperatives are more generally correct second person singular forms; but the plural is also used, especially in rural regions and along the Argentine border.

The *voseo* forms current in Chile are found also in the westernmost Argentine provinces of Cuyo: Mendoza, San Juan, and San Luis (Selva, *Crecimiento*, p. 163). From Carrizo's *Viento de la altipampa* we cull such forms as "*sabís, tenís, ponís,* pa que *acabís* de sanar, *querís, entendís,* no quiero que *llorís,* cuando vos *lleguís,*" etc. Forms in *-éis*, deemed the most rustic, are disappearing (Vidal, p. 120).

Occasionally, of course, one hears other forms in Chile besides those mentioned above: such as *amá(s)* for the more general *amái(s)*, *so(s)* for the more general *soi(s)*, etc., forms probably due to Argentine influence. Again, certain unlettered folk, in an effort to avoid what they have heard to be a grammatical incongruity, use *tú* + a second plural verb form: *tú tomáis;* or *vos* + a second singular verb form: *vos tomas* (Echeverría y Reyes, p. 77).

[13] Menéndez Pidal (*Gramática*, § 115) believes that *comís* is not an assimilation to verbs in *-ir*, because we find *-ís* also in the present subjunctive of *-ar* verbs: *juntís*, etc. Nevertheless, the analogy theory is supported by the fact (not recorded by Menéndez Pidal) that in Chile the first person plural of *-er* verbs is popularly *-imos* (*comimos* instead of *comemos*), most probably by analogy.

[14] Alonso and Henríquez Ureña suggest (*Gram.*, II, 99) that the *-ís* ending is due to the regular future formation: infinitive + present endings of *haber*. Therefore, they argue, since in eastern Argentina *vos has* is the present, the future ends in *-ás* (*vos andarás, verás*); since in Chile the present is *vos habís*, the future there ends in *-ís* (*vos andarís, verís*); and, since "in Colombia *vos habés* is used," the future there ends in *-és* (*vos andarés, verés*), etc. This may or may not be the true explanation. One might also argue thus: If the form *vos has* is common in Argentina, it means that the singular verb form was preferred there in the future, as well as in other tenses; and if the plural *habís* (for *habés*) is current in Chile, it means that here the plural predominated in all verbs and the same analogical form was transferred to the future (*andarís, verís*), since the same analogical *i* was also transferred to the first plural of *-er* verbs: *tenimos* for *tenemos*, etc.; and if *vos habés* were general in Colombia, it would show that the plural here, too, held sway, in this case the archaic form. While the future in *-és* is the more usual in Colombia, the regular *-ás* also exists. Furthermore, *vos habés* is so rare there that Henríquez Ureña did not find it registered. I have found it, but the current form remains *vos has*, as in Argentina. Again, the future in Guatemala ends in *-és*, but the present of *haber* is *habís* rather than *habés;* the future in El Salvador ends in *-ás* and the present of *haber* is *habís* as well as *has;* and even in Argentina the *-és* future is found in the older writers (Tiscornia, *La lengua*, p. 121 n.).

CENTRAL ZONE (SANTIAGO): —*Vos gozay* tanto cuando *comís* choro cruo, que no te *fijay*, niño (Godoy, p. 124). —No lo *tomís* a mal ni *pongai* esa cara (Alberto Romero, *La viuda*, p. 30); Como *vos tenís* sangre de rica, *despreciáis* al pobre (p. 33); Y *vos te atrevís* a hablar ... *vos te podís* imaginar (p. 73). ¿Qué *estás* pensando? *Debís* correr ... *vos sos* niño ... *cómete* todos los chupes que *poday* y *verís* qué gloria ... pa que *vos* no *pongay* esa cara ... *¡mira! te* voy a contar (Sepúlveda, *Hijuna*, p. 70); *vos* que *sos* tan callado ... *has* de saber ... si *vos defendí* a tu Patria, *afíjate, defendí* a tu madre ... *vos* no *tenís* na madre. ¿Es fuerza que lo *digay?* (p. 72). ¿No *vis?* Aquí al lao corri'otro. ... *¿Vis* como se va viendo toitito el Puerto? (Romanángel, p. 87); *¿vis?* —Sí, las veo (p. 89).

CENTRAL ZONE (RURAL): No *creay* ... *dejálos* no más ... ¡no *seay* bruto! Las cosas que se *te* ucurren ... ¿qué *habís* visto? ... Tan fregao que *sois* ... *te sujetay* ... ¿qué *decís vos?* ... antes no *éray* tan sinvergüenza. ... Tan hablaor que *soy vos*. ... ¿Qué *vay* hacer? ... *Vení* p'aca. *¿Ve?* ... Y *vos*, ¿cuándo *vay* a ir a trabajar? ... no *saliay* ... *¿tay* [= estáis] armao? ... ¡No *seay* embustero! *Vos querís* a la Mariana. ... *Sacúame* más ... *¡Tené* cuidao! ... *Te* repito que *tengay* cuidao. ... *Cállate vos* ... ya *stás* aquí ... ya no *t'irís* más (Acevedo Hernández, *La canción rota*, I, 1); *Te* pago lo que *queray*. ... *Vos sabrís*. No *inoray* ... *vos* me *debís* ... *sois*. ... *Mira*. ... Muy por bien que le *busquís* (I, 2), etc.

Manuel Guzmán Maturana, in his *Don Pancho Garuya* (1933), which Lenz called "el libro más chileno que he visto" and "una verdadera enciclopedia del lenguaje vulgar chileno," writes (2d ed., 1935):

CENTRAL ZONE (RURAL): —¿Qué *decíh, niña?* ... —¿Cuánto *valrí* [= valdrás], pelotita dioro? (p. 22); —¡Pero, niña por Dios! Tuavía no *habíh* tréido vino. ... *Andá* a buscar unas botellas y *tréy* ... un buen peazo de queso del mejor que *encontrí*. ... *Sírvele*, niña, un trago de vino (p. 23); Agora *veríh* (p. 30); —*¿Teníh* hambre? ... *Toma* ... por si *sentíh frío* (p. 64); —Te lo presto; *llévatelo* ... después me lo *devolveríh* (p. 70); —Ayer *te andábay* escondiendo de la policía. ... ¡Me alegro de que *volvay* a ser hombre honrao! (p. 99); *Hiciste* bien en defenderte. Debían fusilarte ... pa que no *atentáray* a la vía de las personas (p. 100); *Vení* pa acá pa escond*ete* (p. 101); *Métete* aentro. ... No *te movay* ... *vos* no *atravesíh* una palabra con él (p. 102), etc.

It will be noticed that this author generally represents final aspirated *s* with an *h* (*decíh, habíh, veríh*, etc.), but occasionally omits it from spelling (*valrí* for *valrís, encontrí* for *encontrís*).

In Acevedo Hernández's *Por el atajo* (p. 58), there is a conversation between two sisters, Chabela, a country girl, and Rosario, who has had a city education and uses correct *tú* forms in place of the rural *vos:*

Ño Justo (*the father*): —Chabela, anda a comprarle queso a tu hermana.
Chabela: —¡Qué señorita! ¿Tiene sirvienta? ¡Que vaya ella!
Rosario: —Y yo voy, pues. No me estés pidiendo no más.
Chabela: —No te dé cuidado; ya sé que pa mí no se han hecho las cosas güenas. Yo soy una huasa ordinaria, no sé ni hablar.
Rosario: —Ya, Chabelita, no *seas* así; tanto que me *haces* sufrir; no le puedo decir nada.
Chabela: —Ná me *tenís* que decir *vos*, ni naide, porque yo no doy que hacer.

In her short rural novel *Montaña adentro* Marta Brunet spells as follows:

No *tenís* ojos *vos* ... *echáis* ... *serías vos* ... *vos cerráis* tu hocico (p. 11); a *vos te* va pasar ... *estáis* segura ... *tú sabís* (p. 20); no *seáis* ... sí que *soís* canalla (p. 21); no *estaís* (p. 23); te *ponís* (p. 30); te *juiste* (p. 31); no *m'estís* levantando testimonios (p. 45); *vos te calláis* tu hocico (p. 57); *vos sos* (p. 63); *vos sabrís* (p. 64); ¿qué *te habís* imaginao *vos?* (p. 69); *hácele* (p. 85); *estaís* (p. 88); *estaís* loco (p. 91); *vos serís* (p. 93); si *fueras* cobarde *serías* ... *soís vos* ... *vos sos* (p. 96); *vos* te *callaís* (p. 103).

There seem to be many inconsistencies in the foregoing passages by Marta Brunet. The scene is set in the mountains of the province of Malleco, so that some of the forms may be southern. The position of the written accent in *estaís, soís, callaís,* is probably an attempt to indicate the aspiration of final *s* and the consequent reinforcement of the preceding *i*. The use of *tú sabís* is to be questioned. Though *tú* may be heard in the cities, it is doubtful whether it is an authentic rustic form. This passage shows the necessity of recording popular speech according to some consistent and more or less phonetic system.

Such peculiar rarities as *tuz* and *tis* are reportedly used in the country in an effort to imitate the cultured classes who use the correct forms of *tú* (and never *vos*). Román (I, 398) gives the form *tuz* both as subject and as prepositional form: *tuz, a tuz, de tuz, con tuz,* etc. Elsewhere it is found spelled *tus*. The *s* is merely aspirated in pronunciation and is added, no doubt, by analogy with *vos.*[15] Else-

[15] Another analogical form is *yos* for *yo:* "quien soy *yos*" (p. 120), aquís toy *yos*" (p. 160), etc., in Muñoz, *Don Zacarías Encina.*

where we find also *tis*, which is the same form (plus the aspiration or *s*) that Cuervo (§ 332) speaks of for Colombia: "el vulgo mira como insultante el *ti*"; cf. also Uribe (*Dicc.*): "más feo sos *ti*." *Tos* for *vos* (or *os*) is found in Aragon (Menéndez Pidal, *Gram.*, § 94).

¿Son acaso los Ministros del Señor descendientes de turcos o de gitanos, o de chinos, que al primero que pillan a mano, se lo echan al hombro y lo tratan de *vos* y de *tus*, y sin más ni más, tratan de arrancarle sus ahorros? (Muñoz, p. 244); —Eres *tis*, Adancito mío (p. 120); —¿Llegastes *tis* de Chillán? Pu allá me tirastes *tis* con tus desprecios: ¡cara de pan con anís! (p. 179).

BOLIVIA

The cultured generally use standard *tú* forms (*tú hablas, tú vienes*). In popular and colloquial urban speech, the rule is *vos* + the singular verb (*vos hablas, vos vienes*), except (1) in the imperative, where the plural holds sway (*hablá, vení*), and (2) in the present indicative of *ser* (often *vos sois* beside *vos eres*). In rural regions, particularly in Santa Cruz de la Sierra and in the departments of Potosí and Tarija, sections bordering on Chile and Argentina, *vos* is heard with the plural verb form (*vos habláis* or *hablás, vos venís, vos sabés*, etc.).

La Paz: Es mejor que lo *leas vos* ... *¿vos crees?* ... *tú te encuentras* (Arguedas, *Vida criolla*, p. 221); *¿irías vos?* ... *¿has* ido? (p. 22); *oí* ... tengo que hablar*te* ... ¿qué *quieres? hablá* pronto, *che* (p. 256); no *hables* así, *che* (p. 257); Es *a vos* que no *te* quiere (p. 258). *Vos* ... me *sigues* ... me *has* seguido ... *estás* ... *sois* ... *escucháme* (Díaz Villamil, *La Rosita*, p. 10); no me *interrumpas* ... *dejáme* hablar ... con *vos* ... te *acuerdas* ... a *vos te* han dejado en la calle ... me *quieres* (p. 11); *abríte* nomás una botella ... *quedáte* (p. 13); *vos* ... *servíte* (p. 15); *vos sois* una guagua (p. 89) ... *eres* (p. 90); *andá acostáte* (p. 92); *Andá acabálo* (*Cuando vuelva*, p. 15); *vos* no *conoces* (p. 21); *vos* no *eres* hombre (p. 23); *Vos eres* ... *perdé* cuidado (p. 50). (Panchita, a *chola*): —*Vos eres* ... *dejáte* de cosas ... *oíme*. (Raquel, representing the cultured class, replies): —*Óyeme*, Panchita ... *tú sabes* ... *tú eres*, etc. (Rodrigo, p. 22); qué feliz *sois* (p. 29) ... ¿y de *vos?* (p. 31) ... ¿por qué no *hablas vos* con ella? (p. 41).

Rural: No *serías vos* quien lo dijo (Céspedes, p. 51); *¡Salí, salí!* (p. 56); *Aguardá* la azotera, *te* mato. ... *Vos soltá, soltáme*. ... *Cálmate*, doña Trini. Trinica, *vos* me *conoces* (p. 57); *¡Tendéte*, mi Coronel! (p. 117); ¿Dónde *te perdiste, voj*, camba? *Te pierdej* otra *vej*, *te* mato.

Ayá en Santa Cruz maté mucho camba como *vos* (p. 120); *vení tú. Andá* pa adelante (p. 125); *lleváte* ese queso (p. 215). ... *Che, oyé,* ps, *che.* ... Dicen los otros que *te debés* desertar (Toro Ramallo, p. 34); *Andáte* ... *pasáte* (p. 35); *Andá* a ver si *traés* alguno (p. 51); *¿Tomás* otro trago, *che?* (p. 104).

Santa Cruz de la Sierra: *¿Vos* lo *conocés* a don Hermógenes Parada? ... *decíle* (Alfredo Flores, in *ACB*, p. 67); Al escuchar esto don Hermógenes ... dirigiéndose a un peón, le ordenó: —A ver, *che, traé* pronto mi sillonero ensillao ... , y no *perdás* tiempo (p. 68); —¿Qué *querés,* hija? ... *andá* no más (p. 69); *Tenés* que conformar*te.* ... No *sos* hombre, *che* ... *permitíme* (p. 71); *vos sabés* (p. 73).

Tarija: —Güen día, *che. Pasá. Sentáte.* ¿Qué se *te* ofrece? ... *Aguardáte,* hombre. No *te aflijáis* (Alberto Rodó Pantoja, in *ACB*, p. 96); Lo que *debés* hacer es vicharlos y cuando *sepáis* quién es el buen mozo, le *tiráis* una planiada. ... Después la *lleváis* a tu mujer (p. 97). *Peláte* las papas. ... Y *vos,* Higinia, *andá* deschalando los choclos (Luis Azurduy, in *ACB*, p. 108).

PERU (LIMITED ZONES)

For Peru we find some data, not all fully confirmed or clearly explained, in Benvenutto Murrieta's *El lenguaje peruano* (1936). The *voseo* is used in southern Peru, especially in Arequipa, in rustic as well as in popular urban speech. Furthermore, it appears archaically and with decreasing vigor in the Spanish-speaking towns of the province of Pallasca (Ancash) and to a still less degree in the department of San Martín and among certain Indians along the northern coast. In Huánuco (Pulgar Vidal, p. 816) *vos* is not a familiar form; on the contrary, it is used by the majority to replace the less ceremonious *usted:* "¿Para quién son estas flores? —Para *vos,* doctor." In the central areas of Lima and Cuzco, the *vos* had probably been completely replaced by *tú* by the end of the eighteenth century. But that *vos* had in the earlier period been in vogue there as everywhere else may be inferred by the expressions still current in Peru as elsewhere: "hablarse de tú y vos" and "el ser de tú y vos": "Se han destapado conmigo con una familiaridad grande, *tratándonos de tú y vos,* como si desde la más tierna infancia hubiéramos comido del mismo choclo" (Corrales, p. 49).

The characteristics of the Arequipan *voseo* are essentially those found in Chile, as explained under our caption "Chile" (p. 67), with exceptions like *tomás, estás, vas, has,* etc., that correspond to the Chilean *tomái(s), estái(s), vai(s), habís,* etc.

> Si vos me *querís, quereme*
> Y no me *engañís* bandíu,
> No me *dejís* despancada
> Que para *vos te* he paríu
> —F. Mostajo, cited by Benvenutto, p. 139.

In the northwestern provinces of Pataz (La Libertad) and Cajamarquilla (Cajamarca) the *voseo* is limited to the use of the pronoun *vos,* the verbs being correct second person singular forms. In this region, along the River Marañón, is set Ciro Alegría's *La serpiente de oro,* from which we glean:

—Y *vos tias* [= te has] güelto mentiroso (p. 32); —La cosa va con *vos* (p. 45).

The same author's *Los perros hambrientos* has:

... como *vos quieres* (p. 51); —Wanka, Wankita, *vos sabes* lo ques cuanduel pobre yel animal no tienen tierra ni agua. ... *Has güelto* como la lluvia güena" (p. 168).

López Albújar's *Matalaché,* from the northern department of Piura, shows:

—Es que *vos,* José Mañué, *sos* aquí l'único después del amo, a quien ese bandido respeta. Con dos palabras que *vos* le *digas* no golverá a tocarme ... como *vos estás* un poquito más arriba que nosotros, no *sabes* (p. 88); ¡Qué mal pensao *sos!*" (p. 104).

Voseo usage throughout Peru, as well as in many other regions, needs scientific investigation before linguistic facts can be satisfactorily explained.

ECUADOR

As far as the *voseo* is concerned, Ecuador may be divided into two regions: the Inter-Andean (northern and central parts), including Quito; and the coastal region, including Guayaquil. In the Inter-Andean region the *voseo* is general in both rural and urban daily speech, even among a large group of cultured persons. Among the more puristic groups there, however, the correct use of *tú* is the rule. In all classes of the coastal and south-central region (including Cuenca) the use of *tú* is much commoner than in the highlands. The predominating forms of *voseo*[16] are, in the main, those most generally used in Chile (but final *s* is pronounced in the highlands): the *-áis* ending for *-ar* verbs, and the *-ís* ending for both *-er* and *-ir* verbs (*querís, habís, decís,* etc.). To be sure, in a few verbs the *-és* ending for *-er* verbs (*sabés,* etc.) may occasionally be heard in certain rural sections, but the *-ís* ending (*sabís,* etc.) is the general form for both country and city. The future is very often formed on the Chilean pattern (*tomarís, comerís, dirís,* etc.)—and this is considered the more vulgar form—or more commonly on the Argentine pattern (*tomarás, comerás, dirás*).[17] The imperative is sometimes singular (*toma*) and sometimes plural (*tomá*) in form. As in the urban centers of other countries, so in the cities of Ecuador, the semicultured classes are prone to use a second person singular verb with *vos* (*vos eres, vos sabes,* etc.).[18] (Such agreement, however, is never made by peasants.) *Tú* with the correct singular forms occasionally alternates with *vos* and the mixed forms. Confusion is widespread, and therefore we find no definite or general tendency toward unification as in Argentina and Chile. As elsewhere, too, the expression *tratarse de tú y vos* signifies affection and close friendship. *Vos* is used familiarly among equals and in addressing younger people and those of "inferior social or economic category" (Pérez Guerrero, § 180). While parents may address their children with *vos* (or *usted*), the children very frequently use *usted* (more rarely *su merced*) to their parents. In Ecuador, as elsewhere, the unlettered Indians use *vos* promiscuously, even in addressing their masters—a practice which proves that the form thus used is archaic in application as well as indicative of inurbanity.

[16] Care must be exercised in interpreting texts, not only for human inconsistencies of the author, but for deliberate falsification of forms. In his *Cantares del pueblo ecuatoriano* (1892), J. León Mera substitutes *tú* + a singular verb for *vos* + a plural verb, as the latter seemed to him "barbaridades repugnantes" (p. 240). He reasoned (p. ix): "Con tal que se conserve puro el espíritu ... ¿por qué no ha de corregirse su lenguaje? ¿En qué se menoscaba, por ejemplo, al quitarle la mezcla del *tú* con el *vos* y en sustituir el *vení* con el *ven* y el *tenís* con el *tienes?*" Nevertheless, he was unable to purify the whole text, for he was obliged to allow some of the forms to stand (*tenéte,* etc.) because of the exigencies of rhyme and meter. The same type of editing is unfortunately also that of Antonio José Restrepo in his *El cancionero de Antioquia* (Colombia).

[17] Lemos (*Barbarismos fonéticos del Ecuador,* § 29) mentions the tendency of *-ís* for the future endings, but by far the greater number of examples encountered show *-ás* for the future. A limited number only have *-ís* and occasionally *-éis* (*vos tendréis*).

[18] In a sample of verbs used in familiar conversation, F. J. Salazar ("La pronunciación del castellano en el Ecuador," *Revista Ecuatoriana,* I [1889], 210) gives two verb forms for each tense, the *común* and the *vulgar: común* = *vos* (por *tú*) *has, hubiste, vienes, veniste, ven; vulgar* = *vos* (por *tú*) *habís, hubistes, venís, venistes, vení.*

Except in the coastal region, *tú* is used exclusively by persons of a certain degree of culture (though often affectedly), so that Guerrero ventures to say (p. 167) "de quien lo oímos, por este solo hecho, podemos afirmar que habla bien," a statement that appears too sweeping.

INTER-ANDEAN ZONE (QUITO): ¿No *te quedáis?* (Icaza, *En las calles*, p. 6); *te vis* (p. 8); *decís* (p. 19); ¡*Hacé* justicia, amitu! (p. 21); ¿qué más *te querís?* (p. 73); *tomáte* el primer trago de tu vida, ya'*stáis* caminando para viejo (p. 74); ¿Hasta ónde *vais*, hijo? ... *vení* (p. 80); *Verís* como escribir (p. 82); *abrí, ve.* ¿*Estáis* ocupada? (p. 88); Ya *sabís vos* mesmo. ... ¿*Ti' acordáis?* (p. 101); *te presentáis* (p. 114); *Pondrás* yapando. ... *Poné* más trago (p. 165); *Verás* ... *vos* ... *vais* ... mañana *pedirás*. ... *Andá* no más (p. 181); —*Cashá*, no *shores* tanto. ¿Qué más *te querís?* (p. 182); *A vos* ... *te* van a mandar. ... *Tenís* qui'andar*te* con cuidado ... *estáis* poniéndo*te* así agachado (p. 189); *vos* mismo *te' stás* revolcando (p. 225); *venríste* ... *trairás* ... *saludarás* al compadre si le *vis* (p. 242), etc. Payaso que no *valís*, al diablo *te parecís* (García Muñoz, *Estampas*, p. 47); —No *tomés* más, mañana *tenís* que ir al trabajo (p. 54); *vos te chumas* (p. 55); —*Quitaríste, quitaríste*, José. ... No le *insultarís* a la Rosa (p. 182); —*Callá* ... no *digáis quias* estado con cuatro. ... No *vendrís* a hacer*te* la brava (p. 185); *vos* bien fuerte *sois*. *Sentáte*. ... Pero antes *trai* el número de la lotería (p. 199); *Vos* no *has* de salir; —¿*Querís?* no *comprendís* ... no *te preocupáis* (p. 274); *Subíte* a la cama, *ve.* ¿*Tenís* algo? (p. 285), etc.

COASTAL ZONE (RURAL): —¿*Habij* echao er barbajo? ... —¿Y qué *ejperaj* entonces? ¡*Apúrate! Vos sabés* (Aguilera Malta, p. 8); *Tenej* razón (p. 10); —¡*Ven*, hombre, *apriende!* ¿Me *tenés* miedo? ... ¿*Quierés* [*sic*] acompañarme? (p. 27); (father to son): *Tú sabés*. ... ¿*Sabés vos?* (p. 32); (*patrón* speaks): *voj* no *vaj* a poder pagarme. *Tás* muy viejo. *Bebes* mucho. *Te morirás* muy pronto; (son to father): —Yo pago, viejo. No se preocupe (p. 33); —Me *gustás máj* que antej. ... —¿Qué *querés? Bajá* (p. 38); quiero que *te vengas* a vivir conmigo ... no *seas* ... me *gustas*. ... *Tú te venís* conmigo. *Te vas* conmigo. ... Yo vendré por lo que *tú querás* después (p. 39); *voj érej* un pendejo. ... Si *querej te* llevo donde ér [= él] (p. 60); *Oye* ... *vos* no le *conocés* (p. 62); me *habés* fregao ... ya *veraj* (p. 73), etc.

In his collection of short stories called *Yunga* (written in 1931 and 1932), Gil Gilbert generally uses correct second person singular forms with *vos:*

—*Oye*, Pedro, *vos* bien *sabes*. *Vos* que me *enamoraste* primero (p. 65); *vos* no *eres* mi ñaña ... no *comas* en los platos de nosotros (p. 114); *vos te dejas* mandar por tu mujer ... *vos* no *te impones* (p. 76).

This agreement of *vos* with the second person singular of the verb is common among the semicultured of urban centers.

COLOMBIA

The general characteristics of the *voseo* as employed in popular Colombian speech, where it exists in conflict with *tú*, are similar to the Argentine forms (*vos tomás, tenés, vivís; tomastes* or *tomates* or *tomaste*, etc.; *tomá, tené, viví, tomabas, tenías*, etc.); but, contrary to Argentine usage, the future generally ends in *-és* (*verés*), though not, as Henríquez Ureña implies (*RFH*, VIII, 385), exclusively. The present of *haber* is generally *has*, rarely *habés*. In southern Colombia, however, *voseo* forms resemble those used in Ecuador. In Bogotá, as in urban centers in other countries, one frequently hears *vos* + a second person singular verb (*vos tomas*). On the Atlantic coast of Colombia (Barranquilla, Cartagena, Santa Marta) *tú* is general, *vos* being rare (Sundheim, p. 648), possibly limited to the provinces of Mompox and Magangué (Revollo, p. 281). Negroes there use *tú* indiscriminately, rarely employing *usted*. Furthermore, Tiscornia (p. 289) states, according to information furnished Henríquez Ureña by the Colombian eclectic philosopher, Baldomero Sanín Cano, that in Antioquia one frequently hears the combination *tú te callás* (a fusion of *tú te callas* and *vos te callás*). That the word "frequently," however, might appropriately read "occasionally" we may conclude from Tomás Carrasquilla's three-volume novel laid in Antioquia, entitled *Hace tiempos*, a cursory perusal of which does not reveal that particular fusion of forms. And that the popular language is here used authentically we may infer from the fact that the novel was awarded the Vergara y Vergara prize by the Academia Colombiana de la Lengua. In Antioquia *vos* is now largely restricted to rural areas; occasionally it is heard in intimate urban speech, chiefly in stereotyped forms (*caminá, fijáte*, etc.) or for humorous effect.

In Tomás Carrasquilla's *Hace tiempos*, Volume I (*Por aguas y pedrejones* [1935]), we read:

... *vos estás* muy creído ... *sos* un bobo ... no *sabés* ni pelear ... no *acosés* más a Eloy ... ya *venís vos* ... pa que *te* dé comida (p. 27); *entendé* que de hoy en adelante *tenés* que pagar (p. 265); —Porque me *cogites* con una cuerda encaramada. *Dejá* y *verés* (p. 285); *acordáte* ... si *dejás* a este muchacho (p. 282); no *vengás* aquí (p. 317), etc.

In Volume II (*Por cumbres y cañadas* [1935]):

—*Fijáte* ... *ve* ... ahora *verás* ... ¿no lo *alcanzás* a ver? (p. 45); ¿*has* compuesto mucho versos ... ? Bien *podés* decir ociosidades; pueda ser que con eso *te purgués* de todos los papeles públicos que *leés* con tu taita. *Mostrános* el reló ... no lo *cojás*, porque algún daño le *hacés* (p. 263); El día que *te murás*, *conseguirés* juicio ... *irés* a ser obispo ... no *creás* ... *vos* no *has* subido ... *vos sos* tan bobo que no *te has* fijao (p. 266); lo que *entenderés vos* de esas cosas (p. 275); *vos* misma me *enseñaste* (p. 277); *vos*, ¿por qué no me *has* contado bien todas esas peleas? (p. 279); *has* vivido ... *sabé* y *entendé* (p. 308); *vos deberías* ser directora de minas (p. 330); y *vos*, ¿por qué no me *has* mostrado a la negra Loaiza? (p. 336), etc.

In Volume III (*Del monte a la ciudad* [1936]):

Allá *verés* qué tan bueno (p. 43); ¿*vos has* visto? (p. 58); Bien picao que *ti'habrés* quedao (p. 142); *oléme* y *verés* (p. 163); *oí* y *verés* qué tan feo cantan los gallos criollos (p. 197); *vos sabrés* que *hacés* (p. 225), etc.

In Arango Villegas' *Bobadas mías* (1936) we find a common literary use of *voseo* for humorous effect, produced here by way of contrast between the dignity of a supposed diplomat conversing on grave matters of state with the president of the United States and his use of the overconfident and lowly *voseo:*

sentáte ... *creéme* ... (with a mixture of correct *tú* forms) *tú comprendes*, no *tengas* cuidado ... *vos comprendés* ... no *llames*, *vos creés* ... *decí* ... lo que *vos querés* ... no *te calentés* ... *vos trajiste* (p. 140–41).

The same effect is produced later when the Lord uses the *voseo* in addressing a sinner recently arrived in heaven:

... *vos fuistes* ... *temás* ... (with mixture of correct *tú* forms) para que me *hagas* unos trabajitos (p. 182), etc.

From Jaime Buitrago's *Pescadores del Magdalena* (1938) we cull:

—*Mirá* mijo, le decía su padre: Si una muela *te* duele, *te* la *podés* sacar ... no *te encerrés* ... *cogé* la atarraya ... si *vieras* (p. 57); —Qué hubo: ¿no *cogistes* pescao? ... no *te asustés* (p. 58); *vos* no *has* ido ... ni *habés* visto ... *acordáte* ... *vos sos* ... para que *te vas* de mi río y *dejés* de quitarme los peces; *vos podés verte* con Verónica (p. 66); a medida que lo *conozcás* (p. 70); *vos* la *pegastes* (p. 109); esta tarde *irás vos* a pescar (p. 117); a *vos* el que *te* importa es el Vitorio (p. 134), etc.

In Eustasio Rivera's *La vorágine* we find in rustic and familiar speech:

Andá ... *buscále* ... *decíle* ... *dános vos* algo de comé (p. 29); si *querés*, pa *vos* también hay (p. 31); ¿*vos* por qué *te quedás* aquí? ... *vos parecés* picure [= prófugo]; *vos estabas* ... *vos eras* (p. 151); *te referís* (p. 248); ¡*no* me lo *recordés*! ¡*ponéle* conciencia a lo que *decís*! ... *vas* (p. 249); me *pegaste* y *querías* matarnos, y *te fuiste* ... *vos* le *ibas* a meté no sé cuántos chismes ... ya *ves* (p. 250); *vos* ... *sos* (p. 255).

In Álvarez Garzón's *Los Clavijos*, representing southern Colombia (Pasto and vicinity), we read:

—Hambre *dirís* que *tenís* ... si *comís* que *comás* ... si *querís*, *comé* sin sal (p. 55); no me lo *negués*, lo *mirabas* (p. 81); *andá* ... ¿no *vis*? ... ¿no *sabís*? (p. 90); *te hacís* una cruz ... *oirís* bien ... *llevarís* una pala para que *abrás* (p. 103); (higher social level) *vos tienes*, *eres* (p. 135); *vos mereces* (p. 192), etc.

VENEZUELA

The *voseo* is unknown in eastern and central Venezuela, including the capital Caracas. However, there are two large *voseo* regions: (1) The Andean *voseo* forms are *-ás*, *-és*, etc. (states of Táchira, Mérida, and a large part of neighboring Lara and Falcón). However, here the *voseo* is limited (superiors to inferiors, landowner to ranchhand, master to servant, with a possible derogatory connotation) because the familiar form of address is rare (*RFE*, VIII, 389 n.): *usted* is general even within the family (parents to children, between brother and sister, husband and wife, etc.). (2) The coastal *voseo* forms are *-áis* and *-éis* or *-ái* and *-éi*, showing loss of *-s* in pronunciation as in Chile (Maracaibo or Zulia, with an extension to the Andean state of Trujillo). In the Llanos, a possible third zone, the speech of older people contains a few remnants of *voseo*, chiefly imperative forms (*tomá*, *vení*, etc.). Here, however, correct *tú* forms used in Caracas have practically triumphed, and they are making inroads in the Andean and coastal regions.

Rómulo Gallegos uses an exceedingly limited number of *vos* forms in his *Doña Bárbara* (1929), representing the rural sections of eastern Venezuela (the Araucan plains). The plural forms are here accompanied by *tú*. Only the following caught my attention:

—*Salí tú* primero, chica; —¿Gúa y por qué no *salís tú?* (p. 49); —*¡Andá* viendo, pues! ... *Contá,* pues. ¿Qué *has* mirado? —¿Qué *decís tú* a eso? (p. 76).

A cursory perusal of the same author's *Pobre negro* (1940), representing northeastern Venezuela and the coast, reveals no *voseo* but only correct *tú* forms, as was seen to be the case along the Atlantic coast of Colombia. Coastal regions, being more accessible to traffic, are consequently more exposed to linguistic modification from without. Yet the Maracaibo and the Argentine coastal areas are resistant.

The comparatively meager use of *voseo* is further evidenced by its absence in the short stories selected by A. Uslar Pietri and J. Padrón and published in Caracas (1940) with the title *Antología del cuento venezolano (1895–1935).* Of these thirty-five stories, only five use *voseo* forms; and, significantly enough, four of these five are by authors from the so-called *generaciones* of 1928 and 1930, that is, the most modern in the collection. The fifth is from the preceding group of 1920. Not a single *voseo* form is used by the more conservative authors represented in the first two periods: 1895–1910 and 1910. We may conclude that the *voseo* is more widespread in the popular speech of Venezuela than was apparent from the writings of the older, more conservative, and more purist writers. Nevertheless, it probably is much less extensive than in the other *voseo* countries. The following forms are the most important culled from the *Antología:*

—*Mirá vos,* ¿por qué no *queréis* tirála conmigo? ... me *habéis* ganado ... *has* arrasao con mis moneítas ... *tenéis* los daos aquerenciaos ... *tú sabés* ... *aflojá* (González Eiris, "Los Caribes," I, 324). —¿No *querés?* ¿Acaso es lo que *tú quieras?* ... *vos sabés* que sí (Díaz Sánchez, "Veintiuno," II, 57–58). ... *Tenéis razón.* ... *Mirá* ... *te tirastes* ... *te echastes* (Bracho Montiel, "Odio," II, 82–83). —Si *queréi te* pongo aceite e coco. ... *Alevantáte tú* también pa que *cueles.* ... ¿Aquí no *has* vivío? ... *contestá.* ... ¿Por qué no *te morís* aquí? ... Si *queréi* ... *vete tú* ... ¿Qué *tenéi?* ... *¡Quitámela* de encima! (Luis Peraza, "La güira," II, 167–68); (in the words of a song): *Queréme* chinita ... no *sias* remilgada ... *abrazáme* ... *reyíte* ... etc. (II, 190). *Decí,* qué *venís* a hacer. ...

¿Estás reclutando? no lo *apresaste.* ... *¡Sabés! Quedáte* quieto ... si no *querés* ir (Gonzalo-Patrizi, "Queniquea," II, 194, 204).

In Antonio Arráiz's novel of prison life, *Puros hombres* (1938), we find among other forms:

—¿Y *vos?* ¿Qué *tenéis?* ... *Ven* acá (p. 13); *Meté* la cabeza para que *veáis* (p. 30); *te imaginás vos* ... para que *veáis vos* (p. 31); ¿no *veis vos?* ... ¿no *te fijás vos?* ... ¿no *comprendéis vos?* (p. 33); no *servís* ... *vos sos* ... malhaya *te pudrás* (p. 34); *vos estabais* presente (p. 157); *vos* no *has* oído (p. 158); *fuiste vos* y a *ti te* toca ... *¿vos* me *garantizáis* que si *fueras sido vos, vos botaras?* (p. 188), etc.

ANDEAN REGION (SAN CRISTÓBAL): *Vos* me *ibas* a envainar ... *cogé* la cajeta y *echate* una boliada ... no *saqués* (Croce, p. 12); *seguís* (p. 17); *cojé* el camino que *querás* ... no lo *hagás* (p. 18).

PANAMA

In Panama *tú* is used in the capital and in Colón, and *vos* may be heard in the interior, particularly in the area adjoining Colombia. However, that the *voseo* was at one time familiar in the western province of Chiriquí is evident from a popular theatrical performance representing scenes from the so-called *juntas* of Panamanian peasants, who gather together for certain types of communal labor and entertainment. Narciso Garay witnessed such a "bucolic eclogue" in David, province of Chiriquí, and reproduced it in his *Tradiciones y cantares de Panamá* (1930). The following are *voseo* forms gleaned from his book (pp. 40–43):

Cipriana por vía tuyita, *traéme* una poca de agua de la quebrá. ... *Ponélos* acá. ... *Cuenta te quemáis.* ... ¡Jesú, *andá! parecéi* qu'*estái* movía [= rígida].

The province of Veraguas (in central Panama) is the scene of most of the tales in Nacho Valdés' *Sangre criolla* (1943), in which we find these rural forms:

—Es que *vos te habéis* vuelto zoco [= manco] ... *vos* no *sabéis* jugar ... *vos te estáis* creyendo (p. 34); *te dejáis* pegar ... *vais* a tocarme (p. 35); ¿qué *queréis vos* que haga? (p. 64); *decíme* ... *vos querés* (p. 95); no *te dejéis* llevar (p. 104).

It should be noted that the preferred endings are *-áis* and *-éis* and that final *-s* is generally aspirated.

COSTA RICA

The *voseo* is common in all five republics of Central America.[19] Sometimes the forms are like the Argentine, sometimes like the Chilean, and again there seems to be a general confusion, with a mixture of *tú* and *vos* and verb forms of either singular or plural number. In Costa Rica we find such confusion. There are occasional plural futures in *-és*, but the majority conform to the singular *-ás;* we find an occasional plural form *habís*, but more generally the singular *has;* we find both *vos eres* and *vos sos*, etc.; and both *vos pagaste* and *vos pagastes*, the correct second person singular form being considered the more refined; but apparently no forms like *amái(s)*, *queréi(s)*, etc., which we meet in Chile. The *voseo* is so general in Costa Rica that it can be heard even in the schools, and users of *tú* are considered pedantic and presumptuous. We are told that "los ticos [= costarricenses] todos, cultos e ignorantes" are addicted to the *voseo* and always use it in familiar speech: "Resulta muy gracioso oír a personas muy cultas hablar con corrección, y repentinamente, hablando con sus familiares (y aún con las mismas personas, repitiendo una conversación o frase familiar) usan modismos como los siguientes: '*Mira, no hagás vos* eso. ... ¿Cómo *estás vos?* ¿Quién *sos vos?* ... Si *te vas*, iré *con vos*,' " etc. (Salesiano, p. 130).

RURAL:—*Cogé* esa pujienta/y le *jalás* el pescuesco;/*te fritiás* unos frijoles/*hasés* dos tortas de güebo/y ¿pa qué más? (Agüero, p. 28); *Precurá* dormir, hijito .../Cuando *estés* algo más grande/*entenderés* el motibo .../... *Dormíte*, niñó, *dormíte* (p. 35); —¡Ché, no *toqués*, trabieso! (p. 41). *Vos sos tonta.* ... Si *querés te* llevo conmigo (Lyra, p. 38); ¡no me *robés* mis torrejas! (p. 65); no *te hagás* del rogar (p. 102); *eres vos* (p. 104); ¿ya *olvidaste* a lo que *venías?* ... a ver si *vas* al cuarto ... y *te alcanzás* cuanta mesa y silla *encontrés* (p. 115); ¿Con que *vos eras?* ... *Aguardáte* ai y *verás* (p. 122), etc.

The *voseo* is commonly used in folk tales in the mouths of animals for popular as well as humorous effect.

[19] Owing to the general dearth of suitable literary material in Central America and more particularly because local output is difficult to procure or unknown elsewhere, we have been much more generous than would ordinarily have been necessary with examples culled from writings acquired in visits to the countries in question. Because of such lack of documentary evidence, Tiscornia, for instance, was unable to give any information on El Salvador: "No poseemos datos seguros acerca del voseo en San Salvador [*sic*]" (p. 135). He probably meant El Salvador, which is the name of the republic; San Salvador is the capital of El Salvador. And for the same reason Américo Castro makes the partly erroneous statement: "No existe en Centro América una literatura vertida audazmente en la lengua rústica" (*La peculiaridad lingüística rioplatense*, p. 75).

In the *Concherías* of Aquileo Echeverría (†1909), whom Rubén Darío called "the national poet, the regional poet" of Costa Rica, we read:

—¿De qué *te ris?* (p. 111); —*¿Bos biste* eso? (p. 113); —*Bos cantás* lo que *quedrás* (p. 128); —Pos *oyí* (p. 130); —¿Por ónde *te habís* metido? (p. 147); ¿Cuántos *tenés?* (p. 148); ... no me los *pagastes* (p. 149); *Mirá,* por bida tuyita, no *fregués* (p. 189); *¡Adiviná* si *sos* hombre! (p. 190).

Herrera García in *Vida y dolores de Juan Varela* (1939) wrote:

—Hombré, *no te metás* en filosofías. *¿Vos vas* a saber más que el presidente de la república? —*Decidíte* de una vez (p. 11); *Vos te desanimás* de todo. *Sos* muy flojo. *¿Te has* fijado ... ? *Estarías* salvado ... *no te desanimés.* ... Los chiquillos se ponen tristes si *te* ven *a vos* alicaído (p. 12); No *seas* así ... *veme* a mí ... *vete vos* mismo (p. 13); *Salí* y *date* preso (p. 25).

In Fabián Dobles' rural novel, *Aguas turbias* (1943), we read:

—*Vos sabés* que yo miedo no *te* tengo—dijo Moncho, voseando ya a su rival. ... *Date* cuenta (p. 35); (aunt to niece): —*Mirá,* muchacha, yo *te* quiero mucho *a vos* ... pero si *seguís* ... *vas* a tener que busca*te* otra casa (p. 160); (niece to aunt): —¿Por qué *dice* eso, ah? Si *usté* platicara con él lo vería; (aunt to niece): —*¡Vos sos* una chacalina! *¿Crés* que *te* busca pa casase con *vos?* (p. 161); (mother to son): —¿Qué *decís,* hijó? *¿Estás* pensando casa*te?* ... —*Trételа* pa acá ... cuando *te casés* (p. 46); (son to mother): —¡Y como *usté* no quiere a Chela! (p. 47), etc.

NICARAGUA

That about the same confused usage holds for Nicaragua is attested by the following forms taken from Calero Orozco's *Sangre santa* (1940) and common to all social classes (A. Valle, p. 294):

Me *soltás* la mano ... me *decís* ... qué *querés* (p. 46); que me *ayudés* ... *vos sos* (p. 47); *¿oís?* ... *vestíte* y *andáte* ... *¿oíste?* (p. 64); no *serás* manco (p. 81); anoche *acabastes* la plata ... eso es lo que a *vos te* mata (p. 82); *vos fuistes* ... *vos creías* (p. 86); Como cosa tuya *vos* le *levantás* el arresto, y *te arreglás* con él como *querrás* (p. 113); Si lo *has* custodiado ... lo *has* tratado bien ... no se lo *pidás* (p. 114); lo *confesastes* ... *hu-*

bieras visto *vos* ... *vos te perdías* de vista (p. 116); El jefe *sos vos*. Lo que *digás vos* (p. 121); *te llamarás* ... si *querés* (p. 129); *decíme* como *has* pasado (p. 145); quiero que *vos te vayas* (p. 147).

In Juan Felipe Toruño's *El silencio* (1935) we read:

Estás loco. *Crés* que porque *andás* en ese animal. ... *Sos* una desgraciada y me *habís* quitado a mi hombre (p. 69); ¡A ése lo *podrés* fregar, a mí no! (p. 72).

Here, too, children, especially in the country, are likely to use *usted* to their parents and older relatives, who in turn use *vos:*

—Niño ... quién sabe qué *tenés*. ... ¿Cuándo *querés* que vayamos, ah? —Tía ... son preocupaciones *suyas*. ... *Vd. acabará* por enfermarme (Chamorro, *Entre dos filos*, p. 200).

Some of the confusion of forms, particularly the use of *tú* with a plural verb, is undoubtedly due, as elsewhere, to a desire on the part of certain unlettered speakers of conforming to correct social usage. An example of the resulting inconsistency we find in Chamorro's *Entre dos filos:*

(A father to his daughter): —No te vayas, *vení* para acá ... tanto que te quiere tu papacito y *vos* tan mal que le *correspondés*. —Pero, papá, no digas esas cosas. ... —Eso quiere decir que *tú* no *querés* contármelo.

And the author adds: "Como se ve, Robles, en su laudable afán de hablar correctamente, a veces empleaba el *tú*, otras, el *vos*, y las más usaba ambas formas promiscuamente. Esto sucedía, sobre todo, cuando estaba inquieto" (p. 174).

Farther on, we read:

—Hombre Manuel, no te conozco. *Estás* muy cambiado. No, no *sos* ... no *eres* el mismo de antes (p. 296); No es que me *molestés vos* ... no *te vayas, espera, siéntate* ... pero *tú comprendes* (p. 297); no son cosas mías, como *vos* ... como *tú crees* (p. 299). (Later to his daughter): ¿Lo *conocés?* ... que sólo a *vos* toca resolver ... dice que está enamorado de *ti*. ... *Dime*, hija, ... si *tú* le *quieres* ... *decíme* lo que *sientas* (p. 300).

The author adds by way of explanation: "Otra vez la excitación hacía a Robles promiscuar el *vos* con el *tú*" (p. 300).

We note that *has* is the common form for the present of *haber*, but *habís* and *habés* are found: "¿dónde te *habís* escondido?" (*ibid.*, p. 87). The common future ending is *-ás*, and rarely *-és*.[20]

HONDURAS

In Honduras about the same popular usage prevails as elsewhere in Central America, with the usual mixture of singular and plural forms. Membreño (*Hondureñismos* [3d ed., 1912]) gives the forms for *ser: vos sos, fuistes, serés, seas*. That the singular future is likewise often used (as well as other singular forms) may be deduced from the following examples. At times both pronouns *vos* and *tú* are heard together: *vos tú* or *tú vos*.

Andáte a dormir ... para que *te compongas*, y luego *venís* a la casa (Mejía Nieto, *Relatos*, p. 36); *tú* lo *sabías*, ¿no lo *sabías vos?* (p. 42); *entrá* (p. 43); ¿por qué *lloras vos?* (p. 164); *vos creés* ... *¿te acuerdas?* (p. 166); *vos engañas* a tu padre (p. 168); *ándate* para *tu* cama *vos* ... *hacé* como *tu* padre *te* manda ... *andáte* a acostar (p. 169); *acordáte* de nuestros hijos ... malvada que *sos* ... *verás* ... *vos* no *tenés* nada que decirme (p. 171); no me voy aunque lo *quieras vos* ... ¿lo *oís?* (p. 173); ¿Quién *te* ha juzgado a *vos?* ... *Vos* me *rogaste* ... *vos* lo *sabés* ... *vos* lo *sabes* (p. 174), etc. *Tú sos* una mujer susia ... si me *vuelves* a calumniar *vos* o *tu* marido (Mejía Nieto, *El solterón*, p. 47); *¡Soh* hombre raro! (p. 61); *voh maluste* al amigo (p. 67); *voh* no *sabé* nadita (p. 70); ¿cómo *te sentís?* (p. 121); ya *te rís;* ya *podés* comer gallina ... *cométela vos* (p. 125), etc. Si *sos* de la otra vida ... ¿cuáles son *tus* penas? ... *querés* venir (Carías Reyes, *La heredad*, p. 28); —¡Si no *te callás te* rajo! (p. 75); *mirá* (p. 85), etc. *Vos* no *sabés* (Carías Reyes, *Cuentos de lobos*, p. 21); *andáte* (p. 67); *cométela* (p. 89), etc.

EL SALVADOR

El Salvador is no exception to the popular *voseo*. In fact, the *voseo* is here quite widespread in familiar conversation. Less general than in Argentina, its use (not its forms) is perhaps more comparable to that of Chile. Occasionally in the upper classes it is used "de una manera velada," though refined social usage imposes *tú*. Forms: *vos amás, comés, vivís, habís* and *has, amarás* (not *amarés*), *amastes* or *amaste, sos* and *eres*.

[20] Henríquez Ureña (*RFE*, VIII, 385) stated that the future tense in Central America generally ends in *-és*. This seems to be true only of Guatemala; in the other republics, while the forms may fluctuate, *-ás* seems the preferred. Henríquez Ureña rectified his earlier statement, though not completely, in *BDH*, IV (1938), xxii.

Arturo Ambrogi's collection of rural tales entitled *El Jetón* (1936) brings us such forms as the following:

¿Juana? *abrí* ... ¿por qué diablos no *abrís?* ... ¿Qué ... quería usted, señor? (p. 16); ¿qué *hacés?* (p. 21); Ya *sabés*. Si *te mobés* di'hay, *te* tiro (p. 23); —¿Di 'onde *venís* tan temprano? —Ya lo sabe, patrón (p. 32); ... *Ti alistás* ... pa que *salgás* mañana (p. 33); No las *desensillés*. *Aflojálas* nomás las cinchas (p. 49); *ti'amarrás* la mano (p. 119); ¿qué *decís?* (p. 154); *ayudáme* (p. 155); *Bení* apriesa (p. 160); *apuráte* ... *desíle* (p. 161); *sentáti'* aquí (p. 187); *hacéte* la sonsa ¿no *ti'acordás?* (p. 196); o la *dejás* ... o *te* las *tenés* que haber conmigo; hay *ve vos*, *escogé* (p. 197); ¿por qué *te rís? te* quiero ... a naide más qui'a *vos* ... si me *querés* asina como *decís*, ¿por qué no *te casás* di'una vez conmigo? (p. 203); *quedrás* decir ... pué que se los *incontrés* (p. 204); ¿por qué *sos* así? (p. 205); ¿qué *tenés?* ... *desímelo* a yo, a tu nanita, pue (p. 208); ¿cuánto *calculás* que *habís* ajuntado? (p. 213).

Miguel Ángel Ramírez in *Tierra adentro* (1937) gives among others:

Asigún *pintás vos* (p. 17); *quedáte* a ver si *sos* capaz ... *tendrás* (p. 18); el día que me *andés* con sinvergüenzadas ... cuando *te murás* (p. 19); ¡Niña, *habís* dormido con un muerto! (p. 20); *comprenderás* ... que con nosotras no *jugás* ... *cogé* ... lo que *te merecés* (p. 27); ¡Qué *dieras vos* ... ! (p. 43).

Rafael Torres Arjona in *Correntada* (1934) gives:

¿Decís vos, Ña, que *vijiastes* al niño? (p. 22); Conque eso *traés vos*. Mi mujer y *vos* se han compichao pa engañarme (p. 23); *vos podés* fumarlo, si a *vos te* gusta ... no quiero que *tomés* ... *¿querés?* (p. 28); *¿ves vos?* ... *te* lo agradesco a *vos* (p. 29); no *te molestés* (p. 30); que sea cuando *vos querrás*, niño (p. 32); ya lo *verás vos* ... mejor que *vayás*, *vos* ... tamaño susto es el que *vos* nos *has* dao (p. 35); no *hablés* de eso; ahora que *te casarás* con mi niña (p. 37); *vos has* hablado (p. 38); ¿cuándo me *has* enseñado *vos?* (p. 53); que *durmás* bien (p. 55); *vos eres* la hija (p. 72); quizá *tengás* razón (p. 73); ¿no *encontrastes* nada, mi hija? (p. 80); ¿qué *venistes vos* a buscar? ... *acabarás* de decir (p. 88); *vos fuistes* (p. 90) ... *¿*o es que *te has* muerto? (p. 98); (in a letter): y *vos* ¿cómo *estás*, cómo lo *has* pasado? (p. 126); (in a letter): sufro por todo lo que *has* sufrido y *sufrís* (p. 130); *decíselo* (p. 157); mañana *irás* (p. 161).

Salarrué gives in his exquisite *Cuentos de barro* (1934) that smack deliciously of the soil:

Vos vas arando ... *pegás* ... *ti haces* de plata (p. 10); *te metés* ... *habís* perdido lonra (p. 17); *apurá* el paso, *vos* (p. 20); *dormíte* (p. 21); *estiráte* ... *cuchuyáte* contra yo (p. 22); *¿vos his* [= habís] visto ... ? ... —Me vuá quedar con *vos* atrás, y *te golvés* ... (p. 40); *¿Habís* venido? ... —*Date* priesa, si *querés* que *te* les den algo a los cipotes (p. 54); *¿Vos* no *sos* del pueblo? ... *¿entendiste?* (p. 55).

That *vos* alternates with *usted*, as in many other countries, is to be inferred from the following mixture used by Don Nayo in addressing his daughter, Cande:

—*Date* priesa (p. 70); ¡no *téi* dicho que cuando *vengás* a trer lagua, *cerrés* bien la palanquera! ... ¡No *cierre,* animala, *espere!* ... *Traiga* el canasto (p. 71); (and Lupe, Nayo's wife, addresses him): —¿Le *arvertiste* a Nicho de lo que *te* dije? ... *arrecuérdese*, Nayo, de nosotros ... (p. 74).

A mother to her seven-year-old daughter, Santíos:

—*Quitá* ... *bís* [= habís] nacido para muerta (p. 122); —¡Istúpida, bien *bís* oído que *tenés* catarro! ... *Güelva* luego ... si no *quiere* que *la* tundeye como ayer (p. 123).

And that *vos* alternates with correct *tú* forms we see in Torres Arjona's *Correntada*, in a dialogue between two lovers:

—*Ven* ... *siéntate* aquí ... para que *reposés* ... ¿en qué *piensas?* ... *mirá* ... *fijáte* ... mi cielo, mi mundo se centralizan en *ti* ... *toma* (pp. 41–42).

GUATEMALA

Voseo is more general in Guatemala than in El Salvador but not exactly "a la manera del gauchesco," as Tiscornia (p. 134) states, since a future in *-és* is the rule in Guatemala, but a future in *-ás* is the rule in Argentina; and *habís* is the rule in Guatemala, but *has* is the rule in Argentina.

The nineteenth-century *costumbrista,* Salomé Gil (José Milla), tells us in his *Cuadros de costumbres* that the *chapín,* or typical Guatemalan, "habla un castellano antiquísimo: *vos, habís, tené, andá;* and that a countrified *guanaco* from Nicaragua, because he was distantly related to him, addressed him very unceremoniously "de tú y de vos alternativamente." That the *voseo* is still firmly established among the common people in Guatemala we may infer from the words of the young writer, Carlos Alberto Quintana, who in the collection of short stories entitled *Mal agüero* (1937) says: "Por su boca habla el pueblo. Con su vocabulario lleno de extraño colorido ... sus modismos que se burlan de todas las reglas gramaticales. Pretender hacerle hablar de tú [as would the grammarians] es un sueño" (pp. 186–87). Sandoval (II, 603) tells us that the *voseo* is "tan usado entre personas de confianza, como en la correspondencia familiar." He adds (under *vosear*): "Hay personas que por abuso injustificado y que de buenas a primeras o de *primas a primeras*, como decimos nosotros, se permiten dar a uno el tratamiento de *vos* (o de *tú*), sin tener con uno la menor confianza, o sin que uno haya autorizado tal proceder."

—*Andáte* lista ... *te* mato a *vos* (Wyld-Ospina, *Nahuyacas*, p. 92); *te juntás* con él ... para que *veás* ... lo *estás* engañando con que *te casás* más tarde ... *te debés* casar ... no *negués* ... no *jugués* con los hombres (p. 93); *sos* bonita (p. 94); no *salgás* (p. 97); *¿estás* ay? *abríme* ... ¿qué *querés?* (p. 100); *te habís* metido. *Entrá*, pues; pero Dios *te* guarde si *te propasás* ansina (p. 101); no *seás* bruto: así no *lograrés* nada (p. 102); ¿Por qué no *te desidís?* ... *Serías* la reina ... pa que *vos disfrutés* ... *vos sos* patoja (p. 108); ¿onde *dejastes* al Pedro? (p. 113); *¡Vos* lo *matastes, desílo!* (p. 114); no le *vayás* a decir (p. 165); lo que *fuistes* ... si *tenés* pisto ... ya *podrés* pagar ... *creémelo: habís* de cambiar de profesión (p. 284); si no *fueras* tan bruto ... bueno *irías* estando ya pa general (p. 286); *dirés* (p. 288). *Ve vos* ... si no *entendés* y *querés* salir de la Meches y *tus* patojos ... ya *verés*. ... No *siás* papo (Quintana, p. 157); *ve* m'ija, porque *querés te hogás* en un vaso di'agua (p. 183); no *olvidés* (p. 184); no *pongás* esa cara (p. 185); *¿ti 'acordás* del *último* par de medias que me *hiciste* comprar? ... ¿de dónde *sos vos?* ¿cómo *te llamás?* ¿qué *te* duele? (p. 203); ni me lo *acordés* (p. 211).

MEXICO

Mexico is primarily a *tú* country.[21] The *voseo* is used only in a comparatively limited region in the southeast, the region between Guate-

[21] González Moreno (*Manual elemental de gramática histórica hispano-mexicana* [1926], § 275) reported that "en las clases sociales de alguna cultura se confunden las personas y se mezclan los pronombres; *vos eres, vos estás* oímos con alguna frecuencia. Pero el pueblo no participa de esa mezcolanza. ..." How he could have made such an apparently erroneous statement seems a mystery to all Mexicans consulted on this point. F. J. Santamaría agrees with Rafael Domínguez, who replied to the query concerning Moreno's strange statement: "Las clases sociales de alguna cultura no dicen *vos eres* ni *vos estás*. La primera frase (*vos eres*) no la dicen ni los cultos ni los incultos. La segunda (*vos estás*) se oye entre los campesinos de Tabasco y entre mucha gente de Chiapas. ..."

mala and the Isthmus of Tehuantepec. This portion of Mexico has linguistic affinities with Guatemala and during the colonial time was part of the *capitanía general de Guatemala*. The *voseo* region includes both the state of Chiapas and the major portion of the state of Tabasco. Heretofore most scholars have unwittingly limited the *voseo* area in Mexico to the state of Chiapas.[22] However, most of the state of Tabasco must needs be included. The usage there was touched upon in 1933 by R. M. Gutiérrez Eskildsen,[23] who selected from Güiraldes' famous Argentine novel *Don Segundo Sombra* some twenty-seven *voseo* verb forms identical with those used by Tabascan peasants (p. 307); *andá, decíle, dejás, querés, tenés, sabés, conocés vos, andás, mirá, comprometés, tené, amanezcás, podés, decís, sos,* etc. However, the author's exposition of the *voseo* phonetics is not clear. She gives the forms as being identical with the gaucho forms and writes "*tenés,*" "*venís,*" etc. (p. 266). Later (p. 267) she asserts that in Tabascan pronunciation the final *-s* of a word is lost. That this is a misconception is evident from the review of her article by M. E. Becerra (*Inv. ling.*, II, 60), who points out that this *-s* is not lost but is pronounced as an aspiration, which he chooses to record as *j: compraj,* etc.

In a later work, *El habla popular y campesina de Tabasco* (1941), Miss Gutiérrez devotes a chapter to the *voseo*. While some of her comments are open to question, she makes interesting remarks concerning present-day usage, which we may sum up as follows:

The *voseo* exists only in the speech of the Tabascan peasant and popular classes. It is used only in very familiar conversation: by parents to children, by older people to children, between brother and sister and among intimate friends. It is never used to a stranger or to a person who is not on intimate terms with the speaker, or to persons deserving respect, as, for instance, between godfathers (*compadres*). The spiritual affinity between godfathers (the father of a child and its godfather) is so highly respected that "*compadre*" is preferred to "*hermano*" in case the godfather is a brother, and then the respectful *usted* is used rather than the *voseo*.

The *voseo* is used by peasants and the common classes throughout

[22] In 1921 Henríquez Ureña asserted: "El *vos* no existe en México, fuera de Chiapas" (*RFE*, VIII, 390). In 1930, Tiscornia said: "En Méjico el *voseo* está circunscripto al estado de Chiapas" (*La lengua*, pp. 135 and 290). In 1939 Amado Alonso and Henríquez Ureña repeated the substance of this statement in their *Gramática* (II, 81), although Henríquez Ureña had indicated the regions in 1938 (*BDH*, IV, xxi): "Chiapas y parte de Tabasco."

[23] "Cómo hablamos en Tabasco," *Inv. ling.*, I, 266–312.

the state of Tabasco except in the region of Los Ríos, called also Este de Tabasco and including Jonuta, Balancán, Zapata, and Tenosique. However, it is becoming obsolete in the degree that culture has filtered into the remoter parts.

Besides the regular *voseo* verb forms as noted for Argentina, we find the future ending *-és* (as in Guatemala) rather than *-ás*, and also a mixture of *tú* and *vos* forms: "*acordáte* de tu mama, lo *oíste* ... *ven* acá, dijo la mama agüela, *veníme* a dar los buenos días ... *andá, vete* ... si lo *quieres*, arreglado, no me *volverés* a ve. ... Si *quieres, te vas*, si no *querés*, no *te vas*, dijo la madre." The form *habís* is current besides the regular *habés*.

The author has clarified her *voseo* phonetics (pp. 37–40), indicating that *vos* becomes *boh* before a consonant and in final position. But she fails to mention a future in *-ás* (or *-áh*), a form which is regularly used in the Tabascan novel *Los abrasados* (1937) by Alfonso Taracena. The setting of this *novela tropical* is the town of Cunduacán, the so-called "Atenas de Tabasco," the author's birthplace. From his work we glean the following examples (the aspirated *s* is represented by *j*):

Ahora *voj* ... *hacé* algunaj preguntaj ... no *hagáj* chijtej maloj. *Soj* muy pesao ... *voj soj* ... *opináj* igual que elloj ... *dijijte* (p. 37); la manera de que te *larguéj*. Ya *quedáj* notificado (p. 38); ¿qué *vaj* a decí *voj?* ... *dejámelo* de mi cuenta (p. 92); no sea que *vayáj* a atacá a la autoridá ... *tomá*, pa que lo *dejéj* tranquilo ... *volvé* a ponéte a cantá (p. 93); *¿terminajte* ya *voj?* ... no *te creáj* ... no *hagáj* naa, si *voj* no *queréj* (p. 94); *hacé* todaj tuj ocupacionej sin precipitación y *vení* con calma (p. 111); *voj diráj* ... *¿qué te* pasa? ... puej *veráj* (p. 170); ya *habráj* sabío (p. 171); *vení acá*, ya *sabráj* (p. 181); *dijitej* ... *eraj* (p. 186).

THE ANTILLES

In Puerto Rico and Santo Domingo only *tú* is used. In Cuba the *voseo* is known to a very limited section in the eastern part of the island. As elsewhere (notably Mexico and Peru), the regular use of *tú*, rather than of *vos*, reflects the colonial culture of the region, and this culture served to check popular drift in language. Furthermore, Cuba and Puerto Rico remained Spanish colonies for nearly a century after the rest of Spanish America had attained its independence. *Vos* appeared only in the interior of eastern Cuba, principally Camagüey, Bayamo, and Manzanillo,[24] but with a special form: it is here

[24] Henríquez Ureña, "El español en Santo Domingo," in *BDH*, V (1940), 49.

accompanied, not with the pronouns *te* and *tuyo* as elsewhere, but with the correct forms *os* and *vuestro*, which reflect a higher cultural and social environment. In the last century Pichardo (*Diccionario provincial* [4th ed., 1875], p. xi) comments: "En Tierra-dentro, singularmente en Puerto Príncipe y Bayamo, es aun mui usado el antiguo pronombre personal *vos*, mal espresado el verbo que le sigue por una especie de síncopa de rutina, v.g.: *vos habís visto* ... *vos sabís esto* ... por *vos habéis visto* ... *vos sabéis* esto ... etc." He further reports that this manner of address is "el trato de mayor confianza y franqueza," that it is so soft and cordial that the most cultured, in speaking familiarly with members of his family, puts aside the purist forms "que estiman de etiqueta"; but that, directly he becomes annoyed or seriously reserved, the Camagüeyan uses the formal *usted* and the third person singular verb. He adds that the usage was dying out. In 1921, Henríquez Ureña (*RFE*, VIII, 390 n.) reports information furnished him by native Cubans to the effect that the *vos* (pronounced *vo*) in place of *tú* was still used quite frequently among the peasants of Camagüey, who, however, never employ it when in the cities or in addressing strangers. Its use was being limited more and more.

We find evidence of its present use in Luis Felipe Rodríguez' Cuban novel, *Ciénaga* (1937), dedicated to his native Sabana de la Mar, where the verb forms differ from those reported by Pichardo:

—¡Qué cara tan desmejorá *tenéi!* (p. 115); —*tomá*, *dale* bien la cera ... como *sabéis*—le dice a un prójimo (p. 161); —Ahora me *vai* a despresear ... *meteo* [= meteos] el muslo de gallina y no *seái* fascitora, que en *vuestra* casa no *vei* de esto toos los días ... *mirá*, Fengue, *dejaos* de aconsejar a quien puede *haberos* parío, porque yo *os* aguaité escondiendo un maso de tabaco pa llevarlo a *vuestra* abuela. ... Mongo, ¡qué malas influencias *traéi! Os* perdono la animalá por que sé que *estái* osesao ... ni siquiera *reparái* por donde *andái* caminando. *Necesitái* que *os* hagan oraciones y que *os* santigüen (p. 175); —la misma [cara] que *tenéi vo* (p. 179).

The *voseo* has also penetrated into the *papiamento* of the island of Curaçao.[25]

From the foregoing data it seems evident that caustic condemnation on the part of grammarians and purists will not easily eradicate the deep-seated *voseo*, knit into the very fiber of the language.

[25] R. Lenz, *El papiamento* (Santiago, Chile, 1928).

IV

OTHER PERSONAL PRONOUNS

IN ADDRESS

HAVING dealt with the *voseo* or intimate forms of address, we may now discuss polite or respectful forms. As has been said, children, especially in the country, often address their parents with the respectful *usted* + a third person singular verb, and in certain limited rural sections even with *su merced,* a form applied also to other persons of respect and superior social standing. The old form *vusted* (or *vosted*) may still be heard in a few rural sections, as also in dialectal Spain.

CHILE: —Estaba pensando, paire—contestó el cachorro—si habrá en too el mundo uno más guapo que *su mercé* (Así trataban antes los hijos a los padres) (Manuel Rojas, in *LCC,* p. 461). (MALLECO): ¿Quere *su mercé* que l'amarremos las manos? ... no tenimos seguridá alguna con *su mercé* librecito (Brunet, *Montaña,* p. 58). Si *vosté,* paire, tiene que icil un argo en su abono (Muñoz, p. 160); yo me muero por *vosté* (p. 167), etc.

ECUADOR: —A *su mercé* que los indios le quieren como a taita Dios (Icaza, *Cholos,* p. 36). —Traigo un mensaje para *vusté* (Vásconez, p. 202); Así es, aunque *vusté* no lo crea (p. 203). (AZUAY): —¿Cómo te llamas, bestia? —Bestias en patio están, amo. Macario Zhañay llamo yo. —Para servir a Dios y a *su mercé,* patroncito, has de decir, ¡bruto! (Mata, *Sanagüín,* p. 133). Y más para *busté,* comadrita (La Cuadra, *Horno,* p. 27).

COLOMBIA (ANTIOQUIA): —*Sus mercedes* me dispensarán un momentico (Carrasquilla, *Hace tiempos,* I, 206); Y *vusté* sabe cómo es el señor cura (I, 232); *vustedes,* muchachos, bien puedan [see p. 179] ir acostase (I, 233). —¿No son, pues, *sus mercedes* los que estuvieron en el trapiche? (Rivera, p. 15); ¿Qué quiere *busté?* (p. 202).

VENEZUELA (ANDES, LLANOS): No sea *busté* tan malcriado (Machado, p. 216).

EL SALVADOR: —Asina mesmo es, patrón. No 'ba crérme usté: pero el Damián Flores—¿lo conoce *su mercé?* (Ambrogi, p. 176).

MEXICO: —¡Compadrito! ¿Pos qué había pasado con *su mercé?*

(González Carrasco, p. 169). (NOCHISTLÁN): —Buenos días le dé Dios a *su mercé* (*Inv. ling.*, I, 188).

In addition to being a form of respect, *usted* is often used intimately and affectionately for *tú*, especially to children. Frida Weber reports (*RFH*, III, 114) that in Buenos Aires *usted* applied to small children may imply either anger or tenderness, the distinction being clarified by intonation or the addition of other words; but that for older children the use of *usted* can imply only anger,[1] thus coinciding with the usage referred to in the Spanish proverb, "Cuando en mi casa me hablan de usted, cerca anda el palo."

This change of *tú* to *usted* produced by anger is as common in America as it is in Spain. A few examples will suffice:

URUGUAY: La chica dió media vuelta y salió corriendo. Cuando su padre la trataba de «usted» ya sabía ella que había que obedecer de inmediato, «sin palabrita» (Amorím, *La carreta*, p. 21).

VENEZUELA: —Mamá, mamá. —¿No *te* he dicho que eso no se come? *Cállate* la boca y *déjame* trabajar. ... —Mamá, mamá. —Ah, cará: *usted* lo que está buscando es que *le* dé una cueriza. *Cállese* la boca (Arráiz, p. 164). —Lo que es *usted*. ... Mamá, cuando está disgustada, me suprime el *tú* (Briceño, p. 166).

COSTA RICA: (Mother to son): —*¡Llevále* el almuerzo a Moncho! *Corré*. (Son): —¡Adió, por qué no viene él a coméselo aquí? ... La delgada cara de Ninfa se llena de un celaje de cólera. —¡Lencho, qué es eso? ¡*Coja* ese almuerzo y *llévеselo* a Juan Ramón! *¡Haga* caso! (Fabián Dobles, p. 259).

The affectionate *usted*, on the other hand, is apparently an Americanism. It is applied very frequently to children, more generally by mothers than by fathers:

ARGENTINA: Fingía dormir; como el niño que, a la intimación de *duérmase Vd.*, cierra los ojos (an older example from Mansilla, *Entre-nos*, p. 9).

CHILE: (Father to young son): —¡Pero *sosiégate*, mocoso! (Mother to

[1] That this was not always true in Argentina may be supposed from the following passage from Mansilla's *Entre-nos* (p. 104): (Uncle to grown-up nephew) "—Sobrino, estoy muy contento de *usted*. ... Es de advertir que era buen signo, que Rozas tratara de *usted;* porque cuando de *tú* trataba, quería decir que no estaba contento de su interlocutor, o que por alguna circunstancia del momento fingía no estarlo." An older example of the use of *usted* applied to small children we find in the same book (p. 9); we cite it in the text as an example of affectionate *usted*.

young son): —No le *tenga* miedo, mi lindo. *Dígale* Copito. (Father): ¡*Corre*, Tin! (Sepúlveda, *Camarada*, p. 18).

VENEZUELA: (Victoria and her mother have been using *tú* to each other): Acercándose a la madre le echó los brazos al cuello y la cubrió de besos, mientras conduciéndola a su cama, le iba diciendo con aquel juego de papeles trocados [that is, in the language the mother would use to her daughter]: —*Vuélvase* a acostar, mijita. Y *duérmase* tranquila porque a *su* madre no le va a suceder nada malo, *¿sabe?* (Gallegos, *La trepadora*, p. 180).

Conversely, a parent ordinarily using *usted* may, on waxing confidential, adopt the *voseo* exemplified in the following passage:

URUGUAY: (Father to son): —Yo estaba resentido ... porque no había güelto, porque *lo* creía un desamorau con los *suyos*. ... Y el favor ... el favor. ... El muchacho se ha hecho humilde: —No me diga así, tata. El padre, cual si el correr del prólogo lo hubiera animado, se confía, hasta haciéndose más cordial, abandonando el *usted* grave, usado por nuestra gente nativa, hasta con los allegados, en ciertos momentos solemnes. —El favor es que *levantés* la línea, que *trabajés* con la deligencia ... (Montiel, *La raza*, p. 95).

Although the use of *usted* may imply tenderness only to small children in Buenos Aires, elsewhere (Chile, Colombia, etc.) we know it may be applied to persons of any age, alternating with *vos* or *tú*. In Colombia *su merced* is also used affectionately by parents to children and vice versa, between husband and wife, and among intimate friends.

CHILE: (Mother to older son): —Mi hijo, *usted*, y de dónde me *sale* ¡ay! ... *Acérquese*, m'hijo. —Pa usted, mama. ... —Dios *le* pague la delicadeza, m'hijo (Alberto Romero, *Perucho González*, p. 60). —Rosario, hijita, no *olvidís* nunca que *sois* muy pobre, hija de un viejo campesino. Que tóos *te* tienen envidia y que tóos desearían ver*te* en la desgracia. —Padre, yo no soy mala; se lo probaré. ... —Mihijita, *perdone* a su viejo que habla así porque *la* quiere demasiao (*La abraza*) (Acevedo Hernández, *Por el atajo*, p. 23).

COLOMBIA: —Mamá, aquí tengo el brazo de Carlitos. El otro pedazo lo lleva *su merced* (*El Tiempo*, May 8, 1944).

The following passage is enlightening on a frequent Chilean usage of *usted:*

"Ella misma había expresado que llamar al esposo por su apellido [family name], o evoca una diferencia de edad, que entre ellos no existía, o una falta de cariñosa e íntima unión. Igual cosa ocurría con respecto del tratamiento: el «tú» era lo justo, lo natural entre seres que se aman; pero ella prefería el «Vd.» por parecerle más cariñoso, más de acuerdo con su carácter. Llamar siempre a su marido por su nombre de pila, era cosa que ya estaba consiguiendo; pero el tratamiento de «Vd.» quiso conservarlo" (Maluenda, *Venidos a menos*, pp. 12–13).

This use of affectionate *usted*, particularly on the part of a wife to her husband, is widespread in Chile. The husband, however, generally uses *tú* to his wife. (Man to wife): —Vieja ¡leche al pie de la vaca! ¿*Te* gusta? (Wife to husband): —¿No *le* gusta a *usted*, hijo? ... Hijo, no *sea* chiquillo (Sepúlveda, *Camarada*, p. 21).

Analogous practices occur in other countries. In Gallegos' *La trepadora* (Venezuela)we find a revealing scene between Hilario and his wife, Adelaida, whom he addresses with *usted* when especially tender or moved:

(Adelaida speaks): —Tengo un retrato de padrino ... y a él le gustaban tanto estos muebles ... se sentiría más a gusto en su sala amueblada como él la tenía. Y como nombrar a don Jaime era tocar la fibra más sensible del corazón de Hilario, éste accedió: —Tienes razón. ... Y en seguida, quitándole el *tú*, que no se lo daba nunca cuando quería mostrarse tierno o le hablaba conmovido: —*Mire*, mi Blanca: *usted* no *sabe* cómo le agradezco que quiera tener un retrato del Viejo en la sala. Y eso de que él se encuentre a gusto ... ¡Bueno! ¡Eso no se me olvidará nunca! (p. 153).

Usted generally replaces *tú* in Andean Venezuela (see p. 79).

In Toro's *Minas* (Antioquia, Colombia), Don Evaristo telephones to his wife: —Mija, me demoro un poquito. ... *Acuéstate* tranquila. (Wife replies): —Negro, no me puedo dormir sin estar vos aquí. ... (Don Evaristo, evidently moved, adds): —*Acuéstese*, mijita (p. 41).

Beside the affectionate *usted*, especially for children, stands the use of *él* and *ella*, an older form of address (Keniston, p. 47; *Hispania*, XXIII [1940], 336–40) still kept in dialectal Spain (Menéndez Pidal, *El dialecto leonés*, § 20; Llorente, § 125) and in some regions of America. In Buenos Aires, for instance, it is used to express emotional, if not intellectual, sympathy with one who has been reproached or accused: "¡Pobre viejo, lo que le dicen a *él!* (*RFH*, III, 115).

Uruguay: —Tú en ningún caso estarías contra mí. —¡Contra *ella!* ¡Quién podría estar con *ella*, Dios santo! (Sánchez, *Los derechos de la salud*, I, 1).

Elsewhere it is likewise found to express a change of emotion, often anger, occasionally a deliberate show of affection.

Chile: —Mira, tú no sabes hacerlo. —¡Claro, *ella es* [= tú eres] la única que lo hace bien! —¿Quién rompió esto? —Yo. —*Él tenía* [= tú tenías] que ser no más! (Cifuentes).

Venezuela: Mamá, cuando está disgustada, me suprime el tú. Otras veces me trata en tercera persona (Briceño, p. 166).

Colombia: ¡Cómo *él se queda* callao! (Flórez, p. 376).

In the provinces of southern Chile, according to Román (II, 204), a husband uses *ella* in referring to his wife when absent, and the wife uses *él* in referring to her husband when absent: "Pregúntenselo a *ella*, *ella* dirá" says the husband; and the wife "Lo consultaré con *él*, y según lo que *él* diga, así contestaré." He attributes this practice to a natural disinclination on the part of newlyweds to say *mi mujer* 'my wife' and *mi marido* 'my husband.' This practice, probably current everywhere, may be found in dialectal Spain today (for the Salamancan region cf. Sánchez Sevilla, *RFE*, XV, 244). For popular Argentine speech the following example will suffice: "—¿Dónde estás establecida? —Aquí cerca. En un corralón donde *él* guarda el coche con que trabaja. ... —*¿Él?* ¿Quién es *él?* —Mi marido. —¿Te has casado? ¿Cuándo? —Hace más de tres meses. *Él* está esperándome en la esquina" (Laferrère, *Locos de verano*, III).

As an extension of peninsular practice, the third person plural of the verb is often popularly used in place of a first or second person singular to soften statements, particularly reproaches, by impersonalizing the conversation. The speaker hesitates, either through modesty or politeness, to assume the categoric authority implied by a first person, or to employ the abruptness of the direct second person, when a vague, softer, third person plural will convey his meaning in a less stinging tone.

Chile: —Tan cargoso que te *han* de vel, Fidel [= que te ves *or* que te veo *or* que eres, etc.] (Romanángel, p. 9); —¡Déjese *le icen*

[= le digo]! ... Ya, asosiéguese *le icen* [= le digo] ... —¿No *ven* [= no ves]? Pa paliquero no tenís precio (p. 10), etc.

ECUADOR: —Más mudo que te *han* de ver (Jorge Fernández, p. 155). —Tan tragón que lo *han* de ver (Pareja, *La Beldaca*, p. 30).

We find a peculiar usage in Chiloé, the southern insular province of Chile. In respectful address *ustedes* or *usted* + a plural verb is used instead of *usted* + a singular verb; and the third person plural verb is often used respectfully with singular nouns denoting persons: *¿Qué dijeron usted(es)? = ¿qué dijo usted?* (Cavada, *Chiloé*, p. 277; cf. also *BDH*, VI, 24–25). This respectful pluralization of a pronoun in direct address is what occurred in Old Spanish (*vos*), in French (*vous*), in Italian (*voi*), and in English (*you*).

We cull a few examples of Chiloé usage from Rubén Azócar's regional novel *Gente en la Isla* (1938), considered a faithful description of local atmosphere, customs, and language, as recorded by a native of that region:

—Ya me lo sabía yo que *volverían* [= volvería], caballero ... esto *decían* [= decía] su padre; mas no *les maldijeron* [= le maldijo] nunca; don Lorenzo *les querían* [= le quería] como a las niñas de sus ojos. ... *Créanlo* [= créalo], caballero (p. 32); Mas mi amo no *irán* [= irá] ... *anden* [= ande] usted a Quicaví, don; ahora mismo; no *dilaten* [= dilate]. Doña Ignacia me lo *han* [= ha] manifestado (p. 88).

Some seventy-five years ago Mansilla (*Una excursión*, p. 30) observed, among the populace of Corrientes province (Argentina) and of Paraguay, the practice of mixing second and third person pronouns in address: "—Aquí *te* vengo a ver, che Comandante, pa que me *des* licencia *usted*" (p. 32); "—Aquí *te* vengo a ver *V.E.* ... —Che, *V.E.*, *hacé vos* el favor" (p. 50), etc. Untutored Mexican Indians sometimes say: *tú dijo, tú resolverá* (*BDH*, IV, 323). Such practices are common on any Spanish frontier among Indians who have not yet learned the new language.

We learn that, in Castilian, *usted* as a subject form usually occurs at least once in a speech and that its frequent omission may imply discourtesy. Such is not the case generally in American Spanish. Here, as in certain localities of southern Spain, the form *usted* is very frequently omitted,[2] being used only where other subject pronouns are used: *es usted = eres tú*, but *vaya a verme* (Corominas, p. 104).

[2] Lenz had observed this for Chile (*BDH*, VI [1940], 263–64; *La oración*, p. 258).

Its excessive occurrence seems reminiscent of a certain obsolete social or class distinction. Its suppression is particularly common with imperative verb forms,[3] a use which when heard in Spain often reveals the speaker's provenience. In fact it was this frequent suppression of *usted* in parts of the mysterious Avellaneda's spurious *Don Quijote* (1614) that led some to believe its author to be the Mexican-born Ruiz de Alarcón (Vázquez, p. 393).

For Peru, on the other hand, Benvenutto (p. 145) reports a popular dislike for the plural form *ustedes.* Since in certain cases it seems to imply scorn, it is often replaced by *usted y usted* or *a fulano y a usted,* etc.; that is, when both persons addressed are present. This is not true of Huánuco (Pulgar Vidal, p. 817).

Another peculiarity of *usted* (along with *tú*), in American as well as in continental Spanish, is its quite frequent use in impersonal expressions, analogous to our English use of *you* in the sense of 'one':

VENEZUELA: *Mero* equivale, en Venezuela, a uno solo, o solamente uno. Por eso *usted* oye decir: "¿cuántas cochas han sacado?" "Una mera" (Picón-Febres, p. 250).

SANTO DOMINGO: No sabe *usté* qué pensar [= 'you don't know what to think']. Es capaz de decir*te* cualquier cosa [= 'He's likely to say anything to you = to anyone'] (*BDH*, V, § 93).

FIRST PERSON PRONOUNS

Just as the subject form *tú* is occasionally found after a preposition (*a tú*), possibly by analogy with *a él, ella, usted,* etc., in which the prepositional form is identical with the subject form (Keniston, p. 54), so in many rural sections of Spanish America the prepositional form *mí* is replaced by *yo.* This is still heard in some rural regions of Spain, especially Aragon (Borao, p. 95: "para casarte con *yo*"; Kuhn, § 33: "a *tú* ... pa *yo* ... con *yo*"; etc.) and in Portuguese.[4] The preference for *yo* may possibly be explained by the greater psychological emphasis of a subject pronoun. Its geographical area is much

[3] Keniston (*Syntax list,* p. 162) shows that *usted* is less frequently omitted than expressed; but the frequency count cannot be considered here, since the texts used were both Spanish and Spanish American and therefore establish no relative geographical distinction.

[4] "Now in Brazil (and formerly in Portugal) the subject form is incorrectly used instead of the object or prepositional form: *que espere por eu* (*por mim*), etc." (J. Dunn, *A grammar of the Portuguese language,* § 234[*b*]). For Catalan and Valencian, cf. Menéndez Pidal, *Gram.,* § 93.

more extensive than is generally supposed.[5]

Argentina (San Luis, Rustic): Pobre de *yo;* ¿te vas con *yo?* Yo hablo con *yo* mismo; andan preguntando por *yo* (Vidal, p. 381).

Peru (Calemar, Zona del Marañón): Yo soy diaquí, calemarino, anque quién sabe único los viejos sepan de *yo* (Ciro Alegría, *La serpiente*, p. 220). Él duerme aquí acompanao de *yo* y Valencio (Ciro Alegría, *El mundo*, p. 235).

Ecuador: Van a acabar ... con *yo* (Ortiz, p. 92).

Venezuela: Cerquita e *yo* está durmiendo un trigueño (Briceño, in *ACMV*, II, 128). Bueno es que se vaya acomodando cerquita de *yo* (Briceño, p. 112).

Colombia (Antioquia): A *yo* me mandaron trabajar con usté (Posada, p. 40); le gustaba bailar con *yo* (p. 67, etc.). A *yo* la rabia me abre el apetito (Carrasquilla, *Hace tiempos*, I, 30); a *yo* no me da miedo (p. 295). Eso sí que no sería con *yo* (Rivera, p. 221). (South): —¿Vivirás siempre *con yo?* (Álvarez Garzón, p. 59) (Bogotá, Vulg.): Eso es pa *yo;* camine con *yo*, etc. (Flórez, p. 376).

Costa Rica: Él irá alante de *yo* (Agüero, p. 49); a *yo* me picó la cresta (p. 69). Se rieron de *yo* (*Leyendas*, p. 132). —A *yo* no me vengás con cosas ... lo que a *yo* me gusta, etc. (Fabián Dobles, p. 247).

El Salvador: Cuchuyáte contra *yo*, pué (Salarrué, *Cuentos*, p. 22); Síganme a *yo* (p. 59). Asina mesmo me parece a *yo*, patrón (Ambrogi, p. 33); Desímelo a *yo*, a tu nanita, pues (p. 208).

Guatemala: Sé que en mi ausencia hablas de *yo*. Esta casa es de *yo* (Sandoval, I, 366). El mal será para *yo* (II, 198).

There are other rustic malpractices: *yo* for *a mí*, and (*a*) *mí* for *yo:*

River Plate Zone: *Yo* me parece que ... (C).

Chile (Chiloé): *Yo* me gusta la música; tú cantas mejor que *a mí* (Cavada, p. 277).

Colombia: *Yo* no me gusta ir a la plaza (Flórez, p. 376).

Costa Rica: Hay que ser más hombrecito que *mí* (F. Dobles, p. 10).

Cuba (Vulg.): *Yo* me gusta la música (Padrón).

The masculine plural *nosotros* is often used as feminine in place of standard *nosotras* (cf. Lenz, *Oración*, § 156). When the feeling of composition (pronoun *nos* + adjective *otros* or *otras*) is lost, the distinction of gender likewise tends to vanish.

[5] E.g., Tiscornia (*La lengua*, p. 122, n. 2) says: "El gauchesco ... desconoce las formas vulgares que se notan en los rústicos *españoles* y *colombianos*."

ARGENTINA: —*Nosotros* estábamos *desesperadas* por conocerlo (Pico, p. 5). Las madres como *nosotros* (Vidal, p. 376).

URUGUAY: —Será muy lejos, pues *nosotros* no sabemos nada. —Háganse *las mosquitas muertas*. ¡No van a saber! (Sánchez, *Barranca abajo*, I, 4). Ninguna de *nosotros* valemos un pie de los tuyos (Bellán, p. 60). —¡Salgan ligerito, piojosas arrastradas! —¡Pero *nosotros* qué culpa tenemos! (Espínola, p. 48).

PERU: Ya pasaron los tiempos en que *nosotros* [= las mujeres] éramos ceros a la izquierda de ustedes [= los hombres], y que cuando alguno nos burlaba no había más remedio que desbarrancarse por ahí o encerrarse para toda la vida (López A., *Nuevos cuentos*, p. 79).

GUATEMALA: *Nosotros* las mujeres ... (Sandoval, II, 146).

MEXICO: Mientras las mujeres servían la comida, se pusieron a conversar con nosotros. ... Cuando les preguntamos sobre la gente que se quedaba a dormir en ese paraje, su contestación fué rotunda: —Sólo *nosotros* (Mena Brito, p. 232).

The object form *nos* often becomes *los*, and *nosotros* becomes *losotros* (or *lojotros*) in more Spanish-American regions than have heretofore been recorded. *Los* seems to be the exclusive popular and rustic form used in Chile, where final *-s* becomes a slight aspiration: *los vamos* for *nos vamos*, *vámolos* for *vámonos*, etc. Román (III, 340) reports that the use of *los* for *nos* is so deep-rooted among the Chilean untutored that the railroad station *Nos* is called *Lo e No* (= *Lo de Nos*). He must mean *Lo e Lo* (for *lo de*, cf. p. 129). In the popular speech of Santiago *nos fuimos* (as explained on p. 164 for *nos vamos* or *vámonos*), pronounced *loh juimoh*, is jocularly referred to as *ele jota* (*l j*), representing the initials of the expression: *¿ele jota?* = *¿nos fuimos?* = *¿nos vamos?*

However, that *los* for *nos* is not merely Chilean but has a much wider geographical range will be seen from the examples given below. Furthermore, the same is true in rural regions of Spain, notably Murcia (García Soriano, § 66, 3, where *los* = also *os*), Cadiz, and probably elsewhere (cf. *BDH*, I, § 126; II, 139).

The change of *n* to *l* is probably to be explained by analogy with the many pronouns beginning with *l-* (*lo*, *la*, *los*, etc.), although the interchange of *n* and *l* occurs in other words (Menéndez Pidal, *Gram.*, § 54, 2*b*; § 72, 5*a*), and it is common in popular Chilean speech (Román, IV, 1): *frionera* for *friolera*, *penícula* for *película*, *alimar* for *animar*, etc.

ARGENTINA (COASTAL ZONE): Vámo*los* ... *los* vamos (*BDH*, I, § 126, n. 2; also IV, p. 26, n. 5: "En Buenos Aires y La Plata, entre las clases muy humildes, y, por influencia de los sirvientes, entre los niños, se oye *loh* por *nos*"). In San Luis, Cuyo, Córdoba (*BDH*, II, 139).

CHILE: —En carrito mataero tenimos qu'i*los* [= irnos] (Romanángel, p. 22); *los* pasamos a toma*los* una pilsen (p. 23); y *los* juimos (p. 24); ámo*los* [= vámonos] andando (p. 56), etc. *Los* habimos queao paraos (Acevedo Hernández, *Por el atajo*, p. 29); *los* poímos pasar sin ella (p. 62). Si querís *los* casamos (Cariola, I, 1).

COSTA RICA: Si hay alguno que se atreba/a acompañame, *los* bamos (Agüero, p. 69). Por ella *los* vamos a tomar esta botilla de coñá (Dobles Segreda, p. 37); *los* juimos esapartando (p. 38); Ellos creiban que éramos munchos. Si hubieran sabío que *los* podían contar con los dedos, se güelven y *los* deshacen (p. 48); *Losotros* éramos ricos, pero después *los* fregamos (p. 74). Muriéndo*los* de miedo, los cuatro muchachos *los* juimos ... ¿quién iba con *losotros?* (*Leyendas*, p. 116). Al bolber del trabajo/*los* pedía las tinajas (Echeverría, p. 122).

EL SALVADOR: Ya *los* duele el lomo a yo y al Tiburcio Jeta (Ambrogi, p. 66).

GUATEMALA: Si masito [= por poquito] ya no *los* volvemos a ver, pues por poco me muero anoche (Sandoval, II, 31).

MEXICO (TABASCO): Ya *los* vamos (Ramos Duarte, p. 338). Cuando *los* avisaron fimos a onde estaba ... *los* dió orden de que *los* viniéramo a Villahermosa (Gutiérrez Eskildsen, p. 84).

CUBA: Vamoh*loh* [= vámonos], *loh* vamoh, *loh* dijo (Padrón).

In Argentina we find a popular use of *se* for *nos*, which Lafone (*Tesoro*, p. 210) thinks reflects Quechuan influence (Quechuan *ca* being the reflexive for all three persons); in Buenos Aires it may be due to Italian influence. More likely the confusion was inherited from Spain: in Andalusia, Murcia (García Soriano, § 66, 3), etc., *se* is popularly used for *os;* thus *se vais* = *os vais, se la lleváis* = *os la lleváis.*

CATAMARCA: *Se* fimos [= nos fuimos] ... *se* vamos (Lafone, p. 210). *Se* iremos un día del rancho (Carrizo, p. 64); *se* querimos como hermanos (p. 69); —¿Que *se* juntemos pa siempre? (p. 74).

BUENOS AIRES: ¿*Se* ponemo de novio o no *se* ponemo? (Llanderas and Malfatti, *Cuando las papas*, p. 19). ¡Pues así no *se* podemos seguir! (Llanderas and Malfatti, *Giuanín*, p. 17). *Se* tenemo que pasar el día (Last-Reason, p. 14); vámo*se* ... *se* jugamo la cena (p. 25).

OBJECT PRONOUNS: 'LE,' 'LA,' AND 'LO'

The primitive Spanish direct-object pronoun referring to masculine nouns of persons or things was *lo*. By the sixteenth century *le* had become general for both persons and things among writers of Castilian origin especially (called, accordingly, *leístas*), whereas the primitive *lo* was preferred by writers from southern and eastern Spain (called, accordingly, *loístas*). Between those two groups was a still larger group who generally used *le* to refer to persons and *lo* to refer to things. Today this last usage seems to be the most widely current and most widely accepted in standard Castilian, though both *leístas* and *loístas* may be found among well-known Spanish writers. Spaulding (*Hispanic Review*, XIII, 336) proves a wider diffusion of *le* than is generally suspected: in León, Zamora, and even in the south. The latest editions of the Academy grammar, however, recommend to writers the etymological norm: *lo* for direct object of persons and things, *le* for indirect object only.

Lo is the form most widely used in Spanish America, though it is not exclusive, as many have thought.[6] Just as the use of *lo* for things and of *le* for persons is never a rule among Spanish writers, since the name of a thing may be personified and the name of a person "depersonalized" (see Keniston, *Syntax list*, p. 55), so in American Spanish *lo* often alternates with *le* as direct object in the written language and occasionally in cultured speech (but not in popular speech, with exceptions noted on p. 103).

ARGENTINA: —Sí, *lo* vimos ayer ... *le* vimos a nuestro lado (Pico, p. 6).

URUGUAY: —Aquí *lo* dejo, mi amigo. ... ¡He tenido el mayor gusto en acompañar*le!* (Amorím, *El paisano*, p. 43); ¡Cómo *lo* voy a dejar en medio del callejón! ¡No faltaba mas! *Lo* acompaño hasta su tranquera (p. 44).

CHILE: —Y sobre todo, volvería a ver*le* a él; muy de tarde en tarde, pero a ver*lo*, siquiera alguna vez (D'Halmar, *Lucero*, p. 70). ¡Y qué hombre era nuestro capitán! ¡Cómo *le* queríamos todos! (Lillo, p. 92). Afortunadamente fué ella misma quien *le* recibió ... al volverse *lo* vió junto a la puerta (Durand, *Mercedes*, p. 154). Solaguren ... vió a un hombre gordo que *le* observaba (Prado, *Un juez*, p. 148); nadie *lo* observa [al padre] (p. 176); *le* veníamos observando (p. 248).

[6] Cf. McHale, *Diccionario:* "Desde Méjico hasta Chile nadie dice *le vi, le conocí*" (p. 146); "... en América, donde todo el mundo dice *lo vi, lo saludé, lo conocí, lo llamé*" (p. 150); etc.

Bolivia: —¡Sí, sí, yo *le* mato! —repuso el pequeño. ... —No; haz*lo* parar más bien (Arguedas, *Raza*, p. 105). Yo *lo* he esperado ... *le* espero ahora (Díaz Villamil, *El traje*, p. 52).

Ecuador: Yo *le* quería ... yo *lo* había querido ... *lo* quise de golpe (La Cuadra, *Palo 'e balsa*, p. 303).

El Salvador: Braulio, el jefe de los campistos, no *le* quería (Ramírez, p. 9).

Mexico: —¿Pero tú *lo* viste? ... —No. Yo no *le* vi (M. A. Menéndez, p. 34).

Cuba: Salí a emplear toda mi autoridad para salvar*le* a usted, y mentí, ¡y *lo* salvé! (Hernández Catá, p. 151).

In Spanish-American popular speech *lo* is the rule, except in Ecuador and Paraguay (probably a few other limited areas, as in Venezuelan Guiana), where *le* (plural *les*) may be heard among all classes in referring to persons.

Ecuador: —*Les* van a matar (Icaza, *En las calles*, p. 255); ¿*Le* soltaron de la cárcel? (p. 263). La antigua tendera ... empezó a recoger ... los hijos de los cholos indigentes para educar*les* en la santa ley de Cristo y enseñarles a trabajar desde pequeños. *Les* amaba (Icaza, *Cholos*, p. 29); como *les* quería tanto (p. 30). —¿*Los* conoces? La otra noche *les* conocí (Mata, *Sanagüín*, p. 184). *Le* reconoció al indio. ... Con razón *les* quiero tanto a mis señores (Bustamante, p. 124).

Paraguay: *Le* veo a él, *les* veo a ellos (Morínigo).

Furthermore, both in Ecuador and in Paraguay, *le* is very frequently heard as a feminine pronoun object instead of *la* (as occasionally found in older as well as modern Spanish).

Ecuador (Highlands, Urban): Las amigas y parientes de la Petrona, sosteniéndo*le* del rebozo, a duras penas logran detener*le* en sus ímpetus de furia. Asimismo las amigas y conocidas de la Rosa, *le* consuelan y le piden que cese la batalla ... y era de ver*les* ... guiñar los ojos ... a dos cargadores que ... las contemplaban, lanzándolas bromas de color subido (García Muñoz, *Estampas*, pp. 183–85); —Mi comadre Susana, ni sabe el gusto que tengo de ver*le* (p. 243). Mienten los poetas al fingirse enamorados de la luna, a la que ni siquiera *le* conocen (García Muñoz, *El médico*, p. 73). —Tendrán*le* bien [= ténganla bien], a lo mejor me muerde (Icaza, *En las calles*, p. 179). ¡*Le* quiero, Gloria! ... Hoy será usted mía (Salvador, *Camarada*, p. 47).

—¡Porque yo *le* amo, Magdalena! (Salvador, *Prometeo*, p. 117). (AZUAY): *Le* ha tumbado y golpeado a gusto, hasta dejar*le* sin sentido. Entonces fué cuando abusó de la guagüita inocente (Mata, *Sanagüín*, p. 181). Usted es digna de mejor suerte. ¿*Le* engañó algún hombre? ... Cuando la vea envejecida, enferma, *le* botará a la calle (Salvador, *Noviembre*, p. 227). (HIGHLANDS, RURAL): *Le* encontré acostada (Icaza, *Cholos*, p. 176); yo *le* miraba de reojo (p. 177); *le* llamé por lo bajo (p. 178). (COASTAL ZONE): —Muchas gracias, Gertru. Y Cusumbo, que *le* devoraba con los ojos: —Oiga, ña Andrea. La muchacha ejtá güenaza. A usted *le* voy a hacer mi suegra (Aguilera Malta, p. 49).

PARAGUAY: *Le* veo a ella; *le* seguí con la vista hasta ver*le* [a ella] entrar en su casa (Morínigo).

It is generally believed that *la* is not used in American Spanish as a feminine pronoun indirect object, as is commonly done in Spain, especially in Madrid. Cuervo thought the same: "Entre americanos jamás he oído *la* por *le*" (Bello-Cuervo, n. 121, p. 114). True it is that *la* for *le* is not used in speech, but it may be found in literature.

ARGENTINA: Y pronto sus manos ... *la* ofrecieron otros tantos vasos, de los cuales Marta aceptó uno sin mirar de quién venía (Mallea, *Fiesta*, p. 47).

CHILE: Rosaura declaró ser una entusiasta amazona a quien sólo faltaba un caballero que *la* hiciese compañía (Silva, p. 63). *La* dije que fuera a acostarse (Edwards Bello, *La chica*, p. 92). Cuando *la* dieron de alta, la Ufra hizo venir un coche de alquiler y se largó (Alberto Romero, *La viuda*, p. 18); ¿Qué sorpresas *la* traería ese sol? (p. 78).

BOLIVIA: Falleció ayer sin tener tiempo de escribir*la* (Jaime Mendoza, *Memorias*, I, 78).

PERU: Y lo que *la* gritaba aquel pensamiento era la liberación de su alma (López Albújar, *Matalaché*, p. 53).

ECUADOR: Dos cargadores ... las contemplaban, lanzándo*las* bromas de color subido (García Muñoz, *Estampas*, p. 185).

VENEZUELA: Quiso ponerme la mano sobre los labios; yo se la tomé con pasión y *la* di un beso (Romero García, p. 59).

COSTA RICA: Será muy beya mi niña y *la* ponré Juana Amparo (Agüero, p. 50).

EL SALVADOR: Los campesinos, que regresan de sus guatalitos, *la* dicen siempre, siempre: —¡Dios, nanita! (Ambrogi, p. 92).

MEXICO: ¿La chica, Florita, que *la* da por decir versos? (Quevedo, *Las ensabanadas*, p. 103). Como si *la* leyese los pensamientos, Hipólito pidió la botella del catalán (Gamboa, *Santa*, p. 318).

Nevertheless, in American Spanish *la* as a feminine dative for *le* is the exception, and *lo* is by far commoner than *le* as a masculine accusative of persons. The thirty-four River Plate authors represented in the *Antología de cuentistas rioplatenses* (Buenos Aires, 1939), in referring to persons, use *le* 76 times as against *lo* 284 times. In more than 400 pages of prose, then, *lo* is used about four times as often as *le* as a direct object referring to persons. In the *Antología del cuento hispanoamericano* (ed. Manzor [Santiago de Chile, 1939]) over fifty authors, representing some seventeen Spanish-American republics, use *lo* about two and one-half times as often as *le* as direct object referring to persons.

It must be remembered that often it is practically impossible to determine whether *le* is a direct or an indirect object. Analogy and other forces (such as identical direct- and indirect-object forms of nouns referring to persons) have obliterated original distinctions. The situation is rendered even more obscure for American Spanish, in which certain verbs in some localities take a direct-object pronoun where in standard Spanish they take an indirect-object pronoun (*hablar*, for instance), in addition to certain variable verbs (*mirar*, *seguir*, *pegar*, *obedecer*, etc.). In the older language ***hablar*** could take a direct object; Keniston (p. 17) gives [6–9] as its range and frequency for sixteenth-century prose. Today it is frequently so construed in parts of Spanish America, side by side with standard usage. According to the Argentine perceptist, Garrigós (p. 147), speakers who say *lo* (or *la*) ***hablo*** will revert to standard ***le hablo*** if the verb is followed by some sort of complement: *le hablo muy bien de Juan* (and not *lo hablo muy bien de Juan*), *le hablo en francés* (and not *lo hablo en francés*).

ARGENTINA: Esté solo, completamente solo. Tengo que hablar*lo* (Greca, p. 165). El otro *lo* conversaba con los más finos modales ... ponerse a hablar*le* ligerito (Lynch, *Romance*, p. 261). —Vamos, viejo, ... yo *lo* tengo que hablar para ver si me sigue (Yrurzun, p. 18). Los mozos tímidos y los gárrulos mirábanlas y *las* hablaban (Mallea, in *ACH*, p. 84). No *la* he hablado (Güiraldes, *Xaimaca*, p. 49). Si *los* hablas, vendrán y son siete hermanos (Ezquer Zelaya, p. 196). Ella los mira y *los* habla por la ventana (Petit de Murat, p. 95).

URUGUAY: Toqueló en la rienda y hable*ló* (Montiel, *Cuentos*, p. 14).

CHILE: Desde varias camas más allá *lo* hablaron: —¿Viene Ud. enfermo del corazón? (Juan Modesto Castro, *Aguas*, p. 14). —Escúchame, Lorenzo, ¿desde cuándo *la* hablas? (Azócar, p. 259).

PERU: (A *chola* speaks): —Señor, diz que *lo* quieren hablar dos señores (Corrales, p. 146); —Conque oído al parche, que don Corrales *los* va a hablar (p. 191).

COLOMBIA (SOUTH): Cuando Antoñina *lo* habló ... él dormía (Álvarez Garzón, p. 80; but most cases are with *le* [pp. 16, 20, 45, 48, etc.]. For Bogotá, *lo* is not registered [Flórez, p. 376]).

GUATEMALA: Ya no tarda en llegar. ¿Quiere hablar*lo*? (Quintana, p. 108).

The use of direct object *le* in preference to *lo* in most Spanish-American countries seems to be individual. More than half of the 76 *le* forms (as against 284 *lo* forms) used by the 34 River Plate writers represented in the *Antología de cuentistas rioplatenses* are from the pens of only five of them, at least one of whom (Méndez Calzada) had completed his primary and secondary education in Spain, returning to Argentina at the age of seventeen. Benito Lynch, in his tale "Aquel hijo," uses *le* and *lo* with about equal frequency. The same novelist uses *le* and *lo* with about equal frequency in the narrative portions of *Los caranchos de la Florida*, but in the conversation he uses *lo* with exceedingly few exceptions. With the verb *mirar*, he uses *le* and *lo* with almost equal frequency, *lo* slightly oftener. Of the Argentine writers, Benito Lynch and Eduardo Mallea are the two who use *le* oftener than any others. Only four of the twelve Argentine writers represented in the *Antología del cuento hispanoamericano* use *le*, and only one of these (Eduardo Mallea) uses it noticeably more than *lo*. Among the writers from most other countries, we note the limited use of *le* in narrative and the almost exclusive use of *lo* in conversation. This reflects the almost exclusive (with exceptions, such as Ecuador) use of *lo* in the spoken language of Spanish America, as in much of Spain (Andalusia, Navarre, etc.). In literary style, however, Spanish-American writers, remembering peninsular literature, are likely to imitate Castilian usage in employing *le* as the masculine direct object of persons, considering the *le* more elegant and more correct than the conversational *lo*. Román (III, 281) significantly remarks: "Como ac. de *él*, dicen todos los gramáticos y también la

Academia, que, tratándose de personas, es preferible [*le*] a la forma *lo*. ... En Chile somos más *loístas* que *leístas; pero ya nos iremos enmendando*." This feeling of the literary preference of *le* over *lo* is clearly reflected in Edwards Bello's *La chica del Crillón*, written in diary form. The heroine (p. 193) tells of buying a book translated from the English: *How to be charming, o sea El arte de ser encantadora*. She reads a passage from the chapter entitled "La vida social," which is quoted. The object pronouns referring to male beings are all *le*, probably because Edwards Bello desired to give the impression that he was quoting from a literary work:

«Si algún joven fuera a pedirle una vuelta de baile, aunque no haya tenido el agrado de ver*le* nunca, míre*le* fijamente en los ojos durante varios segundos ... y en voz baja, discreta y musical dígale: Su rostro no me es ajeno; yo *le* conozco a usted y no *le* olvido. ¿Dónde *le* vi antes? ...»

Later on (p. 199) when, at a social function, the heroine relates in diary form how she put into practice what she had read, she uses only *lo*, her accustomed conversational form, thus giving greater verisimilitude to the account of her experience, since *lo* (and not *le*) is the form commonly employed in Chile:

«El interés que tuviera por ver*lo*. ... *Lo* miré un instante ... y le dije: —Yo *lo* he visto a usted en alguna parte, y no puedo olvidar*lo*. ...»

Perhaps this is the place to mention the fact that in some Indian regions *lo* is the only third person singular object pronoun used by the untutored Indians in referring to masculine and feminine persons and things. Thus in parts of Peru (Huacho, Eten): "¿Ya se *lo* casó la María? ... la platita *lo* tengo aquicito no más (Benvenutto, p. 143). Ramos Duarte (p. 353) reports for the state of Morelos, Mexico: "Me *lo* saludas a la señorita." In the province of Chiloé, Chile: "¿Viste ayer a Juana? —No *lo* vi (Cavada, pp. 215–77). Likewise in Bolivia, Argentina (Tucumán, Santiago [cf. Moglia, p. 251]), Yucatan (V. Suárez, p. 150).

REDUNDANT INDIRECT 'LE'

The use of redundant *le*, anticipating a plural indirect object, while not infrequent in both Old and Modern standard Spanish, seems to be much commoner everywhere in America. It is probably analogical with invariable indirect object *ge* (Old Spanish) > *se*

(Modern Spanish), and with invariable reflexive pronoun *se*. This pleonastic *le* is sometimes a mere expletive particle which serves to round out the phrase; sometimes it possesses adverbial force and thus is invariable; and again it may well have distributive force with a logical feeling of the singular present in the plural: *le* for *cada uno de*, etc.[7] While grammarians often call this *le* an error for *les*, it is "genial de nuestra lengua" (Cuervo, § 335) in Spain and apparently even more so in Spanish America, probably because here writers are less grammar-minded.

ARGENTINA: Cuídese mucho y dé*le* recuerdos a los viejos (Lynch, *Los caranchos*, p. 121). *Le* tiene miedo a las ánimas (Larreta, *El linyera*, pp. 12 and 14). Pues es porque *le* obedecen a las mujeres (*Fray Mocho*, p. 175).

URUGUAY: ¡A las malas mañas *le* llaman ahora costumbres! (Sánchez, *M'hijo el dotor*, I, 3). A algunos *le* chispearon los ojos (Montiel, *Alma nuestra*, p. 139). *Le* cambiaba el alpiste a los canarios (Montiel, in *ACH*, p. 377). Ahora puedes dar*le* vuelo a tus planes (Reyles, *El terruño*, p. 290).

CHILE: Se estaba hasta el amanecer ... haciéndo*le* el amor a las niñas (Alberto Romero, *La viuda*, p. 17). A la última hora *le* quitan a los enfermos las camas (Juan Modesto Castro, p. 12); cuénten*le* a carneros esta historia (p. 155).

COLOMBIA: Al otro día ya estaba Eva coqueteándo*le* a las manzanas (Arango Villegas, p. 18); Yo no *le* temo a las ideas. *Le* temo, sí, a los decretos (p. 109). *Le* roba a los ricos, para dar*le* a los necesitados (Buitrago, p. 159).

VENEZUELA: No quiso que *le* pegara a los caimanes (Gallegos, *Doña Bárbara*, p. 19). Este animal ... no *le* embiste a los muertos (Romero García, p. 21); ¿por qué no *le* pagará a sus hijas? (p. 79). No pudo poner*le* freno a las palabras (Salazar Domínguez, in *ACMV*, II, 44).

NICARAGUA: Hay que hablar*le* a los muchachos (Orozco, p. 95).

HONDURAS: —Yo no *le* creo a los hombres (Mejía Nieto, *El solterón*, p. 19); no *le* tenía miedo a los muertos (p. 98).

MEXICO: Usted prénda*le* fuego a los carros (Fernando Robles, p. 258). También me sirvió, para ... prohibir que se *le* siguiera llamando a esos pájaros "ladrones" (Mena Brito, p. 69).

CUBA: Huyéndo*le* a los vapores de guerra ... salí con mi familia

[7] Cf. C. Sturgis, "Uso de *le* por *les*," *Hispania*, X (1927), 251–54.

(Luis Felipe Rodríguez, p. 27); ¡A cuántas muchachas *le* habrá dicho usted lo mismo! (p. 98); el campesino no *le* da mucha importancia a esas uniones irregulares y libres (p. 208). Yo no *le* temo a sus amenazas (Ciro Espinosa, p. 208).

'SE LOS (LAS)' FOR 'SE LO (LA)'

We all know that the phrase *se lo dimos* may mean 'we gave it to him, to her, to you, to them,' etc. It is not always clear as to number, since the invariable *se* may be either singular or plural. To avoid ambiguity we are told to add the prepositional phrases *a él, a ella, a usted, a ellos*, etc., to agree with the gender, number, and person represented by *se* in any given case. Since the feeling of number is important and prepositional phrases are often omitted (cf. *usted*, p. 97) in rapid communication, popular speech in many regions of Spanish America generally insists on indicating plurality of the indirect object *se* by adding an *s* to the immediately following direct object, *lo* or *la*, making them *los* and *las*, even though the object referred to is singular. The pluralizing *-s* is added to *lo* or *la*, though the plural number belongs to the other pronoun, because *los* and *las* are thoroughly familiar forms and a form *ses* would be unthinkable. Thus, *se lo digo a ustedes* (where *ustedes* clarifies the relationship) becomes *se los digo* (since *se lo digo* is ambiguous).

This syntactical error, a case of "associative interference," may occasionally be met in Spain but is evidently rare: Cuervo (§ 356) mentions its occurrence in "libros españoles desaliñados"; Gili y Gaya (p. 208) reports for Aragon: *ya se les* [=*los*] *he dicho* for *ya se lo he dicho*. In American Spanish, however, it thrives abundantly in many regions. In some American areas it is a popular usage, in others it is general even among the cultured and in literary style.

Naturally, grammarians and purists inveigh against this solecism. That it is deep-seated and difficult to eradicate is evident from the sometimes lengthy and elaborate expositions of its use and misuse found in the grammars and other linguistic treatises published in countries where it is most flagrant (Lenz, *La oración*, p. 262, n. 1; Santamaría and Domínguez, *Ensayos*, pp. 226, 295, 296; León, *Barbarismos*, II, 87–92; Cascante de Rojas, p. 421; Cuervo, § 356; Alonso y Henríquez Ureña, *Gramática*, II, 109, etc.).

In many regions not only does *se lo* become *se los* when *se* is plural, but the dative *le* may become *les* in imperatives when the subject of the verb is plural: *ábranle ustedes la puerta* > *ábranles ustedes la puerta* 'open the door for him,' etc. While such attractions of number to object or subject are common in American Spanish, I am not aware of attraction of gender of object pronouns to the subject of the verb as reported for the lower classes of Madrid: "ella *la* quiere ayudar a usted"; *usted* is here masculine but *la* (which should be *le*) is feminine, attracted to the feminine subject *ella*.[8]

Whether *se los* (*las*) for *se lo* (*la*) will eventually be accepted, we cannot predict now, but that it is in certain regions well on its way to tacit acceptance no one can deny.

ARGENTINA: Siento venir a hablarles de su comedia ... pero si no *se los* dijera me iría a acostar molesto (Mallea, *Fiesta*, p. 121). No hay mujer que se conforme con ser vaina 'e cuero no más. ... *Se los* dice uno que siempre jué aficionao (Larreta, *El linyera*, p. 93). Los franciscanos ... habían hecho sus camas muy cerca de mí. ... Yo *se los* había recomendado (Mansilla, *Una excursión*, p. 108).

URUGUAY: Yo *se los* permito (Amorím, *La carreta*, p. 38).

CHILE: Los niños pidieron pan y no había quién *se los* partiese (Román, III, 339). Siempre ha de ser necesario decír*selos* todo a éstos (Barros Grez, I, 155); has hablado con las señoras. —I *se los* he dicho todo (IV, 45). —¡Encontraré los asesinos. *Se los* prometo! (Latorre, *Hombres*, p. 98). Cuando andaban payaseando en la góndola yo *se los* advertí: váyanse (Alberto Romero, *Perucho González*, p. 92). Me acuerdo diuna [payasada] muy diablona que *se las* voy a decir (Juan del Campo, p. 7); ¡a vos te pasan cosas que no *les* suceden a naiden! (p. 43).

BOLIVIA: Mis soldados padecen ... pero debe continuar la excavación. *Se los* notifiqué (Céspedes, p. 34).

ECUADOR: Rezaron todos, despacito, tal como *se los* había indicado el señor cura (Pareja, *La Beldaca*, p. 58). Y de haber sabido algo, ya *se los* habría hecho olvidar el trabajo duro, agobiador (La Cuadra, *Horno*, p. 33).

COLOMBIA: Eso pasó como *se los* digo a ustedes (Cuervo, § 356; also Uribe, *Dicc.*) Piden posada. Con todo corazón *se las* doy (Carrasquilla, *Novelas*, p. 18). Nu hay como el trabajo honrao. Yo sé cómo *se los* digo (Arias Trujillo, p. 211).

VENEZUELA: —Y *se los* he dicho (Pocaterra, p. 18). Pero como los demás que están presentes no conocen la historia, *se las* voy a echar (Gallegos, *Doña Bárbara*, p. 81); *Se los* diré así (p. 97); Lo demás

[8] J. Vallejo, "Complementos y frases complementarias en español," *RFE*, XII (1925), 126.

se los diré en Altamira (p. 318). —¡Este cacho es pesao! Pero *se los* voy a echá (Briceño, in *ACMV*, II, 128).

PANAMA: La advertencia *se las* hizo a todos. ... El dinero ... *se los* trajo su cuñado (Espino, p. 139).

COSTA RICA: ¿Y saben lo que calculo? *Se los* digo, y no lo digan (Echeverría, p. 113).

EL SALVADOR: El niño Raúl quedó de un año. Las niñas—las hermanas del patrón—se lo pedían, pero él no lo quiso dar y sólo *se los* mandaba para las ferias (Mechín, *La muerte*, p. 106).

GUATEMALA: —Digo la suerte ... ¿Quieren que *se las* diga a los cavalleros? ... *Se las* echo, señores, por nada (Samayoa, p. 25); Bueno, pues, echánosla (p. 26); les pido que no me desgraceyen. Por favor *se los* pido (p. 108). Nuestros grandes abuelos, los Mayas, pusieron fin a la ya larga peregrinación ... porque así *se los* habían ordenado que lo hicieran Tzacol y Bitol (Barnoya, p. 89). —¡Qué horror, señora! No sabe usted cuánto lo sentimos. —Dios *se los* pague, señores (Arce, p. 29).

MEXICO: Hacía frío pero no lo sentían; el trabajo y el mezcal *se los* quitaba (Fernando Robles, p. 64); de ésta se escapará Carlitos, pero cuídenlo bien, *se los* encargo mucho (p. 155); —¡Pero si es la verdad, *se los* aseguro! (p. 174). A mis hermanas divertía grandemente aquel chiquitín prieto ... y pedían al padre que *se los* llevara ... lo vi llegar con su hijillo ... para dejár*selos* (Ferretis, *Quijote*, p. 31); ¡Qué dieran los periódicos ... por conseguir un retrato mío! ... ¡*Se los* voy a mandar! (p. 94); Y *se los* ofrece en venta a cuantas gentes lo miran (p. 243). *Se los* devolveré más sano y más fuerte que un roble (Azuela, *Avanzada*, p. 30). Mi madre platicó todo lo de la carta a mis hermanas y *se las* entregó para que la leyeran (Núñez Guzmán, p. 96). —Danos una media. *Se las* di (Galeana, p. 68); Salí a buscarlo. Lo tenían encerrado. ... *Se los* quité (p. 111). Yo creía que venían a felicitarme porque *se los* había quitado [al profesor de Ética] (Vasconcelos, p. 136); les censuraba y así *se los* hice presente (p. 146); Bien *se los* merecía un pueblo de visión obtusa (p. 311); Como que el ejemplo *se los* daba su jefe (p. 440). Las bestias se encabritan cuando ven a la culebra; pero él las acaricia suavemente, *se las* pasa por el anca, y termina atándola a la cabeza de su silla (Mena Brito, p. 42). Creí que les estorbaría y *se los* dije (García Roel, p. 78).

NEW MEXICO: Sacó la oreja de su bolsa y *se las* enseñó. Mi agüela me lo contó a mí, y yo *se los* cuento a ustedes. El capitán *se los* agradeció mucho (Rael, in *HR*, VIII, 347).

CUBA: Los ricos no le venden la tierra a los pobres, pa eso *se las* venden a los americanos (Ciro Espinosa, p. 36); De aquí a mañana no hay quien aguante la pehte, yo *se loh* galantiso (p. 114); Muy pronto lo sabrán por este viejo sacerdote, que les dará la buena nueva. Y a ustedes también *se las* doy (p. 235).

ENCLITIC '-N'

Analogy comes into play in another interesting syntactical error: adding an *-n* to pronouns that, as enclitics, are attached to third person plural verb forms used as imperatives: *siéntensen* or *siéntesen* for *siéntense*, etc. The *-n* is added here for the same reason that *-s* was added to *lo* in *se los* (for *se lo*): without it the legitimate feeling for number is frustrated. The sound *-n* satisfies the feeling of plurality for third person verbs, just as *-s* satisfies the same feeling in nouns and pronouns. In *siéntense* that feeling of plurality is unfulfilled for many speakers who see in the combined form a single verbal concept and not a combination of verb and pronoun; these speakers expect the feeling of plurality to be satisfied at the very end of the word, as happens in the majority of such imperative forms: *hablen, vengan, coman.* Apparently, then, the formation was purely analogical. The commonest mode, which is also the oldest, is *-sen* for *-se.* This was influenced not only by plural *-n*, but probably also by the imperfect-subjunctive ending *-sen* (*hablasen, tuviesen*). Later the analogy was extended to *-me, -le, -lo,* etc. Finally, the inner *n*, being superfluous, was dropped. In addition, the plural *-n* is occasionally added to enclitic pronouns attached to an infinitive (*irsen* for *irse*) or even to a gerund (*esperándomen*).

The phenomenon is common in rural sections of Spain,[9] but undoubtedly its social level is higher in American Spanish, that is, it may be used also by the uneducated urban dweller and even by a few cultured speakers. And it has found its way very readily into realistic Spanish-American literature, particularly of the present

[9] Hartzenbusch, "Apéndices al prólogo" (p. lxiii) to Cuervo's *Apuntaciones*, says (1874): *siéntesen, váyasen,* cualquier honrado labriego lo dice muy grave; y alguna vez he advertido esa *n* añadida a un infinitivo referente a un sustantivo plural, diciendo *al irsen ellos*, en vez de *al irse.*" López Barrera, *Arcaísmos y barbarismos de la provincia de Cuenca* (p. 100): "*Siéntensen* ustedes. —*Márchensen* de aquí. —*Váyansen* a pasear. —Esos chicos van a *pegarsen.* —Van a *comersen* un cordero. —¡A *estudiarsen* las lecciones!" Borao, *Dicc. de voces aragonesas* (p. 95): "*querersen.*" Menéndez Pidal, *Gramática* (§ 94, 2): "En el habla vulgar de Castilla, Aragón, América y de los judíos españoles ... : al *marcharsen* ellos, *siéntensen* ustedes, *váyasen.*" See also M. L. Wagner, *Caracteres generales del judeo-español de Oriente*, p. 70; Rosenblat, *Notas*, pp. 229–32.

century. However, it has not been tacitly sanctioned in any region as has the erroneous use of *se los* for *se lo,* although instances of its use by cultured speakers are not lacking. Practice may often vary according to region. Sometimes the *-n* appears only at the end of the word (*siéntesen*), at other times also at the end of the verb proper (*siéntensen*). Furthermore, popular speech (particularly in Argentina) often stresses the enclitic pronoun in a word of more than two syllables: *sientensén, dejenmelón,* etc. Consequently, spellings vary: some writers indicate two stresses (*siéntensén*), others only one (*sientensén* or *siéntensen*). In the rustic or vulgar speech of Spain (Castile, Aragon) the *-n* is added only to *se* and *me* in imperative and infinitive forms, but apparently *-n* is not added to *le* or *lo* as in many parts of America, where, in turn, *-lon* is rare save in the River Plate area.

ARGENTINA: *Cáyensén* los mirones (*Martín Fierro,* p. 307); *créanmenló* (p. 334). Aguarden, *dejenmén* a mí (Lynch, *Palo verde,* p. 135); —*¡Mirenmelán* a la presumida! (p. 143). *Demen* mujeres y caballos (Lynch, *Los caranchos,* p. 103). —Pasen adelante; *sientensén* (Güiraldes, *Don Segundo,* p. 252); *ladeensén* (p. 280). —*¡Sígamen!* (Yamandú Rodríguez, *Cimarrones,* p. 17); —*¡Mirenlón!* (*Fray Mocho,* p. 19); *Mirenlán* a la princesa ... *¡Veanlón* al mozo vivo! (p. 141); *¡Mirenmelón* al doctor! (p. 155). *¡Lárguenlon!* = Orden que da el domador, cuando ya está acomodado sobre el caballo, a la persona que tiene el potro sujeto de la oreja izquierda (Saubidet, p. 206).

URUGUAY: —¡Pasen! ... *Acomódensen* (Sánchez, *M'hijo el dotor,* II, 2). —*Agarremén* ese gurí; *enlacenlón; ¡bolenlón* al perdulario! (Montiel, *Luz mala,* p. 48). —*Demen* juego (Viana, *Gaucha,* p. 229).

PARAGUAY: *¡Demen* una escafandra! (Casaccia, p. 59).

CHILE: *Demen, delen, desen* (Echeverría y Reyes, p. 69; also Román, II, 70). (CHILOÉ): *Vayansén, sientensén, vayasén, sientesén* (Cavada, p. 275); *traigalón, demelán* (p. 276).

PERU: —*Delen, delen* (Ciro Alegría, *La serpiente,* p. 136).

ECUADOR: —*¿Preguntarálen* al doctor, no? (Icaza, *En las calles,* p. 190). *Váyasen, suéltemen, cállesen* (Pérez Guerrero, § 166). *Digamén, cojalén, tengalén* (Lemos, § 36).

COLOMBIA: —*Gánesen* ... y *agárresen* del palo di'arriba (Carrasquilla, *Hace tiempos,* I, 234); Los ángeles tienen que *volvesen* pal cielo (I, 258); *Espérensen* un momentico (II, 249). Ya estaban los músicos *esperándomen* (Buitrago, p. 54); *levantesén* (p. 126). Prendieron otra vela pa *ponesen* a jugar dao muy pasito (Posada, p. 14).

VENEZUELA: A médico célebre y de vasta ilustración le he oído decir: «*delen* las píldoras esta noche» (Calcaño, § 483).

COSTA RICA: Sin que yeguen a *sitamen* [= citarme] lo mandaré a primer grado (Agüero, p. 49); deben *tenesen* las niñas enserradas (p. 51); *demen* campo (p. 62); ¿quieren *casasen* [= casarse]? (p. 85). Y que beban sin *socarsen* [socarse = emborracharse] (Echeverría, p. 127); —*Traiganmén* al Padre Piedra (p. 169). No van a venir endespués a *esquitasen* [= desquitarse] con naide (Fabián Dobles, p. 92); *Siéntesen* por aquí (p. 129); *Bébasen* este poquillo de café (p. 131), etc.

NICARAGUA: Es muy frecuente oír en Nicaragua "*demen* un vaso de fresco," en lugar de "*denme* un vaso de fresco" (Castellón, p. 56).

EL SALVADOR: —*Desen* priesa, que ya tengo sueño (Mechín, *Brochazos*, p. 134). —*Demen* paso, pues, *déjenme* ver quién puede ser (Torres Arjona, p. 71).

GUATEMALA: *Demen* un poco de agua (Sandoval, I, 328).

MEXICO: Es muy común oír hasta en boca de maestros: *Demen café; demen agua*. Debe decirse *denme*, que es lo mismo que *den a mí* (Ramos Duarte, p. 192). «*Delen* ... por *denle*.» Cometiendo el mismo yerro dicen algunos «córralen,» «páselen,» por «córranle,» «pásenle» (León, II, 29).

NEW MEXICO: *Váyasen, dígamen, demen, desen, delen, hágamen* (Aurelio Espinosa, *Estudios*, § 214).

SANTO DOMINGO: *Demen* dulce, *demen* agua (Patín Maceo, *Dom.*, p. 58); Niños, *estesen* quietos (p. 77).

CUBA: *Demen, dígamen* (Padrón).

PUERTO RICO: *Siéntensen ustedes, siéntesen ustedes, demen, dígamen, delen* (Navarro, p. 129).

OBJECT PRONOUNS OMITTED

In standard Spanish *lo* is generally used with verbs of understanding or expression (*decir, saber, preguntar*, etc.), where in English no direct object is used: *lo sé* 'I know,' *se lo dije* 'I told him.' While this *lo* is occasionally omitted in standard Spanish, it is very frequently omitted in American Spanish, particularly in conversation and nearly always so when an indirect-object pronoun is expressed (in this case *lo* often drops with other verbs). There seems to be a disinclination to use two pronoun objects together. This suppression of the third person pronoun is sometimes alluded to as a syntactical peculiarity of the Basque provinces: *Ya le dije* for *Ya se lo dije* (Huidobro, p. 178). Its geographical distribution is wider than that. It is especially diffused throughout South America. We find such omissions characteristic also of Brazilian Portuguese as opposed to standard Portuguese. This same usage is recorded for French and Italian, and it was not unknown in Latin (Meyer-Lübke, § 379).

Some cases recorded below may be attempts to avoid the ambiguous *se lo*, as: *prepararles* = *preparárselo; les quitamos* = *se la quitamos*.

Argentina: —No quiero decir nada. —¿Por qué? ... ¿Qué puedo ganar con decir*le*? [= decírselo] (Mallea, *La ciudad*, p. 41). —¡Vas a ver! Cuando lo vea a tu padre, *le* [= se lo] voy a contar. —Cuénte*le* [= cuénteselo] (Yrurzún, p. 44). Empieza por pedir agua. *Le* [= se la] traen. (Yamandú Rodríguez, *Cimarrones*, p. 66). Sabiendo que ibas a dir, hubiera hecho con gusto un poco e mazamorra pa mandar*le* [= mandársela] (Lynch, *Romance*, p. 34).

Chile: —Mire, vecina, ¿por qué no cruzamos su gatita con mi gato? —Hay que decir*le* a él—respondía Luz Dina. Todo había que decírselo a él (Godoy, p. 25). Les tengo cafecito listo. Pero si les gusta más el té, no me dilato una nada en preparar*les* (Durand, *Mercedes*, p. 193); No olvides de mandar a decir*le* a doña Celia (p. 203).

Bolivia: —¿Y les quitamos la carga a las bestias? —*Les* quitamos (Arguedas, *Raza*, p. 53). —¿Y quién *les* [= se los] ha dado? —El Satuco *me* ha dado (Díaz Villamil, *Cuando vuelva*, p. 68). Si *le* [= se los] devolvemos, creerá que somos unas orgullosas (Ruiz, p. 15).

Peru: —Bueno, por ahora pidan hospedaje en la casa de los colonos. ... *Les* darán. ... Seguro que *les* darán (Ciro Alegría, *Los perros*, p. 108).

Ecuador: ¿Para qué? Ayúdenme primero y luego *les* diré (García Muñoz, *El médico*, p. 32). Apenas llegue *le* voy a decir (Gil Gilbert, *Nuestro pan*, p. 133). —¿Vas a coger flores? Traerás también para mí. No le digas nada: *te* ruego. ... Aunque llores lágrimas de desconsuelo, él *te* secará (Vázquez, p. 335). —¡Ah, caramba! Calla la boca. Y al decir*le* le da un empujón (Pareja, *Baldomera*, p. 32); Claro que no tengo. Si no, *te* diera (p. 34).

Colombia: —Ella siempre era grandecita, ¿para qué *le* voy a negar? (Arango Villegas, p. 166). —Cuánto *le* agradezco (Álvarez Garzón, p. 263). —Lleve este paquete a la señorita Dolly. —¿Y qué le digo? —Nada. Entrégue*le* y nada más (Bernardo Toro, p. 90).

Occasionally popular speech dispenses even with a single object pronoun, especially when the implied substantive immediately precedes:

BOLIVIA: —Pero tampoco yo *he hecho* [= lo he hecho] adrede (Díaz Villamil, *Cuando vuelva*, p. 25). —Tienes que ir a entregárselos ... —¿No ves que él *ha puesto* [= los ha puesto] a propósito en la silla? (Ruiz, p. 15). —Aquí están los medicamentos. —¿Cómo has traído [= los has traído]? (Rodrigo, p. 64).

ECUADOR: —¿Por qué no has hecho el deber, ociosa? —Ya *hice*, pues, mamá (García Muñoz, *Estampas*, p. 273).

REDUNDANT PRONOUNS

Standard Spanish often uses a redundant indirect-object pronoun when the indirect object is a noun or a stressed personal pronoun: *le doy el libro a Juan, le doy el libro a él*. In the case of stressed direct-object pronouns a redundant pronoun is likewise used: *no le veo a él*. But if the direct object is a noun, then the redundant object pronoun is oftener omitted in correct standard Spanish: *veo a Juan*. Nevertheless, its use is frequent in colloquial speech and in individual writers: "... *le* llevó a Zalacaín al cementerio ... *lo* encontró al vasco francés" (Pío Baroja, *Zalacaín*). The construction is attested very early: *priso lo al conde* (*Cid*, vs. 1012), *afelas sus fijas* (vs. 2947). It seems to be a compensative striving for clarity in a language in which exceedingly free word order and frequent suppression of subject pronouns might tend toward obscurity. Today the abuse of these redundant forms is, in general, commoner in American-Spanish writers than in peninsular writers, when the object is direct.

ARGENTINA: Santos *la* miró a Rosa (Ascasubi, p. 137); *lo* han muerto a Vizcacho (p. 154); *lo* vido muerto a Berdún (p. 217). ¡Oígan*ló* al rebelde! (Larreta, *El linyera*, p. 25); Siéntan*lo* al hereje (p. 51); ¡Míren*lo* al sarnoso! (p. 61). *Lo* llamah' a tu padre (Güiraldes, *Don Segundo*, p. 128); La vieja *lo* tomó al llorón de la mano (p. 128); *La* recordaba a su morocha (p. 132). —¿Así que el tarambana de Octavio *la* liquidó su fortuna? (Rodríguez A., *El barro humano*, I, 4).

URUGUAY: —¿No *lo* esperaba a don Eloy? (Florencio Sánchez, p. 67); —¡Está borracho y *lo* ha provocado al señor! (p. 318); —Tú *las* conoces bien a las muchachas (p. 450).

CHILE: —Cárdenas *la* perdona a Adelaida (Azócar, p. 259). Yo *lo* comprendería al pobre (Luis Meléndez, p. 130). —Es que *lo* quieren al árbol y no quieren creer que cayó (Acevedo H., *Árbol*, p. 48).

PARAGUAY: —¿No te da vergüenza llamar*lo* Demetrio a un hombre casi extraño? (Casaccia, p. 106).

BOLIVIA: ¿*Lo* ha visto a Lucas? (Pereyra, p. 176). Los amigos ... *lo* encontraron a Suárez un poco pálido (Arguedas, *Raza*, p. 327). Desde hacía poco *la* notaba a la joven distraída (Arguedas, *Vida criolla*, p. 51); La cita de la joven *lo* traía preocupado al periodista (p. 57).

PERU: ¿Ya *lo* vistes al Ministro? (Gamarra, *Algo del Perú*, p. 81). (HUÁNUCO): ¿Cuándo me *lo* das a la muchacha el traje que le ofreciste? (Pulgar Vidal, p. 816).

ECUADOR: —Ustedes no *lo* querían a Proano ¿no? (La Cuadra, *Guásinton*, p. 21). Viéndo*la* a la luna sin mirarla (Bustamente, p. 61; se *lo* veía al cadáver (p. 121); nunca *las* tratas a las mujeres en serio (p. 169). Quiero ver*lo* al desgraciado ése (Gil Gilbert, *Nuestro pan*, p. 123); hága*lo* al muchacho que sepa ser hombre (p. 170).

COLOMBIA: Ella *lo* amaba a Andrés (Álvarez Garzón, p. 73).

NICARAGUA: Ella no *lo* quiere a don Robustiano (Chamorro, *Entre dos filos*, p. 240).

Among the Andean populace especially, such a redundant *lo* seems to be the rule even when the direct object is a thing. Furthermore, not only illiterate Indians but other speakers, presumably with a degree of culture, at times employ *lo* regardless of gender or number of the direct-object noun, possibly to lend affective value and to round out the phrase.

ARGENTINA (TUCUMÁN, SANTIAGO): Me *lo* va a escribir la carta (Moglia, p. 251).

BOLIVIA: —Traéme*lo* un vaso (Díaz Villamil, *La Rosita*, p. 14); Yo se *los* preparaba unos picantitos (p. 16); ¡Cómo pues *lo* estás tirando así la plata! (p. 57); Cuando a una le han robado todo lo que tenía, cuando se *lo* matan a sus padres (p. 85). —¿Pudiera usted coserme*ló* unas camisas? (Rodrigo, p. 28).

PERU: (*Chola*) —Me *lo* dieron estos papelitos (Corrales, p. 146).

MEXICO (YUCATAN): ¿No te *lo* da vergüenza? Ya me *lo* cansé mis rodillas (Víctor Suárez, p. 150).

In standard Spanish the redundant form is not infrequently found after a relative pronoun used as direct object when the relative stands at some distance from the pronoun reproducing it, and in American Spanish such usage appears to be general. It was not uncommon in the older language (cf. Keniston, p. 85), especially after *que*, since no definite distinction was then felt when *que* was used as a relative pronoun, as a relative adverb, and as a conjunction. Some of this colorless or indefinite quality of *que* may have been inherited by Spanish Americans, making it necessary to use a redundant object pronoun to clarify its relationship to the verb. Wijk (p. 207), who cites early examples, believes a similar construction in Arabic influenced its widespread use in Spanish.

ARGENTINA: —Te voy a hacer una confesión *que* nunca me animé a hacer*la* a nadie (Cuti Pereira, p. 22); ochenta centavos en efectivo, *que* pensó dar*los* de propina (p. 55).

URUGUAY: ... epítetos ... que él lanzaba como una excomunión, y *a los cuales* temía*les* ella más que al fuego (Reyles, *El terruño*, p. 76).

PARAGUAY: Una pregunta *que* nunca se *la* había hecho (Casaccia, p. 64).

CHILE: Traté de buscarle conversación, *la que* no costaba mucho encontrárse*la* a don Pancho Garuya (Guzmán Maturana, p. 57). Cuántos pecaos habré cometío que *los* pagan mis hijos (Acevedo Hernández, *Árbol viejo*, p. 61).

BOLIVIA: Adquirió ... un saco de cuero *que lo* usaba indiferentemente en invierno o verano (Céspedes, p. 186).

PERU: Al único sentido de equilibrio *que* no *lo* afectan las perturbaciones descritas es a la vista (Martínez de Pinillos, p. 161). Pero a veces hay tentaciones *que* uno haría mal en rechazar*las* (Diez-Canseco, *Duque*, p. 66). Pasaré por alto las peripecias de mi viaje hasta Juliaca, *las que* por lo demás *las* tengo anotadas (Corrales, p. 132).

ECUADOR: Dijo cosas *que las* había tenido guardadas durante toda su vida (Icaza, *Cholos*, p. 161); saltó unas cuantas líneas *que* creyó no entender*las* (p. 170).

COLOMBIA: A los ocho días ... se casó con Belisaria *a la cual la* llevó para dicha ciudad (Álvarez Garzón, p. 27).

VENEZUELA: —No hay arbitrariedad *que* no le provoque hacer*la* (Gallegos, *Doña Bárbara*, p. 331).

NICARAGUA: Trae un niño *que* se *lo* dejaron (Toruño, p. 21).

CUBA: Le llevó en un jarro un poco de aguardiente, *que* el paciente *lo* sorbió con avidez (Ciro Espinosa, p. 407).

PREPOSITIONAL CASES

In standard Spanish when the person is the destination of a movement, the preposition *a* plus the prepositional form of the personal pronoun is preferably used with some verbs (*acercarse a, unirse a, oponerse a*, etc.). However, when the direct object is the reflexive *se*, both object pronouns very often precede these verbs in the standard language: "él *se* me acercó"; but "*me* acerqué a él" is generally preferred to the alternate "*me le* acerqué," although usage varies and grammarians are not agreed (Bello [§ 941b] and Cuervo [*Dicc.*, I, ix and 9] consider "me le acerqué" correct when *le* refers to a person, but not when it refers to a thing). Separation (or other relationship) is expressed sometimes with *a* and sometimes with *de* plus the personal pronoun, according to the verb (*escaparse de* but occasionally *a*, *desprenderse de, reírse de, huir de, apartarse de*, etc.). Many of these relationships can be found expressed not by the more usual prepositional construction but by a simple direct or indirect object pronoun, as the case may be.[10] Such usage may be found in accepted Spanish writers, particularly in the older language. However, these alternate practices appear today to be more extensive in the New World than in the *madre patria*, perhaps because of their popular aspect.

ARGENTINA: Pero él se *les* desprendió de golpe, saltando p'atrás (Lynch, *Romance*, p. 256). ¡Me *le* escapé gritando! (Angélica Mendoza, p. 57). —Ayer me *le* juyí al Comisario (Filloy, p. 192). Disparándo*le* a la ley (Martínez Payva, p. 9).

BOLIVIA: ¿Por qué se *te* habrían de reír? (Arguedas, *Vida*, p. 139).

COLOMBIA: Las autoridades del puerto se propusieron seguirle la pista ... pero El Coica se *les* fugaba en la canoa (Buitrago, p. 126). —Me *les* voy (Osorio Lizarazo, *El hombre*, p. 6).

VENEZUELA: *Le* estuvo enamorada (Gallegos, *Canaima*, p. 60); se *le* aparta [= se aparta de él] (p. 228).

MEXICO: Yo pensé que me *les* escaparía a los guardias (Galeana, p. 127); me *les* solté y me puse a repartir patadas a los agentes (p. 154). —Haces bien en retirárte*les*. Son muy peladotes y ordinarios (Azuela, *La Marchanta*, p. 15). —Yo juí l'único que me *les* juyí (Rubín, p. 186). (YUCATAN): Ella se *lo* ríe. Él se *lo* carcajea (Ramos Duarte, p. 337).

CUBA: Me persiguieron a tiros. ... Pero me *les* fuí entre las uñas (Fernández Cabrera, in *CC*, p. 59). A medida que me *les* acercaba, fuí precisando (Carlos Montenegro, *Los héroes*, p. 109).

REFLEXIVE 'SÍ, CONSIGO'

In many regions of both Spain and America, in cultured and in popular speech, the reflexive prepositional form *sí* (*consigo, para sí,*

[10] Cf. the Spanish usage of *quedarse una cosa* for *quedarse con una cosa:* "Te la quedas ... quédate la sarta" (Valle-Inclán, *Opera omnia*, IV, 12, 14).

etc.) is now seldom used. Here the five original Old Spanish forms with *con* (*conmigo, contigo, consigo, connusco, convusco*) have been reduced to two. In *voseo* areas, where *contigo* is likewise lost, the five have been reduced to one: *conmigo*. And in certain rural sections where *yo* is used as prepositional form (*conmigo* becoming *con yo*), not one of the five original forms has survived.[11] The reason for the change of *sí* to *él* (*ella, ellos, ellas*) is merely one of facilitating comprehension, of clarifying gender and number by changing *sí*, invariable in form but multiple in meaning, to something at once unmistakable in number, gender, and often in person. Evidently such clarification suits the perception of all minds who use it and is not restricted to any one social class or to any one region, as some would lead us to suppose.[12] In some cases where the use of *consigo* or *sí* seems inevitable, a variant construction may appear: *habla consigo mismo* 〉 *habla solo* or *para sus adentros; volvió en sí* 〉 *se recobró*, etc.

Strangely enough, the reverse is the case in some regions, as in Colombia, for instance, along the Atlantic coast (Sundheim, p. 171) and probably elsewhere (Obando, p. 34), including Spain (Vázquez, *También en España*, p. 87): *consigo* for *con nosotros, consigo* for *contigo*, etc. The reverse is likewise the case of certain common expressions like *volver en sí*, in which *sí* is very frequently, though erroneously, used for all persons. This use, as Cuervo (§ 345) points out, may be due to the fact that the third person reflexive *sí* is commoner than the reflexive pronouns of other persons. But the more potent influence is apparently the fact that expressions like *volver en sí, estar en sí, fuera de sí, de por sí*, etc., have become stereotyped and felt as one indissoluble and invariable locution, one single concept, *sí* having acquired the connotation of 'one's inner self.' Its perception is therefore easy, and it offers none of the undesirable vagueness sensed in the use of *sí* after other prepositions, which, because of their changing variety, have not been sufficiently associated with *sí* to petrify them as in the case of *volver en sí*, etc. In many regions one may hear "volví en *sí*" for "volví en *mí*" and the like (Román,

[11] Henríquez Ureña (*BDH*, V, 174) reports for Santo Domingo the two curious forms *tigo* (as well as *ti*) and *migo* as nominatives in compound subjects with quoted examples: "Ya yo y *ti* no semo na. ... Ni an lo piense, que yo y *tigo* nos liemos. ... Algún día *tigo* y *migo*."

[12] Tiscornia (*La lengua*, p. 119): "La existencia de la forma sujeto *él* y su empleo cotidiano sepultaron en el olvido a *consigo*, porque *con él* representaba mejor la idea de persona en la mente del gaucho." Román (V, 257): "Muy común es, en los que manejan libros franceses, usar en vez de este pronombre [sí] el personal *él, ella, ellos, ellas*."

V, 257; Gagini, p. 244; Sandoval, II, 602; etc.). An Ecuadorian grammarian (Pérez Guerrero, § 166) laments the fact that "distinguished persons" are not exempt from such usage. Sometimes both *sí* and *ellos* are used standardly (*acordaron entre sí* and *acordaron entre ellos*), but *sí* is preferred (cf. Hanssen, § 512; Meyer-Lübke, § 67, etc.). We find analogous practices in other languages.

ARGENTINA: Doña Julia ... dijo ... con voz quejosa y como si hablase *con ella* [= consigo] mesma (Lynch, *Romance*, p. 15). Cuando no puede hablar mal de nadie, habla de *ella* [= sí] misma (Ezquer Zelaya, p. 147). Abre suavemente la puerta, mira a todos lados, y la cierra *tras ella* [= tras sí] (Wast, I, 11).

URUGUAY: Se la toma con ambas manos ... y la atrae hacia *él* [= sí] (Florencio Sánchez, p. 420).

CHILE: No las tengo todas *consigo* (Román, I, 403).

PERU: Cautelosamente guarda la suma *para él* [= para sí] (María Wiesse, in *ACP*, p. 144). Cuando *volví en sí* ... creí prudente hacerme el sueco (Corrales, p. 43).

ECUADOR: Lo demás ... lo llevaban dentro de *ellos* [= sí] mismos (Pareja, *El muelle*, p. 6). Porque disqué todo lo quería *para ella* [= para sí] (Aguilera Malta, p. 21). Los guardias cívicos se matan entre *ellos* mismos (Mata, *Sanagüín*, p. 188). De pronto *volví en sí* (Vásconez, p. 163).

COLOMBIA (ANTIOQUIA): —Cuando *volví en sí* (Carrasquilla, *Novelas*, p. 123). (ATLANTIC COAST): Vamos a llevarlo *consigo* [= con nosotros] (Sundheim, p. 171). Dije para entre *sí* (Obando, p. 61); estoy fuera de *sí* (p. 77). Lo traen hacia *ellos* (Buitrago, p. 174).

COSTA RICA: No quería tampoco a su hijo para *ella* sola. Quería compartirlo, pero por partes iguales (Salazar Herrera, p. 7). Le cruzó un brazo por la espalda y la atrajo hacia *él* (Fabián Dobles, p. 152); Ninfa le contestó ... en talante de defenderse de un ataque contra *ella* misma (p. 161); estaba entre esas personas que piensan más en su prójimo que en *ellas* (p. 165).

GUATEMALA: Yo siempre llevo *consigo* mi cuhete (Sandoval, I, 245). Llevá de *consigo* tu chispero [= revólver] (CLC, p. 35).

MEXICO: El miedo que sentía la mujer no era ya por *ella* [= sí] misma (Rubín, p. 143). Lo llevamos *consigo* (Ramos Duarte, p. 136).

CUBA: ¿Qué hacer de la hora que aún faltaba para poder quedarse a solas *con él* [= consigo] mismo? (Carlos Montenegro, *Hombres*, p. 187).

POSITION OF OBJECT PRONOUNS

Modern usage for all types of discourse generally prescribes that object pronouns precede finite verb forms, except in affirmative commands; and that, as enclitics, they must follow infinitives, gerunds, and affirmative commands. In the older language, object pronouns were enclitic forms, always following the verb when it began a new breath-group. They might precede the verb only when some other stressed element in the same group went before (Keniston, p. 89). In standard Spanish today postposition of object pronouns is, with rare exceptions (*habráse visto, diríase,* etc.) only literary; it is sometimes used in stage conversation to produce a pedantically comic effect. The general literary practice today is to follow the older usage of postposition only at the beginning of a breath-group or after a pause (Keniston, *Syntax list,* p. 68). Postposition is commoner in Galicia, Asturias, and León than in other regions of Spain. But with a few writers elsewhere, and particularly with many Spanish-American writers, postposition has become a mannerism employed more according to the older traditions, and even going beyond that tradition in that it appears frequently in subordinate clauses. Often this excessive use, or abuse, obstructs the rhythmic flow of a sentence. In some regions (the Antilles, Andean Venezuela, etc.) postposition is often used in conversation (as in Galicia, Asturias, and León), particularly in narration.

ARGENTINA: Desde temprano, su madre *rodrigóle* (Larreta, *La gloria,* p. 22). La misma palabra *macana* tiene entre nosotros otra acepción distinta de la que la Academia *adjudícale* (Cantarell Dart, p. 53). La necesidad *obligábalo* a participar de la mísera ganancia (Leopoldo Lugones, *Filosofícula* [1924], p. 20).

Bello (§ 906) would have called this construction "algo dura"; García Medina (*Disparates,* II [1929], 106) calls it "intolerable: primero, porque el esdrújulo es muy feo; segundo, porque sería, en todo caso, 'obligába*le*,' tercero, porque cualquiera que tenga gusto dirá siempre 'la necesidad le obligaba.' " Bello would have called most of the following constructions "insoportables":

Sus ojos *diríanse* como envejecido [*sic*] de haber contemplado la miseria del mundo, de ese mundo que él *habíase* como apartado durante el tiempo en que *dedicóse* a sus invenciones (Marengo, p. 101). Disimuló su rencor ... como quien *vase* arrimando ... a un arma oculta (Larreta, *Zogoibi*, p. 120). Un incierto tropel *percibióse* distante. ... La luna *perdíase* en el horizonte (Greca, p. 25).

URUGUAY: (In narrating): Ha poco, *díjele* que yo admiro a Madame (Bellán, p. 106).

CHILE: Mi cabeza vacía *llenábala* un tumulto de precipitados latidos (Latorre, *Hombres*, p. 87). Solaguren *quedóse* allí todavía un rato (Prado, *Un juez*, p. 98). —Dicho *habíaseme* que el archipiélago austral era abundoso (Azócar, p. 146). —Creía que todo en el universo *estábale* subordinado (Lillo, p. 19); cuando sus manos *tropezábanse* en las tinieblas (p. 32); toda duda *fuéle* ya imposible (p. 63). Supo también que ya no *quedábale* derecho ni para pensar en él siquiera (D'Halmar, *Lucero*, p. 92). Baltasar *quédase* meditando largo rato. ... El alma de Baltasar *siéntese* conmovida (Santiván, p. 13).

PERU: No desdeña don Ignacio—título que *plácele* sobre manera—ser mandadero (Benvenutto Murrieta, *Quince plazuelas*, p. 79); hecho del cual *préciase* sobremanera (p. 159); y que *remátase* en el cementerio (p. 185); en cuyo centro *osténtase* una vista (p. 200).

COLOMBIA: Verónica *sentíase* una reina (Buitrago, p. 31); Marcelino *díjole* (p. 92).

VENEZUELA: El más locuaz y ocurrente de todos, a quien *decíanle* Arteaguita (Gallegos, *Canaima*, p. 100); por haberse comprado otro, *díjole* (p. 147); —Berenice—*díjole* su mujer (p. 164); —Él tenía que llegá, de tos modos—*repúsole* (p. 174); —Es un espectáculo curioso—*habíale* dicho (p. 294); —¿Qué, chico?—*repúsele* (p. 364).

COSTA RICA: Él y ña Rafaela *hanse* quedado solos (Fabián Dobles, p. 253); En el segundo en que el viejo *tocábale* casi ... (p. 341).

MEXICO: Cuando mi padre *enviábame* al pueblo (Ferretis, *Quijote*, p. 29); Él *escuchábame* (p. 124).

CUBA: Se detuvo de pronto, con los ojos fijos en algo que *veíase* ... y que seguramente *sorprendíale* mucho (Loveira, p. 44). (In narrating): Ayer vi a José y *díceme* "¿No vas al juego?" (Padrón).

SANTO DOMINGO: (Used in narrating): "estaban conversando, y *dícele* ... "; "llega y *vístese* de prisa ... "; "*déjolo* encerrado y me voy ... " (Henríquez Ureña, *BDH*, V, 49). —Espero que esta noche tenga mejor suerte—*díjole* (Requena, *Camino*, p. 26); y *díjole* a ella (p. 59); que acaso sea grave—*díjole* (p. 122).

WITH PAST PARTICIPLES

In the older language a pronoun was not often attached as an enclitic to the past participle in a compound tense. It might occur (1) when the past participle began the sentence: *Leídolo he;* (2) when the verb followed another stressed element: *dicho peón había ya salvádose;* (3) with a second participle when the auxiliary verb was not repeated, or with a past participle when the auxiliary is understood: *han ofrecido sus servicios y dádose por sus súbditos* (Keniston, pp. 102–3).

In modern Spanish most of this usage has fallen into desuetude. Bello (§ 917) states that the enclitic may legitimately be attached to a past participle only with a second past participle when the auxiliary is not repeated ("habíamos aguardado a nuestros amigos y *preparádoles* lo necesario") and when some phrase is intercalated between the auxiliary and the past participle ("habiendo primero en la marina *hincádose* de rodillas"). Ramsey (§ 1382) and Hanssen (§ 505) limit its use to a second past participle when the auxiliary is not repeated ("donde había nacido y *criádose*"). Keniston (*Syntax list*) does not mention such usage for contemporary Spanish. However, the use and abuse of the older construction is still encountered in individual writers, more frequently in certain Spanish-American writers.

Uruguay: Un accidente *ocurrídole* en el corral de yeguas fué el motivo (Acevedo Díaz, *Cancha larga*, p. 80).

Mexico: —Yo lo que siento ... es haber *ayudádoles* a ustedes sin saberlo (Inclán, I, 321). Me habría gustado no haberle sugerido aquel artefacto: así hubiera *interesádose* por los otros (Ferretis, *Quijote*, p. 124); me impresioné yo mismo al hablar de aquel viejo blanco, que de buena gana habría *contempládome* hasta que se le cerraran los ojos (p. 188).

For postposition with future tenses see p. 157.

In Tucumán (Argentina) and probably elsewhere, even cultured speakers place object pronouns before hortatory subjunctives: *lo sigamos* [= standard *sigámoslo*], *nos quedemos aquí*, *nos apuremos* (Morínigo). This stems from the older language. Analogous practices are found in regional Spain: *se siente usted*, etc. (Zamora Vicente [Mérida], p. 73; Llorente [Salamanca], p. 163).

POSITION OF SUBJECT PRONOUN

This is a suitable place to mention a peculiar and rather popular use of the subject pronouns *él, ella*, etc., standing after an adjective or noun, seemingly to reinforce its application, to identify unmistakably the person thus modified. This usage has been neglected in most treatises despite its currency in many regions of America, as well as of Spain: "—Parece listo este Escopeta. —Sí, señora; pero ... muy movido *él*" (Álvarez Quintero, *Doña Clarines*, ed. S. G. Morley, p. 21 [Andalusia]). Cf. English "a fine man *that.*"

ARGENTINA: Era muy peleador *él* (Varela, p. 167).

PERU: Últimamente un diputado, buen mozo *él* ... (Corrales, p. 67); Por culpa de doña Melania Querejazu, escritora *ella* y feminista ... (p. 118); Donato, que es un joven, muy simpático *él* (p. 185); un señor Corrales, tuertecito *él* (p. 222).

COLOMBIA (ANTIOQUIA): Y ai estaba el Enemigo Malo acostao en un colchón, dormido y como enfermoso y aburridón *él* (Carrasquilla, *Novelas*, p. 36); Se golvió el Señor pa su trono, y a un ratico hizo señas a un santo, apersonao *él*, vestido de curita (p. 42). Uno de mis hijos, casado *él*, es el que molesta (Osorio L., *El hombre*, p. 45).

VENEZUELA: —Sí, ése como que es el nombre. Es un doctorcito *él*, muy nervioso, vestido de casimir (Arráiz, p. 136). Si yo creo que lo vi. ¡Trigueño *él!* (Uslar Pietri, p. 159).

MEXICO: ... un muchachuelo, ladino *él*, que iba con la madre, se quedó mirándolo (Valle-Arizpe, p. 380).

SANTO DOMINGO: Es un joven, alto *él;* es una muchacha, rubia *ella* (*BDH*, V, 228; also in Cuba [Padrón]).

In the Antilles especially, in Venezuela, and sporadically elsewhere, a subject pronoun (except *él, ella, ellos, ellas*) is often placed before its verb: *¿qué tú dices?* for standard *¿qué dices tú?* Some wish to attribute it to Negro influence, some to English contamination. It is probably a mere fusion of *¿tú quieres?* and *¿qué quieres?* The same phenomenon is current in Brazilian Portuguese.

RIVER PLATE REGION: ¿Por qué *vos* querés que yo juegue? ¿Por qué *Vd.* dice que yo soy el culpable? (Morínigo).

VENEZUELA (POP.): ¿Qué *tú* dices? ¿Qué *tú* quieres? (Rosenblat).

CUBA: —¿Por qué *tú* quieres que las cosas sucedan así? (Carlos Montenegro, *Los héroes*, p. 108). ¿Cómo *tú* te llamas? (Padrón).

PUERTO RICO: ¿Qué *tú* dices? ¿Qué *usted* quiere? (Navarro, p. 132). —¿Y qué *tú* quieres que uno haga? (Méndez Ballester, p. 36); ¿Por qué *usted* no quiere que yo me case? (p. 58). ¿Dónde *yo* estoy? (C).

SANTO DOMINGO: ¿Qué *tú* quieres? ¿Qué *tú* tienes? (*BDH*, V, 232). ¿Qué *tú* dices? ¿Qué *tú* crees? (Patín Maceo, *Dom.*, p. 143).

POSITION OF THE SUBJECT OF THE INFINITIVE

In standard Spanish today the pronoun subject of an infinitive normally follows the infinitive: *sin saberlo yo* 'without my knowing it.' Only rarely does the subject precede the infinitive: *sin yo saberlo.* The older language, however, manifested a "fairly strong tendency" to place the subject pronoun before the infinitive (Keniston, p. 550). This older tendency, nearly lost in present-day standard Spanish, has lived on in many regions of Spain and America. Occasionally the pronoun still precedes the gerund or the past participle, as in Santo Domingo: *en yo llegando* (less frequent than *en llegando yo*), *después de tú ido* (*BDH*, V, 230). Often a noun takes this position.

ARGENTINA: —¡Cómo ... se me puede morir Luisa en las manos, sin *yo* verlo, sin *yo* sentirlo! (González Arrili, p. 133).

URUGUAY: Sin *él* notarlo, [el caballo] giró sobre sí mismo volviendo hacia las casas (Montiel, *Luz mala,* p. 86).

ECUADOR: Luego de *ella* desnudarse ... apagó la vela (Jorge Fernández, p. 56).

VENEZUELA: Al *ella* hablar, el silencio crecía alrededor de él hasta defenderlo como un baluarte (Díaz Rodríguez, p. 94).

COLOMBIA (ANTIOQUIA): No nos vemos desde antes de *yo* nacer (Arango Villegas, p. 139); Una alma es algo demasiado delicado, demasiado frágil, para *uno* comprometerse a mantenerla limpia de este fangal de la vida (p. 205). (BOGOTÁ): Se fué antes de *yo* llegar; lo hizo sin *nadie* mandárselo (Flórez, p. 377).

PANAMA: Este salón es para *la gente* bailar; no encuentro razón para *la gente* murmurar (L. Aguilar, p. 322).

CUBA: Al poco tiempo de *uhté* habel benío pa acá llegó a Jaricoa el Sargento (Ciro Espinosa, p. 483).

SANTO DOMINGO: *Al yo venir* alterna con *al venir yo;* sin *tú* decir nada (Henríquez Ureña, *BDH,* V, 230). El amigo que encontró en este viaje sin *usted* buscarlo, seguirá siendo su amigo (Requena, *Camino,* p. 33); a los tres meses de *mamá* morir (p. 55).

PUERTO RICO: Para *yo* comérmelo, etc. (*ap.* Navarro, p. 132).

REDUNDANT POSITION

In standard Spanish object pronouns either may be placed before an auxiliary verb (*lo voy a hacer*) or may be attached to the dependent infinitive (*voy a hacerlo*), the former predominating in conversation, the latter in literary usage. In the colloquial or vulgar speech of some regions the pronouns are placed redundantly in both positions, often when the first verb is not an auxiliary. This seems to be especially true of colloquial or vulgar speech in Chile, sometimes for clarity, sometimes for comic effect, often for affective value.

CHILE: *Los* [= nos] pasamos a toma*los* [= tomarnos] una pilsen (Romanángel, p. 23); ¿pa qué *te* voy a menti*te*? ... yo *te* voy a lleva*te* (p. 89); *les* voy a prepara*les* un ajiaco (p. 98); al tiro *le* voy a busca*le* (p. 100); que *le* amos hace*le*, pué (p. 104). Y a vó *te* va a llega*te* tamién ... —¿Qué *te* va a llega*te*, *te* va a llega*te*? Roto tirillúo [= andrajoso]. ¡Ni hablar aprienden siquiera! (Cariola, II, 9). No escupai tan cerca del perro de la iñora, porque *se lo* podís ahogá*selo* (*Tallas chilenas*, p. 45). —¿Otra vez *se lo* voy a dá*selo*? (Rojas Gallardo, *Aventuras*, *2a serie*, p. 9).

V

NEUTER, RELATIVE, INTERROGATIVE, DEMONSTRATIVE, AND INDEFINITE PRONOUNS

NEUTER 'LE'

AN INTERESTING syntactical usage is the suffix or enclitic *le* with certain verbs and interjections. In standard Spanish we find another idiomatic use with the verb *hacer*: *¿qué le vamos a hacer?* in which *le* means 'about it.' Such a neuter use of *le* is extremely rare in older Spanish (Keniston, p. 70), and today in standard Spanish it is practically limited to the verb *hacer*. However, analogous *interjection + pronoun* constructions, probably stemming from *imperative + pronoun* (*dale*, etc.), are found in northern Spain, particularly in Aragon, Asturias, Santander, and probably elsewhere. Here, however, the enclitic pronoun is not the invariable neuter *le* but is apparently felt to be directly personal and, as such, may agree in number and sometimes in gender with the person or persons involved: "¡Redio*le*! ¡Rediez*la*! ¡Cóntra*les*! ¡Repúña*les*!" (Braue, p. 7).

In American Spanish neuter *le* abounds in the familiar speech of certain regions. Román (III, 281) considers it exclusively Chilean in such expressions as *ándale, ándele, ándenle, córrale, camínele, atráquele, dígale, ¡épale! ¡huífale! ¡ópale!* He is inclined to attribute it to Basque influence, since the Basques (and, we may add, the Galicians) insert *le* frequently and unnecessarily in their Spanish conversation. However, Román is quite wrong in believing this *le* to be exclusively Chilean. We find it elsewhere, used to a much greater degree than in Chile. It is exceedingly common in Mexico, and many people have considered it exclusive there. Ramos Duarte (p. 43) reports: "En esta Capital [Mexico] es rara la persona que no diga: *ándale*, en vez de *anda*, o *ve*, a tal lugar." Years ago, the Spaniard Sánchez Somoano (p. 32) explained in verse after his sojourn in Mexico: "Para animar allí a alguno/que no peque de atrevido,/lo mismo para negocios/que para cruzarse un tiro,/ como palabra suprema/en uno y otro sentido,/para decidirle pronto/le dicen *ándele*, amigo." This neuter *le* is current also in parts of Central America and elsewhere in varying degrees. In many Spanish-American countries where it is not current, as well as in some where it is, the adverbial locution *no más* immediately following the verb expresses the same notion as the enclitic *le: pase no más = pásele, ande no más = ándele*, etc. Sometimes the *le* becomes *les* by attraction to a plural subject: *ándenles* (cf. also Rosenblat, *Notas*, pp. 209–11).

ARGENTINA: ¡Meta*lé*! ¡Metél*e*! [= para incitar] (*BDH*, II, 210).

CHILE: —Camíne*le*, pues, señorita (D'Halmar, *Lucero*, p. 199). —Apúre*le*, agüelo, que ya viene aquí (Acevedo Hernández, *La canción rota*, p. 10); —Entonces atráca*le* no más (Cariola, I, 1). —¡Écha*le*, diablo! —¡Baila*lé*, Felipe! (Sepúlveda, *La fábrica*, p. 147).

COLOMBIA: Ánde*le*, córra*le*, ¡úpa*le*! ¡újua*le*! (Flórez, p. 377).

VENEZUELA: —¡Otro palito, mi negro! ¡Éche*le*! (Díaz-Solís, p. 14). ¡Ánde*le*! (Bus conductor to driver): ¡Púya*lo*! (Rosenblat).

PANAMA: ¡Ánde*le*! (Malaret, *Suplemento*, I, 106).

EL SALVADOR: —¡Atráquen*le* juego! (Ambrogi, p. 99).

GUATEMALA: Ánda*le*, que se hace tarde (Sandoval, I, 54).

MEXICO: Entonces, arriesgándo*le*, me bajé por un lado de la cama (Galeana, p. 20); Vete a ver ... cómo *le* hacen para salvar a esos compañeros (p. 147); y entonces el agente ... nos dice a los dos: «Jálen*le*» (p. 182); *le* entramos duro (p. 202); ¿cómo *le* haremos con tu chamaca? (p. 217). —Anda, pues, córre*le* para tu casa (Madero, II, 6); Jále*le*, amigo (III, 4). —¡Cuarenta y nueve! ánden*le*! (Quevedo, *La camada*, p. 16). Pero no más camíne*le* para allá (Magdaleno, p. 50); ¡Jálen*le*, hatajo de desgraciados (p. 103); —¿Cómo *le* hace para estar en todo, don Felipe? (p. 299). —Lo colgamos/con un clavito en la puerta ... —¡*Le* atinates! ¡Sí, mi encanto! (González Carrasco, p. 135). ¿Pos cómo *li* hacías? (Rivas Larrauri, p. 96); Pero, sígue*le*,

¿aluego qui hacías? (p. 99). —Pása*le* aquí, al cuarto, para ver qué llevas (Urquizo, p. 307). — ... ese vendedor de cacahuates, que con su constante: "¡Pásen*le;* tostado y dorado!" ... me distrae (Valle-Arizpe, p. 393). —¿Pasan muy de prisa por aquí los camiones? —¡Úju*le!*—exclamó la chamaca, atropellándose. —Ayer vide pasar uno requeterreciote (Rubín, p. 182); —¡Éje*le!* (p. 218). Y Santiago *le* acertó (Azuela, *La Marchanta*, p. 36). —¡Ánden*les!* —les dijimos cuando vinieron a vacunarnos (García Roel, p. 129). ¡Páre*le!* (C).

CUBA: ¡Méte*le*, Guayabo! = Manifestación de entusiasmo para aplaudir o animar a una persona que canta, baila, etc. (Suárez, p. 564). (Bus conductor to driver): ¡Da*le!* (Padrón).

LO DE = CASA DE

Originally *lo de* was used before a proper name to indicate a country estate belonging to the person named: *lo de Guzmán* 'Guzmán's place, property, house,' etc., with much the feeling of the English expressions 'to go to John's,' 'to eat at Foster's,' etc. Román (III, 323) has shown this practice to be of old standing in Spain (cf. *RFE*, VIII, 358 n.; Álvar [Aragón], § 72; Llorente [Salamanca], § 123c).

In Chile, when the number of inhabitants in rural settlements had increased to a township, the preposition *de* was generally omitted from the expression *lo de*. Thus in the old central provinces are found some 130 names of estates or settlements or small towns (Lenz, *Oración*, § 202) bearing names like *Lo Bravo*, *Lo Guzmán*, *Lo Herrera*, *Lo Abarca*, etc. In some cases the *lo* has likewise disappeared. But *lo de* is used also to mean 'house, residence, store,' etc., belonging to one or more individuals. This usage was previously much commoner in Chile than it is today. Since the first editions of Bello's *Gramática* (mid-nineteenth century), in which he censured the expression, *lo de* has in Chile gradually yielded to *donde* (discussed under prepositions, p. 363), though not entirely: it is still a rustic form and refers principally to *fundos* 'rural estates' (*BDH*, VI, 59, n. 3).

In the River Plate region *lo de* has been vigorously preserved and is used colloquially by all classes as the general term for *casa de*. To be sure, the standard phrase *ir al médico* is frequent in Buenos Aires instead of *ir a lo del médico* (Tiscornia, *La lengua*, § 176). One hears likewise the Italianism, *ir del médico*, and even *dal médico* (or any other word referring to a person) in the mouths of Italians: "Está *dal* escribano" (Sánchez, *La gringa*, II, 3).

We find *lo de* sporadically in other regions of America, principally rural, and in dialectal Spain (Sánchez Sevilla, § 92; Toro Gisbert, "Voces," p. 491), which proves it to be a survival of the older language and not a localism, as some have believed. Sometimes *a lo de* means not 'house' but rather the 'place where the person is' = *donde está* (cf. examples for Bolivia).

Argentina: Para ir *a lo de* Galván tenía que tomar la misma dirección que para *lo de* don Fabio (Güiraldes, *Don Segundo*, p. 37). Su hijo ... no está *en casa el* padrino ... si no *en lo de* esa mujer (Lynch, *Romance*, p. 51). ¡Hay que llevarlo *a lo del* doctor! (Ezquer Zelaya, p. 119). Esta noche cenaremos *en lo de* Rossi (Boj, p. 193). Voy *de* mi madre; voy *del* médico (Joaquín Romero, p. 399).

Uruguay: En la puerta *de lo de* Hardoy descubrió las figuras de Sofía y Dora (Amorím, *El paisano*, p. 76). Mañana ... podemos ir *a lo de* la Perró, nuestra modista (Sánchez, *M'hijo*, II, 3). ¡[El zapato] parecía salido *de lo de* Fattoruso! (Montiel, in *ACH*, p. 377).

Chile: Se fué *pa lo el* capitán (Vicuña Cifuentes, p. 345). Pase *por lo de* mi compaire (Acevedo Hernández, *Por el atajo*, p. 60). —Dile a Mañungo que se pase *por lo de* misiá Desideria (Maluenda, *Los ciegos*, p. 170). Al frente teníamos el camino *de lo Aguirre* (Guzmán Maturana, p. 53). (Santiago): —Entonces anda *a lo de* las González (Alberto Romero, *La viuda*, p. 55).

Bolivia: Olaguibel se fué *a lo de* su novia, donde acostumbraba pasar los domingos, y Luján y Ramírez *a casa de* Elena (Arguedas, *Vida criolla*, p. 65); Luján corrió *a lo de* [= a donde estaban] sus amigos y los presentó al anfitrión (p. 105); salió escapada al convento de los Jesuitas, *a lo de* su confesor (p. 213). Se alojó *en lo de* mi compagre Mateo (Jaime Mendoza, *El lago*, p. 30). —Pues, yo también iré mañana *a lo del* fotógrafo para que me haga algunas copias (Jaime Mendoza, *Memorias*, p. 17).

Colombia (Rare): Voy *a lo de* Pedro (Malaret, *Suplemento*).

Venezuela: Era un salteador ... hasta venir a parar *en lo de* doña Bárbara donde ahora trabaja (Gallegos, *Doña Bárbara*, p. 15).

Honduras: Madame Dugas debería llevar aquel invierno un suntuoso abrigo de pieles. Iría *a lo de* Kreeger o *a lo de* Godchaux (Martínez Galindo, p. 87).

El Salvador: El sol comienza a ispiar detrás *de lo del* ductor Martínez (Salarrué, *Cuentos*, p. 11).

Mexico: Por ai andan por el cerro *de lo de* Ávalos, con veinticinco hombres (Anda, *Los bragados*, p. 49).

ELLO[1]

The neuter pronoun *ello* has enjoyed many usages: (1) referring to a general idea, expressed or unexpressed; (2) referring to a neuter pronoun or adjective; (3) referring to a definite masculine or feminine noun; (4) as an impersonal subject (*ello es cierto que* 'it is true that'), sometimes with *haber;* (5) as an emphatic particle (*ello que yo lo vi*); (6) as a particle expressing unwilling concession, sometimes separated by a pause from the rest of the sentence.

Such usages of *ello* have, apparently from the end of the nineteenth century, been falling into desuetude. Keniston (*Syntax list,* p. 49) gives only two for the contemporary period: (1) summing up an unnamed idea conveyed by a preceding clause, (2) in the set phrase *ello es que* 'the fact is that.' While *ello* is thus still met in the written language, especially in academic and official style, it has almost disappeared from the ordinary spoken language, to which the archaic flavor of *ello* seems distasteful. Daily speech tends to substitute *eso* or *el caso* or *la cosa:* thus *ello es que* generally becomes *el caso* (or *la cosa*) *es que.*

Nevertheless, some of the older usages of *ello* do survive in the popular speech of limited regions in Spain, Mexico, southwestern United States, the Antilles (especially in Santo Domingo, whose speech is characteristically archaic), Colombia, and probably elsewhere. Among these survivals of *ello* are its use as an impersonal subject and as a particle of emphasis and of concession. Moreover, *ello* has acquired, especially in Santo Domingo, these extensions of older usage: (1) an indication of concession and evasion; (2) an indication of hesitancy or probability or acceptance; (3) an emphatic negation equivalent to *no, nunca, ¡qué va!* (Puerto Rico and Santo Domingo [Malaret, *Suplemento,* I, 478]); (4) the combinations *ello sí* (found also in parts of Spain but unemphatic, or in the sense of *eso sí*) and *ello no* as emphatic asseverations in both popular and cultured speech.

COLOMBIA (VALLE DE RISARALDA): —La Rita es pa vusté ... —*Ello no* (Arias Trujillo, p. 47); —Parece que va como triste, el amigo. —*Ello no,* compadre. Estaba apenas recordando (p. 158). (ANTIOQUIA): "ello sí, ello no" ... para afirmar o negar (Fidel S., X, 127).

MEXICO (TEZIUTLÁN, PUEBLA): *Ello* me costó diez pesos. ¿Cuánto pagaste por *ello?* (*RFH,* I, 209).

[1] The discussion is based principally on Henríquez Ureña's history of the different uses of *ello* ("Ello," *RFH,* I [1939], 209–29, with interesting additional examples in "El español en Santo Domingo," in *BDH,* V [1940], 228, n. 1).

Puerto Rico: —¿Lloverá hoy, señora? —*Ello* [expresses negation or negative probability]; —¿Qué remedios ... han administrado ustedes al niño? —*Eyo* [evasive] dotol (Meléndez Muñoz, *ap.* Malaret; and *RFH*, I, 226, as well as Navarro, p. 124).

Santo Domingo: (Impersonal 'it'): *Ello* es fácil llegar (*BDH*, V, 226); (with *haber*): *¿Ello* hay dulce de ajonjolí? *Ello* hay maíz; (concession or evasion): —Esa familia. ... —*Ello* dicen que no es muy buena ... ; (separated from the sentence): —*Ello*, quizás no viene (p. 227); (hesitation, probability, or acceptance): —¿Vas al pueblo? —*Ello* [= 'that depends' or 'perhaps']. ... ¿Quiere bailar? —*Ello* [= 'Yes, since you invite me'] (p. 228). —¿Pero tú no estuviste allí? —*Ello sí* [= 'Indeed I was'] (*RFH*, I, 225).

'QUE' FOR 'A QUIEN(ES)'

The use of the relative *que* in place of the indirect object *a quien(es)* was current in the older written language (sixteenth-century examples in Keniston, pp. 87, 209); but this construction has long since become more or less colloquial in Spain: "Te acuerdas de aquel hombre viejo *que* [= a quien] le di un achuchón" (Aurelio Espinosa, *Cuentos*, I, 146 [Granada]); "Mandó publicá un bando que se casaría con la niña *que* [= a quien] le viniera er chapín" (II, 215 [Granada]); cf. also Beinhauer, p. 239. Its social status again appears slightly higher today in some regions of Spanish America than it is in Spain, thus partially reflecting its older respectability. The Academy grammar (§§ 351, 352) calls this *que* a dative.

Argentina: Pero yo ando como el tigre/*Que* [= a quien] le roban los cachorros (*Martín Fierro*, p. 66). La hija de don Cepeda, esa *que* le dicen Filomela (Lynch, *Romance*, p. 267); el moreno ese *que* le dicen don Motita (p. 295).

Chile: Al fin era una amistá *que* le gustaba harto el mosto (Juan del Campo, p. 9); ésa ... *que* le faltaban los dientes (p. 32).

Ecuador: A su mercé *que* los indios le quieren como a taita Dios (Icaza, *Cholos*, p. 36); Isabel, moza *que* le gustaba tenderse en las cunetas (p. 219).

Venezuela (Rustic): —Yo no sé cómo puede haber cristianos *que* [= a quienes] les gusta vivir entre cerros o en pueblos de casas tapadas (Gallegos, *Doña Bárbara*, p. 367). (Urban): —Pues, hijo, eres el único ejemplar poético que conozco *que* no le gusta el agua picante (Certad, p. 14).

Colombia: Hay gente *que* le gusta vivir así (Flórez, p. 377).

HONDURAS: Era un niño *que* le gustaba la broma (Mejía Nieto, *Relatos*, p. 6); A Dolores *que* le gustaba el trabajo le buscó un puesto (p. 23).

GUATEMALA: Y miraron el campo, temerosos de que apareciese el temido personaje, *que* [= a quien] la leyenda ha dado cuerpo (Quintana, p. 216).

MEXICO: Hay reses *que* les gusta tumbar las cercas de los potreros (Núñez Guzmán, p. 40). Una vez por poco se mata con un inglés *que* no le gustó el mole de guajolote (Gamboa, *Teatro*, II, 13).

SANTO DOMINGO: Era un hombre *que* le gustaba mucho divertirse (Requena, *Camino*, p. 40).

'QUE SU' FOR 'CUYO'

In the older language *que su* was commonly used for *cuyo* 'whose': "Hay sujetos *que sus* [= cuyas] muchas prendas los hacen ser buscados de todos" (Gracián, *El discreto*, chap. xi); "Primos del Rey, *que* bastaban,/no de Granada, de Troya,/ser incendio sus espadas" (Lope, *Peribáñez*, III, 1). In Spain as well as in Spanish America this usage is still preserved in colloquial and rustic speech, though discountenanced in literary style: "El padre, *que su* [= cuyo] hijo trabaja en el campo" (Tiscornia, *La lengua*, § 181); "un árbol *que la* flor es blanca" (Gagini); cf. also *BDH*, II, 148, and Flórez, p. 377.

For New Mexico, Aurelio Espinosa (*Studies*, II, § 73) reports the use of *cuyo* in place of *que*, etc., even in local newspapers: "las leyes *cuyas* [= que] la comisión acaba de revisar"; "sacaron de la mina más de veinte cadáveres *cuyos* no fué posible identificar." This must stem from the semicultured "tengo dos casas, *cuyas casas* ..., etc."

INTERROGATIVE PRONOUNS

To express the possessive interrogative 'whose' in modern Spanish the phrase *de quién* is used. In the older language *cúyo* was regularly employed in this function. For sixteenth-century prose, Keniston (p. 283) registers a single instance of *de quién*. Since then *cúyo* has been practically ousted by *de quién*. However, *cúyo* still lives in limited regions of dialectal Spain (Sánchez Sevilla, § 91) and of Spanish America. Vázquez (p. 119) reports that *cúyo* is regularly employed in southern Ecuador but not in the northern part of the country and that the northerners criticize the southerners for this archaism: "*¿Cúyo* es ese libro? decimos en Cuenca. Debe decirse: *¿De quién* es ese libro? —nos corrigen en el Norte."

ARGENTINA (SAN LUIS, JUJUY, SALTA, etc.): —*¿Cúyo* es este sombrero? (Rosenblat, *Notas*, p. 144).

BOLIVIA: —*¿Cúya* casa es ésta? (Bayo, p. 86).

COLOMBIA (ANTIOQUIA): —*¿Cúyo* eres tú? ¿Es tuyo, Elisa? —No, don Julián: éste es Gamboa (Carrasquilla, *Hace tiempos*, II, 197). (CHOCÓ): ¿Estas sillas *cuyas* son? (*BICC*, VI, 112).

¿CUÁL ES QUE?

A very peculiar locution used in familiar conversation in Chile, even by the cultured, is *¿cuál es que?* (stress on *és*), meaning *¿por qué no?* Román (I, 467) explains that a sentence like "*¿Cuál es que* me pagas lo que me debes?" means "¿cuál es el motivo o la razón por que no me pagas lo que me debes?" He calls the Chilean locution "inexplicable e inadmisible." He found a somewhat similar use of *quale* in the Latin of St. Jerome, but not in a negative sense: "*Quale* enim *est, ut* individuus comes ... hoc solum ignoraverit?" where the use of neuter or adverbialized *quale* is like the Chilean *cuál;* but the sentence is not negative in meaning, as it would be in the Chilean *¿cuál es que?* The expression may well be related to the peninsular colloquialism *¿qué es que ...* ? meaning 'why, for what reason?' (Beinhauer, p. 66); the negation may be a development analogical to that involved in *en mi vida* 'never in my life' (cf. p. 370). *¿Cuál es?* may also stand alone, meaning *¿por qué no? ¿y qué?* etc. Furthermore, the negative idea may be reinforced by *ná* [= nada].

CHILE: —Es pura pica [= burla] con la Rosario porque no los lleva de apunte [= no les hace caso]. *¿Cuál es que* a la Chabela le icen ná? [=¿Cuál es el motivo (o la razón) por que a la Chabela no le dicen nada?] —La Chabela tampoco los lleva. —Pero no es metía a rica (Acevedo Hernández, *Por el atajo*, p. 34). *¿Cuál es que* viene? [= ¿Por qué no viene?] *¿Cuál es que* se acabó? [= ¿Por qué no se acabó?] *¿Cuál es que* me pegay? [= ¿Por qué no me pegas?] (C).—¿Tanto miedo, y a mí *cuál es que* me tocan? —A vos no, porque tenís mango [= dinero] (Alberto Romero, *Perucho González*, p. 66); —Yo; a mí, mi cabo; yo estaba primero y *¿cuál es?* (p. 225). *¿Cualés ná* que yo te pregunto? (J. M. Castro, *Froilán Urrutia*, p. 45).

As in Spain today (Hanssen, § 551; Braue, pp. 66, 67), *¿el qué?* is occasionally found, particularly in rustic speech (in place of the commoner *¿qué?*) in Argentina, Chile, the Mexican and Caribbean zones; in Argentina likewise *¿lo qué?* (*BDH*, V, 232), a retention of popular Spanish (Borao, p. 95), possibly influenced by the Portuguese *o que?* Cf. our colloquial 'the which?' A few examples:

ARGENTINA: —¿Qué? *¿El qué*, mamá? (Lynch, in *ACH*, p. 67). —Che, apropincuate. —*¿El qué?* —Que te acerqués (Filloy, p. 219). —¿Con cuánto hace el mercado por día? —*¿Lo qué?* ¿El mercado? (Saldías, p. 19). —¿Yo, disimular? ¿y *el qué?* (Monti, p. 264).

URUGUAY: —Pero cristiano, si es mi tatita. —*¿El qué?* ... —Mi tatita (Reyles, *El gaucho*, p. 282).

CHILE: —*¿El qué* decía? (C).

COLOMBIA: —¿No oyes? —*¿El qué?* —Pues la orquesta (Efe Gómez, p. 116); serás el único que no sabe. ... —*¿El qué?* (p. 203).

DEMONSTRATIVES

In standard Spanish the demonstrative pronoun (and adjective) *ése* (*ese*), etc., is used to refer to things belonging or related or close to the person addressed in space or time, and *aquél* (*aquel*) to things distant in space or time from both speaker and person spoken to. Furthermore, *ése* is used to refer to objects not very distant from either speaker or person spoken to, and *aquél* is then reserved for objects that are still farther away; the relationship between *ése* and *aquél* in these cases is merely comparative. In American Spanish, however, there is a tendency to neglect *aquél* and to substitute *ése* under most circumstances. Then *ése* does double duty and therefore loses some of its expressiveness. To be sure, such usage may be encountered in peninsular Spanish. It goes back to the older language when *ese* was frequently employed where the present-day standard requires *aquel:* "Por todas *esas* tierras ivan los mandados" (*Cid*, vs. 564; cf. Menéndez Pidal, *Cantar*, I, §139, 1).

The Mexican grammarian, Revilla, in his *En pro del casticismo* (p. 52) relates an interesting anecdote in connection with *ése* and *aquél*. During a visit to Valladolid he asked a humble porter (*mozo de cordel*) this question: "¿Qué edificio es *ése?*" The porter quickly replied: "*¿Aquél*, dice V.? Pues es el frontón." The cultured Mexican writer adds: "De un modesto ganapán, recibí una buena lección de gramática práctica. Aunque desde pequeño supe que el demostrativo *ése* sirve para señalar la cosa cercana del que escucha, y *aquél* para indicar la distante del que habla y del que escucha (y éste era el caso en la ocasión) yo, con mi habitual descuido de expresión, troqué un demostrativo por otro; cosa que no pasó por alto el zafio vallisoletano, aunque sin ninguna malicia, sino guiado tan sólo por su natural buen hablar."

ARGENTINA (CULTURED): En *ese* momento entraba el hijo mayor; os enviaba *ese* caparazón, con que me obsequia el alcalde de Toledo. El lacayo se adelantó a ofrecérselo (Larreta, *La gloria*, p. 84). (RURAL): El coronel las tenía,/según dijo *esa* ocasión (*Martín Fierro*, p. 34); que la gente acobardada/quedó dende *esa* ocasión (p. 39). —¿Ve, allá lejos, adonde parece que se juntan *aquellas* dos líneas obscuras que cierran el horizonte? ¡Bueno ... ! Pues sabrá que *esas* líneas no se juntan (*Fray Mocho*, p. 65).

CHILE: La humanidad pecadora fué redimida por *aquel* hombre que murió en la cruz. ¿Quién fué *ese* hombre? (Acevedo Hernández, *La canción rota*, p. 57); ¿Qué hizo la sociedad de su tiempo con *ese* gran reformador que se llamó Jesucristo? (p. 58). ¡Nunca se me olvidará cuando se la llevaron al Cementerio al amanecer de *ese* día que llovía tanto! (Pepe Rojas, *La banda*, p. 7).

Perhaps, as in two of the preceding examples, the change of *aquel* (or *aquella*) to *ese* (or *esa*) indicates that, after the first mention, nouns may then be considered "related" to the person addressed.

'ESTE' AS A FILLER

The demonstrative *este* is, furthermore, used freely in American-Spanish conversation as a filler word when the speaker hesitates in his expression, the proper word not being readily available, either from lack of vocabulary or from not knowing what to say in an embarrassing situation. This *este* corresponds to peninsular Spanish *esto* or *pues* (cf. our *a* or *uh* or *well uh*). It is sometimes written *estee* or *esté* or even *estééé*, to show a lengthened final *e* in pronunciation.

Such use of *este*, like many other American-Spanish expressions, is often referred to as exclusively local by people who believe it to be such and who do not know that it is current in most of Spanish America. The Argentine grammarian, Monner Sans,[2] calls it "la muletilla cansadora del 'este' *porteño*," thus erroneously limiting its use to Buenos Aires. Some areas, like Cuba, prefer *esto*.

ARGENTINA: —Déjala a ella. Hable usted, Cristina. —(Vacilando) *Este* ... arreglaba la ropa de Aurora en las valijas (Rodríguez Acasuso,

[2] See Cantarell Dart, *Defendamos nuestro hermoso idioma*, 2d ed. (1937), p. 42 n.

La mujer olvidada, p. 12). El profesor vuelve a la carga, dulcemente: —¿Quién es el autor de "Mireya"? —*Este ... este ...* —hace la externa, frotando las yemas de los dedos medio y pulgar. Pero la chispa no brota (Méndez Calzada, in *ACR*, p. 362). —No ... no es eso. ... Soy yo que no tengo ... *estee* ... que me falta ... *estee* ... yo, ¿sabes? (Saldías, p. 5).

URUGUAY: —¿Tienes algo urgente que hacer? —Según y conforme. ... *Estééé* ... se ha muerto un amigo mío (Florencio Sánchez, p. 459). —Diga, *esté* ... ¿tiene tabaco? (Espínola, p. 82).

CHILE: García permaneció silencioso. Había olvidado sus bellas frases y sólo tontas vulgaridades venían a golpear su mente. —*Este* ... iba a decirle, que me encuentro un poco enfermo (Durand, *Mercedes*, p. 70).

ECUADOR: —¿Y cómo te sacó? —¡Ay, niña! *Este* ... me enamoró, pues—decía María del Socorro, bajando los ojos (Pareja, *El muelle*, p. 34). —Vamos, vamos, ¿qué le ocurre? —*Este*, doctor, yo vengo porque *este*. ... —Vamos, hable recto (Pareja, *Baldomera*, p. 124).

VENEZUELA: —Señorita, *este* ... dispénseme, pero ¿usted no sabe, por casualidad, dónde vive la familia Rodríguez? (Díaz-Solís, p. 37).

CUBA: —¿Qué es una isla? —*Esto* ..., una porción de tierra rodeada de agua por todas partes (Padrón).

Este is used locally in other locutions. In not a few regions the phrase *este que diga* is common in vulgar speech and among children as a substitute for standard Spanish *digo, quiero decir, mejor dicho*, etc. (in the sense of 'I mean,' 'or rather,' etc.) in an attempt to correct a mistake just uttered. In Venezuela we find *este que digo* similarly used:

—¿No será poco, Cho ... —*este que digo*—Pantoja? (Gallegos, *Canaima*, p. 87); —Eso es hambre vieja, catire [= rubio]—¡No sea confianzudo, amigo! *Este que digo:* mi jefe (p. 218); —¡Que lo siento, catire! *Este que digo:* mi jefe (p. 219).

Both *qué digo* and *qué diga* are heard without *este* in peninsular and in American Spanish.

'ESTE' AS VOCATIVE

In many regions *este* (*esta, esto*) are used in vocative phrases in familiar and colloquial speech in addressing a person whose name one does not know or cannot recall or does not care to mention.

ARGENTINA: (Frequent in schools): *¡Esta chica*, pero [= expresión de impaciencia y de presión activa], alcánceme el centímetro! ¡Rosalía, *esta chica*, apúrese! Mire, *esta chica*, el libro no se lo puedo prestar (Frida Weber, p. 120).

CHILE: *Don Éste, Doña Ésta, Ño Éste, Ña Ésta* (Román, II, 311). —Asosiéguese, *¡ñor éste!* (Muñoz, p. 164; with a footnote: "Incomodada, no quiere llamarlo por su nombre").

BOLIVIA: —Gracias, *doña Esto* (Díaz Villamil, *La Rosita*, pp. 32, 49).

ECUADOR (CUENCA): —Ocioso *este* ... milagro que te has levantado (Mata, *Sumag Allpa*, p. 12); —Para que estemos juntos los dos, palomita. —Pretensioso *este* (p. 33); —Bruto *este* ... de gana dije (p. 59).

COLOMBIA: (*llamando a una chica*) —*¿Esta niña ...?* (Flórez, p. 377).

VENEZUELA: ¡Ah negro bandido *este*, caray! De perinola [= de remate] que te la pegaste (Díaz-Solís, p. 13).

COSTA RICA: —Ah, muchacho *este* (Fabián Dobles, p. 230).

MEXICO AND ANTILLES: "*Esta muchacha* ... se usa mucho. ... En México y otras partes es sustituto del nombre que no se recuerda" (Frida Weber, p. 120, n. 3).

ESTOTRO

The old adjectives and pronouns *estotro* or *este otro* and *esotro* or *ese otro* are occasionally used today in Spain with a somewhat archaic flavor. In the familiar and popular speech of Chile, *estotro* has been preserved to refer to the future in such expressions as *estotro año* meaning 'next year'; *el otro año* would mean there 'last year' (Lenz, *La oración*, § 186). The same is generally true elsewhere. In dialectal Spain (Salamancan region) we find *sotro* < (*e*)*sotro* in the temporal sense of *siguiente:* "al *sotro* día de venir se puso malo" (Sánchez Sevilla, § 54). For remnants of *sotro* in Puerto Rico cf. Navarro, page 124 n.

CHILE: *Este otro* año dice que va a sembrar solo (Acevedo Hernández, *Por el atajo*, p. 12). —¿Si me quitas la plata, cómo te voy a traer algo mañana? —Te volvís a encalillar [= adeudar] hasta *este otro* mes (Juan Modesto Castro, p. 400). Pienso hacerlo *estotra* semana (C). *El otro mes* le cortaron una pata (J. del Campo, p. 37).

Otro in general may mean 'next' or 'following' in time or space, as often in the older language with nouns of time (Keniston, p. 272): *la otra calle* is 'the next (*or* second) street,' *el otro domingo* is 'next Sunday,' etc.

Argentina: —*El otro* domingo vuelve mi padre de la corte. Vaya vuesa merced a saludalle (Larreta, *La gloria*, p. 218).

Venezuela: —Él no viene hasta *la otra* semana. Espérame hoy, como siempre (Pocaterra, p. 185).

Costa Rica: *El otro* sábado viene un contrastista (Fallas, p. 14).

Mexico: —Vuelvo *el otro* domingo (Gamboa, *Santa*, p. 202).

Cuba: No podré trabajar hasta *la otra* semana (Padrón).

Otro día, as used in the older language (Hanssen, § 555; Keniston, p. 272) beside *al otro día* and *al día siguiente* 'the following day,' is still common in regional and rustic speech in Spain (Aurelio Espinosa, *Cuentos*, I, 87: "Vamos allí mañana de paseo. Y *otro día* fueron de paseo"; also I, 34, 55, etc.) and flourishes in parts of America.

Mexico: *Otro día* Demetrio se quejó mucho de la herida (Azuela, *Los de abajo*, p. 25); Luis Cervantes, *otro día*, apenas pudo levantarse (p. 48); Camila lloró toda la noche, y *otro día*, por la mañana, dijo a Demetrio que ya le diera licencia de volverse a su casa (p. 205).

New Mexico: *Otro día* se levantó muy de mañana (Aurelio Espinosa, *Estudios*, p. 292).

INDEFINITE REDUNDANT 'LE'

A curious redundant use of *le* is found in the popular speech of some regions, quite frequently in Chile and to a lesser extent in Argentina: *se me le cayó* for *se me cayó*, etc. It is probably an analogical formation on *se le cayó*, etc., and is related to the vague "ethical" datives that suggest a degree of concern or possession on the part of the speaker with the event narrated. But it is not to be confused with an ethical dative *le*, because it apparently has no definite point of reference, whereas the ethical dative *le* is a real personal pronoun referring to a definite person (*castíguesemele*, etc.). The present *le* may be merely a meaningless addition to round out the phrase rhythmically and lend affective value.

Argentina: ¡Y quién sabe cuánto tiempo se hubiese quedao ahí como dormido ... si un redepente no me *le* da por estornudar! (Lynch, *Romance*, p. 275).

Chile: A mí no se me *le* da na (Brunet, *Montaña*, p. 63); se me *le* olvía (Romanángel, p. 88); como se te *li* ocurre (p. 91); casi se me *le* sale un garabato ... cuando se me *le* acaba el molío (p. 108); se me *le* va la vista (p. 118). Se me *le* cayó el pañuelo; se me *le* perdió el sombrero; te se *le* soltó la liga (Román, III, 281). —Ésta se me *le* quiso como arrepentir, ¿ah? (Acevedo Hernández, *De pura cepa*, p. 3).

INDEFINITE 'LA' AND 'LAS'

The object pronoun *la* or *las* used with an indefinite force (with antecedent unexpressed, but perhaps occasionally understood) is employed in American Spanish as in standard Spanish and is extended to many such new popular expressions as *la de malas* (*la* = *hora, suerte*) 'bad luck, misfortune'; *echarlas a correr, rasparlas* (Chilean *raspar la bola* = standard *escurrir la bola*); *emplumarlas* (= "irse como el ave que ya emplumó" [?]) (Cuervo, § 570); by analogy with *tomar las de Villadiego; endilgarlas, envelarlas* (= maritime term: *alzar velas*) 'to run away,' etc.; *irla(s) con* 'to get along with'; Chilean (*en*) *la de no* 'otherwise' (for examples, see p. 298); Chilean *la sin pepa* 'la tajada del melón que no tiene pepitas'; etc.

Concerning the last expression, Román (IV, 210) informs us that, according to a popular Chilean saying, whoever gets the 'seedless slice of melon' will marry the king's daughter. Consequently, *sacarse uno la sin pepa* means in familiar speech 'tocarle el premio gordo u obtener cualquier otra suerte'; *tocarle a uno la sin pepa* means 'una buena suerte, una sinecura ...' and, ironically, 'una mala suerte o desventura, un gran trabajo, un mal empleo, etc.'

ARGENTINA: —Después de una buena siestita, *la* voy a trabajar de lo lindo (Draghi Lucero, p. 239). ¡No *las voy con* vueltas! (Angélica Mendoza, p. 57). *La vamos de* cigarrillos (Last-Reason, p. 9).

URUGUAY: —Te he dicho que no *las voy con* la funeraria. ... ¡Mozo! ... ¡Ese champagne! (Sánchez, *Los muertos*, II, 4). Los nietos no *las van con* los agüelos. Ya no se respeta la familia ni nada (Sánchez, *El desalojo*, scene 4).

CHILE: Mañana *la* duermo hasta afirmar*las* bien (Durand, in *ACH*, p. 230). —A tranco largo *las raspó* pa la calle (Guzmán Maturana, p. 20); Al ver esto el que estaba más adelante, *las echó* a correr que se *las* pelaba (p. 80); *las endilgó* derechito para su casa (p. 112). —¡Córte*la*, cambie el disco, pues, salvaje! (Luis Meléndez, p. 88). —Esta mañana Tito Jara *se las emplumó* ... *se las echó* a primera hora (Durand, *Mercedes*, p. 85). Me puse a sestiar*la* (Latorre, *Hombres*, p. 118); —No vaya a ser cosa que on Peiro *se las envele* pa la Rinconá (p. 170); —al tirito *me las endilgo* p'al cerro (p. 223). Si esta semana no trabajay y seguís tomando, *la* [= la amistad] perdís pa siempre conmigo (Romanángel, p. 14). Charo ... hizo güenasa suelte: se sacó *la sin pepa* al carsarse con Hilarión Machuca (Muñoz, p. 35). Se *la* hago [= le invito a beber] (Román, III, 92).

COLOMBIA (ANTIOQUIA): Siempre *la voy* muy bien *con* ellos y siempre me quieren mucho (Carrasquilla, *Hace tiempos*, II, 31). (BOGOTÁ): Fulano no se *la* [= la mona, borrachera] apea; si la miran, *la* [= vergüenza] pasa; *emplumarlas, empuntarlas* [= 'to run away'] (Cuervo, § 570). Saben que no *la voy con* ella (Buitrago, p. 185).

NICARAGUA: *Abrírselas* [= echar a correr] (A. Valle, p. 2).

VENEZUELA: *La* voy a dormir; va a *la* de ganar (Rosenblat).

GUATEMALA: Ir uno siempre a *la* de ganar [= salir uno siempre bien en todo] (Sandoval, I, 715).

MEXICO: Si la revolución no se acaba, nosotros tenemos ya lo suficiente para irnos a brillar*la* una temporada fuera del país (Azuela, *Los de abajo*, p. 174). —¡No *la* amuelas! (Galeana, p. 99); Ahora sí que *la* amolamos—pensé yo. —¡Se acabaron las comidas del Regis! (p. 166). Me persiguió *la de malas* en el juego (Santamaría, *Dicc.*, II, 221). Ustedes *la* van a pasar mal (Urquizo, p. 15); con la resignación que tiene el pobre cuando le llega *la de malas* (p. 24); verás si tengo narices y *las* [= las cosas] huelo bien (p. 343).

CUBA: Juan *se las templó* [= se fué]; Él se *la* busca muy bien (Padrón).

Throughout Spanish America *pasarla* 'to get along' is used, rather than *pasarlo* as in standard Spanish. The *la* is felt to refer to *vida, suerte*, etc. The American-Spanish preference may be attributed to the fact that *la* is the popular variant of *lo*,[3] and, as such, is likely to have a higher social level and greater currency than in Spain.

ARGENTINA: —La suerte que aquí no *la* vamos pasando tan mal tuavía (Payró, in *Hispanoamericanos*, p. 62).

CHILE: Entonces ha dicho mi abuela que como me *la* paso leyendo libritos de cuentos ... no estudio (Barrios, *El niño*, p. 66; see also below, p. 230).

PERU: Es la manera como él cree que puede pasar*la* mejor (López Albújar, *Matalaché*, p. 42). Todo el domingo nos *la* pasamos en planes de inversión del nuevo haber (Corrales, p. 246).

COLOMBIA: —Y en tu casa, ¿qué tal? —Ahí vamos pasándo*la* (Arango Villegas, p. 139). *La* pasé [= fuí tenido] por poeta (Tobón, p. 140).

[3] L. Spitzer, "*La feminización del neutro*," *RFH*, III (1941), 339–71.

VENEZUELA: —Vamos, cuéntelo todo, sin mentiras, porque *la* puede pasar mal (Nelson Himiob, in *ACMV*, II, 73). Si supiera que cantando/mis penas se distraían/cantando me *la* pasara/toda la noche y el día (Machado, p. 3).

GUATEMALA: *La* estoy pasando con muchas dificultades (Sandoval, II, 205). ¡Vieras cómo *la* pasé de alegre! (Arévalo, p. 115).

COSTA RICA: —Y vos, ¿cómo te va? —Voy pasándo*la* (Fabián Dobles, p. 186; also pp. 358, 360); but cf. Tenía un hijo ... que ... se *lo* pasaba en el parque (p. 188).

CUBA: —A Vd. le conviene no meterse en las cosas ajenas, porque puede ser que no *la* pase muy bien (Ciro Espinosa, p. 208).

MEXICO: —No sabemos cuántos días *la* vamos a pasar en despoblado (Azuela, *Las moscas*, p. 44). —¡Buenos días! ¿Cómo *la* ha pasado? (Galeana, p. 70).

INDEFINITE 'UNO'

The indefinite pronoun *uno*, referring to the person speaking (as a substitute for *yo*) is very frequently used everywhere but seems to be more common in American Spanish generally than in Spain, perhaps indicating a tendency, as Tiscornia (*La lengua*, § 100, 2) suggested for gaucho speech, to abandon reflexive constructions with *se*, and thus to emphasize the agent of the action more concretely than does the vaguer reflexive construction.

ARGENTINA: Y después de un güen tirón/en que *uno* se daba maña (*Martín Fierro*, p. 22); si *uno* anda hinchando el lomo/ya se le apean como plomo (p. 35).

CHILE: *Uno* también ha sío chico (Romanángel, p. 68).

COLOMBIA: ¿Qué va a decir *uno?* (Carrasquilla, *Hace tiempos*, I, 176); Es que cuando *uno* es tan solo ... le pasan tantas cosas (II, 326); Pero se lo podían avisar a *uno* (II, 100). El bruto no es el indio; el bruto es *uno* (C). *Uno* nues pendejo (Posada, p. 92).

VENEZUELA: Entonces vamos a tener por pecado el ratico que nos queda para decidir que una cosa sea ajena o de *uno* (Briceño, p. 156).

COSTA RICA: —Ella no es como *uno* [= yo] (Fabián Dobles, p. 250).

HONDURAS: Ellos se creen perfectos y son más corrompidos que *uno* (Mejía Nieto, *El solterón*, p. 119).

MEXICO: Él gana menos que *uno* [= yo] (C).

CUBA: *Uno* también tiene sus ocupaciones (Padrón).

When *uno,* used as an indefinite pronoun, refers to the person speaking, it should agree with that person in gender. But, if a woman is not referring particularly to herself or speaking of exclusively feminine matters, she prefers *uno.* However, occasionally we find in colloquial or rustic speech the use of *uno* where standard Spanish today would probably require *una:*

URUGUAY: —Además *uno* no puede sustraerse a estas persecuciones [referring to girls followed in the street by men] (Bellán, p. 26).

BOLIVIA: —¡Ché, qué malos son los hombres! ¡Cómo la dejan a *uno* plantada a lo mejor! (Díaz Villamil, *El traje,* p. 24).

COLOMBIA: [Los hijos] se van pa lejos, y ¿qué puede saber *el pobre di' uno?* Los hijos hombres siempre dan mucha lidia. ... Ni los maridos le ayudan a *uno* en estas cosas (Carrasquilla, *Hace tiempos,* I, 175). (A widow speaks): —¿Qué va a estar *uno* piensa y piensa en el muerto? (Álvarez Garzón, p. 236). Cuando *uno* es madre (Obando, p. 199).

COSTA RICA: —¡Ay, si no juera porque *uno* tiene esta fe tan granditítica, no sé qué hacía!—termina por decir ña Rafaela (Fabián Dobles, p. 61).

MEXICO: Nunca se puede *uno* sentir segura (L).

CUBA: Está *uno* cansada de tanto hablar (Padrón).

This colloquial or rustic usage probably goes back to Old Spanish, when apparently *uno* as an indefinite pronoun did not refer directly to the person speaking, as it does today, and therefore *uno* was the general form. Cuervo (§ 242) tells us that Santa Teresa always used *uno.* In the older language *el hombre* or *hombre* was current in vulgar and rustic speech, equivalent to *yo,* even referring to a woman speaker (Keniston, p. 42). For indefinite *usted,* see p. 98.

ALGUIEN, ALGUNO: NADIE, NINGUNO

Correct Spanish does not permit the use of *alguien de ustedes* for *alguno de ustedes, nadie de nosotros* for *ninguno de nosotros;* nor is it the best practice to use *ninguno* for *nadie* or *alguno* for *alguien* (in some regions *alguien* is never heard in popular speech). While Cuervo (§ 374 n.) has pointed out a few examples of such usage in the older language as well as in more recent times, it is constantly censured by grammarians. Possibly it is as frequent in regional Spain as in America.

ARGENTINA: —Pensar que cuando *alguien de nosotros* muere, tratan con dos cruces chuecas ... la doble incógnita de nuestra identidad (Filloy, p. 9); —Si *alguien de ustedes* manejara, yo iría (p. 154).

CHILE: *Nadie de los presentes, nadie de nosotros* (Román, IV, 4).

COLOMBIA (CULT.): *Alguien (nadie) de Uds.* (Flórez, p. 378).

COSTA RICA: *Alguien de ustedes, de nosotros, de los presentes* (Gagini, p. 53).

GUATEMALA: *Alguien de ustedes* fué el que gritó en la clase (Sandoval, I, 39); *Nadie de nosotros* tiene la culpa de tu desgracia. ... En *nadie* parte hallo trabajo (II, 114).

MEXICO: No llegaba *nadie de las demás mujeres* (Galeana, p. 103). *Nadie de nosotros* decía una palabra (Urquizo, p. 174); *nadie de nosotros* pensaba en irse (p. 200). *Alguien de ustedes* (Ramos D., p. 34).

The Old Spanish form *nadi* had become *naide* in popular speech by the sixteenth century. Literary usage imposed the present form *nadie;* but *naide, naiden, nadien, nadies,* and *naides* have survived in popular speech (cf. Rosenblat, *Notas*, p. 150).

In the popular speech of limited areas we find the apocopated form *ningún* as an emphatic negative adverb:

CUBA: —María es muy bonita. —*Ningún* bonita [= no es nada bonita]; Tienes que hacer este trabajo. —*Ningún* de eso [= nada de eso] (Padrón).

SANTO DOMINGO: Él no está *ningún* enfermo; ella no parece *ningún* celosa; él no está *ningún* mal (Patín Maceo, *Dom.*, p. 122).

ALGOTRO

By analogy with such forms as *estotro* (for *este otro*) and *esotro* (for *ese otro*), discussed above, a new indefinite adjective and pronoun has been formed and is used in a few Spanish-American countries: *algotro* (for *algún otro*), *algotra* (for *alguna otra*), *algotros* (for *algunos otros*), *algotras* (for *algunas otras*). Malaret (*Dicc.*) indicates only Colombia for this usage (Cuervo, § 948), but it seems much more common in parts of Central America, notably Guatemala and El Salvador, and in areas of the Mexican and Argentinian zones. The Colombian lexicographer, R. Restrepo (*Apuntaciones*), classifies the word as "inaceptable," although "personas de distinción caen en este vulgarismo." Alcalá Venceslada (p. 18) records its use in Andalusia, giving this example: "Todavía ha de venir *algotro* cofrade."

ARGENTINA (SAN LUIS): *Algotro* vendrá cuando yo no esté; es capaz de fijarse en *algotra* (Vidal, p. 115).

COLOMBIA (ANTIOQUIA): A yo no me gusta plantala en tierra,

comu' hacen otros. ... *Algotros* tienen el vicio de ponela en el tejao (Carrasquilla, *Hace tiempos*, II, 150). Eso no pendía de los doctores, sino de *algotra* cosa (Carrasquilla, *Novelas*, p. 30); Póngame *algotro* oficio que hacer (p. 31). Me faltan *algotros* (Buitrago, p. 107).

El Salvador: Después de la comida de la noche, empezó a llegar gente: ... algunas un poco mayores, otras mayores y *algotras* más o menos de su misma edad (Torres Arjona, p. 102).

Guatemala: Si recibes *algotro* aviso, acude al instante ... si te puedo servir en *algotra* cosa, lo haré con gusto (Bonilla, III, 170).

Mexico (Nuevo León): Se ocupa de *algotra* cosa (García Roel, p. 112); A juerza que dabas con *algotro* si quisieras buscarlo (p. 173).

New Mexico: *Algotra* vez; *algotros* cabayos (Aurelio Espinosa, *Studies*, II, § 82, meaning 'alguno que otro' [cf. *BDH*, II, 159]).

AMBOS A DOS

In addition to standard preference *los dos* or *ambos* 'both,' we find stray survivals of the older *ambos dos* and especially *ambos a dos*, either in speech or in literature. A distinction is sometimes made: *ambos a dos* when the action is performed 'between two' at the same time (as with the archaic *entrambos*, etc.). In limited areas are heard: *todos dos*, as in Colombia (Tascón, p. 271) and Santo Domingo (*BDH*, V, 174); *juntos* (Cuervo, § 532) and *de por ambos* (Tobón, p. 24) in Colombia. Cf. also *BDH*, II, 158.

Argentina: *Ambos a dos*, el doctor y yo, preguntamos por la citada (Cione, p. 8).

Chile: Tienen que respetarse y quererse mutuamente, *ambas a dos* (Acevedo Hernández, *Por el atajo*, p. 36).

Peru: Río de agua y río de sangre, *ambos a dos* agitados y convulsos (Ciro Alegría, *La serpiente*, p. 29).

Guatemala: *Ambos dos* vinieron a verme; *ambas dos* son mis hermanas (Sandoval, I, 49).

Puerto Rico: Me echó los brasos a mí y a éste ... a *dambos a dos* (Meléndez Muñoz, p. 148).

CUALESQUIER

The plural of *cualquier(a)* is *cualesquier(a)*: *cualquier hombre, cualesquier hombres, cualquier(a) cosa, cualesquier(a) cosas*, etc. However, the plural *cualesquier(a)*, or *cualisquier(a)*, is often incorrectly used for the singular *cualquier(a)*. The form is evidently not felt to be plural because the sign of plurality is not found at the end of the locution where it normally is expected. Furthermore, the idea of number involved in *cualquiera* is nearly as uncertain as it is in the English 'any.' When we hear *cualquier cosa*, we may think of more than *one* thing. Possibly because of that implied plurality *cualesquier(a)* has so frequently come to be confused with *cualquier(a)*. Furthermore, the singular *cualquier(a)* has been used with plural nouns, showing that the word, whether in its correct plural or in its singular form, is often felt to be indeclinable, possibly by analogy with such similar indeclinable locutions as *quienquiera, qual si quier, dondequiera*, and the like.

While the confusion may not appear in the oldest popular poetry, it is noted in Golden Age literature (Keniston, p. 269; Cuervo, § 197) and is today common in dialectal Spain. Rodríguez Marín (*Cantos populares españoles* [Sevilla, 1882–83], II, *copla* 1716), claims that the singular *cualquier(a)* is unknown in many parts of Andalusia. Cuervo ("Prólogo," p. xxxi) states that *cualesquier* with a singular noun is commoner in Andalusia than elsewhere.

In Spanish America the confusion is general, not only in popular speech but also in that of some cultured persons. In regions where final *-s* is often dropped from pronunciation, the form *cualesquiera* with a singular noun may be ultra-correct, an attempt to restore an *-s* where it is supposed to belong in correct speech. Román (I, 467) says for Chilean usage: "No olviden algunas personas, señoras sobre todo, que por lo demás no carecen de educación, que el pl. de esta palabra es *cualesquier* o *cualesquiera;* pues ellas creen hacerlo mejor diciendo muy repulidas y con pésima concordancia: *cualesquier día, cualesquiera cosita*. Sin duda les parece que el singular *cualquier, -ra*, sólo es para los zafios que acostumbran no pronunciar la *s*." For northern Colombia, Sundheim (p. 187) declares that *cualesquiera* is not a popular form but is found in certain writers ("entes de pluma").

ARGENTINA: He servido en la frontera/... como sirve *cualesquiera* (*Martín Fierro*, p. 291). ¡*Cualisquiera* crería que tenés a tu disposición el Mercado del Centro! (*Fray Mocho*, p. 184).

CHILE: Por esto ... alguno por *cualesquier* motivo que no sea grande se funde en lo que le dé (Acevedo Hernández, *Árbol viejo*, p. 19). Hay que ... unirse para luchar contra las injusticias de *cualesquiera* índole que sean (Acevedo Hernández, *La canción rota*, p. 57). —Yo me espanto de *cualesquier* cosa (Juan Modesto Castro, p. 188).

PERU: —Ya verá, don Fernán, que a todos los habladores los traigo pacá *cualesquier* día (Ciro Alegría, *Los perros*, p. 86).

COLOMBIA (SOUTH): Como *cualesquier* hija sin madre (Álvarez Garzón, p. 17). (ANTIOQUIA): No dejará de llorar/*Cualesquiera* que la vea (Antonio Restrepo, p. 176). Cf. also *BICC*, I, 352.

COSTA RICA: Seguí jalando terreno con l'intención de llegar de *cualisquier* manera (*Leyendas*, p. 132). Después, pa *cualisquier* comisión, yo no sabía otra cantada que dicir (Dobles Segreda, p. 34). —Ningún cristiano está safo de *cualesquier* contingensia (Echeverría, p. 158); Corte uno *cualesquiera* (p. 177). Es como *cualesquier* otro (Fabián Dobles, p. 284).

GUATEMALA: Te advierto que don Sixto no es un *cualisquiera*, para que lo trates así (Sandoval, I, 238).

MEXICO: *Cualesquera*, por maje que sea,/sempre jalla chamba (Rivas Larrauri, p. 43). —*Cualesquier* día los tenemos aquí (Urquizo, p. 217).

PUERTO RICO: Tardan tanto tiempo en llegar ... que el que tarde *cualesquiera* de nosotros en llegar a San Juan en automóvil (Meléndez Muñoz, p. 32).

Other popular forms recorded are *cualquieras* for the plural *cualesquiera* (often meaning 'person of no account': "son dos *cualquieras*") and *cualsiquiera* for *cualquiera*. The form *qual se quier* is found in Old Spanish (cf. Italian *qualsivoglia*). Cuervo tells us (*Dicc.*, II, 628) that "en Castilla el vulgo dice todavía *cualsiquiá*." *Cualsiquiera* is recorded for Aragon by Kuhn (p. 35), for Murcia by Lemos (p. 87), etc.

ARGENTINA: *Cualquieras* sean las dificultades que se presenten, será necesario salvarlas (Forgione, p. 135).

VENEZUELA: *Cualsiquier* día de éstos ... me va rebosá la totuma de la pacencia (Gallegos, *Pobre negro*, p. 22).

UN POCO DE

The indefinite locution *un poco* (or *poquito*) *de* is indeclinable in standard Spanish. In the older language the pronoun *poco* (or *poquito*) occasionally agreed in gender and number with the noun depending on the preposition *de*. In such instances *poco* (or *poquito*) was equivalent to an adjective: "*una poca de* hierba" (Keniston, p. 138); "*una poca* de sal, *unos pocos de* soldados" (Bello-Cuervo, § 853); "*unas pocas de* migajas ... *otras pocas de* tripas cocidas" (*Lazarillo*,

III). In an expression like *un poco de pan*, it is naturally impossible to say whether *poco* is the indeclinable form or whether it is masculine agreeing with *pan*. At any rate, the older usage in which *poco* agreed with the noun following *de*, is still preserved with certain nouns in rural Spain (Aurelio Espinosa, *Cuentos: "una poca de* agua," I, 145 [Granada]; "*una poca de* caridá," III, 448 [Córdoba]; cf. also Sánchez Sevilla, § 93; Zamora Vicente, § 48) and in many parts of Spanish America, with a slightly higher social status in some regions.

CHILE: —Dame *una poquita di'*agua (Brunet, in *ACH*, p. 255).

COLOMBIA: En algunos puntos de Colombia se oye todavía decir *una poca de agua* (Bello-Cuervo, n. 111).

VENEZUELA: —Lo sorprendieron enterrando una barreta de jabón, una vela de seba y *una poca de* sal (Gallegos, *Pobre negro*, p. 204); *Una poca de* agua (p. 311). *Una poca de* agua ... en el pueblo venezolano (Calcaño, p. 54).

MEXICO: Merecían *una poca de* atención (Payno, I, 6); tengo *una poca de* más libertad (I, 10). Yo, si la anemia me hubiese dejado *una poca más* de sangre ... habría enrojecido de rabia (Ferretis, *Quijote*, p. 18); Lo único que pude reunir fué *una poca de* saliva (p. 227). Adrede no habían querido llevar consigo nada; *una poca de* ropa (Ferretis, *San Automóvil*, p. 35). Hasta *una poca de* lástima ante un pobre diablo metido entre rejas (Gómez Palacio, p. 77). —*Una poquita de* alegría (Azuela, *Avanzada*, p. 209).

CUBA (RURAL): *Una poca de* agua (Padrón).

Another way of expressing 'a little' in some regions, notably Mexico, is the use of *tantito*, not in the capacity of a pronoun as often in the older language and even today ("con *tantico* de curiosidad," *Don Quijote*, I, pról.), but generally as an adjective (as also in the older language: "con *tantica* verdad," Gracián, *Criticón*, III, 3). (For *tantito* as an adverb of quantity, see p. 329.) In continental Spanish we find an analogous construction with *poco: una poca hoja, una poca leña, una poca madera* (Alarcón, *El sombrero de tres picos*, chap. iii; cf. Keniston, p. 274).

MEXICO: Eso se quita con *tantita* árnica y aguardiente (Azuela, *Los de abajo*, p. 213). —Denme *tantita* agua (Benítez, p. 128). *Tantita* carne una vez al mes (Urquizo, p. 83).

COLOMBIA: Páseme *tantica* agua (Flórez, p. 378).

In Colombia, Panama, and elsewhere we hear, even among the

cultured, *un poco de* in the sense of '(quite) a few' (often with augmentative force), where standard speech uses *unos pocos, unos cuantos* or *unas pocas, unas cuantas.* Similar usage seems to be current elsewhere: "le das a cada uno ... *su poco de* vacas" (La Cuadra, *Los Sangurimas,* p. 36 [Ecuador]). Analogous *una poca de* is rare.

COLOMBIA: Compré *un poco de* libros; escribí *un poco de* cartas (C). —Por áhi están *un poco de* viejitos (Buitrago, p. 13). Había allí *un poco de* muchachos gritando (Sundheim, p. 530). Se encontró *un poco* [= un montón] *de* dinero (Revollo, p. 216).

PANAMA: Voy a comprar *un poco de* naranjas; Tengo que contestar *un poco de* cartas (C). Vinieron *un poco de* soldados (*BAPL,* VIII, 86).

PARAGUAY: Voy a comprar *un poco* de bananas (Morínigo).

VENEZUELA: *Una poca de* esos pertrechos (Gallegos, *Pobre negro,* p. 356); *una poca de* ganado (*Cantaclaro,* p. 176).

SANTO DOMINGO: *Una poquita,* —repetía a todo el que le preguntaba como cuántas reses tendría. —Una migajita (Moscoso, p. 29).

CON TODO Y

The locution *con + noun + y todo* was current in the older language as it is today in peninsular and in American Spanish: *con caballo y todo.* The phrase *y todo* had two meanings: (1) *también* 'also,' indicating mere addition, and (2) *también, hasta* or *aun* 'also, even,' indicating corroboration or emphasis of what immediately precedes—a greater heightening of the meaning of the preceding substantive than is implied by the simple adverb *también.*

Meaning (1) *también* 'also,' not mentioned in Keniston, is found in the classical period: "—Estoy celosa. —Yo *y todo* [= yo también]" (Tirso); "—Así lo ofrezco. —Yo *y todo* [= yo también]" (Calderón).[4] This usage has almost fallen into desuetude. The Academy dictionary registers it as antiquated.

Meaning (2) *también, hasta,* or *aun* 'also, even,' was likewise used in the classical period, contrary to Castro's implication (*RFE,* IV, 287). Keniston (p. 142) mentions this use, explaining it as having "the force of *todo lo demás,* like childish English 'nevrything": "¿cómo avía de comer el rocín con el freno *y todo* en la boca?" (Lope de Rueda; cf. also Cejador, *La lengua de Cervantes,* II, 1081). It is frequently found in nineteenth-century Spanish literature and is exceedingly common in the spoken language: "se lo expliqué *y todo* pero no me lo ha creído." In American Spanish today this use not

[4] A. Castro y S. Gili, "Miscelánea," in *RFE,* IV (1917), 288.

only is common in the spoken language but is also found in writing. The negative counterpart is *ni nada:* "no sabe leer *ni nada.*"

Now in many regions of Spanish America the locution *con* + *noun* + *y todo* has undergone a curious reciprocal metathesis in popular speech: *con caballo y todo* > *con todo y caballo* 'horse and all,' in which the noun and *todo* have exchanged places. By anticipation *todo* has been put in a more emphatic position.[5] On the other hand, the locution may be a development from another found in regional Spain, *con todo y con eso* (or *ello*), meaning *a pesar de eso* 'despite that': "Los cinco sentíos del alma le pone uno encima, y *con todo y con eso* no se la pué meter por vereda" (Pereda, *Obras,* V, 363); "Pero *con to y con eso,* ganas me daban muchas veces de echarme a corré" (Muñoz Seca, *El roble de la Jarosa,* p. 80). In fact, *con todo y* + *noun* often has the meaning of *a pesar de* 'despite.'

With an infinitive, *con todo y* likewise means *a pesar de* 'despite,' used especially by Catalan writers (Morales, *Apuntes,* p. 353) and in parts of Spanish America. It may be a transposition and extension of the usual Spanish phrase *con ser y todo.*

While purists have inveighed against *con todo y,*[6] the many examples given below will show not only a wide geographical distribution of it but also its use by recognized writers, as well as in colloquial speech. It seems especially common in Mexico and Central America, but is also recorded in Colombia and Venezuela and is not unknown farther south.

COLOMBIA: Recuéstase en un taburete, se pone a fumar muy tranquilo y me hace sentar a su lado, *con todo y* perro (Carrasquilla, *Hace tiempos,* I, 44); La muchachuela se va; mas siempre vuelve el cuerpo atrás, *con todo y* tarro, para mirarnos (III, 32). Lególe la imagen de mi padre San Roque *con todo y* nicho (Carrasquilla, *Novelas,* p. 129); ¡Ésta sí era la que se iba a ir pa el cielo *con todo y* ropa! (p. 139).

VENEZUELA: Usted no dió en el blanco, *con todo y ser* [= a pesar de ser] muy buen tirador (Gallegos, *Doña Bárbara,* p. 19); A ese espanto lo desvisto yo solo, *con todo y* [= a pesar de] la fama que tiene (p. 341). *Con todo y* [= a pesar de] *no tener* los contornos firmes del pri-

[5] For the three pronunciations of *todo y* (tǫ́i̯, twí, and tí) in New Mexico, see Espinosa in *Inv. ling.,* II (1934), 195–99.

[6] Cf. A. Ayón, *Filología al por menor* (León, 1934 [Nicaragua]): " '*Fulano cayó con todo y caballo,* por *Fulano cayó con caballo y todo,* es un disparate, pues después de *todo,* no puede quedar otra cosa.' Esta observación es del escritor mejicano Dr. Francisco Pimentel, y me parece muy razonable," etc.

mero vale mucho en mi ánimo (Briceño, p. 75); Pero ahí mismito, *con todo y* [= a pesar de] la bulla de la quebrada y del agua, se escuchó un rezo (p. 91).

PANAMA: *Con todo y* [= a pesar de] que es pesado, me gustaría mucho hacerlo (C).

COSTA RICA: Llamó al zopilote y le habló para que lo llevara *con todo y* pieles adonde Tatica Dios (Lyra, p. 105). Pos se pudo haber ido al río *con todo y* carga (Fabián Dobles, p. 82; also p. 116); Mas, *con todo y* [= a pesar de] que en la casa se manejaba con desenvoltura, frente a la gente extraña la oprimía una timidez profunda (p. 139). *Con todo y* el miedo (Fallas, p. 75); *con* miedo *y todo* (p. 77).

NICARAGUA: *Con todo y* [= a pesar de] mi anuencia ante su propuesto pacto de protección mutua, mi compadre no se marchaba (Orozco, p. 4). *Con todo y* [= a pesar de] su renquera, Juan iba al riachuelo a lavar los trapos (Toruño, p. 135). ¡Qué buena sos; te vas a ir al cielo *con todo y* zapatos! (Chamorro, *El último filibustero*, p. 65).

HONDURAS: Stokowsky *con todo y* su nombre eslavo, es un valor yanqui (Martínez Galindo, p. 22). Esas palabras, *con todo y* [= a pesar de] lo que expresan, son poco (Carías Reyes, *La heredad*, p. 6).

EL SALVADOR: Pero, *con todo y* [= a pesar de] su explicación ella no lo creía (Torres Arjona, p. 31); la correntada me arrastró *con todo y* caballo (p. 31). Carretas ... transportaban una familia entera, *con todo y* ajuar (Ambrogi, p. 113). Le regaló la vaca, *con todo y* la cría (Mechín, *Brochazos*, p. 47). *Con todo y* la esperada (C).

GUATEMALA: Ni Bello, ni Irisarri, ni D. José Joaquín de Mora, *con todo y ser* [= a pesar de ser] muy celosos defensores de la independencia, jamás creyeron que al cambiar de instituciones, debiéramos haber cambiado de manera de hablar (Batres, p. 41).

MEXICO: Es evidente que al encumbrar rodemos *con todo y* caballo en cualquier desfiladero (Inclán, I, 42); fué conducido entre filas *con todo y* mulas a la aduana (I, 89); no le han de valer sus respetables canas, sino que, *con todo y* ellas, lo pongo a columpiarse un rato en cualquier roble (I, 191). Y bien, *con todo y* [= a pesar de] eso, Pascual ha seguido visitándonos como si tal cosa (Azuela, *Las tribulaciones*, p. 38). La señorita *con todo y* [= a pesar de] su bondad no deja de tener su condición (Robles, *La virgen*, p. 91). Había momentos en que ... *con todo y* [= a pesar de] su dolor, sentía el deleite del descanso lejos de su mujer (Gómez Palacio, p. 107). ¡Me llevará presa, pero *con todo y* propaganda! (Galeana, p. 122). Irse como el mayate ['beetle'] *con todo y* hebra (Rubio, *Refranes*, I, 265). ¿Es que son capaces de metérsele *con todo y* caballo? (García Roel, p. 108).

NEW MEXICO: Se jué *contui* [= con todo y] familia (Aurelio Espinosa, *Studies*, II, 77).

SANTO DOMINGO (MOCA): *Con todo y* carga; (elsewhere in Santo Domingo) tiene novia *y todo*, con eso *y todo* (*BDH*, V, 238).

PUERTO RICO: *Contui*'l agua pasa la gente (C).

VI

VERBS: TENSES; REFLEXIVES

PRESENT LOCUTIONS FOR FUTURE

IN SOME Spanish-American countries one frequently hears the remark that the future tense is being lost and that in conversation it is all but obsolete, being replaced by the present or by various circumlocutions. Unaware of linguistic change elsewhere, such speakers are likely to consider the partial disappearance of the future as purely local. This is not the case. Furthermore, the present tense is not always to be considered a replacement of the future but rather the continuation of an older usage, since it was probably favored in popular Latin (as it is today in popular speech), the future being the more literary form (Meyer–Lübke, § 102; Hanssen, § 575).

It will be remembered that the old Latin future was lost and new formations were devised in the Romance languages with the aid of so-called auxiliary verbs. The auxiliary *haber* (*de*) had and still has a number of meanings: obligation (ethical necessity), compulsion, commitment. These meanings are not always sharply distinguishable and, losing their affective expression, they easily slip into the realm of simple futurity. That step brought about the future tense in Spanish: *ha* (*de*) *hablar* ⟩ *hablará* 'must speak, is to speak' ⟩ 'will speak.' The English future has a parallel development. Since there was at first no future, the auxiliary *will* ('to have the will to') and *shall* ('to be obliged to') were used, both of which, having become intellectualized, may now express simple futurity. And today new combinations, restoring lost emotional content, are often substituted: 'to be about to,' 'to be going to,' etc.

In Spanish, *haber de* + *inf.* with its several meanings continued to be used side by side with the newborn future and probably in popular speech was always more vigorous than the new locution. As late as the sixteenth century the future tense even in the literary language was still felt as a combination of the infinitive and the present tense of *haber; haber de* and *haber* were felt as practically equivalent since "the hesitation between the pure infinitive and the infinitive with *de* was characteristic of the time" (Keniston, p. 461). Today *haber de* + *inf.* in many regions, particularly in American Spanish, represents a simple future. Occasionally the *de* is still omitted. The real future of probability or conjecture, therefore, is less often heard in Spanish America than in Spain. It is replaced with *haber de* + *inf.* or with some other locution. Similarly, too, in American English, such a future has been lost, while still retained in England. Cf. England: "It *will be* about five o'clock"; America: "It *is* about five o'clock."

ARGENTINA: Mejor *he de ir* yo [= iré yo] a sorprenderlos ... esta tarde ya *he de arreglar* [= arreglaré] todo para ir allá (Ezquer Zelaya, p. 38); —Después te *hemo de contar* bien (p. 67). —¡No se atropellen, señores, que pa todos *ha de haber!* (Lynch, *Palo verde*, p. 16); ¿Y caso que te hagan juerza en contra, *has de decir* que si no te dejan casar conmigo, *has de matarte* con cuchillo, veleno u lo que sea? (p. 161). —¿Me parece que si no vine antes no *ha de haber sido* [= no habrá sido] e vicio? (Lynch, *Romance*, p. 426). Pero dende la otra vida *hay volver* [=ha de volver = volverá) mi ánima en pena en tu busca (César Carrizo, p. 146; cf. also Vidal, p. 388).

CHILE: Seña es que *li' ha de poner* [= le pondrá] toas las impedías pa que sea enterrá en sagrao (Latorre, *Hombres*, p. 23); ¡nunca si' *ha de saber* quién ha sío! (p. 97); Nu' *ha d'estar* lloviendo, porque nu' hay nubes. Cuando vi la tierra medio colorá: Nu' *ha de ser* sangre, igo (p. 118); —Un entierro *ha de ser* (p. 131); No *ha de estar* estudiando (p. 179); Lo vide de pasá. Él *ha de ser*, digo yo (p. 225).

BOLIVIA: Los del pueblo *no han de comprarnos* gran cosa, pero *han de venir* de las haciendas (Arguedas, *Raza*, p. 25). —¿Quieres ofrecernos hospedaje por esta noche en tu casa? *Hemos de pagarte* (p. 72); Oye, madre; *has de encontrar* en el atado un poco de maíz (p. 229). —¡Pero chica, te *has de matar!* (Arguedas, *Vida criolla*, p. 70).

PERU (HIGHLANDS, RUSTIC): Comues temprano *han querer* [= querrán] pasar (Ciro Alegría, *La serpiente*, p. 148).

ECUADOR: —Y por esta porquería el clérigo te *ha de haber sacado* lo menos unos veinte sucres (Icaza, *Cholos*, p. 34). ¿*Ha de ser* [= será] posible? ... *¿Ha de haber* [= habrá] paciencia? ... Ya *han de ser* las cuatro (Bustamante, p. 112). Todas las familias *han de venir;* apenas yo llegue a la otra hacienda, le *he mandar* (Mata, *Sanagüín*, p. 207). —Ve, monstruo, no me llames hijita porque *he de tener* iras y no *he de poder* tomar el chocolate (García Muñoz, *Estampas*, p. 32); Papacito, no tomes porque te *has de chumar* (p. 40); Éste le *hemos de dejar* en cuatro «riales» (p. 65); —¡Vamos pronto, hijita, que los bebés *han de estar* llorando! (p. 74); —¿Verdad que una color verde me *ha de sentar?* (p. 79).

EL SALVADOR: —Ésos *han de ser* Mateyo y Julián. —Palomas *han destar matando* (Salarrué, *Cuentos*, p. 146).

MEXICO: —¿Oye, curro, y tú *has de saber* contar cuentos? (Azuela, *Los de abajo*, p. 50). —No, mal no, *he de haber cogido* frío (Gamboa, *Santa*, p. 254). —*Ha de ser* un diplomático. Yo alcancé a fijarme en la placa (Gómez Palacio, p. 22). Usted la *ha de haber* escondido (Urquizo, p. 57); se lo *he de agradecer* (p. 150).

The locution *tan* (or *más*) + adj. + *que lo* (or *la* or *te*) *han de ver* [= verán] is used in familiar and popular speech in a semi-jocose vein: *tan tonto que lo han de ver* meaning *tan tonto que te ves* (or *eres*). In this phrase *han de* seems to have a bit of "ethical-necessity" force and the feeling of the whole expression is present in time; the vague third person plural appears to be used to make the statement less incisive, that is, to mitigate the sting of reproach or irony or jest inherent in this locution. It may well be related to the phrase *hay que ver* and to such usage as "Mirad si no han de ser locos ... " (*Don Quijote*, II, 32), etc. But Román's explanation (V, 656: "Es tan tonto que hay que verlo para creerlo") is not always applicable today. The feeling of it has become less complicated, being now generally equivalent to "eres muy tonto, qué tonto eres" with overtones of playful irony.

CHILE: *¡Tan* tonto *que lo han de ver! ¡Tan* mezquina *que la han de ver!* (Román, V, 565). —*Tan* cargoso *que te han de vel. ... Tan* cargao a las riendas *que te han de vel* (Romanángel, p. 9). —*¡Tan* cínico *que lo han de ver!* (Maluenda, in *ACH*, p. 204). —¡Gilidioso [= molesto] *que te han de ver*, mirá! (Durand, *Tierra*, p. 47). Lo largo e manos *que lo han de ver* (Guzmán Maturana, p. 21).

ECUADOR: —*Tan* tragón *que lo han de ver* (Pareja, *La Beldaca*, p. 30). —*Más* mudo *que te han de ver* (Jorge Fernández, p. 155).

The locution *ir a* + *inf.* to replace the future is common everywhere, but in popular American Spanish it has extended its domain beyond its normal usage in Spain. Occasionally we find it used with an infinitive to give it a sense of futurity (see Mexico below), a curious survival of Latin feeling, if not form. Cf. Canellada, p. 33.

CHILE: Y lo pior es que no «sabimos» en qué estación *va a ir a parar* [= parará] este tren (Pepe Rojas, *La banda*, II, 3).

PERU: —¡Caramba! hom. ... Ya *va usted a querer* pelear con nosotros por semejante porquería (Barrantes, p. 153).

COSTA RICA: El Moncho es hombre de pantalones y *no va haber estao dormío* estos meses atrás (Fabián Dobles, p. 239).

HONDURAS: —La muchacha ... se dirigió al cuarto de las bebidas. —¿Cuánto *va a querer*, señor? (Mejía Nieto, *El solterón*, p. 122).

EL SALVADOR: Si baila con vos, todos *van a querer* lo mismo (González Montalvo, *Don Benja*).

MEXICO: Después de la sopa, ¿qué *va a querer* usted? (C; waitress in a restaurant). Ni crea que *va a querer* (Urquizo, p. 15); A poquito llegó mi mamá de prisa, temerosa seguro de no *ir a encontrarme* ya [a kind of future infinitive] (p. 19).

In many regions we encounter the use of auxiliary *ir* + *a* + *inf.*, *haber* + *de* + *inf.*, etc., the tense used in the auxiliary being that of the locution as a whole: *iré a querer* = *querré; hubo de ir* = *fué*, etc. ("Temo si *iré a ponerme* tísica" Benavente, *El automóvil*, I, 3).

RIVER PLATE ZONE: Han llamado a la puerta. ¿Quién *irá a ser* [= será]? (Morínigo).

CHILE: —Su mercé *habrá de ver* [= verá], pué, patrón (Durand, in *ACH*, p. 227). *Irá a llegar* a las nueve (C).

COLOMBIA: ¿Se *irá a aburrir?* (Carrasquilla, *Hace tiempos*, I, 68).

MEXICO: ¿Cuándo *iré a querer* a un hombre? (Galeana, p. 63).

CUBA: ¡Está herida! *¿Irá a morirse* [= se morirá]? (Cuca Quintana, in *CC*, p. 221).

Such usage is, however, more characteristic of the preterite.

The future of probability is further avoided by using *deber* (*de*) + *inf.*, as everywhere.

ARGENTINA: *Deben de ser* como las jonce (Lynch, *Las caranchos*, p. 27); *Deben ser* como las cinco (p. 100).

PRESENT FOR PRESENT PERFECT

Often a present tense in the negative (generally after *todavía* or its equivalent) takes the place of a present perfect, probably in an effort to shorten and vivify the expression by bringing it into the realm of actual happening. The construction is current in Spain.

ARGENTINA: El perro ... paró las orejas ... y quiso gruñir. —No hay pa qué. ... Calma y güen discurso, que entuavía *no pasa* [= no ha pasado] nada (César Carrizo, p. 63).

ECUADOR: Todavía *no me devuelven* [= no me han devuelto] los pesos. Dicen que ya mismo habrá algo (Pareja, *El muelle*, p. 5). —Vea, chapita. ... —No tengo fósforos—me respondió. —Si todavía *no le pido* [= no le he pedido] nada (García Muñoz, *Estampas*, p. 74). *No viene* [= no ha venido] (Rosenblat).

MEXICO: —Date priesa, Pifanio. ... Ya se metió el sol y todavía *no bajas* [= no has bajado] al agua a las bestias (Azuela, *Los de abajo*, p. 190); ¡Trabaja dende que Dios amanece! ¡Qué ha que se metió el sol ... y mírelo, *no para* [= no ha parado] todavía! (p. 192). *No nace* todavía el hijo de la ... que tenga que derrotar a mi general Villa (p. 233). A pesar de su carta ... a esta hora *no recibo* [= no he recibido] aviso del ... banco (L). Toavía *no me bautizan*, ni siquiera me han echao l'agua (García Roel, p. 32).

IMPERFECT FOR PLUPERFECT

Similarly, the imperfect tense is found in the same type of construction where the pluperfect is standardly expected.

CHILE: El capitán todavía *no se vestía* [= no se había vestido] cuando llamé a la puerta de su cabina (Délano, p. 120).

ECUADOR: Estaba viviendo sola ... porque su tía aún *no regresaba* [= no había regresado] (Ortiz, p. 41).

COSTA RICA: Media hora larga había pasado y la morenilla *no parecía* [= no había parecido] (Magón, p. 107).

MEXICO: Rodrigo, con la inexperiencia de sus pocos años, todavía *no aprendía* [= no había aprendido] a engañarse a sí mismo. Ni siquiera lograba disimular discreto (García Roel, p. 294). —No, me dejó su padre cuando *no nacía* [= no había nacido] la niña (Galeana, p. 92). Oíamos ... el ruido de la fusilería ... pero todavía no *entrábamos* [= no habíamos entrado] en juego nosotros (Urquizo, p. 227).

IMPERFECT FOR PRESENT

Standardly the present tense is used to indicate that an action begun in the past continues in the present: "hace mucho que no le *veo*" 'I haven't seen him for a long time.' The perfect tense may be used especially when the verb is negative: "hace mucho que no le *he visto.*" By extension, the imperfect tense has come to be used instead of the present, especially when the object of the dependent verb is in plain sight and the action has therefore just recently ended. Such usage is common both in America and in Spain. One constantly hears: "hace tiempo que no te *veía,* hace tiempo que no *venía* usted," and the like. Random examples are given below.

CHILE: —Aló, Carmencita. ... Hace un mes, por lo menos, que no la *veía* (Luis Meléndez, p. 159). ¡Cuánto me alegro de encontrarlo! ¡Qué tiempo que no nos *veíamos!* (Guzmán Maturana, p. 60). —Hace mucho que *deseábamos* mudarnos a Providencia (Edwards Bello, *La chica,* p. 66).

COLOMBIA: —Hace tiempo que no te *oía* hablar (Buitrago, p. 224).

VENEZUELA: —Hace tiempo que no te *oía* ese grito (Gallegos, *La trepadora,* p. 127).

GUATEMALA: ¡Qué milagro! Endequiaque [= hace mucho tiempo que] no lo *veíamos* por acá, don Domingo (Samayoa, p. 112).

MEXICO: —Hace cinco años que no lo *probaba* (Azuela, *Avanzada,* p. 20).

CUBA: —Compadre ... no te *veía* desde hace mucho tiempo. ¿Qué haces por aquí? (Ciro Espinosa, p. 177).

PUERTO RICO: Hace veinte años que no *veía* un campo (Meléndez Muñoz, p. 189).

Quite frequent, too, in popular speech is another construction in which *hacer* appears in the present (*hace*) instead of the imperfect (*hacía*) to express past time. It reflects a more vivid contrast between the present (time of speaking) and the past.

ECUADOR: Como supe que se hallaba enferma volví a la casa. *Hace* [= hacía] muchos meses que no había ido por allí (Icaza, *Cholos,* p. 177); No tenía luz eléctrica desde *hace* [= hacía] algunas semanas; le habían cortado por falta de pago (p. 180).

FUTURE FOR IMPERATIVE

The future has been used in Spanish from earliest times, following Latin usage, to express an authoritative command. Thus in the *Cid* we read "por Molina *iredes,* i *yazredes* una noch" (vs. 2365). It is used in laws, as in the English "Thou shalt not kill." This usage, which gives the command a narrative tinge, continues today, but apparently nowhere so vigorously as in Ecuador, where in this form the object pronoun has retained its older enclitic position (except when the verb is negative) not only in popular speech but also in the familiar speech of the cultured classes. It has the feeling of a softened imperative. In the older language: "*Dirásle,* buena vieja, que ... quise más dexarle por loco que publicar su grande atrevimiento" (*Celestina,* IV); "busca a Lisardo, y *dirásle*/como mi afecto le avisa/que a verme vaya esta noche (Calderón, p. 92). The construction may be considered a local retention of a good classical form probably fixed and extended under the substratum influence of Quechua which, in addition to a present imperative, has one or more future imperatives.

ECUADOR: —Entonces *prepararáste* [= prepárate] (Icaza, *En las calles,* p. 76); —*Acordaráste* [= acuérdate] de nosotros ... *¡Cuidarás* [= cuida] al guagua! ... —*Escribirás* pes (p. 81); —*Casharáste* [= cállate], perra corrompida (p. 174). ... —*Tendránle* [= ténganla] bien, a lo mejor me muerde (p. 179). —*No te harás* [= no te hagas] el chistosito (García Muñoz, *Estampas,* p. 223); *Harás* [= haz] desaguar el arroz, Lucrecia (p. 247); —Entonces, *dirále* [= dígale] a su mujer que mande a sacar las cucharas (p. 266); —*Daráme* [= déme] unos diez sucres (p. 314). —*Daráse* [= dése] prisa, que de no le multo (Pareja, *Baldomera,* p. 12); —¡Mata a la vieja! —*¡Matarás* [= mata] a tu madre, desgraciado, mal parido! (p. 21); Uno de ellos ... le da una tremenda patada en el estómago: —*¡Tomarás* [= toma] este dulce, negrita! (p. 23). —Mamacita, ... *irán* [= vayan] pronto allá. —¡En seguida te seguiremos, hijito mío! *Cuidaráste* bien, *abrigaráste* bien en el páramo, *tomarás* quinina para el paludismo, por si acaso (Mata, *Sanagüín,* p. 50).

COLOMBIA (SOUTH): —Bueno, pero *tendrás* [= ten] cuidado (Álvarez Garzón, p. 60); —*Vendrís* [= ven] a avisarme el resultado (p. 106).

A LOCAL IMPERATIVE LOCUTION

In the popular speech of highland Ecuador and southern Colombia the imperative is softened also by another construction modeled after the Quechua: that is, the use of *da* or *dame* (*cuy* in Quechua) plus a gerund. A form like *dame trayendo,* for instance, is a polite request or entreaty, which is preferred to the abrupt *tráeme* or *tráemelo.* Vázquez (p. 127) gives other examples of this Quechuan-style Spanish: *dame llevando = llévamelo; dame escribiendo = escribe* [*sic*]; *dame hablando a mi favor = habla a mi favor, recomiéndame; dame leyendo = léeme.* This locution not only is characteristic of rustic Indian speech but is not uncommon among the untutored urban population of Quito and is heard even in familiar conversation among those possessing a degree of culture. A superior may be heard saying to his stenographer, for instance: "*Déme escribiendo* esta carta" for the more abrupt and less polite "*Escríbame* esta carta" or "¿Quiere *darme corrigiendo* esto?" for "*Corríjame* esto," etc.

Ecuador: —¿Qué es pues, cholita? —Nada, don Luquitas ... quiero que *dé haciendo* [= haga] un favorzote bien grande por lo que más quiera, linditico. —¡Habla claro y pronto! —Vay *dé rogando* [= ruegue] en el Estanco que se porten mejor con mi Julián (Mata, *Sanagüín*, p. 96); Vay *dé hablando* [= hable], bonito, y *no se enojará* [= no se enoje] (p. 97); Vaya ... *dé preguntando* [= pregunte], señor Diez de Jijón (p. 124); Oye, ... *da dejando* [= deja] esta carta a algunos de los Fernández (p. 216).

Colombia: Cf. p. 211.

CONDITIONAL FOR IMPERFECT SUBJUNCTIVE

In contrary-to-fact conditional clauses after *si*, the conditional is in some regions used incorrectly for an imperfect subjunctive. In the sixteenth century Keniston (p. 412) notes one example only ("si en algo *podría*"), though the conditional is sometimes found instead of a past subjunctive in other dependent clauses.[1] Such incorrect usage may be found colloquially in northern Spain and in parts of Spanish America: *si yo vería* for *si yo viera; si yo diría* for *si yo dijera*. Evidently these forms are used by attraction with the conditional of result clauses. Senet (p. 133) remarks that the subjunctive has almost disappeared in the popular speech of Buenos Aires (cf. "lo recibiré el día que nuestras tropas *entrarán* en Madrid" [Martínez Zuviría, p. 384]). Joaquín Romero (p. 399) states that the conditional is becoming more and more frequent in Argentina ("si yo *tendría*").

Argentina: Si *tendría* tiempo, iría; si *estudiaría* más, aprendería (Tiscornia, *La lengua*, § 173, according to whom such sentences are heard in the schoolroom). (Popular): —Mirá, ché, por compadre [= por arrogante] me *gustaría* [= me hubiera gustado] que le *ganarían* [= ganaran] (Senet, p. 133; cf. also Vidal, p. 389).

[1] Common today in the province of Burgos and elsewhere. Cf. A. Espinosa, "The use of the conditional for the subjunctive in Castilian popular speech," *Modern Philology*, XXVII (1930), 445–49. "Yo le dije que si le *encontraría* un piojo que le mataría" (A. Espinosa, *Cuentos*, III, 408); "Mi madre me dijo que *iría* [= fuera] a misa y que *haría* [= hiciera] lo que los demás" (p. 404); "quería ... llevárselo al león pa que se lo *comería*" (p. 444), etc. Cf. also G. Fernández Shaw, *El caserío* (1926), I, 8; II, 6.

CHILE (CHILOÉ): Si *tendría* dinero, compraría aquel terreno (Cavada, p. 284).

ECUADOR: Hernán piensa cuál sería su situación si él *caería* bajo el hacha del terror (Salvador, *Noviembre*, p. 106); si ella *llegaría* a morir, ¿a dónde iría la niña? (p. 119); Si me *acariciarías* ahora, serías un hombre más en mi vida (p. 156); —Serías una ingrata si te *disgustaría* el quedarte conmigo (p. 206); ¿qué importaría, si *podrían* conseguir un cargo en el exterior? (p. 210).

COLOMBIA (SOUTH): Y si no *podría* hacerlo, ¿cómo se las arreglaría? (Álvarez Garzón, p. 103); y si así lo *vería* la Alegría, cómo se burlaría de él (p. 222).

GUATEMALA: El médico recetó a una enferma delicada/darle media cucharada de un elixir cada día,/hasta que él lo *indicaría* (Bonilla Ruano, III, 156).

SANTO DOMINGO (CIBAO): Ajolá que sucediera/Que yo *sería* tu mujer (Brito, *Dicc. de criollismos*, p. 38, *ap. BDH*, V, 177).

CONDITIONAL IN NEWS REPORTS

Occasionally the conditional is used in news headlines and items with the approximate meaning of 'it has been reported that, it is rumored *or* supposed that, it is said that,' etc. This is a variety of the conditional of probability or conjecture. It is especially common in Chilean and Argentine newspapers and is probably a Gallicism, a reflection of French (and possibly Italian) usage, in which the conditional frequently expresses doubtful assertions or doubtful inquiries. While Spanish usage requires the future tense for conjecture in present time and the conditional in expressed or implied indirect discourse, this is not frequent in newspaper headlines as it is in French.

CHILE: El vapor chileno Copiapó *se estaría hundiendo* en la bahía de Cristóbal (*Mercurio*, July 7, 1940). No cabe la menor duda que el teatro chileno *estaría* a punto de entrar en una fase definida de su desarrollo (*Prólogo* to Pedro de la Barra's *La feria* [Santiago, 1939]).

CONDITIONAL IN BUENOS AIRES SLANG

In Buenos Aires slang we find a peculiar use of the conditional, which expresses incredulity or irony: *¡estaría!* meaning *no está, aunque tú lo creas* or *¡a quién se le ocurre pensar que está!* In *El problema de la lengua en América* (p. 94) the Spanish philologist, Amado Alonso, inveighs against the excessive stereotyping of modes of emotional expression in the Argentine capital, the poverty of individual linguistic resources, as exemplified in this slang use of the conditional. He affirms, for instance, that in answer to the statement "me parece que me van a subir el sueldo" the common reaction and reply would invariably be *¡subirían!* (or distorted to *¡subiriólan!*), expressing a mixed feeling of incredulity, sarcasm, and irony: "—Sí, hermana. Tu marido ha dormido todas las noches como un bendito en casa de Ferruccio ... —¡Fu! ¡Tiempos idos! Ahora ... *¡dormirióla!*" (Llanderas, *Giuanín,* p. 24). This linguistic vagary, first heard in Buenos Aires in 1928 and thence spreading as far as Paraguay, has now fallen into innocuous desuetude, as is the fate of most linguistic whims of this type.

PRETERITE FOR PRESENT PERFECT

In the early language the simple preterite (*vine* 'I came') must have been well distinguished from the present perfect (*he venido* 'I have come'), since the latter tense had arisen to fill a definite need (the Latin perfect combined both meanings). Modern Spanish (as based on best usage and precept) employs the preterite (*vine*) to express a completed act in the past. It employs the present perfect (*he venido*) to express a past act whose effects reach into the present, the effects being either real or merely imagined by the speaker. Consequently, it is used to express a recent past act (*he venido* = 'acabo de venir'), or an act that has taken place within a period of time not yet ended (*hoy, esta semana, este año,* etc.). These distinctions are made quite faithfully in Navarre, Aragon, and part of Old Castile. Elsewhere the people have sometimes refused to accept the usage. In some regions of Galicia, Asturias, and León (Menéndez Pidal, *El dialecto leonés,* § 21; Garrote, § 77) only the preterite is current—an archaic survival of Latin usage—to express both meanings: *vine* 'I came' and 'I have come.' Elsewhere in Spain the two uses have tended to fuse. In Madrid, for instance, the present perfect is preferred to the preterite and is often used in cases where only the preterite was previously considered legitimate: "ayer *he ido* [= fuí] a verlo." Such usage is rare in American Spanish: it is current in Bolivia (see below), as well as in northwestern Córdoba (Argentina) according to Moglia (p. 251), and occasionally elsewhere. The simple preterite, on the contrary, is frequently used in most of Spanish America in cases where a purist insists on the present perfect: *no vino hoy* for *no ha venido hoy, ¿qué pasó?* for *¿qué ha pasado? ¿Qué* *hubo?* (generally pronounced with synaloepha: *quiubo*, in Mexico often *quiúbole*) is current in a number of regions not only in the sense of *¿qué ha habido?* = *¿qué ha pasado?* = *¿cómo te ha ido?* = *¿cómo estás?* 'how are you? what's up?' and of *¡hola!* 'hello!' but also in the sense of 'what do you say? do you agree? how about it?' (Perhaps formulas like *¿qué hubo?*, in which the verbal feeling has almost disappeared, should not be included here.)

It must be remembered that distinctions are not rigid but that, in general, the popular preterite is much more commonly used than the present perfect in Spanish America (with less frequency in Peru, Bolivia, and other limited areas, as in San Luis, Argentina). The short, clipped preterite with its feeling of abruptness and finality is paralleled with familiar American English ("did you do it?" rather than "have you done it?").

ARGENTINA: —¿No se halla mejor?—le pregunté. —Igual no más. —*¿Durmió?* —Hasta aurita, no más (Güiraldes, *Don Segundo*, p. 206); —*¡Reventó* la yegua el lazo!—comenté (p. 250); —*Ganaste* una—me dijo el patrón (p. 264). —Hoy *pasé* por ese pueblo (Larreta, *El linyera*, p. 44); don Nazario me *vendió* hoy el cuchillo (p. 103); Los *retiré* hoy mismo (p. 161). —¿Le *compraste* algo? (Rodríguez Acasuso, *La mujer olvidada*, I, 1); *¿Cerraste* todo? (III, 12). —Hoy *se fueron* papá y mamá. —Por eso *vine* (Boj, p. 219; cf. Vidal, p. 387).

URUGUAY: —¡Qué suerte que *viniste!* ... Te *gané* (Acevedo Díaz, *Cancha larga*, p. 12); *Saliste* aprovechao como tu padre (p. 45); ¿Y *viniste* nada más que pa dar las gracias? (p. 51); ¡Pero! ¡No te *mostré* la sobrecincha! (p. 52); ¿Se te *pasó?* (p. 69); *¿Lloraste?* (p. 120); —*Viniste* como anillo al dedo (p. 158); ¡Le *acertaste!* (p. 161).

CHILE: —Buenos días. ¿Cómo *pasó* la noche? (Maluenda, in *ACH*, p. 204). —*¿Comió* el forastero? —Sí; y está durmiendo (Acevedo Hernández, *Por el atajo*, p. 12). —Güenos días. —Me *curé* pue, eñor (p. 23); —¿Por qué no *vino?* ... Hoy *fué* el olio del niñito nuevo (p. 49); —Se *fué* (p. 54); —Ya 'stá el desayuno. —Yo me *esayuné* (p. 57); —Vos lo *quisiste* (p. 66); —Jorge, ¿a qué *vino?* —*Vine* porque tenía necesidad de verte (p. 70). —*Llegué* hoy (Prado, *Un juez*, p. 232). —*¿Qué hubo*, cómo te *fué*, conquistador? (Acuña, *Huellas*, p. 115). Nuevamente en su cama se acerca el doctor: —*¿Qué hubo*, 21? ¿cómo le *fué?* —Bien, doctor (Juan Modesto Castro, *Aguas*, p. 76). Me *devolví* [= he vuelto] (C). Esa tarde estábamos comiendo cuando *se ha estremecido* [= se estremeció] la tierra (Pino, § 146).

BOLIVIA: Este chico *ha tenido* un mal sueño anoche. ... ¿Qué *has soñado*, chico? ... —¿Quién me llama? —*he preguntado* angustiosamente.—Te *ha llamado* la mina (R. U. Peláez, in *ACB*, p. 163). Ayer *ha solicitado* audiencia del viejo (Arguedas, *Vida criolla*, p. 126); la otra noche la *hemos esperado* inútilmente a su hija (p. 204); Cuando l'*e visto* antes de ayer, daba miedo y m'*a dicho* que no saliría (p. 217); Anoche *he soñao* con toros (p. 258). —¿Te acuerdas de esa tarde que *has roto* la jarra? (Díaz Villamil, *Plebe*, p. 51). De repente *hemos oído* ... el sonido (Leitón, p. 30).

PERU: ¿En dónde *compraste* hoy los huevos? (Ricardo Palma, in *ACP*, p. 39). —*Vine* pa despedirme, vidita (Diez-Canseco, in *ACP*, p. 178).

ECUADOR: Lo *gastó* hoy en necesidades urgentes (Salvador, *Noviembre*, p. 117). Hoy *estuve* con Beatriz (García Muñoz, *El médico*, p. 61). —Y el chico, *¿vino?* (Gil Gilbert, *Nuestro pan*, p. 171); —*¿Qué hubo*, aparcerito? (p. 217); —¿Dónde *estuviste* hasta esta hora? (p. 271). —*¿Qué hubo?* (Pareja, *Baldomera*, pp. 56, 64, etc.). —¿Ya *trajeron* el pan? (García Muñoz, *Estampas*, p. 223); ¿Y los guaguas? ¿Y por qué no les *trajeron?* (p. 243).

COLOMBIA (ANTIOQUIA): —Estoy deshecha, Cantalicia; *¿qué hubo?* —Todo lo *arreglé*, mi Niña. ¿Y qué *fué*, Cantalicia? Cuénteme (Carrasquilla, *Hace tiempos*, I, 31); Me examina los dientes. ... —Te *salieron* muy bonitos y muy parejos. No te *dañaste* nada con la muda: siempre *quedaste* el negrito Eloy (p. 44); —¿Por qué *se volvió* él de allá, Jerónimo, yéndole tan bien? —No *se ha vuelto* (p. 50); —¿Y entonces por qué *se vino* para acá la tal Pastora? (p. 103); —¿Sí le *gustó*, Nicanor? —Muy sabrosa, Pastora (p. 118); —Pa eso *truje* los zapatones (p. 151); Tan siquiera no *perdí* el tiempo. —¿Cómo le *parecieron?* —Muy simpáticas (p. 194). —*¿Qué hubo?* Aurelio; ¿por qué no te *fuistes* a chinchorriar ... ? (Buitrago, p. 34); Saltando de contenta entró María Trina a la sala. —*¿Qué hubo?* mija. *¿Convidastes* a Verónica? (p. 85). (ATLANTIC COAST): *¿Qué hubo?* (Revollo, p. 226, who thinks this locution was brought into northern Colombia at the turn of the century by soldiers from the interior).

VENEZUELA: —*¿Qué hubo*, Juan Primito?—solían preguntarle los peones de la mujerona (Gallegos, *Doña Bárbara*, p. 174); —*¿Qué hubo*, pues, vale? (p. 236). —*¿Qué hubo?*—inquirió roncamente uno de los hombres (Díaz-Solís, p. 24).

PANAMA: *¿Qué hubo?* (Herrero Fuentes, p. 97). —*¡Quiubo!* —*Quiubo*, pues (Nacho Valdés, *Sangre criolla*, p. 100).

COSTA RICA: —Hoy nada *traje* (Noguera, p. 46); —¿Qué tal *quedé?* (p. 63). —¿Por qué *dilataste* tanto? (Fabián Dobles, p. 162).

EL SALVADOR: —¡Hijo: abrí los ojos; ya hasta la color de que los tenés se me *olvidó!* (Salarrué, *Cuentos*, p. 9); —*¿Qué lihubo*, Nayo? —Los *casaron* (p. 75); *¡Oyó* ... tréme la bolsa! (p. 95).

MEXICO: —*¿Quihúbule*, amigo? (López y Fuentes, *¡Mi general!* p. 36); —¿Qué no acostumbra tomar? Pues, entonces, ¿a qué *vino?* A preguntar la hora (p. 88); —Voy de regreso para mi casa. *Estuve* en la ciudad tratando algunos asuntos comerciales (p. 169). Hoy *hubo* mucha gente de fuera (Madero, I, 2). —*Veniste* tarde. Todo ese personal está completo (Azuela, *Avanzada*, p. 167). —¿Qué tal *pasó* la noche? —Muy mal, jefe (Anda, *Juan del Riel*, p. 223). —Pos entonces, ¿a qué *vino?* (González Carrasco, p. 73); —¿Qué, *¿golviste* sin permiso? (p. 77). Te lo compro pero te vas conmigo esta noche, *¿qu'iubo?* ['what do you say?'] (Galeana, p. 162). —*¿Quiubo*, qué *pasó*, compadre? —Pues ya lo ve (Urquizo, p. 13); —*¿Quiúbole?* —*¿Quiubo?* —¿Ya *despertastes?* (p. 186). —Te voy a hacer capitán. ... —*¿Qué hubo?* ['what do you say?']. ¿La aceptas de capitán? (Rubín, p. 158).

SANTO DOMINGO: —¿Tú por aquí? —*Llegué* ahora mismo. ... —*Vine* a ver cómo está esto por acá (Requena, *Los enemigos*, p. 29).

CUBA: ¿Qué *pasó?* ¿Cómo *amaneciste* hoy? (Padrón).

PRETERITE FOR PRESENT OR FUTURE

Standardly the preterite is sometimes used with the adverb *ya* with the force of a present perfect or, better, a present tense: *ya se acabó, ya pasó* 'it's all over'; *ya se fué* 'he is gone'; etc. Because of the Spanish-American predilection for the preterite, this usage has been considerably extended to other verbs. It is especially common with *estar: ya estuvo* for *ya está*. Furthermore, since the present tense is frequently used for an immediate future, so a preterite like *ya estuvo* has in many regions likewise come to indicate a sudden action in the immediate future. Popular in Chile, Colombia, Mexico, Cuba, and elsewhere is the preterite *nos fuimos* (occasionally *fuímonos*) for *nos vamos*, meaning 'we're leaving, we shall go now, let's go,' etc.

In Chile (*nos* ⟩ *los* in popular speech, cf. p. 100) *nos fuimos* is popularly pronounced *loh juimoh* and, probably as a passing fad, is jocularly referred to as *ele jota* (*l j*), representing the initial sounds of each word in the locution: *¿ele jota?* = *¿nos fuimos?* = *¿nos vamos?* For Mexico, Henríquez Ureña (*BDH*, IV, 222, n. 1) describes *¡nos* *fuimos!* for *¡vámonos!* as "uso fantasístico, tal vez humorístico en su origen." Cf. Mexican *¡nos vimos!* for *¡nos vemos!* [= *¡hasta luego!*].

In such expressions the preterite really anticipates the act, like a future, but vividly describes it as already accomplished and irrevocable (as in standard *se acabó*).

ARGENTINA: —Va a leernos algo. (*A Pastora*) A ver, trai. (*Pastora trae la vela. Don Ladislao saca del bolsillo de su pantalón unos papeles*). *Ya estuvo.* Nos va a leer la sentencia como a los condenaos (Larreta, *El linyera*, p. 143).

URUGUAY: —Les jugamos yo y usted a don Pedro y al doctor. —¡Cómo no! *Ya estuvo* (Sánchez, *La gringa*, II, 1). El ayudante dió media vuelta ... y de súbito ... se desplomó. —*Ya estuvo*—exclamó el comandante;—¡pobre muchacho! (Pérez Petit, p. 161).

CHILE: —¡Cinco al caballito! —¡Uno al chancho! —¡El pescado me tinca; voy tres pesos! —*¡Nos fuimos!*—gritó el fondero. El disco giró rápidamente y todos los ojos se abrieron (Silva, p. 22). —¡Ya está, *nos fuimos!*—dijo el viejo. Los dos entraron al cuarto de Don Juan (Ernesto Montenegro, p. 236).

PERU: Si te dan la beca para el colegio de la Magdalena, *te armastes* (Benvenutto, p. 146).

ECUADOR: —Págame tú la comida y el trago. —*Ya estuvo.* ... —¿Quieren tomarse un puro? [= copa de aguardiente de caña]. Yo pago. —*Ya estuvo* (Pareja, *Baldomera*, p. 70); —Oye, Lamparita, vámonos casando. —*Ya estuvo*, Baldomera (p. 87). —Oye, nos vamos atrás del tiburón. —*Ya estuvo*, pues (Pareja, *La Beldaca*, p. 75).

COLOMBIA: —Es que si pedís cosa mala, va y el maestro te la concede; y, una vez concedida, *te amolaste*, porque la palabra del maestro no puede faltar (Carrasquilla, *Novelas*, p. 23). El peje que caiga, *cayó* (Álvarez Garzón, p. 86). *Nos fuimos* [= *nos vamos*, etc.] (Flórez, p. 376).

EL SALVADOR: Por fin ... vido brillar un objeto extraño. —*¡Yastuvo!* —gritó (Salarrué, *Cuentos*, p. 18). La masa endurecía paulatinamente. ... Julián la fué acolochando y levantándola ... hasta darle el toque final. ... —*¡Tuvo!* [= estuvo] (Ambrogi, p. 70).

GUATEMALA: —Buscar un mujer. Si el jefe dal permiso yo lo busque en mi pueble. ... —*¡Ya 'stuvo!* (Samayoa, in *CLC*, p. 70).

MEXICO: —Fíjate dónde hay buenos caballos. Que en diciendo «*nos fuimos*,» todo eso nos va a servir (p. 12). ... Me despedí con un garboso «¡nos vemos!» Al ganar el camino, con mis vaqueros y con el que del rancho me llevara, les dije apretando los talones a mi caballo: —*¡Nos* *fuimos*, muchachos! (López y Fuentes, *¡Mi general!* p. 31). Ese arroz *ya estuvo* [= ya está caliente] (Rubio, *Refranes*, p. 202). Cuando terminen ustedes, *ya sonó* la trompeta del juicio final; Al ratito *ya se compuso* [= ya se compondrá] el tiempo (C). *¡Nos vimos!* (C).

CUBA: —*Te fastidiaste* [= te voy a fastidiar]; —*Te moriste* [= te vas a morir], en son de amenaza (Padrón).

'HUBO DE' + INFINITIVE

Both in Spain and in America the preterite of *haber* + *de* + *inf.* often expresses no more than the preterite of the main verb, as in the older language; that is, the sense of obligation associated with *haber de* is practically lost, probably by analogy with *ha de* to express a mere future and *había de* to express a conditional: "Le persiguieron y *hubieron de capturarle* [= le capturaron]" (Romero García, p. 84); "Era inexacta la versión de que ... el Líder Máximo *hubo de resbalar* [= resbaló] al cruzar un río" (Taracena, p. 57).

For Argentina, however, Capdevila (pp. 109 ff.) mentions a peculiar usage of *haber de* which he deems a localism. He explains that in current Argentinian speech *hube de viajar a Europa* means 'I was on the point of going to Europe (but did not do so),' equivalent to standard *estuve a punto de viajar a Europa;* and, since this locution indicates an attempted act, it is followed by the adversative conjunction *pero*, introducing the reason why the act was not completed. This, of course, is just the reverse of the standard meaning as used by the best speakers and writers everywhere: namely, that the act was completed, often with an implication of necessity (*haber de* often = *tener que*). No doubt this usage is an extension into the preterite tense of such locutions as *he* (or *había*) *de hablar*, in the present (or imperfect) tense. Thus, *he de hablar* 'I am to speak'; *había de hablar* 'I was to speak'; *hube de hablar* 'I was to speak (at a definite time)' > 'I was on the point of speaking.' We find the same in dialectal Spain: (Galicia) "Por poco *hube de* caer al río" (Robles Dégano, *Gram.*, p. 112); (Asturias) "hubo caer" [= *casi se cae*] (Canellada); cf. Salvá, *Gram.*, p. 206).

HABÍA SIDO, HA SIDO

Interesting is the popular use of the pluperfect *había sido*, generally plus a noun or pronoun or adjective, in the sense of a present or imperfect indicative to express surprise or admiration: *¡había sido usted!* meaning *¡conque es* (or *era*) *usted!* 'so it's you!' This locution seems to represent a sort of ellipsis of the speaker's thought: *era usted* *y yo no lo sabía*, or *yo no creí que era usted*, or *que había de ser usted*. Since *ha de ser* expresses a future, so *había de ser* could express the feeling of a present, as it does in indirect discourse.

The expression *había sido usted* is commonly heard in Argentina. Tiscornia (*La lengua*, p. 264) implies that it is a typically or exclusively gaucho usage: "esta forma verbal que ... tiene expresión admirativa en el gauchesco corresponde a una afirmación española," "la frase del paisano," "al imperfecto simple *era* el paisano prefiere la perífrasis *había sido*," "la expresión gauchesca," etc. To be sure, it seems much more abundant in Argentina (both in literature and in speech) than in other regions. However, the examples given below will show that it is quite common, too, in Uruguay, Bolivia, Peru, Ecuador, and probably elsewhere, and with the following variations: in Ecuador (and in southern Colombia) the present perfect tense, *ha sido*, is used much more frequently than *había sido* with the same sense of the present; in Ecuador and Bolivia it is very frequent with other verbs, not only in popular speech but also in the speech of the cultured. The speakers feel that such a tense softens the statement and therefore prefer it to the more blunt present.

Perhaps *había sido* and *ha sido* (= *es*) arose by analogy with the future *ha de ser*. Since *ha de ser* in many regions takes the place of standard *será*, the present of *haber* (*ha*, etc.) has been felt to reflect the future. Consequently, to reflect the present, the next tenses removed one degree back in time, the imperfect *había* or the present perfect *ha sido*, have been vaguely associated with the present. Furthermore, softening a statement by using a tense removed one degree back may well be an extension of the common "imperfect of modesty" (*¿qué deseaba usted?* 'what did you wish?' etc.), in which the abruptness of the definite and closely clipped present tense is tempered psychologically and acoustically by dwelling more leisurely on the form itself: the longer form *deseaba* having the advantage of polite leisure over the blunt *desea*.

Another consideration: the present perfect expresses two aspects, (1) a past act and (2) the present extension of that past act. Now it is possible that one aspect be felt as more important than the other. The feeling of the present extension of the act becomes more dominant than the mere act itself. Then, after the dominant aspect (2) has submerged aspect (1) into insignificance, the present perfect tense as such becomes equivalent in feeling and to all practical purposes to a present: *ha sido* = *es*, *ha tenido* = *tiene*. Some such process must underlie the peculiar construction common in Ecuador (*ha sido* = *es*) and its sister-locution (*había sido* = *es* or *era*) common in Argentina, Bolivia, Peru, Ecuador, and sporadically elsewhere.

ARGENTINA: A su amigo cuando toma/se le despeja el sentido,/y el pobrecito *había sido*/como carne de paloma (*Martín Fierro*, p. 112). —¡Cha que *había sido* salame [= es tonto]! (Lynch, *De los campos*, p. 50). —¡Ay! Pero. ... ¡Vean quién *había sido* [= es]! ¡Qué bueno! ¿No? ¿Cómo le va, señor? —Ya lo ve, señora (Lynch, *Palo verde*, p. 35). —¿Conque usted *había sido* [= es] la madre del mayor González? —Sí, señor ... para servirle (*Fray Mocho*, p. 130). —A ver, enseñe las manos. —¿Y por qué se las vi a enseñar? Caprichudo *había sido* [= es]. —Dale no más el gusto. Te va a decir la suerte (Larreta, *El linyera*, p. 48); Con que *había sido* [= es] usté (p. 147). Dos paisanos se encuentran en Buenos Aires después de mucho tiempo de no verse. —Cha, digo. ¿Pues no *había sido* [= es] don Pedro? —Don Mariano. Tantos años que no nos vemos (*Fogón de las tradiciones*, p. 153). —Mañana, con su licencia, vendré a buscarlo y le traeré la plata. —*Había sido* redondo pa los negocios (Güiraldes, *Don Segundo*, p. 60); —¿Sos vos Pedro? —Barrales de apelativo. Yo mesmo soy. ... —Y es claro que vos no más *habías sido*. Con razón cuanto te vide las viruelas me dije: Ésa es cara con hocico (p. 106); Cuando malició que ella iba a salir del agua, abrió los ojos a lo lechuza porque no quería perder ni un pedacito. —*Había sido* como mosca pa'l tasajo—gritó Pedro (p. 125).

URUGUAY: —¿No quiere darme un poco de carne? Aunque sean las achuras. —¿Conque le gustan las achuras? *Había sido* [= es] delicado —dijo Ireno (Acevedo Díaz, *Cancha larga*, p. 342). —¡Pucha qui *habían sido* [= son] flojo los nacione! (Montiel, *Luz mala*, p. 155). —¡Sabe que es muy gracioso, amigaso, muy gracioso! ¡La pucha que *había sido* vivo usté! ... ¡Ja, ja, ja, que *había sido* bicho! (Amorím, *La carreta*, p. 40).

CHILE: —Miren qué yunta 'e novillos *ha tenido* [= tiene] este Benito (Acevedo Hernández, *Árbol viejo*, p. 36).

BOLIVIA: —Dicen que para ser comandante de batallón se necesita tener actos de machismo. —¿Machismo? ¿Cómo *había sido* [= es] eso? —¿Qué será, pues? Deben ser seguramente hazañas ... (Augusto Guzmán, p. 27). Hoy mismo tienes que desocupar la hacienda ... tu hijo *había sido* [= es] un mañudo. No saben en La Paz qué se ha hecho, porque se ha fugado ... a lo mejor robando (Hugo Blym, in *ACB*, p.

183). Miranda se levantó de su asiento exclamando: —¡Huá! *Había sido* [= es] ya tarde. ... Los gallos están cantando (Jaime Mendoza, *El lago*, p. 57). —¡Bravo!—aplauden. —Usté *había sido* [= es] un artista (Blym, *Puna*, p. 37). —¡Ah, qué cholita tan simpática *habías tenido* [= tienes], eh! (Díaz Villamil, *La Rosita*, p. 17); —¡Qué ricas humintas! —*¡Habían estado* [= están] como de sus manos! (*Plebe*, p. 31); ¡También *había habido* [= hay] mujeres verdaderas! (p. 174). —Esta carta no más *había habido* [= hay *or* había], señorita (Rodrigo, p. 53). —¡Ah! llokalla [=muchacho], *habías venido* [= has venido] (Unzueta, p. 31).

Peru: —¡Qué mal pensado *había sido* [= es] usted, don Juan Francisco! (López Albújar, *Matalaché*, p. 7); ¡que se me caigan los ojo horita mesmo si en mi vida e visto nada más mejó! ¡Jesú, la mesma Virgen! —¡Vaya, que todas ustedes *habían sido* [= son] igualmente aduladoras! (p. 46); —Y ya mía, te dotaré para que te cases con tu godo. Ya verás. La mulatilla ... cayó de rodillas y ... la decía, con sincero alborozo: —¡Ah, qué buena y generosa *había sido* [= es], niñita María Luz! (p. 58). —*Habías sido* [= eres] tan zorro y madrugador como tu padre Rufino (López Albújar, *Nuevos cuentos*, p. 110).

Ecuador: —*Nu' a sido* [= no es] mudo. ¿Veremos la cabeza? Uuu, con piojos, con sarnas (Icaza, *Cholos*, p. 53); —Grandote *ha estado* [= está]. Ahora que estoy solo quiero que le mandes a casa para que me sirva (p. 39). —Bastantes muebles *ha tenido* [= tiene]—dijo la Petrona. —Sí, hija, y eso que hemos empeñado algunos (García Muñoz, *Estampas*, p. 125). —Me muero, ya *ha sido* [= es] tarde—apuntó—ya han de ser las cuatro cuando ya viene su hijo, señora Rosita. Y ... se despidió y bajó a sus cuartos (Bustamante, p. 112). — ... Lo que m'icieron a mí ... los chumados [= embriagados] de un automóvil, eso es cosa. *Habían sido* [= eran] los hijos de unos señores de las haciendas de Machachi (Icaza, *En las calles*, p. 169); ¿Qué te parece? La cosa va arreglándose. El pobre Landeta *ha sido* [= es] leproso (p. 188); si esto ca *ha sido* [= es] páramo. Sí, pes ... estamos en las faldas del Pichincha—murmuró arrebujándose en el capote y en la toalla (p. 195); Luego la hembra ... examina la dentadura del soldado y exclama: —*Nu'a tenido* [= no tiene] ni un diente güeno (p. 269). Sacó su pistola y apuntó. Pero una risa clara ... la detuvo. —Brava *había sido* [= es] Ud. ¿no? —Como andamos cerca de los Aragundi (Gil Gilbert, *Nuestro pan*, p. 115). Vaya, me dije, *n'ha sido* [= no es] este sitio para dormir, y comencé a ver de dónde venía el viento pero no *había habido* [= había] huecos en la roca. ... Creyendo que era sueño mesmo, me despierto y resulta que *había sido* [= era] un indiecito conocido (Vásconez, p. 168). Los espectadores comentaban: —Piernas gordas *ha tenido* [= tiene] la Laura, ¿no? —¡Y blancotas! —Pero más mejores son las de la Mariana, ¡fíjense! (La Cuadra, *Los Sangurimas*, p. 138).

COLOMBIA (SOUTH): —Buena jugadora que *ha sido*—dijo Andrés. Buena suerte es lo que tengo—repuso Alegría (Álvarez Garzón, p. 131); —Tamién *ha sabido* hablar. ... Ambos pueden hablar (p. 148); qué horrible *ha sido* la vejez, y con mayor razón una vejez como la mía ... esto es insoportable (p. 254); Me acerqué, oí que me saludaban. *Había sido* [= era] una mujer, una india, pero era una mujer (p. 258).

PLUPERFECT INDICATIVE IN '-RA'

The *-ra* verb forms used as pluperfect indicatives are generally classified under the subjunctive heading, with some explanation like "the *-ra* subjunctive is sometimes used with the value of a pluperfect indicative." Thus Keniston (p. 441; *Syntax list*, p. 191), Alonso and Henríquez Ureña (II, § 199), and the comparatively few of our many local Spanish grammars that mention the *-ra* indicative at all. But this apparently still important form should receive more careful treatment. Why can it not be called by its proper name and be classified as such?[2] Everyone knows that the *-ra* form in question derives etymologically from the Latin pluperfect indicative, that from the beginning it was used as a pluperfect indicative, that in the fifteenth century it was felt also as a preterite or an imperfect (as in the ballads), that its new subjunctive function (beside the true *-se* subjunctive) superseded its indicative meaning, that its indicative use gradually declined until it was vigorously revived by the romanticists in the nineteenth century, and that it is still used to varying extents in parts of Spain and in most of Spanish America.[3] In Spain the *-ra* form (as a pluperfect, occasionally as a simple past) is limited chiefly to subordinate clauses (relative and adverbial) and is found most frequently in northern speakers and writers (Galicia, Asturias): *el libro que le diera* = *el libro que le había dado* (or *dió*). The use of *-ra* forms in main clauses is found in Galician and Asturian writers and is consid-

[2] The form in question is possibly still vaguely felt as an indicative in the apodosis of conditional sentences, where it may be replaced by the conditional tense or the indicative, but not correctly by the *-se* subjunctive (at least the *-se* form is here not universally accepted as correct though it is frequently used): *si tuviera dinero, lo compraría* or *comprara* or *compraba* (but not correctly *comprase*).

[3] Cf. Leavitt O. Wright, *The -ra verb form in Spain* (1932); also *Hispania*, XII, 259–78; XIV, 109–14; XXIX, 355–62; XXX, 484–95.

ered dialectal (Spaulding, §44, *b*): *jamás se le viera más alegre* = *jamás se le había visto* (or *se le vió*) *más alegre.*

Spanish preceptists frown upon the *-ra* indicative forms, especially in the preterite or imperfect meanings. Bello (§ 720) considered the *-ra* indicative an archaism "que debe evitarse, porque tiende a producir confusión. ..." The best writers, except in Galicia and Asturias, seemingly agree with Bello. Even poets, who generally indulge in archaic expressions, are prone to eschew this particular tense. Its excessive use is considered characteristic of neophytes whose style lacks elegance (Cortejón, p. 206).

The case is somewhat different in Spanish America. Keniston (*Syntax list*, p. 191) records the *-ra* form as found in "some" Spanish-American writers. This is at best a great understatement. It would be more accurate to say "in many" or even "most Spanish-American writers." To be sure, preceptists here too, not guided by local usage but by peninsular practice and precept, are likely to condemn the usage. Martín Aldao (p. 83) refers to it as "el empalagoso imperfecto de subjuntivo en *-ra* usado en lugar del pluscuamperfecto." Alonso and Henríquez Ureña (II, § 199) speak of it as surviving now "como afectación" and that "en general lo evitan los mejores escritores." This last statement may apply to peninsular usage, but surely not to American Spanish where some of the best stylists indulge in it, as will be seen in the examples that follow. The use of the *-ra* form with the value of a simple preterite is even more bitterly denounced in such examples as *desde que saliera* for *desde que salió, los aplausos que le prodigaran* for *los aplausos que le prodigaron.* The Mexican lexicographers, Santamaría and Domínguez (*Ensayos*, p. 154), remark: "A esta forma verbal le llama Robles Dégano caso errante o polícrono, porque desempeña el oficio de varios tiempos. Pero este uso es indebido, y, por tanto, las frases antes indicadas son repudiables."

In *El problema de la lengua en América* (p. 52) Amado Alonso seems more conciliatory toward the much-used *-ra* indicative in Argentina. He mentions it as particularly frequent there in newspaper writing, primarily for ornamental effect. He thinks he perceives a tendency in the local written language to fix the syntactical use and meaning of the *-ra* form: to refer to something well known to the reader. In the sentence "la noticia que este diario *diera* tiene confirmación," the verb *diera* is equivalent to "ya ha dado" or "como sabe el lector, ya ha dado." But, he cautiously adds, the *-ra* is used also to give information not already known to the reader. The vogue of the *-ra* indicative seems to be of relatively recent date. Older living writers, as is still the case even with younger writers, used the *-ra* indicative as a stylistic means of lending historical solemnity to the narration. But today it has become so generalized among most writers that it has lost much of its earlier archaic flavor.

The use of the *-ra* form is common not only in Spanish-American newspapers (Wright, *Hispania*, IX [1926], 288–93) but also in their best stylists, and not only as a pluperfect indicative but often as a preterite or imperfect indicative. It is found most frequently in relative clauses, not rarely in adverbial clauses, and occasionally in main clauses. However, it is not used in familiar conversation, a fact which seems to disprove close relationship with dialectal practice in northern Spain.

ARGENTINA: Un jinete, que *viera* [= vió] venir al Cura, quedóse reteniendo la tranquera automática (Larreta, *Zogoibi*, p. 12); Hacía más de tres años que doña Rosario *dejara* [= había dejado] aquella costumbre del saludo mañanero (p. 293). En su vida el pueblo *sintiera* [= había sentido] más profunda división espiritual (*ACH*, p. 38).

URUGUAY: Renovó la simpatía que lo *impulsara* a padrinarlo años antes (Acevedo Díaz, *Cancha larga*, p. 31); Ella *viera* al padrillo correrla, dominarla a mordiscos (p. 77); Él *se apeara* [= se apeó] confiado en que les daría la voz de «¡juera!» (p. 184); La nieta le cubrió el pecho con el poncho de su juventud, bajo el que *alentara* su corazón de varón recio (p. 375). Pancho Aguilar ... volvía de la capital, donde *hiciera* estudios (Amorím, *El paisano*, p. 7).

PARAGUAY: Desde que *se sentara* no había pronunciado una sola palabra (Casaccia, p. 140); el regodeo que ... *se prometiera* (p. 64).

CHILE: Lorenzo saboreaba la agradable bebida que le *ofertara* Adelaida (Azócar, p. 313). Allí sobre la mesita de noche *dejara* desde días atrás varios libros (Prado, *Un juez*, p. 44); El juez desea darse cuenta cabal del daño que usted *recibiera* [= ha recibido] (p. 76). La primavera que *comenzara* luminosa y casi ardiente, habíase tornado nebulosa y fría (Durand, *Mercedes*, p. 127). A las palabras duras que le *dirigiera*, contestó la joven con otras ásperas e incisivas (Lillo, p. 31); Está en el sitio y muy cerca del escollo junto al cual se *hundiera* la rubia cabeza del náufrago (p. 38). Esta manera de apreciar la vida sorprendió a Lucía; nunca *oyera* hablar así en su casa (Edwards Bello, *Criollos*, p. 63); Nunca *escuchara* hablar a su madre de manera tan rectilínea y precisa; nunca la *viera* interviniendo en sus asuntos íntimos con tanta pasión (p. 105); Nunca *fuera* a los toros y le alteraba la proximidad de ese espectáculo (p. 269). Nacimos años y años después de que él *perdiera* la vista (Ernesto Montenegro, p. 8). No *viera* antes ... aquella cerca de recortados álamos (Maluenda, *Los ciegos*, p. 124).

Bolivia: Tuvo ganas de besar a su mujer, cosa que *olvidara* hacerlo desde hacía la mar de años (Arguedas, *Vida criolla*, p. 212).

Peru: Más de una vez los *viera* preparar la mixtura de hojas con un poco de cal (García Calderón, in *ACP*, p. 91). Gaviria excusó gratitudes y dijo que *hiciera* [= había hecho] su deber. ... El mozo contó entonces que *estuviera* embarcado (Diez-Canseco, *Estampas*, p. 51). Todavía hay eco del ruido que *metiera* usted en sus mocedades con eso de los pesos (López Albújar, *Matalaché*, p. 4); En la carta que ésta le *escribiera* y le *entregara* María Luz ... él no quería entenderlo así (p. 22).

Colombia: Impuso fuertes contribuciones y recogió bastante dinero, que, según la voz pública, *destinara* [= destinó] en gran parte para su provecho, etc. (Cuervo, § 319). *Asistiera* [= asistió] en la mañana al entierro de un amigo (Efe Gómez, p. 10); *Subiera* [= subió] esa tarde a esperar la salida de sus amigos (p. 80).

Venezuela: Era extraño; precisamente esa misma semana *tuviera* un altercado con el general Estranón (Pocaterra, p. 8).

Ecuador: Cuando *llegara* [= llegó] el Presidente ... el doctor Sandoval ... fué a encontrarlo (Gil Gilbert, *Nuestro pan*, p. 255); Una mañana se *sorprendiera* [= sorprendió] por el saludo frío de Eusebio. ... *Viniera* él vestido con aire de ausencia y ... le *dijera*. ... Se *quedara* jugueteando con el cinturón (p. 268).

Costa Rica: Quisiera ... sacudir el aire, como nunca lo *hiciera* hasta ahora (Fabián Dobles, p. 52); Moncho está luego contándole cómo le *fuera* hace unas horas en la Candelaria, p. 65).

Nicaragua: Alcanzó a oír el toque de ángelus que le *llegara* [= llegaba] como en un eco, y se santiguó. ... Al internarse en el camino penumbroso, oyó un débil llanto de niño, a modo de maullido, que *saliera* [= salía] del enmontado terreno que a su siniestra mano *quedara* [= quedaba] (Toruño, p. 7); preparó agua de azúcar en uno de tantos frascos que *llevara* [= llevaba] en su provisión de fugitivo (p. 8).

El Salvador: Diez veces *desapareciera* [= desapareció] del convento durante muchas horas, sin que nadie pudiera decir a dónde iba (Salarrué, *El Cristo negro*, p. 16).

GUATEMALA: ¡Como si él pudiese trabajar ahora, viejo y enfermo, cuando jamás *trabajara* [= había trabajado *or* trabajó] en sus días de mocedad robusta! (Wyld Ospina, in *ACH*, p. 136). Marchó aquella tarde el viejo José María a la ciudad. *Pensara* [= había pensado] largo en ello (Wyld Ospina, *Nahuyacas*, p. 95).

MEXICO: Por la tarde me acosté a dormir en la cama que *ocupara* [= ocupaba] el patrón durante sus visitas al rancho (López y Fuentes, *¡Mi general!* p. 41); Tan sólo una de las alhajas que yo le *comprara* [= había comprado] ... bastaría para mis gastos más urgentes. La misma casa, que yo le *regalara* [= había regalado], bien podía ser hipotecada (p. 215).

CUBA: Y encendí el tabaco que me *obsequiara* (*CC*, p. 37).

Because of the frequency with which *-ra* and *-se* subjunctives may correctly alternate, some writers are led to substitute the *-se* form in the pluperfect indicative function of the *-ra* form, as also in Spain.

ARGENTINA: Se encontró con la nueva casa, que *hiciese* [= había hecho] construir su amoroso padre (Heredia, p. 110).

CHILE: La sepultó donde mismo la *encontrase* [= había encontrado] (Fernando Alegría, *Leyenda*, p. 11).

MEXICO: Ni rastros del muchacho paliducho y enclenque que, cinco años antes, *hubiese* [= había] partido rumbo al Canadá (Azuela, *Avanzada*, p. 13). Vió que la mujer, a quien unos momentos antes *dejase* dormida allí, había desaparecido (Rubín, p. 21).

PRESENT SUBJUNCTIVE, HORTATORY

In standard Spanish the present indicative in the first person is used in asking for orders or directions: *¿entramos?* 'shall we go in?' The first person plural of the present subjunctive serves as an imperative: *entremos* 'let's go in.' A combination of these two meanings we find in an interesting locution used in some regions of America, especially in Chile and Argentina: *¿entremos?* This is the subjunctive as imperative used interrogatively, thus combining the meanings 'let's go in' and 'shall we go in?' The fundamental feeling is probably that of the imperative, softened by its interrogative intonation. But that a reply is often expected is clear from the examples given below. The same thing may occur in other forms: *¿déme un cinco?* 'give me a nickel?'

Questions can thus function as wishes in other languages: *Send me a postcard?* softens the command *do send me a postcard* by combining it with the question *will you send me a postcard?*; German *gehst weg?* softens *geh weg!*

A similar interrogative intonation is given to the command form *mande*, equivalent to *¿qué manda usted?*, in asking for a repetition of what one has not heard or understood in conversation ('I beg your pardon?' etc.); this usage is current notably in Mexico, Central America, southern Chile (Román, III, 409), northwestern Argentina (Solá, p. 185), and the Antilles, as well as in Spain.

ARGENTINA: Otro respondió: —*¿Entremos?* ... La contestación no se hizo esperar como si todos hubieran estado pensando exactamente lo mismo (Marengo, p. 103). —*¿Corramos?* —Ya está ... *¿Entremos?* —*Entremos* (C). ¿Lo *matemos?* (Morínigo).

URUGUAY: *¿Formemos* una patria ... ? ¿Sí ... ? No tenemos patria (Horacio Quiroga, IV, 120).

CHILE: —*¿Comamos?*—dijo ... ambos se dirigieron hacia el comedor (Prado, *Un juez*, p. 11); *¿Entremos?*—insinuó Mozarena, consultando a su amigo (p. 111); —*¿Volvamos?* —¡Para qué!—replicó Solaguren (p. 237). *¿Hagamos* un convenio? (Moock, *Cuando venga el amor*, p. 21). —*¿Bajemos* a almorzar?—dijo Mercedes amablemente, deteniéndose en el umbral de su vecina (D'Halmar, *Lucero*, p. 144). —*¿Hagamos* collera, niños? —¡No! Pa los agentes no desenvaino yo mi cuchillo (Mery, I, 2). —*¿Saquémosle* la miel? —¡Chis! ¿Pero dónde se la vamos a encontrar? (Durand, *Mi amigo*, p. 92); —*¿Galopemos* un poco? —Bueno, Pancho (Manuel Rojas, *Travesía*, p. 7). Mateo lo invita con entusiasmo de niño. —*¿Sigámosla?* El pequeño no oye más (Latorre, *Zurzulita*, p. 73).

BOLIVIA: —¿Lo *matemos?* —Matálo vos (Céspedes, p. 136).

COSTA RICA: —*¿Apostemos* a que aquí no entra Ud? (Lyra, p. 59). —Ma, *¿déme* un cinco? —Y sus ojillos se unieron, suplicantes, con los de Ninfa. —¿Pa qué lo querés?—le respondió ella (F. Dobles, p. 194).

CUBA: —Tráeme la montura del caballo. —*¿Mande?* (Padrón).

VÁMOSNOS, ETC.

As everyone knows, the final *-s* of the first person plural is lost by dissimilation before enclitic *nos: vamos + nos > vámonos*. This is the standard practice today. In the older language there are instances of the full form (Keniston, p. 367). Thus we find: —*Tornémosnos* (*Primera crónica general*, chap. 1084); *contentémosnos* (*Celestina*, XII). Today in popular speech and even among cultured persons it is not rare to hear *sentémosnos*, and the like. It is evident that this cacophonous form is much more common in Spanish America than in Spain. It appears especially widespread in regions where final *-s* is exceedingly weak, aspirated, or lost, since it is thought that the lost *-s* is merely a faulty pronunciation. In Chile the case is a little more complicated, since *los* is current in popular and rustic speech for *nos*, and before *los* the *-s* is normally retained. This is true also of Costa Rica and elsewhere in Central America. Again the *-s* may be lost where standard speech retain it: *escribámole*, etc.

ARGENTINA: *Vamosnós*, amigo Cruz (*Martín Fierro*, p. 126). *¡Dejemosnós* de pavadas! (*Fray Mocho*, p. 21); *Dejémosnos* de roñas (p. 174). *¡Vamosnós* pa "la Estancia"! (Lynch, *Romance*, p. 18). —Ché Jorge, *vámosnos*—dijo la de ojos inquietos (Petit de Murat, p. 17).

URUGUAY: ¡Hija, *vámosnos!* (Sánchez, *M'hijo el dotor*, II, 7); *Sentémosnos* (III, 4).

CHILE: —Güeno; *dejémoslos* [= dejémonos] de pensar en leseras (Acevedo Hernández, *Por el atajo*, p. 12); —Vaya, *dejémosnos* de tonterías (p. 40). —*Preparémosnos* mejor (Luis Meléndez, p. 34). —*Limitémosnos* a analizar (Muñoz, p. 14).

BOLIVIA: —*Acerquémosnos* para estar seguros (Pereyra, p. 118).

COLOMBIA: *Quedémosnos; unámosnos* (Obando, p. 129). *Dejémolo, cojámolo* (Flórez, p. 378). *Tumbémolo* (Posada, p. 40); *saquémola* (p. 43).

VENEZUELA: *Perdonémosnos* (Blanco F., p. 118); *dediquémosnos* (p. 204).

PANAMA: —Pues, *volvámosnos* ... contestaron los cargadores (Nacho Valdés, *Cuentos*, p. 36).

COSTA RICA: *Empujémoles* (Fallas, p. 175).

VAMOS, VAYAMOS

Among present subjunctive forms that are misused more frequently in Spanish America than in Spain is that of the verb *ir: vamos* and *vayamos* and occasionally other persons of this tense. The form *vamos* derives from Latin *vadamus*, while *vayamos* stems from Vulgar Latin **vadeamus*. Both are, then, subjunctive in origin, and in the older language both could be used as such, particularly in the imperative sense of 'let us go.' Today standard speech generally limits the meaning of 'let's go' to *vamos*, reserving *vayamos* for other uses of the subjunctive. However, the older usage, involving confusion of the forms, has survived in some Spanish-American regions, as will be seen in the following examples, *vayamos* being occasionally used for 'let us go' in spite of Bello's admonition that "En el optativo no se dice nunca *vayamos*, sino *vamos* (Bello-Cuervo, § 582). Examples are also found in regional Spain: "Mas, por de pronto, *vayámonos* con calma" (Pereda, *Obras*, VI, 442), as well as occasionally in continental literary usage (Spaulding, § 71, *e*).

ARGENTINA: Apóyate en mí para que *vamos* [= vayamos] hacia nuestra noche (Güiraldes, *Xaimaca*, p. 149). —Saltemos el alambrado y *vayamos* a verlo (Boj, p. 202). (NORTHWEST): —Pero no son pa que *vas* a pastoriar (César Carrizo, p. 112).

CHILE: ¿Quiere que *vamos* [= vayamos] hasta la oficina, señor? (Durand, *Mercedes*, p. 23). —Bueno, apúrate para que *vamos* (Maluenda, *Escenas*, p. 5). —¿Quiere que nos *vamos* pal bajo? (Acevedo Hernández, *Árbol viejo*, p. 14). —¿Quiere que *vamos*, misiá Juanita? (D'Halmar, *Lucero*, p. 88); —¿Está lista para que *vamos* a ver a la matrona? (p. 174).

BOLIVIA: Bien, *vayamos* por ahí (Céspedes, p. 47). Y *vayamos* al hígado (Jaime Mendoza, *Memorias*, p. 43).

COLOMBIA: A ver si quiere que *vamos* con los indios (Uribe Piedrahita, in *Hispanoamericanos*, p. 169). No es posible que nos *vamos* a marchar así (Arango Villegas, p. 193). No, no es para que nos *vamos* de esta tienda (Osorio Lizarazo, *La cosecha*, p. 10); ¿Quieres que *vamos* por el cafetal? (p. 120).

HONDURAS: —Tengo hambre; *vayamos* a comer (Martínez Galindo, p. 14).

MEXICO: —Bien, bien ... *vayamos* a prosternarnos ante César (Ferretis, *Quijote*, p. 81).

QUERRAMOS, QUERRÁS

In the older language the future indicative was not uncommon (subjunctive usual now) in subordinate clauses referring to an indefinite future time: "miedo han que y *verná* (*Cid*, vs. 2987), quando los gallos *cantarán* (*Cid*, vs. 316), "pide lo que *querrás*" (*Celestina*, VI, 80), "comenzá por do *querréis* (Lope de Rueda, *Comedia Eufemia*, I), "Se hará como *querrás*" (Torres Naharro, *Comedia Himenea*, II), "responderé como mejor supiere a todo lo que esta tarde me *querréis* preguntar" (Valdés, p. 2). While the usage was especially common in Aragonese texts, it was not infrequent in others. It may have influenced a peculiar form current in much of Spanish America: *querramos, querráis* (or *querrás*, the *voseo* form, and popular *quedrás*), etc., used in place of the correct subjunctive *queramos* and *queráis*.

The double *-r* forms instead of the standard single *-r* forms may be explained as due to the influence of the future *querremos* and *querréis*. The fact that the future indicative in some constructions yielded to the subjunctive helped to bring about the present anomalous forms, which have survived only in this one verb. Employed even by the cultured, they can be found in outstanding authors, especially in the phrase *querramos o no querramos* (for *queramos o no queramos*).

The Salvadorian grammarian, Salazar García (p. 230), in correcting the form *queráis tú o no* indicates that this should be properly singular and gives "*querrás* tú o no" (!). The Argentine lexicographer, Segovia (p. 610), includes *queramos* in his list of *barbarismos* and adds "Dígase *querramos*" (!) Such statements attest the frequency of *-rr* (cf. also *BDH*, IV, 254, n. 4). The popular forms like *quedría* are evidently so common in the colloquial speech of some regions that local grammars admonish: "El pospretérito es *querría* y no *quedría*," etc. (Cascante, p. 263; cf. also **BDH, II, 234**).

ARGENTINA: —Cuando *querrah* 'ermano (Güiraldes, *Don Segundo*, p. 78).

URUGUAY: —¿*Quedrás* creer? Ni un beso le pude dar (Acevedo Díaz, *Cancha larga*, p. 121).

PERU: —Sobre todo, de la libertad de comerciar con quien *querramos* (López Albújar, *Matalaché*, p. 210).

COSTA RICA: —Como *quedrás*, Pelegrino; si biene siendo la mesma (Agüero, p. 54). ¡Salí por lo que más *querrás!* (Lyra, p. 62).

NICARAGUA: Onque *querrás*, no podrás llegar a la hacienda en toda la noche (Robleto, p. 68).

EL SALVADOR: Y tei [= te he] de topar, aunque no *querrás* (Salarrué, *Cuentos*, p. 13). —Que sea cuando vos *querrás*, niño,—repuso el padre (Torres Arjona, p. 32).

GUATEMALA: Todas las supersticiones absurdas, que *querramos o no*, se nos pegan como mariscos al casco de los buques (Santa Cruz, p. 123). Tanto en la una como en la otra lengua [Spanish and Portuguese], caso que no las *querramos* tener por una misma en su origen, tuvo este artículo [lo] una verdadera declinación parecida a la latina (*Publicaciones de la Academia guatemalteca*, IV, 175).

MEXICO: Cuando morimos les dejamos nuestros bienes a los hombres, *querramos o no querramos* (Lizardi, p. 105).

CUBA: Aquí también es corriente en el habla popular el uso de *querramos* por *queramos* (Padrón).

PRESENT SUBJUNCTIVE FOR INDICATIVE: 'PUEDA (SER) QUE'

The present subjunctive *pueda* is often colloquially used in the locution *pueda (ser) que* 'it may be, perhaps,' etc., in place of the standard and cultured *puede*. It is so much commoner in Spanish America than in Spain that it has often been considered an Americanism. This belief, however, is erroneous, for the expression is current, too, in Spain in the forms *pueda (ser) que, puá (ser) que, ¡pueda!* and *¡puá!*:[4] "—Será la cría, padre ... *¡Puá que,* hijo: no te diré yo que no lo sea" (Pereda, *Obras,* VIII, 281); "*Puá ser* que esté yo denquivocao" (Lemus, p. 261 [Murcia]). However, the popular *pueda* is generally avoided in peninsular literature, whereas examples of it abound in Spanish-American literature. It is considered of lower social status in Spain than in America, where it can be heard in the familiar speech of cultured persons. The expression *¡Bien pueda!* 'go right ahead' is used in some regions in answer to a request for permission to do a thing.

Pueda ser que has another, more interesting, use: to express a wish, with the meaning of *ojalá*. This meaning is easily developed from that of 'perhaps,' as has happened with many other similar locutions (discussed on p. 264); 'perhaps,' 〉 'it may be that' 〉 'I hope that,' etc. The transition was especially easy when *puede* became *pueda,* which may be felt as 'may it be that.' However, that transition has apparently not occurred in all Spanish-speaking territory. While exceedingly common in Chile, Colombia, Panama, parts of Ecuador, and probably elsewhere, its meaning is more purely one of doubt (= 'perhaps') in Spain, Argentina, Bolivia, Venezuela, Mexico, and elsewhere (judging from literary examples and from the personal reactions of many natives consulted from these countries). From a given example it is often impossible to decide which meaning predominates. Only the feeling of the speaker can be decisive, and even that frequently lacks clarity. For this reason examples with both meanings (doubt and desire) are given below.

ARGENTINA: *Pueda que* [desire?] Dios la perdone (Lussich, *Los tres gauchos orientales,* II, 228); *Pueda ser que* [?] ansina sea; *pueda ser que* [?] el muy sotreta/se olvide hasta de comer (*P. Collazo,* vs. 19, *ap.* Tiscornia, *La lengua,* p. 263).

URUGUAY: —Y vea, don juez: *pueda ser que* [doubt] yo al tirarle a

[4] The development of *puá* from *pudiera,* as Pietsch suggests (*Mod. Lang. Notes,* XXVI [1911], 98: *pudiera* 〉 *pudiá* 〉 **puiá* 〉 *puá*), is not impossible. In fact, *pudiera* is used in this sense: "¿Sería posible? *Pudiera*" (Arguedas, *Vida criolla,* p. 109); "—*Pudiera* que no todos" (p. 121); —¿Crees? —¡Psh! *Pudiera*" (p. 205).

un carancho le haiga pegao al pobre mozo, pero lo que es aldrede, ¡eso sí que no! (Viana, *Abrojos*, p. 142). Viá dir rejuntando güevos guachos y *pueda ser que* [?] enllene tuito el poncho con el rosario (Viana, *Tardes*, p. 33); *Pueda ser que* llueva (p. 39).

CHILE: —Interróguelo, *¡pueda ser que* [desire] tenga más suerte que nosotros! (Juan Modesto Castro, p. 104); —Haga Ud. una tentativa, *pueda ser que* [desire] tenga mejor suerte (p. 270); —Voy a ver, *pueda ser que* [desire] encuentre algo (p. 364). *¡Pueda ser que* [desire] se acabe la guerra pronto! (C.) —¿Usté quiere que los hombres se levanten pa que los lleven presos y los pongan a la barra? ¡Si a usté no le hace falta mi marío, a mí me hace falta y a sus hijos! —*Pueda ser que* [doubt, 'perhaps'] usted tenga razón (Acevedo Hernández, *La canción rota*, p. 62). —Yo quiero ver una mujer fea en este pueblo; *pueda ser* [desire] (Sepúlveda, *Camarada*, p. 6).

PERU: *Pueda ser que* [doubt] en otras partes no sea así (Llokje Runa, *Sara cosecho*, p. 28).

ECUADOR: —¡Ah, viejo Vega, que nos conocemos! ... —*Pueda ser* [doubt: 'perhaps'], Capitán (Gil Gilbert, *Nuestro pan*, p. 84).

COLOMBIA (ANTIOQUIA): *Pueda ser que* [desire] le haiga ido go le vaya bien en la cuenta (Carrasquilla, *Hace tiempos*, I, 208); *Pueda ser que* [desire] te haya asomado el juicio (II, 251); Habrá que casarte pronto; *Pueda ser que* [desire] yo alcance a ver los tataranietos (II, 281); *Pueda ser que* [desire] aquellos muchachitos lo alcancen. —Mediante Dios, Ignacita. ... Ahí está rezando Ignacio porque lo alcancen (III, 193–94). —Pero en verdá la creciente estuvo blanda. *Pueda ser que* [desire] no vengan las duras, porque ésas sí nos hacen salir en estampida (Buitrago, p. 52; also p. 118). Also Bogotá (Flórez, p. 378). *¡Bien puedan* ['go right ahead'], muchachos! (Jaramillo, p. 48).

VENEZUELA: *Pueda ser que* [doubt] presente examen (Rosenblat).

PANAMA: *¡Pueda ser que* [desire] llueva! (C). —*Pueda ser que* [desire] haya algo para que vean ustedes la puntería que tengo (Cajar, p. 90).

COSTA RICA: —*Pueda ser que* [doubt] nada ... y *pueda ser que* mucho (Fallas, p. 237).

EL SALVADOR: *Pueda ser* ['perhaps'] que una sobada ... (Salarrué, *Cuentos*, p. 89).

MEXICO: Si él mi abandonara/por no ser yo güena/... *pueda ser* ['perhaps'] qu'estuviera conforme (Rivas Larrauri, p. 109). *Pueda ser que* [desire] dejemos el pueblo por obscuro, lodoso, sucio (Núñez Guzmán, p. 17).

PRESENT SUBJUNCTIVE FOR IMPERFECT

In a few regions of Spanish America we find a present subjunctive often used in a subordinate clause where an imperfect subjunctive should be employed according to the rule of sequence of tenses. According to this rule, a present subjunctive may be used following a past tense when the concept of the subordinate clause continues to have force in the present: "le dije que lo *haga* mañana." This was true also in the older language. For sixteenth-century prose Keniston (p. 456) notes the use of a present subjunctive in subordinate clauses depending upon a present participle, in which the "effect of the original past verb is forgotten." Such usage we still find, particularly in local speech and familiar writing (see examples below from Icaza, *Cholos*).

Local practice in much of Spanish America goes beyond the few allowed exceptions to the general rule of sequence of tenses: that present tenses be followed by present (or perfect) subjunctive and that past tenses be followed by past (or pluperfect) subjunctives. Such infractions are naturally commoner in speech than in writing and may be heard in the conversation of cultured persons. The process has here a parallel in spoken French, where all the forms of the past subjunctive have been lost. Even a future subjunctive may be found for a past (see Venezuela below).

ARGENTINA: Fuí a verla para que me *preste* un libro (C).

CHILE: Lo auscultaron uno tras otro, y mientras ellos discutían, el enfermo seguía hablando sin que ninguno le *escuche* [= escuchara] ni lo *tome* [= tomara] en cuenta (Juan Modesto Castro, p. 366).

BOLIVIA: Era preciso que *sea* [= fuera] un hombre de porvenir ... pero era preciso que *corra* [= corriera] tiempo para el ingreso de Arturo al cuartel. ... Arturo despojóse de ella [la capa]; pero supo sobre qué echarla, sin que se le *descubra* la treta (Abel Alarcón, in *Hispanoamericanos*, p. 123). —Habría que ir a ver lo que rondan los cuervos allá abajo: pudiera que *sea* él (Arguedas, *Raza*, p. 59).

ECUADOR: Sin que el jinete le *obligue* [= obligara], la mula paró frente a la tienda «El Descanso». ... Con el cólico cro que'está—informó la mujer *alzando* la bujía para que el patrón *vea* mejor y no *vaya* a tropezarse (Icaza, *Cholos*, p. 28); Empezó a guardar encierro por las noches *buscando* la tranquilidad que *pueda* dar contestación (p. 35); Hizo una pausa *dando* tiempo al muchacho para que *formule* la queja ahogada en lágrimas y en hipos (p. 41); Le gustaba que le *manden* a ver la chicha y los picantes (p. 53); Peñafiel ordenaba le *preparen* el caballo a toda prisa y huía al galope hacia la capital (p. 54); Mas en aquella ocasión no había trazas de que los insultos *lleguen* (p. 57). Cerca de las diez, sin que nadie le *llame*, ... llegó el ciego ... se sentó en un rincón, ... (Icaza, *En las calles*, p. 73). Los chicos querían que les *haga* conocer el Panecillo (García Muñoz, *Estampas*, p. 24); Por no entablar una pelea me aguanté que me *diga* ratero (p. 66); Esperé que *sean* las siete de la noche y, a pie, emprendí el viaje hasta Quito (p. 90); Los cargadores ... tiraban de los muebles sin importarles que se *rompan*. ... En la cocina, la Patrona, para que el «guagua» no *llore*, le había hecho sentar sobre un retrato de mi suegra (p. 126); las voces de mis «guaguas» que deseaban que *mande* a comprar pan, llenaron mi cabeza (p. 222).

VENEZUELA: —Yo sí ... dijo, bajando la cabeza como para atender a la limpieza del sombrero que tenía en las manos y del cual sacudía el polvo que realmente *hubiere* y el que no existía (Gallegos, *Pobre negro*, p. 47); Deseaba terminar solo ... sin despedidas definitivas que le *frustraren* la ilusión (p. 379).

IMPERFECT SUBJUNCTIVE

According to the Keniston count (*Syntax list*, p. 174), the *-ra* form of the imperfect subjunctive is used about twice as often in conditional sentences as the *-se* form (written evidence). The ratio is quite different for American Spanish. It has been variously estimated. Wright (*Hispania*, IX, 170–73) has shown that in Spanish-American newspaper writing, the *-ra* form appears about six times as often as the *-se* form. We know that in most Spanish-American countries *-ra* has practically ousted *-se* in the spoken language. Many years ago, Cuervo noted the rarity of *-se* in Spanish-American speech (Bello-Cuervo, p. 94), as opposed to its supremacy in Spain. Since then the *-se* form has apparently been losing ground in Spain: Gili y Gaya (§ 137) believes that in Spain *-se* still predominates in ordinary conversation, but that *-ra* is used considerably by the cultured and in the written language, though strict boundaries cannot be fixed. On the other hand, *-se* has become all but lost in most Spanish-American speech. For Chile, for instance, Lenz (*Oración*, § 289) reports that the people use *-ra* exclusively save in some of the old southern provinces where *-se* is also known; cultured persons in Central Chile prefer *-ra* and many use it exclusively; some writers use *-se* frequently because "being rarer, it is believed more elegant," which is in accordance with the universal principle that, of two similar forms, the one in most common use is likely to be avoided in cultivated and literary style. For Argentina, Tiscornia (*La lengua*, § 123) counted in *Martín Fierro:* 76 forms in *-ra* as against 9 in *-se*; in other gaucho texts, a total of 353 in *-ra* as against 131 in *-se*. He notes a growing predilection, from the middle of the nineteenth century, for forms in *-ra;* and his personal observation indicates that the *-ra* form is practically the only one used in the familiar and popular speech of Argentinians. For Costa Rica, Gagini (p. 96) remarks: "son perfectamente desconocidas las formas en *-se*." For Mexico, González Moreno (p. 180) asserts that the subjunctive in *-se* "apenas si se usa en la conversación familiar."

To be sure, academic precept still prevents some authors from transferring correct local usage to the written page. The last twenty years of literary emancipation from European models has also brought a certain emancipation of linguistic forms, not the least of which is the preference of *-ra* over *-se* subjunctives. The *-se* form may eventually disappear completely.

In some regions, as in Bolivia, the *-ra* subjunctive seems to be preferred in cases where standardly the conditional tense is general. Likewise in Bolivia, as well as in some other areas, the *-ra* subjunctive often supplants the more usual present indicative in phrases asking for orders: standard *¿qué hago?* 'what shall I do?' etc.

BOLIVIA: —¿Qué *hiciera?* [= ¿qué hago?]. —Botálo, como el perro (Díaz Villamil, *La Rosita*, p. 82); —¿De cómo le *dijera* [= digo] ahora al Protasio? ... porque si ahora no aprovecho (*Cuando vuelva*, p. 26); —¿Qué *hiciéramos?* [= ¿qué hacemos?] (p. 56); —Joseso, ¿qué *hiciera?* (*Plebe*, p. 51). ¿Adónde *fuéramos* [= vamos] esta noche? (C).

COSTA RICA: —¿Qué más le *pusiéramos* [= ponemos]? decía Secundino, dictando su misiva (Fallas, p. 273).

IMPERFECT SUBJUNCTIVE IN WISHES

Quite common is the use of the imperfect subjunctive in *-ra* to express a wish, as also in Spain (but more particularly in the older language). In some regions, notably in Central America, such a use of the verb *ver* (*viera*) has become so generalized that its real force has been lost (cf. *acabáramos* and its exclamatory value) and it serves merely to round out a phrase, with some such vague adverbial or interjectional connotation as 'unfortunately' or 'strange to say' or 'indeed' or 'you won't believe it, but,' etc. In daily speech one hears snatches of conversation like: " —¿Van al cine? —*Viera* que no sé ... ¿Cuál es el mejor hotel de aquí? —*Viera* que no sé ... —¿Podría usted ir en barco? —*Viera* que no," etc.

In the older language we find many examples like: "la *viérades*, ¡o hermosas Nimphas! fingir una risa tan dissimulada" (Montemayor, *Diana*, II); and as an imperative to soften a direct command: "*Dexássedesvos*, Cid, de aquesta razón" (*Cid*, vs. 3293; cf. Menéndez Pidal, *Cantar*, Vol. I, § 156, 2). Dialectal today: "lo *hubieses hecho*, lo *cantaseis* mejor" (Zamora Vicente, p. 43 [Mérida]).

In standard usage some introductory word (*si*, *que*, *ojalá*, etc.) would normally accompany the forms in the following examples.

ARGENTINA: —¿Exagerado? ¡*Hubieras visto* a tres loteros que yo llevé! (Laferrère, *Locos de verano*, p. 49). —¡*Vieran* los sermones! ... Era cosa de perecer de risa (Payró, p. 29); ¡Le *vieran* los ojos al fraile! Parecía que se quería tragar la plata (p. 31).

URUGUAY: —*Vieras* qué alegrón cuando recibimos el anuncio de tu venida (Sánchez, *M'hijo el dotor*, III, 4).

PARAGUAY: ¡*Vieras* cuánto hemos sufrido! (Morínigo).

CHILE: Allí tenemos nuestras casas. ¡Las *viera!* son pequeñas (Prado, *Alsino*, p. 91). *Viera* cómo brillan las arenitas (C). ¡Los *hubiera oído* Vd. lo enojados que estaban! (Juan Modesto Castro, p. 130). —*Supiera* la alegría con que me muestra sus cartas (Durand, *Mercedes*, p. 169). ¡Me *tragara* la tierra si nues cierto! (Juan del Campo, p. 40). —*Estuviera* aquí José Luis. —¡Me *condenara!*[5] (Acevedo Hernández, *Por el atajo*, p. 24).

BOLIVIA: —*Vieras* tú las pruebas que hizo (Abel Alarcón, in *Hispanoamericanos*, p. 130).

ECUADOR: Estoy en pelotas, *viera*, mama (La Cuadra, in *ACH*, p. 265). El cerrito tiene la forma de una cabeza de gato, *vieran* (La Cuadra, *Guásinton*, p. 98).

COSTA RICA: —Papacito, dígale a esa señora que se venga a vivir en nuestra casa; *viera* qué buena es (Noguera, p. 138).

NICARAGUA: —*Viera* usted lo que me ha costado convencerlo (Chamorro, *Entre dos filos*, p. 204). —*Vieras*—le dijo—que no han podido hacer las instalaciones (Toruño, p. 201). —*Viera* que el hombre que anda en campaña sin mujer, ni el café negro lo puede tomar caliente (Orozco, p. 37).

HONDURAS: —*Vieras* cuánto me preocupo por tu hermano (Mejía

[5] The apocopated form of *¡me condenara!* or *¡me condeno!* is *¡mecón!* used in Chilean popular speech as an oath (see p. 418).

Nieto, *El solterón*, p. 25). —*Viera* usted, Piíto, cuántas cosas buenas por aquí (Martínez Galindo, p. 99).

GUATEMALA: —*Viera:* un chivito cruzado mero chulo (Quintana, p. 19). —*Vieras* que te riagradezco (Bonilla, p. 46).

MEXICO: —*Viera*, compañero, qué mal me estoy sintiendo (Anda, *Los bragados*, p. 83). Una cuchara chica tenía que tomarme en cada vez. Pero *viera* usté qué pronto me alivié (García Roel, p. 50). ¿Es cierto que ya va haciéndose el trabajo? —*Viera* que sí—dijo (p. 73). ¡Ah, *pudiéramos* mandar a Juanito al colegio, el año que viene!—dijo suspirando Elena (Azuela, *Los caciques*, p. 8). —¡Te *callaras!* (C).

FUTURE SUBJUNCTIVE

The use of the future subjunctive is so rare in Spain today that we may say it has practically disappeared (Gili y Gaya, § 140), though grammarians continue to mention it because of its frequency in Golden Age authors and up to the early nineteenth century and its lingering use in legal documents, ecclesiastical writings, and a few stereotyped phrases ("sea lo que *fuere*," "venga lo que *viniere*," etc.). Elsewhere in writing and in speech it has now yielded almost completely to other tenses. Nevertheless, in Spanish America the future subjunctive has survived in a few regions. For Santo Domingo, Henríquez Ureña reports its common use by the cultured, especially in writing (*BDH*, IV, 326, n. 1; V, 49), as in highland Ecuador and elsewhere (*BDH*, II, 216). The following examples show its retention in the written language, if not in speech:

ARGENTINA: —Yo le dejaré nuestra dirección para lo que *fuere* (Filloy, p. 248); sea lo que *fuere* (p. 520).

URUGUAY: Si ello le *resultare* a Vd. violento, yo estoy dispuesto a callar (Bellán, p. 101); Y si no lo *consiguiere*, ¡ya verás! (p. 127).

CHILE: No aparecía nada, si no *hubiere* la misma imagen ... mejorada a su manera (Luis Meléndez, p. 65); lo que *fuere* (p. 169).

BOLIVIA: Lo recibe el criollo cordialmente y se ratifica una vez más en su propósito de que las cuentas *estuvieren* listas para la transacción (Blym, p. 17); —Ven mañana por la noche y te indicaré lo que *hubiere* resuelto (p. 85).

PERU: Como vuelva con la gracia de ir donde el presidente u otro sujeto cualquiera, ya sea a título de religión o de lo que *fuere* ... (Corrales, p. 124).

ECUADOR: Todos son niños y niñas ... infeliz del que se *atreviere* a decir señor o señora (Mateus, p. 276).

COLOMBIA (ANTIOQUIA): Y si asina no *fuere*, ¿no haberá con qué pagar? (Carrasquilla, *Hace tiempos*, I, 172). Botín colorao, perdone lo malo que *hubiere* estao (Carrasquillo, *Novelas*, p. 47).

VENEZUELA: En la paneta gobierna el patrón ... vigilante al aguaje que *denunciare* la presencia de algún caimán en acecho (Gallegos, *Doña Bárbara*, p. 9). —Aunque así *fuere*, que no será (Gallegos, *Canaima*, p. 146); si realmente *hubiere* sentido alguna vez la verdadera necesidad de ello (p. 173; also pp. 179, 187).

COSTA RICA: ¡Siempre que no se le *fuere* a ocurrir volver! (Fabián Dobles, p. 142); algún día, si las cosas *siguieren* su rumbo ciego ... (p. 299); más tarde, si *sucediere* la desgracia ... (p. 301).

MEXICO (NUEVO LEÓN): Y si así *hubiere* sido, ¿habrían estado éstas al alcance de sus escasos recursos? (García Roel, p. 114). (NORTH. MEX.): Bajar por donde se pudiera y como *hubiere* lugar (Urquizo, p. 90); —¿Aunque sea mujer? —Lo que *fuere* (p. 236).

REFLEXIVES

GENERAL

American Spanish, like popular peninsular speech, uses the reflexive pronoun with intransitive verbs more frequently than does the standard language with verbs like *venir*, *subir*, *bajar*, *entrar*, *huir*, *amanecer*, *aparecer*, *volver*, *tardar*, and others. Whether the reflexive pronoun is here employed by analogy with that of transitive verbs or whether it is a manner of indirect object, ethical dative, dative of interest, "pseudo-reflexive," or the like, is not easy to determine. In any case it shows interest or volition on the part of the subject, with a certain nuance of vigor or intensity, of familiarity or spontaneity, a point not yet sufficiently studied by grammarians.

Such reflexive pronouns were very frequent in the older period when the written language resembled the vernacular more closely than it does today. We find many examples like: "*Huyóse* luego con su mujer (Lope de Vega, *Peribáñez*, III); "Cómo *se pasa* la vida,/ Cómo *se viene* la muerte (Jorge Manrique, *Coplas*), etc. Lope de Vega and other Golden Age dramatists frequently used *entrarse* (*éntrese*, *éntrense*) in stage directions to indicate the exit of characters, reserving *entrar* (*entre*, *entren*) to denote their entrance. (Calderón and later playwrights preferred *salir* to *entrar* and *irse* to *entrarse*.)

In modern Spain we find similar examples, especially in the spoken language, many of them in speech of a lower social status: "la aconsejó que *se huyera* con ella al monte" (A. Espinosa, *Cuentos*, II, 207

[Zamora]); "*se había tardado*" (II, 213 [Granada]); "Y ya el diablo determinó *robarse* a la muchacha" (II, 180 [Zamora]); "*me he soñado* contigo" (Zamora Vicente, p. 44 [Mérida]), etc.

Such constructions, with numerous extensions, have survived vigorously in Spanish America with a more liberal social status. The frequency of the reflexive in these expressions has allowed its local acceptance in others which are rare or are construed somewhat differently in the standard language (*ganarse en* = *ganar, saludarse con* =*saludar*, etc.).

ARGENTINA: —Ya sabe que a mí *se* me importa un pepino de todo (Petit de Murat, p. 47). Gómez ... *se* habría robado el dinero (Mansilla, *Una excursión*, p. 43); *me* saludé con Mariano (p. 161). *Se* ganó [= se ocultó] en una casa (Garzón, p. 222). (SAN LUIS): soñar*se*, trasnochar*se*, amanecer*se*, sanar*se* (Vidal, p. 134).

URUGUAY: ¿Y a usted qué *se* le importa? (Sánchez, *La gringa*, I, 2).

CHILE: ¿Qué *se* amaneció? (Juan Modesto Castro, p. 204); Hay noches que *me* amanezco quejándome y sin poder dormir (p. 215). Fulano *se* amaneció jugando, y yo *me* amanecí leyendo (Román, I, 52). (In Chile and elsewhere, *amanecerse* is used in the sense of 'to stay up all night.') A él no *se* le importaba nada (Edwards Bello, *Criollos*, p. 119). *Me* soñaba que hacía un viaje (C). Gáne*se* Ud. [= venga Ud.] para acá; *me* gané [= me fuí] a la cama (Román, III, 8). Podían hacer el ruido que *se* les diera la gana (Alberto Romero, *Perucho González*, p. 23). Él *se* arrancó (C).

BOLIVIA: La pelada no *se* juye con éste (Alfredo Flores, in *ACB*, p. 72). Quiere ir no para robár*se*la a la Filomena ... (Jaime Mendoza, *El lago*, p. 52). [El avión] *se* despega ... *se* ha volcado (Augusto Guzmán, p. 50). *Me* he soñado anoche con él (Díaz Villamil, *Cuando vuelva*, p. 51); después de haber*se* amanecido los dos (*Plebe*, p. 221).

PERU: El muchacho *se* apareció con las copas (Diez-Canseco, *Estampas*, p. 29). *Se* han amanecido (C).

ECUADOR: Ya *se* crecen las mareas (Gil Gilbert, *Nuestro pan*, p. 45). *Nos* amanecimos (Salvador, *Prometeo*, p. 47). —¡Ya quieren que [el muchacho] *se* robe otro chivo! (La Cuadra, *Horno*, p. 106).

COLOMBIA: ¡Y aparecer*se* a la media noche! (Rivera, p. 20). Tiene el malvao vicio de roba*se* [= robarse] las gallinas de cualquier casa (Carrasquilla, *Hace tiempos*, I, 34); Pero éntre*se*, el negrito, para que lo vean (I, 156). —¿Quién creés vos Aurelio que *se* nos robó la canoa del embarcadero? (Buitrago, p. 70); —Háble*se* con el alcalde, don Pioquinto, a ver qué le dice. —Si ya *me* conversé con él (p. 111); —Entre*sén* (p. 130); Entrá*te* (p. 178); Este fenómeno ... *se* sucede con frecuencia (p. 162); *se* sucede el fenómeno conocido (p. 165); el piloto la siguió y al llegar al ruedo ... *se* le desapareció ['she got away from him'] (p. 196). Anoche *me* soñé que estábamos en Bogotá (C).

VENEZUELA: Los de Altamira *se* cambiaban sus impresiones acerca de todo aquello (Gallegos, *Doña Bárbara*, p. 186). Una tarde *se* apareció con Trino (Briceño, p. 96).

COSTA RICA: —Ni siquiera *se* apareció a la hora de almorzar (Fallas, p. 113); —Usted, Chepón, cuénte*se* un cuento (p. 46); *Me* soñé con Caimán (p. 274).

EL SALVADOR: —Vénga*se*, chero; usted tiene una buena voz. ¡Tóque*se* algo! ¡cánte*se* algo! —No me acuerdo de nada esta noche (Torres Arjona, p. 4). Tráiga*se* [= tráiganos] dos botellas (C).

GUATEMALA: *Se* soñaba con ser presidente (Sandoval, II, 455).

MEXICO: ¿La chamaca [= muchacha]? Mire que *se* huye (Quevedo, *La camada*, p. 343). —¿Y si *nos* juyéramos de aquí? (Urquizo, p. 14); *se* huyen de la casa (p. 201); las viejas soldaderas les enseñan a robar*se* las gallinas (p. 96). Juan *se* trasnocha (V. Suárez, p. 153).

SANTO DOMINGO: Todos *se* huyeron (Requena, *Camino*, p. 27). *Me* hablé con él; *te* hablas con ella y la convences; *se* habló conmigo (Patín Maceo, *Dom.*, p. 90); el carro *se* volcó; allí *se* volcaron algunos automóviles (p. 179). —No me faltará ... descuíde*se* (Moscoso, p. 158). —Horita *se* crecen todos esos caños (Bosch, *Dos pesos*, p. 14).

CUBA: "Págá*te* algo" se usa cuando una persona desea que otra la invite a tomar algo; ¡tóque*se* algo! (Padrón).

DEVOLVERSE = VOLVER(SE), REGRESAR

While *volverse* 'to return' is also used in standard Spanish (besides the more cultured *volver*), the form *devolverse* is primarily a Spanish-American usage (countries as given in the examples below). In the older language *volver una cosa* 'to return a thing' and *volverse* 'to return, come back' were the correct locutions. In the modern standard language *volver una cosa* has been replaced by *devolver una cosa*, and *volver(se)* has been retained as an intransitive verb used with persons. American Spanish uses *devolver* (as well as the older *volver*) for things, but has taken one step further in applying *devolverse* to persons, thus paralleling the older *volver* and *volverse*, respectively. As noted by Cuervo (§ 501), *devolverse* is analogous to Latin *reddere se* and French *se rendre*. It must be pointed out, however, that the meanings of *devolverse* do not always correspond to those forms. Cuervo adds that, while in poetry *devolverse* may sound elegant, in ordinary usage "sabe a vulgaridad." In Chile the vulgar form *revolverse* for *devolverse* may be heard among "la parte más indocta del pueblo" (Román, II, 133); it has a similar status elsewhere, such as the Cordillera of Venezuela, for instance (Picón-Febres, p. 146).

CHILE: Salieron algunas gentes ... y como no viesen nada, *se devolvieron* a sus lechos (Azócar, p. 216). Los barcos ... llegan casi hasta la playa misma y *se devuelven* después de grandes saludos y aclamaciones (Délano, *Procesión de San Pedro*). *Me devolví* (C).

COLOMBIA: Estábamos allí parados, esperando que abrieran ... —«Que *se devuelvan*» (Arango Villegas, p. 180). Casi la oye, pues torna a entrar: *se ha devuelto* del comedor de los empleados (Carrasquilla, *Hace tiempos*, II, 318). —*Devolvámonos*, Laura (Carrasquilla, *Novelas*, p. 85).

VENEZUELA: A las dos horas ... oyóse tumulto de tropa. —Debe ser papá que *se devuelve*. Pero no, no era el papá que *se devolvía* (Blanco Fombona, in *Hispanoamericanos*, p. 80). No *se devolvió* temiendo perder tiempo (Pocaterra, p. 285). La mujer *se devolvió* al llegar a la puerta (Calcaño, § 491). (CORDILLERA): Del Alto de la Cruz *me regolví*, porque la noche estaba muy oscura ... (Picón-Febres, p. 146).

COSTA RICA: Pero no siguió adelante ... y *se devolvió* (Lyra, p. 93); Mejor será que *se devuelva*, mano Lagarto, y me deje aquí. Yo no puedo dar un paso (p. 104). Caminó hacia ellas; luego quiso *devolverse* (Fabián Dobles, p. 171; also pp. 38, 365, 382).

MEXICO: *Devuélvanse* por esta misma calle, tuerzan sobre su mano zurda (Azuela, *Los de abajo*, p. 98).

PUERTO RICO: *Me devolví* a casa (Malaret, *Vocabulario*, p. 156).

SANTO DOMINGO: Llegué hasta la esquina y *me devolví* (Patín Maceo, "Amer.," V, 434). Muchas noches llegué a pedir posada a algún bohío y *me devolví* de la puerta (Bosch, *Dos pesos*, p. 111).

REGRESARSE

Standard intransitive *regresar* 'to return' is not used reflexively, but it is often so used in most of Spanish America. The reflexive usage is probably by analogy with some common verbs of motion as *volver(se)*, *ir(se)*, *devolver(se)*, etc. Generally both forms (*regresar*, *regresarse*) may be heard, and speakers often feel a real difference between the two in meaning and application. They will say that the reflexive form (as with *volverse, salirse, quedarse,* etc.) indicates volition on the part of the speaker, an indication of the analytical role played by the speaker in the verbal action. However, this distinction often appears more theoretical than actual. Santamaría (*Ensayos,* p. 288) establishes a difference which seems to be a diametrically opposite view but which, when carefully analyzed, actually supports the volition aspect. He asserts that the sentence *fuimos a Puebla y regresamos al día siguiente* implies that the return was wholly voluntary on our part; but that *fuimos y nos regresamos* implies that the return was due to some fortuitous circumstance which obliged us to make that decision. True, it obliged us to make the decision, and in making it we exercised our will power. This distinction is often valid, and some of the examples given below have been selected to indicate attendant circumstances. However, that the volition aspect is not always applicable may be seen in some of the other examples.

The reflexive *regresarse* is so common in certain areas of Spanish America that occasionally local grammarians (such as Bonilla Ruano, III, 209, for Guatemala) class it along with other verbs (*ir, venir, llegar, estar,* etc.) which may be used with or without the reflexive pronoun, the former being the more emphatic. Others do not accept it fully. Gagini (Costa Rica) says: "no hay necesidad de hacerlo reflejo, diciendo *me regresé, se regresa,* pues basta decir *regresé, regresa.*" Still others condemn the reflexive use, since it is not so found in the Academy dictionary (Román, V, 61, for Chile), or dub it "vicio común y censurable" (Batres, p. 491, for Guatemala). The lexicographer, Darío Rubio, amusingly writes of Mexican usage: "Y con tal barbarismo [*regresarse*] cargan orgullosos entre nosotros muchos, pero muchos que andan por esas calles de Dios luciendo algún título que les da derecho a parecer ilustrados, en tanto que la Gramática, sonriendo maliciosamente, va tras ellos rogándoles que *se regresen* a la escuela de primeras letras" (*La anarquía,* II, 184).

However, *regresarse* is so widely used today that its condemnation will probably prove of little avail. Santamaría pleads for the Academy to authorize *regresarse* because the differing volition-aspects he feels in *regresar* and *regresarse* cannot help enriching the language.

CHILE: Podía pasarse allí el verano, y en invierno, época en que alma alguna se aventuraba por esos lugares, *se* regresaría al rancho familiar (Manuel Rojas, *Travesía,* p. 165).

BOLIVIA: —Tatay, *me* he regresado (Díaz Machicao, in *ACB*, p. 210).

PERU: Es difícil respirar. Acaso el aire no exista. —*Nos* regresaremos, mejor (Ciro Alegría, *La serpiente*, p. 84). Estos sitios no deben ser buenos para la pescana. Regresémo*nos* algo más atrás (Emilio Romero, p. 101). Yo *me* regresé a las peñas para recoger mi bolsa de pejesapos (Corrales, p. 233).

ECUADOR: Cansado, ganoso de sueño, *se* regresó a su casa (Bustamante, p. 122). *Se* regresó a mirarlo con sus ojos (Gil Gilbert, *Nuestro pan*, p. 25). *Se* regresó a la montaña (Aguilera Malta, p. 42); Regresaría a su casa (p. 45). Si no fuera por su caballo ... *se* regresaría en ese mismo instante a la hacienda (Icaza, *Cholos*, p. 58). Ahorita resolví que dentro de una semana, mi familia y yo, *nos* regresemos a Cuenca (Mata, *Sanagüín*, p. 183).

COLOMBIA: Mañana *me* regreso (Cuervo, § 347). —Vengo de Pasto. ... —Sería mejor que *se* regrese a Pasto (Álvarez Garzón, p. 168). —Yo cogí mi canoa y me fuí a recibirlo ... y me tomé dos copitas antes de regresar*me* (Buitrago, p. 53).

VENEZUELA: Don Crisóstomo regresó a los pocos días. ... *Se* regresó de la Guaira (Pocaterra, p. 51). —Ahora *te* regresas a tu casa (Gallegos, *Doña Bárbara*, p. 117); Si resuelvo ... regresar*me* a Caracas ... ¿qué hago con Marisela? (p. 248); Pero al regresar a la casa ... (p. 252). Y en seguida *se* regresó a la Casa Grande (Gallegos, *Pobre negro*, p. 38). Tengo que arreglar mis cuentas con los Hanssen. *Me* regresaré dentro de dos o tres días (Gallegos, *La trepadora*, p. 232).

PANAMA: Al llegar a un extremo de la barandilla, el señor cura ... *se* regresa al altar (Nacho Valdés, *Sangre criolla*, p. 90; also p. 80).

COSTA RICA: *Me* regresé; *se* regresa (Gagini, p. 214). Una bes quél *se* regrese (Echeverría, p. 172).

NICARAGUA: Me chocó tanto aquella frescura de este señor que no reparé más en los detalles del aposento ni seguí mi exploración. *Me* regresé al despacho particular (Orozco, p. 19); Pensando a qué color político habría pertenecido mi señor padre en vida, regresé a mi casa a tomar el desayuno (p. 20).

GUATEMALA: El correo que iba al Petén, *se* regresó de Cobán, porque se enfermó (Sandoval, II, 343).

MEXICO: Recoge los platos y hace ademán de regresar*se* por la izquierda (Madero, I, 2). ¿No *te* regresas conmigo? (González Carrasco, p. 20). (YUCATAN): Fuí a Izamal i de Tixkokob *me* regresé (Ramos Duarte, p. 434; cf. also V. Suárez, p. 153).

The intransitive verb *regresar* is sometimes found incorrectly used as a transitive in place of *devolver*, or even in place of *volver*, which likewise serves in this double capacity.

PERU: Voy a *regresar* [= devolver] el libro mañana (C).

ECUADOR: —*Regresa* [= vuelve] la cara y ríe (Pareja, *La Beldaca*, p. 37). En el camino estiró la pata el angelito ... lo *regresé* donde la mama (La Cuadra, *Los Sangurimas*, p. 27). Estuvo a punto de *regresarla* donde su padre (Ortiz, p. 109).

PANAMA: —*Regrésame* el libro (C).

NICARAGUA: *Regresamos* nuestras cabalgaduras (A. Valle, p. 250).

GUATEMALA: Vamos a *regresar* muchos alimentos (Arévalo, p. 126).

MEXICO: ¡*Regresa* lo que te ha dado! (Galeana, p. 41).

ENFERMARSE

Another verb which in standard Spanish is intransitive and in American Spanish is widely used reflexively is *enfermar* 'to become ill.' To be sure, the reflexive form may be found in the classics, but it was comparatively rare. It was probably formed by analogy with semasiologically related words, such as: *resfriarse*, *constiparse*, *curarse*, and the like. Román (II, 241) suggests a partial explanation in the Latin passive form of *infirmare* 'to make weak': *infirmor*, *infirmari*. We know that some Latin deponents became Spanish reflexives (such as *morirse* [Hanssen, § 514]). However, most Latin deponent verbs became active in form, and *enfermar* may be a later formation from *enfermo* (Hanssen, § 390). *Enfermarse* may be heard today in Spain, particularly in popular speech, rural areas, etc. (Aurelio Espinosa, I, 40 [Burgos]; I, 166 [Cuenca]; III, 376, 379 [Granada]), but in Spanish America it has practically ousted the correct form *enfermar*. It is likely to prevail, particularly since *enfermar* may also be used transitively in the sense of causing or communicating a sickness. Monner Sans (p. 175) thinks *enfermarse* is justifiable if the illness is brought upon a person by himself, by overwork, bad habits, etc.; but if the person is not responsible in any way, the form *enfermar* is indicated. Needless to say, this distinction is not made, *enfermarse* being practically the only form used.

ARGENTINA: Pero era necesario que se quedara para no enfermar*se* otra vez (Monner Sans, p. 174). A los pocos días *se* le enfermó la madre (Güiraldes, *Don Segundo*, p. 127).

CHILE: *Me* enfermé de fiebre; El niño *se* enfermó de muerte; *Te* enfermarás si comes tanto (Román, II, 241).

Bolivia: Los hombres *se* enferman (Céspedes, p. 39).

Ecuador: —Nosotras *nos* enfermamos pronto (Salvador, *Noviembre*, p. 227). ¿Por qué *me* enfermaría ahora? (Gil Gilbert, *Nuestro pan*, p. 293).

Colombia: El niño *se* enfermó (Cuervo, § 347).

Venezuela: —Ay, no me pegues así, que *me* enfermo (Pocaterra, p. 317). Éste como que *se* nos enfermó también (Uslar Pietri, p. 138).

Guatemala: Mi madre, como ya es anciana, *se* enferma frecuentemente (Sandoval, I, 473).

Mexico: He sabido que usted *se* enfermó; *Nos* enfermamos de calenturas (Ramos Duarte, p. 232).

Cuba: *Se* enfelmó la mujel de Don Geraldo Lope (Ciro Espinosa, p. 59); —¿Y *se* enferman muchos así? (p. 405).

TARDARSE, DILATARSE, DEMORARSE

Tardar, in standard speech, may be used both intransitively and reflexively: *he tardado* and *me he tardado*. The first is the more general standard form, the second is found more frequently in Spanish America. In the older language *tardarse en* was rare as compared with *tardar en* (Keniston, p. 523).

Peru: Si *me* tardo, el gramalotal me va ganar (Ciro Alegría, *La serpiente*, p. 25).

Ecuador: Y Uds. sabrán dispensar el que *me* haya tardado tanto (Gil Gilbert, *Nuestro pan*, p. 112). ¿Por qué *te* has tardado tanto? (Salvador, *Camarada*, p. 33).

Venezuela: Ya *te* has tardado bastante y podrían notar tu falta (Padrón, in *ACMV*, II, 115).

El Salvador: El portador de la carta no *se* tardó (Torres Arjona, p. 125).

Mexico: Por eso *me* tardé más (Quevedo, *Las ensabanadas*, p. 13). No *me* tardo (González Carrasco, p. 29). ¿*Me* tardé? (Gamboa, *Teatro*, II, 35).

However, *tardarse* has ceded much ground in American Spanish to the verbs *dilatarse* and *demorarse*, which, however, are not used according to Academy dictates.

In standard Spanish *dilatar* and *demorar* are transitive, meaning 'to delay, put off.' Intransitive *demorar* may mean 'to sojourn, remain.' In American Spanish, however, *dilatar*(*se*) and *demorar*(*se*) are both used to mean 'to delay, take a long time,' etc., usurping the office of *tardar(se)*. This usage has been much discussed by grammarians and lexicographers. Cultured circles favor *demorarse* rather than *dilatarse,* which Román (II, 149) reports is disappearing among the educated in Chile, though heard a great deal among the common people, as elsewhere (for Nochistlán, Mexico, cf. *Inv. ling.*, I, 171).

ARGENTINA: —Cuando se dice a las nueve ... se interpreta a las once. ... *Demorarse, demorarse:* ¡qué hermoso compendio de filosofía! (Filloy, p. 480).

CHILE: *Me demoré* en llegar; *me demoré* en el viaje; el viaje *demoró* veinte días. ¿Por qué *te has dilatado* tanto? No *me dilaté* sino lo necesario (Román, II, 88 and 148). —¿No ha venido ño Manuel? —No, pero ya *no dilata* (Maluenda, *Escenas,* p. 20); cuando uno es solo *se demora* más en mejorarse (p. 72).

PERU: —*¿Te demoraste* mucho? (Diez-Canseco, *Estampas,* p. 101).

ECUADOR: No *te demores,* que te pueden jugar una mala pasada (Pareja, *La Beldaca,* p. 146). *Se demora* en los mandados un mundo (Pareja, *Baldomera,* p. 181).

COLOMBIA: —No *te demores* (Restrepo Jaramillo, p. 148). (SOUTH): —Me voy, máma, no *me dilato;* con la tarde hey de regresar (Álvarez Garzón, p. 99); —¿Y *te vas a demorar* allá? (p. 135).

VENEZUELA: Mal ... *te dilataste* mucho (Romero García, p. 77); —No *te dilates;* mira que no puedo estar sin ti (p. 161). Sí, fuimos a bañarnos. ... *Nos dilatamos* por eso (Pocaterra, p. 19).

PANAMA: —Por favor, no *te demores* ... (L. Aguilera, p. 177).

COSTA RICA: El tren *se dilató* mucho (Gagini, p. 125).

GUATEMALA: La cocinera *se dilata* mucho cada vez que va a compras al mercado (Sandoval, I, 371).

MEXICO: —Arranque para el pueblo y tráigase lo que necesita, no *se dilate,* por vida suya (Inclán, I, 44); Vayan a ver a Manuel, pero no *se dilaten* (I, 200). —No *te dilates* mucho, que miro a esto muy feo (Urquizó, p. 93); —Pues ándale, vete para que no *te dilates* (p. 193).

CUBA: —Podía haber estado ya hace días; pero *me he demorado* a propósito (Martínez Villena, in *CC,* p. 73).

SANTO DOMINGO: Él fué a comprar cigarrillos, pero *se dilata* demasiado (Patín Maceo, "Amer.," V, 435; cf. also *BDH,* V, 61).

PUERTO RICO: ¡Anda, avanza; no *te demores!* (Navarro, p. 210).

ATRASARSE, ADELANTARSE

The verb *atrasar* or *retrasar* 'to be late' and *adelantar* 'to be fast, ahead of time' may be used both with and without the reflexive pronoun, that is, both intransitively and reflexively. The intransitive forms are generally used in Spain: *el reloj atrasa, adelanta,* etc. In Spanish America, on the other hand, the reflexive form is the current usage: *el reloj se atrasa, se adelanta,* etc.

RECORDARSE

In current standard Spanish *recordar* 'to remember' is not used reflexively. One says correctly *recordar una cosa* or *acordarse de una cosa.* Examples of *recordarse de,* however, may be found in the classic writers of the fifteenth and sixteenth centuries: "Ya *me* voy recordando della" (*Celestina,* IV). Such usage, now found only sporadically in Spain, has lived on more vigorously in Spanish America, in the mouths of cultured persons as well as of the people, much to the distress of purists and grammarians.

ARGENTINA: Ahura *me* recuerdo bien, doña Julia (Lynch, *Romance,* p. 43).

CHILE: No *me* recuerdo. Ya *me* recordé (Román, V, 45). No *me* recuerdo naíta (Juan Modesto Castro, p. 224). *Se* recordaba con bastante mala intención del Torito (Muñoz, p. 43).

PERU: No recuerdo *de* haberla perjudicado (Corrales, p. 71).

VENEZUELA: De vez en cuando *se* recuerda *de* su importancia (Arráiz, p. 17).

PANAMA (RURAL): —Usted *se* ricuerda (Nacho Valdés, *Sangre criolla,* p. 79); ¿*Se* recuerda usté de la carta? (p. 109).

EL SALVADOR: —Francamente no *me* recuerdo. —¡Ah! no *si*'arrecuerda (Ambrogi, p. 19).

MEXICO: ¿*Se* recuerda usté *de* cuando corrieron de la escuela a Rosario? —¡No me he de acordar! (Madero, I, 3).

The verb *recordar* has another meaning, current in the classics but now archaic or dialectal in Spain: that of *despertar* 'to awaken': *Recuerde el alma dormida* 'Let the soul awake' (Jorge Manrique, *Coplas* [1476]). The Academy dictionary has called this verb intransitive, and consequently many grammarians have refused to accept its transitive use. Since the transitive use is still common in the popular speech of much of Spanish America, it has been dubbed an Americanism. But Cuervo (§ 453) has long since shown that the transitive use of *recordar* 'to awaken' was far from unknown among the classics: "Y si duerme mi niña,/No la *recordéis* (Lope de Vega, *La niña de plata,*

II, 20). Therefore its usage in popular and rustic Spanish America today is not to be considered a new invention but merely an archaism (Santo Domingo, *BDH*, V, 75; Mexico, *ibid.*, IV, 67; Bolivia, see p. 381, under *ojalá;* Spain, Corominas, p. 90, etc.).

ARGENTINA: Hágame el favor de *recordarmeló* a su esposo, si está sestiando (Lynch, *Romance*, p. 277). *¡Recuérdese* que es tarde! (Lynch, *Los caranchos*, p. 26).

URUGUAY: Sería mejor prepararlo ... cuando *se recuerde* (Sánchez, (*M'hijo el dotor*, III, 4). Aquella noche ... se habían acostado. El *se recordó* dos o tres veces, inquieto (Montiel, *Cuentos*, p. 8); *Se recordó* mal, con dolor de cabeza, con un sabor agrio en la boca (p. 74).

CHILE: —Coman calladitos, pa que el taita no *se recuerde*—advirtió (Alberto Romero, *Perucho González*, p. 32).

ECUADOR: —Han de estar acostadas ... ¿No *se habrán recordao?* —No ... ¡qué va! El sueño del muchacho es como el sueño del chancho (La Cuadra, *Horno*, p. 164).

VENEZUELA: Para hacer saber que estoy despierto pregunto a só voz: —¿Es Chicho? ... —No. Soy yo. ... ¿Ya cómo que *se recordó?* (Briceño, p. 146).

COSTA RICA: Tío Conejo que estaba bien privado *se recordó* con sobresalto (Lyra, *Cuentos*, p. 134).

OMISSION OF REFLEXIVE PRONOUN

The opposite tendency, that is, the suppression of the reflexive pronoun with verbs which generally require it in correct standard speech, is also occasionally encountered in American Spanish. Thus: *desayunar* (current also in Spain), *disparar* (archaic in Spain), *llamar* for *llamarse* (as occasionally in Colombia), *casar* (more frequently *casarse* in Spain), etc. Likewise in dialectal Spain: *voy* for *me voy; marchó* for *se marchó* (Llorente, § 128).

ARGENTINA: Según él, se había traído el animal cuando *disparó* de Leubucó (Sáenz, p. 34). *Dispararon* las yeguas chúcaras que andaban con el matungo y él *disparó* también (Lynch, *Romance*, p. 390). Todos los roedores *dispararon* (Larreta, *La gloria*, p. 297).

URUGUAY: Las yeguas vienen *disparando* (Sánchez, *M'hijo el dotor*, I, 3). El animal *disparó* campo afuera (Acevedo Díaz, *Cancha larga*, p. 80).

BOLIVIA: El cachorro *disparó* como una flecha (Alfredo Flores, in *ACB*, p. 67). *Desayuno* rápido y voy a la oficina (A. Guzmán, p. 83).

Ecuador: Jaime ha comenzado a *desayunar* (Salvador, *Noviembre*, p. 115).

Venezuela: Mientras *desayunamos* observo a Rosa (Briceño, p. 85); ¿no *te* vas a *desayunar?* (p. 173).

Colombia (Antioquia): Con huevos pericos [= revueltos], chocolate, arepa de pelado y quesito, *se desayunó* nuestro hombre (Bernardo Toro, p. 56); Paco *desayunó* (p. 69); *Desayunaron* trancado (p. 81). ¿Cómo *llama* [= se llama] el niño? (Tobón, p. 116).

Guatemala: *Casaron* al iniciarse la época de la recolección de los frutos (Wyld Ospina, *Nahuyacas*, p. 109). No *he desayunado* todavía; Don Fulano *embarcó* ayer. Juan *casó* hace pocos días (Bonilla Ruano, III, 23).

Mexico: ¿Ya *desayunaste* tú? (Gamboa, *Teatro*, II, 27).

Santo Domingo: El otro hermano *casó* joven (Moscoso, p. 23).

VII

VERBAL LOCUTIONS (*a*)

AUXILIARY VERBS OF ASPECT

Auxiliary verbs are generally classified according to the nature of the modifications they effect in verbal concepts. While the auxiliaries of mode (*deber*, *poder*, *haber de*, etc.) express the speaker's interpretation or state of mind and the auxiliaries of tense (*ir a*, *haber de*, *acabar de*, etc.) express the time of an action, the auxiliaries of aspect express some part or aspect of an action. Auxiliaries of aspect may reflect a great variety of qualifications of the main verb: they may stress the beginning of the act (*ponerse a*, *echar(se) a*), the end of the act (*acabar de*), a single repetition of the act (*volver a*), habitual repetition (*soler*), progression (*estar* and present participle), attainment (*llegar a*), etc. Such auxiliary verbs are likely to crop up at any stage of linguistic development. It is not surprising, therefore, that they abound in American Spanish with many regional variations. Some of these reflect usages in the older language or in dialectal peninsular Spanish, others are purely local.

AUXILIARIES OF UNITARY ASPECT

One of the more general auxiliaries of aspect is *ir y* used in familiar conversation in the present, in the preterite, and in commands: *voy y lo tomo* 'I go (*or* up) and take it,' *fuí y lo tomé, vaya y tómelo*. The idea of physical motion disappears, and the verb *ir* serves merely to express more forcefully the meaning of the verb to which it is auxiliary. Keniston (*Syntax list*, p. 203) calls *ir y* an auxiliary of "unitary aspect"; as is sometimes the case with *ir a*, it stresses the "unitary character of an action." Alvarado (p. 242), in mentioning its use in popular Venezuelan speech, describes it as "*ir* histórico, y diríamos, casi bíblico, que se emplea como conjuntivo en una serie de actos indicados por verbos en presente o pretérito." Sandoval (II, 575) calls the *va y* a "frase pleonástica e invariable que da idea de fatalidad, de algo casual e inevitable." Gagini (p. 161) remarks that the locution "envuelve la idea de posibilidad y riesgo."

This auxiliary is used colloquially in Spain, as well as in Spanish America, but modern realistic literature in America has made greater use of an expression whose social level, as is the case with many other constructions, is higher in some countries of America than it is in Spain. In peninsular Spanish we find examples like: "Y *jué y* la encontró ... y *jué y* entráronle unas tercianas a la otra" (Pereda, *Obras*, VI, 150); "Y entonces *fué* La Serrana y *va y* me dise ... y *fué y* me hiso asín ... (Muñoz Seca, *El roble de la Jarosa*, p. 20).

We find an apparent peculiarity in the use of the first person *juí* with the third person of the main verb (see examples below under Costa Rica). However, this merely represents a fusion: *jué y* > *juí*. In Yucatan (Mexico) *ir a* is an auxiliary of unitary aspect.

ARGENTINA: Él, entonces ... *jué y* trujo dos platos y dos cucharas y dos galletas (Lynch, *Romance*, p. 434). —*Vaya y* tráigame el rebenque (Martínez Payva, p. 4); Tome, *vaya y* cuélguelo (p. 5). Colmar *fué y* llamó, y el mozo vino (Mallea, in *ACR*, p. 335).

COLOMBIA: ¿Y si *va y* el Señor lo sabe? ¿Y si *va y* las tiene contadas? (Arango Villegas, p. 18). *Va y da* = also 'dará,' etc.

VENEZUELA: *Fué y* cogió una piedra del suelo (Alvarado, p. 242).

COSTA RICA: No se levante porque *va y* se cae. No llevamos los anteojos, porque *va y* los rompemos. Si suelto los perros, *va y* me muerden (Gagini, p. 161). *Juí* [fusion of *jué* and *y*] se trujo los trastos/del cuarto de mi mama (Echeverría, p. 123); *juí le cojió* ese mal/anteayer en la cama ... *juí y* abrí la ventana (p. 124).

GUATEMALA: —Te traía una carta; pero *va y* se me cae de la bolsa. No vendió su casa Efraín, porque *va y* se la bota el terremoto (Sandoval, II, 575).

MEXICO (YUCATAN): ¿Cómo *te fuistes a* caer? (V. Suárez, p. 152).

Another auxiliary of unitary aspect is *coger y: cogió y se fué*, cf. 'he up and left, he took and left.' It has much the same meaning of *ir y* but expresses possibly greater determination, so that *coger y* is sometimes explained as meaning "resolver hacer algo." It was used in the older language and has survived in rustic speech: "Conque entonce *coge y* se va de pira par palacio" (Aurelio Espinosa, *Cuentos*, I, 41 [Córdoba]); "*cogió y* se fué" (I, 98 [Santander]; II, 200 [Ciudad Real]; II, 249 [Soria]; etc.). The Academy dictionary mentioned its use until the eleventh edition but has rejected it since, possibly as a vulgarism. Cuervo (§ 548) calls it a "muletilla de muy mal gusto."

As is well known, *agarrar* 'to seize' has in many Spanish-American countries almost entirely replaced *coger* 'to take, pluck' and *tomar* 'to take.' One reason for this may be the natural weakening in force that many words undergo in time; the other may be a secondary obscene meaning that *coger* has acquired in parts of America (particularly Argentina, Uruguay, Venezuela, Mexico), where scrupulous individuals are prone to avoid it in speech.[1] Thus, one may hear *agarrar* (for *tomar*) *una mala costumbre; agarrar* (for *coger*) *frutas de sus árboles; una cometa agarra* (for *toma*) *vuelo; me agarra* (for *coge*) *el sueño; agarró* (for *tomó* or *se fué*) *para abajo*. Therefore, it is not strange that *agarrar* should replace *coger* also as an auxiliary of aspect. We find *agarrar* also in rural Spain: "entonce va er chico y *agarra y* le dice a su hermano ... " (Aurelio Espinosa, *Cuentos*, III, 424 [Sevilla]).

ARGENTINA: *Agarró y* se sentó (*BAAL*, XVII, 585).

PERU: *Agarré y* le dije; *agarró y* dió su examen (Benvenutto, p. 151). *Agarró y* se murió la niña (García Calderón, in *ACP*, p. 93).

ECUADOR: —Y *agarramos y* salimos (La Cuadra, *Los Sangurimas*, p. 20); *agarró y* dijo (p. 26); *agarras y* le das (p. 36).

COLOMBIA: *Agarró y* se fué (Cuervo, § 548). (ANTIOQUIA): *Agarré y* me fuí p'al monte (Antonio Restrepo, p. 279).

[1] ARGENTINA: "En el Río de la Plata *coger* es palabra malsonante y hay que reemplazarla siempre por *agarrar*" (Bayo ,*Vocabulario*, p. 58); "La inmoralidad y malicia precoces de la juventud han llegado a tal extremo, que no puede uno hacer uso de este verbo tan castizo, en las aceps. que le son propias, sin exponerse a provocar la risa de los que lo toman en doble sentido" (Garzón, p. 113); "En la República Argentina ninguna persona medianamente culta emplea dicho verbo" (Sundheim, p. 159). VENEZUELA: "En Caracas ya no se puede usar el verbo *coger*" (*ap.* Alvarado, p. 117). MEXICO: Santamaría (*El provincialismo*, I, 369) repeats Bayo's statement as applicable here; "en Méjico lo evitan a veces personas remilgadas, pero nunca la gente culta" (*BDH*, IV, 49, n. 1). Rosenblat reports *coger* still common in Venezuela: "voy a *coger* el autobús." Llorente (§ 128*g*) attributes to Argentine influence the use of *agarrar* for *coger* in a few Salamancan villages.

PANAMA: Y *agarró y* dijo [= a phrase commonly used in folk tales] (Garay, p. 105).

MEXICO: Yo *agarro y* me largo (González Carrasco, p. 46).

In Puerto Rico we find *saltar y* used with the same meaning as *ir y* or *coger y* (as in *saltó y dijo; saltó y bebió*) to express determination or resolution, according to Malaret (p. 456), who quotes a Spanish example: "Y oyéndolo el otro, *salta y* le dice" (Pereda, *Obras*, VI, 406). In the older language *tomar y* was thus used (Keniston, p. 467): "*tomé y* víneme," which Valdés (*Diálogo*, about 1535) called "un malo y feo arrimo;" Correas (p. 652), on the other hand, describes "*tomó y* fuése; *tomó y* murióse" as "donosa manera: poner esta palabra *tomar* antes de lo que se va a decir." For American-English analogies, see Torres Naharro, *Aquilana* (ed. Gillet, note to *Introito*, vs. 104).

In Chile particularly (probably elsewhere) one often hears *llegar y* in colloquial speech: "Juan y yo estábamos bebiendo cuando él [Juan] *llegó y* me pegó ['up and struck me']; "Yo le dije que no saliera pero él, como es testarudo, *llegó y* salió" (C). For Chiloé (Chile), Cavada (p. 282) mentions constructions with the verb *pasar*, which seems to perform the duty of an auxiliary of unitary aspect in such sentences as: "Antonio *pasó a* ganar [= ganó] a Juan en la carrera," "El caballo *pasó a* morir [= murió] en el camino," etc. He mentions also the use of *dejar* as an auxiliary in such popular and energetic expressions as "Antes de venir *dejé tomado* leche [= tomé leche]" and "*¿Dejaste* ya *comido?* [= ¿ya comiste?]." Strangely, *pasar a* in Yucatan is recorded in the sense of *estar a punto de*, under Mayan influence: "me *pasé a* caer; *pasó a* quemarse su casa; lo *pasé a* atropellar con mi automóvil" (Víctor Suárez, p. 152).

AUXILIARIES OF INCEPTIVE ASPECT

The common standard auxiliaries of inceptive aspect are *empezar a, comenzar a, echar(se) a, ponerse a, romper a, soltarse a*, etc. These inceptive or inchoative auxiliaries express a certain degree of violence in the beginning of the act of the main verb. In the older language we find still other auxiliaries of inceptive aspect, such as *tomarse a, acogerse a, meterse a, dar a, apretar a, decir a*, etc. (the last not recorded by Keniston). Thus we read in the *Cid:* "tomáronse a quexar" (vs. 852); in Quevedo: "agarréle y *di a* correr" (p. 83), "*dió a* correr" (p. 247), "*apretó a* correr" (p. 234); in the *Celestina:* "¿ ... no puedes *decir* corriendo *a* abrir la puerta?" (V).

The last-mentioned, *decir a*, is still very common in some parts of Spanish America. It is possibly related to Old Spanish *deçir* 'descender' (*Cid*, vs. 974: "*diçe* de una sierra").

COLOMBIA (ANTIOQUIA): Entre los tres arrimamos y montamos los palos, y *dijimos a* [= empezamos a] echar serrucho ... se escureció de presto ¡y *dice a* [= empieza a] llover, mi padre, y *a* hacer huracán!" (Carrasquilla, *Novelas*, p. 117). Also in Bogotá (Flórez, p. 379).

VENEZUELA: *Dijo a* [= se echó a] llorar. Él entonces *dice a* [= echa a] correr. *Decía a* [= se ponía a] hablar en seguida (Alvarado, p. 162). Eso me tiene preocupado, porque la sangre es una cosa seria cuando *dice a* [= empieza a] dar lo suyo (Gallegos, *Doña Bárbara*, p. 331). *Dice* [= empieza] él *a* sostenerme que era lana y yo a replicarle que era algodón y así estuvimos más de una hora larga (Gallegos, *La trepadora*, p. 277). Usted cuando *dice a* empujar, todo se lo lleva de pecho (Gallegos, *Canaima*, p. 214); cuando *dice a* trabajar no hay quien lo iguale (p. 360).

COSTA RICA: *Dijo a* desir pachotadas (Echeverría, p. 198). Desde ese día no paró en su casa, sino que *dijo a* correr por todo ... paró el rabo y *dijo a* correr y correr (Lyra, p. 133). —Uno ve cuando lo están esplumando [= criticando] los demás, pos *dicen a* miralo con cierta malicia (Fabián Dobles, p. 253; also p. 85).

NICARAGUA: Pero *dije a* caminar, a caminar, por el lado del deshecho para llegar más pronto (Robleto, p. 69).

EL SALVADOR: *Decir a* reír, *a* correr, *a* llorar (Salazar G., p. 98).

GUATEMALA: Pue cuando se vió dentro las tripas de la culebra, *dijo a* hincharse hincharse, hasta que la culebra reventó (Quintana, p. 132). En cuanto anocheció, *dijo a* llover. No se puede contrariar al nene ... porque luego *dice a* gritar ... cuando era yo niño, *decía a* dormirme en la silla después de cenar. Al verme la lora *dijo a* reír, *dijo a* cantar, *dijo a* llorar, alternativamente (Sandoval, I, 315).

SANTO DOMINGO: *Dije a* bailar como a las diez de la noche, y estuve bailando hasta las seis de la mañana; *dijo a* llover, y estuvo lloviendo hasta la madrugada (Patín Maceo, *Dom.*, p. 56).

The older *dar a* is occasionally found:

BOLIVIA: Berta ... echó ... en su mandil cuanto quedaba en la mesa y, *dando a* andar a tropezones, tomó el camino que había traído (Pereyra, p. 37).

Coger a and *agarrar a* are common in popular speech:

ARGENTINA: Y de áhi no más ya *agarró a* acordarse de todo (Lynch, *Romance*, p. 114); *Agarró a* caminar con el recao al hombro (p. 500).
COLOMBIA: *Se agarró a* llorar; *cogió a* insultarme (Flórez, p. 379).
VENEZUELA: La familia *cogió a* llamar médicos y más médicos y no le curaban (Romero García, p. 247, *ap.* Alvarado, p. 117).

While *pegar a* is registered for the Canaries (Millares, p. 130) and Cuba (Malaret, *Suplemento*, II, 277), *pegarse a* is used at least in Guatemala: "con sólo mirarlo *se pega a* llorar; cuando *se pegaba a* cantar la cocinera, era mejor irse de la casa" (Sandoval, II, 218).

Arrastrarse a is found as an auxiliary of inception:

ARGENTINA: El rubio subió en un alazancito malacara que, ni bien sintió el peso, *se arrastró a* bellaquear [= corcovear 'to buck'] (Güiraldes, *Don Segundo*, p. 177).

Largarse a, synonymous with *soltarse a,* may be used as an auxiliary of inception.

ARGENTINA: Dentra al centro un indio viejo/y allí *a* lengüetiar *se larga* (*Martín Fierro,* p. 148).
COLOMBIA: Me vió y *se largó a* llorar (Bueno, p. 27). *Se largó a* reír (Obando, p. 99).

We find *dentrar a* in the gaucho language: "Y *dentra a* crusar el mundo/como burro con la carga" (*Martín Fierro,* p. 77). "Cuando *dentra a* no querer llover, puede ir arriando la hacienda" (Güiraldes, *Don Segundo,* p. 217); "a la mula ... se le perdió una herradura y *dentró a* manquiar" (p. 246).

Malaret (*Suplemento,* I, 47) records for Cuba: *abrirse a correr* meaning 'emprender la fuga'; and for Puerto Rico: *abrió a correr, abrió a cantar* 'empezó a,' etc. Also in Colombia (Flórez, p. 379).

AUXILIARIES OF EFFECTIVE ASPECT

Catar de is used as an auxiliary of effective aspect or of attainment (like *llegar a*) at least in Venezuela; and *catear a* (especially with *ver*) at least in Colombia. Both verbs retain a shade of their original force of *mirar, buscar, procurar,* etc., but *catear* leans toward *intentar* and might be construed as an auxiliary of attempt.

VENEZUELA: En esto *cato de ver* [= alcanzo a ver, etc.] el cepillo del Santísimo (Briceño, in *ACMV,* II, 129). Lo que pasa es que como estamos hundíos en el fondo de ella no la *catamos de ve* (Gallegos, *Pobre negro,* p. 199). —No te creas que no *caté de* pensarlo; pero. ... —Pero es que hay personas que, entre pensar y hacer, le salen canas (Gallegos, *Doña Bárbara,* p. 76). Me fijo bien y *cato de ver* patente que son los mismos hombres (Briceño, p. 91); anduve por esos tunales cuando *caté de ver* un camino trillaíto (p. 93).

Colombia (Cauca): *Catee a ver* ['see,' 'try and see'] si puede con esta llave (Tascón, p. 73). —Voy a *catear a ver* (Buitrago, p. 70).

Hallar a and *merecer* are occasionally found as auxiliaries of effective aspect.

Argentina: Cuanto más subía, más contenía los resuellos para no ser sentido. Al fin *mereció* llegar a una hendidura donde hizo pie (Draghi Lucero, p. 123).

Costa Rica: Tiempo atrás, una vez que iba la india por el interior de la selva, *halló a* mirar a un manigordo [= leopardo] con su hembra (Salazar Herrera, p. 6).

We have already discussed (under nouns of action, pp. 15 ff.) the Spanish-American predilection for replacing a verb with a periphrastic locution consisting of some auxiliary (*dar, echar, pegar,* etc.) plus a noun of action in *-ada* or *-ida: me dió una insultada = me insultó; se pegó una magullada = se magulló.* We also mentioned the fact that such noun formations are congenial to the Spanish language but in Spain more abundant in the older language than today. Other combinations of *dar* with a noun of action are also congenial to the language: *dar un salto, un grito,* etc., for *saltar, gritar,* etc. This practice we may consider a kind of substitute for a verb, consisting of an auxiliary (*dar*) and a noun. The auxiliary commonly used in standard Spanish is *dar,* although *pegar* is not infrequent. In American Spanish the *auxiliary + noun* locution is very widespread and, in colloquial speech, *pegar* in general has developed much further than in Spain. The following examples will attest the vigor and extent of such usage:

Argentina: Mis tías *me pegaron un reto serio* [= me retaron seriamente = me riñeron] (Güiraldes, *Don Segundo,* p. 33). El patrón *le pegó unos rebencazos* (Lynch, *Los caranchos,* p. 30). —Mañana *pegamos la vuelta* (Chiarello, p. 43). *Pegáte* también *una güelta* po el corral (Larreta, *El linyera,* p. 35). Algún bicho de las selvas *pegaba un alarido* que le enfriaba la sangre (Castelnuovo, in *ACR,* p. 126); ... el vehículo *pegó un barquinazo* (p. 129). *Pegó un resuello* tan fuerte que algunos ... alzaron la vista para mirarlo (Lynch, *Romance*, p. 49).

URUGUAY: —Eso está crudón, señorita; *pegue* [= tome] un tajo de acá (Montiel, *Alma nuestra*, p. 138).

PARAGUAY: *pegar un reto, un julepe* [= un susto] (Morínigo).

CHILE: *Pegué la carrera* [= corrí] pacá (Moock, *Un crimen*, p. 10).

ECUADOR: ¿Quieres *pegarte* [= tomarte] un trago, cholito? (Icaza, *Cholos*, p. 134). Vamos a *pegarnos unos tragos* (Sergio Núñez, p. 9).

COLOMBIA: *Pegué patas* pa la puerta y me boté a la calle (Carrasquilla, *Hace tiempos*, I, 36); *pegan patas* agua arriba (I, 138). Los vecinos ... *se pegan los grandes sustos* y se echan a correr (Arango Villegas, p. 91).

VENEZUELA: ¿No se le quiere *pegar* [= tomar], dotolcito? —No, Pancho, no tomo licor nunca (Cabrera, *ap.* Alvarado, p. 345).

PANAMA: Los chiquillos ... *pegan* mentiras [= mienten] (Mangado, p. 110).

COSTA RICA: Cada vez que pasaba el joven, ella *pegaba un suspiro* o le hacía ojitos (Lyra, p. 87); vamos a *pegar una carrera* en esa cuesta (p. 127).

NICARAGUA: —Ay, niña, qué *susto nos ha pegado* (Chamorro, *Entre dos filos*, p. 346).

GUATEMALA: Meleció *pegó la carrera* de regreso. Don Enrique creyó *pegar golpe* [= dar golpe] con el discurso. ... *Pegó volido* [= alzó el vuelo] mi pijije (Sandoval, II, 218, 219).

MEXICO: —¡Qué *chasco me he pegado* [= llevado]! (Inclán, II, 285). Aquí cada uno hace lo que *se le pega* [= da] *la gana* (Azuela, *Las moscas*, p. 65).

Such locutions have given rise to other local and popular expressions with the use of some vicarious or auxiliary verb and a noun (not of action), the combination standing for a verb of action. The construction is a kind of auxiliary of aspect, for the locution expresses progressive, sustained, or continued action of the verb for which the periphrasis is a substitute. The verb *volar* is thus locally used, and variously explained: *volar ojo* (*vidrio, anteojo*) = 'ver, mirar, observar'; *volar lengua* = 'hablar, murmurar'; *volar máquina* = 'escribir en máquina'; *volar canilla* = 'bailar'; *volar diente* = 'comer'; *volar espalda* = 'estar muerto' (Sandoval, II, 598, and Bonilla Ruano, III, 69 [Guatemala]); *volar lengua* = 'trapalear *or* parlotear'; *volar canilla* = 'viajar, caminar, andar, trotar' (Salazar García, p. 288 [Central

America]); *volar bala* = 'tirotear'; *volar cuchillo* = 'acuchillar'; *volar lengua* = 'charlar'; *volar reata* = 'azotar'; *volar cincha* = 'dar cintarazos'; *volar espalda* = 'estar sepultado'; *volar pluma* = 'escribir mucho'; *volar pata* = 'caminar'; *volar biscocho* = 'dar coces'; etc. (Gagini, p. 243 [Costa Rica]); *volar bala, volar reata, volar cincha, volar lengua, volar chilillo (látigo), volar pluma, volar pata,* etc. (Castellón, p. 124 [Nicaragua]); *voliar (volar) pala, azadón, cocas, la angarilla,* etc. (Flórez, p. 379 [Colombia]).

COSTA RICA: El viernes muy de mañana se puso en camino con cinco mulas y todo el día no hizo más que *volar hacha* [= cortar leña] (Lyra, p. 29); estaban a la ventana ... *volando ojo* para la esquina (p. 57); Tío Conejo ... estaba *volando ojo* para todos lados (p. 124).

HONDURAS: De las torres nos *volaban bala* que era un contento (Carías Reyes, *Cuentos*, p. 19).

GUATEMALA: Puede que la bribona/me *vuele vidrio* ella a mí (Bonilla Ruano, III, 69). —Aquélla ... querrá imitar a Chaplin: *volá ojo,* cómo se ha embadurnado la cara con colorete (Guzmán Riore, p. 35).

In Colombia we find, among others, *aventar* thus used; in Santo Domingo *dar:*

COLOMBIA: —Ya me ve usted aquí *aventándole martillo* [= martillando] a esta suela para ganarme el bocado de comida (Arango Villegas, p. 19); ... tal vez vernos mañana empastillando chocolate, fregando trastos, y *aventando escoba* [= barriendo] (p. 40).

SANTO DOMINGO: *dar ojo* 'curiosear'; *dar pata* 'caminar'; *dar lengua* 'murmurar' (Patín Maceo, *Notas*).

AUXILIARY OF MODE

A peculiar auxiliary of mode is *tomar* in the future or conditional plus the infinitive, to express inference or possibility in present or past time, respectively. Such usage exists in the popular speech of Costa Rica and probably elsewhere: "—*Tomará tener* [= tendrá] veinte años,/según dice ña Sotera" (Echeverría, p. 134); "—*Tomarían ser* [= serían] más o menos/las sinco, más bien pasadas,/cuando llegó Cocobola" (p. 197); "*Tomaré llegar* a medio día" (Magón, p. 84).

AUXILIARY OF CUSTOMARY REPETITION

We find misconceptions and conflicting opinions concerning the use of *saber* as an auxiliary of aspect, indicating customary repetition of an act, expressed in standard Spanish with the verb *soler: sabía decirlo* = *solía decirlo* 'he used to say it.' This use of *saber* is found most abundantly in Argentina and hence has been considered by some to be a purely Argentine phenomenon. Thus Malaret (*Dicc.*) indicates only Argentina; Alonso and Henríquez Ureña (*Gram.*, II, § 146) at least imply the exclusive use of this "vulgarismo" in the River Plate region. Tiscornia (*La lengua*, p. 263) speaks of it as "el giro verbal gauchesco" and "el argentinismo," as indicated by Segovia (p. 281) and Garzón (p. 44), especially common in the interior of Argentina. Tiscornia mentions its use both in rustic speech and in familiar urban speech and adds: "No conocemos construcciones análogas de *saber* en el español popular de otras partes." Ciro Bayo (*Manual*, p. 222), on the other hand, goes to the opposite extreme in stating that *saber* takes the place of *soler* "en toda América." This is likewise too sweeping but nearer the truth than its restriction to Argentina. We find *saber* current in Ecuador, Bolivia, Peru, Venezuela, and Central America, but only to a limited in Chile,Colombia, Mexico, Paraguay (Morínigo), and other regions.

Since local lexicographers are not always aware of its use elsewhere, they sometimes try to explain it as due to local influence. Vázquez (p. 362), at least, seems to suggest that the usage may derive from Quechua, since the Quechuan verb *yachana* has the two meanings of 'to know' and 'to be accustomed to.' Semasiologically the step from 'knowing how to do a thing' and 'doing a thing habitually' is logical and easy. As a matter of fact, examples of this semantic change, completed or in the process, have been found in literary and popular Greek and Latin, in Spanish from an early period through the Golden Age, and likewise in other Romance languages, including modern Brazilian Portuguese.[2] It may be deemed, then, a continuation of Latin usage or merely a sporadic development from "knowing" to "doing habitually." We read: "Onbre corto de rasón, muy alegre y de grant conpañía con los suyos, ca jamás *sabía* estar solo, sino entre todos los suyos" (Pérez de Guzmán, p. 51); "Los unos que no *saben* ser vencidos,/los otros a vencer acustumbrados" (Ercilla, *La Araucana*, IV); "con razón con su hermosura [de la mujer] reynos se *saben* perder" (Mira de Amescua, *El esclavo del demonio*, II; cf. Américo Castro, p. 148); "el bien no *sabe* parar" (*El arpa de David*, ed. Aníbal, vs. 2575).

The tense usage of *saber* is, for the most part, that of *soler*, that is,

[2] Cf. María Rosa Lida de Malkiel, "*Saber* 'soler' en las lenguas romances y sus antecedentes grecolatinos," *Romance Philology*, II (1949), 269–83.

usually the present or the imperfect indicative. Nevertheless, *saber* is often found in the preterite and occasionally in the perfect tenses. To be sure, some of these examples may reflect an inexact reproduction of popular speech. However, repeated instances lead us to believe that, in some cases at least, *saber* is no longer felt as indicating customary repetition but has been weakened to an auxiliary of unitary aspect, in which the meaning of the locution is not much affected by the meaning of the auxiliary as such, and the tense to be associated with the main verb is that of the auxiliary: *supo ser* = *fué; supe tener* = *tuve; había sabido ayudar* = *había ayudado,* etc. In many instances this total loss of force is incontrovertible. *Saber* can have no possible meaning of its own in these sentences that refer to one particular occasion: *sabía ser* [= era] *alto, juerte; sabía estar* [= estaba] *amiedentao;* etc. This loss of force must have come about partially through the naturally progressive weakening of its active content and partially because accompanying adverbs and adverbial phrases, which at first intensified the content of the auxiliary, gradually usurped this content. Possibly such adverbs were not used until the auxiliary force had been spent: *saben decir siempre* = *dicen siempre; sabe venir todos los días* = *viene todos los días; sabía decirle siempre* = *le decía siempre; no sé ir con frecuencia* = *no voy con frecuencia;* etc. Such loss of content is evident also in the verb *soler* (*solía venir* = *venía*), *poder* (*podrá ser* = *será*), *querer* (*quiso huir* = *huyó*), etc. Binary combinations are favored in Spanish.

ARGENTINA: Y son tantas las miserias en que me *he sabido* ver (*Martín Fierro,*[3] p. 104). Los mejores domadores son los menos jinetes, *saben* decir siempre los hombres (Lynch, *Romance*, p. 20); su Pantalión ... *sabe* cair allí todos los días de visita (p. 51); ninguno se movió, ni siquiera un viejito ya muy bichoco que *supo* estar en «La Indiana» (p. 95); un tal Floriano que *supo* ser pión en «La Estancia Grande,» pero que ahura andaba sin conchabo (p. 109); Pero doña Cruz se había puesto, como *saben* hacer las señoras en el caso, a cortar unas rodajas de papa pa pegárselas en las sienes (p. 248); don Pacomio, al que *había sabido* ayudar en otras ocasiones, me lo quiso conchabar (p. 254); no *sabe* haber dificultá cuando dos quieren lo mesmo (p. 311); Dicen que lo *supo* conocer muy mucho al finao mi padre (p. 380); Vea, yo *supe* conocer a un vasco que tenía una pierna

[3] Strangely, this is the only instance of the use of *saber* for *soler* in *Martín Fierro*. Twenty-eight times the author allows his cultural habits full sway in preferring *soler* to the popular *saber* (see Tiscornia, *La lengua,* §§ 186 and 187, 3).

seca (p. 437). ¿Vago? No, él nu' es un vago como le *supieron* decir [= le dijeron] l'otro día en Fortín Miñana (Sáenz, p. 7); casi todas las noches *sabíamos* dormir con alguna tropilla en nuestro corral (p. 33). A principios de año ... la clase *sabe* llenarse ... los padres ... *suelen* acobardarse a los pocos días ... para fin de año, me *saben* quedar muy poquitos (Lynch, *Los caranchos*, p. 138); Yo *supe* conocer ... a uno ... El finao don Isidro, mi padrino, *sabía* decirle siempre al padre (p. 175). (Catamarca): Aquí no *sabe* llover/Todo se *sabe* secar/ (J. A. Carrizo, p. 91); Al darle maíz a mis pavos/Me *sé* acordar de vos (p. 221). —Yo *he sabido* encontrarla algunas tardes por ese mismo sitio (Pico, p. 14). —*¿Sabe* verlo al muchacho, viejo? ¿Cómo está de alto? ... ¿Así? (Yrurzun, p. 10). Es un tal Tomás que *supo* ser cabo de bomberos y que aura tiene a su cargo una manguera e las aguas corrientes (*Fray Mocho*, p. 23); El señor es sobrino mío ... que *supo* vivir frente a tu casa (p. 163). —Yo *supe* tener un naranjo, el mejor del pueblo. A su sombra tomaron mate mis agüelos, mis padres y yo mismo (Draghi Lucero, p. 249).

Uruguay: Cuando el Dotor supo lo que me había pasao se rió, como se *saben* reír todos los puebleros (Montiel, *Cuentos*, p. 131). —Yo *supe* tener un amigo llamao Dionisio Lafuente. ... Era mozo guapo (Viana, *Leña seca*, p. 262).

Bolivia: Fulgían intensamente las estrellas ... como sólo allí, bajo el trópico, en la altura de los yermos, *saben* brillar (Arguedas, *Vida criolla*, p. 99). —¿Por qué me lo has matado [al perro]? Nunca *sabía* morder a nadie (Arguedas, *Raza*, p. 323).

Peru: —Él no *sabe* molestarse, al menos conmigo, ¿no es cierto, padrecito? (Barrantes, p. 42); Dizque en la Costa los sucios costeños *saben* comer estas tripas de gallina (p. 101). (Arequipa, Popular): ¿A qué hora *sabe* usted almorzar? ... La preparación de esta chicha *sabe* ser difícil (Tovar, *BAAL*, *X*, 186).

Ecuador: Usted *sabe* equivocarse frecuentemente; N. *sabe* irse por esa calle (Vázquez, p. 362). En guango [= en multitud] mismo *saben* ir todos los años, para prepararse a la fiesta de la Virgen (Icaza, *Cholos*, p. 75); se recargó de joyas imitando al altar mayor de la capilla de su pueblo donde le *supieron* cegar de veneración flores y festones dorados y plateados (p. 160). Mete las hierbas en la olla de barro donde la Cunshi *sabe* hacer la mazmorra (Icaza, *Huasip.*, p. 38).

Colombia (Southern Zone): Los duendes que ya tarde de la noche dizque *saben* subir a esta torre (Álvarez Garzón, p. 12). (Santander): N. *sabía* venir a visitarnos (Flórez, p. 379).

VENEZUELA: Segundo *sabe* pensar estas cosas (*ACMV*, II, 154).

NICARAGUA: *Sabe* cambiarse de ropa de vez en cuando; *Sabe* ir al cine; *Sabe* echarse sus copas (A. Valle, p. 257).

HONDURAS: En esoh díah' e calor asomó en el pueblo un joven 'e nombre Florencio Aguilar. *Sabía* ser alto, juerte, galán muchacho (Mejía Nieto, *El solterón*, p. 60); La casa 'el muerto *sabía* sé al otro lao el cerro (p. 64); Al momento 'e levantá el brazo, se topó con una hacha. —¡Diaglo! Aquí *sabe* estar la hacha con que le rajaron la cabeza al viejito (p. 65); Florencio *sabía* estar [= estaba] amiedentao: —Yo no lo hei matao (p. 66); Duro trabajo *sabía* ser llegar ande el rancho (p. 74). Y una estela de negro humo se *sabe* dibujar en las claras mañanitas rubias (Coello, p. 10); los lupanares se *saben* abrir para todos los gustos (p. 14); las mujeres, que *saben* llegar los días de cupón o de pago (p. 24); su machete sin vaina, al que *sabe* prodigar caricias de amante (p. 26).

GUATEMALA: Cuatro años antes, él *sabía* llegar mucho por aquella casita (Samayoa, p. 115). El finado Julián Penagos *sabía* contarme de cuando estuvo en las monterías (Samayoa, in *CLC*, p. 65); *Sabe* haber algunos muy enconosos (p. 66). No *sé* ir con frecuencia al teatro; A veces *sabe* venir a casa mi suegra (Sandoval, II, 393).

MEXICO: —¿Por qué corren, curros? ... ¡No *sabemos* comer gente! (Azuela, *Los de abajo*, p. 211); Valderrama, poeta romántico, siempre que de fusilar se hablaba, *sabía* perderse lejos y durante todo un día (p. 234); con aquella confianza súbita que a todo el mundo *sabía* tener en un momento dado, le dijo al oído ... (p. 240).

CUBA: (As a reproach) —Cuando Juana vivía aquí, bien que *sabía* venir todos los días (Padrón).

That the import of the auxiliary *saber* is often vague is confirmed by its varied use and often by diverging explanations. Guatemalan preceptists, for instance, seem to feel the meaning of *gustar* as well as *soler* or *acostumbrar*. Thus Sandoval (II, 393) explains that the sentence "no sé ir con frecuencia al teatro" means "no acostumbro (o no me gusta) ir con frecuencia al teatro." Bonilla Ruano (II, 334) explains that "sé comer de todo" means "me gusta comer de todo." In both of these instances, however, we feel a special meaning of *saber*, not connected with *soler*, but rather with *poder*, since *saber* and *poder* as auxiliaries have a close affinity, that of mental ability and physical ability, respectively. That the two are often confused in application is understandable. Examples of *saber* for *poder* follow.

PERU: —Matías, no fastidies ... ¿No *sabes* [= puedes] dormir? (Emilio Romero, p. 95).

ECUADOR: Ella, agotadas las fuerzas, apenas *sabe* llorar o queda desmayada (Gil Gilbert, *Nuestro pan*, p. 82).

Again we find a Gallicized use of the conditional phrase *no sabría ser* (French: *ne saurait être*) in place of *no debe ser* or *no puede ser*. Uribe (*Dicc.*) gives these examples: "La virtud *no sabría ser* tímida ante los perversos" and "este sacrificio *no sabría ser* costoso para un patriota."

To add to the complication we find confusion between *saber* and *conocer*. Mexican preceptists inveigh against the expression *saber un lugar* instead of *conocer un lugar:* "¿*Sabe* usted Toluca?" (Ramos Duarte, p. 447); "¿*Sabe* Vd. Guadalajara? Yo no *sé* Vera Cruz, querría *saber* Tabasco" (Santamaría, *Glosa*, p. 266); "—Me gustaría *saber* por allá" (Galeana, p. 91). In Santo Domingo and elsewhere we find such constructions as "¿*sabe* a casa de Juan?" or "¿*sabe* adonde Juan?" (*BDH*, V, § 94), elliptical for "¿sabe el camino a casa de Juan?" or "¿sabe ir a casa de Juan?" etc. Most of these expressions are found also in Spain, in rustic or popular speech: "—¿*Sabes* a casa de la bruja?" (Concha Espina, *La esfinge maragata* [1914], chap. xvii). The usage is apparently old (Malaret, *Suplemento*, II, 381).

AUXILIARY 'MANDAR'

The auxiliary *mandar* very early became so weakened, especially in the command form, that it resulted in a less abrupt periphrasis for the simple verb: "mandedes ensillar" (*Cid*, vs. 317) = *ensillad;* "mandes lo tomar" (*Fernán González*, vs. 570) was a mere formula used in inviting a person to accept a gift, meaning *tómalo*, etc. (cf. also Menéndez Pidal, *Cantar*, I, § 160, 2). In the early sixteenth century Hernan Cortés wrote (*Segunda carta-relación*): "A V.S.M. suplico me mande perdonar" meaning 'suplico me perdone,' etc. (Keniston, p. 464). The use of *mandarse* in the sense of *servirse* 'please' has survived colloquially in certain areas of Spanish America; in Central America and probably elsewhere it is current with verbs like *entrar*, *sentar*, *apear*, etc. (*mándese entrar* 'please come in'); in Argentina, Chile, Ecuador, and probably elsewhere we find it in the colloquial expressions *mandarse cambiar* (or *mudar*) meaning *largarse*, *irse*, *marcharse* (*mándese mudar* o *cambiar* 'get out, beat it').

ARGENTINA: —A ver si *te mandás mudar*, muchacho, y dejás tranquilos a los mayores (Güiraldes, *Don Segundo*, p. 17). *Mándate mu-*

dar; mándese Vd. mudar; mándese mudar = ¡largo! ¡largo de ahí (o de aquí)! (Garzón, p. 295). Cf. *mandarse a mudar*, p. 335.

CHILE: En un Jesú arreglaron los chirpes [= pingos 'rags'] que tenían y *se mandaron muar*, porque no querían seguir viviendo con este bandío miserable (Guzmán Maturana, p. 201). Dile a esa mujer que *se mande mudar* en el acto ... ¡Te he mantenido y ahora vienes a pedirme plata! *¡Mándate a cambiar* de aquí! (Medina, p. 223). Esa gente no avisa; *se manda cambiar* (Latorre, *Zurzulita*, p. 233).

ECUADOR: Sin conocerlo y nadie *te mandaste a cambiar* (Pareja, *El muelle*, p. 27). —Te ha de *mandar pateando* [= patear] (Icaza, *Huasipungo*, p. 137). —¿Y la gente de aquí no les *mandó pateando?* (Mata, *Sanagüín*, p. 210).

EL SALVADOR: —Güenas tardes déle Dios, ño Goyo. —Güenas, ña Jacinta. *Mándese dentrar* (Ambrogi, p. 79); —*Mándese sentar*, señor Tin, que debe usted estar cansado (p. 175).

GUATEMALA: *Mándese apear*, don Casimiro, y pase adelante (Sandoval, II, 55).

AUXILIARY 'DAR'

In Ecuador and in adjacent southern Colombia we find, in addition to *mandar* + a gerund, also the use of *dar* as auxiliary followed by the gerund: *dar vendiendo* = *vender*, *dar matando* = *matar*, etc. This construction is current not only among the populace but also in colloquial speech among persons of some degree of culture. It is less abrupt, and therefore more courteous, than the simple verb. Used more especially in the command form, the imperative force of the expression is softened to a courteous request (for discussion cf. p. 158).

ECUADOR (HIGHLAND ZONE): —Así *des matando* [= aunque mates], amito, ca no hemos de ir (Gil Gilbert, *Yunga*, p. 50). Yo y mis hermanos le *damos vendiendo* [= vendemos] su trago (Mata, *Sanagüín*, p. 177). —*Haciendo* favor ca *dé* [= si usted quiere hacerme favor] (Mera, p. 266). —Ya dije al vecino Amador que haga la caridad de *dar trayendo* [= de traer] (Icaza, *Media vida*, p. 31); —Por Dios vecinita, venga' *dar viendo* [= venga a ver] (p. 178). —Aura, Conchita, te *daré acompañando* [= te acompañaré] a tu casa (La Cuadra, *Horno*, p. 18); —Te he de *dar amarcando* [= te amarcaré = te llevaré en brazos]. Chazo [= campesino] recio soy (p. 20); —Él misu [= mismo] *dió enseñando* [= enseñó] esos juegos del diablo (p. 21).

COLOMBIA (SOUTHERN ZONE, PASTO): —Como siempre me voy a

demorar en Pasto, le ruego *me dé teniendo* [= me tenga] aquí en su casa esta platica (Álvarez Garzón, p. 135).

Other auxiliaries used with the gerund in Quechua are the verbs for *poner, dejar,* etc., which are likewise transferred to the Spanish spoken in that region: "De rabia, *puso rompiendo* [= rompió] la olla," "Antes de cerrar la puerta, *dejarás apagando* [= apagarás *or* dejarás apagado] el fuego" (Vázquez, p. 127).

IMPERSONAL 'HABER'

In standard Spanish the impersonal *haber* (*hay* 'there is' or 'there are,' *había, habrá, hubo,* etc.) is always singular, since the noun accompanying it is the direct object, not the subject. Cuervo (§ 378) suggests that this construction may have arisen from a blending of such locutions as: *fueron grandes fiestas en la ciudad* and *la ciudad hubo* [= tuvo] *grandes fiestas* > *hubo grandes fiestas en la ciudad.* However, this development goes back to Latin (Bourciez, § 233): *in arca Noë habuit homines.* Nevertheless, there was from the beginning an evident discrepancy between the psychological concept (the noun as subject) and the grammatical expression (the noun as object). It is not surprising, therefore, that speakers should often allow the psychological concept to dominate, making the impersonal verb agree with its grammatical object as if it were a grammatical subject. (Compare an analogous development in the series: *el reloj dió las tres* > *dió las tres* > *dieron las tres.*) We find examples in the older language: "Algunos *ouieron* que ... quisieron disfamar al rey de Navarra" (Pérez de Guzmán, p. 144); "en ella *hubieron* cosas dignas de memoria ... *hubieron* palabras (*La Pícara Justina* [1605]), etc.

Needless to say, the speaker who said *habían muchos* for *había muchos* would likewise incorrectly pluralize auxiliary verbs used with *haber:* thus *pueden, deben, suelen haber muchos* instead of the correct *puede, debe, suele haber muchos,* etc.

This faulty agreement, occasionally encountered in the older language, is still found today in Spain, though it is comparatively rare in literature: "—¿Pero y los centinelas? —No *suelen haber* muchas veces" (Baroja, *Zalacaín*). Also in Portuguese: *haviam* (for *havia*) *muitas senhoras* (E. C. Pereira, § 313). In Spanish America, on the other hand, it is extremely common everywhere, in speech and in writing, and the lashing of grammarians seems to have done little to eradicate it. Its frequency naturally differs from country to country;

in some it is tolerated more than in others. But, on the whole, the examples given below will show that very few regions have escaped this popular usage and that in a good many it can be found side by side with the correct form among cultured folk and in some of the foremost writers. It seems to be particularly widespread in Argentina, Chile, and Central America. In the rustic speech of Argentina, for instance, the plural sign is felt to be so imperative, that an *n* is sometimes added to the singular *hay* (*hain*, *hayn*) to satisfy this feeling.

ARGENTINA: —Bueno, ¿y quiénes hay en lo de Sandalio? —En lo de Sandalio *hain* doña Rosa, Jacinto, y Pedro (Lynch, *Los caranchos*, p. 27). *Habían* varios caballeros en el palenque (Lynch, *Romance*, p. 251); ¿ ... quiénes *hayn* adentro? (p. 253); Si te pregunta quiénes *hayn* en la Estancia, le decís que está la Filomela (p. 320). *Habían* 25 plateros, 7 lomilleros. ... Los *habían* por robo ... (*BAFA*, I [1939], 45). —¿Y quién sabe los que *habrán* dentro? (Lynch, *Palo verde*, p. 132). —En el mar *deben de haber* hombres así (Carlos Quiroga, p. 107). ¿Qué novedades *han de haber*, pues? (Draghi Lucero, p. 206); En la plaza *hubieron* bodegones bulliciosos (p. 215); *iban a haber* fuegos de artificio (p. 277).

URUGUAY: El paisanaje supuso que *habrían nuevas elecciones* (Montiel, *Alma nuestra*, p. 166). *Hubieron* más pasajeros de los supuestos (Montiel, *La raza*, p. 63). En el seno del helenismo *hubieron* tan distintas escuelas como la de Platón, la de Aristóteles, la de Zenón, la de Epicuro (Zum Felde, p. 155).

PARAGUAY: Si no *hubieran* evidencias histológicas (*ap.* Malmberg, p. 104).

CHILE: En el suelo *habían* dos hermosos gallos (Lillo, p. 51). A esa hora los leñadores y carboneros que *pudieran haber* en los buques duermen fatigados (Prado, *Alsino*, p. 67). Largo rato miraba frente a las ventanas iluminadas, donde *habían* montones de galletas (Durand, *Mercedes*, p. 12); —No se imagina Vd. la cantidad de interesados que *habían* (p. 162). Pero don Zacarías ... era rehacio al matrimonio como los[4] *hubieron* pocos (Muñoz, p. 55); ¡con tal que no *hubiesen* presos ni azotes! (p. 213). Vamos al alto y pobres de ustedes como *hayan* piedras (Brunet, *Montaña*, p. 12). —En sus estantes *habían* las más diversas ... mercaderías (Manuel Rojas, *Hombres*, p. 105); ¡Cuántas monedas *habían* en aquella petaca! (p. 153). ¿Es posible que *haigan* cobardes ... ? (Acevedo Hernández, *La canción*, p. 74).

[4] Constructions like *los hubo* prove that what appears to be the subject of the verb *haber* is really the object. In this case, for instance, the subject form *ellos* is unthinkable.

BOLIVIA: Ya no *habían* para ella las cabalgatas fragantes a cebada (Céspedes, p. 75); *Deben haber* otros. ... *Había* muchos pilas heridos (p. 163). (Mistress speaking to maid servant): —Sacá del cajón los botes vacíos que *haigan* (Arguedas, *Vida criolla*, p. 217). —Bien *pueden* no *haber* lesiones materiales en el edificio celular del cerebro (Jaime Mendoza, *Memorias*, I, 42); saqué un paquete en que *habían* papeles de distintos tamaños. ... *Había* hojas sucias (I, 80); No *habían* entonces en el Prado, como *hubieron* posteriormente hileras de eucaliptus y de sauces (III, 28).

PERU: Y las nuevas ideas vinieron a decirle que *habían* dos clases de hombres en el mundo (López Albújar, *Matalaché*, p. 96). No *habían* manos para desenvolver la soga; y aunque *hubieran habido* ... (Emilio Romero, p. 11). *Hubieron* muchas niñas con mantilla (Benvenutto, p. 152).

ECUADOR: *Habrían* culebras (Gil Gilbert, *Nuestro pan*, p. 176); En el interior de la lancha *habían* ya algunas hamacas (p. 192); Sí, *han habido* otros hombres ... (p. 267). *Habían* tantas zarpas que era toda precaución pequeña (Mata, *Sanagüín*, p. 103). En la fiesta *habían* artistas (Salvador, *Noviembre*, p. 81); Ahora *habrían* muchos ejecutados (p. 309). Siempre *han habido* dueños, siempre *han habido* indios (Icaza, *En las calles*, p. 69). *Deben de haber* muchas alas de pájaros heridas sin conciencia (Andrade, p. 39). *Habían* otras cosas en su vida (La Cuadra, *Horno*, p. 28; also pp. 33, 42, 168).

COLOMBIA: Yo no sé que *hayan* más modos, misiá Rosita (Carrasquilla, *Hace tiempos*, I, 72); pelean bastante y *han habido* muchos muertos (I, 74). Pero no pudo contar/Las que *habían* amancebadas (Antonio Restrepo, p. 185).

VENEZUELA: —Antes, por dondequiera *habían* casas (Gallegos, *Doña Bárbara*, p. 122). —En Venezuela *han habido* infinidad de revoluciones de este tipo (Briceño, p. 216).

PANAMA: *Habían* («*habían* muchas cosas») es un solecismo bastante usado, aun entre gente culta y se encuentra en diarios y revistas (Herrero Fuentes, p. 98, n. 7).

COSTA RICA: —*Han de haber* más hombres como ése (Fabián Dobles, p. 391); *Hubieron* bastantes envitaos (p. 114). Recorrían ... las calles preguntando ... si *habían* muertos que llevar (*Leyendas*, p. 163).

NICARAGUA: Ahí no *habían* más que unas pocas botellas escondidas (Toruño, p. 14); Lástima que no *habían* osos por aquellos lados (p. 43).

Honduras: Casi no *habían* hombres (Mejía Nieto, *Relatos*, p. 7); no le importaba que *hubieran* cielos (p. 127). En medio de los pinares *habían* manchas de robles (Carías Reyes, *La heredad*, p. 9).

El Salvador: —Mama, ¿y en el injierno *habrán* hoyitos para mirar lo que andan haciendo en el cielo? (Salarrué, *Cuentos*, p. 129). En la cubierta de proa *habían* muchos marineros (Torres, p. 18).

Guatemala: *Habían* más de mil hombres en la frontera. ... *Habrían* cien parejas en el baile. ... *Comienzan a haber* desagrados en el matrimonio que vive enfrente. ... *Deben haber* mil soldados. ... *Podrán haber* cien alumnos en la escuela. *Suelen haber* niños desobedientes, etc. (Sandoval, I, 601–2). La tercera equivocación es dar por regla de buena concordancia poner el verbo en plural siempre que *hayan* dos o más substantivos con la partícula disyuntiva (*Pub. acad. guatemalteca*, VII [1940], 225).

Mexico: *Hubieron* toros en Santiago (Ramos Duarte, p. 301). *Habían* hombres tan cultos, tan eminentes (Santamaría, *Americanismo*, p. 64); ¡Como si entre la plebe *hubieran* unas personas más despreciables que otras! (p. 247).

Cuba: Se dirigió a la Alcaldía, donde *habían* varias personas (Ciro Espinosa, p. 111); a mí me gusta que siempre *hayan* personas entendidas (p. 199); Le preocupaba el número de personas que *habían* allí (p. 327); Allí *había* dos camas (p. 404).

Puerto Rico: No *habrían* cedros (Meléndez Muñoz, p. 27). En la puerta *habían* dos palmas; *hubieron* muchas lluvias (*ap.* Navarro, p. 131).

The agreement of the subject with *haber* is carried over to the first person plural: the archaic *habemos cuatro* for standard *somos cuatro* 'there are four of us,' etc. Hartzenbusch ("Prólogo" to Cuervo's *Apuntaciones*, p. lxii) says: "*habíamos muchos* por *éramos* o *estábamos muchos* lo tengo oído en lo mejor de Castilla la Vieja." When thus used in Spain *haber* is considered an incorrect and very popular or rustic usage. In Spanish America, in spite of constant and sometimes scathing criticism by grammarians and preceptists,[5] *haber* in this locution is extremely widespread not only among the populace but also among the cultured. The Mexican preceptist Fentanes (*Espulgos*, p. 131) tells us he has heard such constructions in the mouths of "profesionales de algunas polendas"; and so have we all, not only in

[5] "No es posible condescender con errores tan crasos y manifiestos" (Román, III, 83 [Chile]); "Igualmente incurren en gravísimo yerro los que emplean el verbo *haber* como personal en oraciones existenciales, diciendo: *habemos muchas personas aquí* (Fentanes, *Tesoro*, p. 117 [Mexico]).

Mexico but in almost every other region of Spanish America. To be sure, writers try to abide by what is the accepted form in academic circles. Those who use *habíamos* in their conversation will force themselves into the artificiality of *éramos* when penning their thoughts with a literary view. The advantage of *habíamos* is that it includes the speaker explicitly, while *había* does not. The added clarity may explain the persistence of *habíamos, habemos,* etc.

ARGENTINA: Aquí no *habemos* [= hay] hombres (Heredia, p. 159). (SAN LUIS): ¿Cuántos *habimos* acá? (Vidal, p. 391).

URUGUAY: —*Habemos* [= somos] cristianos que con un dedo o dos tocamos algo en la guitarra (Viana, *Tardes*, p. 77).

CHILE: Aquí en el hospital *habíamos* cuatro (Juan Modesto Castro, p. 230).

PERU: *Habíamos* cinco alumnos y el catedrático (Benvenutto, p. 152).

ECUADOR: Aquí *habimos* [= habemos] de vez en cuando algunos más mejores que los abogados mismos (La Cuadra, *Guásinton*, p. 42). —Es que mismo *habimos* hombres así (La Cuadra, *Horno*, p. 180).

COLOMBIA (BOGOTÁ): *Habíamos* treinta en la asamblea; *Hubimos* muchos heridos (Cuervo, § 378). —Pero estése tranquila que aquí *habemos* machos (Buitrago, p. 185). (ATLANTIC COAST): *Habíamos* [= éramos] pocos al comenzar la reunión; al salir *habíamos* [= estábamos] muchos bien disgustados por lo que allí se resolvió (Sundheim, p. 346). (ANTIOQUIA): Aquí no *habemos* sino unos poquitos (Carrasquilla, *Hace tiempos*, I, 67); —Aquí *habemos* muchos locos (II, 185). (SOUTH): Entre todos los que aquí *habimos* no hay uno solo que no esté de acuerdo con nosotros (Álvarez Garzón, p. 149).

VENEZUELA: Aquí *habemos* cuatro hombres y un rifle (Gallegos, *Doña Bárbara*, p. 16); Lo que sucede es que *habemos* personas que le damos fiebre a la calentura (p. 50); Aquí ... no *habemos* un amo y un peón, sino un hombre ... y otro hombre (p. 340). Aquí no *habemos* sino dos hombres (Gallegos, *Canaima*, p. 81).

HONDURAS: *Habíamos* unos veinte y cuatro (Membreño, p. 89).

COSTA RICA: *Habíamos* muchos en la sala; *Habremos* unos veinte vecinos (Gagini, p. 155).

EL SALVADOR: *Habemos* tantos que amamos algo porque en realidad ignoramos su condición única y precisa (Miranda Ruano, p. 213). ¿En qué consistió esa libertad? En que *hubimos* muchos candidatos en cada pueblo (Mechín, *Candidato*, I, 2).

GUATEMALA: Sólo *habíamos* 125 en el paseo cívico (Sandoval, I, 602).

MEXICO: Entre los pocos que *habíamos* teníamos que hacerlo todo (Galeana, p. 159). *Habemos* muchas personas que anhelamos el mejoramiento de la educación (Fentanes, *Espulgos*, p. 131). En el pueblo *habíamos* como treinta familias de agricultores con casas de piedra, con uno o dos caballos y ocho a diez bueyes (Ferretis, *Quijote*, p. 33). En México *habemos* varias clases de vivos (Gómez Palacio, p. 7). En las dos partes *habíamos* forzados (Urquizo, p. 340).

CUBA: —Sólo dos pescadores *habíamos* allí (Hernández Catá, p. 142). Aquí *habemos* cuatro hombres (Padrón).

IMPERSONAL 'HACER'

The same mistaken agreement of *haber* we find also in the verb *hacer* in expressions of time: "*hacen* [= hace] dos días que estoy aquí." This impersonal usage probably arose from the use of *hacer* in the sense of 'to complete,' first with a personal subject (as in Latin usage), then with an expression of time as subject (Bello-Cuervo, n. 104): "el día de hoy *hace* [= completa] cuatro meses que no la veo." The fact that Cervantes and occasionally other classical writers concurred in the popular error of pluralizing *hace* makes grammarians chary of condemning it wholeheartedly (cf. the analogous *el reloj da las dos* 〉 *da las dos* 〉 *dan las dos* 'it is striking two'). Cervantes' example so often quoted is: "Hoy *hacen*, señor, según mi cuenta, quince años, un mes y cuatro días, que llegó a esta posada una señora en hábito de peregrina" (*La ilustre fregona*, ed. R. Marín [1917], p. 115). Grammarians are likely to say today "although classical writers sometimes used impersonal *hacer* in the plural, that usage should not be imitated today." Cortejón (p. 274) goes to one extreme in saying "en este caso es permitido ... la conversión del acusativo en sujeto." Others are unnecessarily scathing in their denunciations, as is Fentanes (*Tesoro*, p. 117), for instance, who says: "Incurren en enorme y vulgarísimo disparate quienes, refiriéndose al transcurso del tiempo, usan el verbo *hacer* en forma personal." The Academy grammar admits that impersonal verbs are sometimes used in the plural: *amanecerán mejores días*, etc. We find the same solecism in Portuguese: "já *fazem* vinte dias" for "já *faz* vinte dias" (E. C. Pereira, § 313). Occasionally the same mistake is made in expressions of weather: *hacen frío y viento*.

ARGENTINA: *Hacen* años o siglos que los temidos vientos que soplan de la costa ... (*BAFA*, II [1940], 66). Donde estaba el patroncito/de cura *hacían* tres años (Ascasubi, p. 222). En tan dura servidumbre/ *hacían* dos años que estaba (*Martín Fierro*, p. 177). Ya *harían* muchas horas que estaba ayí (Güiraldes, in *ACH*, p. 49). Me ocurrió en estos mismos campos, *harán* ahora cuarenta años más o menos (Sáenz, p. 27); *Hacen* meses que no te veo (Yamandú Rodríguez, *Cimarrones*, p. 103); Recién *hacen* dos años (p. 106). ¡Pa San Pedro *hicieron* dos años que le aconteció lo mesmito! (Lynch, *Romance*, p. 49); Está enferma dende *hacen* días (p. 290); *hacían* frío y viento (p. 332). *Van* [= va] *a hacer* dos años (Tiscornia, *La lengua*, p. 220). *Iban* [= iba] *a hacer* dos años que yo me había marchado. ... —*Van a hacer* dos años, mi tío (Mansilla, *Entre-nos*, p. 106).

CHILE: Ya *hacen* tantos años que pasaron (Juan Modesto Castro, p. 302). Como *hicieron* seis semanas, no pudo dudar que el embarazo existía (D'Halmar, *Lucero*, p. 98); aunque apenas *hiciesen* tres años que no la viera (p. 187).

BOLIVIA: *Hacen* dos horas que estamos averiguando de un lado para otro (Arguedas, *Vida criolla*, p. 206). Ya *hacen* seis días que estamos por aquí (Toro Ramallo, p. 99). *Han de hacer* dos años que caí prisionero (Céspedes, p. 156). Pero de esto *deben de hacer* algunos años (Jaime Mendoza, *El lago*, p. 94).

PERU: *Hacen* tres meses de tu promesa y hasta hoy nadie te ha visto (López Albújar, *Nuevos cuentos*, p. 96). Quince años *hacían*, desde que murió la madre (Diez-Canseco, *Estampas*, p. 20). *Hacen* ya cuatro años (Benvenutto, *Quince plazuelas*, p. 185). *Hacen* siete años que no te veo (Benvenutto, p. 152).

ECUADOR: *Hacen* diez años ya (La Cuadra, *Guásinton*, p. 194). No *hacían* muchos meses ... el patrón mandó clavar las estacas (La Cuadra, *Horno*, p. 93).

COLOMBIA: *Hacen* siglos (Sundheim, p. 347). Rare in Bogotá.

VENEZUELA: —*Hacen* días se los vide en su baúl (Gallegos, *Pobre negro*, p. 92); Me lo topé asina ... *hacen* cosa de dos meses (p. 340); *Hacen* días que está en nuestro poder. ... ¿De modo que *hacen* días? (p. 353).

PANAMA: *Hacen* muchos años que pasó eso (C).

NICARAGUA: *Hacían* ya días que don Robustiano estaba en Santa Bárbara (Chamorro, *Entre dos filos*, p. 60).

GUATEMALA: La mesma llegó al rancho de La Tomasa *hacen* ocho días ... *hacen* treinta años que vivo en la costa (Barnoya, in *ACH*, p. 142).

PUERTO RICO: *Jasen* días que estoy a pique [=expuesto] a güelvelme loco (Meléndez Muñoz, p. 107; cf. also Navarro, p. 131).

HACE TIEMPO A QUE

In the older language the verb *haber* (and not *hacer*) was used in the temporal locution under discussion, and the verb either preceded or followed the noun (Keniston, p. 426): "*ha* muchos días que" or "muchos días *ha* que," etc. So we read: "hoy *ha* seis años" (Torres Naharro, *Comedia Aquilana,* IV); "*ha* poco que comenzaron a nacer" (Teresa de Jesús, *Moradas,* 2d ed. ["Clás. cast."], p. 36), "catorce años *ha*" (*ibid.*, p. 65); "yo estoy mejor que *ha* años que estuve," "yo llegué aquí a Valladolid cuatro días *ha* y buena ..." (Teresa de Jesús, *Cartas,* Nos. 101, 282); "veinte y dos años *ha* que ando tras hallar el punto fijo" (Cervantes, *Coloquio de los perros*), etc. In sixteenth-century prose Keniston (p. 433) found only one example of *hacía* ("*hacía* quince años que no oía misa") and therefore thinks that *hacía* in this instance "is almost certainly an error of the editor." It may not be an error, for the letters studied (Bernardino de Mendoza, *Correspondencia*) cover the year 1579, comparatively late in the century.

Since *ha* could stand either at the beginning or at the end of the locution, in the spoken language it was probably not infrequently used twice: "E *ha* dos meses *ha* que llueve" (Juan del Encina, *ap.* Bello-Cuervo, n. 104). Later, *hace* came to be used in such temporal expressions: *ha dos días que* or *dos días ha que* 〉 *hace dos días que.* When this occurred, speakers probably missed the customary *ha* and, to make sure, often inserted it at the end of the locution in addition to the *hace* which preceded: *hace dos días ha que no lo veo.* At least, such constructions are now current in the popular speech of some Spanish-American countries. The speaker, not realizing the value of *ha*, then thought it to be the preposition *a*. Some of the earlier grammarians, too, were misled. Thus Bello (Bello-Cuervo, § 782 n.): "Otro vicio comunísimo en Chile, en este uso impersonal de *haber* [also *hacer*] es el intercalar la preposición *a* antes del *que: Habían cuatro meses a que no le veía.*" So also Cevallos (p. 41) and Echeverría y Reyes (p. 96).

Bello was wrong in considering this a purely Chilean error (if he did) and in considering *a* to be the preposition. Today we know the construction to be used elsewhere (Argentina, Ecuador, etc.), and it is safe to assume that the *a* goes back to original *ha*. Cuervo (in n. 104 to Bello) suggested that the (so-called) Chilean expression "Habían o hacían cuatro días *a* que no le veía" may be due to a fusion of "cuatro días *ha*" with "*hace* cuatro días" and that such a redundant process may possibly be seen in Juan del Encina's "E *ha* dos meses *ha* que llueve."[6] Since Bello's time, *haber* has in such constructions yielded almost completely to *hacer*, so that today the sentence would generally be heard as "hacen cuatro días a que no lo veía" (cf. *BDH*, VI, 58, n. 2). Since Bello's time, too, this use of *ha* has, according to Morales (I, 39), disappeared to some extent. He relates that Bello one day congratulated Mariano Casanova for preaching a notable sermon, adding that all was well except for one *a:* Casanova had said "*Hace* un siglo *a* que, etc." From time to time, he remarks, one still hears and reads such examples as (quoting from a Santiago newspaper) "Al haberlo conocido oportunamente, haría ya muchos días *a* que se encontraría (el asunto) finiquitado."

ARGENTINA: Hace poco/*a* que un día estuve yo/contemplando una tapera (Ascasubi, p. 119); Y no hace mucho *a* que un viejo/... me dijo que ... (p. 143); hará hora y media/*a* que han pegao el malón (p. 179). (SAN LUIS): Cumplió mes *ha* que se jué (Vidal, p. 390).

CHILE: —¿Cuánto tiempo dice que hace *a* que le vendí esos huevos? (Ernesto Montenegro, p. 99). Hacen algunos días *a* que lo vi (Echeverría y Reyes, p. 96). Hace *a* que murió seis meses (Vicuña Cifuentes, p. 324); Ha tres meses *a* que no lo veo; Hace un año *a* que lo espero (*ibid.*, n. 9). Hacían algunas semanas *a* que aguardaba su llegada (Ortúzar, p. 182).

ECUADOR: Hace un año *a* que nos encontramos (Vázquez, p. 5). Hace mucho tiempo *a* que vino Sempronio; hace ya un mes *a* que se lo advertí (Cevallos, p. 41).

AHORA UN AÑO

Since the adverb *ahora* was very frequently used in the older language before the temporal locution *ha que*, the *ha* readily fused with the final *a* of *ahora*, becoming an '*a* embebida': *ahora ha dos años que* > *ahora dos años que*, etc. Thus we read: "*ora* un año me robaste"

[6] Tiscornia (*La lengua*, § 157, 4) is wrong in saying that Cuervo considered this *ha* an "acortamiento de *hace*." *Hacer* was not common in such constructions until a much later date. Lenz (*La oración*, p. 370 n.) calls attention to the fact that no Chilean would say *le veía* but only *lo veía*, an observation that does not affect the main point of contention.

(Juan del Encina, *Égloga 5*); "antes que yo entrase en el colegio, *agora* cuatro años" (Avellaneda, *Don Quijote,* chap. xxii). To prove that these are not cases of ellipsis but of synalepha (or fusion), Cuervo remarks that one never says "ayer un año" or "hoy dos meses," etc.

Gradually the verb *hacer* ousted *haber* in temporal clauses of this type; and, since *ahora* was consequently no longer felt as *ahora* + *ha,* locutions like *ahora dos años* were considered curious cases of syntax. They continued in comparatively rare use in Spain, where they are registered for some regions (Toro y Gisbert, "Voces," p. 323 [Andalusia]). Today they are still found occasionally in literary Spanish and are extremely common in the popular speech of many regions in Spanish America, and in some areas are used by the cultured. The use of *ahora* [= ahora ha] is especially common at the beginning of popular tales: *Ahora muchos años,* etc. The rustic form is *agora,* sometimes *hora,* often spelled *ora.*

Sundheim (p. 18), as well as Alonso and Henríquez Ureña (*Gram.,* II, § 215), speaks of a curious *ahoras días* in which *ahora* is made to agree like an adjective with *días.*

ARGENTINA: *Ahora* poco le robaron (Ascasubi, p. 162). Dentró 'e polecía *aura* quince años (Sáenz, p. 49); con esa misma sonrisa sería con la que *ahora* cuatro años ... amarró ... a la china Liboria (p. 101). Mirá, te vi a contar un sucedido de *ahora* treinta años (González Arrili, p. 37).

CHILE: *Ahora* dos años hubo aquí un rosario muy ruidoso (Barros Grez, I, 11); no se le volvió a ver más la cara, hasta *ahora* poco tiempo (I, 72); aquí tuve yo un bodegoncito *ahora* tiempo (I, 112); he estado hablando con aquel mister inglés que *ahora* tiempos quiso hacer un molino (I, 208); esa linda niña era yo, *ahora* veinte años (III, 170). Doña Lucrecia tiene muchos deseos de irse a Concepción, según le contó a mi madre *ahora* tiempo (Durand, *Mercedes,* p. 160).

PERU: *Ahora* muchos años no corría en Lima esta voz (Arona, p. 254); Hallándonos en España *ahora* muchísimos años recibimos una carta de un joven amigo nuestro español (p. 299). Fué a dar en aguas del Callao *ahora* un mes (López Albújar, *Matalaché,* p. 2); Así se lo dije *ahora* días (p. 3). Mi padre estuvo allí escondido *ahora* años (López Albújar, *Nuevos cuentos,* p. 108).

ECUADOR: El hecho es que *ahora,* cosa de dos años, me vino Torres a decir ... (Gil Gilbert, *Nuestro pan,* p. 107).

COLOMBIA: En esos laos cundía el oso *ahora* años (Carrasquilla, *Hace tiempos*, I, 180); Pero *ahora* años le gustaban mucho los cachumbos (II, 122). *Ahora* tiempos (Obando, p. 90).

VENEZUELA: El cura dijo en la plática, *ahora* dos años, que todas las niñas debían usarla (Romero García, p. 155). Le parecía no ser la misma, la otra, la de *ahora* meses (Pocaterra, p. 126). —Porque lo resolví *ahora* rato (Gallegos, *La trepadora*, p. 231). Ya van dos veces con ésta de *ahora* poco (Gallegos, *Doña Bárbara*, p. 331).

EL SALVADOR: —No nos apalearán como *hora* dos años en el pueblo (Mechín, *Candidato*, III, 2). En el primer momento pienso en los zeppelines, que *hora* cinco años me "echaron" de Londres (Mechín, *La muerte*, p. 53).

GUATEMALA: ¿Y la que se trajo de Escuinta *ora* un año? (Flavio Herrera, p. 50). Vió una tertulia de las de *ahora* cuarenta años (Salomé Gil, *Cuadros*, p. 267); ¿Pues no estoy yo vestido a la moda? —Sí, a la de *ahora* quince o veinte años (p. 304). El vulgo dice: "*Hora* un año me casé," por "ahora hace un año me casé" (Sandoval, I, 638).

MEXICO: No vaya a ser aluego que me pase/lo mesmo qui *ora* un año en esta fecha (Rivas Larrauri, p. 159). *Ahora* un mes (C).

CUBA: He visto *ahora* poco algo que me ha entristecido (Castellanos, p. 100); cantaba una de ustedes *ahora* rato (p. 116).

CUANTO HA

In reproducing popular speech, writers often use *cuantuá* for *cuanto ha*. Grammarians inveigh against this form, not realizing that *cuantuá* is the normal pronunciation of *cuanto ha* in ordinary rapid conversation. Though the modern locution is *cuanto hace* (= *cuanto tiempo hace* or *hace mucho tiempo*), *cuanto ha* may still be heard in popular speech nearly everywhere, in Spain as well as in America. In Costa Rica, however, *cuanto ha* or *cuantuá* or *acuantá* has a diametrically opposed meaning. There its sense is not 'a long time ago' but 'a short time ago, recently': *vine acuantá* means *vine poco antes, ha poco, hace un rato, hace un instante* (Gagini, p. 47).

Possibly because *cuanto ha* came to mean *hace poco tiempo*, it was felt necessary to make a kind of superlative, *cuantísimo ha*, to express the original meaning of *hace mucho tiempo*. The form *cuantisimá* has been recorded for Nochistlán, Zacatecas (*Inv. ling.*, I, 73) (and it exists elsewhere in rustic speech): "—¿Arreglaste lo que te dije? —*Cuantisimá*." The form *cuánta* is found beside *cuantuá* in northwestern Argentina, where the diminutive *cuantita* means *no hace mucho* (Avellaneda, in Lafone, p. 294; cf. also Vidal, p. 391).

ARGENTINA (NORTHWEST): Tenís que ser el de *cuánta*, cuando te venías con las alforjas llenas de aves del campo (César Carrizo, p. 165); —Y diz que *cuánta*, muy *cuánta*, en tiempo de los indios y de los españoles ... ha muerto mucha gente por allá (p. 176).

CHILE: —Pero esto pasó *cuantu' há* en vía del finao mi paire (Latorre, *Hombres*, p. 32). Ese filtrao que llevé *cuantuá* no aguanta mezcla (Durand, *Tierra*, p. 80).

BOLIVIA: El marica de mi compagre ya *cuanto ha* pudo haber llevado fuera del país a don Andrés y su familia (Jaime Mendoza, *El lago*, p. 49).

COSTA RICA: —Pos como le venía diciendo *acuantá* [= hace un rato] ... (Fabián Dobles, p. 199).

GUATEMALA: *¡Cuánto ha* que no te veo! (Sandoval, I, 240).

MEXICO: —Ya *cuánto ha* que quero venir a contesta [= charla] con usté (González Carrasco, p. 49).

DESDE QUEAQUE, ¡DESDE CUÁNDO!

In addition to *cuanto ha que*, one hears (*ya*) *qué ha que* (or *quiaque*) at least in rural areas of Mexico: "¡Trabaja dende que Dios amanece! *¡Qué ha que* [= hace mucho tiempo que] se metió el sol ... y mírelo, no para todavía!" (Azuela, *Los de abajo*, p. 192). Based upon *qué ha que* is another popular and rustic locution *desde* (or *dende*) *queaque* (or *quiaque*) current at least in many regions of Mexico and Central America. Icazbalceta (p. 169) calls this expression "frase del ínfimo vulgo" and explains it as "desde hace mucho tiempo (*desde que ha que*)."

MEXICO: —¿Ha tenido usted relaciones amorosas con ella alguna vez? —Sí, señor, *desde queaque* (Inclán, II, 1); Sí, ya pasaron, señor amo, *dende queaque* (II, 4); —Qué, ¿conoces a ese caballero, Chepe? —Toma, le contesté, *dende queaque;* somos amigos viejos (II, 5), etc. —¿Ya hizo eso? *Dende quiaque* (*Inv. ling.*, I, 76). —Esta boda no tiene madres; la de Samuel, doña Casilda Peral, falleció *dende queaque* (Quevedo, *Las ensabanadas*, p. 127). —Si no, *dende anquiaque* [*sic*] me biera largado con mi hijo a otra tierra (González Carrasco, p. 44); *dende quiaque* sé que todas son ansina (p. 87). —¿Siempre está "tomado"? —Sí patrón, *desde qué ha que* (Gamboa, *Teatro*, III, 23).

—¿Pos qué ya antes de que se casaran tú y Diego ... ? —*¡¡Dende quiaque!!* ... —la interrumpió (Rubín, p. 191).

GUATEMALA: *Dendequeaque* he estado esperándote, sentado en esta banca del parque (Sandoval, I, 329). —¡Ah, don Domingo! ¡Qué milagro! *Endequiaque* no lo veíamos por acá, don Domingo (Samayoa, p. 112).

In some localities *¡desde cuándo!* in reply to the question *¿desde cuándo?* means (*desde*) *hace mucho tiempo:* "—Juanita, *¿desde cuándo* no vas al teatro? —¡Pú! *¡desde cuándo!*; —Publio, *¿desde cuándo* no bailas? —¡Quiá! *¡desde cuándo!*" (Venezuela, *ap.* Alvarado, p. 164); likewise in Cuba (Padrón) and elsewhere.

¡QUÉ AÑOS! ETC.

In some elliptical expressions the verb *ha* has been lost: *¡qué años!* = *¡qué años ha* (or *hace*)*!*; *¡qué rato!* = *¡qué rato ha!*; *¡qué tiempo(s)!* = *¡qué tiempo hace!*

CHILE: *¿Qué tiempo* que salió? ¡Salió *qué tiempo!* (Román, IV, 517). —*¡Qué rato* que pasaron los otros! (Latorre, *Hombres*, p. 54). —Ya debiérai habert' ido *qué rato* (Romanángel, p. 14).

ECUADOR: —*Desde tiempísimo* que quería hablar con usted (Gil Gilbert, *Nuestro pan*, p. 71). *Tiempísimo* que no me harto de una buena cocada (Ortiz, p. 179).

COSTA RICA: Si no en la cama/dende *qué rato*/roncando estará (Agüero, p. 84).

NICARAGUA: —Don Sinforoso, ¿usted ya puso? ¿No ha puesto? —*Quiaños* [= qué años] que puse; yo soy de los primeros (Chamorro, *Entre dos filos*, p. 138).

GUATEMALA: *¡Qué años* que te estoy esperando! (Sandoval, II, 300); *¡Qué tiempos* que te estoy esperando en esta banca! (II, 311).

(DESDE) DOS AÑOS ATRÁS

In the best standard usage today *hace dos años que lo vi* is the recognized way of saying 'I saw it two years ago'; that is, *hace* indicates the period of time that has elapsed between a past act and the present time. Also *hacía dos años que no lo veía* means 'I had not seen it for two years'; that is, *hacía* indicates the time of duration of an act or state begun in the past and continued to a subsequent moment in the past. Both of these types are often avoided in many regions of Spanish America. The temporal idea involved is expressed by the adverb *atrás* (occasionally *antes*) following the element of time: *dos años atrás* (for *hace dos años* or *hacía dos años*). Similarly *desde dos años atrás* often takes the place of *desde hace dos años* or *desde hacía dos años*. The same construction may be found in the older language (for the sixteenth century, Keniston, p. 433) as the equivalent of *ha dos años* or *había dos años:* "figura y trato no visto por luengos tiempos *atrás* en aquella tierra" (*Don Quijote*, II, 16); and it is still used in Spain to a limited extent: "Pero como usté me tenía alvertíu de tiempus *atrás*" (Pereda, *Obras*, XV, 358). American Spanish seems extremely partial to such constructions. Occasionally *hace* is added for good measure: "*hace* un año *atrás*" (see examples for Chile).

ARGENTINA: Y esta vez Marta adivinaba la índole del asunto, lo venía sospechando *desde meses atrás* (Mallea, *Fiesta*, p. 68). Serena Barcos llevaba *desde tres años antes* esa vida. ... Entonces, *tres años atrás*, tenía veintiocho (Mallea, in *ACR*, p. 324). Me decidí llevar a cabo algo que *de tiempo atrás* tenía resuelto (Sáenz, p. 31). Aunque lo conocía *desde muchos meses atrás* (Boj, p. 28).

URUGUAY: Eran co-partícipes *desde varios años atrás* (Acevedo Díaz, p. 149). *Desde dos meses atrás* no tronaba la lluvia (Horacio Quiroga, III, 53); *Desde una semana atrás*, la chica no estaba bien (III, 103).

CHILE: No tardó Gastón en levantarse y saludarme, como si no me hubiera visto *desde mucho tiempo atrás* (Edwards Bello, *La chica*, p. 213). Se encontró con ... Retamales, a quien no veía *desde muchos años atrás* (Silva, p. 105). ... unos despojos óseos ... de algún ser humano sucumbido *tiempo atrás* (Zañartu, p. 73). Se manifestaba enfermo *desde días atrás* (Manuel Rojas, *Travesía*, p. 123). Yo llegué mucho peor que Ud. *hace siete días atrás* (Juan Modesto Castro, p. 15); lo que me pasó con mi hijo mayor *hace tres o cuatro años atrás* (p. 173; also pp. 293, 295, 311, etc.). La Tránsito era *desde cinco años atrás* como de la casa (D'Halmar, *Lucero*, p. 36); seguía tan ignorante de Santiago como *tres años atrás* (p. 110).

BOLIVIA: Sabían que *de meses atrás* venía acumulando el viejo toda suerte de provisiones (Arguedas, *Raza*, p. 271). El ayer y el anteayer le parecían tan distantes como *un año atrás* (Céspedes, in *ACB*, p. 154).

PERU: ... lo que José Manuel venía haciendo *desde un tiempo atrás* (López Albújar, *Matalaché*, p. 119); pensamientos, que, *desde veinticuatro días antes*, no le dejaban dormir (p. 251). Conocía yo *desde dos años atrás* a Chale (César Vallejo, in *ACP*, p. 119).

ECUADOR: Aquello que *un tiempo atrás* hubiera parecido absurdo era ahora una tremenda realidad (Salvador, *Noviembre*, p. 188); *Desde mucho tiempo atrás* no me conmovía (p. 229).

COLOMBIA: Han sido mineros a través de varias generaciones *desde quinientos años atrás* (Arango Villegas, p. 110). Aurelio demostraba *desde algunos días atrás* un decaimiento muy notorio (Buitrago, p. 56).

COSTA RICA: Y ellos no han observado la pequeña figura de Lorenzo, que *desde unos momentos antes* está mirándolos (Fabián Dobles, p. 250).

GUATEMALA: Cogiéralas [las fiebres] en las "chiclerías" del Petén, *años atrás* (Wyld Ospina, in *ACH*, p. 136).

MEXICO: Aquello no se veía *desde muchos años atrás* (Taracena, p. 259). Se le ha hurtado el reloj que *de tiempo atrás* ostentaba (Gómez Palacio, p. 52). La muchacha andaba inquieta *de días atrás* (Azuela, *Los de abajo*, p. 63).

VAN PARA DOS AÑOS

Another locution commonly used in popular and rustic speech of both Spain and America to express the same temporal relation explained above contains the verb *ir* (rather than *hacer*) together with the preposition *para*. The verb *ir* (in present, imperfect, or future tense) frequently agrees in number with the expressed noun of time, but it should be invariable, as in the correct use of *hacer: van* (for *va*) *para dos años* or *para dos años van* (for *va*) 'it's going on two years' or 'it'll soon be two years.' Cf. *van dos años que estoy aquí* 'I've been here for two years.' Such expressions are often preceded by the adverb *ya*.

ARGENTINA: —*Pa* [= para] *quince días van* que no lo agarrás (Lynch, *Romance*, p. 12); *Iban pa unos cuatros* [*sic*] *días* que Zoilo ... estuvo en «La Julia» (p. 287); se acordaron en la pulpería de que don Pedro había güelto *iban pa días* (p. 426); *iba pa años* que estaba de agregao en «La Estancia» (p. 245); *¡Pa dos años van*, patrona, que la mía no me ve a mí! (p. 476); Se lo dije, patrona, *irán pa meses* (p. 478); el esposo se le murió, *van pa unos quince días* (p. 492). Creo que *van pa quince años* que no voy a lo de ningún vecino (Sáenz, p. 24).

URUGUAY: *¡Pa dos meses van*, hijo! (Sánchez, *M'hijo el dotor*, III, 4). —*Va pa sais días* que no vemos a naides (Pérez Petit, p. 164).

CHILE: *Ya va una semana* larga que lo veo en igual traza (Prado,

Un juez rural, p. 72). *Ya va p'al año* qu'estoy aquí (Romanángel, p. 77). —¿Cuánto tiempo hace, don Pancho, que no andábamos juntos? —*Va para cuatro años* (Manuel Rojas, *Travesía*, p. 17). —*Va poco más de un año* que perdí tu inolvidable madre (Juan Modesto Castro, p. 208); *Ya van para los siete años* que estamos casados (p. 301).

ECUADOR: *Iba para un año* que vivían en la parroquia (Icaza, *En las calles*, p. 96).

MEXICO: *Ya va pa cinco años* que dejé mi tierra (Rivas Larrauri, p. 41). *¡Ya va pa las tres semanas* ... ! (González Carrasco, p. 130).

MISCELLANEOUS

In García Muñoz's *Estampas* (p. 257) [Ecuador] we read: "—Pase, pase, comadre Timotea. *A los tiempos que le* [= la] *vemos por aquí.* —Así es, compadrito. Sabe que he estado un poco enferma."

We find the same construction in southern Colombia, in the area bordering on Ecuador: "—*¡A los cuántos tiempos nos vemos*, Sebastían!" (Álvarez Garzón, p. 239). Also in San Luis, Argentina: "—*A los tiempos* (or *al tiempo*, occasionally *a los muchos tiempos*) *recién cayó por acá* (Vidal, p. 170).

In these examples *a los* (*cuántos*) *tiempos* is equivalent to *después de cuánto tiempo* 'after how long a time,' which corresponds to the more usual standard *hace cuánto tiempo que no nos vemos* (or *que no nos hemos visto* or *que no nos veíamos*) with a negative verb. That is, instead of expressing what has *not* happened, the phrase emphatically affirms what *is* happening for the first time after the lapse of a certain period. The introductory *a* may represent the verb form *ha* formerly common, today rare, for *hace*.

Such usage is current in limited regions only and because of its rareness is generally misinterpreted. In Arguedas' *Raza de bronce* (Bolivia), for instance, we read: "—¿Qué tal, Clorinda? *Te veo de algunos años.* Seguramente ya tienes novio, ¿verdad?" In this passage *te veo de algunos años* means *te veo después de algunos años* and corresponds to *no te veo desde hace algunos años* or *hace algunos años que no te veo* (or *que no te he visto* or *que no te veía*); that is, the positive verb form is employed in place of the normal negative, and *de* supplants *desde* (*hace*). The sentence does not mean, as some might interpret it: 'I see you've grown up.'

In the same author's *Vida criolla* (p. 17): "—Ya llegamos, hija. *¿Sabes de cuánto tiempo estoy viniendo a Obrajes?* [= *¿sabes después de cuánto tiempo vengo a Obrajes?* = *¿sabes cuánto tiempo hace que no* *vengo* (or *he venido*) *a Obrajes?*] ¡Admírate, hija! De tres años. La última vez que vinimos, Amelia Montenegro destrozó su lindo vestido ... ¿te acuerdas? ¡el crema! ... queriendo trepar a un manzano ... Reímos al morir."

An excellent example of this usage is presented in Augusto Guzmán's *Prisionero de guerra* (p. 168): A returning soldier on hearing piano music in the distance asks his companion: "—¿Oyes esa música?" (Companion): "—¡Sí, el vals Ondas del Danubio!" (Soldier): "*—De qué tiempo oigo un piano y ese vals.*" More examples follow:

BOLIVIA: —Buenas tardes, Raquel. ¿Cómo está usted? —¿Y usted, Panchita? *De mucho tiempo la estoy viendo,* ¿no? (Rodrigo, p. 56). —¿Hace mucho que estás aquí? ... —¿Cómo está, Julio? *Lo veo de mucho tiempo.* ¿Cuándo llegaste? (Salas, p. 27). *—Nos vemos de dos años.* ¿Qué fué de usted todo ese tiempo? (Unzueta, p. 71).

Often the only change necessary to make the locution standard is that of *de* to *después de;* and this is actually done in the third example below:

BOLIVIA: —¡Y ahora que lo he de ver *de* tanto tiempo! ¡Cerca de cuatro años! (Díaz Villamil, *El traje*, p. 2); —¡Cómo voy a rechazarte [un trago] pues, hijo, en esta ocasión en que volvemos a encontrarnos *de* tanto tiempo! (*Plebe*, p. 207). —Quédate un momento más; nos vemos *después de* tanto tiempo y me haces una visita de médico (Rodrigo, p. 6).

MEXICO: Se conocieron *de* muchos años atrás que fueron insurgentes (Inclán, I, 4, p. 59). Todo ha cambiado *de* hace unos meses a la fecha (López Fuentes, *Huasteca*, p. 13).

The forms *pasa* and *pasan* appear as variants of *hace:*

BOLIVIA (COCHABAMBA): Antes ... *pasa* ya mucho tiempo ... vivía muy lejos (Unzueta, p. 7); *Pasan* ya dos semanas que me dejó (p. 10); Dos años *pasan* desde que el abuelo lo sacara de la casa (p. 15); —De eso ya *pasa* mucho tiempo (p. 107).

A peculiar construction is the substitution of *de lo que* for *que.* This we find in Álvarez Garzón's *Los Clavijos,* set in and around Pasto, southern Colombia. The use of *de lo que,* whether it represents a local or merely a personal usage, is probably by analogy with standard *de lo que* replacing *que* in certain types of comparison: *era más fácil de lo que había creído* 'it was easier than he had believed.'

Cuanto tiempo *era de lo que* [= hacía que] las había comprado (Álvarez Garzón, p. 140); Cinco días ya *de lo que* [= hacía que] se encontraba en la ciudad (p. 162); —¿Y cuánto tiempo hace *de lo que* [=que] viste a don Jaime? (p. 231); A ella la conocí personalmente al otro día *de lo que* [=que] llegué a ese lugar (p. 265).

For other local expressions having the force of *hace poco* 'a short time ago,' see the adverbial locutions *denantes, desde hoy, recién,* etc.

'TENER' FOR 'LLEVAR'

The standard locution *llevo dos años aquí* 'I have been here two years' is used about half as often as *hace dos años que estoy aquí,* according to Keniston's *Syntax list* (p. 180). The construction is slightly more frequent in the past tense (p. 184): *llevaba dos años aquí* 'I had been here two years.' *Llevar* is the verb employed in Spain and also in Spanish America. However, in most of Spanish America, the verb *tener* is by far commoner than *llevar,* particularly in speech: *tengo* [= llevo] *dos años aquí.* This usage is no doubt influenced by phrases like *tengo veinte años* 'I am twenty years old,' etc. In Mexico *tener* is so widespread that it not only replaces the personal verb *llevar* but also the impersonal *hacer.* One hears such constructions as: "—¿Cuándo fué eso? —Ya *tiene* [= hace] un año." The excessive use of auxiliary *tener* for normal *haber* is reported for Yucatan: "*tengo* leída tu carta; me *tiene* sucedido eso; *tengo* trabajado mucho" (Víctor Suárez, p. 151).

ARGENTINA: ¡Dos años *tengo* vividos de agregao en una vizcachera seria! (Lynch, *Palo verde,* p. 138).

BOLIVIA: *Tengo* ya dos años y medio de campaña (Céspedes, p. 21).

PERU: —Castillo *tiene* siete años de empleado (María Wiesse, in *ACP,* p. 136).

ECUADOR: *Tengo* aquí más de dos horas (Gil Gilbert, *Nuestro pan,* p. 271). *Tengo* dos horas esperando (Pareja, *El muelle,* p. 5); Algunos meses *tenía* ya María del Socorro de cocinera en casa de la familia Arana (p. 33). — ... Que cuántoj añoj *tenía* ujté de vivir por ejtoj laoj (Aguilera Malta, p. 104).

COLOMBIA: —Hay unos quince mineros ... que ya *tienen* años de vivir de eso allí (Buitrago, p. 146); este cadáver ... *tiene* cuatro días de ahogado (p. 230). El cadáver ya *tenía* varios años de enterrado (Álvarez Garzón, p. 112).

VENEZUELA: Cuatro años *tenía* sin verlo (Gallegos, *Pobre negro*, p. 116). *Tenían* ya muchos días en Macuto (Pocaterra, p. 91). Pues apenas *tengo* un año de casado (Romero García, p. 26). *Tenía* un año de haber terminado sus estudios de abogado (*ACMV*, I, 257).

COSTA RICA: Ya *tenía* varias semanas de ser el compañero del Padre, y también *llevaba* varios días sin comer (*Leyendas*, p. 166). —*Tiene* como diez años de ser agente (Fabián Dobles, p. 284).

NICARAGUA: *Tenían* tres meses de no cobrar sueldo (Orozco, p. 4). *Tenía* ya dos días de caminar por matorrales (Toruño, p. 16).

GUATEMALA: Varios días *tiene* ya/la señora Casimira/de estar gravemente enferma/donde la niña Chon Silva (Arce, p. 103). Cuando apenas *tenía* un día de nacido, quedó huérfano (Santa Cruz, p. 13). *Tenía* tiempecito de vivir en los Estados Unidos (Arévalo, p. 95).

MEXICO: *Tengo* más de un mes de estar mal durmiendo a raíz del suelo frío (Inclán, I, 100). Ya *tenía* ocho días sin venir a verla (López y Fuentes, *¡Mi general!* p. 42); Ya *teníamos* una semana con el pie en el estribo (p. 111). Ya *tenía* como cinco meses con mi hermana (Galeana, p. 88); *Teníamos* un mes de estar viviendo juntos (p. 209). No *tiene* ni un año de subsecretario (Gómez Palacio, p. 47); Ni un año *tiene* de berse casado (González Carrasco, p. 51); ¿Murió? ... —¡Ya *tiene* ocho meses! (p. 79). En sesenta años que *tengo* de vivir en estos terrones nunca se me presentó el problemazo (Azuela, *Avanzada*, p. 45); *Tengo* muchas semanas aquí de estar viviendo como los cerdos (p. 210).

SANTO DOMINGO: *Tenía* un año de haber llegado de su costeña ciudad de Puerto Plata (Requena, *Los enemigos*, p. 92); Más de dos meses *llevaban* trabajando (p. 119).

In Chile we find among all classes a peculiar use of *llevarse* in a closely related construction with the meaning of 'to spend one's time': *me llevo estudiando, él se lleva paseando.* In these expressions no time element is indicated as might be expected grammatically (*me llevo* [una hora] *estudiando* or *él se lleva* [el día] *paseando*), nor is the neuter *lo* (as in *me lo paso bien*). The gerund is often omitted in the Chilean expression: "Este niño *se lleva* [= se lo pasa] en la calle" (Román, III, 370). "*Se llevaba haciéndole* cariño a un potrillo [= vaso grande]" (Juan del Campo, p. 90).

For verbal expressions patterned on English (*no sabía mejor* 'he did not know better,' *tomar cuidado* 'to take care,' *tomar un viaje* 'to take a trip,' etc.) see Alfaro's *Diccionario de anglicismos.*

VIII

VERBAL LOCUTIONS (*b*)

'NO LE HACE' AND VARIANTS

THE phrase *no le hace* (= *no importa* 'it makes no difference') is generally considered an Americanism, and perhaps justifiably, but only in the sense that its use today is considerably greater in America than in Spain, where it is restricted. The Academy dictionary gives one meaning of *hacer*, intransitive, as "importar, convenir. *Eso no le hace; al caso haría.*" But this idea of suitability is not exactly that of the present-day American-Spanish *no le hace*, nor is the special nuance of *importar* the same in both cases. In Andalusia and elsewhere in rural areas (Borao, p. 95), however, one hears *no le hace* with the same meaning as in America, though it is not considered an elegant expression and is restricted to familiar conversation. Generally, the majority of peninsular Spaniards today say *no importa* where a large number of Spanish Americans would say *no le hace* (or *no li hace* in popular and rustic pronunciation). Many lexicographers have felt this distinction. Some have gone so far as to declare *no le hace* a local form. Ortúzar (p. 182), for instance, registers it as a *chilenismo*. Later, Román (III, 100) disagrees with his fellow-countryman, considering *no le hace* to be "de lo más castizo" and basing his claim on the Academy's definition. Apparently he did not feel the distinction that appears to exist between the American-Spanish usage and the Academy's explanation. Nor did Membreño (1st ed., p. 79) do much better when he remarked: "*No le hace.* —Por *no importa*, no es provincialismo ni de la América Central ni de Chile: lo que hay en la frase expresada es una elipsis del demostrativo *eso*. El Diccionario de la Academia dice 'eso no le hace.' " By the third corrected and enlarged edition of his book ([1912], p. 119), Membreño reduced the paragraph to: "No le hace = Eso no le hace." That the word *eso*, however, was not necessary we see from examples in the older language. A few examples illustrating present-day American-Spanish usage follow:

ARGENTINA: —Mirá—agregó—que el oficio es duro. —*No le hace* (Güiraldes, *Don Segundo*, p. 56). —¡Pero, Marcelina!—exclama.

¡Lleva la cincha bailando! —¡Ah, ah! *No li hace* (Lynch, *Los caranchos*, p. 115).

CHILE: *No le hace* que estés lejos (C). *No le hace* (*no li hace*) es como decir *No importa*. Es frase usada en todo Chile (Laval, I, 174).

PERU: —¡Habré pagado de más! —*No le hace*, viejo, *no le hace* (Diez-Canseco, *Duque*, p. 68).

COLOMBIA: *¡No le hace* que me dejes solo! (Rivera, p. 58). *No le hace* que nos quebremos (Carrasquilla, *Hace tiempos*, II, 117).

GUATEMALA: *No le hace* que se vaya la cocinera (Sandoval, II, 140).

MEXICO: Pero *no le hace* que sean muchos (Azuela, *Los de abajo*, p. 98). Esta tarde saldremos a pasear. —¿I si llueve? —*No le hace* (Ramos Duarte, p. 369).

In rustic and extremely popular Mexican speech the general locution *no le hace* (= *no importa*) is occasionally supplanted by the locution *no li* (or *le*) *aunque* or *nada li aunque:*

—¡Vieja desgraciada! ¡A que te arrimo unos leñazos! ... «*No le aunque*» nomás me decía la condenada ... y a mí me daba ya más risa que ganas de pegarle (Robles Castillo, p. 188). *No liaunque* qui ora sia un esqueleto (García Jiménez, p. 119). *¡No li aunque* que nazcan chatos, con tal que tengan risuello! (Rivas Larrauri, p. 37); *no li aunque* qu'ella mi olvide y *nada li aunque* que ella se ría (p. 173). —¿Y si hay trifulca? —*No le aunque;* es la obligación (Urquizo, p. 158).

SE ME HACE, SE ME PONE

Another locution which, though used in the older language, is not common in Spain today but is quite extensive in Spanish America is *se me hace* (= *se me figura, me parece*) 'it seems to me.' Lexicographers used to consider this expression an Americanism because it did not appear in the Academy dictionary. Tiscornia (*La lengua*, § 187) suspected its use in other Spanish-American countries in addition to Argentina. It now has found its way into the dictionary: "Hacérsele una cosa a uno. fr. Figurársele, parecerle. *Las manadas que a don Quijote se le hicieron ejércitos.*" Consequently, it will no longer be deemed an Americanism. Nevertheless, it may be ranked as such in the sense that, although current in the older language, its frequency has diminished greatly in Spain but has increased in most of Spanish America. We still find it in Andalusia and probably elsewhere in regional Spain, but examples in literature seem to require explanation there, an evidence of its rarity. Thus Rodríguez Marín (*El alma de Andalucía* [1929], p. 121) in a footnote to the verses "*se me hace* que no hay/hombre como tú ninguno" explains "hacérsele a uno una cosa, figurársele, representársele, parecerle." In popular and rustic pronunciation *se me hace* > *se mi hace.*

In many areas *se me pone* (cf. *suponer*) is used in the sense of *se me hace,* as in Andalusia; in Colombia we also find *se me propone.*

ARGENTINA: ¡Cuando la devisé dende lejos, *se me hizo* una muchacha mesmamente! (Lynch, *Romance,* p. 48); —Porque *se me hace* que esta noche se pueden ganar algunos pesos (p. 85); A doña Julia *se le hacía* a cada rato que doña Cruz se iba a levantar de la cama (p. 342). Si el diablo sabe andar suelto, *se me hace* que es a la siesta (*Fray Mocho,* p. 125).

URUGUAY: —*Se me hase* que te llevo en el cuerpo (Reyles, *El gaucho,* p. 219).

CHILE: *Se me pone* que lo va a hacer (C). A mí *se mi hace* que li hace (Laval, I, 174).

PERU: —Y *se me pone,* por la voz, que debe usted estar en sazón como para mi diente (Corrales, p. 221).

ECUADOR: —A mí *se me pone* que el tipo éste anda buscando un acomodo (Gil Gilbert, *Nuestro pan,* p. 112). *Se le puso* que era un mosquitero de fina gasa la llovizna (Ortiz, p. 54).

COLOMBIA: —*Se me pone* ... que jué la ánima del dijunto (Rivera, p. 72). Ese día [mamá] *se me hace* más hermosa que siempre (Carrasquilla, *Hace tiempos,* I, 186). *Se me hace* que el Andrés te miraba (Álvarez, p. 80). *Se me propuso* que se iba a caer (Tobón, p. 151).

VENEZUELA: —A mí *se me pone* lo que es (Briceño, in *ACMV,* II, 127); Pero a mí *se me pone* que eso tiene su puntica tapá (p. 130).

GUATEMALA: A mí *se me pone* que tal vez seya Juan el hermano de Francisco (Quintana, p. 53). *Me se pone* que no lo engaño (Zea Salguero, in *CLC,* p. 51).

MEXICO: —¡Que *se me hace* que usté está enamorado, curro! (Azuela, *Los de abajo,* p. 60). A mí *se mi hace* que ya no es la misma (González Carrasco, p. 51). (NUEVO LEÓN): *Se le puso* y *se le puso* que 'bía sío Lugo el que se 'bía robao las reses. ... Como si no pudiera 'ber juntao él algo de su maíz, ¿no *se le hace?* (García Roel, p. 100).

SANTO DOMINGO: Cuando a mí *se me pone* una cosa, casi siempre sucede (Patín Maceo, *Notas*).

In Guatemala the phrase has an additional meaning, according to Sandoval (I, 609): "Hacérsele a uno una cosa = satisfacer uno un deseo. Cumplírsele a uno algo que anhelaba conseguir, poseer, etc." He gives as an example of this meaning: "A Celmira *se le hizo* al fin casarse con Paco."

According to Aurelio Espinosa (*Apuntaciones*, p. 621), the adverb *meramente* in New Mexican popular speech has extended its meaning to 'exactamente' or 'exactamente como,' then to 'igual a' or 'idéntico a,' and still later to 'es igual a' or 'se parece a' and 'parece.' It is conjugated as if it were the verb *meramenter*, *meenter*, *menter*, or *enter* (for loss of initial *m*, cf. *mi mamá* > *mi amá*, etc.): "*Meramente* [= parece] un payaso. *Menten* [= parecen] unos locos. *Ente* [= parece] que eres rico. ¿Qué quieres que *meramenta* [= parezca] que estoy loco? *Entía* que staba embolau [= parecía que estaba borracho]. *Meentemos* [= parecemos] hermanitos. *Meramentíanos* [= parecíamos] idiotas" (cf. also Rosenblat, *Notas*, pp. 308–10).

HACE SED, HAMBRE, ETC.

Occasionally the personal *tener sed*, *hambre*, etc. (*tengo sed* 'I am thirsty') is used impersonally (*hace sed*, *hambre*, etc.) by analogy with expressions of weather (*hace frío*, *calor*, etc.), and possibly for the sake of impersonalizing bodily appetites. Furthermore, expressions like *hace sed*, *hambre*, *sueño*, for *tengo sed*, *hambre*, *sueño*, etc., are, because of their relative simplicity, characteristic of the speech of young children.

CHILE: —*Hace sueño* (C).

BOLIVIA: —*Hace sed*—dijo Amiceto. Yo le di a beber un poco de agua caliente (Céspedes, p. 162).

ECUADOR: —Apura, pues, que *hace hambre* (Pareja, *La Beldaca*, p. 27).

COLOMBIA: —*Hace hambre* (C). El comer cuando *hace hambre*,/el beber cuando *hace sé* (*Folklore santandereano*, p. 135).

PANAMA: Es medio día y *hace hambre* (Nacho Valdés, *Sangre criolla*, p. 52).

NICARAGUA: Volvimos al cuartel. «*Hace hambre*,» dijo el general. «Desayunemos porque quién sabe si va a haber almuerzo» (Orozco, p. 71).

NO TE HAGAS, NO SEAS, TÚ (SÍ) ERES

In many regions we find a sentence like *no te hagas el tonto* 'don't pretend to be stupid,' etc., shortened to *no te hagas*. The disagreeable portion of the phrase is omitted, for politeness' sake, and its completion is left to the listener's imagination. The indefiniteness of the locution increases its expressiveness and suggestiveness. We find the same ellipsis with the verb *ser* when the predicate adjective or noun expresses some defect or reprehensible quality: *no seas* or *tú* (*sí*) *eres* (*tonto, bruto, perezoso, descuidado*). Román (III, 90; V, 247) erroneously considers such usage purely Chilean; Garay (p. 109) thinks it Panamanian. However, the same usage is found in other regions as well. *Hacerse* may be translated 'to pretend, make believe,' etc.

River Plate Zone: —¿Sabe ella que llegó su marido? Sí, pero *se hace* (Morínigo).

Chile: ¿Para qué *te haces* [= el tonto, el·disimulado, como que no entiendes]? *No te hagas*, porque sé que entiendes bien lo que te digo (Román, III, 90); Te castigo para que *no seas* ... [= tonto, bruto, descuidado, perezoso] (V, 247). —¿Es tonto Ud. o *se hace?* (Juan Modesto Castro, p. 350).

Peru: —Dizque en la Costa los sucios costeños saben comer estas tripas de gallina. ... —*¡No se haga usted!* (Barrantes, p. 101).

Ecuador: —Vamos adentro, Baldomera. —¿Qué es que dice? —*No te hagas;* vamos adentro, negra. ... Vente no más para adentro y *no te hagas* la cojuda [= tonta, sueca] (Pareja, *Baldomera*, p. 85); —No agarre, don Eleuterio. Se lo voy a decir a la señorita. — ¡Boba! ¡Elé, la guambra [= muchacha], *haciéndose* no más! (p. 177). Es que a mí no me vienen a visitar. —A mí tampoco. —¡Ay, vecina! *No se haga.* Anoche oí hablar en su cuarto. ... —¡Ah! Sí. Un amigo de mi marido que acaba de llegar y me traía noticias de él. —Véanla, véanla, cómo *se hace* (Pareja, *El muelle*, p. 103); —De esto no me habías dado. ... *Te estabas haciendo* no más (p. 157). —¿Enterrarlos? ¿Es que *eres* mismo, o *te haces?* (La Cuadra, *Horno*, p. 170).

Colombia: —*Tú sí eres*, ¿no? (Flórez, p. 380).

Venezuela: —*¡Tú sí que eres!* (Andean Zone): *¡Vos sí que sos!* (Rosenblat).

Panama: ¡Niña, *tú sí* que *eres!* (Garay, p. 109; L. Aguilera, p. 323).

Mexico: —¡Ahora vamos a brindar por su conquista! —¡Cuál conquista! —*No se haga*, amigo. ¡Ya me lo dijo Benita! (Galeana, p. 99).

Santo Domingo: ¿Él borracho? ¡Mentira! *Se está haciendo.* A ella no le ocurre nada; no tiene ningún dolor de cabeza; *se está haciendo* (Patín Maceo, *Dom.*, p. 77); Ya se lo dijiste. *¡Tú sí eres!* [indiscreto];

¿Y volvió a decírtelo? *¡Él sí es!* [necio, majadero]; Saben que no me gusta, y me lo repiten. *¡Ustedes sí son!* [malos, perversos, mortificadores] (p. 157).

CUBA: —*¡Tú sí que eres!* ¡Mira *que tú eres!* (Padrón).

HACE = SÍ

The use of *hace* as an equivalent for *sí* is reported for Costa Rica: "—¿Vamos a pasear? —*Hace.* —¿Cenas conmigo? —*Hace*" (Salesiano, p. 81). However, we find this word used in the same meaning but in interrogative form elsewhere in America (as well as in Spain). (CHILE): "—Esta noche podimos alojar en Púa ... *¿Hace?* —Sí, ... cuanto más lejos mejor" (Brunet, *Bestia dañina*, p. 37). (ANDALUSIA): "—Despacha la señora; pero un servidó es el encargao de sacarle er corasón por la boca a to er que la mire con segunda. *¿Hase?* [= ¿comprende, sí?" (Álvarez Quintero, *La mala sombra*).

SOME USES OF THE GERUND

Standardly the progressive forms of certain verbs (such as *ser, ir, venir*) are very seldom used. This was not the case in the older language, however, where we find *id yendo, iremos yendo, vámonos yendo*, etc., in which a finite form and a gerund of the same verb stood together to emphasize the progressive element (*Homenaje a Menéndez Pidal*, I, 43). This older usage has survived in parts of Spanish America not only in popular and rustic speech but also in the mouths of the more cultured. Most preceptists condemn the practice, but others (Vázquez, p. 229), cognizant of its older prevalence, maintain that it should not be dubbed incorrect today.

ARGENTINA: —Pase adelante, Ramallo,/diga, ¿cómo le va *yendo?* (Ascasubi, p. 145). —Se acordó de que iba *diendo* [= yendo] pa lo de don Santos Santos (Lynch, *Romance*, p. 42); ¡Y vayan *viniendosé!* (p. 97). —Si quieren ... podemos ir *yendo* (Güiraldes, *Xaimaca*, p. 178). —Durante estos últimos quince años he estado *yendo* a su pieza a cada rato (Laferrère, *Las de Barranco*, p. 19). Todos se han ido *yendo* unos tras otros (Lynch, *Palo verde*, p. 9). —Y si le sale mal el negocio, ya mismo recoge sus cacharpas y se nos está *yendo* (Draghi Lucero, p. 122); ¿Y para dónde es que va *yendo?* (p. 218).

URUGUAY: —Güeno, ¿vamos a dormir? —Vaya *diendo*, ya lo sigo (Viana, *Abrojos*, p. 74). Don Fausto ... se asercó pa preguntarle cómo le diba *diendo* (Reyles, *El gaucho*, p. 146).

CHILE: ¿Cómo le va *yendo?* (Maluenda, *Escenas,* p. 71). Creo que la que se sale *yendo* soy yo (Acevedo Hernández, *Por el atajo,* p. 59). Bueno, me voy ... y vayan *yéndose* ustedes también (Sepulveda, *Hijuna,* p. 67).

BOLIVIA: —Sigan *yendo* (Arguedas, *Raza,* p. 35). ¿Sabes de cuánto tiempo estoy *viniendo* a Obrajes? (Arguedas, *Vida criolla,* p. 17); —Estaba *yendo* ande la señorita Carlota pa pedirle el traje (p. 215).

PERU: Y estoy *yendo* hacia ella agazapado como un puma (Ciro Alegría, *La serpiente,* p. 210). *Estoy yendo* [= voy] a Huancayo. Aquí *estoy viniendo a verlo* [= he venido a verlo] compadre (Benvenutto, p. 156).

ECUADOR: Cuando se estén *yendo* al infierno tan (Icaza, *Huasipungo,* p. 35). Los Sandoval estaban *yendo* a la perennidad (Gil Gilbert, *Nuestro pan,* p. 232). Se fué *yendo* ... se van *yendo* (Vázquez, p. 229). El viernes por la mañana me estaba *yendo* a cuger leña (Vásconez, p. 217).

COLOMBIA: —Se está *viniendo* la montaña sobre el río (Buitrago, p. 49). Melito se ha ido *yendo* (Efe Gómez, p. 78); había ido *viniéndose* ... en dirección a su casa (p. 146). (RURAL): —¿Dónde queda eso? —*Iyendo* pa la plaza (Flórez, p. 380).

VENEZUELA: —¿Cómo está, Capitán? ¿Cómo le va *yendo?* (Arráiz, p. 69). —Yo me estoy *diendo* (Gallegos, *Canaima,* p. 88).

PANAMA: Ya está *viniendo;* me estoy *yendo* (C).

COSTA RICA: ¡Upe! Tío Coyote. ¿Cómo le va *yendo?* (Lyra, p. 12). En la siguiente semana, estuvo *yendo* a la capital (Fabián Dobles, p. 174); en estas cuatro semanas ha estado *yendo* sin falta y muy a menudo (p. 48).

EL SALVADOR: —Ya tesperan. Ite [= vete] *iyendo* [pop. for *yendo*] (González Montalvo, *La cita*).

GUATEMALA: Todas las noches estoy *iyendo* a ver a Isabel, quien ha estado gravemente enferma (Sandoval, I, 747).

MEXICO: Vi cómo el cantinero se fué *yendo* de lado (López y Fuentes, *¡Mi general!* p. 90). (NUEVO LEÓN): Vámonos *yendo* allá (García Roel, p. 144); te andas *yendo* p'allá (p. 146). (YUCATÁN): La luz se va *yendo;* Ya me voy *yendo* (Ramos Duarte, p. 275).

PUERTO RICO: Me estoy *diendo* ya (Meléndez Muñoz, p. 111).

Progressive forms of *ser* (*estar siendo*), not unknown in Spain, are unusually common in many parts of America in passive constructions: *el puerto está siendo bombardeado* (= están bombardeando el puerto, se sigue bombardeando el puerto, el puerto es bombardeado, etc.). Some cases may be translations of English news reports.

CHILE: Estaba *siendo* vencido por dos enemigos terribles (Fernando Alegría, *Lautaro*, p. 83).

COLOMBIA: Rojas está *siendo* curado ... los soldados están *siendo* acosados (*El Tiempo*, April 12, 1944); Una división de policía está *siendo* trasladada al edificio del Seminario (*ibid.*, April 26, 1944).

MEXICO: El importante puerto ... está *siendo* bombardeado (*Excelsior* [Mexico City], December, 1940). Las otras fueron *siendo* llamadas sucesivamente (Gamboa, *Santa*, p. 255). Muchos eran los católicos que estaban *siendo* pasados por las armas (Fernando Robles, p. 86). Mi padre está *siendo* visitado con frecuencia (Benítez, pp. 39, 98, 110).

CUBA: Estoy *siendo* menospreciada por mi esposo (Ramos, p. 170).

Particularly in Andean regions '*estar* + gerund' may replace any simple verb form of standard speech: *estar teniendo* = *tener*, *estás pudiendo* = *puedes*, etc. (cf. *dar*, p. 211). Current for the most part only in popular speech, it may be considered an extension of Old Spanish progressive constructions carried to unsuspected limits under the influence of local Indian tongues. Sometimes the form is inceptive in feeling; that is, it stresses the beginning of an act: *estoy yendo* (cf. English 'I'll be going, I'll be getting dressed'). Sometimes it expresses the feeling of 'still, yet' as: *estoy teniendo* = *todavía tengo*. Again it may have no idea of progression or incompleteness.

CHILE: —Déjate de *estar molestando* (J. M. Castro, p. 16).

BOLIVIA: Yo me *he de estar sirviendo* [= he de servir = serviré] otro (Díaz V., *La Rosita*, p. 29); Pero lo que es la Rosita, algo *está teniendo* (p. 30); Ha de *estar habiendo* tiempo para bailar (p. 48); —Si ya no te *estás pudiendo* mover (p. 59); —*¿Está habiendo* en la jarra? (*El traje*, p. 28); —¿Qué más nos *estuviéramos queriendo?* (*Cuando vuelva*, p. 14); —Por pura chiripa *había estado habiendo* [=había, cf. p. 166] todavía este vasito (p. 30); Pero mejor no me hubieran *estado haciendo* cambiar de balde (p. 38); —¿Acaso tenemos siquiera hijos? —Por flojo no *estarás teniendo* (p. 43); —¡Si son las cosas de mi mama! —*Estarán* pues *siendo* (p. 57).

PERU (HIGHLANDS): *Estamos* pues *queriendo* una beca para nuestra hija (Benvenutto, p. 156); Tú no más *estás sabiendo* las penas que estoy pasando (p. 157).

ECUADOR: —Ah, *viniendo* ha *estado* mismo el Inspector (Mata, *Sanagüín*, p. 225).

VENEZUELA: —¿Ni qué necesidá tiene de *estar llevándose* estos bochos? ... Ya no voy a *está recogiendo* mis trapos (Gallegos, *Pobre negro*, p. 231).

A peculiar use of the gerund is found in Ecuador in such locutions as *¿qué haciendo? ¿qué diciendo?* which mean *¿por qué causa? ¿cómo?* etc.: "*¿Qué haciendo* me ha de hablar la niña?" The gerunds of *hacer* and *decir* are most frequently employed in this so-called Quechuan locution, which reaches to Catamarca, Argentina (Lafone, p. 106). The original meaning of *¿qué haciendo?* and *¿qué diciendo?* was *¿por haber hecho qué?* and *¿por haber dicho qué?* But the expression has been reduced to the force of a mere *¿por qué?* (Cevallos, p. 68). We find *¿qué haciendo?* also in Chiloé under the influence of Mapuche.

ARGENTINA (CATAMARCA): *¿Qué diciendo?* [= ¿Qué razón hay para ello?] (Lafone, p. 106).

CHILE (CHILOÉ): *¿Qué haciendo* [= por qué] viniste? *¿Qué haciendo* [= cómo] se cayó el niño? (Cavada, p. 282).

ECUADOR: —Así, Rosita, quítale nu más el marido a la Pitrona—dijo uno de ellos, por hacer una broma. —*Qui haciendo* ha de quitar pes mi marido—protesta la Petrona (García Muñoz, *Estampas*, p. 181). —No olvidarán la carabina. —¡Ni *qué haciendo* pues! Bendición nuestra es en montaña (Mata, *Sanagüín*, p. 75); —He aquí la plata. Pero devuelvan siquiera los mulares. —Ni *qué haciendo* pues. —Há-bleles, niño Jaime, que devuelvan las mulitas (p. 171). Con su licencia, patroncito. ¿No les dará ya los cinco barriles a los indios? —¡Ni *qué haciendo* pues, Diego! Nosotros nos entendemos de todo (p. 179).

THE GERUNDIAL IMPERATIVE

To denote continuity of action, particularly of a persistent or even irritating duration, standard Castilian uses a characteristic popular locution. The formula consists of the singular imperative of the verb + *que* + the imperative or the second person future (with or without *te*): *llora que* (*te*) *llora* or *llora que* (*te*) *llorarás* 'weeping and weeping, weeping away,' etc.[1] Thus we read in Pereda's *El sabor de la tierruca* (*Obras*, X, 39): "la moza de arriba, *acalda que te acalda*, y otras, desde abajo, *peina que te peina* la carga con la rastrilla; y la carga, *sube que sube* y *crece que crece*, hasta que debajo de ella no se ven ni el carro ni los bueyes."

[1] Occasionally we find the infinitive in place of the imperative, as in the following example from Santa Teresa (*Cartas*, No. 253): "Ternísima estoy; y el primer día *llorar que llorarás*, sin poder hacer otra cosa."

Another way of standardly expressing continuity of action is with gerund + *y* + gerund. Thus we read in Pereda (*ibid.*, p. 209): "apartaba las malezas y, *apartando y apartando*, llegó a un campuco."

In some parts of Spanish America (especially frequent in Mexico) we find another locution, possibly a blending of the two just mentioned: *llora que llora* + *llorando y llorando* > *llora y llora.*[2] The verb form in this expression is sometimes felt to be a third person singular or even a reduced form of the gerund (whence it has been called a gerundial imperative) rather than the singular imperative, and regularly has an impersonal value. This is evident in examples given below, like "había venido *auméntase y auméntase.*"

Occasionally a noun takes the place of the verb, as in *risa y risa;*[3] or the preposition *a* precedes the expression, as in *a trabaja y trabaja;*[4] or the formal imperative is used impersonally, as in *mátenos y mátenos;* rarely *más* is added: *trabaja que más trabaja, repite y más repite* (see Colombia); occasionally the infinitive is used.

CHILE (CENTRAL ZONE): ¿Y las chiquillas? ¡Va a quedar la pelería, *lloriquea y lloriquea!* (Juan Modesto Castro, p. 79). (SOUTHERN ZONE): ¿Hasta cuándo ha de hablar la señora? Menudita como es, parece en sus ires y venires un abejorro, *zumba y zumba* (Azócar, p. 257). Parecían moscardones ... *zumba que zumba* (Juan del Campo, p. 83).

PERU (CALEMAR AND NORTH HIGHLAND ZONES): Éste quiere armarle conversación pero él se limita a responder parcamente, *masca y masca* la coca buena (Ciro Alegría, *La serpiente*, p. 79); ... los hocicos en la corriente, entre una lluvia de chicotazos, pedradas y gritos. La resistían a pie firme *bebe y bebe* (p. 232). Llegaban más vacas ... un gran grupo que estaba allí ... *brama y brama* (Ciro Alegría, *El mundo*, p. 43); y el bruto *corta y corta* (p. 235); Mi patrón Linche, *tiro y tiro*

[2] Not necessarily a blending, however; possibly an attempt to clarify the expression. Spitzer (*Aufsätze*, pp. 180 ff.) cites a number of examples of the same construction in other Romance languages, notably Italian, where locutions with *e* [= y] are found side by side with forms with *che* [= que]. But he gives no corresponding dual forms for peninsular Spanish and has apparently disregarded American Spanish (see also Spitzer's discussion in *RFH*, IV [1942], 253–65).

[3] We find this form in the older language: "Yo, por lo desapresar,/Entrometo la camisa;/Ella *risa, y risa, y risa,*/Que se quier desternillar" (Sánchez de Badajoz, *Recopilación* [*ca.* 1554], I, 89).

[4] In regional Spain we find a popular locution with *venga* + *a* + *infinitive:* "Y aquel pobre *venga a chillar y venga a chillar* (Aurelio Espinosa, *Cuentos*, I, 32 [Toledo]); *Y vengan a vení* conde y duque *y vengan a vení* conde y grande personaje (I, 48 [Granada]; also I, 83 [Granada]; I, 91 [Toledo]; I, 104 [Sevilla]; II, 218 [Cuenca]; II, 232 [Ávila]; II, 236, 283 [Toledo]; II, 326 [Soria]; II, 337 [Granada]; etc.).

con la mina (p. 355); *Golpe y golpe:* la peña era dura (p. 359).

COLOMBIA (SOUTH): —¿Qué va a estar uno *piensa y piensa* en el muerto? (Álvarez Garzón, p. 236). (BOGOTÁ): *hable que hable, hable y hable, llueva y llueva* (Flórez, p. 380). (ANTIOQUIA): *Aguarda que más aguarda* (T. González, p. 16); *trabaja que más trabajarás* (p. 128); él perdía *que más perderás; andar y andar* y casi llegan (p. 18).

PANAMA: Su mujer era *gomitar y gomitar* (Nacho Valdés, *Sangre criolla*, p. 42). Cf. p. 239, n. 1.

MEXICO (CENTRAL ZONE): Pero no furioso, sino que no más está *risa y risa*, sin contestar a nadie ... mi prima Dolores la grande está *llora y llora* junto a la cama (Inclán, II, 227). Ése sería su triunfo, cubrirla de amor, del que había venido *auméntase y auméntase* dentro de su estropeada envoltura de ciego y de pobre (Gamboa, *Santa*, p. 233). ¿Qué tienen los perros/qu' están *ladra y ladra?* (Rivas Larrauri, p. 145); la chamaca/se las pasa a tod' hora *chilla y chilla* (p. 175); me he pasado la vida *sueña y sueña* (p. 188). —¿Qué piensa ... no va contenta? —Sí, cómo no! *Camina y camina. Piensa y piensa* (Galeana, p. 73); Ella seguía *habla y habla* (p. 195). La idea se maduró *a vuelta y vuelta* en la cabeza (Azuela, *La Marchanta*, p. 121; also p. 150). Desde la tarde ha estado *vueltas y vueltas* una señorita o señora joven a buscarlo (Robles Castillo, p. 49); —Ha estado *pregunta y pregunta* por usted (p. 60). —¡Pero apenas me dió campo de hacerme de la esquina, cuando aistá *a bala y bala!* (Azuela, *Los de abajo*, p. 134); Los dedos callosos de Demetrio iban y venían sobre las brillantes monedas, *a cuenta y cuenta* (p. 173); —Desquitas bien el sueldo, hijo—le interrumpió Demetrio con mansedumbre. *A reniega y reniega*, pero *a trabaja y trabaja* (p. 193); No paraba de rezongar de su patrón, pero no paraba de trabajar tampoco. Y así estamos nosotros: *a reniega y reniega* y *a mátenos y mátenos* (p. 245). ¿Ven cómo está *tiembla y tiembla?* (Magdaleno, p. 188); Está *rebuzna y rebuzna*, y da patadas como los burros (p. 195). (NUEVO LEÓN): —Pos, también pa' qué'stás ai *friegue y friegue* (García Roel, p. 305); Luego en la cárcel sigue *dice y dice* qu' él era inocente (p. 100).

Another way of expressing this continuity of action colloquially is with the imperative of *dar* and the pronoun *le: ¡dale!* The Academy dictionary explains that this interjection "se emplea para reprobar con enfado la obstinación o terquedad." It gives as alternate, but more expressive, the following extensions: *dale que dale, dale que le das*, and *dale que le darás*. It is more characteristic of familiar speech than of cultured speech, and its geographical extension has not been determined (*RFE*, XIX, 189 ff.)

In American Spanish we find *dale que dale* in familiar speech, and in some regions *dale y dale*, *déle que déle*, and *déle y déle.*

ARGENTINA: Y ahora, usted, *dale que dale*, empeñado en perderlo todo por junto (Larreta, *Zogoibi*, p. 143).

CHILE: Enteraban la semana *déle que déle* ... hasta que todo era un enredo y nadie sabía cuál era su mujer (Prado, *Un juez*, p. 152). Ahí estaba *dale y dale*, en su manía de buscar entierros (Azócar, p. 277). Y yo sin chistar, como me ha aconsejado don Carlos; pero ella, *dale y dale* (Barrios, *El niño*, p. 79).

BOLIVIA: Asaltos en descubierto, matanzas, asaltos, y *déle y déle* con Nanawa (Céspedes, p. 106).

COLOMBIA (SOUTH): —Y todavía en después de estar *déle y déle* con el machete cortando palos, se le hace poco que traigo ese guango e leña (Álvarez Garzón, p. 54). (BOGOTÁ): *Déle que déle* (Flórez).

COSTA RICA: Y luego las dos mujeres están otra vez, como la víspera, *déle que déle* al trabajo, una atizando el fuego y la otra con la masa para las tortillas entre las manos (Fabián Dobles, p. 118).

In Spain this *dale* is often followed by the preposition *con* + a noun: *¡Y dale con el llanto!* In parts of Spanish America another form, not unknown in Spain, is generally preferred: *déle* (as well as *dale*) + a noun or an infinitive. This is true notably of rural Argentina (Tiscornia, *La lengua*, § 187, 2): "y ansí andaban noche y día/*déle bala* a los ñanduces" (*Martín Fierro*, p. 36), in which *déle bala* expresses a continuous firing of guns. Again we read:

Él me siguió menudiando/mas sin poderme acertar,/y yo, *déle culebriar*, hasta que al fin le dentré/y ahí no más lo despaché/sin dejarlo resollar (*Martín Fierro*, p. 100); y pedía siempre al resar,/la estirpación de mis tías./Y *dale* siempre *rosarios*,/noche a noche y sin cesar;/*dale* siempre *barajar*/salves, trisagios y credos (p. 263).

URUGUAY: —En cuanto Carlos sale, ya está ella *déle que déle* cepillo a su ropa (Florencio Sánchez, p. 33).

Another verb sometimes found with the force of *¡dale!* or *¡déle!* is *meter: ¡métele!* or *¡métale!* or *¡métanle!* Román (III, 499) explains these forms as equivalent to "¡ea! ¡adelante! ¡vamos! ¡no hay que temer!"

He might have added "¡dale!" to which they more accurately correspond. In the River Plate region and elsewhere this use of *meter* is current in popular speech in the locutions: *meta y meta* + a finite verb or + an infinitive, and *meta* + an infinitive, a noun, etc.

ARGENTINA: —¡Güenas tardes! ... Pero el viejo como si juera sordo, siguió *meta y meta* sobar la guasca (Lynch, *Romance*, p. 36); ¡Y *meta* sobarse la pera! —¡Y *meta* comer nueces! (p. 84); Y aquellos hombres serios ... como si endeveras hubieran sido fulleros y tramposos, *meta y meta:* «¡Cálmese, Rozales! ... ¡Cálmese que no es pa tanto!» (p. 265); Y *meta* rogarlo la señora y *meta* meniar él la cabeza (p. 403); y ella, con los ojos bajos *meta* trabajar su media (p. 428); pero se calló y sin decir palabra siguió *meta y meta* acomodar su camita en el suelo (p. 437). Y así andan, *meta* cine y *meta* boite. Y como dicen que no hay tiempo ni comodidá pa cocinar, a la hora de comer, ¿qué comemos? (Chiarello, p. 43). Después, fotos; *meta* fotos. No ven nada, pero se llevan lo que ve la máquina (Filloy, p. 413).

URUGUAY: —Pero si en cada rancho tiene una chinita, *meta* suspirar (Reyles, *El gaucho*, p. 141); vide al patrón cortau con las boleadoras en la mano, *meta* espuela (p. 231; also pp. 146, 214).

PERU: En seguida le añadíamos pan frío ... poníamos la sabrosa materia en unas cajas o moldes ... y *métale usted* vueltas al tornillo hasta que se formaba un considerable bloque de chicharrón (Corrales, p. 238)

'VENGO DE' FOR 'ACABO DE'

It is frequently stated by preceptists that the Gallicized construction *vengo de* (< French *je viens de* 'I have just') is often and wrongly employed in Spanish for *acabo de* of similar meaning.[5] That this is occasionally done cannot be denied, but one must guard against considering every *vengo de* as an imitation of the French idiom. When *vengo* in this construction is taken in its real sense of motion, there can be no objection to it. For instance, "vengo de comprarlo en la tienda" may correctly mean "vengo de la tienda donde lo compré." However, *venir de* means *acabar de* in sentences like "Y le conté lo que vos *venís de* contarnos" (Reyles, *El gaucho*, p. 207 [Uruguay]). Such Gallicisms may be heard in Spain, as well as in Spanish America.

[5] The same is true of Portuguese: "venho de receber um telegrama" for "acabo de receber" or "recebi há pouco" (J. Dunn, *Portuguese grammar*, § 453*g*).

'DIZQUE' AND VARIANTS

The good Old Spanish form *diz* (< impersonal *dicit ?*) *que* stood for *dicen que* or *se dice que* 'they say, it is said that,' etc. The form *diz* occasionally was a mere apocopation of *dice*, sometimes used for the preterite *dijo* or *dijeron;* but in this sense *diz* is now rare, though examples may be found in dialectal Spanish (Menéndez Pidal, *Dialecto leonés*, § 18, 2). Common in the old language, *diz que* was not discountenanced by Juan de Valdés, who, about 1535, wrote: "También dezimos *diz que* por *dizen*, y no parece mal" (p. 121). However, it apparently began to decline shortly after: of the eleven examples counted by Keniston (p. 344) in that century, only two were found in the second half. Nevertheless, *diz que* did not become obsolete; it became dialectal, provincial, or rustic. At the beginning of the seventeenth century, Covarrubias registered it as "palabra aldeana, que no se deve usar en Corte. Vale tanto como *dizen que*." It lingered on in regional literature, and evidently in speech, into the nineteenth century. Even today it is occasionally heard in Spain, but only as an archaism in familiar or jocose style.

The case is different for Spanish America. In most regions, *dizque* (generally written as one word) still flourishes vigorously, in some areas even in cultured speech. Furthermore, divergent forms have come into use, all of which are in varying degrees considered popular or rustic and some of which may be traced to dialectal Spain (*es que*, *is que*, and *y que* [*RFE*, XV, 248]). These variants and their geographical distribution are as follows:

The form *izque* with loss of initial *d* is found in Mexico, Colombia, Ecuador, Chile, and probably elsewhere. It is pronounced *ihke* in New Mexico (*BDH*, IV, 15), Tabasco (Gutiérrez Eskildsen, pp. 83–85), and in other regions where *s* in the weak final position has become aspirated (Chile, coastal zones of Colombia, Ecuador, etc.). In Venezuela and part of Colombia this weakening has progressed until the aspiration itself has disappeared in popular speech, where we find *i que* (spelled also *y que*). Alvarado (p. 7) tells us that "*y que* es manera vulgar de pronunciar *diz que*." Sánchez Sevilla (*RFE*, XV, 248) reports *y que* as well as *is que* for limited areas in the Salamancan region of Spain; and we know they are used in other areas.[6]

The form *es que* is found in Mexico, Central America, Colombia,

[6] RURAL CASTILE: "¿Conque dices *y que* su hijo se casa?" (Benavente, *Señora ama*, I, 1); "ya me he convencío *y que* no es así" (I, 6); "demasiado *y que* lo sé" (II, 1). NORTH EXTREMADURA: "Dice *y que* vendrá" (Corominas); and in Andalusia. Cf. also *BDH*, II, 311–12.

Chile, rural Argentina, etc. Cuervo (§ 441) mentions it for Colombia, though he fails to include other popular variants: *quesque* for Bogotá, *izque* and *quizque* for Antioquia. He thinks that the two correct locutions *diz que* 'they say that' and *es que* 'the fact is, the reason is, it's because,' have become confused in popular speech to form *es que* with the meaning of *diz que*. Correct *es que* introduces the speaker's opinion, whereas popular *es que* (like *diz que*) expresses someone else's opinion. For instance, in answer to the question "¿Por qué no ha venido?" the reply "*Es que* está enfermo" would express the speaker's reason, and "*Diz que* (or popular *Es que*) está enfermo" would express someone else's opinion. As a matter of fact, while *diz que* and *es que* may have become fused in form, they have also blended their meanings, so that *diz que* frequently means no more than a weak *es que*. There is a difference of stress between popular *es que* [= *diz que*] and correct *es que:* the former *es* is much weaker than the latter. This weakly stressed popular *es que*, according to Cuervo, is commonly used in Colombia in relating folk tales. We find the same to be true elsewhere. For Guatemala, for instance, Sandoval (I, 515), without indicating that *es que* is equivalent to *diz que*, correctly remarks that *es que éste era* is equivalent to *érase que se era* 'once upon a time,' etc. A Chilean folk tale begins "*Es que* le 'ijo/La madre al hijo" (Román, II, 300). However, we also find the correct form *dizque* in folk tales: "Éste *dizque* era un hombre que se llamaba Peralta" (Carrasquilla, *Novelas*, p. 17 [Colombia]). In Ecuador and southern Colombia we find the form *desque*, probably a fusion of *dizque* and *es que*, and of lower social status than *dizque*. In Chiloé, Chile, we find besides *es que* the form *si que*, considered a *corrupción* by Cavada (p. 281), but more probably it is analogical with double forms like *cualesquier* and *cualsiquier* (cf. p. 147), etc.

The form *quizque* (< *que* + *izque*), together with *que dizque*, is found in Colombia, Mexico, and probably elsewhere. Its meaning is not *que dicen que*, as one might suppose, but a vague *dicen que*. Following Spitzer's lead in dealing with narrative *que* (*RFH*, IV, 123), we might call *dizque* a type of 'narrativo' or 'charlativo,' and *que dizque* (or *quizque*, etc.) might then be a blending of two types of 'narrativo': *que* and *dizque*. We find *que dizque*, as well as *dizque que*, used in Santo Domingo (*BDH*, V, 240). The form *quizque* is not mentioned by all preceptists, but it frequently appears in recorded popular speech. Aurelio Espinosa (*Apuntaciones*, p. 619) reports also the form *queisque* for New Mexico.

The variant *quesque* (< *que* + *esque*) is a similar formation found in Mexico (*BDH*, IV, 308), Central America, Colombia, rural areas of Argentina (for San Luis cf. Vidal, p. 396), and probably elsewhere.

Now *quizque* (or *que izque*) and *quesque* (or *que esque*) and *y que*, as well as *dizque*, have in turn become weakened and are often used with the force of the simple conjunction *que* 'that' rather than with the original meaning of 'they say that.' This weakened meaning is related to the correct use of *es que*, a fact which corroborates the theory of confusion of *dizque* and *es que*. For Mexico, Ramos Duarte (p. 425) calls *que es que* [= *quesque*] an "estribillo de la gente del pueblo," remarking that "*que es que* dice mi tía *que es que* no puede venir" means merely "dice mi tía que no puede venir."

Spitzer (*RFH*, VII, 299) suggests that *dizque Antonio se casa* was in popular speech conceived as *diz-que: Antonio se casa*. That is, *dizque* indicates a shade of irresponsibility on the part of the narrator, and the new division bespeaks the popular preference for direct discourse, which is here superimposed, as it were, upon indirect discourse: *diz que se casa* > *diz-que: se casa*. This would explain ubiquitous *dizque* as an adverb of doubt ('supposedly') as well as the elliptic and independent *¡qué dizque!* ('¡ca!') mentioned below.

In the following examples the meaning of *dizque*, or its variants, is indicated only if it is other than impersonal *dicen que* or *se dice que*. It will be remembered that *dizque* may mean *parece que* = "is supposed to" or "apparently" or "I understand that": *él dizque lo hizo* = 'he is supposed to have done it,' 'he supposedly (*or* apparently) did it,' etc.; its force may be further developed to a doubt and even to a negation: *él dizque lo hizo* = 'he is supposed to have done it' > 'it is doubtful whether he did it' > 'he probably did not do it.'

ARGENTINA (NORTHWEST): *Diz que* andaba la Virgen por el mundo. ... —*Diz que* andaba curando enfermos (César Carrizo, p. 17); Y *diz que dicen*, y dicen la verdá, *que* Dios castiga muy juerte al desamor (p. 109). (SAN LUIS): *quesque, esque, que* (Vidal, p. 396).

CHILE (CENTRAL ZONE, RURAL): Cuando estaba en pañales, *iz que*, ... como si hubiera tenido empacho (Muñoz, p. 40); Y *diz que* ... se había permitido el lujo (p. 54); una catervada de veces, *iz que* se habían encontrado (p. 132; also pp. 155, 157). A misa *es que* iba un galán/por la calle de la iglesia (Vicuña Cifuentes, p. 113). (SOUTHERN ZONE): Yo estaba chiquichicho cuando murió el finao Juan

Barrios. De repente, *es que* (Latorre, *Hombres*, p. 132). (CHILOÉ): El rey *si que* (o *es que*) llegó al palacio en que su hija estaba encantada (Cavada, p. 281).

BOLIVIA: *Diz que* en San Ignacio no hubo «elesión» porque se robaron los libros (Alfredo Flores, in *ACB*, p. 64); *diz que* don José está empeñado en llevársela a Matilde (p. 68).

PERU (especially the HIGHLAND ZONE): Este sabio *dizque* se metió a publicar pasquines contra don Guillermo y su familia (Corrales, p. 50). —¡El puma azul ... , *dizque* puma azul! ... ¡Si es como todos ... , medio pardo, medio amarillo! (Ciro Alegría, *La serpiente*, p. 170).

ECUADOR (COASTAL ZONE): La llamaban la agalluda. Porque *dizque* todo lo quería para ella (Aguilera Malta, p. 21); Vienen los blancos. *Izque* han comprao una isla. ... *Dizque* por arriba todo lo arreglaban a látigo o a bala (p. 102). Y *dicen que diz que* [= dicen que] hasta las cuatro de la tarde no más trabajan en el campo (Pareja, *Baldomera*, p. 138); *Diz que* tiene bastantísima plata (p. 151). —Pero, oye, ¿y la Eudosia? —*Iz que* se jué par Guayas (Gil Gilbert, in *ACH*, p. 277). (HIGHLAND ZONE): Y por ahí *dizque dicen que* es el alma de mi patrón (Vásconez, p. 52); bien grande *desque* era el toro (p. 152).

The form *desque* (probably a fusion of *dizque* and *es que*) is current among the populace in the Ecuadorian highland zone, both urban and rural, while *dizque* is felt to be the more correct and elegant form, used even by the cultured. In *Huasipungo* (1934), Jorge Icaza wrote *dizque*, but in his later novels, *En las calles* (1935) and *Cholos* (1938), he wrote *desque*, probably in an attempt at a stricter adherence to the language of the lower classes:

(HIGHLAND ZONE): Y el indio ... *dizque* se viene pes toditicas las noches (*Huasipungo*, p. 30); esto *dizque* va a ser pantano (p. 66); *Dizque* son generosos (p. 133). Hasta con los aventadores *desque* negocea, ¿ha de creer compadre? (*En las calles*, p. 232); —Y éste no *desque* se quiere ir (p. 233); Ya *desque* están formando los comités. —Nu'e sabido pes. ... Cerveza *desque* 'stán repartiendo (p. 234), etc. —No *desque* van a dejar salir a la Virgen (*Cholos*, p. 130; also pp. 138, 147, 148, 149, 216, etc.)

COLOMBIA (BOGOTÁ): *Dizque* te vas al campo ... *¡Quesque* te vas a casar! (C). (ANTIOQUIA): Usté *isque* nesesita piones y me dijo que sí ... (Posada, p. 10); me dijo qui Andrea *isque* quedaba debiendo 2 pesos (p. 28; also pp. 37, 65). Determinaron descargarme *dizque* ['supposedly'] pa que descansara (Carrasquilla, *Novelas*, p. 122). —*Dizque* [= que] no sabía bailar, me dijo usté, Crispín (Buitrago, p. 89). No te ponen en l'escuela, *quizque* pa que no te ayuntés con nosotros: *quizque* te pegamos los piojos (Carrasquilla, *Hace tiempos*, I, 27; also 65, 170, etc.); Dos *izque* son labradores (I, 171); un perro que tenían *izque* [= dijeron que] se los habían envenenao (I, 172); Yo *dizque* [= dice que] soy la reina; que no *dizque* [= dice que] hay una mujer más bella y más querida que yo (II, 108). (ATLANTIC COAST): —Dice la lavandera que *y que* mandó por la ropa sucia. ... Como usted *y que* se va, será ésta la última (Sundheim, p. 555). (SOUTHERN ZONE, PASTO, etc.): —Tamién *dezque* estaba prendado de la hija de ñora Belisaria (Álvarez Garzón, p. 219).

The form *y que* so commonly encountered in Venezuela is reported (Rosenblat) as being used there not only in cultured speech but also in newspaper writing.

VENEZUELA: Florencia me dijo que la esperara mientras llenaba la tinaja porque *y que* le tiene miedo al encanto (Gallegos, *La trepadora*, p. 213); —Me dijo el peluquero que no era necesario, porque *y que* [= dijo que] las tengo muy bonitas y como se usan ahora (p. 267). Su ocupación *y que* es brujear caballos, como también aseguran que *y que* tiene oraciones ... (Gallegos, *Doña Bárbara*, p. 15). —Capitán, ¿usté *y que* va a comprar este barco? (*ACMV*, II, 40); —¿No *y que* no tienes virtud para traerlo? (p. 151); Tú *y que* tenías una cosa peligrosa, que eso que tú tienes *y que* es de cuidado, y tú *y que* eres muy disparatero. ... —¿Dijo eso mamá? —Sí (Pocaterra, p. 84). ¿Será por la parte de blanco que *y que* tiene? (Gallegos, *El pobre negro*, p. 27); Unos periódicos de ésos que *y que* salen en la capital (p. 92); —Eso *y que* contaba mi máe, a quien no conocí (p. 348). Me dijeron *que y que* [= que] me andaban buscando (Briceño, p. 93); ahí mismo se le cuadró ... diciendo *y que* [= que] ... (p. 156).

PANAMA: —¿Qué haces? —*Dizque* estudio ['I'm supposed to be studying']; ¿Qué tocas? *Dizque* ['supposedly'] una sonata (C). Dijo aquello, *di que* para que le creyeran; Antonio es hombre *diz que* panameño (Mangado, p. 91). *Dizque* el veinticuatro es la fiesta; me dijo *que dizque* venía a visitarme (L. Aguilera, p. 314).

COSTA RICA: Pos también dicen *quesque* [= que] una vez mató a uno (Fabián Dobles, p. 93); el mestro ... decía a ña Rafela *quesque* [= que] el chacalín era un poco raro (p. 293; also pp. 85, 167, 226, etc.); *diz que* la sangre nunca es del todo roja (p. 298).

GUATEMALA: *Dizque* habrá guerra europea (Sandoval, I, 421).

MEXICO (CENTRAL ZONE): Josefa se tiró de cabeza a un pozo *dizque* porque estaba loca (José Romero, p. 14); seguían surtiendo las recetas *dizque* para preservarse de todo género de dolencias (p. 50); metiéronme a la cárcel *dizque* por robo (p. 121). —Yo les traigo de comer, indios amolados ... contaban las voces que *dizque* oyeron a un emisario del rebelde (Magdaleno, p. 38; also p. 66, etc.); —*Quesque* se aparecen por aquí muchas ánimas (p. 50); *Quesque* un lucas le pegó un golpazo al señor general Díaz, en México ... ¿será posible? (p. 100); ¿Ya supo *quesque* [= que] hay bolas? (p. 101); *Quesque* se quieren casar (p. 180), etc. *Que dizque* yo era maderista y que me iba a levantar (Azuela, *Los de abajo*, p. 76); en carta que me pone mi mujer me notifica *que izque* [= que] ya tenemos otro hijo (p. 90). (EASTERN COASTAL ZONE): —¡Ay, Comadre! Una orden del juez ... *¡Esque* acá tienen escondido un hombre! ... *Esque* ustedes lo tienen escondido aquí ... (Delgado, *El desertor*, in *Obras*, I, 205). (TABASCO, ESCUINAPA): Cuando supo *izque* a mi hermano lo habían nombrao del Comité Agrario. ... Ansina que lo vido malherido *izque* parti huyendo (Gutiérrez Eskildsen, p. 83); cómo se puede pedir ayuda para la señora *izque* quedó con sei niño (p. 85).

NEW MEXICO: *Esque* no hubo na. ... *Isque* no. ... *¿Isque* [= es verdad que] ya vinieron? ... Dicen *quesque* [= que] no. ... *Quisque* ya se acabó too (Aurelio Espinosa, *Apuntaciones*, p. 619). Dijo *quisque* [= que] ya no vinía; no igas *quisque* no [= no digas que no] (Espinosa, *Studies*, II, 91).

SANTO DOMINGO: ¿No *dique* anda atrás de la hermana? (Bosch, *Dos pesos*, p. 108). Dicen *dizque* [= que] llegará el vapor esta tarde (Patín Maceo, *Dom.*, p. 61). Lola dise *que dique* se parese a mí (Bosch, *Camino real*, p. 45).

Locally the locution *dizque*, with its variants, may assume special functions. Thus, for Ecuador, Vázquez (p. 147) reports two particular uses: (1) To indicate an emphatic protest or great surprise: "—¿Aceptas la invitación que N. te hace? —*¡Dizque* he de ir, después de lo que me ha hecho!" In this example *dizque he de ir* means something like "What! Can anyone possibly say or believe that I shall go?" (2) As a strong exclamatory negation: "¡Qué *dizqué!*" The first meaning is apparently the one attributable to *dizqué* in the following passage: "—¡Señorcito, a mí prefiera pes! Dé un litrito. —¡Pish ...

para un litro *dizqué* molesta al señor! —¡A mí más mejor dé dando veinte litros!" (Mata, *Sanagüín*, p. 81). The second meaning of exclamatory negation we find in both Ecuador and Peru (also under the guise of *quesqué*):

ECUADOR: Yo seré tu cualquier cosa,/Tú serás mi no sé qué;/En pares podrás ganarme,/Pero en nones *qué dizqué* (Mera, p. 265).
PERU: Una cuitada lo creía improbable, diciendo este modismo de más fuerza negativa que si estuviera cargado de noes y verbos: —*¡Cuándo, ya, dizqué!* (Barrantes, p. 192). —¿Le duele la mano? —*Quesqué,*—gruñó (Ciro Alegría, *La serpiente*, p. 92).

This strong negation is the reinforced feeling of doubt previously mentioned. For instance, *dizque se casa* may have developed through the following series: 'they say he's to be married' > 'it is doubtful that he will be married' > 'he surely will not be married'; that is, 'they say he will be married (but I am sure it is not true).'

In Chiloé, Chile, we find the local form *si que* used as an exclamation of surprise, with the force of *diz que* in Ecuador: "¡Eso contó *si que!*" = "¡Es posible que haya contado eso!" (Cavada, p. 281).

For Mexico Icazbalceta (p. 202) mentions a special popular use of *esque* in questions, with the meaning of *¿es así? ¿es verdad eso?*: "—*¿Esque*, niña? dijo la nana. —No, Susana, te están engañando" (Inclán, I, 15).

A related force is given to *esqué* by the boy Rudecindo, a rustic in Latorre's *Zurzulita* (Chile); but, to judge from the author's comments, this *esqué* is merely a personal linguistic habit ("curiosa forma interrogativa de sus respuestas" [p. 26]) which invariably provokes the risibilities of listeners (pp. 26, 34, 68, etc.): "—¿Cómo m'había de llamar, *es qué?* ¡Rudecindo me llamo pú!" (p. 26); "—¿Qué no' sta viendo qu'es un picaflor, *es qué?*" (p. 68); etc.

ES QUE

Many constructions containing *es que* involve the so-called Gallicized *que*, current in most regions. Cuervo (§ 460) treats at great length such expressions, which he considers due to French influence, particularly through poor Spanish translations from the French. Among his examples are: "*fué* entonces *que* nació" for "entonces fué cuando nació"; "*es* por esta razón *que* escribo" for "por esta razón escribo" or "por esta razón es por la que escribo"; "en la paz *es que* florecen las artes" for "en la paz es cuando florecen las artes"; "¿de dónde *fué que* vino?" for "¿de dónde vino?"; "para Europa *es que* se va" for "para Europa es para donde se va"; "mañana *será que* me voy" for "mañana será cuando me voy"; "*es* a usted *que* me dirijo" for "es a usted a quien me dirijo"; etc.

Cuervo admits not only that such usage is found in newspapers, in the writing of "poetastros, filosofastros y la innúmera caterva de los demás corruptores de la lengua castellana, y aun en los de autores por otra parte estimables," but that it is gaining ground in familiar and popular speech. But, as Henríquez Ureña has pointed out (*RFE*, VIII, 358, n. 3), the phenomenon is encountered in popular speech in regions where few people read and where there have been very few translations from the French. Some are inclined, therefore, to consider the locution as not due to French influence but rather as a purely popular usage. Furthermore, it is occasionally found in the older language from the thirteenth century on, a circumstance which led Cuervo to believe, with his unerring acumen, that the construction had its origin in Spain and that thus the way was prepared for its more abundant Gallicized modern usage. There seems to be no reason, however, why in some regions it may not be due in part to French influence among the lettered, and in others a merely popular form of expression among the untutored, harking back to a genuine characteristic Castilian mode. Thus the same phenomenon may conceivably exist on two distinct social levels, though anchored in different sources.

Argentina: Entonces *fué/que*, al verlo, reconoció Berdún a Luis (Ascasubi, p. 170). Y aura *es que* [= es cuando], en habiendo dejao el cuerpo pa los bichos, Miseria pensó lo que le quedaba por hacer (Güiraldes, *Don Segundo*, p. 258). *Es* entonces *que* [= cuando] descubre por entre uno de los huecos ... (Lynch, *De los campos*, p. 39).

Uruguay: *Fué* aquí *que* [= donde] le dió el ataque (Amorím, *El paisano*, p. 97). Por eso *es que* esta gente lo mira con tanta atención (Trías du Pre, p. 108).

Chile: *Fué* en medio de este júbilo *que* conoció el bando del rey (Fernando Alegría, *Leyenda*, p. 42). —Por eso *es que* no me hallo con los viejos (Alberto Romero, *Perucho González*, p. 39).

Bolivia: Por eso *es que* hay bandidos aquí (Alfredo Flores, in *ACB*, p. 66). *Es* aquí *que* le he aconsejado a Andrés que haga uso de la prensa (Arguedas, *Vida criolla*, p. 214).

PERU: Luego *es* el barbero *que* [= quien] lo rasura (María Wiesse, in *ACP*, p. 138). —Pues ahora *es que* la rueda se ha puesto cuadrada (Corrales, p. 242). Por eso *es que* concluyo, como comencé ... (José Gálvez, *ap.* Corrales, p. 278).

ECUADOR: Pero si ahora no más *es que* se ha vuelto así (Pareja, *El muelle*, p. 27); Un muchacho *es que* [= quien] ha venido (p. 35; also pp. 39, 132). —El ocho mismo *fué que* me diste los cinco sucres (Icaza, *En las calles*, p. 180).

COLOMBIA: ¿Y a ese marchante *fué que* lo bombiaron [= despidieron]? —No, Amalia. Él *fué que* se apretó la iraca [= se ajustó el sombrero = huyó] (Carrasquilla, *Hace tiempos*, III, 87).

VENEZUELA: Ahoritica *fué que* [= cuando] comenzó el invierno (Arráiz, p. 13). Ahora *es que* vengo a darme cuenta de que se hallaba aquí (Gallegos, *Doña Bárbara*, p. 86); Ahora *es que* estoy en un peso (p. 319). Entre esos campesinos *fué que* [= donde] llegó Simón (Croce, p. 24). Pa la casa *es que* voy yo (Díaz-Solís, p. 67).

NICARAGUA: Por vos *es que* [= por quien] me yecho hasta baboso (Toruño, p. 89).

EL SALVADOR: *Fué* entonces *que* [= cuando] la india ... entró una noche ... en el palacio (Salarrué, *El Cristo negro*, p. 14).

MEXICO: *Fué* entonces *que* nació; Con él *fué que* peleé (Ramos Duarte [p. 422], who gives many other examples, which challenge Henríquez Ureña's statement "en México no existe semejante empleo del *que*" [RFE, VIII, 358, n. 3]).

SANTO DOMINGO: Así *es que*, ahora *es que*, allí *es que*, por eso *es que* (*BDH*, V, 178). Con esto *es que* me pagas (Requena, *Camino*, p. 16); *Es* Dios *que* se ha acordado de mí (p. 28); —Por esto *es que* muchos hombres prefieren no trabajar (p. 34).

PUERTO RICO: Allí *es que* lo vi; así *es que* se hace (Navarro, p. 132).

In Mexico, and probably elsewhere, we find an *es que* in locutions like *de modo es que* [= *de modo que*], in which the *es* is intrusive by analogy with such expressions as *así es que*, etc. Such usage is not unknown in provincial Spain. In Pereda's *Escenas montañesas* (*Obras*, V, 266) we read "—De modo y manera *es que* ... la paré bien tiesa se estaba."

MEXICO: ¿De moo *es que* usté iba a ser dotor? (Azuela, *Los de abajo*, p. 49); ¿De moo *es que* no le cierra el balazo? (p. 53); De modo *es que* si por este corral pudiéramos atravesar, saldríamos derecho al callejón? (p. 103).

¿ES QUE?

In some regions, particularly the Andean zone, *es que* abounds in questions, a locution which again reminds us of the French usage but which again is very probably a popular development found also in Spain. Its divergence from standard Castilian is evident after the interrogative adverbs *por qué, dónde,* etc.

ARGENTINA: ¿Quién *es que* habla? (C).

CHILE: —*¿Es que* esta guerra no habrá de terminar jamás? (Fernando Alegría, *Lautaro,* p. 198).

BOLIVIA: —*¿Es que* no has recogido más que eso? ¡Uy, qué vergüenza! (Arguedas, *Vida criolla,* p. 38); —*¿Es que* ha bailado usté mucho, mascarita? Parece que está cansado (p. 107); —*¿Es que* usted me insulta? —¡No, señor! (p. 132).

ECUADOR (COASTAL ZONE): ¿Por qué *es que* Inocente pelea con mi papá? (Pareja, *Baldomera,* p. 112); ¿Y qué *es que* [= es lo que] te pasa también en el brazo? ... ¿Dónde *es que* está Lamparita, hágame el favor? (p. 121); ¿Qué *es que* [= es lo que] mismo te pasa? (p. 131); ¿Y adónde *es que* te vas? (p. 132); ¿Quién *es que* [= es el que] te anda rondando? (p. 180).

COLOMBIA: ¿Adónd'*es que* va? ¿Cómu *es qu*'es? Por esu *es que* lo digo; A ust'*es que* li hablo (Flórez, p. 380).

VENEZUELA: ¿Cómo *es que* es, compa? (Briceño, p. 32).

CUBA (ORIENTE): ¿Dónde *es que* está Juan? (Padrón).

For Mexico, Ramos Duarte (p. 425) reports a peculiar local usage in Sinaloa and Chihuahua, *qué si quí* for *qué:* "*¿Qué si quí* vendes?" for "*¿Qué* vendes?" This is probably due to a desire to emphasize by rounding out the question formula.

ES (ERA) DE QUE

We have previously noted (p. 157) the special Ecuadorian predilection for the use of the future tense to replace the more abrupt imperative: *escribirásme* for *escríbeme.* This inclination to avoid the direct and apparently harsh imperative is manifested further in an interesting locution of a number of areas: *es* (or *era*) *de que* + the subjunctive (*es de que te levantes*). Since this locution expresses a softened command or a necessity idea (*hay que*), the sentence *es de que te levantes* is equivalent to *hay que levantarte* or an attenuated *levántate* and may sometimes be rendered in English with 'should': 'you should get up.' It is exceedingly common in popular speech and in familiar conversation among the cultured.

CHILE: (*de* omitted): *Era que* me dieras uno; yo te lo crío (Acevedo H., *Árbol,* p. 39). *Era que* los [= nos] juéramos (Durand, *Campesinos,* p. 61).

ECUADOR: —*Es de que* les hagas dormir a los longos en otro cuarto; ya no se puede ni andar por aquí (Icaza, *Cholos,* p. 31); *Es de que* te vayas a Quito y l'exijas al viejo (p. 32). ¡Algo siquiera *era de que* vayas shevando [= llevando]! (Icaza, *Media vida,* p. 45); Vos tan *es de que* les des duro (p. 54); —Vos tan *es de que* vayas sabiendo (p. 115); —Entonces nu'*es de que* digas que no ti'a dicho nada, pes (p. 163); —A nosotros *era* pes *de que* grite vecina Matilde (p. 176).

COLOMBIA: *¡Es de que* lo llames! *¡Es de que* vaya cuantu antes! *¡Es de que* li hag'el reclamo! (Flórez, p. 380).

VENEZUELA: Ya *es de que* trabajes; ya *es de que* ganes dinero (Rosenblat).

MEXICO: —Con tanto tiempo que llevas de trabajar, *era de que* ya fueras cuando menos jefe de la estación (Anda, *Juan del Riel,* p. 123). —Lo peor del cuento, observó Cándido, es que está volviendo como ella a Doña Tomasa la cocinera. Ya *era de que* estuviese dándole a la cena (Quevedo, *La camada,* p. 175).

A form with the subjunctive like *es de que veas* might be elliptical for *es hora de que veas.* Or it might be a mere extension of impersonal *es de ver.* The finite form of the verb (*veas*) preceded by *que* is used for the purpose of indicating person and number, which the impersonal infinitive alone (*ver*) cannot do. The infinitive form (*es de notar,* etc.) itself is an old usage. Keniston (p. 527) records a good sixteenth-century example from Jiménez de Cisneros' *Cartas:* "*es de dar* ynfinjtas gracias a nuestro señor." This older usage, limited in the modern standard language, survives in some regions.

BOLIVIA: *Sería de* agradecerle a ese caballero tanto interés que toma por nosotros (Ruiz, p. 35).

ECUADOR: *Era de* haberlo enterrao allá mesmo (*ACH,* p. 272). —Caray, *era de* cobrarle un poquito más (Icaza, *Media vida,* p. 83). —¿Por dónde *será,* pues, *de* hallar trabajo? (Gil Gilbert, *Nuestro pan,* p. 187); ¿Hasta cuándo *será de* estarnos cojudeando [= haciendo el tonto] aquí? (p. 45).

COLOMBIA: *Era di* haberlo comprao; *era di* haberle cogido la caña (la flota, etc.) (Flórez, p. 380).

TODO ES QUE

A divergent use of *es* (*de*) *que* we find in the expression *todo es que* meaning *basta que*. (In Colombia *el todo es* = *lo deseable es*.)

COLOMBIA: *¡El todu es* que no llueva! (Flórez, p. 380).

VENEZUELA: *Todo es que* lo sepa uno para que los demás lo sepan (Rosenblat).

MEXICO: Pero no le hace que sean muchos ... *todo es que* [= basta que] uno haga por voltearse y dejan a los jefes solos (Azuela, *Los de abajo*, p. 98). *Todo es que* uno de los muchachos empiece a fumar para que los demás lo imiten (C). A la pobre siempre le pasaba igual: *todo era que* se llegara la hora de la fiesta para que se pusiera nerviosa y olvidara lo que ya sabía (García Roel, p. 214); Lo dejaban sin juerzas ... pero, *todito jué que* empezara a tomar la yerbita que San Lorenzo le dió y ya lo ve usté: güeno y sano (p. 283; also p. 320).

COSTA RICA: —Eso se lo arreglan. ... *Todo es que* los de encima se tapen los ojos y le hagan lao. ... *Todo jué que* se apurara en las otras eleciones y echara muchos vivas al candidato, pa que se refrescara (Fabián Dobles, p. 285); *Todo es que* el probe animal ya no pueda defendesc, y ellos [los zopilotes] se encargan de remachalo sacándole los ojos (p. 318).

GUATEMALA: Y *todo era que* dijera eso, para que metiera otros gritos (Arévalo, p. 91).

LO QUE SOY YO

In the standard phrase '*lo que es* + a subject pronoun,' the form *es* remains invariable, agreeing with its subject *que: lo que es yo* 'as for me, as far as I am concerned." In most regions of Spanish America, on the other hand, the verb is made to agree in person and number with the pronoun following it: *lo que soy yo, lo que somos nosotros,* etc. This practice is no doubt by analogy with the common locutions *es él* 'it's he,' *soy yo* 'it's I,' *somos nosotros* 'it's we,' etc., in which agreement in person and number is made between verb and pronoun.

RIVER PLATE ZONE: *Lo que soy yo, lo que somos nosotros* (Morínigo).

VENEZUELA: *Lo que soy yo,* monto el rucio (Gallegos, *Cantaclaro*, p. 213). *Lo que somos nosotros,* levantamos el bollo [= nos vamos sin decir nada] esta tarde (Rosenblat).

GUATEMALA: *Lo que somos nosotros* no podemos ir al baile, por estar mamá enferma de cuidado. ... *Lo que soy yo,* como buen cristiano perdono a mis enemigos (Sandoval, II, 30).

MEXICO: *Lo que soy yo* no vuelvo (Ramos Duarte, p. 568).

EMPHATIC 'SER'

We find an apparently redundant use of the verb *ser* in such expressions as *quiero es pan* for emphatic *quiero pan*. This phenomenon is current in Colombia: Cuervo (§ 431) reports it for Bogotá; Tascón (p. 255), for the Cauca Valley. We find it also in Ecuador, Panama, Andean Venezuela (Rosenblat); and possibly it exists elsewhere.

A sentence like *quiero es pan* may be a blending of *lo que quiero es pan* + *quiero pan* (Cuervo), or it may simply be a loss of the introductory *lo que*.

In Colombia one may hear in popular speech such snatches of conversation as: "—¿Llegó usted con hambre? —No, llegué *fué* cansado"; "¿Tomaste té en el desayuno? —No, tomé *fué* leche"; etc. Cuervo relates such turns of speech to Gallicized expressions like *fué entonces que nació* (< *ce fut alors qu'il naquit*), etc. For his detailed discussion and examples see *Apuntaciones*, §§ 431 and 460. Strangely enough, we find the same peculiar blending in Brazilian Portuguese: Jorge Amado's *Capitães de areia* (1937 ed.) reveals such examples as "Eu só queria *era* ver" (p. 62), "gostava *era* de deitar na areia" (p. 94), "morreu *foi* aqui mesmo" (p. 111), "quero *é* trabalbar" (p. 157), etc. Perhaps an intermediate stage is represented by such an example as the following, from rural Spain: "—Denguno se ha muerto por eso, que los tres que se me desgraciaron *fué* ya criaos y bien crecíos" (Benavente, *De cerca*, scene 4).

Ecuador: Aquí se ha venido *es* pa comer (La Cuadra, *Palo 'e balsa*, p. 294).

Panama: Él vino *fué* hoy; él tiene *son* diez pesos; yo me voy *es* mañana (Espino, p. 206). Hablé *fué* con él; nos encontramos *fué* a las ocho (C).

Colombia (Bogotá): ¿Usted es Sánchez? —Yo soy *es* Pérez. ... ¿Llegó hoy? —Llegué *fué* ayer. ... Yo hablaba *era* de usted, etc. (Cuervo, § 431). (Cauca Valley): Yo quiero *es* que vamos; lo trajeron *fué* amarrado; van *es* al campo; vine *fué* el sábado (Tascón, p. 255). ¡Quiero *es* la ropa que yo le di! (Antonio García, in *ACH*, p. 173). (Atlantic Coast): Yo voy *es* en el automóvil; yo fuí *fué* a las ocho (Sundheim, p. 595). (Central Highland Zone): —Yo necesito *es* jóvenes que no le tengan miedo al agua (Buitrago, p. 13); —Yo quiero *es* trabajar honradamente (p. 133); Ellos buscan *es* los pelotones de bagres (p. 167).

¿(NO) CIERTO?

The verb *es* is often omitted, or absorbed, in expressions like *¿no es cierto? ¿no es verdad?* etc., as sometimes in Spain. Possibly *¿no cierto?* is merely an emphatic expansion of *¿cierto?* used everywhere, though the standardly preferred form is *¿verdad?*

CHILE: *¿No cierto?* (C).

ECUADOR: —Te habías enamorao de la Gertru. *¿No verdad?* (Aguilera Malta, p. 51). —*¿Cierto* que no tienes enamorado? (Pareja, *La Beldaca*, p. 162).

COLOMBIA (ANTIOQUIA): —*¿No cierto* que es muy dichosa ña Melchorita? (Carrasquilla, *Hace tiempos*, I, 215). —Yo también sé nadar. *¿Cierto*, papacito, que yo también sé nadar? (Efe Gómez, p. 10).

VENEZUELA (ANDES): *¿No cierto* que ... ? (Rosenblat).

COMO SER

The locution *como ser* 'for example' is now frequently used instead of the standard *como es;* that is, the infinitive *ser* is preferred to the finite form of the verb. Because of its extensive use in Chile, even by writers of note, Román (I, 374), failing to note its divergence from standard Castilian, erroneously called it "expresión usada por todos los buenos escritores." We have no evidence of *como ser* in the older language, and it is rarely used in Spain today.

ARGENTINA: Siempre habrá derecho a suponer que la similitud o identidad de algunas de esas voces con otras arábigas se debe a causas muy ajenas a la Conquista española: —*como ser* un origen común del quichua y el árabe ... u otros motivos parecidos (Lizondo Borda, p. 8). —¿Querés penuria mayor que la de trabajar en cualquier oficio *como ser* de lavacopas o cuidador de automóviles? (Boj, p. 190).

CHILE: Este París tiene aspectos falsos, *como ser* los cabarets, los bulevares, los conciertos para tentar a los rastacueros (Edwards Bello, *Criollos*, p. 23).

PERU: Tengo un Folleque [= auto viejo] ... que he usado ... en mis menesteres domésticos y hasta industriales, *como ser* el trasporte de cuchis [= cochinos] (Corrales, p. 238).

VENEZUELA: Hago cualquier trabajo, *como ser* ... (Rosenblat).

PANAMA: De orden espiritual, *como ser* sufrir ... (L. Aguilar, p. 160).

¡YA ESTÁ!

This expression is general in familiar speech. It is an elliptical locution standing for *ya está hecho* and generally means *entendido, con-*

venido, de acuerdo, etc., implying the acceptance of a proposition considered as already completed: "—¿Vamos al cine? —*Ya está.*" In standard Castilian this *¡ya está!* would generally be *¡vamos!* or *¡muy bien!* or *¡está bien!* etc., since colloquial *¡y ya está!* is generally restricted to the meaning of *y ya está hecho* (cf. Beinhauer, p. 243). However, it is heard in Andalusia. For *¡ya estuvo!* see p. 164.

ARGENTINA: Si me lo pedís, *ya está* (César Carrizo, p. 108).

URUGUAY: —¿Queré, mi negro? —*Ya está* (Reyles, *El gaucho,* p. 141).

CHILE: ¿Vámonos al campo hoy? *Ya está* (Román, IV, 725).

ECUADOR: Cualquier otra cosita que usted encuentre ... traeráme no más, le he de pagar bien. —*¡Ya está,* viejito! (García Muñoz, *Estampas,* p. 315). Vamos a ver quién vence. —*Ya 'stá,* patrón (Icaza, *Cholos,* p. 64); —¿Querís darte? —*Ya 'stá.* ¡Vamos! (p. 80).

GUATEMALA: Te doy cinco mil quetzales al contado. ¿Aceptas? —*Ya está,* Narciso (Sandoval, II, 612).

Ya está is used in familiar speech to exhort a person to cease doing something which may be annoying. When a child cries, the parent says "*ya está*" to silence him. In this sense the standard equivalent would be *¡basta!*

'YA ESTÁ' + GERUND

The locution '*ya está* (*estás, estáis,* etc.) + gerund' is occasionally used to express a peremptory command, the urgency of which is shown by implying action as already in progress. The usage occurs in popular peninsular Spanish: "—Bueno, *ya me la estáis pagando* [= pagádmela]" (Aurelio Espinosa, *Cuentos,* III, 406 [Palencia]); "Pues *ya estás yevándolas* [= llévalas] al río" (Castro, *Luna lunera, ap.* Toro Gisbert, "Voces andaluzas," p. 445). In fact, it may have helped to establish the use of the simple gerund in colloquial commands (*¡andando!*) in which the relatively unimportant auxiliary is dropped (cf. Braue, p. 48; Spitzer, *Aufsätze,* p. 226).

ARGENTINA: —Y si le sale mal el negocio, ya mismo recoge sus cacharpas y *se nos está yendo* (Draghi Lucero, p. 122).

MEXICO: *Ya te vas largando; ya están saliendo* (C).

PUERTO RICO: Ejémonos e contumelias, y manda a buscal papel al pueblo, y ya mesmito *les tás escribiendo,* ¡y se acabó! (Meléndez Muñoz, p. 59).

LO LAVÓ BIEN LAVADO

This type of construction is common in popular and rustic speech in Spain: "Preparó la gallina y la guisó muy bien guisada" (Aurelio Espinosa, *Cuentos,* I, 100 [Valladolid]; cf. also Beinhauer, p. 200). Probably because of the abundance of modern regional literature in Spanish America, the expression seems more widespread here than in Spain and its social level often higher. It is especially frequent with verbs that express mechanical acts performed on an object, like *lavar, fregar, teñir, torcer, picar,* etc. To indicate the efficacy of the procedure the repetition of the same verb in past participle form suggests the action as already completed; that is, the act is vividly conceived as successfully accomplished (as in the case of *ya estuvo,* p. 164). Furthermore, the mere echoing of the basic verb greatly intensifies its force by reflecting on the mind the spatial and temporal lengthening of the concept. Intensifying the action by widening or lengthening the word itself is congenial to the Spanish language.

Our expression may best be rendered by 'thoroughly,' etc.: *lo lavó bien lavado* 'he washed it thoroughly,' 'he gave it a thorough scrubbing,' etc.

CHILE: Se la lavaba *bien lavá* con jabón y [la mancha] no salía (Vicuña Cifuentes, p. 517); la tiñó *bien teñida;* la fregó *bien fregada;* la miró *bien mirada* (p. 519, n. 8). Va a comer aquí solita, y después va a reposar *bien reposada* (Edwards Bello, *La chica,* p. 102); lo que compro es para gozarlo *bien gozado* (p. 106). Lo insultó *bien insultado* (C).

PERU: Una vez ... vide quial cura le sonaron *bien sonao* ... y yo también le di sus cuantos quiños [= golpes fuertes] (Ciro Alegría, *La serpiente,* p. 133). Había que poner una buena carga de dinamita ... y ... la pusimos *bien puesta* (Ciro Alegría, *El mundo,* p. 359).

ECUADOR: Aura tarde [= hoy por la tarde], usted les ha de vender *bien vendidos* (García Muñoz, *Estampas,* p. 318).

COLOMBIA: Li' aseguro que lo que sus padrecitos han pedido en el cielo, se los ha oído mi Dios *muy bien oído* (Carrasquilla, *Hace tiempos,* III, 93).

VENEZUELA: —Le traigo este vagamundo para que ... lo pele *bien pelao* (Gallegos, *Cantaclaro,* p. 262).

EL SALVADOR: Metió en el hoyo el cántaro, lo tapó *bien tapado* (Salarrué, *Cuentos,* p. 14).

MEXICO: Pensaba tomarse *muy bien tomada* su revancha (Rubín, p. 77).

SANTO DOMINGO: Lo cogí *cogío;* lo maté *muertecito* (Jiménez, p. 22).

QUIERDE, QUISTE, QUESE

A peculiar popular form apparently restricted to Ecuador is the verbal or adverbial expression *quierde,* a puzzle to all who do not use it daily. Ecuadorians fail to agree as to its exact meaning. Cevallos (*Breve catálogo*) considered *quierde* equivalent to the adverb *dónde.* Cevallos' critics proposed *¿dónde está?* as a more accurate equivalent. Tobar (p. 399) believes that neither Cevallos nor his critics gave sufficient thought to the meaning of *quierde* as used in popular speech. He asserts that the form is always interrogative and he supposes it to be a development of *¿qué es de?* To be sure, the sense is *¿dónde está?* but *¿qué es de?* would explain both the meaning of the form and its provenience. Popular Ecuadorian pronunciation, with its similarity of *s* and fricative or assibilated *r*, might account for the change of *s* to *r* in rapid speech. As examples of *quierde,* Tobar gives *¿quierde el dinero?* = standard *¿qué es del dinero?* and *¿quierde Antonio?* = *¿qué es de Antonio?*

Though generally called interrogative, punctuation will be found to vary (*¡quierde!* or *¿quierde?* or *quierde*). This is because, as heard colloquially in Quito, the word has both interrogative and exclamatory force.

Icaza uses *quierde* (*En las calles,* p. 233: "—*Quierde* pes"); but he also uses *¿qué es de?* (*Cholos,* p. 34: "—*¿Qué 's de* los cien sucres?"; *En las calles,* p. 140: "—*¿Qué 's de* la longa Mariana?" and p. 210: "*¿Qué's del* Rafel? —¿Acaso está aquí?"). La Cuadra writes *quiersde* in his collection of short stories called *Horno:* "¿Podrás dir a pata? Ella lo intentó. No consiguió levantarse. —*¿Quiersde* [= dónde = cómo] he de poder?" (p. 20); "—*¿Quiersde* el Saquicela? —Ahí" (p. 25); "—¿Y l'agua? *¿Quiersde* l'agua? —En Manantial venden" (p. 105).

There can be little doubt about the derivation of *quierde* from *qué es de,* as used in the older language and occasionally today. We find similar formations in other regions. In Bolivia one hears *quiste: ¿quiste mi sombrero?* (= *¿qué es de mi sombrero?* = *¿dónde está mi sombrero?*). Bayo (p. 212) reports the form for Santa Cruz, but it probably has a more extensive geographical area. The unvoicing of the *d* to *t* in *qué es de* > *quiste* is an unusual case of progressive assimilation.[7] We find it also in "*¿qui éste* [= dónde está] el chico?" reported for Salta (Argentina) beside "*¿quié de* Juan?" (Solá, p. 243).

In New Mexico (*BDH*, I, 139) and Mexico (Ramos Duarte, p. 425) we find the form *quese*, whose development is probably *que es de* > *quez de* > *queze* > *quese*, since the form *queze* (with voiced *s*) is still heard in northern Mexico. Aurelio Espinosa (*BDH*, I, 139) gives these examples for New Mexico: "*¿quése* Juan?" [= *¿dónde está Juan?*], "*¿quése* mis guantes?" [= *¿dónde están mis guantes?*], "*¿qués'* ellos?" [= *¿dónde están ellos?*].

EXPRESSION OF WISHES

Wishes may be standardly expressed by *ojalá que* or *ojalá* alone: *ojalá (que) no viniera* 'I wish he wouldn't come.' However, *ojalá y* is common in some regions of Spain, particularly in Andalusia (where also: *ajolá, anjolá, ojalay* [Braue, p. 36]), and even more so in many parts of Spanish America. How old this usage is has not been determined. Rosenblat (*Notas*, p. 197) relates it to exclamatory *y* (cf. "¡Sant Juan *y* ciégale!" [*Lazarillo*, II] and "¡Santiago *y* cierra España," etc.); and he rejects Cuervo's explanation (§ 407), namely, that this "superfluous" *y* originally joined two optative phrases and was then extended to cases where only one wish was expressed. We find an analogous *y* in other locutions: *ahora y verá* (= *ahora verá*) which Cuervo bases on *aguarde y verá, molésteme y verá; hágame el favor y dígame* (= *hágame el favor de decirme*) based on *atiéndame y dígame, moléstese y dígame* (Cuervo): "—*Hori verís* [= ahora y verás]" (Álvarez Garzón, p. 65 [Colombia, South]); "—De modo *y* es ... que no vuelvo mañana" (Carrasquilla, *Hace tiempos*, I, 24 [Colombia, Antioquia]). Expressions like *cuidado y, quién quita y, Dios quiera y* are common in Mexico: "—*Cuidado y* me contradigas, ¿oyes?" (Gamboa, *Santa*, p. 12).

COLOMBIA: *Ojalá y* venga (Uribe, *Dicc.*).—*Ojalá y* regrese (Buitrago, p. 184).

GUATEMALA: *Ojalá y* sea (Sandoval, II, 167).

MEXICO: *¡Ojalá y* lo reviente un toro! (Gamboa, *Santa*, p. 201).

[7] Since voiced occlusive *d* is lacking in Quechua and Aymara, its pronunciation is difficult for the highland Indian and *mestizo*. When *d* immediately follows their characteristically unvoiced intensely sibilant *s*, speakers are especially prone to reinforce their unvoiced *t*: "—Me *haste* [= has de] esperar" (Díaz V., *La Rosita*, p. 11); "*deste* [= desde] ayer" (Rodrigo, p. 19); "vaya *traste* [= tras de] ella" (p. 27).

¡Ojalá y el bien que Procopio ha sabido hacer nos salve de la catástrofe! (Azuela, *Las tribulaciones*, p. 120).

NEW MEXICO: *Ójali* [< *ójala y* < *ojalá y*] que vengan (Aurelio Espinosa, *Apuntaciones*, p. 622; *BDH*, I, 53, n. 4).

SANTO DOMINGO: —*Ojalá y* no llueva (Bosch, *Dos pesos*, p. 93).

The stress of *ojalá* oftens shifts to the penult (*ojála*) in the popular speech of Chile (Román, IV, 63), southern Ecuador (Tobar, p. 349), northern Guatemala (Sandoval, II, 167), Argentina and Uruguay (Tiscornia, *La lengua*, § 5), and probably elsewhere. Occasionally in Spain (also in the classics) and very frequently in Mexico (Ramos Duarte, p. 378; *BDH*, IV, 387) and New Mexico (*BDH*, I, § 12) the stress falls on the antepenult (*ójala*).[8] In rustic Colombian speech we find such variants as *ojolá* (Tascón, p. 207), *ajolá* (as elsewhere), *ajualá* (Sundheim, p. 20), etc.: "*Ajualá* que lo tumbe" (Arias Trujillo, p. 160); "*ajualá* que se largara del pueblo" (p. 180), etc.

In Santo Domingo one hears *¡ojalalo* (or *ojalala*) *yo!* meaning *¡ojalá que fuera mío* (or *mía*)! but *¡ojalala tú!* means *tú la quisieras*, etc. (Patín Maceo, *Dom.*, p. 124; *BDH*, V, 229).

For *ojalá* with the conjunctive force of *aunque* 'although,' see p. 381. Finally, for northern Colombia, Revollo (p. 189) registers *ojalá* with the interjectional meaning of *¡cuidado! ¡Dios te libre!* : "*Ojalá* te muevas de ahí, *ojalá* hagas tal cosa" (cf. also Flórez, p. 380; *ojalita* is so used in Salta, Argentina [Solá, p. 207]).

Other methods of expressing wishes are found locally.

In rural areas of many regions, *amalaya* is commonly used for *ojalá* (for discussion see p. 406).

In Antioquia, Colombia, *ah bueno si* is current as an equivalent of *ojalá*: "—*Ah bueno si* Elisa me lo prestara" (Carrasquilla, *Hace tiempos*, II, 298); "*Ah bueno si* estuviera aquí don Ceferino pa que pusiera en el cepo a este Princés" (III, 168).

In Costa Rica, New Mexico, the Antilles, and probably elsewhere, we find rural survivals of a peculiar Old Spanish usage of expressing a wish with *tomaría* or *tomara*. It may be heard in regions of Spain, as in Andalusia: "*Tomara yo* que viera usté eso que suena" (Muñoz Seca and Pérez Fernández, *Trianerías* [1919], p. 133).

COSTA RICA: ¡Pos hombre, está hecho un altar! *Me tomara* [= ojalá] que lo biera (Echeverría, p. 155).

[8] For a possible explanation of stress shift cf. A. Alonso, "Problemas de dialectología hispanoamericana," *BDH*, I (1930), 363. For the etymology of *ojalá* cf. M. Asín Palacios, *Bol. acad.*, VII (1930), 360–62.

NEW MEXICO: *¡Tomaría* yo nu aberte conosido! [= ¡ojalá no te hubiera conocido!] (*BDH*, IV, 40).

SANTO DOMINGO: *¡Tomara* yo morirme! (*BDH*, V, §94). *Tomaría* yo sacarme el premio mayor; *tomaría* tú casarte con ella; *tomaría* él que lo nombraran comisario (Patín Maceo, *Dom.*, p. 170).

CUBA: *—¡Tomaría* (o *tomara*) yo tener dinero, pues entonces viajaría mucho! (Padrón).

PUERTO RICO: *—¡Tomara* que tú fueras como él! (C).

In Costa Rica *aviaos que* is sometimes used in the sense of *ojalá que no, no vaya a ser que*, etc. Gagini (p. 66), who records also *aviados*, interprets the meaning as *arriesgando, a riesgo de:* "Voy a mandar la loza en una carreta; *aviaos* que se quiebre." The locution seems to be a mere ellipsis of the familiar phrase *aviados estamos* 'we're in a nice fix.'

—¡Aviaos que nos agarre tata y nos rezongue! (Fabián Dobles, p. 51); *—¡Aviaos que* le pase algo a mi hijo!—está diciendo casi en voz alta (p. 59); *—¡Aviaos que no* me reciba [= ojalá que me reciba] ña Rafela!—va diciéndose Ninfa (p. 126); Aquí la viuda se pone sombría, y continúa: *—Aviaos que* un día me lo traigan malquebrao de por ahi (p. 226).

In some regions, *ánimas que* may replace *ojalá*, the souls in Purgatory being invoked to fulfil the wish (cf. *Dios quiera que*, etc.): *¡ánimas que llueva!* = *¡ojalá que llueva!* In his novel, *Las ensabanadas* (p. 16), Quevedo y Zubieta in referring to Flora Boves, one of the characters, remarks that her speech was "el lenguage indígena tapatío, tomado seguramente en el medio familiar donde había crecido y alentaba todavía. Decía *pos sí, diatiro, dizque* y expresaba un deseo con *ánimas que*." However, we know that none of the locutions indicated, including *ánimas que*, may be labeled exclusively *tapatío*, that is, belonging to Guadalajara or the state of Jalisco in general. In Magdalena's *El resplandor*, set in the state of Hidalgo, we read:

¡Ánimas que llegara ahorita y acabara con todos estos sardos [= soldados de vigilancia] que no hallan qué maldades hacernos! (p. 37); *¡Ánimas que* lleguemos al Mesón de la Providencia! (p. 50); *¡Ánimas que* acabe todo esto para volver a mi tierra! (p. 120), etc.

COSTA RICA: *—Ánimas benditas, que* no llueva. —¡Dios mío, que no llueva! (Herrera García, p. 20).

COLOMBIA (ANTIOQUIA): *¡Ánimas, que* cante el gallo,/Ánimas, que ya cantó,/*Ánimas, de que* amanezca,/Ánimas, que amaneció! (Antonio Restrepo, p. 117). (Tolima): ¡*Ánimas* [= cuidado] que se caiga! ¡*Ánimas benditas* que se moje! (Flórez, p. 380).

Venezuela: ¡*Ánimas benditas,* que no venga el profesor! (Rosenblat).

A wish is often colloquially expressed with a locution that originally signified doubt and that usually retains much or some of this original force: 'perhaps' > 'I hope, I wish'; 'maybe he will come' > 'I hope he will come, I wish he would come'; etc. The doubt is psychologically colored in favor of the speaker. This process has taken place or is taking place with such locutions of doubt as: *quizás* (Vázquez [p. 339] warns the Ecuadorians that *quizás* and *quizá* express doubt and not desire); *pueda ser que,* expressing doubt in some regions like standard *puede ser que* (see p. 179) and desire in others; *quién quita* = standard *tal vez* (Central America, Mexico, the Antilles, Colombia, Venezuela, etc.). In Mexico the form is generally *quién quita y* (cf. *ojalá y,* etc.), and occasionally *quién quite.*

Of these expressions *pueda ser* and *quién quita* enjoy wider geographical extent than the others. *Pueda ser* has already been discussed (p. 179) and examples cited. The psychological trend of *quién quita* seems to be 'who can prevent?' > 'can anyone prevent?' > 'it is probable that no one can prevent' > 'I hope no one can prevent' > 'I wish,' etc. In most cases the feeling is still midway between possibility and desire. Probably this fluctuating emotion accounts for uncertainty in punctuation: ¡*quién quita!* ¿*quién quita?* etc.

Colombia: Aunque sea tu enemigo, *quién quita* que quisiera hacerte ese favor (R. Restrepo, p. 430). —*Quién quita* que yo pueda acompañarte (Buitrago, p. 43); —Vení, Julita, bailemos los dos, porque *quién quita* que de aquí a mañana vos y yo seamos novios (p. 89).

Venezuela: —Sí, y *quién quita* que en el ínterin nos pongamos en comunicación con otros movimientos (Briceño, p. 160); —La cosa es que ya estoy viejo ... pero ... ¿*quién quita?* (p. 170). —Parece que lo estuvieras viendo como en un espejo. —¡Jm! ¡*Quién quita,* don Manuel! (Gallegos, *Canaima,* p. 45).

Costa Rica: Este mes me saco la lotería, ¡*quién quita!* (Gagini, p. 211). —*Quién quita* ... que te pase lo mismo (Lyra, p. 29); *Quién quita* que pueda yo sacarlos a ustedes de jaranas [= deudas] (p. 50); ¡*Quién quita* que le salga un marido nonis [= sin par]! (p. 109); ¡Pobrecitico! Pero no está muerto, todavía resuella. Le voy a echar en la carreta y *quién quita* que vuelva en sí (p. 152). —¡*Quién quita* que con esto se le vaya esa idea de la cabeza! (Fabián Dobles, p. 58); *¡Quién quita, quién quita* que pueda quedarse allí! (p. 128); *Quién quita* que si lo pasturiamos bien, se apegue a la casa y siga trabajando aquí (p. 257).

HONDURAS: *Quién quita* que yo también/Sin colegios y sin maestros,/Llegue a ser un Bachiller (*ap.* Membreño, p. 141).

GUATEMALA: *¡Quién quita* me saque la lotería este mes! *¡Quién quita* que el juez te mande a la cárcel, por las injurias que le dices en tus escritos! *¡Quién quita* que le vaya bien! *¡Quién quitucha!* or *¡Quién quituche!* = *¡Quién quita!* (Sandoval, II, 317). —*¿Quién quita* que me lo saque?—dice el sujeto ... empleando una frase que usamos y abusamos no poco los guatemaltecos (Salomé Gil, *Cuadros*, IV, 185).

MEXICO: ¡El número de la suerte! *¡Quén quita y* que se la saque! (Rivas Larrauri, p. 91); *¡Quén quita y* que te dicidas! (p. 127), etc. (NUEVO LEÓN): —Suerte que Raúl nos hizo el favor de avisarnos pronto. *¡Quién quita y* toavía haiga en qué ayudar! ... —Eso es casi seguro (García Roel, p. 52); —Ándele, *quién quita y* pronto los suelten. —Quiera Dios que asina sea (p. 163). (NORTHERN ZONE): *Quién quita y* en un descuido nos tocara ser mandones (Urquizo, p. 207).

CANTAMOS CON ÉL = ÉL Y YO CANTAMOS

We know that a singular subject immediately joined to another with the preposition *con* may take a plural verb: "El padre *con* el hijo perecieron" (Bello-Cuervo, § 838; Hanssen, § 486; Cuervo, *Dicc.*, II, 296). In such cases *con* is felt to have the conjunctive value of *y*. This ancient practice, harking back to Latin ("pater cum matre veniunt") is the starting point of an ambiguous and frequently baffling development: *cantamos con él* [= *él y yo cantamos*]; that is, the first subject (*yo*) is not expressed but is implied in the plural verb form (*cantamos*), and the second subject (*él*), introduced by *con*, generally follows the verb. Since such phrases are easily misunderstood, their use is subconsciously avoided. They are not frequent in the spoken language and are rare in literary style (except cases involving the so-called "royal we"). An early example occurs in the *Cid* (vs. 1860): "*con* diez de sus parientes [= él y diez de sus parientes] davan salto." We find sporadic examples of this usage in parts of Spain and Spanish America (as well as in other languages), but it is seldom recorded in grammars.

ARGENTINA: Durante los días subsiguientes *hablamos* mucho *con* Ferrier [=Ferrier y yo hablamos] (Mallea, *La bahía de silencio* [2d ed.], p. 399).

Chile: *Jugamos con* Carmen [= Carmen y yo jugamos] (C). *Yo con* mi General Baqueano aelante no *aflojábamos* un pelo (Romanángel, p. 17).

Colombia: Carmen *con* Pedro *son* primos (Sundheim, p. 166).

Guatemala: La cocinita la *compramos con* tu papá [= tu papá y yo] en un paseíto que fuimos a dar hoy en la mañana (Arévalo, p. 69); *Con* ella [= ella y yo] *nos vamos* a diferentes partes (p. 117); *Con* Anita *nos quedamos* viendo [= Anita y yo] (p. 119); *Nos fuimos con* mi hermano [= él y yo] (p. 153).

VERB POSITION

Sometimes after the adverb *ya* the verb follows the subject (or some other phrase) contrary to preferred standard practice: *ya usted verá* for standard *ya verá usted,* etc. This verb position is common not only in popular speech but also in the written language.

We find the same phenomenon not infrequently in peninsular speech: "Hasta que *ya* er sacristán tuvo que cerrá la iglesia" (Aurelio Espinosa, *Cuentos,* I, 104 [Sevilla]); "*Ya* yo me voy" (I, 110 [Zamora]); "Y como *ya* la mujer estaba desesperada ... y *ya* su mujer no lo volvió a ver" (I, 164 [Ciudad Real]); "Cuando *ya* la niña estaba en el palacio" (II, 180 [Zamora]), etc. In the older language *yo* frequently followed *ya: "ya yo* os conozco, fementida canalla" (*Don Quijote,* I, 8).

Argentina: *Ya* mis tías no hacían caso de mí (Güiraldes, *Don Segundo,* p. 13); *Ya* la gente se había amontonado por demás (p. 107); *Ya* el corredor del alazán había convidado dos veces (p. 240).

Bolivia: *Ya* usté sabe (Jaime Mendoza, *El lago,* p. 52); *Ya* usted comprenderá (p. 90).

Peru: —*Ya* usted sabe, que hay que pagar por adelantado (Corrales, p. 218).

Colombia: *Ya* usté sabe lo qui hay qui hacer (Flórez, p. 380).

Venezuela: —Pues *ya* usted verá si será agradable la fiesta (Gallegos, *Canaima,* p. 51); Dice que *ya* su mandato está hecho (p. 53); —*Ya* los negros pasaron y deben de ir lejos (p. 108); *Ya* mis amigas ... me han traído el cuento (p. 147).

El Salvador: *Ya* hasta la color de que los tenés se me olvidó (Salarrué, *Cuentos,* p. 9); —*Ya* el padre tá cabando [= está acabando] (p. 54).

Mexico: *Ya* el vino no le interesaba nada (Valle-Arizpe, p. 377).

Santo Domingo: —Pero *ya* usté está acostumbrado (Bosch, *Dos*

pesos, p. 19); *Ya* usté ve el tiempo que hace de eso (p. 63).
CUBA: *Ya* usted verá (Padrón).

Another peculiar phenomenon among the untutored of some regions is verbal repetition at the end of a sentence or phrase. This appears to be done for emphasis generally, but occasionally merely to round out the rhythm of the phrase. Cf. colloquial English: "*He won't* do that again, *he won't*," etc. In Argentina this is called "hablar en sángüiche" (Costa Álvarez, p. 45).

ARGENTINA: ¿Son muchas las yeguas? —No, señora. *Son* ocho no más, *son* (Güiraldes, *Don Segundo*, p. 46). *Será* pa que no se ponga demasiado pedigüeña, *será* (Larreta, *El linyera*, I, 27). Y *te has tomao* diez y seis, *te has tomao*. ... Pero *si me buscan* las broncas, hermano, *si me buscan* (Manuel Romero, I). *Tené* pasensia, *tené* ... *soy* un desgraciao, *soy* (Last-Reason, p. 13).
URUGUAY: *Tengo* sentimientos, *tengo* (Sánchez, *La gringa*, IV, 5). *Me hacen* un caso bárbaro, *me hacen* (Montiel, *Montevideo*, p. 118).
CHILE: Otra vez que te pille gritando, *te voy* ... *a llevate* pa la carabinería, *te voy a llevate* (Rojas Gallardo, *2a serie*, p. 50).

IX

ADVERBIAL LOCUTIONS

THIS is not the place to discuss such divergencies from standard forms as *agora* or *aura* or *hora* for *ahora; ansí* or *ansina* for *así*, *tuavía* or *entuavía* for *todavía*, *nuncamente* for *nunca*, and *casimente* for *casi;* or diminutives, characteristic of popular and rustic speech nearly everywhere, such as *acasito* for *acá*, *ahorita* for *ahora*, *allasito* for *allá*, *alguito* for *algo*, *apenitas* for *apenas*, *ayercito* for *ayer*, *casitico* (Costa Rica) for *casi*, *detrasito* for *detrás*, *endeveritas* for *de veras*, *lueguito* or *lueguichicho* (Chile) for *luego*, *nunquita* for *nunca*, *reciencito* for *recién*, *siemprecito* for *siempre*, *yaíta* for *ya*, etc.; or augmentatives, such as *asinote* for *así*, *abajenque* (Peruvian highlands, where *-enque* is a common augmentative ending used by cholos or mestizos and Indians); and the like. The majority of such forms are survivals from the older language (cf. *BDH*, II, 180; Flórez, p. 381).

We are concerned here with adverbial expressions involving relationship with other parts of speech and other elements in the sentence, that is, a syntactical relationship. We mention also a few adverbs notable for some new semasiological development in Spanish

America, although establishing meanings belongs primarily to the field of lexicography.

Some of these adverbial phrases are common to several Spanish-American regions; others are local or have a relatively restricted geographical area. They are so numerous that only a limited number of the most important and most frequently encountered can be included in our list. The order will not be strictly alphabetical, since adverbs closely related in form or meaning will sometimes be grouped together.

ABSOLUTAMENTE

The adverb *absolutamente* (as well as the phrase *en absoluto*) is often used elliptically for *de ninguna manera, de ningún modo,* etc.; that is, the negative element *no* or *nada,* while understood, is often omitted. Such usage is in accordance with that peculiarity of Spanish whereby certain originally affirmative expressions have acquired negative value through constant use with *no* or some other negative word: *no lo he visto en mi vida* > *en mi vida lo he visto.* Because such practice is so congenial to the Spanish language, preceptists are often inclined not to consider as incorrect the use of *absolutamente* for *absolutamente nada* or *absolutamente no.* Hanssen (§ 641) states that *absolutamente* may be negative. It seems more frequent in America than in Spain.

RIVER PLATE REGION: Yo dudé un rato. —¿Una humorada, Quiroga? —¡*Absolutamente!* (Espinoza, in *ACR*, p. 220). —¿Estás dormido? —*En absoluto.* —No puedo agarrar el sueño en este catre (Filloy, p. 146). —Tú no puedes hacerlo? —*En absoluto* (Florencio Sánchez, p. 459).

CHILE: —¿Tienes veinte pesos que prestarme? —*Absolutamente.* —¿Oíste lo que dijo Pedro? —*Absolutamente* (Román, I, 9). Así que mi enfermedad ¿no es de cuidado? —*Absolutamente* (Pepe Rojas y Fernández, *La hoja de Parra*, p. 6).

COLOMBIA: —¿No son, pues, sus mercedes los que estuvieron en el trapiche? —*Absolutamente* (Rivera, p. 15); —¿Y podrán describirnos? —*Absolutamente* (p. 69).

VENEZUELA: —Usted habla en un tono que parece que fuera la autoridad. —*En absoluto,* Coronel. Hablo en el tono de quien reclama ante la autoridad el cumplimiento de una ley (Gallegos, *Doña Bárbara*, p. 157).

COSTA RICA: ¿Me das permiso? *Absolutamente* (Salesiano, p. 32).

GUATEMALA: ¿Lo molesto? —*Absolutamente* (Flavio Herrera, p. 61). *Absolutamente* consiento, hija mía, en que te cases con Ramiro (Sandoval, I, 5).

The form *todavía* is likewise heard in many regions for standard *todavía no:* "—¿Ya vino tu padre?—*Todavía*" (Garay, p. 109 [Panama]). Also in rural Spain: "Entodavía ha venido = aún no ha venido" (*RFE*, XXVII, 241 [Albacete]).

ACÁ, ALLÁ

The standard adverbs of place *acá* and *aquí*, both meaning 'here,' differ in that *aquí* indicates more definite location, whereas *acá* indicates vague location or motion. Colloquially in the River Plate and Andean zones and elsewhere, *acá* is now used almost exclusively to indicate 'here' whether definite or indefinite. This usage stems from the older language. Santa Teresa was extremely partial to *acá*. The form *aquí* is being replaced by *acá*, of greater affective value, as is *allí* by *allá*, *donde* by *adonde*, etc.

The phrase *ven acá*, as used in the older language, is still employed in some regions (Antilles, Mexico, etc.) to attract the attention of an interlocutor who may be standing close by, as we sometimes say: 'listen, say, do you hear?' etc. For instance: "*Ven acá*, ¿qué fué lo que te pasó ayer?" (V. Suárez, p. 67 [Yucatan]).

In the popular and rustic speech of some regions the adverb *acá* may take the place of the demonstrative pronoun *éste* or *ésta*—another indication that adverbs of place and demonstrative pronouns are logically related. In this sense *aquí* is popularly used in Spain (Beinhauer, p. 204).

COSTA RICA: Cuando *acá* y yo nos casamos,/los [= nos] dieron una ternera,/dos quintales de café,/tres bejigas de manteca (Echeverría, p. 157). *Acá* tiene razón, *acá* me lo dijo (Gagini, p. 45).

SANTO DOMINGO: *Acá* le contará lo sucedido; *acá* lo sabe; *acá* me conoce (Patín Maceo, *Dom.*, p. 8).

CUBA: *Acá* me lo dijo (Padrón).

The common Spanish *daca* (*da* + *acá*) 'give me' may by analogy become *déque* in formal address. Although Cuervo (§ 290) calls *déque* "tan dañino como asqueroso avechucho," Lope de Vega did not hesitate to use it for *déme* ("*Déque* presto o matarélo," *Los locos de Valencia*, I, 3, cited by Cuervo). For Mexico, Icazbalceta (p. 165) reports the form *déquen* as a plural. In addition to *déque* for Santo

Domingo, Henríquez Ureña (*BDH*, V, 176) reports both *dácame* and *daca acá;* that is, *daca* is felt to be a form of the hypothetical verb *dacar*. A survival from the older language (Correas, p. 551), *daca acá* is current in Guatemala (Batres, p. 237; Sandoval, I, 294), in Quito and elsewhere (*BDH*, IV, 100, n. 3).

COLOMBIA: —*Déque* aprisa. —No vendo, oyé? (Antonio García, p. 177). *Déque* tantica agua (Tobón, p. 170).

MEXICO: —*Déque* dos mil papeles por todo (Azuela, *Los de abajo*, p. 199). —¿Quiubo amigos? ... *Déquen* un cigarro (Urquizo, p. 34).

SANTO DOMINGO: —*Déque* la mano (Patín Maceo, *Dom.*, p. 58).

AHÍ, ALLÍ, DE AHÍ

In standard Castilian the adverb of place, *ahí* 'there,' corresponds to the demonstrative *ese* and refers to things near the person spoken to; *allí* 'there' corresponds to the demonstrative *aquel.* In American Spanish (sometimes in Spain) *ahí* may replace *allí*, as *ese* often supplants *aquel.* Now the adverbs of place (*ahí*, *allí*, and *allá*) may become adverbs of time, meaning 'then' and sometimes the combination 'then and there.' But in such temporal usage *allí* generally refers to past time ("*allí* fué Troya"), and *ahí* to future time. In Spanish America and in Andalusia, however, because of the confusion of *allí* and *ahí*, we often find *ahí fué* instead of the standard *allí fué* in referring to past time. Colloquially *ahí* is often monosyllabic, with the stress on *a*, and is spelled variously: *áhi*, *ahi*, *ai*, *ay*, etc.

As an adverb of time, *ahí* is used in the popular speech of some regions with the connotation of *pronto, en seguida* 'soon': *ahí vengo* = *pronto vendré* or *luego volveré; ahí voy* = *en seguida voy.*

It is found likewise as an expletive or emphasizing particle:

COLOMBIA: —¿Quién es ese tipo? —Un italianu *ai;* ¡Bueno, *ahí* se les avisa! (Flórez, p. 381).

NICARAGUA: Sírvase *ai* unas copas (A. Valle, p. 7).

GUATEMALA: *Ay* regreso mañana; *ay* te conduces bien (Bonilla Ruano, p. 48).

MEXICO (YUCATAN): Trae *ai* esa silla (V. Suárez, p. 61).

CUBA: Despácheme una caja de fósforos *ai* (Padrón).

As an adverb of place, *ahí* in the expression *por ahí* is used generally (as in the older language and also colloquially in Spain today, although the dictionary does not explain the usage) with the meaning of 'anywhere at all,' involving a feeling of indifference or even scorn on the part of the speaker as well as a disinclination to mention the exact location (cf. Beinhauer, p. 53 n.). A few examples will suffice.

URUGUAY: —¿Y de ánde salís? —De *por ai* (Reyles, *El gaucho*, p. 196).

ECUADOR: Tengo que ir a un negocio *por ahí* ... los encontré *por ahí* (García Muñoz, *Estampas*, pp. 161, 314).

VENEZUELA: Lo he oído *por ahí* (Gallegos, *Pobre negro*, p. 256).

EL SALVADOR: El negro Nayo era de *porái:* de un *porái* dudoso, mezcla de Honduras y Berlice, Chiquimula y Blufiles de la Costelnorte (Salarrué, *Cuentos*, p. 164).

GUATEMALA: —¿Y Julián? —*Por ay* anda, ya no tarda en llegar (Quintana, p. 108).

We find the temporal meaning of *ahí* in the common expression *de ahí*, which in popular speech is reduced to two syllables (often spelled *de áhi* or *de ai*, etc.) or even to one (often spelled *deay* or *diay;* and especially in Chile: *(en) dey*, *dei*, *d'hey*, or *d'ehi*). This adverbial phrase has the temporal connotation of *luego, en seguida,* etc.

ARGENTINA: *De áhi* Rufo picó tabaco/y dos cigarros armó (Ascasubi, p. 106).

CHILE: Y *di'ai* m'entró recelo (Latorre, *Hombres*, p. 118); —Éjalo que se seque primero y *d'ey* le preguntay (p. 164). —Es un gurto que se me le pone por aquí ... y *en d'ehi* me agarra l'estomo (Brunet, in *LCC*, p. 489).

COLOMBIA: Y *di ai* me dijo que ... (Flórez, p. 381).

COSTA RICA: De pronto/se puso a oler la perruja/*d'iay* a ladrar y ladrar (Echeverría, p. 111); Coja por este saguán/y *d'iay* crusa a la derecha (p. 180). —En un prencipio me jodía la cosa. ... Pero, *¡diay!* se me quitó (Fabián Dobles, p. 255).

EL SALVADOR: Arrojaba un piro [= desperdicios en la fabricación de alcohol] espumoso y hediondo y *diay* se desmayaba (Salarrué, *Cuentos*, p. 48).

Combined with the conjunction *y*, the expression *¿y de ahí?* is equivalent to standard *¿y bien? ¿y por fin? ¿y luego? ¿y entonces?* As such it may be found spelled variously by writers attempting to reproduce popular and rustic speech: *y deay*, *y di-ay*, *ydiay*, *idiay*, *y di'hay;* and especially in Chile: *y dey*, *dei*, *d'hey*. This locution serves to encourage the speaker to finish what he has been saying, with this implication: 'You have stopped there; what comes next?' Again it corresponds to our 'what of it?' or our slang 'so what?'

ARGENTINA: Vea, Pantalión—dijo al fin. ... Antiayer ... se dejó cair de visita por aquí ... doña Casildra. —¡Ah! ¡ah!, la curandera. ¡Ah! ¡ah! *¿Y de áhi?* (Lynch, *Romance*, p. 43). Ella se pudo casar conmigo ... —*¿Y de áhi?* —*Y de áhi*, que no quiso (Lynch, *Palo verde*, p. 153). A eso del anochecer le cayó el patrón. —*¿Ydiay?* (Draghi Lucero, p. 239).

URUGUAY: —No vayás, chino querido. Es cosa de duendes y ánimas en pena. —*¿Y d'ai?* (Reyles, *El gaucho*, p. 126).

ECUADOR: —Llegué. —*¿Y deay?* —Le reconviene. —*¿Y deay?* (Vázquez, p. 227). Yo ca iba a trepar el carro di pasajerus, cuando dando tirón al poncho me manda pur un ladu ... cay en sangradera. Toditico poncho estaba hecho lástima. ¿Nu olís? ... —*Y di'ay* ca. —Él se trepó pes (Icaza, *En las calles*, p. 95).

PERU: —Güeno, *¿idiay?*—prosiguió el viejo—aquí corre pa siempre nuestro río (Ciro Alegría, *La serpiente*, p. 228). Le escribí una carta. —*¿Y de áhi?* —Nunca me contestó (Benvenutto, p. 149).

MEXICO: Asigún nuestras dotrinas/l'acuso de riacionaria/—*¿Y di ai* qué? (Rivas Larrauri, p. 17). Yo también me pongo avispa/—*Y diai*, ¿qué? —Que te denuncio (González Carrasco, p. 22); Esta parte a ti te toca,/y est'otra mitá es la mía/—*¿Y di ai*, ¡qué? —¡Que ... lo que hablamos/jué purita fantasía! (p. 24).

Elsewhere, particularly in Central America, *y de ahí* or *de ahí* is used to attract a person's attention, as in a greeting.

COSTA RICA: Tío Coyote, donde oyó gente, por quedar bien comenzó a decir: —*¿Idiai*, a qué hora viene la princesa? (Lyra, p. 123). —*¡Diay*, muchacho! ¿Estás dispierto? Yo te creiba bien dormío (Agüero, p. 34). —*¡Diay*, Chano, cómo vamos a hacer con esa mujer? (Fabián Dobles, p. 116).

NICARAGUA: Esta vez, al llegar nosotros al cuartel, el jefe salía con dos de sus ayudantes. Cuando nos vió, nos dijo «—*¿Idiay*, muchachos? ¿Vamos?» (Orozco, p. 69).

EL SALVADOR: —¡Canelóo! ¡Buchinche! *¡Y diay!* (Ambrogi, p. 79).

The expression *de allá soy* (*somos*) is used in Chile beside standard *allá voy* (*vamos*), as in: "—¿Vamos al parque? —*De allá somos* [= vamos seguramente]" (C); "Y a propósito de ovejas, anda a rodiarlas. —*Di allá soy*. Hasta luego" (Acevedo H., *Canción*, p. 8).

ACASO

The adverb *acaso* 'perchance, perhaps' has come to indicate a simple negation or denial: *¿acaso yo lo sé?* = *no sé*. The ironical usage is common enough in Spain. Thus in Pereda (*Obras*, V, 314): "—Hola, Tomasa, ¿qué es eso? ¿Ónde echastes la otra jarra? —¿Pues *acaso* yo la tengo ni la he visto, deslenguada?" Such usage has been extended in parts of Spanish America and its ironical and interrogative force subsequently weakened to such a degree that it is now felt to be an equivalent of *no*.

BOLIVIA: —¿Está en casa don Pancho? —*¿Acaso* regresó de la ciudad?; —¿Puedes prestarme el hacha? —*¿Acaso* está sana? (Bayo, *Manual*, p. 16; *Vocabulario*, p. 9).

PERU: *¿Acaso* la señora le había pagado la cuenta del mes anterior? (María Wiesse, in *ACP*, p. 139).

ECUADOR: *¿Acaso* he podido dormir? —Yo tampoco (Icaza, *Cholos*, p. 33); —¿Ya'stará despierto el cura? —*Acaso* nos ha de dar nada (p. 88). —¿Otra [copa]?—protesta el visitante. —Qu'es pes. *Acaso* hace mal (*Icaza*, Huasipungo, p. 20). —¿Ónde está la vela? —*Acaso* hay (Icaza, *En las calles*, p. 126); —¿Y el huambra Rafel? —*¿Acaso* tiene nada? —Veamos—decía el médico, apartando los obstáculos (p. 209).

COLOMBIA: *Acaso* sé; *acaso* me dijeron [= pues si no me dijeron] (Uribe, *Dicc.*).

VENEZUELA: —¿Y a ti por qué te preocupa? —¿A mí? *¡Acaso* es lo mismo! (Pocaterra, p. 139); —No tuve tiempo; figúrate que ... *¡acaso* es fácil! Y además, no tuve tiempo (p. 204).

SANTO DOMINGO: —Préstame cinco pesos. —*¿Acaso* tengo dinero? (Patín Maceo, "Amer.," IV, 411; cf. *BDH*, V, 57).

A DIARIO, DIARIO

Some thirty or forty years ago, Gagini (p. 125) condemned the phrase *a diario* (= *todos los días, diariamente*, etc.) claiming it to be restricted to "el vulgo madrileño," although it was considered "el colmo de la elegancia" when used in the Costa Rican newspapers. About the same time, Mir (*Frases de los autores clásicos*, under *llorar*) wrote: "Los periodistas presentes dicen *a diario*. Mañana dirán *a semanario ... a mensual, a anual*, etc." The phrase was not then entered in the Academy dictionary, and many preceptists considered it an Americanism because of its frequent use and its social status in Spanish America. Despite its apparently anomalous formation, it has, since then, gained a firm foothold in Spain, being used there by outstanding writers,[1] and has recently found a haven in the Academy dictionary. To be sure, it probably is still more extensive in Spanish America than in Spain. A few examples will suffice.

COLOMBIA: —Hace como dos meses que nos vemos *a diario* (Carrasquilla, *Hace tiempos*, I, 190).

GUATEMALA: —Me escribirás *a diario*, ¿sabes? (Wyld Ospina, *La gringa*, p. 130).

MEXICO: Casi *a diario* visitaban al ex-ministro (Gómez P., p. 34).

What is now troubling purists and preceptists is the use of the adjective *diario* (sometimes *de diario*) as an adverb in place of *diariamente* or *todos los días* or even *a diario* (since this form is now accepted as standard). *Diario* is used adverbially in Bolivia (Malaret, *Suplemento*), Colombia (Sundheim), Peru, Central America, Mexico (Rubio, *Anarquía*), Puerto Rico (Malaret), and probably elsewhere.

PERU: —Existen indios ... que *diario* andan de tarro y leva [= sombrero de copa y levita] (Barrantes, p. 84).

VENEZUELA: Esperaba *de diario* a que saliese (Blanco F., p. 135).

COSTA RICA: Ahí lo veo pasar *diario* (Fabián Dobles, p. 238; also pp. 243, 283, 293). Voy *diario* a la suidá (Gagini, p. 125).

NICARAGUA: Y cuando se fué la viejita se fijaron donde estaba la sandilla y *diario* la iban a ver y la tanteaban (*Centro*, I, No. 3, p. 19).

GUATEMALA: Don Pepe *diario* se afeita (Sandoval, I, 367).

EL SALVADOR: *Diario* va a la finca (Salazar García, p. 108).

AFUERA, FUERA, ADENTRO, DENTRO

The best standard usage of the adverbs *afuera*, *fuera*, and *adentro*, *dentro*, seems to be this: the longer forms, *afuera* (< *a* + *fuera*) and *adentro* (< *a* + *dentro*), are used alone (*afuera* 'outside,' *adentro* 'inside'); the shorter forms *fuera* and *dentro* are preferred with prepositions, both in constructions like *hacia fuera* and in the compounds: *dentro de*, *fuera de*. Keniston's count (*Syntax list*, pp. 39, 61) implies this preference. While the standard language prefers the shorter forms after prepositions, the contrary seems to be the case in Spanish America, especially after *hacia*. In ordinary conversation, of course,

[1] Benavente, *La otra honra*, I, 3: "Cuando considera uno estos espectáculos que *a diario* nos ofrece la Humanidad." Américo Castro, *La peculiaridad*, p. 113: "Fuera de ellas se organizan *a diario* cursos de ortografía." And it appears much earlier in Pereda (*Obras completas*, XV, 68): "Bajo las coberturas sencillas que usamos *a diario* los simples mortales."

hacia fuera sounds exactly like *hacia afuera,* and those who write *hacia afuera* probably consider *hacia fuera* a case of '*a* embebida,' which it may have been in many cases. *Afuera de* and *adentro de* are popular, but *hacia afuera* and *hacia adentro* are also literary.

ARGENTINA: *Afuera* de la ramada había colgado un cuarto de carne (Payró, p. 13). *Adentro* de la ciénaga (Petit de Murat, p. 67).

URUGUAY: *Hacia afuera* ... se abría el campo (Viana, *Gaucha,* p. 180). ... La gallina ... tenía la pollada *adentro* de la cocina (Pérez Petit, p. 22).

CHILE: Y su angustia creció al advertir que *desde afuera* alguien hacía presión sobre la puerta (Maluenda, *Los ciegos,* p. 150); dió un paso *hacia afuera* (p. 151). Ya están aprendiendo castellano *adentro* de la cáscara (Díaz Garcés, in *Hispanoamericanos,* p. 120).

PERU: La gente ... mira *hacia afuera* (Barrantes, p. 74). Los pastores se endurecieron ... llorando *para adentro* sus lágrimas (Ciro Alegría, *El mundo,* p. 107).

COLOMBIA: Sálgome al punto *hacia adentro* (Carrasquilla, *Hace tiempos,* I, 261); bota *hacia afuera* sus copos (II, 7).

COSTA RICA: Poco después ya viene *hacia adentro* (Fabián Dobles, p. 122; also pp. 135, 158); siguió *hacia afuera* (p. 171).

HONDURAS: La lengua pastosa yacía *afuera* de la boca (Mejía Nieto, *El solterón,* p. 128).

GUATEMALA: Pegastes centro [= acertaste] para calmar mi aflición,/por más que la procesión/la llevemos *por adentro* (Bonilla Ruano, III, 74).

MEXICO: Yo traigo media docena de plomos *adentro* de mi cuerpo (Azuela, *Los de abajo,* p. 16). En eso vi a un hombre ... mirando *para adentro* (Galeana, p. 103). Se formó una línea de soldados *adentro* del zaguán (Urquizo, p. 45). *Adentro* de la choza ... yacía una mujer joven tendida sobre un petate (Rubín, p. 139).

CUBA: Después que el viejo marino hubo mirado un momento *hacia adentro* de sí mismo (Ibarzábal, in *CC,* p. 42).

A CADA NADA

The locution *a cada nada,* 'a cada rato, a cada instante' is heard in Chile (Román), Colombia, Venezuela, Central America (Malaret, *Dicc.*), and probably elsewhere. Cuervo (§ 398) bases it on the meaning of *nada* in such phrases as *nada ha que vino* ('muy poco, un momento'). Variants are: *a cualquier nada* (Chile, where *a cada nada* is pronounced *a caa na*), *cada poco* (Mexico), *cada nonada* 'de vez en cuando' (New Mexico), *cada manada* 'a menudo' (Honduras), etc. (cf. *BDH*, II, 131).

A GATAS

Standardly the adverbial locution *a gatas* means 'on all fours.' The figurative and colloquial expression *salir uno a gatas* means 'to extricate one's self with difficulty from a dangerous plight.' This figurative sense of *a gatas* has been extended colloquially in the River Plate region to the simple meaning of *apenas* ('hardly'). The phrase (*a gatas, agatas, a gatitas, agatitas*) is used both as an adverb of manner and as a temporal conjunction. There seem to be traces of this extension of meaning in popular peninsular Spanish (Tiscornia, *La lengua*, p. 204, n. 1), in Bolivia (Malaret), and elsewhere.

As an adverb: *Agatas* andaría por los once [años] (Lynch, *Romance*, p. 105); el hijo e la viuda ... *agatas* si le contestó uno que otro «¡ah, ah!» (p. 245); pa la madre *agatas* si el mozo tuvo un pensamiento (p. 255). —¿No te podeh' enderezar? —*A gatitas*—contesté mientras lograba tomar posición de gente (Güiraldes, *Don Segundo*, p. 91); *a gatas* aguantó las ganas que tenía de echársele encima, ahí no más (p. 134). Aquí *a gatas* sabemos lo que pasa en el pago y eso mismo a veces por puro vicio (Larreta, *El linyera*, p. 44). El boleto *agatita* alcanzó pa mí solita (Chiarello, p. 15). La tierra ardía bajo el sol terrible, cubierta *a gatas* con un ponchito de gramillas (Espínola, p. 25).

As a conjunction: —El patrón se jué *agatas* llegué yo (Lynch, *Romance*, p. 318). *A gatas* la vi, me fué simpática (Payró, p. 22).

AHORA, HOY

In the popular speech of some regions, confusion exists in the use and meaning of the adverbs *ahora* 'now' and *hoy* 'today.' In the first place, popular and rustic usage often shows *hora* (beside *aura*) for *ahora*. On the other hand, the monosyllable *hoy*, apparently felt to be of insufficient force, has been lengthened in various ways (cf. *oy en este día* in the *Cid*, vs. 754; French *aujourd'hui*). Thus *ahoy* may be heard especially in provincial Mexico, probably by analogy with *ahora*.

MEXICO: —*Ahoy* me ha tocado ser de los de la legalidá (Madero, I, 7). Lo que es yo te quedré siempre lo mismo que *ahoy* (Delgado, p. 64).

The form *hoy día*, which in standard speech generally means 'nowadays,' is heard in many areas in the sense of *hoy*, an old usage.

ARGENTINA: *Hoy día* iremos al cine (Morínigo).

CHILE: Está bueno que te vayas *hoy día*, te doy quince días para que te repongas (Juan Modesto Castro, p. 100); Levántate *hoy día* un par de horas (p. 127); —Ud. ya se puede levantar *hoy día*, y si sigue bien, irse el lunes (p. 396).

BOLIVIA: *Hoy día* se ha vuelto usté a perder (Jaime Mendoza, *El lago*, p. 70).

ECUADOR: —Será *hoy día* que estará bueno, pero mañana ... (Pareja, *La Beldaca*, p. 27). —Desde *hoy día* te voy a dar ocho sucres al mes (Pareja, *Baldomera*, p. 176).

COLOMBIA (SOUTH): *Hoy día* estamos a siete de mayo (Alvarez Garzón, p. 158); *hoy día* la pagarán (p. 177); aunque fuera *hoy día* mismo, p. 199).

The form *todoy* (< *todo* + *hoy*) is apparently used in the coastal zone of Ecuador:

—¡Ah! ¿Tanto cuesta? —Sí, don Jesús. Todo está caro *todoy* (Pareja, *La Beldaca*, p. 183); —Le dió un ataque, Jesús. Todito temblaba *todoy* (p. 184). —No sé. Pero no me gusta argo que ejtá pasando *todoy* (Aguilera Malta, p. 107).

What is particularly baffling about *ahora* and *hoy* is their interchange of meanings: in some regions *ahora* means 'today' and *hoy* means 'now'! The use of *hoy* for *ahora* 'now' evidently goes back to the older language: "quesiste casar/A tu hija, *hoy* ha seis años" (Torres Naharro, *Comedia Aquilana*, IV); "Bien parece que no me conosciste en mi prosperidad, *oy* ha veynte años" (*Celestina*, IX). In Central America particularly, one hears "*hoy* (= ahora) ha llovido más que el año pasado," "*hoy* mismo (= ahora mismo) voy," "*hoy* (= ahora) los inviernos son más fríos que antes." The Ecuadorian, García Muñoz, uses *hoy* for *ahora* in *El médico que pretendió la gloria* (p. 44): "—¿Desde qué horas está usted con esa intranquilidad, señora? —Hace una hora, doctor. —¿Una hora? Entonces, los dolores han empezado a las diez, porque *hoy* son las once." The same author uses *ahora* for *hoy* in *Estampas de mi ciudad, segunda serie:* "—¿Por qué no he de beber, pes? Si *aura* es día de chumarse (p. 54); Y como necesito plata para *aura* de noche [= hoy por la noche] (p. 317); *Aura* tarde [= hoy por la tarde] usted les ha de vender bien vendidos" (p. 318).

This same use of *ahora* for *hoy* is encountered nearly everywhere beside the standard usage. Bonilla Ruano (III, 49) attests it for Guatemala with the example "*ahora* llegaré a verte" for "*hoy* llegaré a verte." The Mexican lexicographer, Santamaría (*El provincialismo tabasqueño*, p. 70), makes this revealing statement: "*Ahora*, propiamente, se refiere a la actualidad durante el día o la fecha en que se habla; así, se dice *iremos ahora, ahora en la noche*, esto es, 'hoy'; en tanto que *ahorita* es 'en este momento,' en el instante mismo en que se habla." The Academy dictionary gives *por ahora* as an equivalent of *por hoy*.

The use of *hoy* for *ahora* is especially frequent in the colloquial phrase *desde hoy* (rustic *dende hoy*) meaning *desde ahora*, that is, *desde hace rato* or *poco antes* or *hace un momento*.

ARGENTINA: ¡Al fin, mujer! ¿De dónde salís? *Desde hoy* te estoy llamando (Laferrère, *Las de Barranco*, p. 19). —¡*Desde hoy* te estoy esperando! Tengo que hablarte (Laferrère, *Locos de verano*, p. 24).

URUGUAY: —*Desde hoy* le estoy diciendo que vaya a acostarse, pero ella por esperarte. ... —¡Caramba, y yo que he tardado tanto! (Florencio Sánchez, p. 39).

GUATEMALA: *Dende hoy* vino a buscarte el carretero, quien trae para ti un certificado urgente (Sandoval, I, 329); Vine *desde hoy* a buscarte y no te encontré (p. 342). —¿Pero dónde puse las tijeras? Dios mío—dice la costurera—Si *desde 'oyito* las tenía en la mano (José Valle).

A HUEVO

The much-discussed *a huevo* has again been recorded in the Academy dictionary. It is found in the older language[2] and apparently is still used in regions of Spain, though not so freely as in parts of Spanish America. The dictionary explains the phrase as indicating "lo barato que cuestan o se venden las cosas." In addition to the general meaning of 'cheap,' the phrase has acquired extended meanings in several different regions. In Venezuela, *huevo* means *centavo de cobre* 'a copper cent,' stemming from the custom of using eggs in barter at the value of a cent apiece, at a time when there were no coins smaller than the *medio real*, worth five *sueldos*. Lavayasse, a French traveler to Venezuela, says in 1807: "If you enter a store to buy something worth less than five *sueldos*, you are given two or three eggs in return" (cited by Alvarado, p. 238). Standard *a huevo*

[2] Cf. the proverb "En Toledo el abad *a huevo*, y en Salamanca a blanca," quoted in Lope's *Dorotea* (1632), II, 3.

becomes *de a huevo* in Venezuela and elsewhere. In Cuba (Tierradentro) the popular expression *de a huevo* means "una cosa mui fácil o mínima" (Pichardo, p. 197); "una cosa ... insignificante, o sumamente fácil de preparar, resolver, etc." (Macías, p. 692); "la escasa importancia de algo: un traje *de a huevo*" (Suárez, p. 287).

Elsewhere *huevo* may have the opposite sense, that of great importance or value. Thus for Puerto Rico "costar una cosa un huevo" means "costar un ojo de la cara" (Malaret, *Dicc.*, p. 292). In Guatemala *de a huevo* is applied to "la persona valiente, esforzada y apta para muchas cosas, entre otras para el estudio." Sandoval (I, 311),[3] for instance, gives these: "Rufino es *de a huevo* y le pega a cualquiera"; "Tú fuiste *de a huevo* para las matemáticas."

In Mexico *a huevo* means *por fuerza* 'by force':

—Nosotras no salimos de aquí, y si salimos vamos juntas. —¡Pues ustedes salen *a huevo!*—contestó el oficial. Y ordenó a los soldados que nos sacaran. —*A huevo* no nos sacan, y si nos sacan, nos sacarán muertas! (Galeana, p. 187).

The phrase *a chaleco* has the same meaning in Mexico (Rubio, *Anarquía*, I, 54). Ramos Duarte (p. 156) gives *al chaleco* with the meaning "A ufo, a la fuerza, porque le dió la gana." This phrase is probably related to *chaleco de fuerza* 'strait jacket.'

A LA DISPARADA

This expression is apparently restricted to the River Plate region, Chile, and Peru. The verbal noun *disparada* (from *disparar*) meaning *fuga desordenada* 'disorderly flight' is used with *a* or *de* (*a la disparada* or *de disparada*) to mean *con mucha urgencia* (Tiscornia), or *a todo correr* and, figuratively, *precipitada y atolondradamente* (Acad. dict.). It is used even by well-known Argentine stylists:

Antes de echarse a bajar precipitadamente la escalera, se paró ante un espejo, se miró, alisó *a la disparada* la parte derecha del peinado (Mallea, *Fiesta*, p. 46).

A LA DISTANCIA, LARGO

Standard *a distancia*, meaning *lejos*, often becomes *a la distancia* in American Spanish as in Andalusia, probably by analogy with *a lo lejos*. A few examples will suffice:

[3] Other Guatemalan slang phrases registered by Sandoval with the same meaning are: *de a pichinga, de a pipián, de a sombrero, de a pozol*, etc.

URUGUAY: Había descubierto *a la distancia* a Juan de Dios (Pérez Petit, p. 72).

CHILE: Tropezó con la dura mirada del viejo que le interrogaba *a la distancia* (Azócar, p. 314).

PERU: Una tarde el cholo ... distinguió *a la distancia* a dos reses trabadas en lucha (Ciro Alegría, *El mundo*, p. 41).

ECUADOR: *A la distancia* sólo se veía una misma mancha negra (Vásconez, p. 164). *A la distancia* latían los perros (Icaza, *Media vida*, p. 228).

COLOMBIA: Andrés las seguía *a la distancia* (Álvarez Garzón, p. 91).

VENEZUELA: Un toque de corneta *a la distancia* y luego otro más cerca (Gallegos, *Pobre negro*, p. 309).

NICARAGUA: *A la distancia* se apreciaba el bloque apretado de las montañas (Toruño, p. 17).

In some regions, as in Costa Rica, *largo* has the meaning of *lejos*, as is also the case in some rural regions of Spain: (TOLEDO): "Ahora vamos a ver quién coge un canto y lo tira más *largo*" (Aurelio Espinosa, *Cuentos*, III, 360); (LEÓN): "tenemos que ir a muy *largo* por ella" (*Cuentos*, I, 111).

COSTA RICA: Así que anocheció, vieron allá muy *largo* una lucecita (Lyra, p. 65). Las mujeres y los curas, hijito,/hay que ispialos *de larguito* (Dobles Segreda, p. 74). —¡Llévesenlo *largo!* (Fabián Dobles, p. 384). —Ya va *largo* Felipe (Fallas, p. 58).

The standard expression *de largo a largo* (= *a todo su largor* 'full length') becomes *largo a largo* (Román, III, 271 [Chile and elsewhere]), or *de largo en largo* (Vázquez, p. 235 [Ecuador]), etc. Standard *a lo lejos* is occasionally found as *al lejos* (by analogy with *a lo menos, al menos*) and *a los lejos*.

A LA FIJA

This locution (variant: *en fija*) is common in the River Plate region, Chile, Peru, Colombia, and probably elsewhere. It means *con seguridad, seguramente*. Standard is the adverbial phrase *de fijo* (= *seguramente, sin duda*) and the colloquial expression (*ésa*) *es la fija* (= *es seguro*); *estar en la fija* (for *es la fija*) is registered for Andalusia (Toro Gisbert, "Voces," p. 451).

ARGENTINA: Era algún remedio *a la fija* (Lynch, *Romance*, p. 95); *En fija* que hizo mal en humedecerse ansí los pies (p. 247).

URUGUAY: —Ha de ser Ciriaca. —Ésta, *a la fija*, mañana va a denunciarnos (Pérez Petit, p. 40).

CHILE: Vete con el caballero a la hacienda, que irás *a la fija* [= perfectamente, con la deseable comodidad o seguridad]: no sale de ella administrador que no salga con Don por delante i con el riñón tapado (Zorobabel Rodríguez, p. 3).

COLOMBIA (VALLE DEL CAUCA): A las dos lo encuentra *a la fija* (Tascón, p. 21). (ANTIOQUIA): Iban *a la fija* (Jaramillo, p. 89).

A LA MEJOR

The standard phrase *a lo mejor* meaning 'maybe, when least expected, possibly' often becomes *a la mejor* in Mexico, Venezuela (Rosenblat), in areas of Cuba (Padrón), and possibly elsewhere.

MEXICO: —¿Por qué no? ¡Tanto ha visto uno! —*A la mejor*, el día de mañana nos depara algo a nosotros (Gómez Palacio, p. 31); decíase a sí misma que *a la mejor* hay tiros, bomberos, excesos políticos, y que vale más no salir de casa (p. 32). ¡Quién sabe! *¡A la mejor* aquel muchacho que tenía buenas ideas y tan firme carácter, triunfaba! (Fernando Robles, p. 76); todo se va a ir en alegar y *a la mejor* ni se hace nada (p. 58).

A LAS CANSADAS

In the River Plate zone, Puerto Rico, Peru, Mexico, and possibly elsewhere, *a las cansadas* is used in the sense of "muy tarde, después de mucha demora, a las mil y quinientas" (Malaret), with overtones of 'tired from waiting.'

ARGENTINA: Se descansó, se tomó mate, se durmió y *a las cansadas* llegaron las mulas de carga (Mansilla, *Una excursión*, p. 57). *A las cansadas*, cayó la policía con el médico (Güiraldes, *Don Segundo*, p. 282). Güeno, por fin, allá, *a las cansadas* ... se abría de golpe ... la puerta (Lynch, *Romance*, p. 358).

'AL ÑUDO' AND SYNONYMS

The locution *al ñudo* (variant: *al divino ñudo*), meaning *en vano, inútilmente* 'in vain,' is commonly used colloquially in the River Plate region. It is used also jocosely by the cultured. The Argentine proverb *Al que nace barrigón es al ñudo que lo fajen* corresponds to the well-known *Genio y figura hasta la sepultura* 'You cannot change a leopard's spots.' The form *ñudo* for *nudo* 'knot' was influenced by *añudar* (< Latin *annodare*). Reciprocal contamination resulted in the double forms *añudar—ñudo* and *nudo—anudar* (*BDH*, I, 159).

Frequently found in Golden Age writers, *ñudo* is now considered archaic but has survived (in addition to *nudo*) in Spanish dialects and in popular speech in Spanish America. Tiscornia (*Martín Fierro*, p. 52 n.) thinks the meaning stems from the difficulty of untying a knot, which closes more and more tightly when an attempt is made to pull it apart. Rossi (Folleto No. 21, p. 21) considers it to be "porque deshacer un nudo es menos práctico que cortar el hilo, y es tiempo y paciencia malgastados en obsequio exclusivo del nudo."

ARGENTINA: Pero *al ñudo* fué. El mozo no contestó palabra (Lynch, *Romance*, p. 192). Pensó que era *al ñudo* buscar su caburé [= ave de rapiña] a esas horas (Güiraldes, *Don Segundo*, p. 130); —No *al ñudo* te has criao como la biznaga (p. 299). Lo demás es calentarse/El mate *al divino ñudo* (Del Campo, *Fausto*, p. 281).

URUGUAY: Hacen mal en dir a gastar plata *al ñudo* (Sánchez, *M'hijo el dotor*, III, 2). —Porque a mí no me gusta gastar la plata ni las palabras *al ñudo* (Viana, *Tardes*, p. 31); —Está *al ñudo* la alvertencia (p. 33).

The phrases *al cohete* (spelled also in imitation of rustic speech: *al cuhete, al cuete*), *al botón*, and *al pedo*, synonymous with *al ñudo*, are used in the rustic and vulgar speech of the same region. Sometimes the adjective *divino* (also *santo*) is used with the noun (*al divino botón*), as is also the case with *ñudo* (*al divino ñudo*). The phrases *al botón* and *al cohete* mean also *sin razón, sin motivo* 'for no reason,' 'without a reason,' etc. In this sense *al botón* is not unknown, at least in some regions of Chile, especially in the phrase *hablar al* (*divino*) *botón* meaning 'hablar por hablar, sin concierto ni objeto alguno' (Medina, p. 44). Malaret (*Suplemento*, I, 206) records *al* (*divino*) *botón* for Peru.

ARGENTINA: —Cuando yo te digo que no vale la pena, no lo digo *al cuhete*. ¡Sé lo que son! (González Arrili, p. 37); No lo hago porque se me hace que todo va a ser un puro perder tiempo y saliva *al cohete* (p. 50). ¡Caramba, yo no quiero hacer un sacrificio *al cuete!* (Martínez Payva, p. 11). Una vez entre otras muchas,/tanto salir *al botón*,/nos pegaron un malón (*Martín Fierro*, p. 39). ¡Paisano hereje, *al pedo* cansó el caballo! (Saubidet, p. 12). —Su sermón no fué *al divino pedo* ... sino un ataque certeramente dirigida (Filloy, p. 430).

URUGUAY: —Es *al cohete*. ¡Al viento no se asujeta como a la yegua por los garrones! (Acevedo Díaz, *Soledad*, p. 147). —No, no mire p'atrás. ¿Pa qué? Si es *al pedo*. Con mirar p'atrás no se gana nada (Montiel, *Cuentos*, p. 14). —Están hablando *al santo botón*. ... Más valiera seguir como hasta aura (Viana, *Tardes*, p. 68). —Me parece que nos hemos alarmao *al cuete* (Pérez Petit, p. 141). —Allí hay que llegar temprano si no se quiere hacer el viaje *al botón* (Florencio Sánchez, p. 284).

CHILE: Pero 'chacra' tiene en cambio la variante 'chácara,' como suelen decir ciertos puristas *al divino botón*, que se imaginan que para hablar castizo con apartarse siempre del vulgo basta i sobra (Zorobabel Rodríguez, p. 140).

A LO MACHO

The phrase *a lo macho* is particularly common in Mexico in familiar conversation, meaning 'firmly, truthfully, reliably, wholeheartedly,' etc. Cf. our 'like a man' and Cuban 'de a hombre' (Padrón).

CENTRAL ZONE: Échele encima los pleitos en que me he metido *a lo macho*, sin conseguir nada (Magdaleno, p. 15). Quero que me dé un consejo/*a lo macho* y a lo amigo. ... Lo que les dije, compadre,/y lo sostengo *a lo macho*/jué qu'es usté sinvergüenza (Rivas Larrauri, pp. 85, 157).

Elsewhere the opposite meaning is sometimes conveyed in the phrase *a lo hembra;* that is, 'unreliably, treacherously,' etc. In Yamandú Rodríguez's *Cimarrones* (Argentina), Valerio complains to his friend who treacherously robbed him of his love, Pastora: "Te portaste *a lo hembra*. Como Pastora. Son parejos. ¡Entre los dos me han echado del rancho, del pago, de mí" (p. 105).

'AL TIRO, AL GRITO,' AND RELATED PHRASES

The adverbial phrase *al tiro* with the meaning of 'immediately,' 'in a jiffy,' etc. (= *al instante, al momento, en el acto, inmediatamente, de golpe*) is current particularly in Chile (Román, V, 477), while not unknown in Bolivia, Argentina (though *al grito* is preferred here), Peru, Ecuador (Malaret), Colombia (Tascón, p. 25), Costa Rica (Gagini, p. 55), Honduras (Membreño, p. 7), and probably elsewhere, but examples are not abundant. The meaning of *al tiro* may be compared to our 'quick as a shot.' The closest standard expressions are *de un tiro* and *de un tirón* 'with one pull, quickly, suddenly,' etc. It may well have been influenced by standard *a tiro*, whose meaning 'within (a stone's) throw,' 'within (shooting) range,' etc., developed into 'within close range' and 'near'; and then by a common transferral of spatial to temporal values: 'soon, quickly.' Thus in the Canaries *a tiro*, or *a tirito*, is used in the sense of *en seguida, a escape, inmediatamente, sin dilación* (Millares, p. 17).

Variant forms of *al tiro* are *al tirito, alretirito, altirichicho, al tiro liro*, etc.

ARGENTINA: Le soltó/las bolas, con tal certeza,/que, *al tiro*, se las ató/en las manos al rocín (Ascasubi, p. 168).

CHILE: Vistámonos *al tiro* y veamos qué ha sucedido (Laval, II, 90). *Al tirito* me las endilgo p'al cerro (Latorre, *Hombres*, p. 223). —Voy a volver *altirito* (Acevedo Hernández, *De pura cepa*, p. 8); Quiero peliarte, pero *alretirito* (p. 10). —Cuente lo que le pasó con mi compadre. —*Al tiro liro* (Guzmán Maturana, p. 198). —¡Me duele tanto la cabeza, hijito! Con un par de puchaditas ['puffs'] se me quita *al tiro* (Juan Modesto Castro, p. 17); No se hizo rogar, pagó *al tiro* (p. 147); me calman *al tiro* el dolor (p. 214); Empezaron *al tiro* con sus pruebas (p. 375). ¡Yastá! *¡Altirichicho!* ¡Los juimos! [= nos vamos] (Muñoz, p. 232).

BOLIVIA: Retiraron la bolsa y comprobaron que en el ángulo de la vivienda había un hueco. ... —Tápalo *al tiro*, che. La vida es imposible con estas malditas [ratas] (Céspedes, p. 215).

The River Plate expression *al grito* (not entered in the Argentine dictionaries) has the same temporal value as *al tiro*. Tiscornia (*Martín Fierro*, p. 111 n.) remarks: "Ambos modos [*al grito* and *al tiro*] parecen tener origen a principios del siglo XIX, en las guerras de la independencia: les es común el sentido bélico de las voces 'grito' y 'tiro,' a las cuales acudían prontamente los soldados." While the alleged circumstances may have had their share of influence in the life of these expressions, they do not necessarily or even probably represent the source.

Al grito salió de adentro/Un gringo con un jusil (*Martín Fierro*, p. 111). Y, en cuanto esto se concluya,/*al grito* nos descolgamos (Hidalgo, p. 74); al galope llegó arriba/y, *al grito*, ya le echó mano/a la chuspa (p. 88). Haga el favor/de acollararlos. —*Al grito* (Del Campo, *Fausto*, p. 261).

Related to *al tiro* are the locutions *del tiro* and *de a tiro*, with the variants *de al tiro* and *dialtiro*, used by the populace in Venezuela (*del tiro*), most regions of Central America (*de al tiro* and *del tiro*) and

Mexico (*de a tiro, de al tiro, dialtiro*), with the meaning of *en absoluto, por completo, de un todo* (Alvarado); *de golpe* (Gagini); *enteramente, de golpe o zumbido* (Batres); *de una vez, enteramente, totalmente* (Sandoval); *de una vez, enteramente, de un tirón* (Ramos Duarte). Darío Rubio (*Refranes*, I, 128) reports that the phrase *de a tiro* is very commonly used in Mexico "para calificar la conducta de una persona, cuando nos parece que dicha conducta merece reprobación" with the general meaning of *completamente*, although the expression may have additional and subtle connotations.

VENEZUELA: No es tan *del tiro* así. *Del tiro* dejé mi oficio (Alvarado, p. 431).

EL SALVADOR: Por más que se hizo, el niño Raulo ya no tuvo compostura y se perdió *de al tiro* (Mechín, *La muerte*, p. 107). Éste salió medio rajado y aquél boliado [= astillado] *dialtiro* (Salarrué, *Cuentos*, p. 7); La barranca ... se despejaba *dialtiro* y se véiyan clarito los morados del guarumal (p. 134).

GUATEMALA: —La Toña es una igualada. ¡Y tan *dialtiro* orgullosa! (Wyld Ospina, *Nahuyacas*, p. 88). *De al tiro* se me rompió el pantalón (Sandoval, I, 311). Ya estaba esperando que el animal se le juera encima y ... la dejara muerta *dialtiro* (Quintana, p. 130). Pero ahura sí que cambió en un *dialtiro* (Barnoya, p. 26).

MEXICO: —No me pareció tan *de atiro* despreciable (Inclán, II, 166). Eres *de a tiro* sinvergüenza; —¿Qué te pareció la tiple que se presentó anoche? —*De a tiro* mala. (Proverb): *Dealtiro* la tronchan verde, no la dejan madurar (Rubio, *Refranes*, I, 128). La suerte/con los que son güenos/*dialtiro* la troncha,/en l'ínter qui hay munchos/ que son puras mulas y son los que gozan (Rivas Larrauri, p. 10); se quedó *dialtiro*/sin un solo jierro (p. 59); pero es que t'equivocas *dialtiro* si te fias/nomás de l'aparencia (p. 62); Mi mamacita está muy mala *dialtiro* (p. 92); ¿Ti has güelto loco *dialtiro?* (p. 114), etc. —¡No, hombres! Ustedes sí que la amuelan ... *¡diatiro!* —Este "diatiro," interjección provincial, precedió a otra crudez (Quevedo, *Las ensabanadas*, p. 129).

A MANO

The Spanish-American phrase *estamos a mano* 'we are even,' 'we are quits' (in games, accounts, actions, or words) corresponds to standard *estamos en paz* rather than to *estamos mano a mano*, since the latter is restricted in application, according to the Academy dictionary: "entre jugadores y luchadores, sin ventaja de uno a otro o con partido igual." Román (III, 417) considered *estar a mano* to be a *chilenismo* and thought it derived from the custom of shaking hands to indicate that two persons are even or quits. Far from being such a localism, *estar a mano* (or *a manos*) is heard practically throughout Spanish America (cf. Malaret, *Dicc.*). A few examples will suffice:

ARGENTINA: (Terencio, who has already answered a wrong-number telephone-call): Hola. ... No, señor. ... Belarmino no está ... [fibbing]. Se fué a la casa de su agüela. ... Bueno. *¡Estamos a mano!* (Chiarello, p. 42). *Está a mano* con él (Y. Rodríguez, *Bichito*, p. 70).

PARAGUAY: *Estamos a mano* (Morínigo).

CHILE: —Agora sí qu'es cierto que no le debo ni cobre. —*Tamos a mano,*—me ijo (Romanángel, p. 73).

VENEZUELA: Ya *estamos a mano* (Alvarado, p. 274).

GUATEMALA: Nada nos debemos, porque *estamos a mano* (Sandoval, I, 47).

MEXICO: —Lorenzo, *estamos a mano,* tu cuenta está saldada (Inclán, I, 89).

A POCO

A peculiarly Mexican usage is the locution *a poco (crees que)*, etc., meaning approximately 'you probably think (that)' or 'I suppose you think (that)' or 'do you perchance think (that),' etc. Occasionally its meaning has been weakened to a simple negation: *no* (cf. *acaso*, p. 272). Apparently the verb *creer* was an essential part of the expression originally, but it is often now lacking, though the connotation remains the same. The intonation is that of a combined question and exclamation. For this reason some writers punctuate it as a question, others as an exclamation. The phrase is generally ironical in that its affirmative statement is in reality negative: while we may translate the sentence *A poco crees que me asustas* as 'You probably think you're frightening me,' a more accurate rendition might be 'You don't think you're frightening me, do you?' Standard equivalents generally given for the phrase are *acaso* (ironic), *a lo mejor, por casualidad, que te crees que,* etc. (León, II, 15); it sometimes means *yo sospecho, malicio, recelo que,* etc. Cf. also p. 319.

With *creer* (or *pensar*): —Pulmonía. ¿Por qué no llevó al médico? —¡Ah, qué doña Chole! *¿A poco usted cree* en ésos? (Ferretis, *San Automóvil*, p. 23). ¿Pero *a poco piensas que* sin sindicatos, sabiendo trabajar, nos muramos de hambre? (Ferretis, *Quijote*, p. 239). *¿A poco crees que* puedo correr más fuerte [= más de prisa] que un coche? (C). —Ay, desgraciados, yo también ya los conocí; *a poco creían que* andaban muy bien disfrazados (Galeana, p. 164). —¡Mmm! *¿A poco creen que* el Coyotito no anda en todo esto? (Magdaleno, p. 38).

Without *creer: ¿A poco* es tuyo? [= 'I suppose you think it's yours?]; *¿A poco* no me sienta bien el negro? [= 'I suppose you think black doesn't become me' = 'Black certainly is becoming to me']; *¿A poco* tienes tan limpia la conciencia? (C). *¡A poco* [= acaso] son los mochos! (Azuela, *Los de abajo*, p. 71). —Sí, doctor, su futuro suegro, don Ezequiel Casanova, de la familia de los Casanova. ... *¿A poco* no? ¡Hora niéguemelo! Si aquí todo se sabe (Robles Castillo, p. 19). Porque dígase lo que se diga, lo decente se ve, se siente, se huele. *¿A poco* ustedes no han adivinado que no toda mi vida he sido una pobre cocinera? ¡Cocinera! Tal como se los digo (Azuela, *Avanzada*, p. 238). Ya nomás el aroma quedó. —¡Cómo! *¡A poco* ya comieron! —Pues sí, figúrate. Llegaste tarde (Galeana, p. 120). *¿A poco* cualquiera de las muchachas le iba a decir que no? (García Roel, p. 200); ¿A que nunca han matao una gallina? —¿Y *a poco* tú sí? (p. 303).

A SABER

A saber is especially common in Central America in the sense of *tal vez* as well as of *no sé, no se sabe,* etc. Its use corresponds to that of *quién sabe* elsewhere, especially in Mexico. Occasionally *al saber* is heard in popular and rustic speech in parts of Mexico. The Academy dictionary explains that *a saber* as an exclamation means *vete a saber*. However, it appears much less frequently in Spain than in parts of America: "—*A saber* si ella hará lo mismo" (Benavente, *Señora ama,* I, 5). It is often written as one word: *asaber*.

VENEZUELA (ANDES): *A saber* quién se robó el dinero (Rosenblat).

COSTA RICA: ¡Y *a saber* si ya endenantes/me bía fabricao muñeco! (Agüero, p. 13).

NICARAGUA: *A saber* de qué mujer suya será y quiere venirnos con que lo recogió (Toruño, p. 37). No hay uno que no lamente el cambio de patrón. —*¡A saber* cómo irá a ser el que venga! (Robleto, p. 66).

EL SALVADOR: —¿Nuha yegado? ¿y eso? —*A saber*, patrón. —¿Qué li habrá sucedido? Ladislao respondió maquinalmente, como de costumbre: —*Asaber* (Ambrogi, p. 62). —Pero, ¿no van al Cielo los que se portan bien en la Tierra? —*A saber* ... a veces quizá (Salarrué, *Eso y más*, p. 29). En seguida puso al fuego un tiliche que quizás tenía agua, y *a saber* qué vió (Mechín, *La muerte*, p. 55). —Ende que le entró *asaber* qué, se propuso hacer pisto (Salarrué, *Cuentos*, p. 12).

GUATEMALA: ¿Cree usted que vendrá Juan? *A saber* [= quién sabe]; *A saber* [= no se sabe] quién se robó el dinero; *A saber* [= no sé] si volveré a ver a mi madre (Batres, p. 63). *A saber* Dios cómo estarán a esas horas en su casa (Samayoa, p. 27); —*A saber, a saber,* donde está el hombre del monte (p. 69).

MEXICO: —¿Luego es decir que este invierno/te lo pasas sin cobija? —Pos, *¡al saber!* (González Carrasco, p. 87); ¿Ya se siente igual que antes? —*¡Al saber!* (p. 170).

AVANTE

The adverb *avante*, meaning *adelante*, is registered in the Academy dictionary as antiquated but as still in use in Salamanca (Spain) and as a strictly nautical term: "Hoy tiene uso en *Sal.* y en la marina." However, under *salir*, we find the phrase *salir adelante* or *avante* meaning, figuratively, 'to succeed in an undertaking, to overcome some great difficulty or danger.' The adverb *avante* (= *adelante*) is current in many regions of America and has been considered a localism (especially the phrase *salir avante*) by some lexicographers: Ecuador (Mateus, p. 22), Chile (Echeverría y Reyes, p. 131), Central America (Salazar, p. 43), Guatemala (Sandoval, I, 96), etc. The last two erroneously consider it a vulgarism for *ovante* 'triumphant, victorious. Occasionally it is made to agree like an adjective: "los niños podrán salir *avantes* en sus estudios" (Coen, p. 28 [Mexico]).

URUGUAY: Pero hemos ido *avante* y aquí estamos (Manuel Bernárdez, *ap.* Martínez Vigil, p. 10).

VENEZUELA (ANDES): Llevamos los mulos *avante; Avante* lo topará; Siempre *salgo avante* en los exámenes (Rosenblat).

MEXICO: En la prueba clínica ¿sabes cómo *salí avante?* (Quevedo, *La camada*, p. 291). Pero el ingeniero supo sacar *avante* la aprobación de sus trabajos (Azuela, *Mala yerba*, p. 96); algo había hecho Julián: dos homicidios calificados de los que supo *salir avante* y cuando no cumplía veinte años (p. 107).

PERU: Si para algo se necesita desplegar actividades es para sacar *avante* la candidatura de don Antero (Corrales, p. 172).

CASUALMENTE, TAN LUEGO

The adverb *casualmente* (= *por casualidad* 'by chance') is often used ill-advisedly for *precisamente* 'exactly': "*casualmente* por eso he venido" = standard "*precisamente* por eso he venido." Such usage has been criticized as an Americanism, but we find the same, less frequently however, in peninsular Spanish.

ARGENTINA: Parece que la recogió uno de los transeúntes, según lo declaró un señor Cabello, que es un corredor rengo, casado *casualmente* con una sobrina (*Fray Mocho*, p. 180). —Pues podemos repartírnoslos, como buenos hermanos. —*Casualmente*, el dormitorio que tengo está pasado de moda (Rodríguez Acasuso, *La mujer olvidada*, III, 9). La virtud del automóvil reside *casualmente* en la nerviosidad del pique y la constancia de la velocidad (Filloy, p. 229).

URUGUAY: El caballo te haría mucho bien. *Casualmente*, el overo ... está pidiendo que le pongan el basto (Reyles, *El terruño*, p. 78).

CHILE: No es que Latinoamérica tenga una producción teatral que pueda compararse en valor y trascendencia a su poesía o a su novela, sino *casualmente* por lo contrario: por su deficiencia (Fernando Alegría, in *Atenea*, XX [1943], 162).

COLOMBIA: —¿Y don Florentino vió al bandido? —*Casualmente* eso es lo que voy a contarles (Buitrago, p. 73).

VENEZUELA: *Casualmente* no hace mucho que [el Padre] me acaba de casá con una blanquita (Gallegos, *Pobre negro*, p. 340).

MEXICO: *Casualmente* por eso he venido (Santamaría and Domínguez, *Ensayos*, p. 133). —Sí, de veras, todo eso es cierto; yo temo. ... —¿Eh? Pos *casualmente* por esto te lo advertimos (Robles, *La virgen*, p. 94).

With about the same meaning of *precisamente* we find the locution *tan luego*, but apparently only in restricted areas. Examples abound for the River Plate region. The standard value of *tan luego* is temporal; its transferral to the new connotation is similar to that of temporal *desde luego* ('immediately' > 'undoubtedly, surely, inevitably').

ARGENTINA: ¿Por qué él, *tan luego* él, debía enredarse? ... ¿por qué él, *tan luego* él, que intervino en los furiosos entreveros ... debía abandonar la ciudad por la sola insinuación de un colega? (Filloy, p. 45). —Dos personas ... quieren hablar con usted. —¿Conmigo? ¡*Tan luego* ahora! (Laferrère, *Locos de verano*, p. 43).

URUGUAY: —¡Qué rareza! Todo eso para escribir un libro. —¡Figúrense! *Tan luego* él que nunca tuvo aficiones literarias (Florencio Sánchez, p. 538).

'CÓMO' + ADJECTIVE

In modern standard Castilian our exclamatory *how* + an adjective or adverb is commonly expressed by *qué* + an adjective or adverb: *¡qué bella es la vida!* Besides this locution, there existed in the older language another less common way of expressing the same type of exclamatory phrase: *cómo* + verb + adjective or adverb. Thus one could say "¡qué bella es!" or "¡cómo es bella!" One recalls Gil Vicente's famous *canción* from *El auto de la Sibila Casandra:* "Muy graciosa es la doncella;/*cómo* es bella y hermosa!" According to the Keniston count (p. 158), the *qué* construction was encountered nearly twice as frequently as the *cómo* construction in the sixteenth century. In the standard language *cómo* has here generally ceded to *qué;* but it has survived in the popular speech of certain regions, more extensively in Spanish America than in Spain.

ARGENTINA: *¡Cómo* somos desgraciadas las mujeres! (Manuel Romero, p. 13). *¡Cómo* estaría arrepentido de sus burlas y sus risas! (Cuti Pereira, p. 123).

URUGUAY: *¡Cómo* es difícil vivir! (Trías du Pre, p. 79). —*¡Cómo* estoy cansada! (Sánchez, *La gringa* [1941 ed.], II, 3); *cómo* están caras las cosas, ¿eh? (II, 4).

The Sánchez examples just quoted are interesting because previous editions (1920, 1926, 1939) have another construction (discussed below): "*¡cómo* estoy *de* cansada!" and "*cómo* están las cosas *de* caras." The editor of the 1941 Claridad edition, Dardo Cúneo, derived his readings from popular editions appearing at the time of the first performances.[4] María, for instance, who uses the expressions cited, is supposed to have a marked Italian accent (Piedmontese dialect) and occasionally is made to lapse into Italianisms ("está dal escribano" [II, 3]; "roba de gente, povero diavolo" [IV, 3]).

[4] According to his reply to my inquiry. His letter reads in part: "Existe por cierto algún desorden en los textos de Sánchez. Su autor nunca se interesó en unificarlos pues se desprendía de los originales en el momento en que los vendía a los empresarios. Incluso alguna vez, no faltó director de escena que resolviera modificar expresiones y pasajes. A falta de ediciones perfectamente corregidas por su autor, debemos—y así lo hice yo en la organización del 'Teatro Completo'—servirnos de las ediciones más inmediatas a los estrenos, incluídas en colecciones populares y cuyos ejemplares salían al público al mismo tiempo que se levantaba el telón para la representación de la pieza."

Other Italianisms or colloquialisms originally written by Sánchez were either misunderstood or considered faulty by later editors and were consequently tampered with. Such tamperings have resumed their original forms in the 1941 edition (original "ma es caro" [II, 4] for "mas es caro"; original "que lo haga de la modista el vestido" [II, 4] for "que le haga la modista el vestido," etc.).

In other countries the construction has been called a Gallicism. It resembles both French and Italian, but one must remember it existed in the older language and is used today in popular and rustic speech into which Gallicisms could hardly penetrate.

Bolivia: Mire, señorita, *¡cómo* está bonito el guindal! (Arguedas, *Vida criolla*, p. 10); —¡Jesús! *¡Cómo* son inmorales estas indias! (p. 188); ¡Pero *cómo* es puerca la vida! (p. 234).

Colombia: —*¡Cómo* había sido feliz en la soledad! (Efe Gómez, p. 153).

Mexico: *¡Cómo* eres ruin y bajo! *¡Cómo* eres tonto! *¡Cómo* eres bobo! (C). *¡Cómo* eres hablador! (Rivas Larrauri, p. 140). *¡Cómo* eres malo! ¿Para qué los incomodas? (Ferretis, *Quijote*, p. 254). *¡Cómo* he sido tonto! (Anda, *Juan del Riel*, p. 59). *Cómo* serán atascados (Urquizo, p. 62). *¡Cómo* eres lenguaraz, hermano mío! ... —Y tú, hermana mía, *¡cómo* eres cándida! (Gamboa, *Teatro*, III, 177).

The same construction with the preposition *de* preceding the adjective is prevalent in America as well as in Spain.

Argentina: *¡Cómo* le parecía *de* bien! (Lynch, *Romance*, p. 43). ¡Ay, Jesús, *cómo* son estos hombres *de* ciegos! (González Arrili, p. 54). ¡Sos *de* loco que da asco! (Y. Rodríguez, *Bichito*, p. 79).

Uruguay: *¡Cómo* estoy *de* cansada! (Sánchez, *La gringa* [1920, 1926, 1939 eds.], II, 3); *cómo* están las cosas *de* caras, ¿eh? (11, 4).

Chile: *¿Cómo* estaré *de* grave? (Juan Modesto Castro, p. 370).

Bolivia: *¡Cómo* fué *de* enorme su consternación! (Arguedas, *Raza*, p. 79).

Colombia (Antioquia): Figúrese, *cómo* es mi niña *de* hacendosa (Carrasquilla, *Hace tiempos*, I, 40); *¡Cómo* viniste *de* bien puesta y bien peinada! (II, 107); *¡Cómo* suena *de* extraño aquel golpeo! (II, 142). ¡Ya ve—empezó el maestro Feliciano—*cómo* son *de* orgullosas las mujeres! (Arango Villegas, p. 15); *¡Cómo* es la vida *de* cruel, *de* miserable, *de* ruin! (p. 92). (South): *Cómo* le estoy *de* agradecido; *Cómo* es *de* bueno (Álvarez Garzón, p. 197). Bogotá (Flórez).

Venezuela: *¡Cómo* soy *de* distraído! (Gallegos, *Pobre*, p. 256).

NICARAGUA: *Cómo* es *de* bueno y *de* ingenuo el soldado nicaragüense (Orozco, p. 127).

GUATEMALA: *Cómo* era *de* alegre el Pedro (Barnoya, p. 26); vos sabés *cómo* son *de* águilas los muchachos para dar coba (p. 42).

MEXICO: *¿Cómo* estarían *de* asustados sus habitantes? (Núñez Guzmán, p. 101). —Pero ¿qué es eso, Borita? *¡Cómo* vienes *de* revolcada! (Quevedo, *Las ensabanadas*, p. 107).

CUBA: Ustedes bien saben *cómo* andaba *de* enamorao de Conchita (Luis Felipe Rodríguez, p. 204).

In some regions, as in Colombia, *como* is used adverbially in the sense of *un poco, algo, más bien* 'somewhat, fairly, rather.' Thus:

—Estoy *como* cansada. —¿Qué tal es esa película? —Es *como* buena, es *como* cansona; Fulano es *como* tan simpático (Flórez, pp. 382, 384).

CONTIMÁS

Standard *cuanto más* = *con mayor razón* '(all) the more, so much the more, especially,' acquired the more emphatic form *cuanto y más*, possibly by a fusion of *cuanto más* with *y más* (Cuervo, *Dicc.*, II, 658*b*). Current in the classics (see examples in Cuervo), *cuanto y más* apparently simplified in familiar speech to *cuantimás*, a form used frequently by Santa Teresa and others. At any rate *cuantimás* derives more likely from *cuanto y más* (A. Espinosa, *Language*, IV [1928], 111–12; and *BDH*, I, 102, n. 2) than from *cuanto más* (Keniston, p. 660). Be that as it may, today both *cuanto y más* and *cuantimás* are familiar and popular locutions in Spain and, with a slightly higher social status, in Spanish America. The popular and rustic *contimás* is found only once in Aurelio Espinosa's peninsular *Cuentos* (II, 192 [Zamora]: "el diablo *contimás* iba creciendo la chica más se enamoraba de ella"). It is probably used elsewhere, as in Navarre (*BDH*, V, 88 n.). However, it appears to be much commoner in Spanish America, and is sometimes pronounced *cotimás* (Picón-Febres, p. 84). There is some truth in Santamaría's remark about *contimás* (*Dicc.*, I, 390): "forma popular tan generalizada, que casi nadie usa de la forma castiza [cuanto más] ni la conoce." But the statement is too sweeping (unless it applies strictly to rustic usage), for in Mexico itself *cuantimás* is the form most current among the populace both in the capital and in towns of the interior.

The reduction of *ua* in *cuantimás* to *o* in *contimás* may be due to the analogical influence of such parallel forms as stressed Old Spanish *uo, ue, ua* (< Latin stressed *ŏ*) and *o* (< Latin unstressed *ŏ*): stressed *nuove, nueve, nuave* and unstressed *novecientos*, stressed *cuento* and unstressed *contamos*, etc. On the other hand, as has been suggested, *contimás* may well be a syntactical cross between *contra más* and *cuantimás.*

In negative sentences *cuanto y menos, cuantimenos* and *contimenos* are sometimes found as the counterpart of *cuanto y más: cuanto y menos = con menor razón; cuanto y más = con mayor razón.*

Argentina: *Cuanti más* se lo regalonea, *cuanti más* mañero y más idioso se hace (Lynch, *Romance*, p. 16). —*Cuanti más* me mire ... más seguro que me compra (Güiraldes, *Don Segundo*, p. 113).

Chile: Es difícil de hacer, *contimás* durante la guerra (C). Somos gente trabajaora ... y *contimás* que ya los [= nos] tiene anotaos (Romanángel, p. 36).

Peru: Usté no tiene necesidá diandá con esos revuelos, *cuantimás* que don Pompeyo no se va' quedar con esa pirigalla (Diez-Canseco, *Estampas*, p. 167). —Yo no me dejo robar ni de mi abuela, *cuantimás* de usted (Corrales, p. 247).

Venezuela: Pero un hombre no tiene precio, *contimás* como don Manuel Ladera (Gallegos, *Canaima*, p. 88); Pero no crea usted que le sirvió de poco, *contimenos* de nada (p. 284). Es de los hombres más necesarios aquí, *contimás* ahora que doña Bárbara se va a abrir en pelea (Gallegos, *Doña Bárbara*, p. 73). *Contimás* ahora que hemos derrotado a esa gente (Briceño, p. 160).

Guatemala: Eugenia dice que no topó al Doctor Zárate, *contimás* al sastre Dávila; No le tengo miedo a Tobías, *cuantimenos* a usted (Sandoval, I, 216).

Mexico: Sobre que apenas los envía a traer medio de cigarros, *contimás* manteca, ni chiles, ni pulque, ni carbón ni nada como acá (Lizardi, *Periquillo*, I, 24, 149). El miedo lo tienen hasta los animales, *cuantimás* la gente (Urquizo, p. 229).

Puerto Rico: Pero como la hoja del árbol no se mueve sin la voluntad de Dios, *contimás* catorce astas con setenta arrobas de carne (Morales Cabrera, *ap.* Malaret, *Voc.*, p. 134).

Santo Domingo: Horita se crecen todos esos caños que yo he dejado atrás, *contimás* que 'tá lloviendo duro en las cabezadas (Bosch, *Dos pesos*, p. 14).

DE GANA, DE GUSTO

The standard locution *de* (*buena*) *gana* means 'willingly, voluntarily, with pleasure,' that is, 'with a good will.' In Ecuador, at least, this sense has developed into *por capricho, inútilmente* (Vázquez, p. 192) or *sin razón ni motivo, porque sí* (Tobar, p. 183) 'wilfully, just for fun, as a prank, out of stubbornness, etc., that is, 'with a bad will'; it is often interchangeable with *por gusto*.

—¿Por qué has caído en la ratonera?—me preguntó uno de ellos. —*De gana*—respondo, temeroso (García Muñoz, *Estampas*, p. 94); —Oigan "guambritos," ¿por qué están aquí? —*De gana*—me respondió uno de ellos, con un mohín de infinita hipocresía (p. 95); —¿Qué haces, pues, hijita? —Nada. —¿Y por qué estás triste? —*De gana* (p. 121). —*De pura gana* no entró en el Colegio (Mata, *Sanagüín*, p. 176). —*De gana* te ponís a moquiar (Icaza, *Media vida*, p. 137); Don Manuel Clavijo mató. *De gana*, porque el monte onde juimos a sacar la madera nues d'él (p. 146).

In the River Plate region we find *de gusto* used with the foregoing meanings of *de gana*, that is, *sin motivo, por gusto, por capricho, de vicio*, etc.

Argentina: —¡No, no ... zonzo! ¡Si te digo *de gusto!* Ya sabés que soy la que menos te reprocha tus trasnochadas (Laferrère, *Locos de verano*, p. 13); —¡Lucía! Te llama Elena. —¡Lo está haciendo *de gusto* (p. 49).

Uruguay: —La gente no es tan mala para hacer un daño así, *de gusto* (Florencio Sánchez, p. 359).

DE INMEDIATO

The phrase *de inmediato* is commonly used in many regions, as occasionally in Spain, for *inmediatamente*. It is probably by analogy with *de improviso* and other similar locutions.

Argentina: Esa noche no pudo conciliar el sueño *de inmediato* (Boj, p. 73); *de inmediato* cambió de parecer (p. 76); *de inmediato* se recupera (p. 114); iré *de inmediato* (p. 173).

Paraguay: Luciano quedó *de inmediato* prendado de una de ella (Casaccia, p. 96).

Uruguay: Se presentó *de inmediato* a su jefe (Pérez Petit, p. 179).

Chile: Si algo más deseas, todo lo tendrás *de inmediato* (Fernando Alegría, *Leyenda*, p. 42). Saldrás *de inmediato*, luego, luego (Azócar,

p. 229). Se habría hundido de inmediato (Luis Meléndez, p. 10).

BOLIVIA: La recibieron con placer, pues podían entregarse *de inmediato* al reposo (Arguedas, *Raza*, p. 16).

ECUADOR: *De inmediato* un calorcillo galopaba en las arterias del mayordomo (Mata, *Sanagüín*, p. 180).

VENEZUELA: *De inmediato* hizo dibujar por un experto un hermoso árbol genealógico (Díaz-Solís, p. 61).

COSTA RICA: Hay que contestar *de inmediato* (F. Dobles, p. 241).

In Panama *juntamente* reportedly means *inmediatamente*, as in: "*Juntamente* iré a tu casa" (L. Aguilera, p. 300).

DE JURO

The locution *de juro* is now registered in the Academy dictionary with the meaning *ciertamente, por fuerza, sin remedio*. It is found in the older language and is still used today in rural Spain and in some rural regions of America, where it replaces such common adverbial locutions as *naturalmente, por supuesto, sin duda*, etc. The Peruvian Arona (p. 180) described it as "palabra ordinaria y grosera usada por los negros y nadie más." We find also the rustic forms *dejuramente* and *de jurito*. The forms *de juro* and *dejuramente* are probably confused with *seguro* and *seguramente*. The form *a juro* is reported for Colombia (Tobón, Flórez) and Venezuela (Malaret, *Dicc.*).

ARGENTINA: ¿Y eso? —No sé. ... Zoilo *de juro* o el chico (Lynch, *Romance*, p. 13); ¿Y *dejuramente* que habrá fiesta en lo de don Santos? (p. 31) —*Dejuramente*. ... Yo no podía saber (p. 41).

URUGUAY: —*Dejuro* no has comido. ¿Querés? (Reyles, *El gaucho*, p. 196); —¿Y estará? —*Dejuramente* (p. 138).

CHILE: —¡Si no calla la boca, amigazo, le rompo la cabeza a culatazos! *¡De jurito!* (Barros Grez, I, 11).

PERU: Naides pasaba de miedu al Colluash, que *dejuro* andaba viendo comu alimentarse di algún cristiano (Ciro Alegría, *La serpiente*, p. 22); —Lindo ai [= ha de] ser. —Como no, *dejuro* (p. 42).

COLOMBIA: Hacer una cosa *de juro;* ir *a juro* (Flórez, p. 381).

The flavor of Latinity in the phrase *de juro* suggests religion and ritual in the popular mind, which results in local variations like *de juro amén* (Guatemala), *de juro a Dios* (Cuba), etc.

GUATEMALA: Para ir sin dificultad a El Salvador *de juro amén* debes obtener pasaporte (Sandoval, I, 324).

Cuba: *De juro a Dios* que era Mongo Paneque. Se lo decía el corazón, pero ya la pagaría el maldito (Luis Felipe Rodríguez, p. 210).

DEMASIADO

The standard meaning of *demasiado* is *en demasía, excesivamente* 'too, too much, excessively,' etc. However, since the Spaniard is often inclined to express an excessive degree with a merely high degree, he prefers *muy* or *mucho* to *demasiado* for the expression of 'too,' and sometimes dispenses even with *muy:* consequently, *llegué demasiado tarde* > *llegué muy tarde* and even *llegué tarde* 'I arrived too late,' *es demasiado* > *es mucho* 'it's too much,' etc. In most of Spanish America, on the contrary, *demasiado* has, through excessive use, frequently become weakened to the sense of *muy, mucho,* or *bastante* 'very, much,' etc.: *él es demasiado amable* = standard *él es muy amable* 'he is very kind.' (Cf. *vous êtes trop aimable* 'you are too kind' = 'you are very kind,' and Pidgin-English *too* for *very:* 'I like you too much,' etc.). This meaning seems to have been known in the older language, though more generally the adverbial construction was then *demasiado de* ("hizo *demasiado de* bien" [*Don Quijote,* I, 25]) or *demasiadamente* ("debe de estar *demasiadamente* cansado" [*ibid.,* I, 7]).

Argentina: El jefe es *demasiado* bueno. Nuestro médico es *demasiado* sabio (Forgione, p. 158). El amor mandaba inscribir un mote *demasiado* indeleble (Larreta, *La gloria,* p. 345). —Ya arreglaré mis asuntos en forma, por si muero, para que a usted no le falte nada. —No piense en cosas *demasiado* remotas (Rodríguez Acasuso, *La mujer olvidada,* III, 11).

Chile: Es *demasiado* discreto, ya sabemos (Luis Meléndez, p. 146).

Bolivia: Fulano es *demasiado* sabio; la quiero *demasiado;* soy *demasiado* honrado, etc. (Bayo, *Vocabulario,* p. 85).

Ecuador: —Agradezco a Ud. *demasiado;* —*Demasiado* lo siento; —Está Vd. *demasiado* bien (Tobar, p. 184).

Venezuela: Con *demasiado* gusto escribo para U. esto (Alvarado, p. 163). Rancho = casa de paja muy pequeña y *demasiado* humilde (Picón-Febres, p. 292).

Nicaragua: Siento *demasiado* (Castellón, p. 56).

Guatemala: Dios es *demasiado* bueno; Pedro es *demasiado* honrado; Julia es *demasiado* virtuosa (Batres, p. 248).

Mexico: Decía que las maestras ... deben ser *demasiado* vigilantes y prevenidas. ... Su conversación siempre me era *demasiado* agradable (Pensador, *Quijotita*, chap. iii, *ap.* Icazbalceta, p. 164). Era verdad que se habían conocido mucho en la escuela ... pero nunca habían intimado *demasiado* para hablarse a lo macho, como ahora hablarían (Taracena, p. 170). La costilla no se rompió, cosa que yo hubiese lamentado *demasiado* (L). La quiero *demasiado;* es *demasiado* honrado (Santamaría, *Dicc.*, I, 559; cf. also Rubio, *Anarquía*, I, 170).

Santo Domingo: Era *demasiado* sincera y amarga su queja (Requena, *Los enemigos*, p. 61); Por primera vez se sintió *demasiado* solo (p. 92); lo encontró *demasiado* triste (p. 110); el resultado, un poco cruel, pero *demasiado* cierto (p. 111), etc. Hace ya *demasiados* años que las mujeres dominicanas no se adornan con ellas (Patín Maceo, "Amer.," V, 436).

Sometimes the adverb *demasiado* is in popular speech attracted into the gender of the adjective modified, as was apparently the case in the older language (Keniston, p. 533). However, this agreement (like "*media* muerta, de *pura* tonta") is considered incorrect today. A Costa Rican preceptist, in an effort to rectify this mistaken agreement, failed to note the impropiety of *demasiado* in the sense of *muy:* "es incorrecto decir *Demasiada culta es mi maestra.* ... Debemos decir *Demasiado culta es mi maestra*" (Cascante de Rojas, p. 237).

Sometimes *por demás* and *demás* are inadvisedly used today in their older sense of *mucho, muy:* "El viaje es *por demás* interesante" (L); "actitud *por demás* desairada" (Heredia, p. 233).

DE NO

The phrase *de no* (sometimes written *denó*, and *dinó* in the mouths of mestizos and Indians) 'if not, otherwise,' though not registered in the Academy dictionary, is not unknown in Spain. Standard equivalents are *de lo contrario, si no, donde no,* etc. Causal *de* (expressing at first origin) has quite naturally evolved into a conditional meaning: '*from* doing A, the result is B' > '*because* of doing A, the result is B' > '*if* one does A, the result is B.' Found in the older language, *de no* is comparatively rare today: "Se admitirá la postura; y *de no*, allá va mi niño" (Estébanez Calderón, p. 16); "Que *de no*, y le mataban" (Benavente, *Señora ama*, II, 3).

It is extremely frequent, on the other hand, in the popular and rustic speech of many regions in Spanish America. Because of its excessive use in rural Argentina, it has been erroneously considered by some to be an Argentinism. To be sure, the phrase preceded by *y* and written as an interrogation (*¿y de no?* rarely *¿y si no?*) has developed another sense in Argentina: that of an affirmation equivalent to *sí* or *claro* or *por supuesto* 'of course.' The semasiological development was probably 'and if not?' (that is, 'what would happen otherwise?') becoming 'of course, certainly,' etc. For illustrative examples of this usage see page 414.

In Chile, *de no* is less frequent than the expanded form (*en, de*) *la de no,* in which the indefinite feminine *la* stands for 'circumstance, situation, case,' etc.

ARGENTINA: Ya se lo imaginarán, y *de no,* poco importa (Payró, p. 6). —Y dejáme que te diga cómo has de hacer, porque *denó* va siendo tarde (Güiraldes, *Don Segundo,* p. 129).

URUGUAY: —Tome antes un trago 'e caña; *de no,* se va' pasmar (Reyles, *El gaucho,* p. 102); asegurenló, *de no* voy a tener que chusearlo (p. 140); ¿Me querés, mi chino? —¿Y *de no,* diba a estar aquí? (p. 218).

CHILE: —Ud. debe estudiar a fondo las cosas y *de nó* que lo digan los compañeros, ¿tengo razón o no? (Juan Modesto Castro, p. 62); tiene que ser mandaruna, *en la de no* cualesquiera le atropella el 'contra' (p. 278); lo encontraba emponchado o *la de no* con chaleco (p. 359), etc. —Monte en mi mula y vaya corriendo a la botica, o *la de no* su amigo pasa a pérdida en poquito tiempo (Ernesto Montenegro, p. 147). Hay que pegar como negro ... *en la de no,* se quea uno a ventestate [= ab intestato] (Guzmán Maturana, p. 103). Hagan el favor d'irse al tiro, *de la de no,* ya verán (Ramírez, *Del mar y la sierra, ap.* Braue, p. 108).

BOLIVIA: Mejor será que no largue los animales, *de no,* a la madrugada me va a costar pillarlos en el potrero (Flores, in *ACB,* p. 64); Ahorita mismo; *de no,* dejamos el cuero en el camino (p. 68).

PERU: —Aura, vamos a ver si surte el otro negocito. ... Si *de no,* ¡a la porra! (Barrantes, p. 32). —No quedó *dinó* la balsita el Rogelio (Ciro Alegría, *La serpiente,* p. 19); anque no le paguen *dinó* un ochenta po cada cristiano (p. 20). Juraría que te ha sembrao. *De no,* ¿cómo t'ibas a rebajá tanto, niña? (López Albújar, *Matalaché,* p. 150). Dime si aceptas el cargo; *de no,* buscaré a otro (Benvenutto, p. 148).

ECUADOR (COASTAL ZONE): Y fué bueno, porque *de no,* no hubieran esos retratos de los periódicos (Gil Gilbert, *Yunga,* p. 110). (HIGHLAND ZONE): —Hay qui aprovechar de la mañanita siquiera. *De no* ca, tarde ya nu adiaber [= no ha de haber] agua (Icaza, *En las calles*, p. 7). Si la pesco la enamoro, *de no* me voy al cine (Salvador, *Camarada*, p. 101).

Colombia (Antioquia): Sí, que le calcen; que *de no* el querido se presentaría como un zarrapastroso (Rendón, p. 37); él amaba a Inocencia, y Ángel la amaba también. ¿Cómo dudarlo? Y *de no*, ¿a qué ese ir a la casa de Jacinta? (p. 88). En seguida pienso ir a Iquitos a preguntar si a las señoras ya se les contuvieron las aspiraciones y, *de nó*, para ver si se les puede hacer algún remediecito (Arango Villegas, p. 59). (South): —Pero harís las cosas como te las hey ordenado; *de no*, si las hacís mal, no salen bien tus planes, ¿oíste? (Álvarez, p. 106).

Venezuela (Llanos, Andes): Iré mañana, *de no* te llamaré por teléfono (Rosenblat).

Guatemala: Viene una tormenta, lo moja y se abajera, o *de no* se pudre en la arpillada (Acevedo, in *CLC*, p. 249).

DE PIE

This phrase, meaning *constantemente*, seems to be restricted to Central America and Mexico. The thought development may have been 'on foot' > 'on a sound, permanent footing' > 'constantly, daily,' etc. Salazar García (p. 100) gives the equivalents *diariamente* and *constantemente* for Central America, particularly El Salvador; Ayón (p. 147) gives *de continuo* for Nicaragua; Sandoval (I, 330) gives *frecuentemente, constantemente, periódicamente*, and *sin interrupción* for Guatemala; Membreño (p. 64) gives *constantemente, sin interrupción*, and *de permanencia* for Honduras.

Nicaragua: *De pie* está enojado; *de pie* se ausenta (Ayón, p. 147).

Honduras: El niño está *de pie* en la escuela (Membreño [1895 ed.], p. 37).

El Salvador: *De pie* voy; *de pie* viene (Salazar García, p. 100).

Guatemala: *De pie* voy a las sesiones de la Sociedad de Obreros; *De pie* se queda Gilberto castigado en el colegio (Sandoval, I, 330).

Mexico: Las personas que en los mesones, posadas o casas de huéspedes vivan *de pie* [= 'as permanent guests'], y no como pasajeros [= 'transients'], se sujetarán a lo prevenido en la fracción III del artículo que precede (Art. 335 del *Código penal del distrito federal*, etc., *ap.* Membreño, p. 37).

DE REPENTE, EN UN DESCUIDO

The standard meaning of *de repente* is *prontamente, sin preparación, sin discurrir o pensar*, that is, 'suddenly,' etc. In many regions of

Spanish America the phrase is often used with the meaning of *de vez en cuando, algunas veces* (or more rarely *por casualidad,* and *a lo mejor* 'probably, when least expected'), often with a concomitant feeling of original 'suddenly.' The transfer of meaning may have been approximately this: 'it happened suddenly' > 'it used to happen suddenly' > 'it used to happen,' etc., but the idea of suddenness is always looming. Probably because of this semasiological development of *de repente* the notion of 'suddenly' is often expressed by (*de*) *un repente,* where the definite article *un* returns the thought to one definite occurrence, that is, 'suddenly.' Rustic forms of *de repente* are *redepente* (by metathesis), (*en*) *un redepente,* etc. In some regions the meaning of *luego* (also *de pronto*) develops like that of *de repente: luego > a veces, algunas veces, de cuando en cuando.*

Argentina: ... hasta que *un redepente* ['suddenly'] don Santos ... se levantó (Lynch, *Romance,* p. 96); Puede ser que *redepente*/véamos el campo disierto (*Martín Fierro,* p. 118).

Uruguay: —Pero *de un repente* ... clavaron la uña (Reyles, *El gaucho,* p. 15); —*De un repente,* no sé qué me dió (p. 200).

Chile: No me atrevo ya a mirar a la ventana, porque *de repente* [= 'at times,' also 'suddenly'] me quedo sin poder quitar la vista de la cordillera (Barrios, *El niño,* p. 94). El hombre se enfermó *de un repente* ['suddenly'] (Ernesto Montenegro, p. 51).

Bolivia: —No es de descuidarse, porque *de repente* [= a lo mejor] lo zurdean a uno (Céspedes, p. 82).

Peru: *Derrepente* [= a lo mejor] es aprista y tú ni lo sospechas (Benvenutto, p. 151). Ya vendrá, porque *luego* pasa por aquí (C).

Ecuador: *De repente* [= alguna vez] salgo a la calle. *De repente* tomo una copa (Mateus, p. 101). *De repente* [= de vez en cuando] no es malo divertirse (Tobar, p. 189). *De repente,* no siempre (C).

Colombia: *De pronto* blanquiaba los ojos (Posada, p. 106).

Costa Rica: —¿Me acompañas, Pelegrino? —No, *de repente* [= a lo mejor] se queda/enganchao con una mis (Agüero, p. 59).

Nicaragua: *De repente* [= algunas veces] eran cosas gratas, de sorpresa: conciertos, músicas ambulantes (Robleto, p. 92).

Guatemala: *De repente* [= a lo mejor, por casualidad] lo sabe el gobierno, y por él nos josemaría [= molesta] a todos (Acevedo, in *CLC,* p. 254). La tarde cayó, *di un repente* ['suddenly'], como dijo ella (Barnoya, p. 54). Yo soy así. ... *En un derrepente* [= cuando menos se piensa] me duele la cabeza, como cuando estaba recién curado de la bebida. Así me pongo en veces y me siento como chucho con rabia (Samayoa, p. 104).

MEXICO: Luego empecé a ponerme mala de la vista. ... No podía mover los ojos. *De repente* [= a lo mejor, also 'suddenly'] se me paraban y entonces no podía caminar (Galeana, p. 189).

PUERTO RICO: Lo conozco porque pasa *luego* por aquí (Malaret, *Dicc.*)

SANTO DOMINGO: Él pasa *luego* por esta calle (Patín Maceo, "Amer.," VII, 58).

Related to *de repente* is the locution *en un descuido* used in Mexico, the Caribbean, River Plate, and Andean zones, in the sense of *cuando menos se piensa,* or *es de temerse* if the reference is to something disagreeable. The thought process seems to be that in a moment of carelessness or negligence (*descuido*), unexpected and often disagreeable things may happen; whence 'in a moment of carelessness' may become 'when least expected' or 'it is to be feared' and then 'probably.'

MEXICO: —Déjeme, no se apure, ya verá cómo salgo bueno para estas cosas y hasta *en un descuido* me dan mi águila—añadió Carlos bromeando (Fernando Robles, p. 78). Dieciséis años había dicho Patricia que tenía; *en un descuido* eran menos (García Roel, p. 32); —Este Blas ha de 'star creyendo qu'es la gran cosa ... oye, pos si *en un descuido* hasta 'stá esperando que mandes a los meros gallones del pueblo a pedir a Chonita (p. 330). Lhinda Palma no me importa a mí y *en un descuido* hasta me voy (Azuela, *La Marchanta,* p. 97).

DE SEGUIDO, SEGUIDO

In many regions of Spanish America (to a limited extent in Spain) *de seguido* is commonly used instead of standard *en seguida* 'immediately,' and also for standard *de seguida* 'continuously.' However, in the sense of *seguidamente* or better *frecuentemente* 'frequently' one finds *seguido* the preferred form in familiar speech. This usage was not unknown in the older language: "Muchos no hablaban *seguido,* y muy pocos se mordían la lengua" (Gracián, *El criticón,* I, vii).

ARGENTINA: Don Fabio dejó de venir *seguido* (Güiraldes, *Don Segundo,* p. 19). —Negrita ... ¿por qué no venís más *seguido?* (Petit de Murat, p. 212).

URUGUAY: —¿Salen *seguido,* así? (Montiel, *Cuentos,* p. 90). Nos veíamos muy *seguido* (Sánchez, *La gringa,* III, 4).

CHILE: El jutre había agarrao e venir aquí *seguiíto* (Acevedo Hernández, *Por el atajo*, p. 56). —Es que yo podría venir más *seguido* (Guerrero, p. 40).

COLOMBIA: Cuando ... lo miran muy *seguido*, dice ... : —Hasta después, mis amigos (Buitrago, p. 67).

EL SALVADOR: Lo recordamos *seguido* (L).

GUATEMALA: *Seguido* viene Victoriano a pedirme dinero prestado (Sandoval, II, 412). Yo voy a ver muy *seguido* al patrón (*CLC*, p. 34).

MEXICO: —Me molesta que ese hombre venga tan *seguido* a la casa (Azuela, *Avanzada*, p. 211). Mis primos y yo nos lo encontramos *seguido* (Núñez Guzmán, p. 36). —Y ¿has visto a tu novia *seguido?* (Robles Castillo, p. 154). Pregunté si había bailes muy *seguido* (García Roel, p. 44); yo escribo bien *seguido* (p. 119).

CUBA: Antes venías más *seguido* por aquí (Padrón).

DESPACIO, DESPACIOSAMENTE

The standard meaning of the adverb *despacio* (< *de* + *espacio*) is *lentamente* 'slowly.' Its original spatial concept (measuring space) became temporal (measuring time), and still later it became an adverb of manner (measuring sound) with the meaning of *bajo, quedo, en voz baja* 'low, soft, in a low voice.' While this meaning is not registered in the Academy dictionary, it is possible in the older language in passages like: "aunque sea un lindo compuesto/que hable melifluo y *despacio*/y aunque galantee en palacio/que es peor que todo esto" (Calderón, *Casa con dos puertas*, II); "El buen filósofo Diógenes vió en la plaza hablar muy *despacio* a un discípulo suyo con un mancebo" (Guevara, *Epístolas*, *ap*. Américo Castro, p. 146). This meaning is found in parts of Spain (Corominas, p. 95; Llorente, p. 170) and in Spanish-American regions: the River Plate, Chile, Bolivia, Peru (Arona, p. 183), Ecuador, Colombia (Sundheim, p. 233), Venezuela, and Nicaragua. The semasiological change of 'slow' to 'low' is the same change that evolved from the adverb *paso* 'slowly' to *paso* 'in a low voice.' Covarrubias gives *hablar passo* as meaning *hablar quedo*, and we read in *Lazarillo* (III): "Con mejor salsa lo comes tú, respondí yo *paso*." The form *apasito* is still used in the sense of *en voz baja* in Cuba (Suárez; Dihigo, *Léxico*), *pasito* in Colombia, etc.

ARGENTINA: Le dije *despacito* porque noté que había gent' en la sala y no quería hacer ruido (*Fray Mocho*, p. 133). —¡Chist! *Despacito* ... no lo vayan a sentir (Lynch, *Romance*, p. 345). Me dijo *despacito*, como para que nadie lo pudiese oír ... (Payró, p. 30). —Váyase nomás ahura ... ¿*despacito*, no? que no la vayan a sentir (Lynch, *Palo verde*, p. 161).

URUGUAY: Éste al salir la mira y le dijo *despacio*. ... La chinita ... le articuló quedo ... (Montiel, *Cuentos*, p. 28). Al levantarse el telón, aparece don Zoilo encerando un lazo y silbando *despacito* (Sánchez, *Barranca abajo*, III).

CHILE: —Conversen más *despacio*. Va a pasar la guardia (Juan Modesto Castro, p. 312). De pronto oyó que alguien tocaba *despacito* en su puerta (Durand, *Mercedes*, p. 103). —No siai indiscreto y habla más *despacio*, mira que se puee dar cuenta el marío (*Tallas chilenas*, p. 92).

BOLIVIA: Hable *despacio*; tosa *despacio* (Bayo, *Manual*, p. 108).

ECUADOR: No grites, habla *despacio*, pues pueden oírnos. Habla tan *despacio* que no se le oye (Vázquez, p. 142). —No haga bulla. Hable *despacio*. Oyen de aquí al lado (Pareja, *El muelle*, p. 107).

COLOMBIA: Le decí' unos secretos *pasito* (T. González, p. 19).

VENEZUELA (LLANOS): Canta *despacio* pa oírte yo solo (Rosenblat).

Despite the fact that *despacio* has acquired the meaning of 'in a low voice,' it is also used, though less frequently, in its standard sense of 'slowly.'

ARGENTINA: —Ahura [= más tarde] se lo contaré más *despacio* (Lynch, *Romance*, p. 106).

CHILE: Se fué caminando *despacito* (Durand, *Mercedes*, p. 66).

However, since this double meaning may lead to obscurity, the form *despaciosamente* is commonly used in the sense of 'slowly,' particularly in regions where *despacio* is widely used for 'in a low voice.'

RIVER PLATE: —¿No sabe, amigo?—dijo *despaciosamente* el Petiso (Eandi, in *ACR*, p. 183).

CHILE: Ha amarrado *despaciosamente* su caballejo a un pilar del corredor (Latorre, *Hombres*, p. 31); Un arreo de mulas avanza *despaciosamente* por el sendero enlodado (p. 207). Se restregaba las manos *despaciosamente* (Durand, *Mercedes*, p. 61); Doña Lucrecia se sacó los anteojos, para meterlos *despaciosamente* dentro de la caja, que al cerrarse sonó tan fuerte que asustó al gato (p. 133).

PERU: El viejo hablaba *despaciosamente* (Ciro Alegría, *La serpiente*, p. 66). Don Cipriano, presidiendo la mesa, comía *despaciosamente* (Ciro Alegría, *Los perros*, p. 157).

DE VIAJE

The expressions *de viaje, de un viaje,* and *de al viaje* mean *de una vez, enteramente, de golpe, inmediatamente,* and are commonly used, one or more of them, in most Spanish-American countries, as they are sometimes in Spain (cf. Borao). One of the standard meanings of *viaje* as given in the Academy dictionary is: "Fam. Acometimiento; golpe asestado con arma blanca corta"; and this meaning is easily expanded to apply to any kind of blow (Román, V, 672).

ARGENTINA: Se mandó el vaso de vino *de un viaje,* sin respirar (Saubidet, p. 134).

COLOMBIA: Me sirvieron un vaso de herradura casi lleno, y me lo tomé *de un viaje* (Arango Villegas, p. 174).

VENEZUELA (LLANOS): Me lo tragué *de un solo viaje* (Rosenblat).

COSTA RICA: Quiso parase, y las piernas/se le aflojaron *debiaje*/y se jué tras (Agüero, p. 35). Llegaron todos *de viaje;* lo mataron *de viaje* (Gagini, p. 125). Al sargento Tomás Miranda le rajó la cabeza *de un viajazo* (Dobles Segreda, p. 31).

NICARAGUA: *De viaje* le arrancaron el dedo (Ayón, p. 279).

HONDURAS: Le dieron un balaso [*sic*] a fulano de tal, y *de viaje* (o *de al viaje*) murió (Membreño, in 1895 ed.; omitted in 1912 ed.).

GUATEMALA: El niño se comió *de al viaje* los dulces y la fruta que le obsequiaste (Sandoval, I, 311).

EL SALVADOR: Dígalo *de viaje* (o *de un viaje*) (Salazar García).

SANTO DOMINGO: Hablaste mal de mí, y vino *de viaje* [= inmediatamente] a decírmelo un individuo (Patín Maceo, *Dom.*, p. 177).

CUBA: Se tomó el vaso de vino *de un viaje* (Padrón).

DE YAPA (ÑAPA)

In its literal meaning the locution *de yapa* (often written *de llapa,* though generally pronounced *de yapa*) and its variant *de ñapa* mean 'as a present, to boot,' etc., applying to any additional bit of merchandise given a customer gratis or 'thrown in for good measure' by a vendor or dealer. The form *yapa* (or *llapa*) prevails in the River Plate region, Chile, Bolivia (Bayo, p. 260), Peru (Arona, p. 507), and Ecuador (Mateus, p. 493); *ñapa* prevails in Colombia (Cuervo, § 977), Venezuela, and in part of the Antilles (Malaret). While Ramos Duarte (p. 371) registers *ñapa* for Vera Cruz, the phrase usually heard in Mexico is *de pilón;* and while Gagini (p. 140) registers *ñapa* (also *yapa* and *llapa* in Salesiano) for Costa Rica, the expression *de feria* (stemming from the custom of presenting gifts at fairs) is apparently commoner there: a person buying meat will ask for "una *feria* de hígado, mondongo, etc." The groceryman gives a bit of candy *de feria* to boys buying groceries. Elsewhere other local phrases are used. While *de ñapa* is current in eastern Cuba, elsewhere *de contra* is used (Pichardo, Macías, Suárez). Besides *ñapa*, Panamanians use *pezuña* 'hoof,' perhaps because butchers were wont to 'throw in' that part of the animal (Garay, p. 104).

Yapa derives from the Quechua. Gillet ingeniously conjectures that *yapa*, originating in the Peruvian Andes, "turned into *ñapa* possibly under the influence of Guaraní, made its way across the southern continent and, reaching the coast east of Panamá, crossed the Caribbean, touched Puerto Rico and the eastern end of Cuba and made a happy landing at New Orleans [as *lagniappe*]."[5] While *ñapa* may be due to Guaraní influence, it must be remembered that the change of *ll* (= *y*) to *ñ*, which means merely the nasalization of *y*, occurs in other words: *llamar* › *ñamar*, etc. (cf. *BDH*, I, 203, n. 1).

The standard equivalents of *yapa* are *adehala*, *refacción*, and the colloquial *pal gato;* figuratively, *además* or *por añadidura*.

ARGENTINA: Tú sabes del dolor de los niños descalzos y andrajosos que piden al hombre *yapa* de caramelos y a la vida *yapa* de felicidad (Yrurzun, p. 13). La crió, la educó, y *de yapa* le dió un excelente esposo (Garzón, p. 511). El hombre ... venía bastante mamao y *de yapa* traiba en la mano una botella (Lynch, *Romance*, p. 278). —Sí, lo vide; está muy enfermo, y tan viejo. —Y *de yapa*, pobre (Martínez Payva, p. 25). Me daba rabia y no volvía en muchos días ... *De llapa* cuando volvía ... no quería ser mi mujer (Mansilla, *Una excursión*, p. 181).

CHILE: Podía comprarse una sandía enorme con otra más chica *de yapa* o *ñapa* (lo último decía en sus bandos don Mariano Egaña) (Vicuña Mackenna, *ap.* Rodríguez, *Dicc.*, p. 482). Fresca la aloja, ¡ay, qué rica,/buena y barata!/si no me la compran toda,/la que sobre doy *de yapa* (Laval, I, 126). Sí, pues, a la Amalia le compran, porque ella da *de llapa* otras cosas (Guerrero, p. 38); —¿Una *llapita* pal gato? —¡Con mucho gusto, caserita [= parroquiana]! ¿Y usted me dará otra *llapita?* —¡Tan bromista, don Pedro, que lo han de ver! (p. 173). Lo examinan tanto que casi rogase uno que hubiese

[5] J. E. Gillet, "Lexicographical notes," *American Speech*, XIV (1939), 93–96.

menos médicos. Y *de llapa* tiene Ud. a los internos (Juan Modesto Castro, p. 137).

PERU: Al darse a la fuga, Choloque, *de llapa*, les aventaba una cornada por los costillares o las ancas (Ciro Alegría, *El mundo*, p. 41).

ECUADOR: Por eso es que cuando las cocineras me piden *yapa* en el azúcar, les ponga un poquito más (García Muñoz, *Estampas*, p. 261); ¡Dará, pes, una *yapita!* (p. 262); Cinco sucres le doy. Y como *yapa*, puede usted escoger alguna de esas corbatas (p. 314).

MEXICO: Al terminar el baile, los músicos nos tocaron una pieza más *de pilón*. Le fuí a cobrar a Pedro; no me pagó, y *de pilón* me insultó (Rubio, *Anarquía*, II, 341).

CUBA: Fulano se arruinó en el negocio, y *de contra* perdió la salud; Me convidaron a comer, y *de contra*, a pasear en automóvil (Suárez, p. 149).

PUERTO RICO: Le va a metel tres patás/y *de ñapa* otras tres más (Cestero, *ap.* Malaret, *Vocabulario*, p. 229).

ENDENANTES

In the older language we find the temporal adverbs *denante(s)*, *en(d)enante(s)*, and *enante(s)* with the meaning of primitive *antes* 'before.' The Spanish Academy dictionary registers *denante* as antiquated, *denantes* as having the meaning of *antes*, *endenantes* as antiquated but still used in popular speech in several parts of Spain,[6] *enante(s)* as antiquated but still used in rural areas. All of these adverbs of time may be found today in nearly all Spanish-American countries but with these differences: (1) they are not always exclusively popular or rustic but are frequently used by the cultured, (2) they do not always mean simply *antes* but very often have the more precise meaning of *hace poco tiempo* 'a short time ago.' This may be true likewise in parts of Spain, since the *Diccionario de autoridades* (1726–39) points out such a difference between *antes* and *denantes* (cf. *BDH*, I, 243, n. 2). In Chile cultured folk use *denante* or

[6] We have found the following examples: ANDALUSIA:—¿De qué peligros me hablaba usté *endenantes?* (Muñoz Seca, *El roble de la Jarosa* [4th ed., 1925], p. 38); *Enantes*, cuando pa él no había más que la Jarosa (p. 44); la copla que tú *endenante* no sabías poné de pie (p. 81). SANTANDER, MONTAÑA: ¿No ajustemos *endenantes* la cuenta más de treinta veces? (Pereda, *Obras completas*, V, 147). EXTREMADURA: ¿Por qué refunfuñabas *andenantes?* (Luis Chamizo, *El miajón de los castúos* [2d ed.; Madrid, 1921], p. 78); *Endenantes* jué la joya de los buitres (p. 153). For Salamanca, see Lamano, p. 415, and Sánchez Sevilla, § 95. Because none of the above forms is found in his *Cuentos populares españoles*, Espinosa concluded they were not so common as previously supposed (*Language*, III [1927], 190). Cf. also *BDH*, II, 173–74; Vicente Zamora, p. 45.

denantes with the meaning of 'a short time ago,' while the populace and rustics use *endenantes* and *enenantes* (Román, II, 89).

The form *endenantes* (< *en* + *de* + *en* + *antes*) represents a successive piling-up of prefixes apparently to maintain affective value; the *en* is often an integral part of temporal expressions (*en ese día*, *en ese momento*, popular *endespués*, etc.).

CHILE: —¿Qué me decía, *denantes?* (D'Halmar, *Lucero*, p. 188). Y yo, *denantes*, vi pasar un cortejo fúnebre (Sepúlveda, *Camarada*, p. 166). —No cambie las palabras, *denantes* dijo que era dije, bonita (Durand, *Mercedes*, p. 57); En eso pensaba *denantes*—dijo Andrés hablando lentamente (p. 198). —¡Jesús, María!—gritó la misma mujercita que había dado la voz de alarma *denantes*, y se puso a correr como una loca (Magdalena Petit, p. 27).

BOLIVIA: ¡Está desconocida, niño! Antes no era así. *Endenantes* m'a dicho que lo quiere al Chungara (Arguedas, *Vida criolla*, p. 252).

PERU: Y ¿cómo, entonces, dijo usted *enantes* que conocía todo el Perú si no ha visitado nunca el interior? (Barrantes, p. 121). —*Enenantes* le dije eso (Corrales, p. 172); lo que dije *enantes* (p. 196).

ECUADOR: —¿Usted mismo no dijo *enenantes?* (Pareja, *La Beldaca*, p. 36). Compadecía a María ... que *enantes* no más visitara (Ortiz, p. 234).

COLOMBIA: Hicieron del *enantes* "gurrerito" [= terreno estéril] un paraíso en miniatura (Arango Villegas, p. 120). Cf. Cuervo, § 374.

VENEZUELA: De esta casa no saldrá nunca una palabra en contra del juramento que *endenantes* le hicimos Eufrasia y yo (Gallegos, *Pobre negro*, p. 40); —Lo sorprendieron enterrando una barreta de jabón, una vela de sebo y una poca de sal, que *endenantico* no más había comprao en la pulpería (p. 204).

PANAMA: —*Enantes* [= antes] me dijo Ud. que sí, y *enantito* [= hace muy poco tiempo] me acaba de decir él que no (Mangado, p. 93). *Enenantes, enenantitos* (Garay, p. 109).

GUATEMALA: Desde *endenantes* estoy aquí esperándote (Sandoval, I, 470).

MEXICO: Vino *endenantes* [= vino hace poco] (Icazbalceta, p. 191). Y digo lo mesmo que dije *endenantes* (Rivas Larrauri, p. 34), etc.

CUBA: —Amos a la plaza. ... *Endenantes* llegaron para el torneo (Castellanos, p. 139).

For Argentina, Garzón (p. 186) asserts that *endenantes* (Segovia gives also *denantes*), used "entre la gente del bajo pueblo, en las provincias del interior," means only "recientemente, poco tiempo antes"; and for Catamarca, Lafone (p. 107) defines *endenantes* as "poco ha, acaba de suceder." That this is not always the case is shown by the following examples, in which *endenantes* means merely 'before' (*antes*) and not 'a short time ago.'

Quiere decir que ansina como *endenantes*, cuando era chiquito, no quiso aprender las letras porque el maistro que daba escuela era un gringo fiero (Lynch, *Romance*, p. 79). Siento un olor raro, un olor que aquí no se ha sentido nunca *endenantes* (Lynch, *Palo verde*, p. 145). Empezó a crecer y, cuando llegó al altor que Dios le había dao *endenantes*, le echó los brazos al pescuezo a Dolores (Güiraldes, *Don Segundo*, p. 135).

Elsewhere, too, *denantes* may have the simple meaning of *antes:* "Había empezao *denantes* que los americanos a regalarles casas" (Gatell, *Flor del cafeto* [1936], p. 97, *ap.* Malaret, *Vocabulario*).

HOY MAÑANA, ETC.

By analogy with the ubiquitous *ayer tarde* (= standard *ayer por la tarde*) and the occasional *ayer noche* (= *anoche*) and *ayer mañana* (= *ayer por la mañana*), such locutions as *hoy mañana* (= standard *hoy por* [or *en*] *la mañana*), *hoy noche* (= standard *hoy por* [or *en*] *la noche*), *hoy tarde* (= standard *hoy por* [or *en*] *la tarde*), etc., are occasionally heard in popular or rustic speech:

BOLIVIA: —¿Y ha parido la «Choroja»? —*Ayer mañana* (Arguedas, *Raza*, p. 131).

ECUADOR: *Aura* [= ahora = hoy] *tarde* usted les ha de vender bien vendidos (García Muñoz, *Estampas*, p. 318).

EL SALVADOR: *Ayer mañana*, mientras leía en el corredor ... he visto llegar al señor Tin (Ambrogi, p. 73).

GUATEMALA: Así ocurrió *el jueves noche; hoy mañana* ocurrió el accidente; *hoy noche* se correrá la película (Bonilla Ruano, III, 229).

'LO MÁS' + ADVERB OR ADJECTIVE

In the colloquial and rustic speech of many regions is found an interesting adverbial, or less frequently adjectival, locution that is rare in standard speech. It is '*lo más* + an adverb *or* an adjective' equivalent to '*muy* + an adverb *or* an adjective': *lo más bien* = *muy bien*, etc. A few examples of such usage are encountered in sixteenth-century Spain, but they are comparatively rare (Keniston, p. 241). The more usual expression involving *lo más* was *lo más que* + some form of the verb *poder;* and our present *estoy lo más bien* (= *estoy muy bien*) is very likely an ellipsis of some form like *estoy lo más bien que puedo estar,* or *lo más bien que es posible,* etc. This construction still survives in rural Spain: "Había en él [paquete] una toalla *lo más preciosa que podía haber*" (Aurelio Espinosa, *Cuentos,* II, 306 [Cuenca]); "Si te los pones en los ojos puedes ver todo *lo más divino del mundo*" (III, 360 [Toledo]). But the elliptical *lo más bien* is apparently not widespread in Spain. García-Lomas (p. 21) registers it as characteristic of the Montaña region: "estamos *lo más bien*" for "estamos muy bien"; and Baráibar (p. 167) records it for Álava: "allí estuvimos *lo más bien*" for "allí estuvimos muy bien."

Argentina: ¿No te lo expliqué *lo más bien* el otro día? (Lynch, *Palo verde,* p. 106). Saludó el hombre *lo más fino* (Lynch, *Romance,* p. 251); Todito anduvo *lo más lindo* pa doña Julia (p. 315); las visitas se despidieron *lo más cariñosos* (p. 389), etc. Aprovecho *lo más tranquilo* aquí mis quince días de vacaciones (Olivari, in ACR, p. 366).

Uruguay: —Este pantaloncito le queda muy ancho. ... —¡No, mentira! ... Me queda *lo más bien* (Sánchez, *Los muertos,* I, 3).

Chile: —Estoy *lo más bien* aquí (Guerrero, p. 35). Ha estado *lo más enfermo* (Durand, *Mercedes,* p. 179).

Colombia: Me recibió *lo más formal* (Arango Villegas, p. 180). Está *lo más entablao* de botines (Carrasquilla, *Hace tiempos,* II, 16).

Puerto Rico: La muchacha contestaba *lo más apurá* (Meléndez Muñoz, p. 138).

Santo Domingo: Allí estaremos *lo más bien* (Patín Maceo, "Amer.," VII, 199).

MÁS NADA, MÁS NUNCA

Occasionally we find the order of standard *nada más, nunca más,* and *nadie más* reversed to *más nada, más nunca,* and *más nadie.* This occurs in many regions of Spanish America, with an apparent preponderance in the Antilles zone. Toro y Gisbert (*L'évolution,* § 183) erroneously implies that it is a Gallicism. The practice is common in León, Galicia, and Aragón (Alvar, § 75) and is characteristic of Portuguese. Cuervo (§ 432) thought the inversion might be due to such double forms as *no pide más* and *no pide nada, que no entren más* and *que no entre nadie.* However, it goes back to the older language (Correas, p. 607). Possibly a pause originally followed *más.*

ARGENTINA: —¿No se le ofrece *más nada*, mama? (Lynch, *Romance*, p. 34); No quiso saber *más nada* (p. 471). Usually rural.

URUGUAY: —No te vamos a poder mandar *más nada* (Montiel, *La raza*, p. 108). —¡Que no te vea *más nunca!* (Espínola, p. 51).

PARAGUAY: No se oyó *más nada* (Casaccia, p. 77).

COLOMBIA: No vi *más nada* (or *a nadie*) (Obando, p. 115).

VENEZUELA: —*¿Más nada?*—preguntó ella ansiosamente. —*Más nada*—repuso (Pocaterra, p. 218); —¡No volveremos a misa *más nunca!* (p. 283). No volvían *más nunquita* (Urbaneja, p. 225).

PANAMA: —No me dijo *más nada* (Mangado, p. 103). ¡Pero no regresó *más nunca!* (Nacho Valdés, *Cuentos*, p. 89).

COSTA RICA: —Sin acordarse de *más nada* (Lyra, p. 115).

CUBA: El doctor no contestó *más nada* (Ciro Espinosa, p. 52). No vuelve a salir *más nunca* (Luis Felipe Rodríguez, p. 198).

PUERTO RICO: —Samuel no se acostumbrará *más nunca* a ese trabajo (Méndez Ballester, p. 5). Cf. also Navarro, p. 134.

SANTO DOMINGO: —¿Qué más se llevó? —*Más nada.* —*Más nunca* vuelvo a salir contigo (*BDH*, V, 238–39).

MEXICO: —¡No güelvas *más nunca!* (Rubín, p. 247).

Corominas (p. 102, n. 3) relates this usage in Argentina to another, likewise current there and partially influenced by French and Italian: *no ... más* (standard 'ya no ...'): *no lo tengo más, no tengo más nada* 'ya no tengo nada.' So *no está más* 'ya no está,' etc.

In some regions *más*, or any other comparative, may precede the relative pronoun: "este libro es el *más* que me gusta" for standard 'este libro es el que *más* me gusta,' etc.:

ARGENTINA (SAN LUIS): Son los *peores* que se portan; Dicen que son los *mejores* que amansan potros (Vidal, p. 397).

PUERTO RICO: El final del artículo es lo *menos* que se entiende (Navarro, p. 133); El más joven es el *mejor* que canta (p. 134). El más viejo no es el *más* que sabe (Meléndez Muñoz, p. 104).

Chilean popular speech uses a related construction in a typically ironical statement, as follows: —"No s'enoje, joen [= joven]; es una groma no má. —Chs. *El más que* s'enoja (Romanángel, p. 72). The statement *el más que s'enoja* ('el que más se enoja') means 'el que más se enoja no soy yo' or 'yo no soy de los que se enojan' or 'yo nunca me enojo,' etc. Again: —"¿Pa qué te aurismay [=te asustas] tanto? —*El más que* se aurisma" (Romanángel, p. 91).

MÁS RATO

The noun *rato* is used as an adverb of time in *más rato,* meaning *más tarde* 'a little later,' current in Chilean speech:

—Con usté voy a tener un palabreo, *más rato.* —¡Cuando quiera! (Moock, *Un crimen,* p. 9). Y ahora me voy, tengo mucho que hacer; *más rato* vengo a bailar (Acevedo Hernández, *Cardo negro,* p. 51). —¿Por qué no le dice que me cante una tona? —*Más rato* (Acevedo Hernández, *De pura cepa,* p. 5). Déjela aquí, compaire; yo se lo voy a dejar *más rato* (Acevedo Hernández, *Por el atajo,* p. 39).

In Yucatan the adverb *masino* (*mas* + *si* + *no*) is used in questions when an affirmative reply is expected: "Todavía me quieres, *masino?* (V. Suárez, p. 62).

MISMO

The adverb *mismo* (the classical form *mesmo* is now rural) is often used with excessive freedom to modify another part of speech with apparently no definite meaning except to reinforce the word modified. Now and then, however, it is an approximate equivalent of *precisamente, siempre, es cierto,* etc., as in: *¿Ella mismo se va mañana?* = *¿siempre se va?* or *¿es cierto que se va?* The use is often paralleled or foreshadowed in Spain: in Andalusia *donde mismo* means *en el mismo lugar* (Toro Gisbert, "Voces," p. 507). Cf. Llorente, p. 171.

CHILE: Donde *mismo* le dejara estaba Keltán (Fernando Alegría, *Leyenda,* p. 31). —La máquina queó onde *mesmo* se averió (Brunet, *Montaña,* p. 11).

ECUADOR: —¿Siempre *mismo* te vas mañana? —¿Ya no te dije que sí? (Pareja, *La Beldaca,* p. 217). —¿Y dónde *mismo* estaba, ah? —Enferma donde una parienta pues (Pareja, *Baldomera,* p. 31); —¿Qué *mismo* dices? (p. 42); —Y nosotros ni sentimos nadita *mismo* (p. 43); —¿Y quién *mismo* es? (p. 96). Often *miso.*

COLOMBIA: ¿Adónde *mismo* lo llevó? (Flórez, p. 382).

VENEZUELA: ¿Vive usted donde *mismo?* (Rosenblat).

Sometimes, as particularly in Argentina, one hears a Gallicized *mismo* (<French *même*) in place of standard *aun* or *hasta;* as in: "*mismo* los españoles hacen eso; no lo haría *mismo* si pudiera."

In rural River Plate areas we often encounter *mesmo* with the equivalence of *eso mismo* or *eso es:* "—¡Paice que el dijunto ha resucitao! —*Mesmo*" (Pérez Petit, p. 80); "—¿Ustedes vienen de allá, por el camino, no? —*Mesmo*" (p. 172).

Compare this use of *mismo* with the adjective *mismo*, which, when placed after the noun, may mean *completo, cabal,* as on the Atlantic coast of Colombia (Revollo, p. 181): "Es hombre *mismo* = es todo un hombre, es hombre cabal; tomó ron *mismo* = puro ron; es un burro *mismo* = un perfecto burro."

For Guatemala, Sandoval (II, 95) records the use of *mismas* with *ser*, as applied to "personas amigas, compañeras, correligionarias." He gives these examples: "Yo soy *mismas* con Sarbelio; el coronel Barrios es *mismas* con el Secretario de Guerra."

MUY MUCHO, NO MUY

While considered incorrect today, the locution *muy mucho* occurs throughout the sixteenth century as an emphatic form of *mucho* (Keniston, p. 591); and Cervantes wrote: "era ... *muy mucho* discreto" (*Don Quijote,* I, 4). Today *muy mucho* is a rustic survival in general use, and occasionally it is found in literary style both in Spain and in America.

ARGENTINA: Ya sabe cómo el finao me quiso, *muy mucho* (Lynch, *Romance,* p. 17); la partida había aflojao ya *muy mucho* (p. 99); ¿Pero has perdido entonces *muy mucho?* (p. 175).

ECUADOR: Extraño era todo. Extraña la casa, extrañas las ideas de don Balón, *muy mucho* lo que ocurríale y etcétera (Pareja, *Don Balón,* p. 163).

Occasionally *no muy* may be found improperly used for *no mucho.* This is an apparently common error in Guatemala, where an additional impropriety is the prepositive use of *muy:* "A Juan *no muy* le gusta [= no le gusta mucho] el trago; Águeda *no muy* quiere a su marido; Ya te dije que *no muy* deseo conciliarme con Rafael" (Sandoval, II, 141).

MUY NOCHE

In the phrase *muy noche* 'very late,' the noun *noche* is used as an adverb, perhaps by analogy with *tarde.* The standard locution is *muy de noche.* The use of *noche* as an adverb is found in the older language: "El padre prior vino tan *noche,* que le pude hablar poco" (Santa Teresa, *Cartas,* No. 294); "a qualquiera parte que el huésped llega *muy noche* halla mal recaudo" (Covarrubias, *Tesoro,* under *güésped*). This usage has survived in rural regions of Spain (examples in Aurelio Espinosa's *Cuentos,* I, 166; II, 189; III, 384) and in many regions of America. Sometimes *oscuro* is used in the sense of 'after dark.'

Ecuador: —Vaya a que repose, señor Segovia. Ya es *muy noche* (Mata, *Sanagüín*, p. 120).

El Salvador: Hasta *bien noche* se jué [= no se fué] quedando dormida (Ambrogi, p. 66).

Guatemala: Me acosté *muy noche* ... me acosté *nochísimo* (Sandoval, II, 131).

Mexico: No pude hacerlo porque llegué *muy noche* (C).

NO MÁS[7]

Golden Age writers frequently used *no más* 'only,' placed after the word modified, and it is still found in modern standard Spanish, but *nada más* is today the form preferred in Spain. Spanish America, on the other hand, has preserved the archaic usage of *no más* and has extended its force to connotations unknown in Spain, though a few classical examples may vaguely imply such extensions.

American-Spanish usages may be classified as follows:

1. *Solamente*, as in Spain—where, however, *nada más* is preferred. This usage is so common that a few examples will suffice. In Mexico *no más* (or *nomás*) is more commonly placed before the word modified.

Argentina: ¡Eso *no más*, compadre! (Lynch, *Romance*, p. 205); pa unas copas *no más* (p. 251).

Chile: ¿Quién es? —Yo *no más* (Latorre, *Hombres*, p. 128).

Bolivia: Fué al arroyo *no más* (Céspedes, p. 55).

Peru: Hace dos días *no más* que se fué (López Albújar, *Nuevos cuentos*, p. 94).

Ecuador: Y dieciséis años *nomás* tiene (Gil Gilbert, *Yunga*, p. 102).

Mexico: ¡Ándale, un tiro *no más!* (Azuela, *Los de abajo*, p. 20); *no más* te pongo esta reata en el gaznate (p. 47). *No más* vamos por ahí (Inclán, I, 21); *no más* voy a traer mi cacaztle (I, 252).

So exceedingly common has the use of *no más* (or *nomás*) for *solamente* become in Mexico, that some employ it ill-advisedly for *solamente* in the locution *no solamente ... sino* (cf. also Pino, § 127):

[7] For fuller treatment cf. C. E. Kany, "American Spanish *no más*," *Hispanic Review*, XIII (1945), 72–79. For Argentina and the language of the gaucho, cf. Tiscornia, *La lengua*, § 144; cf. also *BDH*, IV, 61, n. 3, and p. 387 ; *Filología* (Buenos Aires), I, 23–42.

Y *no nomás* [= no solamente] es eso, sino que no le faltan al médico muestras de agradecimiento ... el médico vive y medra, y se la pasa *no nomás* [= no solamente] pagado, sino mimado por esa gente (Lussa). Ramirito *no* 'staba *no más* enfermo, sino que ... (García Roel, p. 259); antes los señores casaos bailaban con las muchachas y con las demás señoras, *no no más* con sus mujeres (p. 306). *No* había *no más* que carpas (Pino [Chile], p. 71).

2. *No más* is added as a sort of reinforcing suffix to adjectives and adverbs and to other parts of speech used adverbially: "ahí *no más*" = standard *ahí mismo* or *ahí precisamente* or *ahí cerca,* with the additional temporal meaning of *en ese mismo instante* 'right then and there'; "ahora *no más*" = standard *ahora mismo* or *en seguida* or *hace muy poco tiempo;* "mañana *no más*" = standard *no antes de mañana, mañana mismo;* "así *no más*" = standard *así es, precisamente;* "bien *no más,* lindo *no más*" = 'just fine,' etc.; "así *no más*" in reply to a query about one's health is equivalent to standard *así, así* or *regular* 'so, so; middling'; "¡ahí *no más!*" often means 'stop there! hold on!'; "un así *no más*" = *un cualquiera;* etc.

This use of *no más* is comparatively rare in the Antilles.

ARGENTINA: Me preguntaron por mi paseo. —Lindo *no más* (Güiraldes, *Don Segundo,* p. 165). Y ahí *no más* [= 'right then and there'] ya se largó a caminar pa las casas (Lynch, *Romance,* p. 39); al oir esto, áhi *no más* agachó la cabeza la curandera (p. 49); en seguidita *no más* (p. 134). ¡Lindo *nomá!* [= frase de aprobación, aplauso y estímulo] (Saubidet, p. 213).

URUGUAY: —¿Cómo está? —Bien, *no más* (F. Sánchez, p. 138).

CHILE: —Así es *no más* [= precisamente] (Romero, *Perucho González,* p. 24); —Bien *no más* (p. 51). Entonces *no más* [= y no antes; cf. *recién,* p. 324] llegó a mis oídos rumor de pasos (Latorre, *Hombres,* p. 87); ¿Y ahora *no más* [= no antes] te vienes a acordar de tu casa? (p. 235).

BOLIVIA: —Hasta por ahí, *no más* (Céspedes, p. 48); ¿Crees que ahora se puede dejar de ser militar así *no más* [= 'just like that'], como quien se quita las botas? (p. 88).

PERU: Hay que hacerlo tempranito, *no más* (Barrantes, p. 73).

ECUADOR: Atrás de esa lomita *no más* está (Icaza, *En las calles,* p. 199). —A la vueltita *no masito* queda (La Cuadra, *Horno,* p. 20).

COLOMBIA: ¿Cómo sigue el enfermo? Así *no más* (Tascón, p. 36). —¿Cómo te va en la pesca? —Así *no más* (Buitrago, p. 52).

VENEZUELA: Ayer *no más* (Gallegos, *Pobre negro*, p. 52); Trasantier *no más* (p. 315).

COSTA RICA: Vivo ahi *nomasito* (Gagini, p. 50).

GUATEMALA: Podemos ir a pie a mi finca, porque ahi *no más* está (Sandoval, I, 27).

CUBA: Así *no más* (Dihigo, *Léxico*).

3. *No más* is added to verb forms, particularly imperatives, as a sort of emphasizing suffix. It serves to set off the verb and leaves the speaker's thought unfinished, often to be completed from the intonation of the speaker's voice. Its most usual meanings are *sin recelo* 'without fear,' *resueltamente* 'promptly, quickly, without fear,' *libremente* 'freely,' *con confianza* 'trustfully,' *sin tardanza* 'without delay,' or merely *pues: entre no más, siéntese no más, siga no más, diga no más,* are equivalent to our 'come right in,' 'do sit down,' 'go right ahead,' 'just speak up,' etc. Perhaps the closest English equivalent that might well cover the majority of cases is 'just.' This usage of *no más* with command forms of the verb may be heard in all South America, is less frequent in Central America and the Antilles, and rare in Mexico.

ARGENTINA: ¡Diga *no más*, señora! (Lynch, *Romance*, p. 54); cuente *no más* conmigo (p. 70); ¡vaya *no más!* (p. 146); sentáte *no más* (p. 166); siga *no más* (p. 262), etc.

URUGUAY: —Murmuren *no más* (Sánchez, *La gringa*, III, 3); dejen *no más* que me caiga encima (III, 10).

PARAGUAY: Golpee *no más* (Casaccia, p. 20).

CHILE: Siga, *no más* (Latorre, *Hombres*, p. 208). —Fume *no más*, a mí no me hace daño (Juan Modesto Castro, p. 118).

BOLIVIA: Sigan *no más* abriendo el mismo (Céspedes, p. 34).

PERU: —Toque fuerte, *no más* (Barrantes, p. 20); pregunte, *no más* (p. 166).

ECUADOR: Diga, *no más* (García Muñoz, *Estampas*, p. 118); —¿Está arriba? —Sí, suba, *no más* (p. 232).

COLOMBIA (SOUTH): Entrá *nomás*, sentáte en ese asiento (Álvarez Garzón, p. 101); —Vení *nomás*, bebamos un trago (p. 114); Habla *nomás* (p. 135). Rare in Bogotá (Flórez, p. 382).

VENEZUELA: Siga *no más;* tráigalo *no más* (Rosenblat).

PANAMA: —No tenga usted cuidado ... continúe usted *no más* (Nacho Valdés, *Sangre criolla*, p. 18).

EL SALVADOR: —Tráigalo *nomás* (Ambrogi, p. 137); —Pase *nomás* (p. 175).

In Mexico, *no más* is seldom used with imperatives in the foregoing sense. It is common there, however, with certain verbs (like *mirar*, *parecer*, etc.) to connote surprise or admiration: "mire *no más*" = *mire usted qué cosa* 'just imagine! just think of it!' As will be remembered, the enclitic pronoun *le* added to command forms often imparts the same feeling in Mexico as *no más* in the River Plate region, Chile, Bolivia, Peru, and Ecuador: *ándele* = *vaya no más* = standard *vaya usted; pásele* = *pase no más* = standard *pase usted*, etc.

¡Mira *no más* qué chapetes! (Azuela, *Los de abajo*, p. 8); ¿qué te parece *no más*, curro? (p. 66). ¡Mira *nomás* qué vestido! (Rivas Larrauri, p. 124).

4. *No más* is placed between *al* and an infinitive, with the meaning of *apenas, tan pronto como* 'hardly, as soon as': *al no más llegar, lo vi* 'as soon as I arrived, I saw him.' Such usage is common in Central America and not unknown in Mexico; but in Mexico *no más* with this meaning is more general with a finite verb: *no más que llegue, lo haré* 'as soon as I arrive, I'll do it,' which seems to be a rather widespread usage found also in regional Spain.[8]

NICARAGUA: El hueso soldó y al *no más* hacer ejercicio ... ésta se le inflamaba (Toruño, p. 41).

HONDURAS: Al *no más* llegar a la tumba ... se inclinó a llorar sobre ella desesperadamente (Martínez Galindo, p. 18).

EL SALVADOR: Decidió abandonar el hogar al *no más* rayar el día (Ramírez, p. 17).

GUATEMALA: Ya lo presentía yo al *no más* verte de nuevo (Wyld Ospina, *La gringa*, p. 76).

MEXICO: Santa reía al *no más* abrirse la boca de Isidoro (Gamboa, *Santa*, p. 203). Espérate, *nomás* que tenga [dinero], irás por tu hija (Galeana, p. 93); ... con la intención de echarme a correr *nomás* que llegara a la calle (p. 182). ¿Cuándo me va a pagar esa cuentecita? —Pos *no más* que me suelten mi chiva (Madero, I, 7).

NEW MEXICO: *Nomás* se comensó la misa y ... (*BDH*, I, 290).

VENEZUELA: Cuando *no más* se levanta, lo pide (Rosenblat).

[8] We find a *nada más* and *no más* in rural Spain: "*Nada más* que saco la calandria a la puerta empieza a llover" (Aurelio Espinosa, *Cuentos*, II, 222 [Málaga]); "Escríbeme *no más* llegues" (L [Valencia]).

5. The frequent use of *no más* has weakened it and in some cases deprived it of any real connotation. Its function then is merely to soften a phrase. In some countries, like Ecuador and Peru, this function of *no más* may have become popular particularly because it could easily assume the function of the Quechua *lla*, in sentences like: "¿Qué *no más* has traído?" '(Just) what did you bring?'

Ecuador: —Entonces, comadrita, cuente, pues, algo del sermón. ¿Qué *no más* dijo el padre Erazo? (García Muñoz, *Estampas*, p. 245). ¿Qué *no más* has traído? (Vázquez, p. 280).

In Bolivia this feeling of *no más* (or *pues*) is sometimes expressed in popular speech with the particle *jai*. The word corresponds to the harshly guttural Aymara *ja* (or *ka*), originally expressing doubt or uncertainty, but now employed as a postpositive emphasizing particle.

—Es *jay* forastera (Díaz Villamil, *La Rosita*, p. 23); Eso *jay* me tocaba decir a mí (p. 25); Llega una forastera y los jóvenes *jay* como moscas detrás de ella (*Cuando vuelva*, p. 17); —Apaguen ese cirio ... —Si es *jay* para la Virgen, hijo (p. 77).

OTRA VUELTA, VEZ PASADA

The phrases *otra vuelta* (rustic: *güelta*) and *vez pasada* are often heard in familiar and especially in rustic speech for standard *otra vez* and *una vez* (also *no ha mucho tiempo, en cierta ocasión*), respectively. They are both survivals from the older language. For *occasión* meaning *vez*, cf. p. 366.

Argentina: —Dejemé que la abrace *otra güelta* (p. 61). ¿Quieren creer que *vez pasada* la pic' un coral ...? (*Fray Mocho*, p. 131); —*Vez pasada* vivía con su familia en la calle Chile y me llevó (p. 148). ¿Por qué no conchaba un hombre pa que la ayude? ¿No tenía uno *vez pasada?* ¿Qué se le hizo? (p. 248). ¡Vea qui andan cebaos esta *güelta!* ¿Pero si no han dentrao hasta el Vainticinco *vez pasada?* (Sáenz, p. 6).

Paraguay: *Vez pasada* [= hace poco tiempo] le vi a tu abuela (Morínigo).

Peru: Si sobraba gente, *otra güelta* veníamos (Ciro Alegría, *La serpiente*, p. 20).

Venezuela: ¿Viene V. *otra vuelta?* (Alvarado, p. 459). Empiézalo *otra vuelta* (Gallegos, *La trepadora*, p. 199); ¡pero con más ganas de rompé a cantá *otra güelta!* (p. 200).

EL SALVADOR: Miacaban de soplar *otra vuelta* (Salarrué, *Cuentos*, p. 95); se metió *otra güelta* por debajo (p. 126).

GUATEMALA: ¡Bravo! ¡Que se repita *otra vuelta!* Allá viene *otra vuelta* la sirvienta de Mercedes por la contestación de la carta que te entregó ayer (Sandoval, II, 177 and 605).

MEXICO: Dímelo *otra güelta* (Ramos Duarte, p. 285).

CUBA: Fuí *otra vuelta* a casa de Juan (Padrón).

POR LAS DUDAS

The popular expression *por las dudas* (also *por aquello de las dudas*) is common in some regions of Spanish America as an equivalent of standard *por si acaso* 'to make sure, to be on the safe side, just in case,' etc. On the other hand, the standard *por si acaso* may become *por si alcaso* (as sometimes in Mexico and Central America), and shortened to *por si aca* (and even *porsia*) in the familiar and jocular speech of many regions.

ARGENTINA: De repente entramos a pisar algo sonoro y resbaloso. Largué los estribos *por las dudas* (Pico, p. 36). —Y, será por otra cosa. —Yo, *por las dudas* voy a revisar todos esos papeles (Llanderas and Malfatti, *Cuando las papas*, p. 42).

URUGUAY: Bueno, *por las dudas*, ya el jefe le había adelantado algo sobre la conveniencia de ser previsor (Montiel, *Cuentos*, p. 71). Traigo la escopeta *por las dudas* (Sánchez, *La gringa*, I, 15).

CHILE: —Era *por siaca* (Romanángel, p. 103).

PERU (COASTAL ZONE): Añadió la oleografía del Señor milagrero y la chaveta, *por si aca* (Diez-Canseco, *Estampas*, p. 24); —Yo vo'a salir, prienda. ... *Por si aca*, ahí te dejo el machete (p. 157). Dígale que *porsiaca* ocurriera la desgracia ... no tenga cuidado (Corrales, p. 181).

ECUADOR: —Es por un *porsiaca* (Pareja, *La Beldaca*, p. 24). Pero ... por un *por si aca* ... (La Cuadra, *Los Sangurimas*, p. 58).

VENEZUELA (LLANOS, ANDES): *Por las dudas;* (LLANOS): also *por si las moscas* (as in Spain) (Rosenblat). Noun *porsiacaso* 'alforja.'

GUATEMALA: Usté sabe lo qui hace. Pero *por aquello de las dudas*, li aconsejo que se merque una daga de cruz (Barnoya, p. 43).

MEXICO: —Quién sabe si de aquí a la madrugada cambie de opinión el general, y no te fusile. —¡Hum! *por las dudas*, no se te olvide

(Ferretis, Quijote, p. 64). Lo más probable era que no se tratase de ningún agente policíaco. Pero *por las dudas*, Nelly resolvió despistarlo (Ferretis, *San Automóvil*, p. 32). Yo me había llevado, *por aquello de las dudas*, unos cuantos huevos podridos, porque sabía que se iban a necesitar (p. 154).

CUBA: Me parece que ya no va a llover, pero me pondré la capa de agua *porsia* (Padrón).

POR POCOS, SI MÁS

A variant of standard *por poco* (= *casi* 'almost') is *por pocos*, as in: *por pocos me caigo* for *por poco me caigo* 'I nearly fell.' Cuervo (§ 439) records it for Bogotá, but I have heard it also in the speech of educated *antioqueños*. I find it in popular use elsewhere, particularly in Central America. Quesada (p. 56) records it for Costa Rica. Sandoval (II, 268) records *por pocos* ("por pocos te caes") as well as the form *por poco y* ("por poco y me caigo"). Cuervo thinks the *s* of *por pocos* stems from the older form *por pocas* used from early times apparently through the sixteenth century,[9] though not recorded by Keniston. One thinks, too, of the very commonly used analogical adverbial *s: en ciernes* for older *en cierne;* the sporadic use of *corrientes* for *corriente, adredes* for *adrede, cercas* for *cerca, de corridas* for *de corrida, a poquitos* for *poco a poco, a seguidas* for *de seguida*, etc. The form *por poca* is registered for Argentina (Segovia, p. 609).

Furthermore, in addition to the older *por pocas*, another synonymous form was *a pocas*[10] (not recorded in Keniston). Therefore, if we relate modern *por poco* to the older *por pocas*, we may do the same with Mexican *a poco* (cf. p. 286) and the older *a pocas*.

Another equivalent of standard *por poco* 'almost' is the expression *si más* (written also *simás*) or *si masito* (written also *simasito*) current in Mexico, Central America, Colombia, and probably elsewhere.

COLOMBIA: *Simasito* me rajan en el examen (C). Anoche ... me cogió un rematador y me quitó el cóngolo [= red de boca circular].

[9] It is found in Lucena's *Libro de vida beata* (1463) and in the *Pícara Justina* (1605). We find *en pocas* recorded for dialectal Spain: the Salamancan region (Sánchez Sevilla, § 95).

[10] "*A pocas* me hubiera muerto" (Sánchez de Badajoz, *Recopilación en metro* [about 1554] ["Libros de antaño," Vol. XII (Madrid, 1886)], p. 179). —*A pocas* me farían reyr tus donaires. ... *A pocas* se me cayera nuestra questión dentre manos, etc. (Juan de Lucena, *Libro de vida beata* [1463] ["Opúsculos literarios de los siglos XIV a XVI," Vol. XXIX, ed. Paz y Melia] [Madrid: La sociedad de bibliófilos españoles, 1892], pp. 164, 167).

Si masito me ahoga el gámbito ese (Buitrago, p. 110); *Simasito* nos soba [= desuella] una raya ['skate-fish'] (p. 124).

CENTRAL AMERICA (especially EL SALVADOR): *Si más* or *si masito* me caigo (Salazar García, p. 254).

GUATEMALA: *Si más* me saco la lotería. *Simás* me caigo, por bajar muy ligero la escalera. *Simasito* me caso con Ambrosio (Sandoval, I, 439–40). *Si más* me voy de espaldas (Arévalo, p. 69).

MEXICO: *Si más* me agarra el tren (C).

The idea of *por poco* 'nearly' is expressed by *escape* or *escaparse* and also by *antes* (or *anantes*) *no:*

COLOMBIA: *Escape* (*escapito*) lo mata (Obando, p. 63). *Escapitas* que me ahogo al pasar una laguna (cf. Tobón, p. 82).

NICARAGUA: ¿No vió a la pobre doña Ritana, cómo *se escapó de* ir para atrás?" (Chamorro, *Entre dos filas*, p. 63). El muchacho cayó y recibió un gran golpe; *antes no* se desnucó (A. Valle, p. 14).

Other popular equivalents of *por poco* are the locutions *por áinas* (Colombia) and *en áinas* (Colombia and Costa Rica), etc. The adverb *aína* or *aínas* was used in the older language with this meaning (in addition to that of *presto* or *fácilmente*). Covarrubias explains that *aínas que cayera* meant *poco faltó que no cayese. Aínas* has survived in some rural regions of Spain, as in Salamanca: "Cayó la escopeta ... se disparó y *ainas* me mata" (Maldonado, *La montaraza, ap.* Lamano, p. 201). In popular speech *aínas* becomes dissyllabic and is written *ainas* or *áinas* (cf. Garrote, García Soriano, etc.).

COLOMBIA (BOGOTÁ): *Por ainas* me caigo (Cuervo, § 136). (VALLE DEL CAUCA): *En ainas* me caigo (Tascón, p. 20). (ANTIOQUIA): *Por ainas* te traigo un peine (Antonio Restrepo, p. 353).

COSTA RICA: *En áinas* se mata (Gagini, p. 130). *Enainiticas* me pega,/y me yamó fariseo,/mentiroso y poca pena (Echeverría, p. 187). —¡Carachas! ¡Que me he visto en alitas de cucaracha! ¡*Enainas* me almuerza! (Lyra, p. 125). Si dilata un poquillo más, *enainas* se lleva un sopapo (F. Dobles, p. 82); ¡*Enainas* se me muere! (p. 91).

MEXICO (YUCATAN): *Áinas* me deja el tren (V. Suárez, p. 62).

Fabián Dobles (p. 395) gives "en la de menos" as the equivalent of *enainas*, but it also means *a lo mejor, fácilmente, pronto,* etc.

COSTA RICA: —Pero no sé ónde escondelas [alforjas] ¡*En la de menos* nos quen [= caen] los guardas y quién sabe ónde vamos a parar vos y yo! (p. 44); Juan Ramón es muy suscetible a la cólera, y, con ese genio, *en la de menos* le mete al viejo y el viejo puede sacar cuchillo (p. 61); —Quién sabe. *En la de menos* le vuelve a pasar lo del otro día (p. 226); Ese hombre *en la de menos* no era un crestiano. Tal vez no era un güen hombre (p. 326).

QUIZÁ, QUIÉN SABE, QUIÉN QUITA

Standard *quizá(s)* is now an adverb of doubt, meaning 'perhaps.' Probably stemming from *qui sapit* 'who knows,' it evidently lost the force of its component parts early. Covarrubias (1611) explains *quiça* as "vocablo antiguo, vale por ventura, Lat. forte, fortasse, forsan. Dizen traer origen del termino Italiano quisa, quien sabe." Lamano (p. 592) registers *quizaes* for popular Salamancan speech and *quizayes* for Galician. We encounter *quizabes* in Concha Espina's *La esfinge maragata* (1920 ed.): "*Quizabes* no sea cierto" (p. 267); "—Y *quizabes* esta noche dormamos en la trilla toda la mocedad" (p. 306).

In certain parts of Spanish America we find today a confusion of the full form *quién sabe* 'who knows' and the adverbial *quizá(s)* 'perhaps'; that is, *quién sabe* may mean 'perhaps' (as does standard *quién sabe si*), and *quizá* may mean *¿quién sabe?*

Argentina: *Quizá* qué oyó y cómo lo interpretó Terreros ... (Rossi, Folleto No. 19, p. 39).

Chile: *Quizás* hasta qué hora siguió el 20 llamando a Adolfo (Juan Modesto Castro, p. 35); —*Quizás* si el hombre ha ido a la mina abandoná (p. 310); ¡*quizás* por qué será que me equivoco! (p. 394). *Quizá* si vaya mañana a verte (Román, IV, 562).

Peru (Coastal Zone): Y así comenzó su nueva vida, anclado otra vez, *quizá* si para siempre (Diez-Canseco, *Estampas*, p. 48).

Venezuela (Perijá): *Quizás* qué le pasó (Armellada, p. 196).

On the other hand, *quien sabe* (generally without accent and often as one word) is frequently found for *quizá*:

Bolivia: —Yo le hubiera sabido vengar *quiensabe* (Díaz V., *Plebe*, p. 88); —*Quiensabe* ya ha muerto (p. 198).

Peru: —*Quien sabe* iban a decir algo (Ciro Alegría, *La serpiente*, p. 96); —*Quien sabe* lo contó en el sueño (p. 143); *quiensabe* único los viejos sepan de yo (p. 220); —¿Cuándo va pa los lavaderos? —*Quien sabe* esta misma tarde (p. 200). *Quien sabe* los gobernantes comiencen a comprender que a la nación no le conviene la injusticia (Ciro Alegría, *El mundo*, p. 501). Su pareja, que parece aturdida, *quiensabe* por súbitos escrúpulos (Barrantes, p. 191).

CUBA: —¿Dónde está mi sombrero? —*Quien sabe* Juan lo haya cogida (Padrón).

Furthermore, the full form *¡quién sabe!* is used as an adverbial locution of doubt in many regions, but it is especially notable among the Indian and rustic population of Mexico (rustic, *quén sabe*), Venezuela, Peru, Ecuador, and Bolivia. In this use, rather than the sense of *quizá* 'perhaps,' it has the connotation of *lo ignoro* or *no sé* 'I don't know,' and is used most frequently as an answer to a question implying future time: "—¿Lloverá? —*¡Quién sabe!*" It is said that, when an Indian is disinclined to answer any question put to him, he will invariably reply: "Pues *¿quién sabe* (rustic *pos quén sabe*), señor?" Sánchez Somoano (p. 67) has explained this attitude of the Mexican Indian:

> Si se le pregunta a un indio
> por el año en que nació,
> o quiénes fueron sus padres,
> o que si se bautizó,
> se rasca tras de la oreja,
> mira con cierto candor,
> y levantando los hombros
> dice *¡quién sabe,* señor!

This peculiarity is common to the Bolivian and Ecuadorian Indians and has invaded the speech of other social groups.

BOLIVIA: —Pero ¿estarás allá mucho, mucho tiempo? —*¡Quién sabe!* (Céspedes, p. 68).

PERU: —¿Así es que no creen en Dios? —*Quién sabe,* señor (Ciro Alegría, *La serpiente*, p. 75); —Bueno, don Oshva, ¿no trabaja las minas? —*¡Quién sabe!* (p. 195).

ECUADOR: —¿Lloverá hoy? *¡Quién sabe!* (Mateus, p. 367).

MEXICO: —¿Y qu'es eso? —Pos ... *quén sabe* (Rivas Larrauri, p. 20). —¡Una mujer se llevó a tu hija! —¿Quién sería? —¡Pues *quién sabe!* (Galeana, p. 105).

Another form found in the popular speech of Mexico is *quí sabe.* Ramos Duarte (p. 426) erroneously limits this phrase to Hidalgo.

—¿Pero no se queja? —*¡Quí sabe*/si con esas viejas con que se arrejunta! (González Carrasco, p. 51); Mi razón era/que, al no golver por aquí,/*quí sabe* si no tuviera/algo que sentir de mí (p. 169). *Quisabe* en qué artes está esto (Ramos Duarte, 426).

The meaning of possibility in *¿quién sabe?* (= *puede ser, ¿por qué no? quizá, tal vez,* etc.) is often expressed in popular and rustic speech with *¡quién quita!* 'who can prevent?' in Mexico (Rubio, *Anarquía*, II, 168), Central America (Gagini, p. 211), Puerto Rico, Cuba (Malaret, *Suplemento*), Venezuela (Alvarado, p. 381), and elsewhere: "Y por ser enteligente/y d'injluencia mi muchacho,/*¡quién quita* que llegue a ser/autoridá o diputao!" (Agüero, p. 50 [Costa Rica]); "—Deje d'esbariar. *¡Quién quita*/benga su mujer!" (p. 77).

More often, however, the expression has the added meaning of a wish, an equivalent of *ojalá*, and as such is treated under the expression of wishes (p. 264): "*¡Quién quita* me saque la lotería este mes!" It is sometimes used as a noun meaning 'slight possibility, hope': "Lino lo desasusió [*sic*]/apenas bido la lengua,/y sólo por un *quién quita*/jué que liso [= le hizo] deligensias" (Echeverría, p. 171 [Costa Rica]).

RECIÉN[11]

The adverb *recién* is not an apocopation of *recientemente*, but is an apocopated form derived from Latin *recēns, -tem*, which meant 'newly arrived, fresh, recent.' This apparently participial form is used as an adverb in Spanish, primarily to modify past participles: *recién nacido* 'newborn,' *recién casado* 'newly wed' (cf. French *nouveau-né, nouveau venu*, etc.). Occasionally it is found before an adjective or a noun used participially: *recién libre* = 'recién libertado,' *recién sacerdote* = 'recién ordenado de sacerdote.'

Apparently the original *reciente* was occasionally used in the older language with the meaning of *hace poco tiempo* (Román, V, 40). While such usage has fallen into desuetude in Spain, it has developed greatly in certain regions of Spanish America, where the shorter form *recién* (rustic *ricién*) has acquired additional meanings. These meanings, with some overlapping, correspond in general: (1) To English 'just,' 'a short time ago,' etc.: *llegó* (or *ha llegado*) *recién* or *recién llegó* (*ha llegado*) = standard *acaba de llegar, llegó hace poco tiempo; ¿cuando llegó?—recién* = standard *¿cuándo llegó?—hace poco tiempo* or *poco tiempo antes* or *ahora mismo* or *recientemente*. Sometimes *recién* is used redundantly: *recién acabo de llegar* = standard *acabo de llegar*.

[11] For fuller treatment cf. C. E. Kany, "American Spanish *recién*," *Hispanic Review*, Vol. XIII (1945), 169–73.

(2) To English 'only,' 'only then,' 'not before': *recién hoy, recién ahora* = standard *sólo* (*solamente*) *hoy, sólo ahora; ¿recién?* = standard *¿sólo ahora? ¿tan tarde?; recién mañana llegará* = standard *no llegará hasta mañana, sólo mañana llegará*, etc. (3) To English 'hardly,' 'no sooner . . . . than,' etc.: *lo vi recién* (*que*) *llegó* = standard *lo vi apenas llegó* or *a poco que llegó.*

Meaning No. 2 seems to be the commonest of all. This sense often implies a particular state of mind, a feeling of surprise, particularly when the verb is present or future. For instance, the sentence *recién llego* means not merely the temporal *acabo de llegar* 'I have just arrived' but implies also 'I should have *or* might have arrived sooner'; the sentence *¿recién llega usted?* means not only *¿acaba usted de llegar?* but implies 'you should have arrived sooner' or 'we expected you sooner.' These meanings, however, are not always clearly differentiated one from another. That senses often overlap is evident when the same writer sometimes uses *recién me daba cuenta* and again *recién entonces me daba cuenta;* or *recién se fué* and *reciencito no más se fué.*

Now such constructions have often been considered Argentinisms.[12] This is a misconception. While, to be sure, the usage is most widespread in the River Plate region, it is common in Chile, Bolivia, Peru, and Ecuador. Elsewhere it is rare, but a stray example may be found today among writers as far north as Mexico.

While this usage has been condemned by grammarians, it has nevertheless persisted in certain regions not only among the untutored but also among the cultured classes, not only in familiar speech but also in elevated literary style. So essential has it become, in fact, that one writer on the subject affirmed that Spanish Americans could not speak without it.[13] It therefore seems appropriate that the use of *recién* instead of being anathematized should be accepted in those countries where outstanding writers do not hesitate to employ it in their serious literary output. A few examples follow, as recorded in the writings of various Spanish-American regions.

Argentina, with meaning No. 1: —*Recién* pasó para su cuarto (Laferrère, *Locos de verano*, p. 45). *Recién* había terminado la lectura

[12] "En el Río de la Plata se usa [*recién*] en lugar de *recientemente*. ... Estos usos son *desconocidos* en las otras naciones de lengua española" (Alonso and Henríquez Ureña, *Gramática*, II, § 204); "es uso argentino" (Santamaría and Domínguez, p. 153), etc.

[13] Eduardo Wilde, *Idioma y gramática*, of which extracts are cited in Garzón's *Diccionario*, p. 425.

de un libro que llevaba debajo del brazo (Marengo, p. 69). La escena ... fué interceptada por el pesquisa joven de *recién* (Filloy, p. 39).

With meaning No. 2: —*Recién* cuando vendiese los animalitos les completaría la cantidá (Lynch, *Romance*, p. 274); Y jué *ricién* ['only then'], que al mirarlo a Pantalión, doña Julia se dió cuenta de la cara tan seria que tenía el mozo (p. 395). *Recién* cuando estuve dentro me di cuenta (Güiraldes, *Don Segundo*, p. 18). —*Recién* mañana sabré (Güiraldes, *Xaimaca*, p. 104).

With meaning No. 3: *Recién* salía de casa cuando llegó mi viejo amigo (Forgione, p. 28). *Recién* se descubrió el incendio volaron los bomberos (Bayo, *Vocabulario*, p. 198).

Uruguay, with meaning No. 1: —Cómo no, si *ricién* me dijo el carrero Juca que lo vido (Montiel, *Alma nuestra*, p. 189). —Lo que no hizo la pasión ... lo hará esa grandeza de alma que descubres *recién* (Sánchez, *M'hijo el dotor*, III, 12).

With meaning No. 2: *Recién* con el sol alto concilió el sueño (Acevedo Díaz, *Soledad*, p. 131). —Cuando el vaso esté colmado, *recién* entonces te permitirán ir a buscar un poco de paz (Sánchez, *Nuestros hijos*, III, 4).

Paraguay, with meaning No. 1: —*Recién* estaba abierta [la puerta] (Casaccia, p. 20).

With meaning No. 2: *Recién* por la noche vendría Sarita con la comida (Casaccia, p. 73); como si *recién* después de diez años notase algo (p. 129).

Chile, with meaning No. 1: ... tal si deseara sacarse el freno que el mayordomo *recién* le había puesto (Durand, *Mi amigo*, p. 10). Un hombre que *recién* llega a la ciudad ... tiene un montón de necesidades que satisfacer (Alberto Romero, *La viuda*, p. 131).

With meaning No. 2: A las cinco, a la hora de comida, *recién* llegaba el andariego (Juan Modesto Castro, p. 53). —Pero ella habría jurado que *recién* ahora conocía la riqueza de esos objetos, que *recién* ['only now'] apreciaba el encanto del lujo (Fernando Alegría, *Leyenda*, p. 24).

Bolivia, with meaning No. 1: Fué cuando *recién* principiaba en este negocio (Pereyra, p. 46); donde *recién* había ingresado (p. 334).

With meaning No. 2: *Recién* ['only now'] nos vamos dando cuenta de la magnitud de la guerra (Toro Ramallo, p. 94). Su marcha ... motivó que, *recién* al mediar el segundo día, comprobasen que la senda ... estaba en poder de los pilas (Céspedes, p. 127). *Y recién* ['only then'] se explicó Ramírez esa despreocupación, la dureza y el coraje que había observado en las gentes de esos valles. ¡Claro! (Arguedas, *Vida criolla*, p. 169).

PERU, with meaning No. 1: Yo fuí uno de sus primeros amigos cuando *recién* llegó a Lima (Velarde, in *ACR*, p. 153).

With meaning No. 2: Una tarde se incorpora mirando a todos lados. Detiene sus ojos en nosotros como si *recién* ['only then, for the first time'] nos viera en su vida (Ciro Alegría, *La serpiente*, p. 116).

ECUADOR, with meaning No. 1: Balladares se había curado *recién* una enfermedad (Gil Gilbert, *Nuestro pan*, p. 23); *Reciencito* no más subió la lancha (p. 84). *Recién* la perdieron (Salvador, *Camarada*, p. 60). —Y eso que Ud. *recién* viene (Mata, *Sanagüín*, p. 131). Caray, quejtaj flaco. —Ej que *recién* sargo er hospitar (Aguilera Malta, p. 60).

With meaning No. 2: *Recién* ahora, don Cruz se daba cuenta de cómo era el río (Gil Gilbert, *Nuestro pan*, p. 36). Porque Vicenta tiene *recién* una semana en casa de don Rodolfo (Pareja, *La Beldaca*, p. 69).

COLOMBIA, with meaning No. 3: Lo vi *recién* que llegó; Se fué *recién* murió su hermano (Cuervo, § 400).

VENEZUELA (LLANOS only, not CARACAS), with meaning No. 1: Recién lo comprendió; *recién* lo acabo de ver (Rosenblat).

COSTA RICA, with meaning No. 2: *Recién* entonces (Salesiano).

GUATEMALA, with meaning No. 1: El rostro de la tierra *recién* se libra de espantosas arrugas (Leiva, in CLC, p. 27).

MEXICO, with meaning No. 2: Y *recién* entonces se iniciaron los combates (Robles Castillo, p. 166).

SANTO DOMINGO, with meaning No. 1: El capitán Naranjo había *recién* pasado los cincuenta años (Requena, *Camino*, p. 20).

SIEMPRE

The adverb *siempre*, in addition to its more general use of *en todo tiempo* 'always,' may also mean *en todo caso* 'in any case' or *cuando menos* 'at least': "Quizá no logre mi objeto, pero *siempre* ['in any case, at least, still'] me quedará la satisfacción de haber hecho lo que debía" (Academy dictionary). Current in American Spanish is an apparent extension of the meaning of adversative 'still' (= *sin embargo*) to that of temporal 'still' (= *todavía*) 'at length, definitely, certainly, surely' (= *al fin, de todos modos, resueltamente*, etc.) and other connotations difficult to translate. In Mexico the word *siempre* is often used immediately before *no* or *sí* as a sort of reinforcing particle. The essential meaning of *no* or *sí* would not suffer with the omission of *siempre*. Ramos Duarte (p. 457) gives this example: "¿Va usted, o no? —*Siempre* no voy." He explains that if *siempre* were omitted, the sentence would then be correct. Sánchez Somoano (p. 29) commented in verse: "Allí [in Mexico] es la palabra *siempre*/negación y afirmación; así dicen *siempre*, sí,/como dicen *siempre*, no." We find in Colombia, as elsewhere, *siempre* meaning *sí* (Revollo), *un poco* or *más bien* (Flórez) 'yes, more or less,' etc.

Argentina: Mi próxima separación de Clara va siendo más incierta. ¿Bajaré *siempre* ['really'] en Mollendo? (Güiraldes, *Xaimaca*, p. 53). —Te vas a la madrugada, *¿siempre?* ['definitely']. Él asiente (Mallea, *La ciudad*, p. 99).

Uruguay: —*¿Siempre* se va mañana? Él sonrió y dijo: —¡De juro! (Viana, *Leña seca*, p. 124). —Manda decir don Horacio que el tilburí está pronto. ... Que si *siempre* piensa irse (Sánchez, *La gringa*, IV, 9).

Chile: —Me habían dicho que tú habías resuelto no casarte ya. —Mentira, yo no he dicho nada. ... —¿Entonces *siempre* ['definitely'] te casas? —*Siempre* (Maluenda, *Escenas*, p. 76–77). —¿Tú *siempre* [= todavía] queriéndola?—*Siempre* (p. 168).

Bolivia: Ante todo, ¿estás *siempre* ['definitely'] decidido a casarte? (Arguedas, *Vida criollo*, p. 151); —¿De veras se va usté *siempre* a Europa? (p. 265).

Ecuador: —*Siempre* [= todavía] mismo me queda debiendo ese resto (Icaza, *Cholos*, p. 12). —Yo *siempre* ['definitely'] mismo tengo qu'irme (Icaza, *Huasipungo*, p. 102). Despierto ya, le preparó ella el desayuno. ... —¿Se va, *siempre?* (La Cuadra, *Horno*, p. 191).

Colombia: Aunque la mañana del domingo es lluviosa, *siempre* ['nevertheless'] se ha levantado mamá (Carrasquilla, *Hace tiempos*, I, 185). *Siempre* [= al fin] se escapó el herido del hospital (Sundheim, p. 597). (Mompox): ¿Ganaste algo en el negocio? —*Siempre* [= sí]; ¿Te fué bien en el viaje? —*Siempre* [= sí] (Revollo, p. 247). (Bogotá): —¿Es muy lejos? —*Siempre* [= más bien]; (pop. and rustic): *¿Siempre no* se fué? (Flórez, p. 382). —¿Muy grande? —Pues *siempre* es grandecito (Arango, p. 148).

Panama: —¿Se decidió Ud. a venir *siempre* [= por fin]? —¿Lo hizo Ud. *siempre?* (Mangado, p. 116).

Guatemala: *Siempre* me casaré el sábado (Sandoval, II, 437).

El Salvador: —¿Y aquél tomó? —No, señor. Lo dejó. —Pero llevåselo *siempre* ['nevertheless'] (Ambrogi, p. 25).

Mexico: ¿Conque *siempre* ['finally'] se murió? *¿Siempre* se mató?

(C). —¿Nos vamos, o te esperamos? pues no dilata en reventar la aurora. —*Siempre* ['anyway'] vete yendo, compadre (Inclán, II, 145). —No la querían recibir. ... Se despertó y gritaba mucho. *Siempre* ['anyway, finally'] la dejamos (Quevedo, *La camada*, p. 64); —A pie no podrá. —Que vaya en coche. —*Siempre* ['in any case'] se tendrá que llevarla a él y sacarla en peso (p. 126). Confiados en los rebeldes no nos fuimos a huir *siempre* [merely emphatic] (Núñez Guzmán, p. 100). Los mismos mensajeros de las buenas nuevas, fueron a decirme que *siempre no* (López y Fuentes, *¡Mi general!* p. 135). —¡No le hace, no te cases, dile que vaya al diablo! Tanto me dijeron que así lo hice. Al día siguiente que fué le dije: —*¡Siempre no* me caso con usted! (Galeana, p. 41). (YUCATAN): Le dije que *siempre no* se lo vendía (V. Suárez, p. 62).

Sometimes, as along the Colombian Atlantic coast (Sundheim, p. 466), the negative sense of this *siempre* is expressed by *nunca*, which then means *al fin no, por fin no, de ningún modo*, etc: "Sabrá Ud. que *nunca* se fué mi tía; *nunca* vendo el caballo."

TAMBIÉN NO

One finds *también no* for standard *tampoco* 'not either' in the popular and rustic speech of many regions. It was so used by Cervantes and others in his day (*Don Quijote*, I, 17 and 40).

PERU: El cristiano ya no lo vió y los otros pajaritos *tamién no* lo vieron poque subió pa las nubes (Ciro Alegría, *La serpiente*, p. 142); Mi compañerito se quedó sin pasar el río y como que siento que *no* lo pasaré *tamién* (p. 161). —Yo *también no* tengo inconveniente (Corrales, p. 157).

ECUADOR: Yo *también no* quiero (Vázquez, p. 401). *También* yo *no* quise concurrir; *ni* él *también* quiso venir (Cevallos, p. 79).

MEXICO: *También no* tenían mamá (Galeana, p. 34).

SANTO DOMINGO: *No* faltaba allí *también* la buena longaniza, como *tampoco* ... un par de cesinas (Moscoso, p. 23).

TAN, TANTITO, QUÉ TAN

The apocopated form *tan* (from the adverb *tanto*) is in modern correct usage placed only before an adjective or another adverb (*tan malo, tan mal*), and the full form *tanto* is used before verbs (*tanto es así, tanto comí*). The use of *tan* before verbs is a grammatical impropriety stemming from the older language. While it is committed in Spain, it seems to be much commoner in Spanish America. Both in Spain and, more frequently, in Spanish America *tan* is used also with the equivalence of *tan cierto es que.*

ARGENTINA: El señor Batet se marcha. *Tan* [= tan cierto es que] se marcha que llegaron unos hombres para llevarse sus cosas (Cerretani, in *ACR*, p. 150).

URUGUAY: El mozo no es malo, como le digo y *tan* lo creo así, que veo que le anda arrastrando el ala a Sara (Sánchez, *M'hijo el dotor*, I, 12). *Tan* se embebía en sus peroraciones que ellos lo arrancaban de la silla del café ... (Acevedo Díaz, *Argentina*, p. 51).

COLOMBIA: *Tan* es así; *tan* es verdad. Ya hoy no llueve. —*Tan* [= tan cierto es que] llueve, que ya veo lloviznar. *Tan* no está enfermo Gregorio, que anoche no hizo sino bailar (Cuervo, §§ 402, 403).

VENEZUELA: Yo me olvidaré de todo, *tan* me olvido que he venido a hablar contigo aquí (Pocaterra, p. 175).

NICARAGUA: —Dicen que tiras muy bien con pistola. —No es tanto como aseguran. Y *tan* no tiro bien que si así fuera ... (Toruño, p. 189).

GUATEMALA: No crees lo que te estoy refiriendo, pero *tan* es así que no cabe Jerónimo de duda (Sandoval, II, 478).

MEXICO: —¿Qué, tú crees en los ofrecimientos de este pillo? —*Tan* no los creo, que ahora más que nunca debemos poner en juego las vigilancias (Inclán, II, 12). Lo habían leído. ... Y *tan* lo habían leído, que le habían dado su parecer por escrito (Gómez Palacio, p. 98). *Tan* lo trataba bien que el chico había llegado a quererla como a su propia madre (Rubín, p. 74).

SANTO DOMINGO: *Tan* no vino, que ... ; *tan* no está enfermo, que ... ; *tan* lo sabe, que ... (Patín Maceo, *Dom.*, p. 163).

The adverb *tan* as used in Ecuador, chiefly among the Indian and mestizo populace, is in many cases equivalent to *también* (of which it is a reduction) or is merely an intensive particle:

Ojalá aura *tan* dé trago el patrón Lucho ... tengo que 'star corriendo por aquí *tan*, por ashí *tan*. ... ¿Qué *tan* irá' pasar? (Icaza, *En las calles*, p. 6). —Yo *tan* voy a ver si la semana del lunes cojo mis trapos y me voy con los guaguas. —Si querís, t'e de shevar no más a vos *tan* (p. 76).

The adverb of quantity, *tantito*, is current in Mexico, Central America, and probably elsewhere. The standard form, which, however, is not widely used, is *tantico*. Since the diminutive ending *-ico* is not popular in America (except in special zones, such as Costa Rica, Colombia, etc.), *tantito* has apparently taken the place of *tantico* and of the commoner *un poco* or *un poquito*.

COLOMBIA: Había quedado *tantico* caldo en la olla (*Folklore santandereano*, p. 176). Espere *tantico* (Tobón, p. 170).

EL SALVADOR: El bote coleó, libre, descantillándose *tantito* (Salarrué, *Cuentos*, p. 32).

GUATEMALA: —Apartáte *tantito*, que voy a saltar (Quezada Silva, in *CLC*, p. 187). Por *tantito* me caigo; la enferma amaneció *tantito* aliviada; espéreme usted *tantito;* espéreme *tantitito* (Sandoval).

MEXICO: Mi madre ... lloró *tantito* cuando le hablé de mi regalo (Benítez, p. 164). Ai nomás *tantito* pa' su derecha 'stán dos o tres pollas (García Roel, p. 92). Cuestión de no sulfurarse y de pensar *tantito* (Urquizo, p. 106).

The adverbial locution of quantity *qué tan* (*tanto*) 'how (much)' is current in many regions of Spanish America in preference to the more generally used standard *qué* or *cuán* (*cuánto*) or some other phrase. The usage is a survival from the older language: "¿Y *qué tanto* tiempo ha? ... *qué tanto* ha que tiene el mal" (*Celestina*, IV); "¿Preguntando a un maestre de una nao *qué tan* lejos de la muerte van los que nauegan? antes que les respondiesse dixo: ¿*Qué tan* gruessa es una tabla de esta nao? y señaló como tres dedos. Respondió entonces: Tan cerca vamos de la muerte" (Melchor de Santa Cruz, *Floresta española* [ed. "Biblióf. madril.," Vol. III], p. 157); "¿Queréis ver *qué tan* malos son los letrados?" (Quevedo, *Visita de los chistes*).[14]

Because the locution is now rare in the standard language and therefore unfamiliar, modern editors of older works have occasionally misinterpreted and mispunctuated passages like "¿qué tan privado estás?" by writing ¿qué, tan privado estás?" To be sure, as Keniston (p. 158) points out, such interpretations are possible. Spanish-American editors would not be thus misled since they are quite familiar with the construction.

ARGENTINA: Yo no sé *qué tantos* meses/esta vida me duró (*Martín Fierro*, p. 113). (SAN LUIS): ¿*Qué tanto* gana? (Vidal, p. 396).

URUGUAY: ¡*Qué tanto* amolar por dos mujeres! (Espínola, p. 15).

CHILE: *Qué tanto* será ... (Acevedo Hernández, *Por el atajo*, p. 10). ¿*Qué tanto* será, ije? (Latorre, *Hombres*, p. 117).

[24] For medieval examples cf. D. L. Bolinger, *Hispanic Rev.*, XIV, 167–69.

PERU: No sé *qué tanto* le pagan (Benvenutto, p. 150).

COLOMBIA (ANTIOQUIA): Verá *qué tan* a gusto juegan (Carrasquilla, *Hace tiempos*, I, 22); *¡qué tan* bobos y brutos serán! (I, 168); ¡Allá verés *qué tan* bueno! (III, 43); —A ver *qué tanto* ha aprendido (III, 45); *¡Qué tanto* cuidan a estos sinvergüenzas! (III, 74). (Also Bogotá; and the Atlantic Coast [Sundheim, p. 554].)

GUATEMALA: *¿Qué tan* lujosa ha de ser que valga la pena de ir a verla? (Salomé Gil, *Un viaje*, III, 282).

MEXICO: *¿Qué tan* grande es? *¿Qué tan* grave está el enfermo? (C). ¿Saben ustedes *qué tanto* les cuesta? (Azuela, *Los caciques*, p. 174). *¿Qué tanto* se te debe? (Azuela, *Los de abajo*, p. 213). —*¿Qué tanto* nos falta para llegar? (Anda, *Los bragados*, p. 82). —*Qué tanta* prisa tráin (Menéndez, p. 74).

PUERTO RICO: *¡Qué mucho* llora esta niña! (*ap.* Navarro, p. 134).

VIOLENTAMENTE, CON VIOLENCIA

In some regions the meaning of *violentamente* has weakened from 'violently' to 'rapidly, quickly.' In Chile *al contado violento* used in familiar speech means *en dinero contante, sin dilación en la paga* (Román, V, 688).

ECUADOR: *Violentamente* se organizó un viaje del rebelde a Chile (Jorge Fernández, p. 153).

GUATEMALA: "El Transiberiano," rápido como el rayo, cruzó *violentamente* hacia el Oeste, en la esquina de la catorce calle (Guzmán Riore, p. 29).

MEXICO: Sentó su caballo, se apeó *violentamente* y cuando Astucia trató de contenerlo, salvó de un brinco la bardita del cementerio (Inclán, II, 94); Le lavó la cara, lo peinó y *violentamente* lo vistió de limpio (II, 353). *Con la violencia* que el caso demandaba, me fortifiqué en las alturas de la población (Azuela, *Los de abajo*, p. 101). *Violentamente* regresó a su alcoba y a poco reapareció modestamente vestida, sin abrigo ni sombrero (Azuela, *La Marchanta*, p. 135).

YA MISMO, DESDE YA, YA ... YA

The phrase *ya mismo* 'right now' (cf. *ya mero* in Mexico) is used much more frequently in many regions of Spanish America than in standard Castilian, which prefers *ahora mismo* except in certain regions, as possibly Andalusia.

ARGENTINA (CUYO, ANDES): —Si es así, ... *ya mesmo* te vas a soltar las poquitas vacas y ovejas que merezco tener (Draghi Lucero, p. 24); *Ya mismo* vámonos yendo (p. 272). (TUCUMÁN): Te hago largar *ya mismo* si entregas dos mil pesos (Cuti Pereira, p. 59). Venga. Le pagaré *ya mismo* (Filloy, p. 252).

ECUADOR: ¡Te largas *ya mismo* de mi casa! (Icaza, *Cholos*, p. 21). *Ya mismo* te largas (Pareja, *Baldomera*, p. 30); —*Ya mismo* no más te pego (p. 34). —*Ya mismo* shega. ... ¡*Ya mismito* shega! (Icaza, *En las calles*, p. 17).

COLOMBIA: Arreglamos esto *ya mismo* (Arango Villegas, p. 140). Se va *ya mismo* di' aquí (Flórez, p. 382).

VENEZUELA: *Ya mismo* te vas de aquí; Acaba de llegar y *ya mismito* se ha ido (Rosenblat).

In the River Plate region, the use of *ya* for *ahora* is common in the phrase *desde ya*, probably influenced by Portuguese *desde ja* (evidence of the Brazilian linguistic influence exercised upon its southern neighbor), although it is not unknown in the older language: "Anda, vete, mamaburras,/*dende ya*, que nos aturras" (Fernández, *Églogas*, *ap.* Lamano, p. 381 [Salamanca]). The phrase *desde ya* corresponds to standard *desde ahora*, *desde este momento*, *desde luego*, etc. Grammarians have heretofore considered *desde ya* as incorrect, "locución en extremo viciosa," says Monner Sans (p. 158), but it seems to be gaining ground. In fact, it has penetrated into Chile, especially in journalistic style. In Spain one hears occasionally *desde ya mismo:* "—Pero hay que hacer, *desde ya mismo*, lo indicado en estos casos (Muñoz Seca, *Todo para ti*, p. 15).

ARGENTINA: —*Desde ya* me obligo (Larreta, *La gloria*, p. 261). La acepto *desde ya* (Cuti Pereira, p. 41). —Quiero carta blanca. —*Desde ya* la tiene (Heredia, p. 161); —Sólo con una condición aceptaría su propuesta. —*Desde ya* aceptada, hijo (p. 174).

URUGUAY: Gurí ... veía el pago ... como la realidad de una vida que, *desde ya*, estaba viviendo de nuevo (Viana, *Gurí*, p. 56). El orden ... hacia el cual tiende y se orienta, de suyo, y *desde ya*, nuestra evolución histórica (Zum Felde, p. 143).

CHILE: *Desde ya* le agradecemos lo que Ud. pueda hacer en nuestro favor (L).

Related to this use of *ya* is the popular *es ya*, which means *inmediatamente*, *en seguida* (cf. *pero que ya* in peninsular speech).

COSTA RICA: Si se decide *es ya* (Salesiano, p. 131); Hoy [= ahora] mismo me voy y *es ya* (Magón, p. 103).

COLOMBIA: —El que no trabaje me desocupa. Pero *es ya*, ¿entienden? (Antonio García, p. 49). ¡Si sale *es ya!* (Flórez, p. 382).

This is a convenient place to mention the curious repetition of *ya* at the end of a phrase or verb (*ya está ya*, etc.) frequently encountered in the popular speech of some regions of Spanish America. It is found in peninsular Spanish, too, but is not nearly so widespread. The reduplication was used in the older language and may stem from Latin *jamjam*.

CHILE: —Miren pué: *ya* me cambió nombre *ya* (Romanángel, p. 9); Y *ya* sabís *ya* (p. 14); —*Ya* te pusistes serio *ya* (p. 16); —*Ya* m'estay cargando *ya* (p. 17); —No siapure, si *ya* me voy a sentar *ya* (p. 20); *Ya* ve *ya* (p. 41); —*Ya* voy *ya* (p. 98).

PERU: *Ya* está *ya; ya* vino *ya*, etc. (Arona, p. 506). *Yastá* muy escuro *ya* (Ciro Alegría, *La serpiente*, p. 100).

CENTRAL AMERICA: *¡Ya* está *ya!* (Salazar García, p. 290).

X

PREPOSITIONS

'A' OMITTED

IN OLD Spanish the preposition *a* was not required with an infinitive, as it is today, to express goal or purpose after a verb of motion. The old practice of frequent omission survived into the first years of the sixteenth century, but thereafter *a* is necessary in the standard language. Examples: (the *Cid* [*ca.* 1140]): "le van çercar" (vs. 655), "vayámoslos ferir" (vs. 676), "vo meter la vuestra seña" (vs. 707), etc.; (*Rimado de Palacio* [end of fourteenth century]): "que vengan rreposteros, que quiere yr cenar"; (*Celestina* [1499]): "abatióse el girifalte y vínele endereçar en el alcándara" (I). The last example is interesting because in the 1501 Sevilla edition of the *Celestina* the passage involved reads "vínele *a* endereçar"; that is, the preposition was apparently then felt to be necessary in a literary document. The older practice of omitting *a* after verbs of motion, however, was evidently kept in popular speech, was brought to the New World, and has survived to this day in the popular and rustic speech of many regions, as occasionally also in Spain: "No me la *van* (?) quitar" (Arniches, *La pena negra*, I, 3); "Ven ver tou padre" (Garrote, § 79 [León]; cf. also Menéndez Pidal, *El dialecto leonés*, § 21, 3).

Only such cases as rule out an '*a* embebida' have been recorded, since the preposition *a* immediately preceding an initial *a* or following a final *a* (especially unstressed) is generally elided in everyday speech, and this omission is often unintentionally reflected in literary texts.

ARGENTINA: —Mañana me *voy ir* pa' allá (González Arrili, p. 87).

URUGUAY: —*Vas ver* (Sánchez, *M'hijo el dotor*, III, 2).

BOLIVIA: Piro no *vas dicir* nada a mi sargento (Blym, p. 142).

PERU (especially HIGHLAND ZONE): Te *voy pegar;* Si no me quieres/me *voy matar* (Benvenutto, p. 147).

HONDURAS: Mejor *voy ir* yo a la casa (Mejía Nieto, *Relatos*, p. 157); *Voy ir* a visitar a Mariana (p. 167).

EL SALVADOR: *Vamos ir* con mucho gusto (Ambrogi, p. 176). ¿Te atreverías a *ir* con alguien *colocársela?* (Torres Arjona, p. 134). *Vamos ir* a que nos pinten el dedo (Mechín, *Candidato*, III, 2).

GUATEMALA: *Vamos ir* (Bonilla Ruano, III, 209 n.).

MEXICO: No creas que te *voy defender* (Galeana, p. 111).

There is a popular tendency to omit *a* (or *con*) after *invitar* (or *convidar*) and before the dependent noun: "te invito una copa" for standard "te invito *a* (or *con*) una copa" or "te invito a tomar una copa." In such cases the noun is felt as direct object of *invitar* and the pronoun object as indirect, as in "te pago una copa."

ARGENTINA: En seguida, indicando taburetes, les *invitó* sentarse (Boj, p. 28). ¡*Invito* un chopp a todos ... ! (Cuti Pereira, p. 112).

CHILE: —¡*Convídame* un pedacito de pan! (N. Guzmán, p. 239).

BOLIVIA: Me ha *invitado* unos tragos de cinzano (Augusto Guzmán, p. 46). *Invitóle* asiento (Chirveches, *Casa solariega*, p. 178).

PERU: Los dueños *convidan* a los visitantes vasos de chicha (Benvenutto, *Quince plazuelas*, p. 13); No falta casi nunca tampoco un compasivo trasnochador que le *invita* una buena taza de café (p. 65). Querían que les *convidara* un pan de Guatemala ... si quieren bizcochos vayan a que se los *convide* su madre (Corrales, p. 47).

ECUADOR: Jaime les *invitó* tabaco (Mata, *Sanagüín*, p. 70). Ellas iban ... a la pesca de algún hombre que ... les *convidara* la cena (La Cuadra, *Horno*, p. 53); En seguida m'*invitó* unos tragos (p. 109).

MEXICO: Te *invito* otra copa (Benítez, p. 95). Si quieren los *invito* unas tortas (Galeana, p. 173). Les voy a *envitar* un trago (Fernando Robles, p. 116). Ahora yo les *invitaré* un cordial orange (Gómez Palacio, p. 100). Les *convidé* de mis gordas [= tortillas gruesas] (Urquizo, p. 30); nos podrá *convidar* lo que consiga de comer (p. 139).

SUPERFLUOUS 'A'

In standard speech *él me mandó llamar* means 'he had me called,' viz., 'he *ordered* me to be called'; whereas *él me mandó a llamar* (or *él mandó a llamarme*) means 'he *sent* someone to call me.' That is, *mandar* without *a* means *ordenar*, and *mandar* with *a* means *enviar*. Since this standard distinction is apparently not always clear to the speaker, and especially to the writer, he is likely to use the preposition when it should be omitted; that is, he uses *a* when the meaning of *mandar* is 'to order.' Such confusion probably goes back to the older language. At any rate it seems much more frequent today in Spanish America than in Spain, and preceptists admonish their readers to make the proper distinction (Cuervo, § 417; Román, III, 407; etc.). Naturally, in normal conversational tempo speakers fuse the preposition *a* ('*a* embebida') with a following *a:* they generally pronounce *mandé a hacer*, for instance, exactly like *mandé hacer*. Therefore, as far as speakers are concerned, only unmistakable cases (*mandé a poner*, etc.) definitely prove the *a* to be superfluous. Probably in many cases the *a* is used by the principle of ultracorrection; and, furthermore, the two meanings often tend to coalesce.

ARGENTINA: —¡Mandesé *a* mudar de aquí, trompeta! (Lynch, *Romance*, p. 367). (For *mandarse mudar* or *cambiar*, cf. p. 210.)

CHILE: —Lárgate ... mándate *a* cambiar (Alberto Romero, *Perucho González*, p. 65).

ECUADOR: Me mandé *a* hacer el vestido de baile (García Muñoz, *Estampas*, p. 12). Ya he mandado *a* hacer otro charol (Icaza, *Cholos*, p. 60).

VENEZUELA: —¿Y quién los manda a ustedes *a* no tener a nadie? (Blanco, in *ACMV*, I, 196).

CUBA: —Por tal razón, continuó el Alcalde, mandé *a* hacer la caja (Ciro Espinosa, p. 118).

In Central America and occasionally in Mexico we find a superfluous *a*, in colloquial speech, used in expressions of time, such as *¿a qué horas son? a las dos, a las cinco* for standard *¿qué hora es? las dos, las cinco*, by analogy with standard *a las dos* 'at two o'clock,' etc.

CENTRAL AMERICA: ¿*A* qué hora [*sic*] son? —*A* las cuatro (Salazar García, pp. 24, 230).

GUATEMALA: Cuando se pregunta ¿Qué hora es? generalmente se responde "*A* las nueve," "*A* las once," etc. (Sandoval, I, 33).

MEXICO: ¿*A* qué horas serían cuando eso pasó, amigote? (Inclán, II, 55).

Sometimes we find *a aquí* and *a allá* for *aquí* and *allá*. These may be examples of "ultracorrección," attempts to restore an *a* erroneously considered absorbed in *aquí* or *allá;* or they may be attempts to supply a feeling of motion 'to' absent in *aquí* and weakening in *allá*.

VENEZUELA: Puedo ir *a allá* (Díaz R., p. 54).

COSTA RICA: Juan vino *a* aquí (Salesiano, p. 32).

For Chile, Román (V, 473) records a superfluous *a* after the verb *tirar* in its sense of 'to attract,' thus making a transitive verb impersonal. This construction may have been influenced by *tirar a* 'to tend toward, lean toward, approach,' etc.: *el color tira a verde*, etc.

CHILE: ¿*A* qué te tira a ti? A mí me tira *a* la milicia. A Juana le tiró *a* casada (o *al* matrimonio) (Román, V, 473).

'A' FOR 'DE'

We find *a* used frequently to express means or instrument in cases in which the standard language now more generally uses *de: máquina a vapor* for the more general *máquina de vapor*. To be sure, examples of *a* may be found in the classics and in contemporary peninsular writers; and since the locution resembles French usage (*machine à vapeur*), it is sometimes dubbed a Gallicism. In Spanish America this construction is most common in the River Plate region and Chile.

ARGENTINA: Trasladados en una lancha *a* nafta a la isla Guaruja (Carlos Quiroga, p. 101). La cocina *a* gas (C).

URUGUAY: Las lámparas *a* kerosene (Montiel, *Alma*, p. 128).

PARAGUAY: ... la lámpara *a* querosene (Casaccia, p. 126).

Chile: Un buque *a* la vela (Durand, *Mercedes*, p. 15). Una lámpara *a* parafina (Latorre, *Zurzulita*, p. 24).

Peru: Buque *a* vapor; cocina *a* electricidad (Benvenutto, p. 147).

Colombia (in newspaper writing): lancha *a* motor, tela *a* cuadros, avión *a* chorro (Flórez, p. 383).

The preposition *a* is used often where *de* or *en* would probably be preferred in the present-day standard language after nouns like *dolor, enfermedad, afección, aflicción, congestión*, etc., and before the part of the body affected: *dolor a los oídos* for *dolor de oídos* or *en los oídos*, etc. Such usage has been defended on the ground that both *a* and *en* are often employed promiscuously to express place (cf. *a la puerta, en la puerta, el caballero con la mano al pecho, los ojos clavados al cielo*, etc.). However, this promiscuity is in general more apparent in the older language and less so in the modern standard idiom. Perhaps the practice we find today in parts of Spanish America is merely a survival of that older usage. In the case of *ataque* the preposition *a* is by some admitted to be correct because the meaning of this word involves a certain movement justifying the use of *a* (Román, II, 175; Morales, I, 30): *ataque al corazón*. Be that as it may, the standard speech in this case prefers a modifying adjective: *ataque cardíaco*.

Argentina: Está con el ataque *al* hígado (Lynch, *Romance*, p. 267). —No tiene nada ... nada *al* pulmón (Petit de Murat, p. 21); Otros están afectados de ... enfermedades *a la* piel (p. 31). Hay que haber sufrido *a* celos por una mujer (Lynch, *Romance*, p. 153).

Chile: Tengo una aflicción *al* corazón (Juan Modesto Castro, p. 353). Ha quedado con una afección *a* los nervios (Casanova Vicuña, p. 7); —Siento también unos dolores *al* hígado y *al* bazo (p. 13). Bebiendo a cada rato a pesar de su afección *al* hígado (Durand, *Mercedes*, p. 17). El guaina había sido medio enfelmón *al* estógamo (Muñoz, p. 35). Dolor *a* los huesos (Latorre, *Zurzulita*, p. 217).

Bolivia: Dicen que es mal *al* corazón (Díaz V., *Plebe*, p. 216).

Ecuador: Mi 'atacado un dolor *al* vientre (Icaza, *Cholos*, p. 31). Una afección *al* corazón (García Muñoz, *Estampas*, p. 211). —Murió con unos dolores *a* la barriga (Jorge Fernández, p. 144).

The verb *aprender* 'to learn' is followed by the dative in the colloquial speech of some Spanish-American regions, that is, by *a* rather than by standard *de*. *Aprender* is not included in Keniston's list of verbs expressing separation or derivation (such as *comprar, preguntar, quitar*, etc.), either for the sixteenth century or for the contemporary period. However, such usage is clearly analogical with other verbs, especially with *prender* in its sense of 'to take, seize,' and possibly influenced by the preposition *a* used after *aprender* 'to learn' before a following infinitive.

ARGENTINA: Y enseguida, mirandolá a la señora con esos ojos de corsario, que le aprendió *al* rubio Cepeda, añidiría muy risueño: "¡Qué doña Julia, ésta!" (Lynch, *Romance*, p. 278).

CHILE: Apréndame *a* mí, el hombre debe ser reservado (Juan Modesto Castro, p. 398); Apréndeme *a* mí que tengo enormes quebraderos de cabeza (C). —Son cosas aprendidas *al* doctor (Luis Meléndez, p. 130).

PERU: Desde hace tiempo, aprendió *a* su abuela (Benvenutto, p. 149).

COLOMBIA: —*¿A* quién *le* aprendió eso? (Buitrago, p. 37).

VENEZUELA: Aprende *a* Lorenzo (Gallegos, *Doña Bárbara*, p. 105).

MEXICO: ¡Mueran los agraristas! ¡Aprendan *a* su padre, caporales de vacas robadas! (Fernando Robles, p. 146); Aprenda usté *a* su papá (González Carrasco, p. 72). —¡Lástima, Torres! Se ha contagiado de la grosería de la gente entre quien vive. Aprenda *a* Margarita y *a* Adolfo (Azuela, *Avanzada*, p. 249). Este sistema de confeccionar chalecos *se* lo aprendí *a* Chente Gutiérrez (Anda, *Juan del Riel*, p. 84).

The prepositional phrase *cerca a* (as well as *cercano a*) is current in some regions for standard *cerca de*. In the older language there was often considerable uncertainty in the preposition which, together with a noun or adjective or adverb, formed a compound preposition (*dentro de* and *dentro en*, *cerca de* and *cerca a*, *junto de* and *junto a*, etc.). Not infrequently some of this variety of usage has survived in the modern standard language. In most cases, however, the standard language has decided on a single form: in the case of *junto de* and *junto a*, the latter is the standard modern usage; but in that of *cerca de* and *cerca a*, the first form, *cerca de*, is considered the correct usage, although *cerca a* is still encountered occasionally in Spain (Hanssen, § 712). The form *cerca a* is rather rare in the older language, so rare, in fact, that Keniston does not register it for the sixteenth century. Cuervo (*Dicc.*) gives a couple of examples. Its extension in Spanish America, then, may be a later development under the influence of such kindred forms as *junto a* and *próximo a* (cf. *en medio a*).

Argentina: Pantalión estaba perdiendo 'e palabra muy *cerca a* dos mil pesos (Lynch, *Romance*, p. 95).

Bolivia: Bara se cubría los hombros con una toalla, *cerca a* unas cambas [= indias] silenciosas que le servían agua (Céspedes, p. 58). Este territorio silvestre ... lo ennoblecían ... con pequeños cuadros de cultivo *cerca a* las cañadas (Augusto Guzmán, p. 29).

Peru: La Hormecinda hace zumbar piedras *cerca a* los animales (Ciro Alegría, *La serpiente*, p. 186).

Ecuador: Emprendió una carrera tendida tras la bestia, hasta que, cuando estuvo *cerca a* ella, se tiró ... (Icaza, *Cholos*, p. 96). Tener *cerca a* sí una mujer (Gil Gilbert, *Nuestro pan*, p. 141).

Colombia: En Junín, *cerca al* Santillana, Paco se encontró con Dolly (Bernardo Toro, p. 11); *cerca a* Cerrobruto se reunieron (p. 81). Nos sentamos en dos poltronas *cerca al* lecho (Lozano). *Cerca al* río Magdalena (Buitrago, p. 9; also pp. 10, 19, 50; *cerca de*, pp. 40, 47); las piedras *cercanas a* los sangreros (p. 126).

Guatemala: Martín y la Toña se encontraron, de atardecida, *cerca al* río (Wyld Ospina, *Nahuyacas*, p. 111).

Frequently one finds *distinto a* for standard *distinto de*, probably by analogy with *diferente a*, which is much less frequent, however, than *diferente de*. A few examples will suffice:

Argentina: ¡Tan *distinto a* Antonio el mayor! (Lynch, in *ACR*, p. 313). Y mi poder es *distinto al* tuyo, más fuerte (Mallea, *Fiesta*, p. 14). Es una musicalidad *distinta a* la verdadera música (Boj, p. 56); —Monti es tan *distinto a* mí (p. 83).

Colombia: —Usted es *distinta a* todas las mujeres (Antonio García, p. 131).

Mexico: Se convertiría en una persona enteramente *distinta a* la que fué (García Roel, p. 284). —Saben muy *distintos a* los que yo formulo (Gamboa, *Teatro*, III, 400).

Santo Domingo: Martín comenzó a vivir en una forma *distinta a* la que estaba acostumbrado (Requena, *Los enemigos*, p. 39); Algo ... le daba a esa comida un sabor *distinto a* las demás (p. 71).

Cuba: Nosotros éramos *distintos al* resto de la tripulación (Carlos Montenegro, *Los héroes*, p. 135).

In Chile, and elsewhere, the expressions *hacerse al rogar* 'to like to be coaxed' and *al todo* 'completely' are colloquially used for standard *hacerse de rogar* and *del todo*.

CHILE: —Ya, no se haga tanto *al* [= de] rogar (Acevedo Hernández, *La canción rota*, p. 53). Hágase *al* rogar, tamién (Acevedo Hernández, *Por el atajo*, p. 31). Me has olvidado *al* [= del] todo (Román, V, 486).

'A' FOR 'EN'

After *entrar* the preposition *en* is today used in the standard language meaning 'into' to express motion: *entró en la casa*. In American Spanish, however, the preposition *a* is the rule. This usage may be considered an Americanism in so far as it differs from present-day standard Castilian, but it is far from new. On the contrary, it is as old as the Spanish language itself. It was general from the earliest literary monuments (*Cid*, vs. 12: "entrando *a* Burgos," etc.) to the end of the Golden Age (Lope de Vega, *Peribáñez*, II, 4: "¿Qué has entrado *a* su aposento?") and less frequently even into the nineteenth century (Larra, *La nochebuena* [1836]: "Me *entré* de rondón *a* mi estancia"). It was apparently also the popular usage, since it has survived so vigorously in Spanish America and sporadically in parts of Spain, not only in Asturias (as already pointed out by Cuervo, § 457), but in many other regions, including Old and New Castile (Segovia, Madrid, Ciudad Real), Andalusia (Sevilla, Granada, Jaén),[1] etc.

While *entrar* is generally the one verb mentioned by preceptists and grammarians dealing with this usage, it is certainly not the only one diverging from the so-called standard construction. Another of equal frequency is *meter a* for *meter en*. The preposition *a* is found with still other verbs having meanings akin to that of *entrar*, such as: *internarse a* (for *en*), *penetrar a* (for *en*), *caer a la cama* (for *en la cama*) *colarse a* (for *en*), *tirarse a la cama* (for *en la cama*), *ingresar a* (for *en*), *introducir a* (for *en*), *zampar a* (for *en*), etc. The phrase *al centro* for standard *en el centro* is frequently encountered; and occasionally others, such as *al almuerzo* for *en el almuerzo; a lo mejor de* for *en lo mejor de* 'in the midst of'; *tener fe a* (Colombia, Venezuela) for *tener fe en; a éstas* (Venezuela) for *en éstas* or *en esto;* etc.

ARGENTINA: Entró *a* una de ellas [pulperías] (Lucero Draghi, p. 122). —¿No gusta dentrar *a* la cocina? (Güiraldes, *Don Segundo*, p. 45). Se tiró *a* la cama, decepcionado (Greca, p. 166 [North Santa Fe]).

[1] Aurelio Espinosa's *Cuentos populares españoles* contains a number of examples from various provinces: "entró er chico *a* la cocina" (I, 112 [Granada]); "le dice que entre *a* la cocina" (I, 97 [Jaén]); "se metió de ermitaño *a* una cueva" (I, 140 [Ciudad Real]); "entra *a* la sala" (II, 303 [Segovia]); "me vi a meter *a* la cama" (III, 425 [Sevilla]), etc. See also *BDH*, V, 234.

Al centro, cinco o seis Salvacionistas cantan su plegaria (Pacheco, p. 2). Recoge los papeles y los mete *al* bolsillo (Boj, p. 136). Estaban *a* lo mejor de ella (Lynch, *Romance*, p. 13). El tipo cayó *a* la cama (Petit de Murat, p. 91).

CHILE: Hay que entrar *al* aula (Sepúlveda, *La fábrica*, p. 23). La noche entró *al* cuarto con su frescor siempre puro (Latorre, *Hombres*, p. 20). Iba ya a penetrar *al* edificio (Alberto Edwards, in *LCC*, p. 285). Suspiraba, cayó *a* la cama (Acevedo Hernández, *Por el atajo*, p. 56). Viviendo más *al centro* (Durand, *Mercedes*, p. 165).

BOLIVIA: Sirpa saltó ... en momentos en que la vieja ... ingresaba *a* la vivienda (Céspedes, p. 56); Nosotros, siempre *al centro* de esa polifonía irritante, vivimos una escasa vida (p. 26). La metimos *a* la cueva (Arguedas, p. 343). Nos internamos *al* Chaco (Augusto Guzmán, p. 14); Yo estoy *al centro* (p. 71; also p. 55).

PERU: —Recojan los muertos y métanlos *a* ese cuarto (Ciro Alegría, *Los perros*, p. 163). —Métanlo *a* la celda (Ciro Alegría, *El mundo*, p. 309). *Al centro* ... está el farol (Benvenutto, *Quince plazuelas*, p. 186). Vilela me amenaza con influencias para zamparme *a* la cárcel. ... Entré *al* cuarto (Corrales, p. 51).

ECUADOR: Entro *a* mi casa (García Muñoz, *Estampas*, p. 318). Se metieron *al* estero (Aguilera Malta, p. 7). Se metió apresuradamente *a* la casa (Icaza, *En las calles*, p. 126). *Al centro* una mesa rectangular (Jorge Fernández, p. 52).

COLOMBIA: Se cuela *a* la sala y grita atragantada (Carrasquilla, *Hace tiempos*, III, 16); me entro *al* cuarto de don Julián (III, 198). Tuvo que ingresar *al* sindicato (Restrepo Jaramillo, p. 156). *Al* almuerzo no estuvo amable y *a* la comida menos (Sundheim, p. 20). Tienen mucha fe *a* tal médico o *a* tal remedio (Tascón, p. 268).

VENEZUELA: *A* éstas, Pedro Miguel se había alejado (Gallegos, *Pobre negro*, p. 353); Entraban *a* sus ranchos (p. 363). Le tengo mucha fe *a* este remedio (Rosenblat).

COSTA RICA: Se meten los dos *al* cuarto (Fallas, p. 37).

NICARAGUA: ¿Entrar *a* la casa? Era arriesgado (Chamorro, *Entre dos filos*, p. 78).

EL SALVADOR: Al llegar, meten las bestias *a* la caballeriza (Ambrogi, p. 49); Dentro *a* la estancia (p. 176).

GUATEMALA: Anochecido, entró don Juan *al* cuarto de Monteros (Flavio Herrera, p. 61).

MEXICO: Conseguí que lo metieran *al* jurado de examen (Quevedo, *La camada*, p. 293); Me metió de nuevo *a* la cárcel (p. 360). Nos metimos *a* su oficina y redactó el mensaje (Menéndez, *Nayar*, p. 62). Penetro *a* un pequeño gabinete (Benítez, p. 118); penetro *en* la iglesia (p. 143); penetro *a* un patiecito (p. 149); Comienzan a entrar *al* teatro (p. 190). El gran templo ... se yergue *al* centro de la ciudad (*El Nacional*, May 26, 1942).

SANTO DOMINGO: ¡Entra, reina del canto, entra *a* la gloria! (in *BDH*, V, 234). Al entrar *a* la habitación sus ojos se alegraron (Requena, *Los enemigos*, p. 71); Entonces entró *en* la barbería (p. 71).

CUBA (prefers *en*): Entrar *en* la iglesia (Padrón).

'A' FOR 'POR'

In standard speech *por* or *que* introduces an infinitive to indicate that the act of the infinitive has not yet been performed, that it remains to be performed: "una novela *por* escribir, está *por* hacer, tengo mucho *que* hacer," etc. In comparatively recent times the preposition *a* has been substituted for *por* by some writers in Spain (where Huidobro dubbed the usage "desaforado galicismo" and "horrible disparate") and to a large extent in the River Plate zone (in Argentina, Garzón [p. 1] calls it "construcción gálica muy en boga"), to some extent in Chile (where Román expostulates [I, 3]: "¡Dios nos libre para siempre de galicismos tan crudos y tan chocantes a los oídos castellanos!"), and frequently elsewhere, particularly in newspaper writing. While, to be sure, such a construction is typically French (*livre à lire*, etc.), it is also characteristic of Italian; and, furthermore, constructions akin to it are found in preclassic writings. Morales (I, 21) is inclined to consider the construction more of an archaism than a Gallicism and as not contrary to the genius of the language (cf. also González de la Calle, *BICC*, II, 535–46).

ARGENTINA: El temperamento *a* adoptarse (Garzón, p. 1). Su cautela, igual que la antena de ciertos insectos, exploraba el camino *a* seguir (Filloy, p. 29).

URUGUAY: De las tres observaciones normales *a* hacer en el día, el encargado suele efectuar únicamente dos (Horacio Quiroga, V, 31). Matacabayo quedó apoyado a un poste del alambrado, acomodando sobre los hombros los arreos *a* reparar (Amorím, *La carreta*, p. 14); era más aún motivo de regocijo la comedia *a* representar por los hombres (p. 49).

CHILE: ¿Qué nos queda *a* esperar? (Concha y Castillo, *Al vivir*, *ap.* Morales, I, 21).

BOLIVIA: No sabían el camino *a* tomar (Céspedes, p. 121).

PERU: El piloto debe conocer exactamente sus rumbos tanto de ida como de regreso *a* seguir (Martínez de Pinillos, p. 47).

COLOMBIA: Problema *a* resolver, camino *a* seguir (Flórez, p. 383).

PANAMA: ... la actitud a tomar (Cajar, p. 105).

GUATEMALA: Para lo cual se procura/todas las armas *a* emplear/; los procedimientos *a* seguir; el punto *a* dilucidar (Bonilla, III, 222).

MEXICO: El sacerdote tuvo el cuidado de hablar ... del camino *a* seguir para obtener nuestra salvación (Benítez, p. 220).

SANTO DOMINGO: Eran bastantes las vacas *a* ordeñar (Bosch, *Camino real*, p. 126).

In Spanish America the preposition *a* is commonly found in locutions like *día a día* 'day after day, every day,' where standard speech generally prefers *día por día* or *día tras día*. The probable explanation for this divergence is analogy with expressions like *uno a uno* 'one by one,' *poco a poco* 'little by little,' *gota a gota* 'drop by drop,' and *de día a día* 'from day to day' (though *de día en día* is commoner). Other examples of this divergence are: *noche a noche, mañana a mañana, vuelta a vuelta, año a año, hora a hora, tarde a tarde, momento a momento,* etc. Such phrases have sometimes been considered localisms. For instance, Martín Aldao (p. 86) dubbed *día a día* an Argentinism. That it is no mere localism but is rather widely distributed in Spanish America is shown by the following examples.

ARGENTINA: Después de visitar *día a día* aquella casa ... (Larreta, *La gloria*, p. 128). Empecé a desconfiar o más bien dicho a desconfiarle a una tipa a la que *noche a noche* encontrábamos en el cine con su marido (Lynch, *Palo verde*, p. 113). El Asilo San Miguel se nutre *mañana a mañana* del material humano que viene en carros celulares (Angélica Mendoza, p. 28). *Vuelta a vuelta* se extraviaban animales sin que volviéramos a verlos (Sáenz, p. 28). Doña Cruz ... sentenciaba endenantes y *güelta a güelta:* «Naides es güeno ni malo ... » (Lynch, *Romance*, p. 110).

URUGUAY: Había quien gastaba *mes a mes* el producto entero de su trabajo (Reyles, *El gaucho*, p. 18).

CHILE: Hey trabajao *día a día* y no tengo mi chapa (Acevedo Hernández, *Por el atajo*, p. 29). Estaba enviando *día a día* una redoma de leche para Lorenzo (Azócar, p. 108). Recordó Solaguren que en las tardes de verano, *año a año*, veía agruparse sobre la mole andina esas mismas eternas nubes (Prado, *Un juez*, p. 99). Allí llegaban *noche a noche* comparsas de remoledores (Durand, *Mercedes*, p. 13).

BOLIVIA: Sirpa hacía lo mismo incorporándose *día a día* al hechizo misterioso de aquellos horizontes vagos (Céspedes, p. 72).

COSTA RICA: *Noche a noche* bían salir una lus junto 'e la sequia (Agüero, p. 68). *Mes a mes* [la gente] se apretuja en la ermita encalada (Fabián Dobles, p. 7).

NICARAGUA: Jugamos *día a día* con la muerte (Orozco, p. 17). *Noche a noche* concurría a las clases (Toruño, p. 84).

HONDURAS: Formaban *noche a noche* una ronda cordial cabe la luminaria (Martínez Galindo, p. 146).

GUATEMALA: La vida transcurre dejando *hora a hora, día a día,* una esperanza, un dolor, un desengaño (Quintana, p. 227).

MEXICO: *Domingo a domingo* causaba las delicias de los aficionados mexicanos en la Plaza (Gamboa, *Santa*, p. 79); *día a día* captábase las voluntades de la moza (p. 142). Los agraristas están cayendo *noche a noche* a los alfalfales (Fernando Robles, p. 190). Es la «peña» que *tarde a tarde* se incrusta contra algún escaparate o puerta de cantina (Gómez Palacio, p. 6); Todo se modifica hora tras hora, *momento a momento* (p. 123).

CUBA: *Día a día* el destino me sorprende con nuevas demostraciones (J. A. Ramos, p. 181).

SANTO DOMINGO: Sólo se destaca el techo grueso, seco, ansioso de quemarse *día a día* (Juan Bosch, in *ACH*, p. 127).

A, POR = PARA

Occasionally we find *a* (also *por*) for *para* in the expression *estar al* (also *estar por*) for standard *estar para* 'to be about to, to be on the point of.' (This *estar al* is not to be confused with *estar a* meaning *haber ido*, as in: "Fulano *está a* llamar al médico" [Robles Dégano, *Gram.*, p. 115]).

ARGENTINA: *Está por* (= para) caer. (SAN LUIS): *está al* llegar, *está al* llover, etc. (Vidal, p. 406).

BOLIVIA: Pronto *estaremos al* pedir limosna (Ruiz, p. 5); *estamos al* morir de hambre (p. 46).

COLOMBIA: *Está al* llegar (Bueno, p. 40).

VENEZUELA: El avión *está al* salir (Rosenblat).

SANTO DOMINGO: Otra vez *estuve al* casarme, pero le salí huyendo al matrimonio (Requena, *Camino*, p. 56); El ardiente deseo de Ramón del Pulgar *estaba al* cumplirse (p. 127). De ser éstos los cacaotales de Vinicio, *estoy al* alcanzar la pulpería (Bosch, *Dos pesos*, p. 141).

CUBA (POP.): Mi primo *está al* llegar (Padrón).

ARRIBA DE

The compound preposition *arriba de*, formed from the adverb *arriba* 'above,' is comparatively rare in standard Spanish in the sense of *encima de* or *en lo alto de*, etc. For contemporary Spanish prose, Keniston (*Syntax list*, p. 264) gives these range and frequency figures: *arriba de* [4–4]; *encima de* [10–14]. Unfortunately, there is no indication as to whether the four cases of *arriba de* were found in American or in peninsular prose. It is commoner in the popular speech of rural regions in Spain than in the standard language (cf. Aurelio Espinosa, *Cuentos*, III, 378, 416, 442, 489, etc.). For the sixteenth century, Keniston's investigation (p. 645) shows *arriba de* as occurring only in the additional material perused (except one example of *arriba de* with the force of *más de* before a numeral), and *encima de* (p. 651) with a range and frequency of [7–12]. Be that as it may, usage in some Spanish-American regions today indicates an abuse of *arriba de* (or merely *arriba*) where standard Spanish prescribes *encima de*, *en lo alto de*, *más arriba de*, or merely *sobre*.

ARGENTINA: ¡Con decirte que bailó el tangón *arriba de* una mesa! (Llanderas and Malfatti, *Giuanín*, p. 26).

URUGUAY: Después lo sangró en la frente, *arriba de* los ojos (Acevedo Díaz, *Cancha larga*, p. 43).

PARAGUAY: Colgaba *arriba de* la cabeza (Casaccia, p. 151).

CHILE: Allá, *arriba de* aquel huerto,/hay un rico naranjal (Vicuña Cifuentes, p. 163).

ECUADOR (CUENCA): *Arriba de* la playa donde se ubicaba la casa de Segovia, la montaña escabritaba chúcara (Mata, *Sanagüín*, p. 73).

NICARAGUA: ¡Cuénteme el asunto! les dijo tío Conejo, *arriba de* una piedra (*Centro* I, No. 3, 23).

GUATEMALA: El asesino se apostó *arriba de* la escalera, y cuando subía el Coronel, le disparó dos tiros (Salomé Gil, *Un viaje*, I, 200); su habitación estaba dos pisos *arriba de* la mía (II, 138).

MEXICO: Frente a mis ojos, *arriba de* Playa del Rey y del Cerro del Castillo, las pupilas del faro comienzan a voltejear sus ráfagas avizorantes (Menéndez, *Nayar*, p. 53); *Arriba del* cerro, cañones viejos (p.

54). La anudó fuertemente al muslo *arriba del* balazo (Azuela, *Los de abajo*, p. 12).

SANTO DOMINGO: —Saltaban las brasas *arriba de* él (Bosch, *La Mañosa*, p. 148).

ATRÁS DE, TRAS DE

In popular and rustic speech we frequently hear *atrás de* for standard *detrás de*. This practice, stemming from confusion in the older language, is quite general, and therefore only a few examples are necessary.

ARGENTINA: Habían estao escondidos/Aguaitando *atrás de* un cerro (*Martín Fierro*, p. 39). *Atrás de* aquel cortinao/Un Dotor apareció (*Fausto*, p. 138). *Atrás de* cada uno de esos agujeritos debía haber un ángel (Güiraldes, *Don Segundo*, p. 166); me colocó unos pellones *atrás de* la cabeza (p. 206).

NEW MEXICO: Se 'scondió *atrás el* barril (Aurelio Espinosa, *Estudios*, p. 290); se 'scondieron *atrás de* un pino (p. 308).

In many regions we find *tras de* followed by an infinitive with the temporal force of *después de*. Standardly, *tras de* in this usage is not temporal but expresses manner, with the meaning of *además*, *fuera de*, etc., 'in addition to, besides,' etc. This is merely a confusion with *tras* (*de*) which, when used with substantives, means spatial or temporal *después de:* "llevaba *tras de* sí más de doscientas personas," "*tras* este tiempo vendrá otro mejor," etc.

ARGENTINA: —Esta mañana tuve un serio disgusto—había dicho el señor Caviedes *tras de* engullir un bocado (Boj, p. 44). *Tras de* un barbotar de carcajadas, todos se callaron (Filloy, p. 233); *tras de* huir al interior ... se asomó de nuevo (p. 326).

CHILE: Hacía algunas indicaciones y se iba, *tras de* mirarlas muy fijo (Brunet, *Bestia dañina*, p. 26).

MEXICO: *Tras de* entrar nuevamente en aquella casona a despedirme del padre de Fernando, me lancé adonde los vientos me llevaran (Ferretis, *Quijote*, p. 188). *Tras de* rasurarse ... vertíase agua por el cuello y la cabeza (Robles Castillo, p. 79); —Hasta celosa la tengo—dijo *tras de* colgar el audífono (p. 89). *Tras de* haberse echado un trago ... empezaron a buscar con todo empeño (García Roel, p. 157); Y *tras de* pasar algunos meses en la cárcel logró salir (p. 283).

CUBA: Y *tras de* doblar cuidadosamente el papel oficial, volvió grupa (Mesa Sanabria, in *CC*, p. 137).

'PARA' FOR 'DE'

We find a peculiar use of *para* for *de* especially in the Andean highlands:

BOLIVIA: —Mi madre era una de las criadas ... llegó a tener una hija *para* uno de los señoritos de la casa (Rodrigo, p. 3).

PERU: La cholita parió un chico *para* don Gómez (Benvenutto, p. 149).

'PARA' FOR 'EN'

The use of *para* for *en* seems local:

CUBA (RURAL): Josefa está *para* el campo; Juan está *para* la sala (Padrón).

'PARA' FOR 'MÁS'

PERU: ¡Qué juego *para* entretenido! ¡Qué día *pa* bonito! (C).

COLOMBIA (ANTIOQUIA): ¡Ah niño *para* necio! ¡Ah don Luciano *para* porfiado! (Fidel Suárez, XII, 126).

CON

In some regions, particularly in Mexico and Central America, there is an apparent abuse of *con* in place of *a* after *presentar* 'to introduce' (rarely after *recomendar*), and after such verbs as *acusar*, *quejarse*, *llevar*, *venir*, *ir*, *llegar*, *volver*, *mandar*, and the like. With most of the latter group *con* is also found in Spain: *ven conmigo* 'come to me,' *llévame con él* 'take me to him,' etc.[2] Perhaps the use of *con* stems from a desire to distinguish more easily the direct from the indirect object or the object of *a* expressing motion from a personal direct object introduced by *a*—that is, a desire to avoid ambiguity and often, incidentally, the cacophony of two *a*'s in close proximity. For instance, "le voy a presentar *a* mi amigo" lacks the clarity of "le voy a presentar *con* mi amigo," just as "lléveme *a* mis amigos" is less readily perceptible than "lléveme *con* mis amigos," and "presenté a Juan *a* mi tío" less euphonious than "presenté a Juan *con* mi tío." Other peculiar uses of *con* in northern Colombia are recorded by Sundheim (see examples below). For *con* meaning *y*, see p. 265.

[2] Cf. "le enviaron sus padres *con* el sacristán" (Aurelio Espinosa, *Cuentos*, II, 284 [Soria]); "el muchacho se fué entonces pa su casa *con* su padre" (II, 325 [Soria]); "Voy *con* mi hijo" (Benavente, *De cerca*, p. 5 [Castile]); etc. Cf. Cuervo, *Dicc.*, II, 297.

ARGENTINA: Cada rico estanciero, cada señorón del pago, venían à hacerse cortar el pelo o la barba *con* él (Lynch, *Romance*, p. 311).

URUGUAY: ¡Mira *con* don Eloy! Ese galleguito podrá tener todos los defetos, pero es rumboso como él solo (Sánchez, *M'hijo el dotor*, III, 2). Me volveré *con* mis padres (Bellán, p. 141).

EL SALVADOR: —¿Me puedes presentar *con* él? (Ramírez, p. 64).

COLOMBIA (ATLANTIC COAST): El Alcalde es muy amigo *con* mi hermano; ¿Se conoce Ud. *con* el doctor X? Julio es compañero *con* mi sobrino; Carmen *con* Pedro son primos hermanos (Sundheim, p. 166). (CHOCÓ): Es hermano *con* fulano (*BICC*, VI, 113).

Revollo (p. 71) explains that *conocerse con* implies friendship, whereas *conocer a* means 'to know by sight'.

VENEZUELA: Te voy a acusar *con* mi papá (Rosenblat).

GUATEMALA: Agapito viene *conmigo* [= a mí] para pedirme un favor (Sandoval, I, 212); Victoriano recurre siempre *contigo* [= a ti] para que lo salves de algún apuro (I, 216).

MEXICO: No nos has presentado *con* el señor (Anda, *Los bragados*, p. 66). ¡Don Antón! ¡Lléveme *con* Don Antón! (Quevedo, *La camada*, p. 215). El doctor Celis ... presentó al recién llegado *con* Septembrino (Gómez Palacio, p. 51). Yo no tengo; pero vaya *con* señá Dolores, a ella no le faltan nunca yerbitas (Azuela, *Los de abajo*, p. 54). —Estás «neuras,» ya sé. Ve *con* un médico (Azuela, *Regina Landa*, p. 24); Flores Marín presentó a su nueva mecanógrafa *con* el señor de Casasola (p. 110). Le voy a presentar *con* mi abogado (Gutiérrez Nájera, p. 104). L'otro día/le dije que juera/*con* el médico (González Carrasco, p. 51). Si alguna persona vende un solar o pide dinero prestado, luego van *con* él para que les escriba un papel (Núñez Guzmán, p. 32). Le recordamos su promesa de llevarnos *con* el general Villa (Azuela, *Las moscas*, p. 53). —Estoy seguro de que en tu casa no te pegarán; al contrario, te dan *conmigo;* hoy mismo te pido (Galeana, p. 38); se convino en que me llevarían *con* un médico (p. 98). Llegué *con* el [= al] pagador y le dije: —Señor, yo quiero trabajar (p. 140). Lo voy a recomendar *con* Plácido, el garrotero mayor (Anda, *Juan del Riel*, p. 53); cuando me presenté *con* el superintendente (p. 77). No te ha de gustar que te acuse *con* el profesor. ... Vuelven a quejarse *con* el profesor (García Roel, p. 305); allá va *con* el profesor: —Oiga, profesor (p. 307). Un mes más tarde se quejó *con* la Marchanta (Azuela, *La Marchanta*, p. 61). (YUCATAN): Lo compré *con* [= en casa de] don Antonio (V. Suárez, p. 154, who sees Mayan influence here).

A related and older use of *con* we find, as in Bolivia, replacing modern standard *por:*

—¡No sé cómo me contengo de hacerlo sacar *con* mis peones! (Díaz V., *El traje*, p. 100); —Ah, es que me daba rabia que se haga vencer *con* el hijo de la Tabla-guitarra (*Cuando vuelva*, p. 8); —Hágame pegar *con* su hijo (p. 58); —¿Por qué no te has hecho leer *con* cualquiera? (p. 73); —¡*Con* esa vieja se había hecho conquistar! (p. 73).

'CON' OMITTED

The verb *obsequiar* means standardly *agasajar a uno con atenciones, servicios o regalos* 'to treat, entertain, or regale someone with, to favor someone with,' etc. That is, in the standard construction the person entertained or regaled is the direct object and the thing is the object of the preposition *con: la obsequié con un libro* 'I presented her with a book.' In Spanish America generally, the construction has become *le obsequié un libro;* that is, the thing given is the direct object of the verb and the person is the indirect object. The meaning of *obsequiar* has weakened to that of *dar* or *regalar* 'to give (as a gift)' and has been attracted into the construction of these verbs: *le regalé* (or *le di*) *un libro* = *le obsequié un libro.*

The semasiological and syntactical development of *obsequiar* follows the pattern of *regalar:* original *la regalé con un libro* 'I regaled her with a book' became *le regalé un libro* 'I gave her a book.' This evolution of *obsequiar* is not unknown in Spain; but it has not been recognized there officially and is undoubtedly much commoner in Spanish America, where drift and change have in general been more facile. It is current everywhere. A few examples will suffice:

River Plate Zone: Me obsequió un mate (Morínigo).

Chile: Pedro me obsequió su retrato (Román, IV, 52).

Colombia: Él me obsequió un libro (Cuervo, § 425).

El Salvador: Obsequiar a Inés un libro (Salazar García, p. 200).

Guatemala: Mis padres me obsequiaron un collar de perlas muy valioso (Sandoval, II, 160).

Mexico: Él me obsequió este libro (Ramos Duarte, p. 373).

Soñar is often used, especially in Mexico and Central America, without the usual prepositions *con* (or *en*).

HONDURAS: El pensarla y el *soñarla* ... (Martínez Galindo, p. 125).
MEXICO: *¡Me soñaste!* (Madero, II, 1). Me sonreía de un modo, que me hizo *soñarla* dos noches (Ferretis, *Quijote*, p. 112).

CONTRA

This preposition is frequently met in the gauchesco poets and is used also in other regions in the sense of *junto a* 'beside.' Such a meaning is closely related to and easily developed from its most current meaning of 'against' and from its other meanings of *enfrente* 'facing' and *hacia* 'toward.' *Contra* means *junto a* also in provincial Spain: Lamano (p. 351) gives it for Salamanca ("—¿Y te fijaste en el cuento de *contra* el camino?"), and Corominas (p. 94) mentions León.

ARGENTINA: Áhi tiene *contra* el recao/cuchillo (*Fausto*, p. 256); vide una fila de coches/*contra* el tiatro de Colón (p. 262); *contra* una máquina hilando/la rubia se apareció (p. 289).
COLOMBIA: Tenía detrás de su trapiche, *contra* un rincón de la bagacera, un cuarto hecho de tabiques (Jaramillo, p. 33).

Román (I, 410) mentions two Chilean meanings of *contra: en* and *para*. He gives these examples: "*¿Contra qué* [= para qué, con qué fin, con qué objeto] estudio si no aprendo? *Contra nada* [= inútilmente] porfías, porque tendrás que hacerlo"; Le clavó contra [= en] la pared." The meaning of "en" is found elsewhere: "Clavó vidrios *contra* la pared" (Schock, p. 16 [Argentina]); "su libreta de apuntes *contra* la que aprisionaba unos pocos billetes" (Jaramillo, p. 143 [Colombia]); etc.

'DE' OMITTED

By the sixteenth century the preposition *de* had become the most general means of changing an adverb into a preposition (*dentro* > *dentro de, fuera* > *fuera de*), as *que* was used to create a corresponding conjunction (*después* > *después de* and *después que*). This *de* was then extended to original prepositions to make of them compound prepositions: *cerca* > *cerca de; delante* (a combination of prepositions) > *delante de*, etc. By the sixteenth century the new forms in general had become established, but in the first half of the century the older forms still survived[3] and usage of compound prepositions involving

[3] Thus we read in the older texts: "asentóse el marido en el banco *delante* la cama ... e púsogela *delante* la cara" (*Corbacho* [1438], II, 10); "hablas entre dientes *delante* mí" (*Celestina*, IV); "*cerca* los muros de una ciudad" (Avellaneda's *Quijote*, XIX).

a noun or adjective was not at all fixed (Keniston, p. 637): *encima* and *encima de* (original noun *cima* > adverb *encima* > preposition *encima de*); *junto, junto de,* and *junto a,* etc.

This confusion of prepositional forms was brought to America and has survived in a number of regions. In Catalonia, too, the preposition *de* is often omitted in *acerca de, cerca de, dentro de,* etc. (Huidobro, pp. 24, 66), and this fact has led some local lexicographers (Calcaño, § 290) to attribute it to Catalan influence. To be sure, it may well have been kept alive in regions in which Catalan colonists abound. On the other hand, the same thing occurs elsewhere in Spain, particularly in rural areas, and occasionally in poetic style.

ARGENTINA: No hay nada como injertar el miedo *dentro* la velocidad (Filloy, p. 44); El corazón ... aleteaba contento *dentro* su alma (p. 62; also pp. 41, 98, 211, 276; but *dentro de* on pp. 6, 245, 277); quiso dar explicaciones *acerca* su demora (p. 197).

URUGUAY: —*Dentro* unas horas traigo a Pedro (Espínola, p. 52).

CHILE: Empotrados *dentro* las cuatro paredes de una cárcel (Muñoz, p. 210).

BOLIVIA: —Son *cerca* las doce (Arguedas, *Vida criolla,* p. 62). El hacendado ... ciñó el ... cuello de ave, *encima* su albo collar de plumas (Arguedas, *Raza,* p. 76); *cerca* el camino (p. 106); *cerca* las yuntas (p. 260); *dentro* el círculo rojo (p. 372). *Delante* los cachorros ... muere la pobre Loca (Augusto Guzmán, p. 155).

PERU: *Dentro* la acequia estaba el sapo; ¿cómo será tener un crimen así *dentro* la conciencia? (Benvenutto, p. 148).

VENEZUELA: *Aparte* lo alegado; *En medio* la matanza (Calcaño, § 290). De *adentro* la casa llegó una voz (Díaz-Solís, p. 39).

EL SALVADOR: *Dentro* el mismo círculo (Salazar García, p. 100).

GUATEMALA: Cuando se vió *dentro* las tripas de la culebra, dijo a [=empezó a, cf. p. 200] hincharse (Quintana, p. 132).

More rarely a *de* is added (by analogy with *dentro de,* etc.) where it does not belong: *sobre de* for *sobre, entre de* for *entre,* etc.

ARGENTINA: Están sobre *de* ellos como una amenaza (Monti, p. 80).

ECUADOR: A ellos, a los negros, los trajeron en rimeros, unos sobre *de* otros (Gil Gilbert, *Yunga,* p. 17).

MEXICO: Después, las medias de algodón, y sobre *de* éstas, las medias de seda (Gamboa, *Santa,* p. 197).

GUATEMALA: Este juego se hace entre *de* varias personas (Sandoval I, 490).

In the older language the preposition *de* was used with many verbs (often interchangeably with another preposition) that later discarded the *de* and today are standardly used with some other preposition or with none at all: *atreverse de* (more frequently *a*) = today *atreverse a; comenzar de* (also *a*) = today *comenzar a; creer de* = today *creer; determinar de* = today *determinar; empezar de* (also *a*) = today *empezar a; obligarse de* (also *a*) = today *obligarse a; olvidar de* = today *olvidar; pensar de* ('to intend') = today *pensar; procurar de* = today *procurar; prometer de* = today *prometer; quedar de* = today *quedar en;* etc.

This older confusion was the American heritage, and today in colloquial speech some verbs omit *de* where standardly *de* is indispensable: *acordarse* = standard *acordarse de; olvidarse* = standard *olvidarse de; gustar* = standard *gustar de; hacerse rogar* = standard *hacerse de rogar;* rarely *han ir* = standard *han de ir* or *irán;* etc. The confusion is undoubtedly furthered by the fact that some verbs, adjectives, and prepositions normally followed by *de* may omit this *de* if followed by *que* + a clause (in this case the prepositions become conjunctions): *acordarse* (*de*) *que, alegrarse* (*de*) *que, dudar* (*de*) *que, olvidarse* (*de*) *que, estar seguro* (*de*) *que, antes* (*de*) *que, después* (*de*) *que, a fin* (*de*) *que,* etc. The omission of *de* in some of the following examples may represent an original absorption of *e* (> *de*) by an adjacent vowel.

ARGENTINA: No me hice rogar (Güiraldes, *Don Segundo*, p. 95). Me hice rogar y cedí (Mansilla, *Una excursión*, p. 77). ¿Gusta un cigarrillo? (Larreta, *El linyera*, p. 63). El viejo Sinforiano gustaba trabajar reconcentrado (Varela, p. 99). —Acuérdate lo que decía el maestro (Martínez Cuitiño, p. 53).

URUGUAY: Era remolona y gustaba decir palabras vanas (Acevedo Díaz, *Cancha larga*, p. 329). El individuo no se hizo rogar (Montiel, *Luz mala*, p. 11).

PARAGUAY: ¿Gusta pitar un negro [= cigarrillo de tabaco negro]?; me acordaba lo que nos pasó en el río (Morínigo).

CHILE: No se hizo rogar, pagó al tiro [= en seguida] (Juan Modesto Castro, p. 147). El señor ... gustaba especialmente la sociedad de los vendedores viajeros (Luis Meléndez, p. 6). Me olvidé avisarle (J. M. Castro, p. 18).

BOLIVIA: Se había olvidado preparar el arma (Arguedas, *Raza*, p. 105); acuérdate lo que nos pasó la última vez (p. 164). —¡Ajai! exclamó ella pasándome el té ... al que no se olvidó agregarle el correspondiente cognac (Jaime Mendoza, *Memorias*, II, 59). Le aconsejan qu no se haga rogar tanto (Rodrigo, p. 32).

Ecuador: El Capitán Sandoval gusta contemplar eso (Gil Gilbert, *Nuestro pan*, p. 141); Los ahogados no gustan estar solos (p. 237). Julia ... gustaba ir por las noches a sentarse unos minutos en el banco (Diez-Canseco, *El muelle*, p. 33). Gustar toros (Cevallos, p. 41). ¡Pish! ¡para lo que han durar! (Mata, *Sanagüín*, p. 97).

Colombia: hacerse rogar *or del* rogar (Obando, p. 86).

Venezuela: Ella se va a dar sus artes para hacerse rogar (Gallegos, *Doña Bárbara*, p. 315).

Nicaragua: —Vas a darte cuenta ahora ... lo que es un rodeo (Toruño, p. 231).

Mexico: Acuérdate lo que cobran de rédito (Núñez Guzmán, p. 34). ¿No gustan tomar algo? (Inclán, I, 331). —Entonces las acompaño,—declaró generosamente el parásito como si se hiciera rogar (Quevedo, *México marimacho*, p. 43).

SUPERFLUOUS 'DE'

DECIR DE QUE, ETC.

The same confusion which is responsible for the omission of *de* also explains a superfluous *de* commonly used in Spanish America before a *que* clause contrary to correct standard usage, the most conspicuous offenders being *decir*, *avisar*, *aconsejar*, etc. One finds it occasionally in the older language and also in popular and rustic peninsular speech today: "Dijo *de* que vió a la moza" (Sánchez de Badajoz, *Recopilación* [1554], p. 3); "lo que sucede es *de* que ... " (Pereda, *Obras*, VIII, 298). Its preference is possibly based on syntactical rhythm.

Argentina: Volvió ... pa avisarle a doña Cruz *de* que ya había cumplido su encargue y *de* que a la mañana siguiente iban a sacar los cien novillitos (Lynch, *Romance*, p. 247); siempre me ha dicho *de* que tenía que quererlo (p. 382); Él me hizo ver *de* que no había ... quien quisiera comprar (p. 387); —Dijo la médica *de* que debe de estar deshecho por dentro (p. 478). Cuando coligió *de* que todo era verdá, el paisanito recogió sus menesteres (Güiraldes, *Don Segundo*, p. 131). ¿Me aconsejás *de* que me siente en el piano? (*Fray Mocho*, p. 106).

Uruguay: Llegó a suponer ... *de* que ... alguna peste había acabado con todos los hombres del globo (Castelnuovo, in *ACR*, p. 126). Por ello dedujo *de* que se trataba de gente pobre y forastera (Amorím, *La carreta*, p. 12); No era posible *de* que saliesen de aquel atolladero de deudas (p. 15). Sucede *de* que ... (Florencio Sánchez, p. 268).

CHILE: Me creo *de* que no (Acevedo Hernández, *La canción rota*, p. 37). Le escribí *de* que estaba casado con una doctora (Malbrán, *El marido*, p. 4). Le contesté *de* que sí (Román, II, 71). Me creo *de* que sí; Parece *de* que no volverá; De manera *de* que llegó tarde (Vicuña Cifuentes, p. 310, n. 1). For *del que* (=*de que* or *que*), cf. p. 379.

BOLIVIA: Me dijo *de* que vendrá (C).

PERU: Yo le dije *de* que no fuera; ya él sabrá *de* que a Luis nadie le pisaba el poncho (Benvenutto, p. 148). Me da el corazón *de* que no nos hemos de ver hasta el día del juicio (Corrales, p. 58).

ECUADOR: No digo *de* que no (La Cuadra, *Horno*, p. 126); —Ya te hey dicho *de* que sí (p. 178); —Puede *de* que no (p. 195).

COLOMBIA: Aseguran *de* que, opino *de* que, etc. (Flórez, p. 383).

PANAMA: Hará ocho días *de* que vi entrar en la iglesia a una mujer (Espino, p. 145).

NICARAGUA: Dijo *de* que no puede (A. Valle, p. 95).

GUATEMALA: Liberato dijo *de* que te espera (Sandoval, I, 315).

MEXICO: Así es *de* que no puedo ir (C). Resulta *de* que ella no viene (C). —(YUCATAN): Dijo *de* que no era cierto (V. Suárez, p. 156).

CUBA: Opino *de* que, me dijo *de* que, etc. (Padrón).

Just as *de* is today often incorrectly omitted after *acordarse*, so *de* is more often inserted after *recordar* than it is in the standard language. Sometimes *recordar*, by analogy with *acordarse*, is inadvisedly made reflexive and then it is used with *de* by the same persons who correctly omit *de* when they use *recordar* alone.

ARGENTINA: ¿Recuerda *de* la primera conversación que tuvimos? (Carlos Quiroga, p. 133).

CHILE: ¡Con qué entusiasmo recordaba *del* regocijo popular en aquellos buenos entonces! (Muñoz, p. 86).

EL SALVADOR: ¿Cómo no iba a recordarse *de* eso? Perfectamente recordó la repugnante escena (Ambrogi, p. 20). Grité, recordándome *de* aquel individuo rollizo (Ramírez, p. 71).

MEXICO: —¿Es decir, que no recuerdas *de* tu mayor? —Sí, recuerdo *de* él (López y Fuentes, *Campamento*, p. 32); no recuerdo el nombre (p. 36). ¿Recuerdas *de* él? (López y F., *Huasteca*, p. 314).

CUBA: No me recuerdo *de* eso (Padrón).

HACER(SE) DE CUENTA

In many regions *hacer(se) de cuenta* (rarely *hacer de caso*) is current for standard *hacer(se) cuenta*, probably by analogy with other locutions containing *hacer* and *de* (*hacerse de nuevas, hacer de portero, hacerse de rogar*, etc.). It is not a localism (Martín Aldao [p. 86] thought it an Argentinism) but is rather widely used throughout Spanish America even by writers of note, and occasionally in Spain. It has been criticized by grammarians, from Cuervo (§ 411) down. Another locution with an analogical superfluous *de* is *hacerse de la vista gorda* 'to wink at' for standard *hacer(se) la vista gorda. Haber* (or *ser*) *de menester* 'to be necessary' for *haber* (or *ser*) *menester* is apparently almost as common in Spain as in Spanish America.[4]

ARGENTINA: —Si tal os sucede, hijo mío, haréis *de* cuenta que os hicisteis herir, una vez más, en servicio del Rey (Larreta, *La gloria*, p. 174). —Hagan *de* cuenta que está soplando el Zonda [= 'north wind'] (Filloy, p. 468).

URUGUAY: Hacé *de* cuenta que todo ha pasao entre vos y él (Sánchez, *Barranca abajo*, II, 13).

PERU: Hago *de* cuenta que no he aprendido (Benvenutto, p. 148). Pues hagan *de* cuenta que no hay nada de lo dicho (Corrales, p. 204).

COLOMBIA: Haga *de* cuenta un matadero de marranos, un viernes (Arango V., p. 176). Hacerse *de* la vista gorda (Tascón, p. 165).

VENEZUELA: Las autoridades se hacían *de* la vista gorda, pues eran tiempos de cacicazgos (Gallegos, *Doña Bárbara*, p. 24).

PANAMA: —Pus hágase *de* cuenta cómo me puse (Nacho Valdés, *Cuentos*, p. 11).

COSTA RICA: Se hace *de* la vista gorda (Fallas, p. 54).

NICARAGUA: Hagan *de* caso que ya están viendo tranvías, teatros (Chamorro, *Entre dos filos*, p. 263).

GUATEMALA: Para juzgar mis acciones, hay que hacer *de* cuenta que vivía atormentado por mis deudas (Sandoval, I, 605); hacerse uno *de* la vista gorda (I, 610).

MEXICO: Hágase *de* cuenta cómo sucedería (Ramos Duarte, p. 292). Haces *de* cuenta que nada has oído (López y Fuentes, *¡Mi general!* p. 10). Herrera, que le conocía admirablemente, no tenía empacho en hacerse *de* la vista gorda (Magdaleno, p. 294).

SANTO DOMINGO: —Pues hágase *de* cuenta que lo tiene (Bosch, *Dos pesos*, p. 129).

[4] A verb *menestar* 'necesitar' is recorded for Colombia (Tobón, p. 123). For *menester* as a verb cf. Cuervo, § 413; "Cuando más los *menesto*" (Rivera, p. 28).

PARTITIVE 'DE'

The use of *de* to express a partitive force, 'some' or 'some of the,' was current in the old language. In the *Cid* we read: 'prestalde *de* aver" (vs. 118), "no nos darán *del* pan" (vs. 673), "dandos *del* agua" (vs. 2798), etc. According to Keniston (p. 266), the partitive indefinite survived in Spanish prose until the last third of the sixteenth century. However, while not usual today, it still exists in Spain, especially in dialects (Garrote, § 73; Sánchez Sevilla, § 88; etc.); but it is more prevalent in America than in Spain. In the standard language *de* is still frequently used after *dar* with nouns expressing blows or injury caused to the body: *dar de palos* 'to beat,' *dar de patadas* 'to kick,' *dar de bofetadas* 'to slap,' etc. This usage has often been extended in Spanish America to examples displeasing to a Castilian ear, which perceives the *de* as superfluous.

PERU: El rematista vuelve a dar *de* nudazos en la puerta (Barrantes, p. 20).

MEXICO: Seguía pegando *de* gritos (Inclán, I, 175); venía dando *de* bastonazos por el corredor (I, 281); partió también pegando *de* chillidos (I, 363); —Por ahí anda una mujer dando *de* vueltas por la ranchería (II, 38), etc. No había siempre *de* trigo y, por lo tanto, escaseaba el trabajo (Fernando Robles, p. 54). Un teniente que mandaba mi pelotón, me tuvo *de* ojeriza desde que me vió, por huero (Ferretis, *Quijote*, p. 66).

DE PARADO, ETC.

By analogy with certain fixed expressions of manner (*de pie, de prisa*, etc.) and with the standard use of *de* before nouns indicating office or profession (*fué de cónsul, se recibió de maestro*, etc.), occasional usages have developed that are strange to a Castilian ear.

ARGENTINA: Estaba comiendo e priesa y *de* parao (Lynch, *Romance*, p. 252); prefirió no decirle nada a naides y dirse *de* callao no más (p. 298). Estoy mejor *de* parao (Sánchez Gardel, p. 7).

CHILE: Estar *de* ocioso (Román, II, 72).

BOLIVIA: *De* sentado cebó el mozo su vieja escopeta (Arguedas, *Raza*, p. 104).

DE A CABALLO, ETC.

The preposition *de* is often superfluous in colloquial usage with other prepositions,[5] particularly in adverbial phrases: *de a caballo* for

[5] This is sometimes the case in Golden Age writers: "Van *de* por fuerza" (*Don Quijote*, I, 22), etc. Cf. also such primitive use of *de* in the formation of *dentro, debajo, donde*, etc.

a caballo, de a pie for *a pie, de aprisa* for *aprisa, de demás* for *demás, de (a) deveras* for *de veras* (cf. *de a verdad* in Santo Domingo, *BDH*, V, 238), *de adrede* for *adrede, de a* (or *por*) *buenas* for *a buenas, de a* (or *por*) *malas* for *a malas*. *De* is apparently added when the force of the original introductory preposition has become spent. The expression *de a caballo* is correctly applied to soldiers or guards on horseback, as a counterpart to *de a pie* applied to persons who do not use horses: *cien hombres de a caballo y trescientos de a pie;* but standardly one says *ir a caballo* (*a pie*) and not *ir de a caballo* (*de a pie*), that is, when *a caballo* and *a pie* are adverbial phrases of manner.

ARGENTINA: ¡No ves que voy *de* a pie! (Güiraldes, *Don Segundo*, p. 58); El patrón se acercaba a nosotros *de* a caballo (p. 267). El visitante pudo llegar *de* a pie (Yamandú Rodríguez, *Cimarrones*, p. 90). Lo mató la policía ... *de* a traición (Ezquer Zelaya, p. 167). Tomó al caballo de las riendas, y *de* a pie inició camino entre la espesura del monte (Cuti Pereira, p. 31).

URUGUAY: —Voy *de* a pie y me hallo cansado (Castelnuovo, in *ACR*, p. 128). —Aunque *de* a de balde que juese quiero trabajar (Acevedo Díaz, *Soledad*, p. 113). El capataz quiso abrirla [la portera] *de* a caballo (Pérez Petit, p. 71).

CHILE: —Venía *de* a caballo tranquilamente (Prado, *Un juez*, p. 160). Pero ¿cómo huir *de* a pie? (Latorre, *Hombres*, p. 80). Las echaba pal Sur ... *de* a pie (Guzmán Maturana, p. 104). —¿Viene *de* a caballo? (Maluendo, *Los ciegos*, p. 121). Esas versainas son más viejas que andar *de* a pie (Acevedo Hernández, *Árbol viejo*, p. 6).

BOLIVIA: —Estos indios son así. *De* a buenas no te han de obedecer. ... Si no se le trata *de* a malas, el indio se subleva (Cerruto, p. 34).

ECUADOR: —*De* a de veras no quería (La Cuadra, *Los Sangurimas*, p. 16).

COLOMBIA: Venía *de* para arriba, cuando ella iba *de* para abajo; Hágalo *de* por amor de Dios; Si no lo hace *de* por buenas, lo hará *de* por malas; Rompió el vaso *de* adrede; Eso no lo dijo *de* de veras; Ya yo estoy *de* demás aquí (Cuervo, § 383); Despácheme, porque vengo *de* aprisa (§ 385). Bibiana la tomó por *de* su cuenta (Buitrago, p. 16).

VENEZUELA: De aquí para alante puedo irme caminando al píritu, como dicen los llaneros cuando van *de* a pie (Gallegos, *Doña Bárbara*, p. 18).

COSTA RICA: —¡Sea *de* por Dios, qué empeño! (Agüero, p. 40); ¡Eso es querer *de* deberas! (p. 59). Es un hombre *de* de veras (Echeverría, p. 136). Me han dado cuatro reales *de* demás (Gagini, p. 121).

EL SALVADOR: Lo hizo *de* adrede (Salazar García, p. 97).

GUATEMALA: No te perdono el machucón que me diste, porque lo hiciste *de* adrede (Sandoval, I, 310).

MEXICO: Y que ahora sí va la *de* deveras (Madero, II, 6). Tiene un aeroplanito, mano, con motor *de* a deveras (Azuela, *La Marchanta*, p. 14). Usted me dió un quinto *de* demás (Ramos Duarte, p. 556).

DE A POCO, ETC.

An apparently superfluous *de* is found in a related type of expression with *de a: de a poco* for standard *poco a poco* 'little by little'; *de a ratos* for standard *de rato en rato* (or *a ratos*) 'from time to time'; *de a dos* for standard *de dos en dos* 'two by two'; etc. Analogy is evident with expressions like *sello de a dos centavos*, as well as fusion of *de dos* with *dos a dos*, etc. *De a poco* is an old usage. The old *de a uno en uno* is still found in some areas (*BDH*, II, 132).

ARGENTINA: Ahura, cuando le pido alguna cosa, me la sabe dir concediendo *de a* poco, como si juera remedio (Larreta, *El linyera*, p. 27). Déle su primer cuota, *de a* poco, todos los domingos (Mansilla, *Entre-nos*, p. 147). Cuando la vieja lo vió calmado a su hijo, le fué diciendo, *de a* poquito, la cuenta de sus noticias (Draghi Lucero, p. 309). *De a* ratos, cuando calma el viento ... se distingue ... el núcleo principal de la población (Inchauspe, *Allá*, p. 112); el silencio de la casa sólo era turbado, *de a* ratos, por los sollozos de la mujer angustiada (p. 129). Como buen gaucho trabaja *de a* ocasiones no más (Sáenz, p. 102). Don Sixto ... venía dándonos *de a* puchitos ['between cigarette stubs'], datos sobre la estancia (Güiraldes, *Don Segundo*, p. 159); el bicherío le va a arrancar *de a* pellizcos la carne (p. 165); *De a* posturas chicas ['with small stakes'], comprometí setenta pesos (p. 241). *De a (en) uno en uno* (*BDH*, II, 133).

URUGUAY: Emilio subió a la cubierta con los cabellos al aire, el paso largo, *de a* tres peldaños por la escalera (Amorím, in *ACR*, p. 11).

CHILE: Primero comenzó a manosearme *de a* poco, como al descuido (Sepúlveda, *La fábrica*, p. 82). Se exprime el limón firmemente, apretando *de a* poco, lentamente (Sepúlveda, *Camarada*, p. 197). Suelen juntarse, según creo, hasta veinte o treinta, i llegan a la casa *de a* dos o *de a* tres; pero nunca *de a* más (Barros Grez, V, 5). Comiendo *de a* pedacitos la galleta que llevaba en las carteras (Guzmán Maturana, p. 56). Los acumulaba *de a* poco en poco en los Bancos del Pobre (Muñoz, p. 23.)

Santo Domingo: A personas a quienes preguntamos familiarmente cómo pasan la vida, es común oírlas responder: "ahí bregandito," "ahí *de a* poquito" (Jiménez, p. 7); Mientras los novios no se hablan ni se escriben, están "*de a* balazo" (p. 15).

'DE' FOR 'EN'

In some instances *de* not infrequently supplants *en*. Such is the case after the verbs *quedar* and *ocuparse* and after the noun *gusto*. The verb *quedar de* 'to agree on' was used up to the seventeenth century ("todos se abraçaron y quedaron *de* darse noticia de sus sucessos" [*Don Quijote*, I, 47]) but is now archaic in Spain, though still current in America, especially in popular and rustic speech, instead of modern standard *quedar en; ocuparse de* for the older *ocuparse en* is a Gallicism used also in Spain to such an extent that many consider it normal today, although purists may still insist on the literary *ocuparse en*. After the noun *gusto*, the preposition *de* is occasionally found in Spain (cf. Aurelio Espinosa, *Cuentos*, III, 462), but *en* is the preferred standard. A few examples will suffice:

River Plate Region: Quedamos *de* vernos aquí (Sánchez, *La gringa*, II, 5); No te ocupes *de* mí, hijo (IV, 2).

Chile: Ellos quedaron *de* hablar con el padre (Barros Grez, I, 6). —Mucho gusto *de* conocerla (Edwards Bello, *La chica*, p. 66). Se ocupan *de* hacer subir los precios (Sepúlveda, *Camarada*, p. 94).

Ecuador: —Mucho gusto *de* saludarle (García M., *Estampos*, p. 136).

Colombia: Mucho gusto *de* (*en*) verlo; quedaron *de* ... (Flórez).

Costa Rica: —Quedó *de* trelas ayer (Magón, p. 206).

El Salvador: Quedar *de* ir al campo (Salazar García, p. 230).

Guatemala: Pío quedó *de* venir a almorzar con nosotros (Sandoval, II, 302). Quedé *de* ir ... con ella (Arévalo, p. 116).

Mexico: Quedé *de* ir a verte; Quedó *de* pagarme pronto (Ramos Duarte, p. 424). Formalmente quedó *de* venir (Santamaría and Domínguez, *Ensayos*, p. 258). Otros se ocuparon *de* dar agua a los caballos (López y Fuentes, *¡Mi general!* p. 41).

Santo Domingo: *Quedar de* ... se usa poco en la clase culta, mucho en las humildes (*BDH*, V, 70); «quedó *de* venir» (p. 234).

Cuba: Quedó *de* venir; mucho gusto *de* saludarte (Padrón).

Preceptists everywhere call attention to *de balde* when used for standard *en balde* 'in vain.' Standardly *de balde* generally means 'gratis, free of cost,' and *en balde* generally means 'in vain, to no purpose.' It seems natural that such closely related forms should become confused in the popular mind. The confusion is not unknown in Spain. In fact, the latest Academy dictionary has recognized the usage by giving *en balde* (= *en vano*) as one of the meanings of *de balde*. A few examples will suffice.

ARGENTINA: *De balde* quiero moverme:/Aquel indio no me suelta (*Martín Fierro*, p. 184). *De balde* porfió contra la tentación (Draghi Lucero, p. 217).

URUGUAY: —Es *de balde*, uno ya no sirve (Espínola, p. 83).

ECUADOR: *De balde* le busca: ya se fué (Vázquez, p. 63).

'DE' FOR 'Y'

In expressions of time, emphatic phrases with *de* are preferred: *horas de horas* for standard *horas y horas* (= *muchas horas*). Such practice may go back to older usage. Correas (*Vocabulario*) explains that the expression *había gente de gente* signifies *multitud*. This usage is not to be confused with a closely related one: *hay hombres de hombres* 'there are men and men, there are many different kinds of men,' etc., as in: "Hay *casas de casas*, hay casas aonde se puee hacer too" (Acevedo Hernández, *Pedro Urdemalas*, p. 187 [Chile]).

CHILE: Allí se lo pasan *horas de horas*, en sus brujerías (Barros Grez, IV, 11). Inmóviles pasaban *horas de horas* (Prado, *Un juez*, p. 26). No es bueno eso de que un niño esté *horas de horas* solo (Barrios, *El niño*, p. 80). Sabía que ésa era la peña consagrada por "el Palmero" desde hacía *años de años* (D'Halmar, *Pasión*, p. 121).

BOLIVIA: *Horas de horas* pasaba ante su cristal ensayando posturas, sonrisas, gestos (Arguedas, *Vida criolla*, p. 33). Sus acémilas ... resultaban inutilizadas, *meses de meses*, y a veces definitivamente (Arguedas, *Raza*, p. 123); ¿Quieres que nos maten o nos pudramos *años de años* en los calabozos de una cárcel? (p. 163).

VENEZUELA: Se pasaba *horas de horas* en la puerta (Rosenblat).

COSTA RICA: Jugaba *horas de horas* con los niños ajenos (Herrera García, p. 19); Caminaron *horas de horas* (p. 26).

GUATEMALA: Se para delante de las tiendas, viendo *horas de horas* cualquiera baratija (Salomé Gil, *Cuadros*, p. 164). Sale al patio y se está *horas di horas* platicando con él bajo la higuera (Barnoya, p. 22).

CONDITIONAL 'DE' + INFINITIVE

The use of *de* with an infinitive to express condition, particularly contrary to fact, is apparently even commoner in American Spanish than in Spain, where it likewise is rapidly supplanting *a* + inf., the preferred form in the older language: *de haber ido* = *si hubiera ido.* Studies on *de* + inf. have revealed that in peninsular Spanish prose it is found about three times as often as *a* + inf.,[6] and in contemporary Spanish American prose, *de* + inf. is used nearly five times as often as *a* + inf.[7] *De* was first used with an infinitive to express origin. The transition of *de* 'from, out of, because of' to *de* 'if' is found in writers of the sixteenth century, who, however, generally used the preposition *a* for this purpose. By the late nineteenth century the tables had turned in favor of *de*, probably under the steady influence of such basically conditional expressions as *de otro modo*, *de lo contrario*, *(en el) caso de*, *donde no*, *de no*, etc. Because *de* is rapidly ousting *a*, preceptists have inveighed against this *abuso moderno* (Mir, I, 5) and tried to establish sharp and rigid distinctions between cause or derivation (requiring *de*) and condition (requiring *a*) (Mir, I, 507–9; Román, II, 73; etc.). However, *de* + inf. to express condition is so common today even in the best writers that it is futile to condemn it any more than other well-established practices that may not agree with past classical usage.

ARGENTINA: *De* haberme atrevido, la hubiera hecho echar abajo (Güiraldes, *Don Segundo*, p. 315).

CHILE: No me hubiese afeitado hasta el domingo *de* no haberme convidado ustedes (Barrios, *Un perdido*, I, 132); *de* hablarle, ... no tendrían respuesta (II, 54). *De* estar solo, se hubiese lanzado sobre él (Edwards Bello, *El roto*, p. 219).

VENEZUELA: Contestó secamente que él, *de* volver a la capital, sería cuando mandaran los godos (Pocaterra, p. 51).

MEXICO: *De* hallar los tesoros, él disfrutaría de una buena parte (López y Fuentes, *El indio*, p. 46).

OTHER USES OF 'DE'

A few other sporadic uses of *de* attract the observer's attention. Among such are *arroz de leche* heard in a number of Spanish-American

[6] C. E. Kany, "Conditions expressed by Spanish *de* plus infinitive," *Hispania*, XIX (1936), 211–16.

[7] C. E. Kany, "More about conditions expressed by Spanish *de* plus infinitive," *ibid.*, XXII (1939), 165–70.

regions (Mexico, Central America, Colombia) for standard *arroz con leche* 'rice pudding.' Cuervo ("Prólogo" to Gagini) explains it as a fusion: *arroz con leche* + *sopa de leche* > *arroz de leche.* Similarly *café de leche* for *café con leche* (Sundheim, p. 113, etc.). The phrase *irse de con* 'to leave, abandon' was occasionally used in the older language in Spain: "Yo *me fuí de con* mi Nuflo" (Lope de Vega, *La Dorotea,* II, 6); cf. also "nunca se quita *de con* él este verdadero amador" (Teresa de Jesús, *Moradas,* ed. Navarro Tomás, p. 33). But *de con* is rare today (Cuervo, *Dicc.,* II, 297), though examples are found: "la sacaron *de con* sus padres," "hasta *de con* sus padres fueron a buscarle" (Gili y Gaya, p. 220). For Guatemala, Sandoval (I, 712) explains that the phrase *irse de con uno* means "retirarse o separarse del servicio de uno el criado o la criada que se ha ajustado por mes: —Quiero, patrón, que me deje *ir de con usted* a fines del presente mes." Such an application shows considerable restriction of its original meaning.

Other more local or restricted usages may be discovered by consulting local dictionaries.

SUPERFLUOUS 'DESDE'

The preposition *desde* (pop. and rustic *dende,* also *denge* or *dengue* in Cuba, apparently *deje* in Puerto Rico[8]) is correctly used to denote a point of time from which some fact proceeds, originates, or should begin to be counted: *desde hoy lo haré, desde ayer está aquí, desde que llegó,* etc. In some regions of Spanish America, *desde* is used superfluously in sentences like "*desde* el lunes llegó." In the standard language a related construction is possible in a sentence like *desde muy antiguo este pueblo tomó tal carácter,* in which the act as well as its effect began at the time indicated and has continued to the present; that is, *desde* indicates the origin or point of departure. But when the verb expresses a single past act the result of which has no essential bearing on the present, that construction is not possible. However, in *desde ayer llegó* the speaker is thinking of the result of the action; that is, he is psychologically fusing two constructions: *llegó ayer* and *desde ayer está aquí.* This phenomenon seems to have escaped the attention of preceptists and lexicographers.

COLOMBIA: Don Jesús, que ha pernoctado en el camino, llega *desde* temprano (Carrasquilla, *Hace tiempos,* I, 124); Diré *desde* ahora quién es Minos (II, 106); *Desde* antier los traje del Sitio (II, 250).

[8] See *BDH,* V, 147; cf. also *lejos* and *lenjos,* the form rejected by Valdés as an equivalent of *lejos* in *Diálogo de la lengua* (p. 81).

—José Félix se va *desde* [= a] las seis de la mañana para su latonería (Efe Gómez, p. 154). —*Dende* el lunes se jué (Rivera, p. 28).

COSTA RICA: *Desde* el lunes llegó (Cascante, p. 170). Ayer *desde* la mañana salió de su casa (C). —Se rasuró *desde* temprano (Herrera García, p. 28).

GUATEMALA: *Desdi* [= *desde*] ayer te advertí lo que debías hacer hoy (Sandoval, I, 343). El tomo se publicó *desde* abril (C).

MEXICO: Lorenzo, *desde* en la tarde, mandó a Simón una copia del decreto (Inclán, II, 348). ¿*Desde* cuándo salió? (C).

CUBA: —*Denge* [= dende] la última vez que vino del pueblo trajo esa mala costumbre (Luis Felipe Rodríguez, p. 114).

DONDE

The use of *donde* (or *adonde*) as a preposition for *en* (*de, a,* etc.) *casa de* has sometimes been considered a localism. Thus Arona (p. 189) thought it was a purely Peruvian locution until he learned it was used not only elsewhere in America but likewise in Castile (Baralt, 1st ed.; in 2d ed. he remarks "muy común entre la gente vulgar de Castilla"). This elliptical construction (*donde estaba mi tío, donde vivía mi tío* ⟩ *donde mi tío*) may stem from the older period (Hanssen, § 661) and is parallel to the elliptical use of *cuando* in expressions like *cuando niño.* Keniston mentions sixteenth-century examples (pp. 53 and 106) that foreshadow modern *donde.* Today it is found colloquially in certain regions of Spain (as well as among Spanish-speaking Jews in the East): Castile (Baralt, p. 190; Huidobro, p. 78); León and Galicia (Cuervo, § 458); Andalusia (Aurelio Espinosa, *Cuentos*); Aragon and northern Navarre (*BDH*, V, 88); and in the Basque provinces (for Bilbao cf. Arriaga, p. 40), as, for instance, in Baroja's *Zalacaín* (chap. v): "En Estella no vaya usted *donde* el ministro de la guerra." Cf. *BDH*, II, 190.

Because of this respectable background, Cuervo was reluctant to attempt the abolition of *donde* in America: "no es de las cosas que afrentan." Nevertheless, for the sake of conscientious purists he explains that it can be replaced in literary language with *en* (*de, a, por*) *casa de, en la tienda* (*oficina,* etc.) *de,* merely *a* (e.g., *ir al médico*) or *para,* and the like. Other and later preceptists appear to be less kindly disposed toward *donde,* calling it "abuso" (Román, II, 178), "barbarismo" (Huidobro, p. 78; Calcaño, p. 98), "uso vicioso" (Batres, p. 258), "viciosa construcción" (Bonilla Ruano, III, 208), etc.

In general, *donde* is erroneously considered in vogue throughout

Spanish America. It is current in Chile (*lo de* is rustic here), Bolivia, Peru, Ecuador, Colombia, Panama, Central America, and the Caribbean zone; but it is seldom heard in Mexico. In Argentina *lo de* reigns supreme (cf. p. 129).[9] In fact, the use of *donde* there smacks of Chilean speech: an Argentine visitor to Chile remarks on his return, "Yo ya' bía' prendido a decir *puj' hombre, al tiro* y *donde Concha* ... como si fuese oriundo de las orillas del Mapocho" (*Fray Mocho*, p. 134). Elsewhere, in rural regions one hears sporadically also *a* (*en*, *de*) *lo de;* the archaic *a* (*en*, *de*) *ca*(*s*) *de* (as in Spain, and often with *de* omitted and occasionally also with no introductory preposition, *ca* then equaling the French preposition *chez*); *con* in parts of Mexico and elsewhere (as in Andalusia: Toro Gisbert, "Voces," p. 395); *en* locally in Chiloé (Chile); *de* locally in Argentina (under influence of Italian *da;* in Venezuela *casa de* (in Perijá *en qué* < *en casa de*) may mean *donde* (*está*), *con*, *hacia*, etc.; cf. also pp. 129, 347.

Other forms of *donde* and *adonde* are rustic and colloquial: *onde*, *aonde*, and *ande* (rustic generally, but also urban in Bolivia). Henríquez Ureña (*BDH*, V, 61) mentions a restaurant in Bilbao, Spain, called "Ande Lusiano" (cf. Arriaga, p. 40).

ARGENTINA: Se olvidaron de un asao que habían mandado hacer temprano *con* el pulpero (Lynch, *Romance*, p. 88).

CHILE: ¿Ud. no ha vuelto más *donde* la Matilde? (Durand, *Mercedes*, p. 179). Me juí entonces *pa onde* el comisario (Juan del Campo, p. 19); ¿vamos *a onde* «La María Piojo?» (p. 66). (CHILOÉ, POPULAR): Alojé *en* un tío [= en casa de un tío] (Cavada, p. 338). (LOW): Er niño jué *ontá* [= donde está] su paire (Lenz, *La oración*, p. 512 n.; cf. *BDH*, VI, 60, n. 1).

BOLIVIA: Anda cuando quieras *ande* doña Brígida (Arguedas, *Vida criolla*, p. 29); El «Chungara» ha venido *ande* papá a pedirla, pero parece que ella no lo quiere (p. 29). Cf. also examples on p. 130.

PERU: Me acerqué *donde* [= a la oficina de] el director (Corrales, p. 143); —Señorita, no contestan de *donde* [= la casa de] Garazátua (p. 221); el alcalde vino *donde* mí [= donde yo estaba] (p. 240).

ECUADOR: Se refugió a la noche *donde* su querida (Icaza, *Cholos*, p. 221). Nunca más mando a poner medias suelas *donde* [= en la tienda de] usted (García Muñoz, *Estampas*, p. 266). Llegaron *donde* don Carlos (Aguilera Malta, p. 107).

[9] However, *donde* is heard in rural Mendoza (Corominas, p. 99 n.) and possibly elsewhere.

COLOMBIA (ANTIOQUIA): Me mandaba a pedir la limosnita *a cas de* ricos y pobres (Carrasquilla, *Hace tiempos*, I, 17); se había metido ... *en cas de* las Vegas (I, 33); Rosana está *en cas de* doña Resfa (III, 133). (BOGOTÁ): Estuvo *donde* mí; voy *donde* mi tío; salió de *donde* su amiga (Cuervo, § 458).

VENEZUELA: Ahora no vamos a tené ni el recurso de presentanos mañana *caj* el de esta hacienda (Gallegos, *Pobre negro*, p. 332). Fuí *donde* él a hacerme un traje (Gallegos, *La trepadora*, p. 277); la misma a quien encontramos hoy *donde* la modista (p. 291). El padre se encaminaba *donde* míster Danger. ... —No, papá. No vayas *casa de* ese hombre (Gallegos, *Doña Bárbara*, p. 298). Me voltié *pa cas'e* Juan [= volví la cara hacia Juan] (Rosenblat). (PERIJÁ): A un niño, que está con nosotros, se le dice para que vaya con su mamá, que está en la misma sala: «ve *en qué* mamá» (Armellada, p. 192).

PANAMA: Voy *adonde* mi tío (Garay, p. 106). —Yo volví *donde* el patrón (Nacho Valdés, *Sangre criolla*, p. 110).

COSTA RICA: Vino *donde* [= a] mí; fuí *donde el* [= al] juez; vamos *donde* [= a casa de] López; compré esto *donde* [= en la tienda de] Romero (Gagini, p. 127). —Iba ... *onde* un tal Barahona (Fabián Dobles, p. 240); Me vine *pa onde* una tía muy güena (p. 248).

NICARAGUA: Lo he visto . . allá *donde* mamá Sara (Toruño, p. 231).

HONDURAS: La misma señora *en donde* Carlos permanecía, recibía las injusticias del señor Rubio (Mejía Nieto, *Relatos*, p. 10); un sobrinito mío vino asustado *a donde* mí (p. 63). Cf. also p. 130.

EL SALVADOR: Como único recurso visible le quedaba irse *donde* su tía (Torres Arjona, p. 85). Él no está ... *donde* el doctor Sevilla (Mechín, *Candidato*, III, 2). Vamos mejor *onde* la Sebastiana (Ambrogi, p. 15).

GUATEMALA: Voy *a donde* mi hermano Sancho ... es bueno que vengas *a donde* mí [= a mí, a mi casa] ... espero que vengas *a donde* yo (Sandoval, I, 13). Ayer fuimos *onde* Juana/de tarde a tomar el té (Bonilla Ruano, III, 45). Los potreros *de lo de* Bran (in *ACH*, p. 142).

MEXICO (especially YUCATÁN): Voy *con* [= a la tienda de] Nicho. ¿Dónde compraste eso? *Con* [= en la tienda de] don Darío (Ramos Duarte, p. 131). (NUEVO LEÓN): —¿Viene de *en ca'* Tomás? (García Roel, p. 28); ¿Verdá que usté 'stá *en ca'* don Rómulo? (p. 37); ai no más vive *ca'* Lourdes la de Blas (p. 120); se jué ... *a ca'* sus papás (p. 139); vámonos yendo allá pa' *en ca'* Tomás (p. 144). Cf. p. 348.

SANTO DOMINGO: —La conseguiremos barato, *donde* un amigo mío

(Requena, *Los enemigos*, p. 34); estoy trabajando *donde* un turco (p. 59); pensó pasar por *donde* su primo Mario (p. 68).

PUERTO RICO: Vamos *donde* mi hermano (*ap*. Navarro, p. 133).

EN

One encounters many isolated examples of *en* that do not agree with standard usage. Some of these reflect a restricted local habit, but others are individual grammatical errors.

The use of *en* for *a* in phrases of motion like *ir en casa* for *ir a casa* is very old (cf. Hanssen, § 693). In *Don Quijote*, I, 24: "quería ... que los dos nos viniésemos *en* casa de mi padre". Today some erroneously consider it a Gallicism (Baralt, p. 204). It is found both in Spain (cf. *BDH*, V, 71, 234) and in Spanish America. "Juimos *en* ca' don Teodoro" (García Roel, p. 187 [Mexico]); "Tenía que ir *en* [an Italianism here] casa de Testaseca" (Sánchez, *La gringa*, II, 10 [Uruguay]); "—Llego *en* el esamen ... me voy *en* el balneario" (Saldías, pp. 7, 8 [Argentina]). A real Gallicism is the use of *casa en madera* for *casa de madera*, *vestido en lana* for *vestido de lana*, etc.

Occasionally we find *en* wrongly used after verbs: *atar en* for standard *atar a* 'to tie to': "—Decíle ... que me ate el tordillo viejo *en* el birlocho" (Sánchez, *La gringa*, I, 6); *apresurarse en* for standard *apresurarse a:* "Bueno, apresúrate *en* traer a la india" (Icaza, *Huasipungo*, p. 30). Also *en medias* for *a medias:* "¿Y quiere que hagamos *en medias* ese negocio?" (Acevedo H., *Árbol*, p. 14).

En is reported for standard *de* by Ramos Duarte for parts of Mexico: "La finca está *en* venta" (p. 227); "Examinar a uno *en* gramática" (p. 560). The use of *en* after *examinar* is current also in other regions and goes back to an older peninsular usage, which has survived in parts of Spain. Gagini (p. 139) mentions it for Costa Rica; Sandoval (I, 541) remarks: "En Guatemala es tan corriente decir *Me examiné en álgebra*, que nos choca la forma castiza *Me examiné de álgebra*"; so also in the River Plate zone, Venezuela, and elsewhere.

Vázquez (p. 171) mentions the popular use of *en* with an infinitive in Ecuador: "Me fuí, *en* ver [= viendo, por ver] que ya no venía," a survival from the classical period. Benvenutto (p. 150) reports *en fuera* for *fuera* in Peru: "*en fuera* de Lima."

'EN' OMITTED

In the popular speech of many regions *en* is omitted with *ocasión* meaning *vez* 'time' (cf. p. 317) and with a few other nouns used as temporal adverbs (*momento, instante,* etc.): *una ocasión* 'once, on one ocasion'; *algunas ocasiones* 'sometimes'; etc. In such cases the standard language now prefers the preposition *en: en una ocasión,* etc. Originally the preposition *a* was current with such temporal locutions: *a aquella sazón* 'at that time'; and since the *a* in this position coalesces with initial *a* of *aquella,* in ordinary speech one heard only *aquella sazón.* Then the *a* was often suppressed in writing, and the double forms arose. When *en* came to be preferred in such phrases, the older duality was simply continued: *a aquella sazón* and *aquella sazón* ⟩ *en aquella sazón* and *aquella sazón,* etc. The omission of *en* today is influenced also by such expressions as *una vez* 'once,' *ese día* 'on that day,' in which *en* is not used. (For *en* omitted after verbs, cf. p. 4.)

ARGENTINA: *Esa ocasión* eché el resto (*Martín Fierro,* p. 32); Estando allí *una ocasión* (p. 176). Claro, *ocasiones* suceden cosas (Sáenz, p. 7).

URUGUAY: ¿No lo había descubierto él *una siesta* ... ? (Montiel, *Luz mala,* p. 85).

ECUADOR: Dos moscas que pasaban *ese momento* ... cayeron fulminadas (Mata, *Sanagüín,* p. 161). El pueblo da *algunas ocasiones* a este modo adverbial [de repente] el significado de «de vez en cuando» o más bien de «alguna vez» (Tobar, p. 189).

COLOMBIA: Aquel hombre ... lo había visto *varias ocasiones* (Buitrago, p. 136). La vi *varias ocasiones* (Obando, p. 133).

HONDURAS: El dios Pan encontró *cierta ocasión* a una ninfa en el bosque (Zúñiga, p. 21).

EL SALVADOR: Pues bien, *una ocasión,* yo lo aceché y lo pesqué (Mechín, *Brochazos,* p. 112).

MEXICO: *Una ocasión* entró el cura a hacer una de esas consultas (Taracena, p. 11); *Esta ocasión* no le cupo la menor duda (p. 263). Se ganó el cariño de mi chiquilla, que *ocasiones* me causa celos al ver que le hace más mimos que a mí (Inclán, II, 132); *varias ocasiones* le promoví conversación sobre eso (II, 166). Hasta lo interrogó *cierta ocasión* (Gamboa, *Santa,* p. 107); esas cosas no se intentan *dos ocasiones* y si *en* la primera no se mata, se concluyó (p. 212); me lo ha probado *cien ocasiones* (p. 228). *Varias ocasiones* recorro la calle (Benítez, p. 152).

CUBA (RURAL): *Una ocasión* me lo dijo (Padrón).

By confusion with the dual *ocasión* constructions, or as a survival of older usage, we occasionally find *en* with *vez,* as in: *en esta vez* for *esta vez; en veces* for *a (las) veces.*

ECUADOR: *En veces* feliz (Pareja, *Hombres sin tiempo*, p. 63).

PERU: En Alemania predomina la novela histórica, y, *en veces*, la novela de pura imaginación (Federico More, "Prólogo" to Diez-Canseco, *Estampas*, p. 10).

COLOMBIA: *En veces* empalidece (T. González, p. 109).

VENEZUELA: *En veces* ... se pasa de punta a punta el bordoneo de una guitarra (Briceño, p. 7).

NICARAGUA: Pero, *en esta vez*, Gabriel no quiere dar su brazo a torcer (Robleto, p. 90).

GUATEMALA: Si el hombre es listo se encarama a un palo, pero *en veces* ni eso lo salva (Samayoa, in *CLC*, p. 65).

MEXICO: Una cuchara chica tenía que tomarme *en cada vez* (García Roel, p. 50).

ENTRE

The use of *entre* for *en* or *dentro de* is current in the popular speech of practically all regions. In the standard language *entre* means *dentro de* in expressions like *pensé entre mí* 'I thought to myself'; but otherwise it is not so used today, except in some parts of rural Spain: "cogió el pollo y lo engolvió en una toalla y se lo metió *entre* su capa" (Aurelio Espinosa, *Cuentos*, I, 112 [Granada]).

ARGENTINA (TUCUMÁN): Trató de alcanzar el cuchillo que tenía *entre* el recado (Cuti Pereira, p. 20).

URUGUAY: —¡Eso sí; usan un lenguaje *entre* casa, esas señoras decentes! (Florencio Sánchez, p. 27).

COLOMBIA (ANTIOQUIA): Se ponen a apostar a ver cuál aguanta más *entre* el agua (Carrasquilla, *Hace tiempos*, I, 70). (ATLANTIC COAST): Está *entre* el baúl (Sundheim, p. 274). (BOGOTÁ): Usted se queda *entre* el carro (C).

VENEZUELA: Están los del gremio docente *entre* un zapato (Jabino, *Verrugas y lunares*, *ap.* Alvarado, p. 181). El viento suspira «*entre* el frío mármol de una tumba» (*ap.* Calcaño, § 283).

COSTA RICA: El papel está *entre* la gaveta (Gagini, p. 134). Estaba *entre* el saco (Lyra, p. 96); lo metió *entre* un saco (p. 122); ya *entre* poco acabamos (p. 127). Caí *entre* la caldera; quedó *entre* casa (Salesiano, p. 71).

EL SALVADOR: *Entre* un mes vendré a verte (Salazar G., p. 123).

GUATEMALA: Espero que *entre* dos días, a más tardar, me traigas el dinero (Sandoval, I, 492).

MEXICO: *Entre* la obscuridad ... había en una de las paredes un socavón negro en el que no serían encontrados (Ferretis, *Quijote*, p. 42). (YUCATAN): Llegará *entre* una semana (V. Suárez, p. 62).

CUBA (POP.): Se lo metió *entre* el bolsillo (Padrón).

In restricted areas, *entre* is often used for *a* in certain locutions: *entre veces* for *a veces* (Colombia, Panama, Guatemala, etc.); in expressions of time, like *entre las ocho* for *a las ocho* (Ecuador, Chile, etc.). The latter is heard in popular and cultured Ecuadorean speech.

PANAMA: —Yo lo hago *entre* veces (Mangado, p. 93).

GUATEMALA: *Entre* veces voy al cine (Sandoval, I, 492).

ECUADOR: *Entre* las diez de la mañana todo está listo para el viaje (García Muñoz, *Estampas*, p. 21); la otra noche, *entre* eso de las dos de la madrugada, oí un «chivo» feroz en el cuarto de al lado del mío (p. 258). Antonio y yo oímos, *entre* las doce, un ruido en el patio de la hacienda (Vásconez, p. 51).

HASTA

In some parts of Spanish America when the preposition *hasta* + an expression of time is used with a verb in a negative sense, the sign of negation *no* is generally omitted, contrary to correct usage: *hasta las tres iré* = standard *hasta las tres no iré* 'I shall not go until three.' This phenomenon is current in Colombia, Central America, and Mexico, and sporadically elsewhere. It has become firmly intrenched in the language of these regions among all classes. In some areas an attempt is made to restrict it to daily speech and to employ the correct form in elevated and official writing. Elsewhere it finds its way even into serious literary style. (Examples given below will show the nature of the style involved.) Where the anomaly has become deeply imbedded in popular consciousness, it is often extremely difficult for the uninitiated to disentangle the conflicting meanings. Then preceptists go to great lengths to explain the conditions under which *no* should be inserted in correct speech. The error is perfectly obvious, on the other hand, to speakers who are accustomed to the standard form.

Cuervo (§ 447) explains the usage as a blending of two phrases of similar meaning: *a las cuatro llega* + *hasta las cuatro no llega* = *hasta las cuatro llega*. But perhaps the actual process was more complicated than that. It seems probable that other constructions with *hasta* have brought their influence to bear. Today a redundant *no* is often found in the dependent clause after the conjunction *hasta que* when the main verb is negative: *No saldré hasta que no llegue* 'I shall not leave until he arrives.'[10] This usage is probably by analogy with, standard *no saldré mientras no llegue* and appears to have come into wide vogue in the eighteenth and nineteenth centuries. The pleonastic *no*, when actually considered superfluous, is often omitted by certain speakers who, conscious of their classics, feel it to be an intrusive element, perhaps a Gallicism. This hesitancy, whether conscious or subconscious, between the use and the omission of *no* after *hasta que* may well have contributed to its omission in phrases like *hasta las tres iré* for standard *hasta las tres no iré.*

Now the omission of *no* is particularly frequent when '*hasta* + time element' precedes the verb (*hasta las tres iré*) and appears less common when '*hasta* + time element' follows the verb (*iré hasta las tres*). Cuervo implies that in Bogotá '*hasta* + time element' practically always precedes the verb ("Cuando el complemento formado con *hasta* va después del verbo, casi ningún bogotano se equivoca en cuanto al uso del *no: no almorcé* hasta las diez"). However, it is very evident that this is not true of other regions. Of the 40 examples given below (excluding Colombia), 25 cases of *hasta* precede the verb, and 15 cases follow. The fact remains that placing *hasta* before the verb favors the omission of *no*, and very probably this was the position in which *no* was first dropped. This circumstance leads us to the following consideration: the loss of *no* may have been partially aided by a process parallel to that entailing the loss of *no* with certain expressions which, through frequent use in negative sentences, acquired a negative force of their own when preceding the verb, making the *no* unnecessary in this position. In other words, the process involved in *no tengo nada* > *nada tengo, no lo he visto en mi vida* > *en mi vida lo he visto*, etc., may well have influenced *no iré hasta las tres* > *hasta las tres iré* (cf. also *absolutamente*, p. 268).

Again, as suggested by Gagini (p. 156), the omission of *no* may have been favored by the fact that in the speaker's mind the affirmative value of the verb predominates over the negation. For instance, when he says "el tren llegó hasta las ocho," the predominating element is the positive act of the train's arrival, and the fact that the train did *not* arrive sooner is secondary in the speaker's thought.

[10] In fact, this pleonastic *no* has become so common in some regions that it is occasionally used when the main verb is not negative: "Le afeitó el rostro hasta *no* dejárselo azuloso y terso" (Gamboa, *Santa*, p. 194); "bajó sus dos manos ... hasta que *no* toparon con un hombro de la muchacha" (p. 219); "a tu lado me tendrás hasta que *no* nos muramos" (p. 316), etc. "Si Ráices se resiste a firmar el contrato de las acciones hasta tanto [= mientras] *no* obtenga una garantía ... ¿qué remedio me queda?" (Mallea, *Fiesta*, p. 23).

Whatever the influence or combination of influences bearing on *hasta las tres iré* 'I shall not go until three,' the important point is that such expressions are often misinterpreted and may lead to serious complications. For instance, a person who is conscious of both usages will not know whether *hasta las tres como* means 'I eat until three' or 'I don't eat until three.' I recall an experience in a doctor's office in Acapulco, Mexico, where the following conversation took place: —¿Está el doctor? —El doctor no está ahora. Al rato regresa. —¿Estará hasta las ocho? (I asked, meaning 'Will he be in until eight tonight?') —No, llega mucho antes (replied the nurse, who understood *estará hasta las ocho* as meaning '*Won't* he be in until eight?'). On a schoolhouse in another Mexican town I noticed this sign: "Las solicitudes de reinscripción serán recibidas únicamente hasta el 15 de febrero." Curious to know what interpretation was here placed on *hasta,* I inquired at a window inside and was told that February 15 was the last date on which petitions were accepted; that is, the statement was correctly expressed. "However," I remonstrated, "since many students here may well think that petitions are *not* accepted until the 15th of February, how can they be sure?" "They can always come here to the window and inquire," was the prompt and courteous reply.

For Guatemalan usage Bonilla Ruano (III, 156–57) relates in verse more serious dangers involved in omitting the *no* with *hasta:* "Por no intervenir el *no*/cuando *hasta* es continuativo,/más de un perjuicio efectivo/en tal forma se causó:/El médico recetó/a una enferma delicada/darle media cucharada/de un elixir cada día,/*hasta* que él lo indicaría. .../¡Pronto aquélla era finada!/En la mortual de Bolaños/—un rico terrateniente—/hay la cláusula siguiente:/'*Hasta* la edad de ochenta años,/para no irrogarles daños .../entrarán los herederos/a poseer sus dineros. ...'/Y un abogado muy listo/reclamó en el acto el 'pisto' [=dinero]/dejando al tutor 'en cueros.' "

Equivalents are often given for *hasta* used without standard *no,* which, however, seem to circumvent the real difficulty by implying that a simple semantic change in *hasta* is involved rather than an unusual syntactical development. These equivalents are *sólo, únicamente, desde,* etc. Thus Quesada (p. 267) and Santamaría and Domínguez (*Ensayos,* p. 246) explain that *hasta,* which marks the end of an action or state, is often used wrongly to indicate the diametrically opposite, that is, the beginning of an action or state. But this explanation applied to Quesada's illustrative example *hasta ayer llegó la carta* is unsatisfactory. Santamaría diverges even further by calling the phenomenon a simple change of preposition: from *desde* to *hasta*. While the illustrative example ("*hasta* el lunes habrá clases en la escuela") may be rectified by substituting *desde* ("*desde* el lunes habrá clases en la escuela"), the psychological attitude is not thus rendered exactly (the meaning is 'not until Monday,' etc.), nor could *desde* be applied to all cases involving the misuse of *hasta*.

CHILE (CHILOÉ): Nuestro hermano llegó *hasta* hoy. ... ¿Cuándo llegaste? —*Hastesto* [= hasta esto = sólo ahora, en este momento]. The diminutive *hastestito* [= ahorita] is also used (Cavada, p. 346).

VENEZUELA (TÁCHIRA): *Hasta* ahora es que se aparece; *Hasta* ahora es que viene a trabajar (Rosenblat).

COLOMBIA: *Hasta* las cuatro llega; *hasta* las doce almorcé; *hasta* ahora vengo; *hasta* ayer comencé a estudiar (Cuervo, § 447). —¿Y todo el tiempo estuvo arriba? —Que *hasta* ahora veo gente, les digo (Osorio Lizarazo, *El hombre*, p. 197).

COSTA RICA: Cancelaré esa cuenta *hasta* el día primero del mes (Cascante, p. 170). *Hasta* hoy he trabajado aquí (Quesada, p. 267). —Bamonós que ya es muy tarde. —*Hasta* que tome otro trago (Echeverría, p. 147). Yo voy *hasta* después (Fallas, p. 56).

NICARAGUA: —¿Qué me pasó? ¿A mí? Nada. ... Sí. Algo ... *hasta* ahorita me doy cuenta (Orozco, p. 91). Es *hasta* entonces cuando acuden a la mesa de Gabriel los paisanos (Robleto, p. 31). El martillo clava la forma a golpes regulares, y *hasta* entonces Gabriel comprende la naturaleza del trabajo: Vicente está haciendo un ataúd (p. 176).

HONDURAS: Jacinto volvería *hasta* el anochecer, y ella quería que volviese pronto (Martínez Galindo, p. 138). Carlos se dió cuenta de esto *hasta* en cierta época (Mejía Nieto, *Relatos*, p. 10); se ausentó de su cuarto esa vez y regresó *hasta* que estuvo cierta de que Juan había ido a cerrar las ventanas de su cuarto (p. 113).

EL SALVADOR: —Todita la santa noche ha sido un quejido parejo. ... *Hasta* bien noche se jué quedando dormida (Ambrogi, p. 66); *Hasta* entonces la nanita puede articular palabra (p. 79). Me parece que *hasta* ahora está empezando (Torres Arjona, p. 59). *Hasta* mañana pagaré a Ud; *hasta* el año entrante volveré; *hasta* las 3 p.m. sale el tren (Salazar García, p. 150).

GUATEMALA: *Hasta* ahora oigo que «pisto» no es palabra castellana (Salomé Gil, *Cuadros*, p. 103). Hace tres horas que hacemos cola, y llegaremos *hasta* el día de juicio, al paso que vamos (Salomé Gil, *Un viaje*, I, 206). Y como si *hasta* entonces se diera cuenta de que Julián permanece de pie, le dice: —Siéntate, hombre (Quintana, p. 112). Puso mi tarjeta al correo *hasta* en la tarde, porque recuerdo muy bien haberla escrito en la mañana (Guzmán Riore, p. 51).

MEXICO: ¿Quién había de pensar que se volviera tan pronto mi tío, cuando siempre [= nunca] viene *hasta* la madrugada? (Inclán, I, 40); —Siempre me vendré [= de todos modos no vendré] *hasta* la tardecita (p. 43); mi padrino se fué a Orocutín y *hasta* hoy volverá (p. 68; also pp. 106, 253). Era tan feliz, que *hasta* entonces se acordó del ciego (Gamboa, *Santa*, p. 166). Asomaron los fulgores del sol, y *hasta* entonces pudo verse el despeñadero cubierto de gente (Azuela, *Los de abajo*, p. 19); *Hasta* ahora puedo contestar su grata de enero del corriente año debido a que mis atenciones profesionales absorben todo mi tiempo (p. 225). Nosotros tuvimos que tomar un coche porque nos aseguraron que *hasta* mañana correrían de nuevo esos trenes (Azuela, *Las tribulaciones*, p. 84). —Yo lo supe *hasta* hoy en la tarde. ... ¿Y de qué murió? (López y Fuentes, *Cuentos*, p. 225). Mi hermana salió el jueves ... y debía regresar *hasta* mañana (Magdaleno, p. 97). —Yo me voy a descansar una temporada a mi tierra y volveré *hasta* que pase el invierno (Azuela, *La Marchanta*, p. 39).

The perusal of the preceding examples may lead the reader to an interesting observation: the fact that in the northern half of Spanish America (Colombia, Central America, Mexico, etc.) the preposition *hasta* has in many instances usurped a place analogous to that of one meaning of *recién* in the southern half (Argentina, Uruguay, Chile, Bolivia, Peru, and Ecuador). Many of the cases cited above from the northern zones would ring true to the colloquial speech of the southern zones by changing *hasta* to *recién:* northern "*hasta* ayer comencé a estudiar" = southern "*recién* ayer comencé a estudiar"; northern "*hasta* ahorita me doy cuenta" = southern "*recién* ahorita me doy cuenta"; northern "*hasta* entonces Gabriel comprende la naturaleza del trabajo" = southern "*recién* entonces Gabriel comprende la naturaleza del trabajo"; northern "Jacinto volvería *hasta* el anochecer" = southern "Jacinto volvería *recién* al anochecer" (cf. p. 324).

PREPOSITIONS OMITTED BEFORE 'QUE'

Popular speech today frequently omits an introductory preposition before the relative *que* (for the omission of *a*, cf. p. 132), as in the older language (Keniston, p. 210; *BDH*, II, 145). This usage often represents a mere substitution of *que* for *donde, cuando,* etc.; again, it is apparently a type of syntactical dissimilation.

CHILE: El fundo está situado a tres horas de camino del lugar *que* vivo (L). Me fuí a Europa con la familia *que* vivo (Román, IV, 519). Con la tijera *que* tusan los caballos (Prado, *Alsino,* p. 143).

NEW MEXICO: El caballo *que* [= en que] vino; la casa *que* [= adonde] va; el lugar *que* vive (*BDH*, II, 32).

SANTO DOMINGO: Allí lo depositaron en un hoyo ... con la misma ropa *que* murió (Moscoso, p. 167).

XI

CONJUNCTIONS

ACASO

THE adverb *acaso* 'by chance' is, at least in Chile, sometimes colloquially used as a conjunction taking the place of *si* 'if.' Its use is probably due to a fusion of the locutions *por si acaso* or *si por acaso,* in which *acaso* is intimately associated with *si,* and (*en*) *caso que* or *dado caso que,* in which *caso* is an integral part of a compound conjunction with a meaning related to *si* 'if.'

CHILE: —¡*Acaso* quieren, hablo! (Sepúlveda, *La fábrica,* p. 82). —¡Eh! ¡Casero! Dos pesos, casero, caserito. —Sesenta cobres, *acaso* quiere. —Ya, casero (Sepúlveda, *Camarada,* p. 10); —*Acaso* quiere lo ve (p. 11); *Acaso* quiere. ... Si no quiere, pediré la pensión (p. 12).

A LO QUE, LO QUE[1]

These temporal conjunctions, used in colloquial and rustic speech, are equivalent to standard *cuando, al punto que, luego que, apenas,* etc. They are current in the popular speech of a number of Spanish-American regions: *a lo que* in Ecuador, Peru, Colombia, Panama, Central America, Argentina (coastal zone), Venezuela (Andean zone), rare elsewhere; *lo que* in Argentina (center and northwest), Uruguay, Chile, Ecuador, and sporadically elsewhere.

The temporal conjunction *lo que* in the older language meant 'however long' > 'while, during the time that,' etc. (*dure lo que durare*).

[1] For fuller treatment cf. C. E. Kany, "Temporal conjunction *a lo que* and its congeners in American Spanish," *Hispanic Review,* XI (1943), 131–42.

From the early part of the seventeenth century we find examples of *a lo que* 'when, as soon as,' especially in Aragonese writers, and it has therefore generally been considered of Aragonese origin. *A lo que* may be a morphological formation by analogy with such locutions as *al tiempo que, al punto que*. Or it may be a semasiological development from *lo que*, since the preposition *a* placed before an expression of time stresses the end of that period (*a los ocho días*, etc.): *lo que* = 'during the time that'; *a lo que* = 'after the time that, as soon as,' etc. Such a development may have been supported by the form *aluego que*, not uncommon in rustic speech everywhere, and in rapid speech often heard as *alo(go) que*. Then, when *a lo que* was established, it may well have been shortened later to *lo que:* a case of '*a* embebida,' that is, the absorption of *a* into the final *a* of a preceding word ("ahor*a lo que* venga," etc.). Again, *lo que* may be a blending of form and meaning of original *lo que* 'during the time that' and *luego que* 'as soon as,' or of *a lo que* and *luego que*. (On the other hand, original *lo que* may even have evolved into *logo* [*luego*] *que*, rather than the reverse.) A purely semasiological development may be involved from the original standard *lo que:* 'during the period that' > 'at the end of the period that' and 'immediately after the period that.' These are all hypotheses, and the probability is that they are all inextricably interrelated. The resulting duality of forms *a lo que* and *lo que* is supported by the analogy of other double forms, such as *en cuanto* and *cuanto* 'as soon as,' Chilean *en la de no* and *la de no* 'if not,' etc.

ARGENTINA: Aura *a lo que* venga, dígale que me llame (Chiarello, p. 42). *A lo que* lo vió, arremetió contra él (Monner Sans, p. 228). *Lo que* todo quedó escuro/Empezó a verse en apuro (*Martín Fierro*, p. 112). Aura, *lo que* se vea ciego, se descuelga (*Fray Mocho*, p. 91); Aura, *lo que* venga doñ' Amalia, los convidaré (p. 130). Al fin, y *lo que* medio se serenó un poco ... se dió cuenta de que ... (Lynch, *Romance*, p. 330). *Lo que* la noche se puso oscura, hice fuerza para levantarme (Mansilla, *Una excursión*, p. 36). (SAN LUIS): *Lo que* llovió se mejoraron los campos (Vidal, p. 394).

URUGUAY: Me debía unos pesos y *lo que* me vió se acordó de lo que me debía y me los pagó (Sánchez, *Los muertos*, I, 5).

CHILE: —Acuérdeme *a lo que* venga mi señora a dejarme el almuerzo (Juan Modesto Castro, p. 244); *Lo que* llegaron los pacos, era finao (p. 95); *lo que* me divisó, me tendió la mano (p. 231); *lo que* sintió el peso que significaba ser dueño de casa, abandonó a la mujer y al hijo (p. 232). Dijo que vendría *lo que* acabase la misa (D'Halmar, *Lucero*, p. 27). *Lo que* estuvo frente a él, sólo tuvo fuerzas para llorar (J. Espinosa, in *LCC*, p. 330). El conde, *lo que* la vido, a un peñasco se arrimó (Vicuña Cifuentes, p. 64 [Santiago]); *lo que* la vío [= vido], de susto abortó (p. 65 [Talca]); *lo que* lo supo, con el susto malparió (p. 67 [Coquimbo]); *lo que* lo vío, como muerta se cayó (p. 71 [Curicó]).

PERU: *A lo que* me vió, se hizo el desentendido y se fué por el callejón (Benvenutto, p. 150). Y *a lo que* bajé la cabeza, se prendió al pallar de una oreja (Corrales, p. 140).

ECUADOR: Se quedó mustio *a lo que* le vió (Vázquez, p. 31). Les vide *lo que* se metían por el monte (Icaza, *Cholos*, p. 36). —Dejarles, pues. —¿Y *lo que* lloran? (García Muñoz, *Estampas*, p. 240). —¿Piensas que no te estaba viendo *lo que* querías robarte esta linda veta? [= cabestro] (Mata, *Sumag Allpa*, p. 1).

COLOMBIA (ANTIOQUIA): Asina hicieron las negras Aramburos, *a lo que* se vieron quedadas (Carrasquilla, *Hace tiempos*, III, 89). *A lo que* me pagaron el sábado, le dije "Camine" (Posada, p. 64). (BOGOTÁ): *A lo que* salía, lo vi; cójalo *a lo que* asome; *a lo que* [= a medida que] va creciendo, se va empeorando (Cuervo, § 364). (SOUTH): Don Jaime se paseaba en el recinto obscuro ... embadurnándose hasta las rodillas *a lo que* caminaba (Álvarez Garzón, p. 40); me salí corriendo y *a lo que* pasé por el zaguán, la cocinera me dió con una escoba en los lomos (p. 141).

PANAMA: *A lo que* vino mi padre, los ladrones huyeron (Mangado, p. 77). *A lo que* sonó el timbre ... (L. Aguilera, p. 305).

COSTA RICA: Lo vieron *a lo que* se asomó (Gagini, p. 55).

NICARAGUA: *Aloque* di la vuelta me robaron (A. Valle, p. 12).

Sometimes the conjunctions *a lo que* and *lo que* are adversative rather than temporal, meaning *mientras* 'while, whereas.' This we find to be the case in Panama and Mexico, and probably it is so used in other regions.

PANAMA: Soy formal y estudioso *a lo que* mi hermano es desaplicado y peleador (Garay, p. 105).

MEXICO: Todo se hace a base de amigos, *lo que* el dinero, te lo quitan o lo pierdes (Gómez Palacio, p. 8).

In regions where temporal (*a*) *lo que* is not commonly used (Venezuela, Mexico, the Antilles) and also in Central America, we find in popular use the conjunction *en lo que* meaning *al tiempo que* 'while, during the time that, by the time that,' etc. It may be a fusion of *lo que* and *en que* (*en que* is found in Old Spanish; *en lo que* appears later, and survives in parts of Spain [Sánchez Sevilla, § 99]).

VENEZUELA: —¿Y qué decían? —Que *en lo que* mejore se iban para Caracas y no volvían más nunquita (Urbaneja, p. 225). —*En lo que* se supo la cosa en el pueblo, el coronel ... quiso cobrarse al Zancudo (Briceño, p. 64). (*A lo que* is heard in the Andean region.)

NICARAGUA: —Yo voy a levantar la rama parriba, y *en lo que* yo empuje, usté se safa—le dijo tío Buey (*Centro*, I, No. 3, p. 23); Y tío Coyote por de afuera abrió la red y *en lo que* se iba metiendo, el Conejo salió en carrera (p. 21).

EL SALVADOR: *En lo que, a lo que* = al tiempo que, al momento que, cuando (Salazar García, p. 120).

MEXICO: *En lo que* llegué ... eran las once (Galeana, p. 117); Pidió la cena. *En lo que* la traían, me di cuenta que entraba mucha gente (p. 195).

SANTO DOMINGO: *En lo que* me detengo, se me escapa el muchacho (*BDH*, V, § 14). —*En lo que* alisto la cena pueden ir a la casa (Requena, *Camino*, p. 48); —*En lo que* le termino ... (p. 67).

In Colombia we find a rare and curious *a no* (*que*) meaning *luego que, tan luego como:* "Lo cogieron *a no que* salió" (Cuervo, § 365); "*A no que* dormí, soñé contigo" (Uribe, *Dicc.*); (VALLE DEL CAUCA): "*A no* me trajeron el caballo, monté" (Tascón, p. 29). *A no que* may be a blending of *a lo que* and phrases like *no bien* (*llegue*), or, more doubtfully, a fusion of *a lo que* and *a na* (or *nada*) *que* (found in Spain). Spitzer has suggested (in a personal communication) that "*a no que llegue* may be *a lo que llegue* + *no que llegue:* 'whenever he comes' + 'he should not come, even then . . . .'; that is, *a no me trajeron el caballo* may originate in a hypothetical *a no me trajeran el caballo* (= *a lo que me trajeran* + *¡no me trajeran!*)." Calcaño (§ 225) picturesquely described Colombian *a no que* "un disparate vulgar, tan estupendo como el Salto de Tequendama."

The relative neuter pronoun *lo cual* is reported as current in popular and rustic speech in Panama as a temporal conjunction, equivalent to *en cuanto, cuando,* etc.: "*Lo cual* yo lo vide, salí huyendo" (Malaret, *Suplemento*, I, 352; Mangado, p. 101). In Cuba *lo cual* is popular and rustic for concessive *mientras que:* "Yo nunca lo hago, *lo cual* ella sí" (Padrón).

The older form *en bien* has become *ambién* in Arequipa, Peru: "*Ambién* [= luego que] amanezca partiremos" (Mostajo, p. 85). The form *entual* (*untual*) or *entualito* (*untualito*), meaning 'mientras, en el momento,' are used by the populace in some parts of Colombia (Antioquia, Boyacá, Cundinamarca [cf. Tobón, p. 81]).

'LO QUE' FOR 'QUE,' 'EL QUE'

Temporal *lo que* must not be confused with a popular *lo que* found chiefly in Bolivia for standard *que*. The pleonastic *lo* (p. 117) was probably a more potent factor in the genesis of this *lo que* than the natural linguistic tendency of expansion, when a word, particularly a monosyllable, has lost its affective value for the speaker. Since *de* often means *por*, the conjunction *de lo que* may mean *porque*.

BOLIVIA: —¡Que venga, que se convenza con sus mismos ojos *lo que* se ha de ir mi hijo! (Díaz Villamil, *Cuando vuelva*, p. 25); Están tan afligidos *de lo que* te estás yendo (p. 27); *De lo que* me he atajado de mis cosas y *de lo que* he sacado la cara, *de lo que* te lo está botando tu ropa, de eso no más me viene a pegar (p. 69); —Joseso, ¿te acuerdas *lo que*, una vez, por mi causa has sufrido una paliza de tu padre? (*Plebe*, p. 10). —Nos tratan mal ... nos roban ... ¿Será por *lo que* somos indios y no sabemos reclamar? (Leitón, p. 104). —¿Por qué pues mi mama va a ser vieja verde? —¿Y *lo que* [= el que] se muda de ropa cada rato? ¿Y *lo que* [= el que] sólo piensa en pijearse [= emperifollarse]? (Díaz Villamil, *Cuando vuelva*, p. 44).

COLOMBIA (ANTIOQUIA): Olvidados y de *lo que* fuera Corina saltando en pos suya (T. González, p. 147).

In Chile we find *del que* as an expansion of *de que* or *que;* that is, the masculine article introduces the *que* clause (cf. standard *el que* 'the fact that') rather than the neuter *lo*, as in Bolivia. This *del que* is current in popular and rustic Chilean speech and has penetrated "las capas de cultura media" (Pino, § 125): "Les dijeron *del que* [= que] llegaríamos; pensaron *del que* era el enemigo; haga cuenta *del que* [= de que] tal hijo ha tenido; yo a gritos con los soldados *del que* [= para que] avanzásemos" (*ibid.*). For *de que* = *que*, cf. p. 353.

A QUE

The conjunction *a que* was used in the older language to indicate purpose, more commonly expressed by *para que* 'in order that,' but apparently only after verbs of motion (Keniston, p. 388). Today *a que* is still so used in the standard language (Keniston, *Syntax list*, p. 166). In limited regions of Spanish America, particularly in the highlands of Peru and Ecuador, we find *a que* frequently employed when the verb is not one of motion.

PERU: —Paga primero y di tu apellido, *a que* yo sepa quién fué tu padre (Barrantes, p. 31).

ECUADOR (AZUAY): ¡Tengo harta plata para comprar al más pintado abogado de Cuenca *a que* me saque libre! Un doctorcito me ofreció hasta llorar. ¡*A que* vea! (Mata, *Sanagüín*, p. 178); tapémonos con hojas, *a que* no descubran (p. 239); Tomen también, *a que* no les traiga desgracia (p. 249). —Linduritas he de hacer, *a que* veya la niña Techita (Mata, *Sumag Allpa*, p. 3); —Toma, perro, *a que* aprendas a golpiar (p. 10); Dejaron sin nadie *a que* las cuide (p. 13).

Standard *a que* (< *apuesto a que*) 'I'll bet that' at first glance appears to be reduced to *a* in Yucatan, and possibly elsewhere, when the phrase connotes a threat: "*A* se lo digo a tu papá; *A* te doy cinco azotes si no te portas bien" (V. Suárez, p. 61). However, in Yucatan, phrases introduced by *a* sometimes connote a promise, a petition: "*A* te lo doy mañana; ¿*A* se lo dices?; *A* jalas la puerta cuando salgas" (*ibid.*). These examples seem to indicate that the *a* may not be a reduction of *a que* (< *apuesto a que*) but merely a reduced form of *ái* (<*ahí*) with its expletive value as indicated on page 270.

AUNQUE, MANQUE, MÁS QUE

In a restricted area in northern Argentina, the province of Catamarca, *aunque* is reportedly used in popular speech with the sense of *supongo que* or *creo que* (Avellaneda, p. 274). For instance, in asking the name of a person or thing, one might receive this reply: "Pedro *aunque* le llaman" or "Callecita *aunque* le dicen," etc. *Aunque* here introduces a statement of doubt. However, the speaker is not really in doubt, but rather he hesitates to assume the responsibility of a categoric affirmation.

The conjunction *manque* (< *más que*) 'although' is found in the rustic speech of many regions (as well as in Spain) as a survival of the older language, beside *aunque* (rustic *anque*, less frequently *onque*, *enque* [*BDH*, I, 73–76]).

CHILE: —Éste sí qu'es perro, *manque* sea un pichín de perro (Latorre, *Hombres*, p. 70).

PERU: *Manque* le quemen el pico (Diez-Canseco, *Estampas*, p. 168). Hay que hacelo *manque* el mundo se abarraje (López Albújar, *Matalaché*, p. 101).

COLOMBIA (ANTIOQUIA): *Manque* creció tanto, siempre es el mesmo (Carrasquilla, *Hace tiempos*, II, 248). (ATLANTIC COAST): Pa lo que mi pae sembró *manque* no llueva (Revollo; cf. Flórez, p. 384).

VENEZUELA: —*Manque* soy de Buscarruidos, no lo formo antes de tiempo (Gallegos, *Cantaclaro*, p. 307).

MEXICO: —*Manque* no te quejes,/s'está viendo claro (Rivas Larrauri, p. 168).

CUBA: Los tendrá ... *manque* tenga que ir arrastrao (Castellano, p. 41); *Manque* se quée paralítica, dotol, pero que no se me muera (p. 168).

PUERTO RICO: *Manque* nos muramos 'e viejos siempre estamos aprendiendo (Meléndez Muñoz, p. 91).

SANTO DOMINGO: —*Manque* sea dudoso, se llega má pronto (Bosch, *Camino real*, p. 99).

Current in the classics, *más que* (‹ *por más que*) 'although,' which was only one of its meanings,[2] is still registered in the Academy dictionary as in standard use; but its frequency and its social status are apparently lower in Spain today than in many regions of Spanish America, where it is sometimes erroneously considered a localism, and its use criticized. Vázquez (p. 255) reports a frequent play on words employed by purists who ridicule speakers using *más que* 'although': "¿Qué masca usted, cuando dice *más que?*" etc. Sometimes (as in Chile) *nunca* reinforces *más que*. In such cases *nunca* does not indicate negation, as it usually does in Spain in the same locution. Román (III, 448) suggests that the affirmative value of *más que nunca* in Chile developed from the habit of using it alone and ironically in the sense of *poco importa*. This occurred also in Costa Rica (Gagini, p. 178), Mexico (Ramos Duarte, p. 350), and probably elsewhere. In Chile *más que* has also preserved the old meaning of (*apuesto*) *a que*.

CHILE: *Más que* haga frío, las mañanas son siempre despejás (Guzmán Maturana, p. 95). No te hablo más, *más que* me busquí (Romanángel, p. 14). Iré a la fiesta, *más que nunca* llueva (Román, III, 448). He de vengar mis injurias,/ ... *más que* sepa que al infierno/

[2] Cf. S. A. Wofsy, "A note on *más que*," *Romanic Review*, XIX, No. 1 (1928), 41–48; E. H. Templin, "An additional note on *más que*," *Hispania*, XII, No. 2 (1929), 163–70; J. Brooks, "*Más que, mas que* and *mas ¡qué!*" *Hispania*, XVI, No. 1 (1933), 23–34.

voy a pagar mi delito (Vicuña Cifuentes, p. 357). —Lo tengo pensado y *más que* me embrome, lo haré (Alberto Romero, *Perucho González*, p. 121). *¡Más que* [= a que] le doy un palo! (C).

PERU: *Más que* no lo vea, para eso lo hemos de amolar (Gamarra, *Algo del Perú*, p. 81). —Yo he sido soldao, *más que* sea montonero (Ciro Alegría, *El mundo*, p. 224). *Más que* nunca haiga nadao, es capaz e pasar cuatro ríos juntos (Ciro Alegría, *Los perros*, p. 60).

ECUADOR: *Más que* me riña, no callaré (Vázquez, p. 255); Me voy *más que* te enojes. *Más que* te duela, camina (p. 256). —Pues me iría, a dormir *más que* sea en plena montaña (Mata, *Sanagüín*, p. 62).

VENEZUELA: *Más que* nunca vuelva (Picón-Febres, p. 247). —Mire joven: *masque* yo no le conozco ... le voy a dar un consejo (Briceño, p. 97).

COSTA RICA: Me embarcaré, *más que* me ahogue (Gagini, p. 178). —¡Dale duro por la trompa! ¡Por la pansa, *más que* sea! (Agüero, p. 62); yo le hablo *más que* me muera (p. 69).

MEXICO: Si no hay vino, *más que* sea agua tomaremos (Santamaría, *Dicc.*, II, 251).

In limited rural regions, including Venezuela (Andes) and Chile (Chiloé), concession is sometimes expressed by *ojalá* (or *ojála*, in Colombia also *ajualá, aojalá*) and the subjunctive. Garzón (p. 338) suggested that this usage may possibly stem from the interjection *¡ojalá!* as a threat, followed by the expression of an adversative idea: "¡Ojalá no llueva! (con todo *o* no obstante) hemos de sembrar." Later this *¡ojalá!* may have lost its force as an interjection and, because of a certain rural intonation, also its final stress: *ojalá* > *ojála*. Possibly the concessive force developed from the wish, as it did with *así*. (The penultimate stress [*ojála*] is common elsewhere: Chile [Román, IV, 63]; parts of Mexico and Guatemala [Sandoval, II, 166]; etc.). *Ojalá* in the sense of *aunque* is occasionally found in the classics: "*¡Ojalá* supiera que me había de condenar, que no hubiera cansádome en hacer buenas obras!" (Quevedo, *El sueño de las calaveras*).

ARGENTINA (NORTHWEST): Me voy *ojála* venga (Vidal, p. 195). *Ojála* no llueva, hemos de sembrar (Garzón, p. 338).

BOLIVIA: *Ojalá* le recuerde [= aunque le despierte] nunca se ha de levantar (Bayo, p. 178).

COLOMBIA (ATLANTIC COAST): No haré tal cosa *ojalá* me maten (Revollo, p. 189).

CADA QUE

The temporal conjunction *cada que* 'every time that, whenever,' was current in the fourteenth century (*Libro de buen amor:* "syempre me fallo mal, *cada que* te escucho" [c. 246*d*]) and to some extent in the fifteenth ("*cada que* me mienbro de qual guisa fiere" in *Cancionero de Baena* [*ca.* 1445; 1851 ed., p. 39]). In the sixteenth century it evidently became a popular or rustic form. About 1535, Valdés (p. 104) reports: "*cada que*, por *siempre*, dizen algunos, pero no lo tengo por bueno." Keniston (p. 360) found no example of the actual use of *cada que* in sixteenth-century prose, nor did Quirarte (*Inv. ling.*, I, 168). It has survived in popular and rustic speech not only in Spain but with special vigor in many regions of Spanish America. Beside *cada que* is found *cada y cuando* (*que*), current in the classics.

ARGENTINA: Pero *cada que* el viejo ese se mete en las cosas, ya arma algún enriedo (Lynch, *Romance*, p. 381).

PARAGUAY: *Cada que* llueve, me ataca el reumatismo (Morínigo).

CHILE: Dende entonce el toro salía a cumplir la misión ... *caa y cuando* sentía que las vacas reclamaban su servicio (Guzmán Maturana, p. 130).

BOLIVIA: *Cada que* le veo así (Díaz Villamil, *Plebe*, p. 80).

PERU: *Cada que* viene provoca pleito (Benvenutto, p. 151).

ECUADOR: *Cada que* llegaba Sandoval la encontraba vestida con blanca tela vaporosa (Gil Gilbert, *Nuestro pan*, p. 131).

COLOMBIA (ANTIOQUIA): Desnuqué la gallinita que les mato *cada que* vienen (Carrasquilla, *Hace tiempos*, I, 179); *Cada que* vienen, prenden las casas (I, 182). (SOUTH): Andrés *cada que* encontraba a Alegría le hablaba con los ojos más que con los labios (Álvarez Garzón, p. 77). (TOLIMA): *Cada que* voy (Flórez, p. 384).

MEXICO (NUEVO LEÓN): «¿Qué tal te sientes?» me preguntaba él *cada qu'* iba (García Roel, p. 185); nos íbanos hasta el pueblo *cada que* podíamos (p. 186); Que *cada que* ella le reclamaba, él se lo hacía ver (p. 200). (GUERRERO): *Cada que* estoy triste te ricuerdo muncho (García Jiménez, p. 33). (For Nochistlán, see *Inv. ling.*, I, 168.)

COMO QUE

The locution *como que* expressing probability ("*como que* quiere llover") or attenuation ("*como que* me voy" = a softened form of 'me voy') has been variously explained.[3] In the older language *como*

[3] See esp. Cuervo, *Dicc.*, II, 238; L. Spitzer, *Aufsätze*, pp. 95–101; Amado Alonso, "Español *como que* y *cómo que*," in *RFE*, XII (1925), 133–56.

alone was used in this sense; then *que* was added as a kind of expletive article. In many cases *como que* seems to be an ellipsis of *parece como que*, but generally the *como que* is a mere formula that has gradually become extended, perhaps by analogy with *como si*, though the nature of *como que* is expositive and that of *como si* is conditional. The expression is heard in Spain as well as in Spanish America, but its use is apparently much greater in some Spanish-American zones, where the observer may hear extensions of it not familiar to the Castilian ear.

PERU: Les alvertiré quial puma *como que* [= parece que] lo vide azuliar (Ciro Alegría, *La serpiente*, p. 162).

ECUADOR: —*Como que* don Antonio anda *atrás* de la ingenierita (Ortiz, p. 91).

COLOMBIA: —Parece que se acerca. —Sí, *como que* [= parece que] llega—replicó el coro artístico (Restrepo Jaramillo, p. 201). —Y el mocito de El Chorro Blanco también *como que* tuvo mal fin; ¿no supo, ña Melchorita? (Carrasquilla, *Hace tiempos*, I, 208); —Usted *como que* es muy leído, señor Hernández. —Un poco, señor cura (I, 306). *Como que* me voy [= a softened 'me voy'] (C). (Cf. Flórez, p. 384.)

VENEZUELA: —Pero *como que* es un poco alocada. ... Por lo pronto, silencio *como que* no va a haber mucho en esta casa de ahora en adelante (Gallegos, *La trepadora*, p. 242); usté *como que* hace mal en dejá que su hija ande sola por esos caminos de montes (p. 219). ¿*Como que* hay pan fresco, Simón? (Croce, p. 22). Oiga, amiguito, ¿usted *como que* se imagina que el whisky se va a acabar en el mundo? (Certad, I). —Ya Melquíades *como que* está perdiendo los libros (Gallegos, *Doña Bárbara*, p. 98). —A doña Bárbara *como que* le robaron sus reales (p. 123); —Allá *como que* viene uno (p. 174); Algo de eso *como que* he oído mentar por ahí (p. 302).

GUATEMALA: *Como que* tocan el zaguán: anda a ver quién es (Sandoval, I, 205).

MEXICO (NUEVO LEÓN): *Como que* obscurecía de prisa (García Roel, p. 140); Al atardecer ... el río pareció querer ensancharse. *Como que* redoblaba sus bramidos; *como que* sus advertencias se tornaban más terminantes (p. 145); *Como que* se oye un caballo. —Sí, por ai viene alguien (p. 149); el río *como que* se reía con descaramiento (p. 156); dizque la panza *como que* le iba creciendo (p. 193); el espectro del hambre dejó de hacer visajes. *Como que* se despintaba (p. 286).

SANTO DOMINGO: *Como que* quiere llover (*BDH*, V, 240). —*Como que* viene de lejos—susurró (Bosch, *Dos pesos*, p. 56). *Como que* sabe a limón (Jiménez, p. 67).

COSA QUE

The conjunction *cosa que* is currently used in most regions of Spanish America to express purpose or result, with the equivalence of standard *para que, de modo que, de suerte que, de tal manera que, hasta tal punto o grado que, a fin de que*, etc. It is not rare in the classics. Lope de Vega was especially fond of the locution, to judge from the abundant use he made of it (*BAE*, XXIV, 118*b*, 134*a;* Academy ed., IX, 102*a*, 105*b*, 116*b;* New Academy ed., I, 151*a;* II, 86*b*, 108*a;* III, 224*a*, 579*b;* IV, 455*b;* V, 684*a;* etc.). Surprisingly, it is not recorded by Keniston. A number of Lope's examples admit the meaning of *para que*, as one in *Peribáñez* (III, 8): "(Luján): —¿Qué señas ha de llevar? (Comendador): —Unos músicos que canten. (Luján): —*¿Cosa que* la caza espanten?" Editors Hill and Harlan (*Cuatro comedias* [1941], p. 169) interpret *cosa que* here as 'Is it likely that? Isn't it possible that?' But simple *para que* fits more easily. In some other Lope passages the meanings suggested by the same editors seem necessary: 'I'll wager, maybe, perhaps, what if . . . . '; etc. Strangely enough, 'in order that, so that,' etc., are not included in these meanings. (For intrusive *de* in *cosa de que* cf. p. 353.)

Argentina: Terminá y venite, *cosa que* yo te encuentre cuando vuelva (Vidal, p. 399).

Uruguay: —Metéle talón, *cosa 'e* [= cosa de] *qu'*el día no nos agarre ajuera 'el monte (Espínola, p. 74).

Chile: Vente temprano, *cosa que* no faltes a la reunión; Trabaja en la juventud, *cosa que* ahorres para la vejez (Román, I, 441). —Aquí hay que apretar fuerte, compañero. *Cosa que* la novia se maltrate a fin de que Arriagada después no se vea tan afligido (Durand, *Mercedes*, p. 140).

Ecuador: *Cosa que* [= de modo que] caí (Mateus, p. 73). —Anoche a un pobre borracho que había estado gritando contra el Mono, no le shevaron dándole palo, *cosa que* gritaba, de dar lástima (Icaza, *En las calles*, p. 233). —Lindos para hacer, amo mayordomito. —*Cosa de que* agradezcan a Ud. (Mata, *Sumag Allpa*, p. 3).

Peru: *Cosa que* nunca sanara (*ap*. Benvenutto, p. 151).

Colombia: —Déle duro *cosa* (*de*) *que* le duela, *cosa* (*de*) *que* coja vergüenza (Flórez, p. 384).

VENEZUELA: Prevéngalo todo bien, *cosa que* no se pierda un instante (Alvarado, p. 131).

EL SALVADOR: *Cosa que* [= para que, a fin de que, a efecto de que] así se arregle todo (Salazar García, p. 73).

GUATEMALA: Te espero mañana a las doce, *cosa que* almorcemos juntos (Sandoval, I, 229).

CUBA: Cierra bien la puerta, *cosa que* no entre el viento (Padrón).

CON ESO

Another curious conjunction of purpose is the familiar locution *con eso*. It is recorded for Chile as an equivalent of *a fin de que, con el objeto de que* (Zorobabel Rodríguez, p. 117), *para que, a fin de que* (Román, I, 390); for Mexico as *a fin de que, para que, de esa manera* (Icazbalceta, p. 200); and it is found elsewhere. It is a slightly distorted application of standard *con eso* 'with that, by that means, in that way,' the determining difference being chiefly one of intonation. For instance, in the example "date prisa, *con eso* podemos ir al teatro," the pause before *con eso* is so short that a comma suffices to indicate it, and the clause becomes dependent, *con eso* being equivalent to *para que* or *con el fin de que:* 'Hurry up, so we'll be able to go to the show.' The standard use of *con eso* might be "date prisa; *con eso* podemos ir al teatro," where the pause before *con eso*, being longer, is indicated by a semicolon, and the second clause is independent: 'hurry up; *in that way* we'll be able to go to the show.'

While *con eso* may appear to mean 'if you do as I say' or 'having done that,' etc., it is apparently felt as a conjunction of purpose by its users, who prefer it precisely for the reason that it obviates the necessity of the subjunctive, which is never the case with *para que* or any other standard conjunction of purpose.

CHILE: Cuando te desocupes de barrer el patio, lávate las manos i ven, *con eso* peinas a las niñitas; Levántate, hijita i ponte el más alegre vestido que tengas, *con eso* vamos a pasear juntos (Zorobabel Rodríguez, p. 117). Vente luego, *con eso* vamos al comercio (Román, I, 390). —¡Levántate guachito, *con eso* vamos a componer el cuerpo! (Durand, *Tierra*, p. 47).

COLOMBIA: Váyase ya, *con eso* vuelve temprano (Flórez, p. 384).

VENEZUELA: Vente a almorzar, *con eso* te cuento una cosa (Rosenblat).

GUATEMALA: ¿Quiere Ud. pasar por mí *con eso* nos vamos juntos?

No me gusta caminar solo y no tener con quién charlar un poco por el camino (Salomé Gil, *Cuadros*, IV, 64).

MEXICO: Ven temprano ... *con eso* tienes tiempo de peinar a las niñas (Icazbalceta, p. 200).

CUBA: Ven esta noche por aquí, *con eso* me ayudas (Padrón).

DEQUE, DESQUE

These temporal conjunctions are sometimes written as one word in accordance with the Academy dictionary, and sometimes as two. *Deque* is defined as a familiar "adverb" of time meaning *después que, luego que; desque* as an archaic "adverb" of time, still used in poetry and by the populace, meaning *desde que, luego que, así que*. They are both conjunctions, however, and not adverbs; and they are often causal as well as temporal. *Deque* goes back to the *Cid* and was used in literary style through the Golden Age. Today it remains in popular usage in Spain (Spaulding, *How Spanish grew*, p. 133; Aurelio Espinosa, *Cuentos*, II, 200) and in regions of Spanish America. In Chile *en de que* is a current rustic form, the *en* by analogy with *en la de no, endespués, endenantes*, etc. *Desque* is equally as old as *deque*. By the sixteenth century it had lost much of its social status: about 1535, Valdés (p. 105) remarks that "Algunos escriven *desque*, por *quando*, diziendo *desque vais* por dezir *quando vais*, pero es mal hablar."

ARGENTINA (CATAMARCA): *Deque* por «desde que,» «toda vez que,» «dando por cierto que ... » (Avellaneda, p. 307). (SAN LUIS): Te quiero *de que* te conocí, etc. (Vidal, p. 405).

CHILE (CENTRAL ZONE): *En de que* llegó, se los [mostachos] llevaba atusando todo el tiempo (Muñoz, p. 11). (CARAHUE): *En de que* ve la vara/echa a correr asustao (Laval, I, 118). (CENTRAL ZONE): Blanca Flor, *de que* la vido,/del susto se desmayó (Vicuña Cifuentes, p. 60); Blanca Flor, *des que* la vío,/con el susto malparió (p. 62).

ECUADOR: —¿Cuándo vendré? —*De que* te llame; —*De que* vió aquello, ya se resolvió; *De que* empieces la lectura, no soltarás el libro (Vázquez, p. 137). —*De que* ya firmó el pacto malo, ño Sangurima podía hablar con los muertos (La Cuadra, *Los Sangurimas*, p. 25); —*De que* me muera, no voy a fregar a naidien con apuros (p. 29); —*De que* tomes tu agua caliente, irás al pueblo con un recado (p. 154).

COLOMBIA (ANTIOQUIA): *Desque* vi tus ojos negros/No quiero quedarme solo (Antonio Restrepo, p. 326).

Mexico: *De que* a mí me cuadra un guiso, como, como, hasta que lo eructo (Azuela, *Los de abajo*, p. 74).

Cuba: *Dehque* le entraron lah calenturah hase ocho díah, no pue casi ni comel (Ciro Espinosa, p. 403).

Santo Domingo: *Desque* a la fosa descendió mi ídolo (Enrique Henríquez [1893], *ap. BDH*, V, 94).

DESDE QUE

The standard conjunction *desde que* 'since' is exclusively temporal. The temporal meaning has, reportedly under the initial influence of French *dès que*, come to assume also a causal force standardly expressed by *ya que*, *puesto que*, or *siendo así que*. This semasiological change is evident to a limited extent in Spain itself (Mir, I, 579) and much more so in regions of Spanish America and among all classes (rustic: *dende que*). Américo Castro (p. 153) assumes that Argentine *desde que* owes its causal force to the Portuguese. This is not wholly accurate, for we find causal *desde que* in countries remote from Brazil. It seems more probable that causal *desde que* was first a Gallicism (as found in Spain) but that its greater currency in Spanish America, particularly in Argentina, is due in part to Portuguese causal *desde que*, for the frequency of causal *desde que* diminishes with the distance from Brazil: River Plate region, Chile, Bolivia, Peru. On the other hand, the causal force may well have developed spontaneously from the temporal force (as it apparently did in English: causal *since* < temporal *since*). The starting-point may have been sentences in the present tense like *Desde que Dios habla, es necesario creer*, which are still susceptible of two interpretations, one temporal and the other causal.

Argentina: Y *dende que* todos cantan/Yo también quiero cantar (*Martín Fierro*, p. 10). ¡Pero *desde que* no hay otro remedio, qué se va a hacer! (Laferrère, *Las de Barranco*, p. 30). Los italianos apresuran el envío de refuerzos ... *desde que*, probablemente, el general ... no permitirá que se retrasen las operaciones (*La Nación*, November 24, 1940). Creemos innecesario comentar mayormente la significación del acto, *desde que* transcribimos en otro lado los discursos que allí se pronunciaron (*BAFA*, I [1939], 45). Nadie podrá desconocer que aporta un eufemismo tanto más valioso, *desde que* difícilmente se hallarán términos que puedan reemplazarlo (Selva, p. 106). No se puede suponer ... máxime *desde que* se trata de una lengua muy grata al oído (Selva, *El castellano*, p. 29).

URUGUAY: El hombre no tuvo reparo en ello *desde que*, sin la colaboración del comisario, sería imposible vengarse (Amorím, *La carreta*, p. 39). *Desde que* se paga, no hay mancha (Sánchez, *M'hijo el dotor*, I, 11). Estarías en tu derecho, *desde que* sos el marido (Sánchez, *Los muertos*, I, 7).

CHILE: *Desde que* tú no me cumples lo prometido, yo tampoco te doy lo que te ofrecí (Román, II, 105). *Desde que* no tenemos aquí nuestros caballos, no podemos ponernos en camino (Barros Grez, I, 44); *desde que* él pidió la confesión, debemos creer que nada ha ocultado (I, 108).

BOLIVIA: —Y así ha de ser no más, *desde que* no hay quien lo ventee (Flores Hurtado, in *ACB*, p. 65).

PERU: —Pero ¡qué vamos a hacer! *desde que* necesitamos que nos presten, no hay más que convidarlas (Gamarra, *Rasgos de pluma*, p. 77). No sé por qué, *desde que* no había pensado en que ... (Corrales, p. 246).

COLOMBIA: *Desde que* Ud. no conviene en ello, me retiro (Sundheim, p. 227).

In Colombia (especially Antioquia) we find a *desde que*, followed by the subjunctive, with the conditional force of 'if, provided that,' etc.; elsewhere, as on the Atlantic coast of Colombia, it often means *cuando, así que, en cuanto*, etc., a usage not unknown in Spain.

COLOMBIA (ANTIOQUIA): ¿Cómo le va pareciendo esto, misiá Rosita? ¿Se irá a aburrir mucho? —*Desde que* no nos enfermemos, creo que no me aburro (Carrasquilla, *Hace tiempos*, I, 68); Berrío es muy bueno, pero *desde que* no vuelva a traer a los jesuitas no se acaba la semilla que sembró Mosquera (II, 129); —Con ella hablaría y creo que nos entenderíamos, *desde que* no intervenga Martina (III, 20). (ATLANTIC COAST): *Desde que* venga se lo digo [= *cuando* venga, *así que* venga o *en cuanto* venga, se lo digo] (Sundheim, p. 227). *Desde que* [= si] las cosas estén así, prefiero no tocar el tema (Roberto Restrepo, p. 189).

DONDE, DEJANTE (QUE)

Old Spanish *onde* derived from Latin *ŭnde* and meant 'from where.' Later, when *onde* had changed in meaning from 'whence' to stationary 'where,' it was necessary to prefix *de* when the original sense of 'from where' was required. Consequently, *donde* contains a repetition of the idea of separation. Nevertheless, *donde,* in turn, acquired stationary force, changing in meaning from 'whence' to 'where'; and today one triples the separation idea in the phrase *de donde* 'from where' (< *de* + *de* + *ŭnde* 'from + from + from where'). The old *dónde* (or popular and rustic *ónde,* which may be a retention of the archaic form or a later development from *dónde* with loss of initial *d*) 'from where' has survived in certain interrogative and exclamatory sentences in parts of Spain and especially in America. In these cases *dónde* is generally interpreted as meaning *cómo* (less often *cuándo*); then it is a conjunctive adverb of manner. Such a transfer is not necessary if the original *dónde* (= *de dónde*) is kept in mind. A few examples will suffice. (For exclamatory *dónde,* cf. also p. 409.)

ECUADOR: *¿Dónde* [= de dónde] sabes que eso es cierto? —Porque lo he visto (Vázquez, p. 149). (For *quiersde* [= *dónde*] in the sense of *cómo,* cf. p. 260.)

COLOMBIA: *¡Dónde* me iba yo a figurar que no me pagarían! (Sundheim, p. 248).

GUATEMALA: Si una persona es invitada para contribuir a los gastos de una fiesta y no dispone de fondos, contesta: «*¡Ónde!* [= ¡cómo! ¡imposible!] si no tengo dinero» (Sandoval, II, 171). *¿Dónde* me iba yo a imaginar? (Batres, p. 259).

MEXICO: Cuando lo vi *¿dónde* iba a figurarme que estaba para morirse (Icazbalceta, p. 181). *¡Ónde* me 'biera pasao si vivo cerca de don Teodoro! (García Roel, p. 191). *¿Dónde* lo sabes? (Ramos Duarte, p. 215).

SANTO DOMINGO: *¡Dónde* había de olvidarlo! (*BDH*, V, 178).

An extension of this force of *dónde* we meet in Chile, where it undeniably expresses manner; that is, *donde* here is commonly used for *como* 'since, as.' Examples do not abound elsewhere with exactly the same meaning. Román (II, 177) thinks to trace the usage to the preclassic period, that is, contemporaneous with the *conquistadores,* who, he believes, must have brought it to America; but the one example he cites (from the *Libro de buen amor,* c. 305) is not wholly convincing.

CHILE: *Donde* [= como] no tomé el desayuno, no me siento bien (C). —Me dió susto *donde* [= como] no te encontré (Juan Modesto Castro, p. 277). *Donde* [= como] me mojé tanto, me vino una enfermedad; Pedro ha perdido la salud, *donde* [= como] trasnochaba tanto (Román, II, 177). *Donde* [= como] ya no podían más de cansados, se bajaron en aquella montaña (Vicuña Cifuentes, p. 510).

Of greater geographical distribution is the use of *donde* to express time (*cuando, en cuanto*), condition (*si*), and occasionally some other relationship (see examples). In Old Spanish (Hanssen, § 661) and in popular and rustic speech today, *donde* is found for *cuando* (*Cid*, vs. 1516: "*Don* llegan los otros, a Minaya se van homillar"); its temporal value probably evolved from its use as a relative (*tiempo donde, día donde*, etc.). In addition, *donde* was used in the Golden Age with the force of *si* (Keniston, p. 400). These older usages have survived in rural Spain (Aurelio Espinosa, *Cuentos*, II, 212) and with seemingly greater vigor in Spanish America. Conditional *donde* must have been influenced by the elliptical phrase *donde no*, which was widely used in the sense of *en caso que no* or *de lo contrario* (see examples in Cuervo, *Dicc.*, II, 1321*f*).

CHILE: Yo iba muy tranquilo, *donde* [= cuando] el caballo se espantó y me echó al suelo. Me entretuve conversando, *donde* [= por lo que] se me pasó la hora y perdí el tren. Me dió Juan un remedio, *donde* [= y] me hizo tanto mal, que por na no me morí (Vicuña Cifuentes, p. 344, n. 3).

ECUADOR: Es mi hijo. *Donde* [= si, en cuanto] le toques un pelo, te rajo (Diez-Canseco, *Baldomera*, p. 111). ¡Y *donde* [= si, en cuanto] intenten sacar las armas ... cuídense, señores! (Mata, *Sanagüín*, p. 111).

VENEZUELA (ANDES, GUAYANA): —Tenía un peso y lo gasté, *adonde* [= por lo cual] me quedé limpio (Rosenblat).

COSTA RICA: Y *onde* [= cuando] tueso, siento un chuso/debajo de este sobaco (Echeverría, p. 164). *Donde* [= cuando] dijo que sí, retumbó la casa (Lyra, p. 39); ¡ya le parecía oír los chiflidos de la gente *donde* [= cuando] vieran salir de la carreta una mica! (p. 47).

EL SALVADOR: *Donde* [= cuando] vuelvas, te diré (Salazar García, p. 111).

GUATEMALA: *Donde* [= cuando] supe tal cosa, no lo hice. *Donde* vengas a verme, te daré una agradable sorpresa (Sandoval, I, 423).

MEXICO: *Adonde* [= si, en caso que] este muchacho no vuelva, ciertos son los toros de estar complicado en ese asunto (Inclán, I, 46); *adonde* [= si, en caso que] me salga bien, creo que cortamos a raíz todos los males (I, 60). —No me diga 'sté esas cosas,/porqui *onde*

[= si, en caso que] me lo repita,/va 'sti a hacer que me ricuerde/de la hermana de su tía (Rivas Larrauri, p. 23).

CUBA: *Donde* [= si, en cuanto, en el momento que] se descuide; *donde* [= si, cuando] se saque la lotería (Macías, p. 475).

SANTO DOMINGO: Tenía yo un peso y cometí la torpeza de gastarlo; *adonde* [= por lo cual] hoy carezco hasta de cigarrillos (Patín Maceo, *Dom.*, p. 8).

Just as *donde* for *como* is most prevalent in Chile, so in Mexico we find a usage apparently not known elsewhere. Both Icazbalceta (p. 181) and Santamaría (*Dicc.*, I, 581) mention a *donde* current among the Mexican populace in the sense of *ahí tiene usted* or *además de eso*. Examples cited by Icazbalceta are: "Yo no sé si nos debíamos ir, decía una fregatriz ... *onde* que ha fregado una todo el día, que todos mis trapos los tengo empapados" (Facundo, *Baile y cochino*, chap. vii). —"¡Qué calor! ¿no, mialmas? No hay gota de sombra. ... *Donde*, que vengo desde lejísimos. ... *Donde* que después tuve que ir al Sagrario" (Micrós, *Ocios y apuntes*, pp. 79, 80). It is apparent that this usage is closely allied to the Chilean: the sense of the first example is completely satisfactory, assuming that *onde* = *como;* the second example diverges somewhat. The structural difference in the Mexican idiom is the use of *que* with *onde* or *donde*, where it is not so used in Chile, and the fact that *donde que* does not introduce the essential dependent causal phrase but rather a nonrestrictive clause, an explanatory afterthought.

The meaning of *además de* associated with *donde* in Mexico we find inherent in another expression generally restricted to popular and rustic speech in some localities: the strange *dejante* (*que*) or, as it is often pronounced, *ejante* (*que*), more usually heard with *que*, as a conjunction. In Colombian usage *no* precedes: *no dejante* = *no obstante* (Cuervo, § 855), *no ejante* = *no obstante* (Tobón, p. 13).

ARGENTINA (CUYO, all classes): *dejante* zonzo, pobre; *Dejante que* tengo mala suerte, nadies me ayuda (Vidal, p. 190).

CHILE: —¿I no te pedía que le buscaras niditos de diucas o chincoles? —*¡Dejante que* se enojaba conmigo porque dejaba que mis niñas sacasen los huevos a los pajaritos del nido! Decía que le daba mucha pena (Zorobabel Rodríguez, p. 182). *Dejante que* no me has pagado, vienes a faltarme al respeto ... [and as a preposition: *Dejante* los trabajos que hay que pasar, no se gana con qué vivir] (Román, II, 83). Unos gracejos, para mofarse de él, a tiempo que se deslizaba un triste cortejo, no *dejante que* venía despreocupado, le priduntaron de manos a boca: —¿Conoces tís al que llevan a enterral? (Muñoz, p. 188). —Espéreme siquiera unos quince días. —¡Quince días! ... *¡Dejante que* me tiene usted avergonzado con mi mamita y las niñas, porque las tenía dicho que a todas les regalaría algo! (Blest Gana, *Martín Rivas*, chap. xxviii).

The form *dejante*, present participle of *dejar*, is parallel with such forms as *no obstante*, *no embargante*, etc. Román found no examples of this *dejante* in the classics but quotes examples of *dejando*, *dejando aparte*, and *dejado* in the same sense.

Both aforementioned Mexican lexicographers record another usage of *onde* or *donde que* which appears to have no exact parallel elsewhere: to indicate some sudden and disagreeable interruption.

MEXICO: Estábamos platicando, y *onde que* llega D. Sinforiano y nos encuentra (Icazbalceta, p. 181). Dormíamos, y *dónde que* un tiro nos despierta (Santamaría, *Dicc.*, I, 581).

The matter of stress is doubtful, if we may judge from the above examples. This unique development of *donde* possibly stems in some circuitous way from the use of *dónde* (= *de dónde*) in the sense of *cómo*, into which has grown a feeling of surprise or astonishment; or, more probably, it is a development of *donde* in the sense of *cuando*. It seems to be equivalent to *he aquí que* 'lo and behold,' etc.

HASTA QUE, HASTA CUANDO

In addition to its standard meaning of 'until,' *hasta que* is reported for Panama and Venezuela (Perijá) in the sense of standard *a que* (= *apuesto a que*) 'I'll bet that,' etc.: "—*Hasta que* [= *a que*] te alcanzo" (Mangado, p. 98); "*Hasta que* sí [= *a que* sí]" (Armellada, p. 194). This double form, analogical to double *a que* and *hasta que* 'until,' may help to explain the use of clarifying *hasta cuando* for standard *hasta que*, as in: "los siguió *hasta cuando* se perdieron" (Cajar, p. 112).

PUES

The illative conjunction *pues* is extremely frequent (sometimes with the force of an interjection) in the familiar speech of many regions when placed after the word or phrase to which it belongs rather than before (though it may also precede, as is more frequently the case in the standard language). It has various meanings of cause, result, and other relationships difficult to define, and in many regions its frequent repetition has deprived it of all significance, save that of its rhythmic and stylistic function. The excessive use of this *pues* is generally considered characteristic of familiar speech in the Basque provinces, Navarre, and Rioja and in many Spanish-American zones. While, in writing, a comma should be placed before *pues*, actually it is often omitted, for in conversation no pause is here made: *vamos pues, sí pues*, etc. Unstressed Latin *pŏst* yielded *pos, po, pus*,[4] *pu, p;* Spanish *pues* yielded *pué, pes, pe, pis, ps, p*. None of these forms has an exclusive geographical area, and two or more of them often alternate in the speech of the same person. In general, it may be said, that *pos* and *pus* are most widely spread (*BDH*, I, 118 n.). Popular and rustic *pes* (*pis, ps, bs*) predominates in the Inter-Andean zone of Ecuador. The Ecuadorian grammarian, Pérez Guerrero (p. 253), describes *pis* (*ps, bs*) and *ca* (probably of Quechua origin), used by the *vulgo* and *la plebe burguesa* in certain regions of the interior, as "rústicos cayados en que apoyamos el macilento y torpe paso de nuestro discurso para que no se caiga y despedace." The forms *pu* and *p* predominate in Chile, *pis* and *p* in Bolivia, etc. In Central America and especially in Mexico prepositive *pos* is current in rustic speech, often followed by a hesitant pause. The region where postpositive *pues* is most commonly heard (*pos sí, pues*) in Mexico is Guadalajara; wherefore, according to Rubio (*Anarquía*, II, 155), the phrase *Guadalajara pues* is often used to refer jocosely to the city itself or to its inhabitants (*tapatíos*). In Colombia postpositive *pues* is most frequently heard in the province of Antioquia. In imitating the local speech of this region, the speaker generously sprinkles *pues* into his discourse. Postpositive *pues* is also frequent in Panama, where Mangado (p. 113) thinks it due to the preponderantly Basque influence in colonization and civilization.

Argentina (Northwest): —¡Es claro, *pu!* (César Carrizo, p. 176).

Chile: —Ya 'sta, *pué*, ¿qué se les ofrece? —Güeno, *pues*,[5] eñor, ta bien (Acevedo Hernández, *Por el atajo*, p. 24); Dejen descansar, *pues* (p. 31); Así es, *pues* (p. 33); A usté qué, *pues* (p. 43); los dejo en su

[4] Rather than deriving from *pues*, "debido a una acentuación originaria *púes*" (as suggested in *BDH*, I, 118 n.), *pus* is probably a reduction of *pos* ⟨ unstressed *pŏst:* the labial element in the initial *p* and the final checking *s* combine to raise *o* to *u*.

[5] Since final *s* is generally aspirated or lost in Chile, *pues* though often written with an *s* is usually pronounced *pueh* or *pué* or, with lower social status, *puh* or merely *p*.

casa, no peleen *pué* (p. 60); ¡Claro, *pué!* (p. 61). —Creí que no s'iba a cansar nunca. —Me cansé, *pué* (Acevedo Hernández, *La canción rota,* I, 1); Pero cuando usté, que sabe de asuntos, lo ice, así será, *pué.* ... —Güeno tenía qu' estar, *pué;* Así dicen que es, *pué* (II, 2). —Miren *pué,* ya me cambió nombre ya (Romanángel, p. 9); Oye, *pus* (p. 12).

BOLIVIA: —Veremos *ps,* ché (Céspedes, p. 212); Lo mismo que en Viacha no más *ps,* ché (p. 244). —Te mata *ps,* hijo, te mata (Augusto Guzmán, p. 76).

PERU: —Veremos, *pues,* qué dice *pues.* —Él, *pues,* nos contará, *pues.* —Hoy, *pues,* sí que estamos bien parados, *pues* (Gamarra, *Algo del Perú,* p. 88).

ECUADOR: ¿Por qué no vienes? —No quiero *pues.* No encuentro el libro que busco. —En la mesa mismo está *pues.* ¿No lo ves? (Vázquez, p. 328). —¡Qué's *pes!* (Icaza, *En las calles,* p. 6); —¡Elé, como no *pes!* (p. 7); —Aquí venimos, *pes* (p. 18); Sí, *pes* (p. 19); —Ojalá *pes* (p. 233), etc. ¿Leyó usted el libro? —Sí, *ps;* y era bonito, *ps.* Venga usted. Eso *ca* no quiero *ps.* ... Para qué *ps;* mañana *ca* si he dir *ps* (Pérez Guerrero, p. 254).

MEXICO: —*Pos* ¡quién sabe! (Quevedo, *La camada,* p. 294). —¿Y cómo son los ferrocarriles? —*Pos* nomás. ... —Quítale el *pos,* Tavito; no está en la gramática—corrigió doña Paz (Quevedo, *Las ensabanadas* p. 66). *Pos* eso sí que ni modo! (González Carrasco, p. 21); —*¡Pos* cuidado, don Ciriaco! (p. 29; *¡Pos* ora voy yo! (p. 33).

COSTA RICA: *¡Pos* hombre, está hecho un altar! (Echeverría, p. 155); —Caramba, *pus* pa que bea (p. 158); *Pos* mirá lo que faltaba (p. 192); *Pos* yo lo bide ¡carastas! (p. 193).

PERO

In the Andean highland zones, the conjunction *pero* 'but' is often placed at the end of a phrase or sentence rather than at the beginning, as in standard speech. This is probably due to widespread postposition of particles, prepositions, and other parts of speech in Aymara and Quechua.

BOLIVIA: —Dame el café ... —¿Y si te ha de quitar el sueño, *pero?* (Rodrigo, p. 14); —¡Ven a ver! Prontito *pero* (p. 31); —¿Y por qué no ha entrado a comer pues, *pero?* (p. 40).

ECUADOR (CUENCA): —¡Esto daremos parte en el Estanco, *pero!* (Mata, *Sanagüín,* p. 111); —¡Mos [= hemos] de sacar tripas de chasos ['white peasants'] *pero!* (p. 167); —No peleen, *pero* (p. 169).

SUPERFLUOUS 'QUE'

The conjunction *que*, the most widely used of all, has come to express almost any type of syntactical relationship. Bello (§ 1006) says of *que:* "No hay palabra que sufra tan variadas y a veces inexplicables trasformaciones." Thus, the borderland between its functions as subordinating conjunction and as relative adverb is impossible to define accurately. Some of its uses have already been discussed under other parts of speech, where they could conveniently be placed (see pp. 117, 132, 133, etc.).

In some regions of Spanish America, *que* is ill-advisedly added to the standard conjunctions (*en*) *cuanto* 'as soon as' and *por cuanto* 'inasmuch as.' The superfluous *que*, so congenial to Spanish, is not unknown in popular and rustic peninsular speech today ("Cuanto *que* entre la pillo" [Aurelio Espinosa, *Cuentos*, III, 447; Toro Gisbert, "Voces," p. 403]) and was frequent in the oldest language ("E quanto *que* pueden non fincan de andar" [*Cid*, vs. 1474]). Cuervo (§ 395) remarks that judges and lawyers are particularly given to *por cuanto que* and some go so far as *por cuanto a que*, all of which he censures.

ARGENTINA: Cuanto *que* la sintió, el vacaje se puso a disparar a la loca (Larreta, *El linyera*, II).

PERU: En cuanto *que* uno se sienta le mete pedal (Corrales, p. 236).

COLOMBIA: En cuanto *que* me vió echó a correr ... (Cuervo, § 396).

MEXICO: En cuanto *que* llegue te avisaré; En cuanto *que* lo vi, lo conocí (Ramos Duarte, p. 231). Cuantito *que* yo pueda, le pago a usted (Santamaría, *Dicc.*, I, 418).

In rural parts of Mexico the superfluous *que* of *en cuanto que* becomes *y* (*en cuanto y*) probably by analogy with other similar uses of *y* (as in *ojalá y* for *ojalá que*, etc.).

MEXICO (NUEVO LEÓN): —Me quiero amparar en cuanto *y* pueda (García Roel, p. 135); en cuanto *y* el río se ponga más bravo nosotros podemos retirarnos (p. 145); en cuanto *y* dan una semana (p. 332).

In popular and rustic speech everywhere, *nada* is used to reinforce a negative: *no vino nada* 'he didn't come at all.' Now when this *nada* precedes the phrase, *no* is omitted (according to correct usage), and a superfluous *que* is added (unlike standard usage). While not registered in the Academy dictionary, this locution is extremely common in rustic peninsular speech[6] and in popular and rustic speech in regions of Spanish America.

CHILE: *Nada que* tengo pena; *Nada que* vino Pedro (Román, IV, 4). En la Pasión de Cristo, ni *nada que* se le pareciera (Muñoz, p. 207). —Como uno es sufrido, *nadita que* se queja, hermano (Alberto Romero, *Perucho González,* p. 182).

COLOMBIA: *Nada que* viene; *nada que* se somete (Roberto Restrepo, p. 353).

MEXICO: Pero *nadítita que* me jallo por acá . ...¡Una tristeza y una murria! (Azuela, *Los de abajo,* p. 195). Mojé toda la pieza y *nada que* lo lavaba (Galeana, p. 88). —Pos bien escondío que ha de 'star ... porque *nada que* damos con él (García Roel, p. 158).

Another type of superfluous *que* is one of a relative nature found in exclamatory sentences like "¡qué bien *que* canta!" This usage, current in the classics, has survived in colloquial speech both in Spain and in America, but it is losing ground under the influence of the written language, which avoids it. In a few regions, however, among them Santo Domingo (*BDH,* V, 240), the superfluous *que* is current even in cultured speech. Locally we find extensions in popular speech like the following:

CHILE: —¡Gilidioso *que* te han de ver, mirá! (Durand, in *LCC,* p. 444). —Tan cargoso *que* te han de vel. ... Tan cargao a las riendas *que* te han de vel (Romanángel, p. 9).

VENEZUELA: Y ya sudé mi calentura. ... ¡Sabrosita *que* estaba! (Gallegos, *Doña Bárbara,* p. 14). Sabrosa *que* está la niña Nieves (Díaz-Solís, p. 26).

MEXICO: Flojita *que* te estás volviendo. ... Gruñona *que* se está volviendo la tía (Madero, I, 2). Pero bueno *que* estuvo el baile (García Roel, p. 203); —Regüeno *qu* 'es (p. 282); Andrea bien *que* las sabe (p. 299); ella bien *que* les entiende (p. 302), etc.

Another use of superfluous *que* involving a degree of relative force is one reported by Román (IV, 515) as being much used in Chile: "Yo *que* entro y él *que* sale." Román was surprised not to find it registered in the Academy dictionary, since it is extremely common in the *Romanceros* and in other authors. It is probably current collo-

[6] Cf. Aurelia Espinosa, *Cuentos,* I, 88 (Ávila): "La Picotera se hizo la que se comía el higo pero *nada que* comía"; III, 373 (Santander): "Quemó al enfermo y echó la benedición a las cenizas, pero *nada que* resucitó"; also III, 369 (Madrid); 375 (Soria); 378 (Santander); 380 (Granada); etc.

quially in regions of Spain, as well as of Spanish America, despite its nonappearance in the Academy dictionary. In this construction the *que*, beyond its force as a relative, imparts a temporal quality, a sense of rapidity, due in part to its own brevity, which gives it an advantage over other ways of construing the same thought. Román mentions such equivalents: "Inmediatamente que yo entré, salió él; Junto con entrar yo, salió él; Todo fué entrar yo y salir él; Entrar yo y salir él, fué todo uno." Naturally, none of these is so "concise, clear, and elegant" as "Yo *que* entro y él *que* sale," with its sense of simultaneity and suddenness. In Chile one hears the proverb "En nombrando al rey de Roma, él *que* asoma (for *pronto asoma*)."

CHILE: L'agua *que* llega a la puerta,/Delgadina *que* moría (Vicuña Cifuentes, p. 34); Antes de que llegue el agua,/Delgadina *que* se acaba (p. 37); Micaela *que* esto dijo,/don Alberto *que* llegó (p. 79).

ECUADOR: Yo *que* salgo a la azotea y veo un hermoso venao (Ortiz, p. 115).

COLOMBIA: Yo *qu'*entro y ella *que* sale (Flórez, p. 384).

VENEZUELA: Yo *que* estoy ensillando ... cuando oigo que llega un viajero (Gallegos, *Doña Bárbara*, p. 67). Yo *que* enciendo un cigarro y una cuaima [= serpiente venenosa] *que* me le tira una mordía a la brasa (Gallegos, *Canaima*, p. 274).

COSTA RICA: Él *que* le apunta el canón, y el Cadejos *que* empieza a bajar la cabeza (Fabián Dobles, p. 24); La mujer *que* lo veya entre las piedras de una quebrada, ella *que* iba a cogelo con sus manos, y el chacalín *que* se esparecía (p. 201).

A peculiar use of *que* is found in the Chilean locution *el* (*la*, *lo*) *que menor* for *el* (*la*, *lo*) *menor* in such sentences as: "No tienes disculpa *la que menor*" for "No tienes *la menor* disculpa."

CHILE: No tengo dinero *lo que menor*. ... No tienes motivo para negármelo *el que menor* (Román, III, 487). Pero como no tenía pruebas *la que menor*, se limitó a indagar la pista y el actual paradero del presunto asesino (Silva, p. 57).

Among other local uses of superfluous *que*, we find the Mexican expression *mucho que mejor* for standard *mucho mejor:* "Y si hay modo de hacer una topada con los agrarios ... mucho *que* mejor" (Fernando Robles, p. 136):

At other times *que* is substituted for some other word of a standard phrase.

After the standard locution *no poder menos* 'to be necessary, not to be able to help,' etc., we find either the preposition *de* or the conjunction *que* before the dependent infinitive: "no pude menos *de* (or *que*) reírme" 'I couldn't help laughing.' This dual construction reflects the same usage in comparisons with *más* and *menos: más* (or *menos*) *de* before a numeral in affirmative sentences, elsewhere *que;* and *más* (or *menos*) *que* (or *de*) in negative sentences before a numeral, elsewhere *que*. In the older language *no poder menos que* is common, but today *no poder menos de* is the standard form and the one generally used in Spain. Spanish America, on the other hand, prefers *no poder menos que*. For Chile, Román (III, 487) mentions "no poder *por* menos" for "no poder menos."

ARGENTINA: La moza no pudo menos *que* rairse (Lynch, *Romance*, p. 182). No pudo menos *que* comentar (Filloy, p. 70).

URUGUAY: —El patrón no pudo menos *que* rirse (Reyles, *El gaucho*, p. 211).

CHILE: No pudo menos *que* expresar el vivo disgusto que tal noticia causaba en su ánimo (Azócar, p. 286). Éstos no pudieron menos *que* retirarse (Fernando Alegría, *Lautaro*, p. 50).

COLOMBIA: No pude menos *que* (*or* de) preguntar (Flórez, p. 384).

VENEZUELA: Yo no pude menos *que* réime (Gallegos, *La trepadora*, p. 200).

MEXICO: Sus compañeros no pueden menos *que* envidiarlo (García Roel, p. 16). Ya no pudo menos *que* preguntarle qué cosa era aquella llamita azul (Rubín, p. 54).

Que sometimes takes the place of *o*, as in the Chilean expression *más que menos* for standard *más o menos* 'more or less': "—¿Y dices que los muertos son ... ? —Sus doscientos más *que* menos" (Riquelme, in *LCC*, p. 216). While this expression has been dubbed a Catalanism (cf. Román, III, 449), it is probably nothing more than an analogical formation after the many alternative expressions in which *que* standardly means 'or.' According to Keniston (p. 681), the origin of *que* meaning 'or' may be found in asyndetic alternative clauses of concession (*que me pesse que me plega*). Since in such clauses the second *que* was felt as introducing the alternative, the first could be omitted (*quiera que no quiera* = *que quiera o no* 'whether he will or no'). Then *que ... que* came to mean 'whether . . . . or,' even without a verb (*que tarde que temprano*); and finally the first *que* was dropped. *Que* for *o* we find also in the standard expression *mal que bien:* "Aquí tienen techo, y *mal que bien* ... reuno un pedazo de pan, que yo comparto con ellas (Gallegos, *La trepadora*, p. 248 [Venezuela]). —¡Por fortuna, mi hija, *mal que bien*, se casó! (Gamboa, *Teatro*, III, 299 [Mexico]).

The expression *mal que mal*, current at least in Chile, Argentina, Puerto Rico, and Santo Domingo, is not a case of *que* meaning *o* but is of an adversative nature as an equivalent of "aunque algo mal, aunque no del todo bien, así así, tal cual, medianamente" (Román, III, 392); "aunque mal, aunque esté mal, aunque lo haya hecho mal"; etc. (Garzón, p. 293). Garzón gives this example: "*Mal que mal* siempre servirá de algo, o no dejará por esto de servir de algo"; cf. Güiraldes' *Don Segundo Sombra* (p. 229): "Traspuesto que hubimos unas cuarenta leguas, pude sonreír *mal que mal* ante lo sucedido;" (p. 287): "... empantanándose en el fondo aquel, corríamos *mal que mal* a impedir que así sucediera." Patín Maceo ("Amer.," VII, 191) gives: "*mal que mal*, él atiende a su familia."

In some regions, *que* popularly supplants *como* in expressions like *tan luego que* for standard *tan luego como* 'as soon as,' etc. This is due (1) to frequent confusion of *como* 'than' after comparisons of equality and *que* 'than' after comparisons of inequality; (2) to the use of either *como* or *que* meaning 'that' to introduce a noun clause: "Sabrás *como* (= que) hemos llegado buenos"; and (3) to conjunctions containing *que*.

Argentina: Ahorita tan luego *que* él comenzaba a endierezarse, le daba por dirse a ese viejo fantástico (Lynch, *Romance*, p. 97).

Ecuador: El ruido ... lo sentían ya por todo el cuerpo. Tal *que* si un abrazo colosal les triturara todas las vértebras (Aguilera Malta, p. 20).

Guatemala: Tan luego *que* haya venido el médico, dígale usted que pase a la habitación del enfermo (Sandoval, II, 478).

At least in Ecuador, *que* is used in place of *ni* in the locution *sin más que más* for standard *sin más ni más* 'without more ado, without any reason.' Vázquez (p. 376), who registers the phrase, gives the equivalents "sin razón, antojadizamente, sin otro requisito."

The *que* in the expression *de que un rato* or *de que un instante*, heard frequently in Chile even among the educated, is not the conjunction *que* but is merely a corruption of *aquí* + *a*: *de que un rato* = standard *de aquí a un rato*, *de que un instante* = *de aquí a un instante* (Román, IV, 516): "*De que un rato* vamos a cenar" (C).

In Chile *que* is likewise heard for *quien* in the expression *como que no quiere la cosa* for standard *como quien no quiere la cosa* 'as if uninterested, nonchalantly,' etc.

SI QUE TAMBIÉN

The conjunction *si que también* 'but also' is occasionally found for standard *sino que también.* It has been called a Gallicism (Román, V, 260), and a Catalanism (Calcaño, § 231). It is more probably a mere development of older *si también,* which, when preceding a clause, might take a *que,* just as *sino también* > *sino que también* before a clause. Then the *que* is often unnecessarily retained (as in *sino que también*) when no clause follows, influenced, perhaps, by the reinforcing *que,* as often used, for instance, after *sí: sí voy* and *sí que voy,* etc. This construction, which Mir (II, 790) calls "digna de eterna reprobación," crops up in popular speech not only in Spain but also in Spanish America. Casares (*Crítica profana,* p. 147) remarks: "hoy no hay ya quien escriba en serio aquello de *si que también.*"

Peru: Como si hablara desde el insondable *si que también* despatarrante abismo del misterio, soltó estas incoherencias (Corrales, p. 52); tan generoso *si que también* laudable empeño (p. 192).

Venezuela: No sólo por deber, *si que también* por respeto al público (*ap.* Calcaño, p. 59).

Guatemala: ... se exhibieron no sólo productos de la América Central, *si que también* de Cuba y Panamá (Sandoval, II, 443).

TRAS QUE

This conjunction is popularly used in some areas as an extension of standard *tras de* in the sense of *además* 'in addition to, besides' and that of *cuanto más que* 'so much the more, especially since.' It is an older usage (cf. *Lazarillo,* ed. Cejador, p. 209).

Argentina (San Luis): *Tras que* no trabaja, se emborracha (Vidal, p. 400, also p. 189).

Bolivia: No me estés ahora con esa cantaleta. *Tras que* ahora estoy no sé como (Díaz Villamil, *Cuando vuelva,* p. 12).

Mexico (Yucatan): *Tras que* no es cierto (V. Suárez, p. 64).

¿Y?

Standardly, the conjunction *y* may be stressed when heading a phrase or clause syntactically unrelated with what precedes, in order to emphasize the expression. This occurs in questions and exclamations: *¿Y tu padre? ¡Y si no llega a tiempo!* etc. This redundant *y*, which reaches far back into the older language (Keniston, p. 662), has in some regions of Spanish America been extended to a new use: it stands alone with interrogative intonation, and in writing is generally followed by suspension points, showing that the expression is elliptical: *¿Y?* ... It means something like 'what's up? what's the matter? what happened? well, uh; oh . . . ; oh, I don't know! and so?' etc. The phrase is often considered a localism, as if it were restricted to Argentina (Alonso and Henríquez Ureña, *Gram.*, II, 194; Segovia, p. 302), or to Peru (Arona, p. 505). It seems most widely employed in the River Plate region, Chile, Peru, and Ecuador, but it is probably encountered elsewhere, though it may have escaped the attention of lexicographers "sin duda por ser tan chiquito" (says Arona). Standard equivalents are: "¿Y pues? ¿En qué quedamos? ¿Conque? ¿En qué paró aquello? Pues ... ¿qué quiere? ¿Qué más? ¿Qué hacemos? ¿Qué resultó? ¡Qué sé yo! ¡Claro! ¡Pues! etc. Arona gives a typical instance of how *¿y?* is used: "Dos amigos han convenido en un asunto; se separan; vuelven a encontrarse de acera a acera: lo primero que el más vivo dice al otro es '—¿Y?' ...

> Con esto y una mirada
> de inteligencia a su modo
> con esto se han dicho todo
> sin haberse dicho nada."

Argentina: ¿Cómo se halla doña Julia ... ? —*¿Y?* ... ¡Qué sabía él! Enferma no estaba (Lynch, *Romance*, p. 31); —¿Y ustedes cómo se hayan? ... —*¿Y?* Ansina nomás (p. 32); Confesá entonces, ¿ánde has estao? —*¿Y?* ... He estao en lo del padrino (p. 60); ¿Cuánto me debe? —*¿Y?* ... ¡Qué sé yo, señor! (p. 93), etc. —*¿Y?*—preguntó la muchacha. —Vi a dir ahurita no más, niña (Larreta, *Zogoibi*, p. 139). Don Segundo se acomodó en el banco como para hablar. Pasó un rato. —*¿Y?* ... —preguntó Perico (Güiraldes, *Don Segundo*, p. 123).

Uruguay: —¡Desalmao! Es que me va a quitar el campo y la casa y todo. ... —*¿Y?* ... —Es que todo eso es tuyo (Sánchez, *La gringa*, I, 14); —*¿Y?* ... ¿Se corta o no se corta? (III, 7). Cuando quedaron solas, doña Justa ... interrogó: —*¿Y ... ?* (Reyles, *El gaucho*, p. 176).

Chile: *¿Y?* ¿No vamos a comer? —¿Y? ¿Cómo les fué? (C).

Ecuador: —*¿Y?* ¿Usted ya habló con la hembra? (Gil Gilbert, *Nuestro pan*, p. 69); —¡Pero con esa facha! —*¿Y?* La cara no es lo que hace al hombre (p. 79); La cara del negro escudriñaba el río. —*¿Y?*

¿Será muy salobre esta agua? (p. 12).

EL SALVADOR: —¿Usted nos conoce?—le preguntó Fina. —*Y* ... cómo no,—respondió el hombre con esfuerzo (Torres Arjona, p. 71).

Quite another thing is Bolivian *¿y?* at the end of a question, heard chiefly in Sucre (Chuquisaca) and current among all classes (possibly a close pronunciation of standard *¿eh?* similarly used): "Creo que Vd. es Joseso, *¿y?* ¿Soltero todavía, *y?* —Podemos estar haciendo programa, *¿y?*" (Díaz V., *Plebe*, p. 123); "Quédate, *¿y?*" (Rodrigo, p. 55).

XII

INTERJECTIONS

THIS is not the place to discuss simple interjections, that is, exclamatory words existing only as interjections that in themselves are syntactically unrelated to the rest of the sentence. But, rather, we shall in the main take up more complete expressions consisting principally of other parts of speech, singly or grouped, used with the force of interjections. This treatment will eliminate, among others, such forms as ubiquitous *¡ahá!* or *¡ajá!* giving approbation or consent, or uttered on surprising a person doing something blameworthy, with its variants *¡anjá! ¡ajú! ¡uhjú! ¡unjú!*, etc.; *¡epa!* or *¡épale!* with the equivalence of *¡hola!* or *¡ea!; ¡chis!* or *¡achís!* expressing disgust, especially in parts of Central America; *¡gua!* expressing surprise, admiration, or fear, in Bolivia, Peru, Ecuador, Colombia, and Venezuela, with its variant *¡güé!* in rural Uruguay.[1] We exclude the endless list of local interjections used in frightening away domestic animals: such as *¡shé!* (El Salvador), *¡so!* (Peru, Venezuela, Puerto Rico, etc.), *¡huche!* (Chiloé, Chile), etc.; *¡zafa!* (Peru, Ecuador, Puerto Rico, Santo Domingo, etc.), *¡ah perro!* (Chile), and *¡zumba!* (Valle del Cauca, Colombia) to frighten away dogs; *¡ochi!* (Valle del Cauca), to frighten pigs; *¡huise!* (Valle del Cauca) and *¡ocio!* (Costa Rica) for chickens, etc. We exclude also the interesting interjections of Quechua origin current in Ecuador, Peru, and in very limited zones of Chile, Bolivia, and Argentina, among them *¡achachay!* to express cold, sometimes approbation; *¡arrarray!* or *¡arrarrau!* to express heat, burning; *¡atatay!* to express disgust, sometimes in-

[1] "Su sorpresa se condensó en esa extraña interjección campera, norteña, de asombro y de pregunta: —¡Güé!? (Montiel, *Alma nuestra*, p. 153).

credulity; *¡ajajay!* to express laughter, ridicule; *¡achalay!* or *¡achallau!* to express admiration; Bolivian *ampe* (*ampesito*) to express endearment or entreaty, etc. Many of these restricted uses can be found in local dictionaries or in general dictionaries of *americanismos*, such as Malaret's or Santamaría's, and in Malaret's *Semántica americana* (pp. 85–89). For Mayan interjections used in Yucatan, see V. Suárez, p. 94.

¿AH? = ¿NO? = ¿EH?

The interjection *¿ah?* usually placed at the end of a phrase or sentence, though it may also stand alone, is used in many regions of Spanish America where the standard language prefers *¿eh?* The form *ah* represents a more open vowel sound, which has greater carrying power. Occasionally one reads *¿eh?* in literature, but generally this spelling is merely an imitation of peninsular practice and does not always correspond to oral usage. When placed at the end of a phrase or sentence *¿ah?* serves to inquire of the listener whether he has heard what has been said; when standing alone, the speaker himself inquires about what he has not heard.

ARGENTINA (NORTHWEST, RUSTIC): —Tenís que salir. —*¿Ah?* (Vidal, p. 195).

CHILE: ¿Cómo sabe usté si el día de mañana me muero sin conocer el amor, *ah?* (Acevedo Hernández, *De pura cepa*, p. 7). ¿Y usted tendrá algunas avecitas que no le hagan falta, *ah?* (Ernesto Montenegro, p. 116). Se casó, *¿ah?* (Délano, in *LCC*, p. 518).

PERU: Viene mañana, *¿ah?* (C).

ECUADOR: —¿Macanuda? *¿Ah?* (Gil Gilbert, *Yunga*, p. 17). —¿Cuándo volverás, *ah?* (Icaza, *Cholos*, p. 95).

COLOMBIA: ¿Qué es, *ah?* ¿Qué te ha sucedido, *ah?* (Uribe, *Dicc.*; also Sundheim, p. 16; and Revollo, p. 1: "*¿A?*").

VENEZUELA: —O te empezaron a comer las patas y te fuistes, *¿ah*, vagabundito? (Uslar Pietri, in *ACMV*, II, 15). —*¿Ah?* —apresuróse a inquirir Enrique (Díaz-Solís, p. 39).

PANAMA: —¿Cuándo vendrás, *ah?* ¿Qué dice, *ah?* (Mangado, p. 76; cf. also Herrero Fuentes, p. 95).

COSTA RICA: —¿Por qué dice eso, *ah?* (Fabián Dobles, p. 161); —¿Y por qué, *ah*, por qué? (p. 204).

NICARAGUA: —¿Quién la mató, *ah?* (Chamorro, *Entre dos filos*, p. 47); ¿Cuándo se casan, *ah?* ¿Vamos a ir al casamiento, *ah?* (p. 362).

Qué sueño el suyo; le hablamos, lo sacudimos, y Ud. sólo decía «*ah? ah?*» (Orozco, p. 60).

The negative particle *¿no?* (at times *¿que no?*) ends a phrase or sentence where the peninsular standard prefers *¿no es verdad?* or *¿verdad?* or *¿no es cierto?* This *¿no?* is common also in Andalusia (Braue, p. 64). Román (IV, 19) erroneously thought such usage a *chilenismo* (as did Lenz [*La oración*, § 350]); and he expostulates: "Ojalá se evite, porque es muletilla harto enfadosa no sólo gramatical, sino también urbana y filosóficamente." The use of this *¿no?* has been extended further to usurp the place of standard *¿eh?* at the end of a phrase or sentence. Despite its interrogative character, *¿no?* is in some regions pronounced with an affirmative intonation. This fact has apparently led Vázquez (p. 278) to insinuate that the frequency of *no* thus used in Ecuador may have been influenced by the analogous use of Quechua *manchu* meaning *¿no es* (*será, habrá sido*)*?* etc.: "Vendrás pronto, *nó;* calla, *nó.*" He suggests that the intonation of *no* should always be interrogative in this usage.

ARGENTINA: ¡Güenas noches! *¿No* [= eh]? (Lynch, *Palo verde*, p. 14). —Adiosito, *¿no* [= eh]? (Filloy, p. 184). —Sí ... *¿no* [= eh]? (p. 351).

CHILE: Ud. me dijo que saliéramos, *¿no?* Pero Ud. no quiere salir, *¿no* [= verdad]? (Román, IV, 19). ¿Tiene gracia, *no* [= verdad]? (Azócar, p. 317). ¡Compadézcase de este pobre pecador! —Pecador, *¿no* [= eh]? (Ernesto Montenegro, p. 148). Hasta mañana, *¿no* [= eh]? (Durand, *Mercedes*, p. 46); —¿Sí, *no* [= eh]? (p. 254). —Sí, *¿no* [= eh]? (Brunet, *Montaña*, p. 90). —Nada tengo yo que hacer contigo. —¿Nada, *no* [= eh]? (Maluenda, *Escenas*, p. 77). —¿Hasta lueguito, *no* [= eh]? (Latorre, *Zurzulita*, p. 99).

BOLIVIA: —¿Quién les pondría ese nombre, *no* [= eh]? —Quién sería; es chistoso (August Guzmán, p. 28).

PERU: No me peguen, questoy malo. ... —Conque malo, *¿no* [= eh]? (Ciro Alegría, *La serpiente*, p. 136).

ECUADOR: Muy bien que te he oído. —¿Sí? *¿No* [= eh]? A ver, dime lo que decía (Pareja, *Don Balón*, p. 96); No le dirás nada, *¿no* [= eh]? (p. 132).

VENEZUELA: ¿Me lo contará todo, *no?* ¿Sí, *no?* (Rosenblat).

PANAMA: —Es Ud. colombiano, ¿sí, *no* [= verdad]? —Es una cosa bella, ¿sí, *no?* (Mangado, p. 117).

MEXICO (YUCATAN): Ayer llegó Tomasa *¿que no?* (V. Suárez, p. 63).

AMALAYA

The locution *mal haya* as used in some regions of Spanish America presents a curious example of semasiological development sometimes referred to as the meliorative tendency of words. Originally used to express a curse, it has acquired an additional and diametrically opposed use: the expression of a wish.

The primitive meaning of *mal haya* was 'cursed be,' and, conversely, that of *bien haya* was 'blessed be.' The verb agreed with its subject in number: *¡mal haya él! ¡mal hayan ellos!* (Such agreement is still occasionally found.) Gradually the verb became invariable, and the original subject was felt as the object: *¡mal haya ellos! ¡bien haya ellos!* Finally, *mal haya* was interpreted as one word (*malhaya*) equivalent to *maldito* and was then construed with the subjunctive of *ser* through a blending of two constructions: *mal haya ellos* + *malditos sean ellos* 〉 *malhaya sean ellos*. This construction, originally very low in social status (Cuervo, § 430) has penetrated into cultured spheres but has not been accepted by grammarians. It is found in Spain, especially in Andalusia, and is general in Spanish America.

GUATEMALA: *¡Mal haya sea* la lluvia que no nos dejó salir! (Batres, p. 88).

MEXICO: *¡Mal haya sea* yo tan bestia! (Inclán, I, 3); *¡Mal haya sea* el tal Carlos, que tiene la culpa de que usted se vea en este estado! (II, 5).

NEW MEXICO: *¡Mal haya siá* dél! [= mal haya sea de él] (Aurelio Espinosa, "Apuntaciones," p. 161; also *alaya* and *laya*).

Then, *mal haya* came to be used as an optative particle equivalent to *¡ojalá tuviera!* or *¡quién tuviera!* followed by a noun: *¡malaya una guitarra!* 'I wish I had a guitar!' That is, the speaker curses the object as lacking when most needed, thus indirectly expressing a desire to have it at hand. This usage is not unknown in the older language. Cuervo cites an example from Lope: "*¡Mal haya* un hacha y tocino!" (*El arenal de Sevilla*, I, 4). It is frequent today in some regions of Spanish America. Both spelling (*ah malhaya, ah malaya, amalaya*) and semantic change arose through loss of the etymological sense, since the popular form is not *haya* but *haiga*.

COLOMBIA: *¡Ah malhaya una escopeta!* (Cuervo, § 430). (ANTIOQUIA): *¡Ah, mal haya una vihuela!* (Antonio Restrepo, p. 292).

One hears a quip about the impecunious student who, on passing a tavern redolent of freshly cooked sausage, remarked "*¡Amalaya* un pan para comer con este olor!"

VENEZUELA: *¡Ah malhaya* una guitarra para cantarles a ustedes un corrido! (Picón-Febres, p. 239). *Ah malhaya* un pajarito/que volara más que el viento,/que llevara mis suspiros/donde está mi pensamiento (Montesinos, *Cancionero popular, ap.* Alvarado, p. 270). —*¡Ah, malhaya* la guerra! Pa probale al compae quién es entoavía el Comandante Rosendo Zapata. ¡Maldita sea la paz! (Gallegos, *La trepadora,* p. 217).

GUATEMALA: *¡Malaya* un buen vino para tan rica cena! (Bonilla Ruano, III, 334).

From this frequent usage the new verb *(a)malayar* has been formed. It means *anhelar* 'to long for,' expressing a desire for things with no possibility of obtaining them. In such a sense it is used in Colombia (Sundheim, p. 30), Central America (Salazar García, p. 28), Mexico (Malaret, *Suplemento,* I, 95), and probably elsewhere.

COLOMBIA (ANTIOQUIA): Está *amalayando* una bonita novia; lo que más *amalayaba* en aquel páramo era un trago de aguardiente (Antonio Restrepo, p. 126 n.).

HONDURAS: Hay personas pobres; pero hay otras que están *amalhayando* (Membreño, p. 13).

GUATEMALA: No me mantengo *amalhayando* lo que por allí dicen nos falta (Salomé Gil, *Cuadros,* p. 72). Vive *amalayando* todo lo bueno que ve (Bonilla Ruano, III, 334).

From the use of *¡mal haya!* or *¡ah mal haya!* meaning *¡ojalá tuviera!* or *¡quién tuviera!* developed the use of '*ah malhaya* + a verb' equivalent to '*ojalá* + the verb'—a meaning we should associate more logically with *bien haya.* The interjection *ah* is prefixed to make the new word *amalaya* (spelled variously: *ah malaya, amalhaya, ah malhaya*). We find *amalaya* for *ojalá* in rural regions of Argentina (Garzón, p. 13; Segovia, pp. 412, 592); Uruguay, Venezuela, Central America (Salazar García, p. 28); Mexico (Ramos Duarte reports *malaya* = *ojalá* for Tabasco, *a mal haya* = *ojalá* in Michoacán and Morelos); it probably exists elsewhere.[2] (The form *mal haya* or *malaya* without

[2] For Ciro Bayo's misstatements concerning the geographical area of *amalaya* cf. C. E. Kany, "American Spanish *amalaya* to express a wish," *Hispanic Review,* XI (1943), 333–37).

ah is generally preserved with its original meaning of 'cursed be.'[3]) In Colombia (Antioquia) '*ah mal haya quién* + verb' is equivalent to '*ojalá* + verb'. This is a redundant usage, perhaps employed first for emphasis; or the sense of *quién* has shifted to *yo*.

ARGENTINA: Stá seria la cosa—dije con malicia. —No. Si todo va a ser chacota. —*¡Amalaya!* (Güiraldes, *Don Segundo*, p. 211). *¡Amalaya* la hubiera visto Pantalión! (Lynch, *Romance*, p. 102); ¡Y *amalaya* no se le hubiera ocurrido! (p. 111); *¡Amalaya* no estuviera don Pedro! (p. 277); *¡Amalaya* yo pudiera! (p. 450). *¡A malhaya* lo podamos complacer! (Larreta, *El linyera*, p. 165). (Cf. Vidal, p. 197.)

URUGUAY: *Amalaya* me saliera bien una idea (Florencio Sánchez, p. 217); *¡Amalaya* fuese tan fácil vivir como morir! (p. 229); *¡Amalaya* tuviera voz yo! (p. 348).

COLOMBIA (ANTIOQUIA): *¡Ah, mal haya quién* pudiera! (Antonio Restrepo, p. 143); *Mal haya quién* fuera perro/Para latirle a la gente (p. 182); *¡Ah, mal haya quién* supiera! (p. 292).

VENEZUELA: *¡Ah malaya* sea verdá! (Gallegos, in *ACMV*, I, 109).

GUATEMALA: *Amalaya* sea usted presidente (Sandoval, I, 47).

Finally, there are two other locutions which seem to be restricted to American Spanish.

One of these is an extended use of *malhaya sea* as an exclamation of praise, a compliment, etc., thus expressing a diametrically opposed feeling to that of the original *mal haya*, a feeling more in accord with *bien haya*. Thus in Colombia *¡malhaya sea la muchacha!* may be a compliment: "*¡Malhaya sea* la china!" (Cuervo, § 430); "—¡Vean al Princés! *¡Malhaya sea!*" (Carrasquilla, *Hace tiempos*, II, 301).

In Spain one occasionally hears *maldito sea* popularly used with this meliorative tendency. A mother fondling an infant may be heard jocosely exclaiming "*Maldita sea tu estampa.*" The same semasiological phenomenon is present in the expression "*¡Qué fea!*" so frequently applied as a *piropo* to a pretty girl.

The other locution is *¡malhaya nunca!* or *¡malhaya sea nunca!* the meaning of which has been rendered in several ways: "maldito sea el momento" (Bayo), "no me importa" or "no me venga usted con ésas" (Picón-Febres, p. 239), etc. Perhaps Román (III, 396) comes closer to the meaning, though his explanation may seem fanciful. He

[3] "Volví a pensar en que iba a ver un hombre rico y que yo era lo que los ricos tienen por la deshonra de una familia. *¡Malhaya!*" (Güiraldes, *Don Segundo*, p. 307). Also *alaya* in Mexico (Ramos Duarte, p. 29 [Michoacán]) and New Mexico (Aurelio Espinosa, *Studies*, II, § 100).

gives *¡malhaya sea nunca!* as equivalent to "¡maldito sea N., esto o aquello!" and explains "por sentimiento cristiano se convierte la palabra *maldito* en *mal haya* y se calla el nombre de la persona o cosa objeto de la maldición, y aun, como corrigiéndose a sí mismo el que la profiere, parece que trata de alejarla agregando el adv. *nunca.*" If the phrase is followed by a *cuando*-clause, it generally means "maldito sea el momento en que. ..."

CHILE: *¡Mal haya nunca* (o *mal haya sea nunca*) cuando te conocí! [= ¡maldito sea el momento en que te conocí!] (Vicuña Cifuentes, p. 324, n. 2).

VENEZUELA: —Vengo en comisión a coger a Queniquea. ¿No se ha asomao puaquí? —Esta mañana estuvo descansando en el mesmo tercio de leña donde estabas sentao. —*¡Malhaya nunca!* ¡Y no lo apresaste! —Pues ... es que ya estoy viejo pa tener camorras (Gonzalo-Patrizi, in *ACMV*, II, 194).

Such a use of *nunca* is not unknown in Spain, where *mal año para* has imprecatory force. We read in Pereda (*Obras*, V, 120): "ese hijo condenao de la Lambiona tiene un aquel ... que malañu pa él *nunca* ni no."

By analogy with *mal haya* we find the New Mexican form *mal redo vaya* or *marredo vaya* beside *a* (or *al*) *redo vaya* (< the older *a redro* or *riedro vaya*), originally 'get thee behind me.' The form *arredro vaya* 'to the dickens with' is recorded for Yucatan (V. Suárez), Tabasco (Santamaría), Guatemala (Jáuregui), Costa Rica (Gagini), etc.

NEW MEXICO: *¡A redo vaya* este tonto! *¡Al redo vayan* con sus bajezas! *¡Mal redo vaya* y su moda! *¡Marredo vaya* el sinvergüenza! *¡A redo vayan* y sus cuidaus! *¡Redo vaya* la tía! (Aurelio Espinosa, "Apuntaciones," p. 616).

BUENA COSA, BUEN DAR, ETC.

Among the current American-Spanish interjections of a more general nature used to express a pleasant or an unpleasant surprise are *¡buena* (popular and rustic: *güena*) *cosa! ¡buen dar! ¡güen dar! ¡bueno con!* (Chile), *¡a buen!* or *¡ah, buen!* (El Salvador), *¡ah cosa!* (Central America), *¡is!* (Costa Rica), etc. Some of these are related to standard ironical *bueno* in such expressions as *¡buena es ésa!* and are, in general, equivalent to standard *¡vaya! ¡vaya con!* etc. Román (II, 69) thinks *¡buen dar!* may be taken from card games in which the manner of dealing the cards (*dar las cartas bien o mal*) is of great importance. Batres (p. 78) registers *¡ah cosa!* for Guatemala, as especially common among women and equivalent to *¡qué idea!* 'what an idea!' Sandoval defines *¡ah cosa!* as a "negación irónica." Gagini (p. 50) explains its use in Costa Rica "en son de reproche, cuando uno, por ejemplo, revela indiscretamente algo que deseábamos tener oculto." Salarrué (*Cuentos*) gives the equivalents of *¡a buen!* or *¡agüén!* in El Salvador as *¡bah! ¡vaya! ¡anda!* or *¡no faltaba más!* which lend it considerable latitude as an interjection. Gagini defines *¡is!* for Costa Rica as expressing "mofa, desprecio, asco," but it is used also for admiration (see examples).

Chile: —*Güena cosa,* Juana Rosa que te ponís mañosa (Romanángel, p. 9); —Salú, viejo hablaor. —Salú, pué, viejo reservao. ... —*Güena cosa,* on Peiro. ... Qué, pus, *güena cosa* (p. 16); —*Güen dar,*— ijo on Juan,—quién ib'a pensar la esgracia (p. 37). *Güen dar con* el niño, tan tierno y ya con ganas de correrla (Alberto Romero, *Perucho González,* p. 43). —*Bueno con* la mujer «ayecahue» [= grotesca, risible] (Durand, *Mercedes,* p. 200). *¡Buena cosa con* la niña! (C).

Costa Rica: —*¡Is!* ¡qué libianos! (Echeverría, p. 174). —*¡Is,* mirá ayá qué bonito! (Agüero, p. 40). —*¡Is,* tío Tigre! No creí que fuera tan mal corazón (Lyra, p. 130).

El Salvador: —*¡A buen!* al chucho ya se lo robaron (Rivas Bonilla, p. 43); —*¡A buen!*—exclamó—¿No serán los que ha traído el chucho? (p. 59). —*¡Agüén,* usté! ¡Asaber qué lián confesado las biatas! (Salarrué, *Cuentos,* p. 118).

'CA' AND EQUIVALENTS

The familiar standard interjection *¡ca!* (or *¡quiá!*) with which incredulity and negation are expressed ('nonsense, not at all,' slang: 'nothing doing,' etc.) is very seldom heard in Spanish America. Its place is taken by other exclamatory locutions, some of which are local. Thus, we hear *¡qué va!* (general in the majority of areas, familiar in Spain), *¡qué esperanza!* (River Plate region, Bolivia, Peru, Ecuador, Mexico, and Puerto Rico), *¡ni modo!* (Mexico and Central America), *¡de dónde!* (general), *¡de ánde!* (rural), *¡qué capaz!* (Ecuador, Mexico, Guatemala, etc.), *¡Je!* (Atlantic coast of Colombia [Sundheim, p. 380]), *¡ni riesgo(s)!* (Colombia, Caldas-Antioquia, along the upper Magdalena), etc. These expressions are not all exact equivalents of peninsular *ca* but are used under similar circumstances. *¡Qué esperanza!* and *¡ni modo!* generally indicate that a desire has not been fulfilled or that an effort has not succeeded, etc. In Panama we find the following familiar and jocose forms: *¡ni esperula!* and *¡ni espe!* (Lewis, p. 10).

Gagini (p. 48) explains that *¡adió(s)!* expresses "negación o extrañeza" corresponding to Spanish *¡ca! ¡quiá! ¡qué! ¡cómo!* But, in addition to negation, it often expresses unhappy surprise, as elsewhere in Central America, Mexico, the Antilles, Colombia, etc., being often equivalent to *¿de veras? ¡no diga!* etc. Equivalents for *¡qué capaz!* are given as "¡absolutamente imposible!" (Icazbalceta, p. 83) and "¡imposible!" (Batres, p. 477; Sandoval, II, 301). Vázquez (p. 335) defines *¡qué capaz!* as an "exclamación con que ponderamos la dificultad para algo." (Cf. *es capaz = es posible*, p. 421.)

ARGENTINA: ¿Quintín habría permitido semejante postura? —*¡Qué esperanza!* (Yamandú Rodríguez, *Cimarrones*, p. 65). —¿Orgulloso el patroncito? *¡De ánde,* hombre! (Lynch, *Los caranchos*, p. 38). ¿Y cuándo llegó usted de allá? —Ahorita nomás. —¿Con alguien de su familia? *¡De ánde!* Si el boleto agatita alcanzó pa mí solita (Chiarello, p. 15); ¿por qué no se va a un hotel? —*Di ánde*, si no tengo ni un cinco (p. 16). ¿Has tenido algún dijusto, alguna alegación con alguno? —*¡De ánde*, mama! ... ¡Con quién! (Lynch, *Romance*, p. 11).

URUGUAY: ¡Oh! ¡señora! ¡Perdón! ¡La he incomodado tanto! —*¡Qué esperanza!* —¡Gracias! (Sánchez, *Los muertos*, III, 1). —¿No tienen caña? —¿Caña? *¡Diánde!* (Pérez Petit, p. 168).

BOLIVIA: —¿Pero no crees que Miranda resultó con algún inconveniente a última hora? —*¡De dónde!* (J. Mendoza, *El lago*, p. 62).

ECUADOR: ¿Te pagó la deuda? *¡Qué esperanza!* (Vázquez, p. 175); ¡Yo levantaré esa piedra! —*¡Qué capaz!* (p. 335). —Cuando él no quiere, no habla. —*¡Ah dios!* ... Nunca para de hablar (Pareja, *La Beldaca*, p. 22); —Pierdo plata, ña Tomasa. —*¡Ah dios!* Si le estoy dando trece sandías, don Ciro (p. 34).

COLOMBIA (CALDAS–ANTIOQUIA): —Sabé, Vitorio, que vos sos capaz de arponiar caimanes. ¿Por qué no ensayás? —*Ni riesgos*. Yo no voy a exponerme a que me trague un burrón de ésos (Buitrago, p. 194); —¿No pensás volver a Río Grande, Vitorio? —*Ni riesgos*. La sociedad me interesa más (p. 221). —Te vas a madrugar mañana con nosotros. —*¡Ni riesgos!* No me dejan en casa (Efe Gómez, p. 29); —No adivinamos. —Piénsenlo. —*Ni riesgo*. Dínoslo tú (p. 134).

COSTA RICA: ¿No le coge caniyera [= desmayo]? —*¡Adió*, si no es primer bes/que li hablo a un muerto! (Agüero, p. 67); y si usted no está vendida/a dos manos me la dejo./ —*¡Adió!* ¿De veras? ¡No diga! (p. 76). Esa Candelaria queda largo [= lejos]. ... —*¡Adió?* ¡Si queda ahi no más! (Fabián Dobles, p. 133).

GUATEMALA: Si supieras lo mucho que me prometió ... y que llegado el momento de cumplir *¡ni modo!* (Sandoval, II, 124); *¡Qué capaz!* Nunca haré lo que usted me propone (II, 301). —¿Pacto con la zumbadora, cómo es eso? —*Adiós,* no lo sabe usté (Quintana, p. 134).

MEXICO: —¡Las probaremos! —*¡Ni modo!* —¿No hay de piña? —¡Ni de fresa! (González Carrasco, p. 130). Yo, si la anemia me hubiese dejado una poca más de sangre ... de seguro habría enrojecido de rabia. Pero *ni modo* (Ferretis, *Quijote,* p. 18). Eran muchos los deseos que tenían de ir, pero *ni modo* (García Roel, p. 165). —¡A que no me ven "mosquiando"/en los trenes, ni pidiendo/en las puertas de los tiatros!/—*¡Qué capaz!* Mi chilpayate/ya se sabe dar su trato/ como gente grande (González Carrasco, p. 133). —*¡Qué va ... !* ¡Ni de groma! (Rivas Larrauri, p. 97); —¿Al fin la ensillo? —*¡Qué va!* (p. 193). —¡No quiero beber y no sé bailar!—contestó secamente Santa. —*¡Adiós!* ¿Y si yo te pago porque te emborraches y porque me bailes ... ? (Gamboa, *Santa,* p. 25). (NUEVO LEÓN): ¿Cómo no se lo trajo Raúl derechito hasta acá? —*Adió,* y a poco l'iba a hacer caso a Raúl ... (García Roel, p. 58); Pero, eso sí: aquello no terminaba bien. —*¡Qué esperanzas!* (p. 205); —Pos a lo mejor ni va la pobre señorita Diamantina al baile. —*¡Adió!* ¿Y por qué no ha de ir? (p. 224). —¿Y con qué fierros [= dinero]? —*¡Adiós!,* con lo que nos paguen (Urquizo, p. 60); ¿pero allí van a ser libres de veras? *¿De dónde?* Allí en el monte van a comerse unos a otros para poder vivir (p. 132). (YUCATAN): *¡Atiós* [= adiós]! ¿a qué hora llegaste que no te vi? (V. Suárez, p. 64).

SANTO DOMINGO: (Indifference): *¡Adiós!* ¿Y qué? (Curiosity): *¡Adiós!* ¿Y tu hermano? (Surprise): *¡Adiós!* ¿Y no lo sabes? (Patín Maceo, *Dom.,* p. 8).

Peninsular *ca* must not be confused with a *ca* current in Ecuador. The *ca* used locally in Ecuador in rustic and popular speech (among mestizos and Indians) is probably a Quechua particle employed to emphasize a phrase or sentence. It has various equivalents in Spanish, according to the context: sometimes it has the force of the adversative conjunction *pero* 'but'; again, according to León Mera (p. 266, n. 2), it may have the adverbial function of *mas* 'but' or *antes* 'rather.' More generally, however, it has no meaning of its own and may best be likened to a continuative or illative particle. Icaza often distinguishes two forms (*ca* and *ga*) in his regional novels. In the 1936 edition of *Huasipungo* (p. 153) he remarks that *ca* is the form employed by the mestizo, whereas *ga* (with voiced consonant) is typical of the Indian's speech. The same emphasizing particle in Bolivia is often written *ja* and is found after nouns and adjectives.

ECUADOR: —El mío *ga* ... vele pes ... gordito está (*Huasipungo*, p. 26); —¿Y nusutras *ga*? (p. 27); —Tenís qu'ir al monte. —¿Y la Cunshi, *ga*? (p. 28); —Aura *ca*, patrona ... difícil ha de ser encontrar (p. 29); Y aura *ca* vos n'as de poder pararte.

BOLIVIA: —¡Tan lisa esta Marcelina *ja!* ... ¡Su lisura *ja!* (Díaz Villamil, *La Rosita*, p. 41).

CÓMO NO

Many believe the phrase *cómo no* to be solely an Americanism, which is not the whole truth. It was used to a limited extent in the older language and is not unknown today in Spain.[4] To be sure, it is employed much more frequently in Spanish America, and this very frequency has changed its original force to such an extent that it now generally means no more than a simple, unemphatic *sí*. The change involves also the intonation: the interrogative and exclamatory elements have been weakened or lost, and the stress has been shifted from *cómo* to *no*. Consequently, instead of the interrogative *¿cómo no?* or the exclamatory *¡cómo no!* the phrase has in many cases become affirmative and is often pronounced *como no*, as if one were pronouncing *sí* or *ciertamente*, although printers frequently follow the traditional punctuation. In many regions the abrupt *sí* is avoided in favor of the longer and more emphatic *cómo no*. This divergence is evident when one compares the fuller force as registered in the Academy dictionary: "¿Cómo no? expr. que equivale a ¿Cómo podría ser de otro modo? Mañana partiremos; y *¿cómo no*, si lo he prometido?" In Spain the phrase is generally used after a negative question or accompanied with a conditional clause, in either case retaining its original and fuller significance. As commonly used in Spanish America, however, its equivalents are *sí* and the more energetic *por supuesto, seguramente, ya lo creo, sin duda, claro, ¿por qué no?, con mucho gusto*, etc. Its semasiological development may be approximately

[4] "—¿Me permiten ustedes ir a la misa? Y le dijo ella que *cómo no*" (Aurelio Espinosa, *Cuentos*, I, 121 [Ávila]); cf. M. L. Amunátegui Reyes, *Observaciones i enmiendas a un diccionario*, II (Santiago, Chile, 1925), 25–31; Keniston, p. 153. For the older language cf. Torres Naharro, *Aquilana*, vs. 135.

this: "—¿Vas a hacerlo? —*¿Cómo* supones que *no* he de hacerlo? > *¿Cómo no* he de hacerlo? > ¿Cómo no? > Como no (meaning *sí*)." Since the usage is general, a few random examples will suffice.

Argentina: —Aura déme la mano. —*¡Cómo no!* (Güiraldes, *Don Segundo*, p. 31); —¿Puedo mirarlo? —*Cómo no*, hasta que se enllene (p. 60); —Y vah' hacer lo que yo te mande.

Paraguay: —¿Me permite entrar? —*¡Cómo no!* (Casaccia, p. 36).

Chile: —¿Podrías acompañarme a pasear? —*Como no* (Morales, II, 105). ¿Y esta noche irá otra vez? —*¡Cómo no!* (Laval, II, 232).

Peru: —¿Es usted aficionado a la chicha? —*¡Cómo no!* (Barrantes, p. 147). —Lindo ai [= ha de] ser. —*Como no* (Ciro Alegría, *La serpiente*, p. 42).

Ecuador: —¿Vendrá usted? —*Como nó*. —¿Conoce usted a fulano? —*Como nó* (Vázquez, p. 94).

Colombia: ¿Y ha rezado mucho por él? —*Cómo nó* (Carrasquilla, *Hace tiempos*, II, 203). —¿Aquí está la señora Bibiana? —*Cómo no* (Buitrago, p. 26).

Venezuela: ¿Y tú crees que se acostumbrará a está en una tienda? —*¡Cómo nó!* (Luis Bello, *Tomasito*, *ap.* Alvarado, p. 123). —¿Sabes nadar? —*¡Cómo no!* (Gallegos, *La trepadora*, p. 339).

Panama: —¿Quieres buscarme el traje? —*Como no*, con mucho gusto, —¿Me prestarás la novela? —*Como no* (L. Aguilera, p. 311).

Costa Rica: Présteme su lápiz. —*Cómo no* (Gagini, p. 95).

Guatemala: —¿Se casará usted al fin? —*Como no*. Me casaré el sábado (Sandoval, I, 204). —Dicen que usted se va a Europa, con su mamá. —*Cómo nó*, señor, nos iremos pronto (Batres, p. 181).

Santo Domingo: —¿Me prestará los tres pesos? —*¡Cómo no!* (Patín Maceo, "Amer.," V, 265; cf. *BDH*, V, 238).

A more emphatically pronounced *¡cómo no!* is often used ironically to express a decided negative, meaning *de ninguna manera, absolutamente no, no faltaba más*, etc. This usage is general.

Costa Rica: Quieres que te preste para no pagarme. *¡Cómo no!* (Gagini, p. 95).

Guatemala: ¿Dicen que te casarás con un vejete, Concha? —*¡Cómo no!* (Sandoval, I, 204).

Mexico: Dice Arturo que le hagas el favor de prestarle cinco pesos. —*¡Cómo no!* (Rubio, I, 114). ¿Le cuadró a usté? —*¡Cómo no!* (González Carrasco, p. 33).

EQUIVALENTS OF 'CÓMO NO'

In the approximate sense of affirmative *cómo no* 'yes, certainly, of course,' etc., we find a number of other locutions the second part of which is *no*, such as *cuándo no*, *y de no*, *si no*, *pues no*, etc. While the *no* is generally stressed, the accent is not consistently written. The phrases *cuándo no* and *y de no* in time became conditional. Through their frequent use as interjections they have lost most of their conditional force and now express an emphatic affirmation. While *cuándo no* is quite general in popular speech, *y de no* is usually associated with *gauchesco* and rural speech in Argentina, though it is occasionally found elsewhere. The following examples show how punctuation and accentuation often vary (see also p. 298).

ARGENTINA: ¿Vah'a trabajar? —*¿Y de no?* —Güeno ... dale agua al petizo (Güiraldes, *Don Segundo*, p. 39); —¿Vah' a ... ensillar tu potrillo? —*¿Y de no?* —Güeno. Yo te vi a ayudar (p. 92). —Pues, amigo, a mí me echaron a las tropas de línea sin razón. —*¡Cuando no!* le dije, ya saliste con una de las tuyas (Mansilla, *Una excursión*, p. 83).

CHILE: —Si no jué ná, señora. Era una copa qu'estaba clisá [= clisada 'cracked']. ... —*¡Cuando no*, pues! (Durand, in *Atenea*, LXXII [1943], 10).

PERU: ¿Ya sabe usted a quiénes-me refiero? —*¡Cuándo no!* A los de Catacaos (Barrantes, p. 158). —¿Lo conoces? —*¡Si no!* Es mi casero (Diez-Canseco, *Estampas*, p. 22).

COLOMBIA: —¿Y la otra ya sabrá todo el cuento? —*¿Cuándo nó*, misiá Rosita? Aquí se sabe todo (Carrasquilla, *Hace tiempos*, I, 178).

VENEZUELA: —*¡Cuando no!* Siempre te saliste con la tuya (Gallegos, *La trepadora*, p. 267). ¡Se casaría *cuándo no!* con aquella mujercita adorable, perfecta (Blanco F., *El hombre de hierro*, *ap.* Alvarado, p. 135).

MEXICO: ¿Y vendrá también la sobrina de Blas? ... Pos, *cuándo no* (García Roel, p. 228).

Sometimes *cuándo no* has a specially reinforced connotation. Sandoval (I, 239) explains that *¡cuándo no!* is used "para vituperar la acción de una persona que en todo se mete, que en todo procede siempre mal y que de ella no puede esperarse nada bueno, con relación al asunto de que se trata." This explanation seems to apply well to the following examples:

GUATEMALA: —¿Y quién te dijo eso de los sueños? —Una adivinadora. —*¡Cuándo no!* Las adivinadoras sólo sirven para explotar la ignorancia de los cándidos (Quintana, p. 42).

COLOMBIA: ¿Quién l'hizu ese vestido, que le quedó tan mal? —Fulana. —*¡Cuándo no* (había de ser)! (Flórez, p. 385).

The phrase *cuándo no* must not be confused with the interjection *¡cuándo!* which is current in many regions in the sense of "¡imposible! eso no puede ser; eso es imposible de realizarse" (Sandoval, I, 238), "¡imposible! ¡nunca!" (Alvarado, p. 135), "negativa rotunda" (Santamaría, *Dicc.*, I, 418), "¡cómo!" (Sundheim, p. 187), etc.

CHILE: —El papá come en la misma hacienda ahora. —¡Síííí, *cuándo!* ... No es cierto (Durand, *Mercedes*, p. 44).

ECUADOR: —¿Te dió lo ofrecido? —*¡Cuándo!* (Vázquez, p. 114).

MEXICO: Creyendo que yo me había de ablandar a los gritos del muchacho; pero *¡cuándo!* (*Quijotita*, I, *ap.* Icazbalceta, p. 130).

PUERTO RICO: Creyeron que yo iba a darle el dinero, pero *¡cuándo!* (Malaret, *Vocabulario*, p. 139).

SANTO DOMINGO: —Me dicen, Elvira, que te casas con él. —¿Yo? *¡Cuándo!* (Patín Maceo, "Amer.," V, 269).

The locution *¡pues no!* like *¡cuándo no!* expresses an emphatic affirmation meaning 'of course.' Though much less common than *como no*, it is more energetic. This interjection was and is used in Spain. Tiscornia (*La lengua*, § 152) in discussing the Argentine use of *pues no* refers to it as a sixteenth-century expression ("valor de afirmación admirativa que tuvo en el español del siglo XVI," "la antigua expresión"). As a matter of fact, though not recorded in the Academy dictionary, it is found today in the peninsula with the same apparent frequency as in Spanish America.[5] In Argentina *pues no* is recorded for rustic speech, whereas *cómo no* is preferred in familiar urban speech. Elsewhere *pues no* is not necessarily rustic but is less used than the ubiquitous *cómo no*. It is the ellipsis of an ironical statement: "¿No lo hace? *¡Pues no* he de hacerlo! > *¡pues no!*" Punctuation varies: *¡pues no! ¿pues no? pues no.*

[5] "¡Además dicen todos que ella es una santa! *¡Pues no!* Como que es la madre de Eduardo" (Echegaray, *O locura o santidad*, I, 4); "—¿Pagaste el aceite de ayer? —*¡Pues no!* —¿Y la tila y la sanguinaria? Todo, todo" (Galdós, *Misericordia*, ed. Nelson, p. 62); "Bien entusiasmados estaban ustedes anoche. —*Pues no*" (Martínez Sierra, *Rosina es frágil*), etc. A classical example: "—¿Piensa vuesa merced esperar, señor don Quijote? —*¿Pues no?* ... Aquí esperaré" (*Don Quijote*, II, 34).

ARGENTINA: Cántemé alguna cosita/antes de nuestro malambo/ *¡Pues no,* cielo! ¡en el momento! (Ascasubi, p. 137). Armemos un cigarrillo/si le parece. ... —*¡Pues no!* (*Fausto*, p. 279). —No les dará de comer, hermano,—le contesté. —*¡Pues no!* —¿Y qué les da de comer? —Lo que sobra (Mansilla, *Una excursión*, p. 445).

CHILE: Deje espresar su opinión a la ciencia. El arte de. ... —*¿Pues no?* interrumpió José: al momento se me ocurrió que había de andar aquí metida la jente del arte (Barros Grez, I, 9).

GUATEMALA: Cuando se pregunta a una persona si le agrada viajar, responde "*Pues no,*" para indicar que sí le gusta viajar (Sandoval, II, 292).

CUBA: ¿Ya la muchacha también se dió cuenta? —*¡Pues no!* (Carlos Montenegro, *Hombres*, p. 85).

In Yucatan, on the other hand, *no' y pues* is an emphatic negation: "¿Vas al cine? —*No' y pues,* no me deja mi mamá; ¿Llega Juan mañana? —*No' y pues,* se le enfermó su hija" (V. Suárez, p. 63). The apostrophe indicates a strong glottal stress on the *o*.

Another expression of confirmation synonymous with *cómo no*, in the sense of *sí*, is the phrase *era que no*, apparently confined to popular and rustic speech in Chile. Possibly derived from *viera que no*, it appears to be one of those ironical locutions, negative in form but affirmative in meaning, like *pues no* 'of course.' It will be remembered that, while the *no* is generally stressed, the accent is not consistently written.

CHILE: —Y mientras tanto llega la cazuela, póngale unos tragullos [= traguitos]. —*Era que no,* mi alma (Acevedo Hernández, *Por el atajo*, p. 30). —¿Tamién hay? —Chi. *Era que nó* (Romanángel, p. 90); —Sírvanse otra por mi cuenta,—ijo on Bartolo. —*Era que nó,* —ijo Quiró,—y antes que se arrepienta (p. 99); —¿Sabís firmar? —*Era que no,* patrón. —A ver, firm' aquí (p. 114); —¿Vaporino, m'hijito?—me ijeron. —Chís, *era que nó.* —¿De qué buque? —Del «Güemul» (p. 116). —¿A vos te ha tocao caer? —*Era que no*—infló el tórax don Vito—; la mar de veces (Alberto Romero, *Perucho González*, p. 49).

In the same sense we find *¡vaya que no!* and *¡vaya si no!* used locally.

PERU (PIURA): —¿Me habla en serio don Baltasar? —*¡Vaya que no!* Y, en negro, porque no puede ser más negro lo que me pasa y lo que traigo entre manos (López Albújar, *Matalaché*, p. 8).

GUATEMALA: ¿Tienes valor de examinarte en aritmética, sin estar bien preparado? —*¡Vaya si no!* (Sandoval, II, 575).

Another expression of assent, registered for Colombia, is *¡de más!* which Restrepo describes as "expresión de cortesía tan común como el aire que respiramos." It is elliptical for "de más está pedirlo," etc.

COLOMBIA: —Présteme su libro, don Pedro. —*¡De más!* (Roberto Restrepo, p. 333). —¿Cree usted que venga? —*De más* (Tobón, p. 71).

In Peru we find *que* occasionally appended to *ya* 'yes, all right,' etc., to lengthen and thereby reinforce the monosyllable in popular and familiar speech, as an emphatic affirmation equivalent to *como no:*

—Quiere decir que o cambia usted de temas y de estilo o. ... —*¡Yaque!* Ni media palabra más: me tiro por lo segundo (Corrales, p. 138); —¿Dónde me quedé ... ? —En la mona. —*¡Yaque!* ... Pues, como decía (p. 157); ¿Se acuerda usted de ese terrorífico descubrimiento ... ? —*Yaque* (p. 207). —¿Quieres embarcarte? Necesito un grumete. —*¡Yaque,* patrón! (Diez-Canseco, *Estampas*, p. 23); —En cuantito salga 'e viaje, me avisas, ¿quieres? —*Yaqu'*ermano (p. 119).

MÁS QUE

The rustic conjunction *más que* (or its variant *más que nunca*) 'although' when used elliptically—that is, when it stands alone—is equivalent to an interjection meaning *no importa*. While the expression has been considered a localism, it appears in one or the other form in Chile, Ecuador, Venezuela, Costa Rica, El Salvador, Mexico, and probably elsewhere. Uses and equivalents as recorded for these countries are as follows: Chile (Román, III, 448): *más que nunca* "se usa ... como respuesta a algo que se desprecia, y entonces equivale a *no importa*"; (Zorobabel Rodríguez, p. 307): "*más que nunca*, equivalente a *suceda lo que quiera, venga lo que viniere*, i aun algo más"; Venezuela (Alvarado, p. 282): "*más que nunca* 'frase vulgar de pésimo gusto, quiere decir *ni por ésas, por ninguna razón, a pesar de eso*' (Medrano). ... En otros puntos de Occ. es interjectiva, en el sentido de: *no me importa, con su pan se lo coma, aunque nunca sea* así"; Costa Rica (Gagini, p. 178): "*más que* ... hácese a veces más enfática la expresión diciendo *más que nunca*"; El Salvador (Salazar García, p. 182): "*más que, más que sea (y a mí qué) = no me importa*"; Mexico (Ramos Duarte, p. 350): "En Zumpango [Central Zone] se oye a menudo en la conversación familiar el estribillo *másque, másque,* por *no importa, aunque,* etc." The phrase *más que* is probably used likewise in Spanish dialects; Garrote (§ 63) seems to indicate it for Leonese in his equivalents of *más que* as *no importa, a pesar de que.*

CHILE: ¿Está Ud. resuelto a casarse? —Resuelto. —¿I con una viuda, pobre i cargada de hijos? —*¡Más que nunca!*

ECUADOR: Hay un rico de Guayaquil que necesita harta gente. Está pagando buen diario. —*¡Más que!* No tenemos plata para el viaje (Gil Gilbert, *Nuestro pan,* p. 190).

COSTA RICA: Puedes ahogarte. *Más que.* Me enojaré si vas. *Más que.* No te querré si vas. *Más que nunca* (Gagini, p. 178).

MEXICO: —Pos ya le he dicho [a mi padre] que ese apodo es italiano, y él dice que *más que,* que si me lo sigue [usted] diciendo, no me deja volver y yo quero seguir (Gamboa, *Teatro,* III, 22).

MECÓN

The inelegant Chilean interjection or oath *¡mecón!* (used only by the populace) is generally believed to be a shortened form of *me condeno* or *me condenara* ('I'll be damned'), variants of this "juramento execratorio." No satisfactory explanation has yet been offered, but it seems more likely that the longer forms are later embellishments of *mecón* (for an unlikely conjecture see Román, III, 468). Other forms heard are *meconcito, me recondenara,* and occasional new varieties like *me consolara* and the facetious *me condenitre.*

CHILE: —Habría que verlo pa crerlo. —*Mecón* ques cierto (Guzmán Maturana, p. 207). *¡Me recondenara!* ¡Cómo no se acrimina uno! Creen que porque son ricos han de mirar al pobre como un perro (Durand, in *ACH,* p. 225). *Mecón,* no miento, tuvimos que sacarlos [= sacarnos] hasta los calzoncillos (Romanángel, p. 37); *¡Mecón* la carreta grande que tiró el pobre finao Feli! (p. 38); —*Me condenara,* por la maire, mire (p. 45); —*Me consolara* qu'el coñá t'apretaor [= el coñac está apretador] como caballo (p. 51); —*Mecón* qu'el pobre Feli si no resucita agora no resucita nunca (p. 53); —*Me condenara,* —ecía,—si hubiera sabío tal, arreo con el jarro lavatorio (p. 54); —*Me condenitre* qu'es entallao (p. 93). —No quito ni pongo con el patrón, *¡meconcito!* (Acevedo H., *La canción rota,* p. 5).

¡O! ¡OH! ¡HO! ¡HOM!

The interjection *¡o!* (spelled *¡oh! ¡ho!,* etc.) is used frequently in the colloquial and rustic speech of some regions at the end of a phrase or sentence as a vocative and often with the equivalence of the interjection *¡eh!* Since the form *hom* (in the Peruvian highlands a plural *homs*) is also current, both *o* (or *ho*) and *hom* are generally thought to be reduced forms of *hombre*, which is likewise common as a vocative, and, as an interjection, expresses surprise or astonishment. This explanation is not convincing. Possibly *¡o!* goes back to the Latin use of *o* with vocatives and was later blended with *hombre* used in this sense. At any rate, we find a similar use of *o* and *hom* in Spanish dialects: Galician (Cuveiro Piñol), Asturias (Acevedo and Fernández), Montaña (García-Lomas), Bilbao (Arriaga), etc. (cf. Corominas, p. 100).

In Catamarca (Argentina) this *o* corresponds to *che* (cf. p. 57) of the coastal zone; Lafone (p. 175) reports that it was formerly "muy general" and that today it is relegated to the populace ("pueblo bajo") and may have come from Copiapó. This seems plausible, since the use of *ho* and *hom* is quite common in Chile, where newsboys in Santiago shout "¡El Mercurio, *ho!*" "*¡El Mercurió!*" etc. In Chile, *ho* is of lower social status than *hom*. In Salta (Argentina) we find the form *hon* (Spanish final *m* is generally pronounced as *n*). For Venezuela, Alvarado (p. 413) defines *¡sí oh!* as "interjección irónica de incredulidad"; but that *¡sí oh!* does not always have such a meaning is clear from the examples given below. Some writers capitalize the *o*.

Argentina (Catamarca): Vea *¡O!* —¿De dónde viene *¡O!?* (Lafone, p. 175). (Salta): ¡Apúrate, *hon!* (Dávalos, p. 12). (San Luis): ¡Pero, *hó!* —¡Peró! ¡Pero, *jo* (with aspirated *h*)! (Vidal, p. 84).

Uruguay: ¡Vamos, duérmase, *oh!*—gritó al nene (Horacio Quiroga, V, 87).

Chile: ¡Mira, *hom! ¡Mirom! ¡Miró!* (Román, III, 130). —¡Y qué diablos querís que diga, pos *hom!* (Rojas Gallardo, *3a serie*, p. 10); —¡Pero vos no poís andal así, pos *hom!* (p. 15); —¿Qué te pasa, *hom?* (p. 18); —¡Oye Tristán, *oh!* (p. 37), etc. —¡Pucha la payasá, Liboria, *oh!* (Romanángel, p. 60). —¡Oye *oh!* Usebio, vení un ratito (Juan del Campo, p. 44); —¡Güeno, pus *oh!* si nues pa tanto pa ponerse ronco (p. 65); —¡Güeno *ho!* (p. 95), etc. —Por la madre, *¡oh* ... Güena cosa, *oh!* (Acevedo Hernández, *De pura cepa*, p. 4). —Anda, *ho* (Latorre, *Zurzulita*, p. 62); —¿Quién ganó ahora, *ho?* (p. 63).

Peru: —Pasa, *hom* ... llega, *hom* ... —suena la voz amistosa del viejo (Ciro Alegría, *La serpiente*, p. 17); ¿Y vos, *hom?* (p. 25); Ta güena, *hom* (p. 31); —*Hom*, vaya con la suerte e ser mayor y hombre e rispeto (p. 34); —Vamos nomá, *hom.* ... —¡Juerte, *hom!* (p. 100);

—*Homs*, a la balsa, a pasar luego ... a ver, cristianos (p. 154); —*Homs* ... —dice el Encarna al círculo voraz de cholos (p. 162).

VENEZUELA: —¿Llegaste esta tarde? —¡Si, *oh!* Nos atrasamos (Guillermo Meneses, in *ACMV*, II, 141); —Tenemos toda la noche para los dos. —¡Si, *oh!* (p. 142); —¿Nerviosa? —¡Si, *oh!* —¿Por qué? —Por nada, negro (p. 155). (Rustic, mother to daughter): ¿Lo viste? (Daughter to mother): —¡Sí *hom!* Si está cambiadísimo (Díaz-Solís, p. 73).

NICARAGUA: ¿Dónde va, *hom?* (C).

EL SALVADOR: —¿Cayen, *O?* —¡Sí, *O!* —¡Ya quizá va maneciendo, *O!* ... ¡Tá haciendo friyo, *O!* (Salarrué, *Cuentos*, p. 95); —¿Qué jué, *O?* —¡Es un palo que siá reido, *O!* (p. 97).

GUATEMALA: No te vayas, *o* [= tú]; ¿Qué dice ése, *o* [= tú]? ¿Cuándo volvés [= vuelves], *o* [= vos o tú]? (Sandoval, II, 156). —¿Quien and'ay, *oh!* —¡Soy yo, Ramón! (Santa Cruz, in *CLCA*, p. 235). —Güen día, nana. —Güen día, *oh* (Quintana, p. 87).

The Argentine *che* (see p. 57) has the same source as a *che* heard in regions of Central America. In Costa Rica (Gagini, p. 110), Nicaragua (Ayón, p. 133; Castellón, p. 49), and Honduras (Membreño, p. 54), *che* expresses displeasure and disgust or scorn (like standard *¡puf! ¡quita! ¡qué asco!* etc.), and is used also "para contener a uno que nos molesta de obra, como la castellana *¡tate!*" (Gagini); "para rechazar algo, o para impedir que una persona lleve a cabo lo que se propone" (Membreño). It is employed, too, as a substantive in the expression *hacerle (el) che a* 'to scorn.'

COSTA RICA: —¡Vea, mi hijita, a nadie hay que *hacerle ¡che!* en esta vida (Lyra, p. 109).

HONDURAS: Paco despertó y ... gritó su protesta: —*¡Che*, hombre, *che!* (Martínez Galindo, p. 100).

In Bolivia *choy* and *cho* are used among *cholos* in the sense of *che* or *hombre* to call a person's attention. In Quechua *chu* is an interrogative particle.

—*Choy*, Francisquito (Díaz Villamil, *La Rosita*, p. 14); —¡Qué rico, *choy!* (p. 15); —*Cho*, al pasar no has reparado (*Cuando vuelva*, p. 24); —*Cho*, dime francamente (p. 29); —*Choy*, Faustino, si me muero, no me has de olvidar, ¿quieres? (p. 51); —*Choy*, apúrense (p. 39).

(ES) CAPAZ QUE

The impersonal locution '*(es) capaz que* + subj.' is used in most regions (Malaret, *Supl.; BDH*, II, 311) in the sense of *es posible, es probable, quizás*, etc. Cuervo (§ 440) considered it of Spanish origin ("... no *es capaz* me acuerde de todas, por ser muchísimas" [1764]), deeming it a contamination: *es capaz de insultarlo* + *es fácil, posible que lo insulte* 〉 *es capaz que lo insulte*. Curiously, Sánchez Sevilla (p. 248) reports a negative meaning for rural Salamanca: "*es capaz que* venga" = *probablemente no vendrá* (cf. also Zamora Vicente, p. 45).

ARGENTINA (RURAL): *Capaz que* llueva en seguida (Vidal, p. 397).

CHILE: *Es capaz que* te salgan al encuentro unos bandidos y te maten (Román, I, 268). *Capaz que* me lo coma todo (C). Eran tan hábiles los montoneros que *capaz que* en las mismas barbas de los carceleros las emprendieran con alguna presa (M. Petit, p. 107).

BOLIVIA: No *es capaz que* haiga otra como usté (Arguedas, *Vida*, p. 216).

PERU: —¿Vendrá Juan a la tarde? —*Capaz* (Benvenutto, p. 153).

ECUADOR: *Capaz de que* no van a llegar a tiempo (Aguilera Malta, p. 10).

COLOMBIA: Si usted me dice una palabra más, *es capaz que* le dé una bofetada (Cuervo, § 440). Si vas a su casa, *es capaz que* te pegue (Sundheim).

MEXICO: ¡Cómo molestan a esta niña! *es capaz que* la vuelvan loca (Inclán, I, 174); *es capaz que* ese charro se figure que todavía eres cerrera (I, 47). Si pierdo esta oportunidad, *es capaz que* yo enloquezca (Santamaría, *Dicc.*; cf. also Icazbalceta, p. 83).

Román (I, 268) implies that *¡Capaz que no me pagues!* may be a threat or challenge, equivalent to standard *¡Cuidado con no pagarme!*

CUIDADO

In standard speech the interjection *¡cuidado!* is used with varying constructions in exhorting a person to proceed carefully and attentively, as a warning of impending danger, or as a sort of threat: "*¡Cuidado*, que se va a caer! *¡Cuidado* que no se caiga! *¡Cuidado* con caerse! *¡Cuidado* si lo hace!" etc. In many regions of Spanish America we find additional constructions unfamiliar to the Castilian ear, some of them involving merely the omission of the connecting *que* or *si* or the omission of the usual pause represented in writing with a comma.

Peru: *¡Cuidado* tropecemos! *¡Cuidado* se queme! (C).

Ecuador: *¡Cuidado* te aplasta un carro! (Gallegos Lara, *Las cruces sobre el agua*, p. 137). *¡Cuidadito* se remoja! (Aguilera M., *La isla virgen*, p. 98). Hable despacio, *cuidado* lo oyen (Gil Gilbert, *Nuestro pan*, p. 71).

Colombia: —Los esperamos a almorzar. *¡Cuidado* no van! (Efe Gómez, *Guayabo negro*, p. 26).

Venezuela: *¡Cuidado* como te oyen decí eso! (Gallegos, *Cantaclaro*, p. 166); Pero *cuidado* como va a darle alcance (p. 216).

Costa Rica: *¡Cuidado* me corta! (Fallas, p. 79). *¡Cuidado* se te ocurre hablar de lo de ayer! (J. Gutiérrez, p. 180).

Mexico: —*Cuidado* y me contradigas ¿oyes? (Gamboa, *Santa*, p. 12).

¡PA(RA) NUNCA!

In Chile the expression *¡pa nunca!* means "mal, incómodo" 'in a sorry plight,' etc. Its usage is rural and popular.

—¡Si estamos *pa nunca!* No me acuerdo naíta cómo llegué. —Pero si venían *pa nunca* ... ¿y cómo se jueron a curarse [= emborracharse] tanto? (Romanángel, p. 95); —Agora sí qu'estoy *pa nunca* ... con el cuerpo malo y en el medio 'e la mar (p. 118). Cuando no juntamos ... taba *pa nunca* (J. M. Castro, *Froilán Urrutia*, p. 24).

¡AMPE!

The word *ampe* (*ampesito*) expresses endearment or entreaty, softening the whole phrase, sometimes in an attempt to curry favor, and often equivalent to *por favor*. In older Aymara *ampi* is recorded as an affirmative particle: "es de uno que afirma alguna cosa";[6] its meaning is defined as "Así es; verdad es,"[7] more recently (1891) by Middendorf as "so ist es."[8]

—*Ampe*, no me vengas con tus malos augurios (Díaz Villamil, *La Rosita*, p. 10); —Me he cansado, *ampe* (p. 13); —¿Qué cosa, mama? —Las gallinas, pues, *ampe!* (p. 23); Este bailecito más pues, *ampe* mama (p. 46); —¡Abrime, *ampe!* ... Ay, *ampe*. ¡Hace un frío! (p. 78).

[6] L. Bertonio, *Arte de lengua aymara* (1603), ed. Platzman (Leipzig, 1879), p. 251.

[7] L. Bertonio, *Vocabulario de la lengua aymara* (1612), ed. Platzman (Leipzig, 1879), p. 16.

[8] *Die Aimará-Sprache* (Leipzig, 1891), § 71.

FORMS OF ADDRESS

The preceding vocative forms *¡oh! ¡che!* etc., lead us to forms of address in general. Our strictly syntactical classification will not include independent forms like *esposo, -a* (avoided by the upper classes), *marido* and *mujer* (avoided by the middle classes); *mamá* (urban) and *máma* (now rural, but the original Spanish form until the eighteenth century, when under French influence *mamá* came to be used in the cities); *tata, taita, tatita* (now fast falling into desuetude, though still current in rural regions in addressing fathers, old men, priests, and God); *nana* ('mother, granny'; in New Mexico *nanita* also 'little sister'), *viejo, -a* (sometimes for 'father, mother,' sometimes for 'husband, wife,' sometimes for 'friend'); *amigo, amigazo* (rural), *compadre* or *compay* and *comadre* or *comay, vale* or *valito, chico,* and *hermano* or *mano* (for 'friend, chum'; also *cuate* in Mexico; *mano* and *mana* in New Mexico for older people: *mano Juan* 'good old John'); *patrón* or *jefe* (for 'sir' to a superior); *señorita* or *joven* ('young lady'); *joven* (for 'young man,' though he may be middle aged); *ñato, -a* (as a term of endearment); the lowly *tío* and *tía;* and other forms, the geographical area of all of these varying sometimes considerably.[9]

The use of the possessive adjective *mi* with the vocative, apparently an archaism, has been discussed (p. 41): *mi hijo, m'hijo* = standard *hijo mío.* In many regions the adjective *lindo, -a,* is frequently added to such expressions in familiar speech to make them more affectionate, with the equivalence of 'dear' rather than of 'beautiful.'

CHILE: Pero, *mi hija linda,* fíjate que tu situación es especial (Durand, *Mercedes,* p. 252). «Aquí no hay ni un alma, *mi amito lindo,*» jilibiaba poniendo tamaña jeta una pícara mulata que habían criado en la casa (Ernesto Montenegro, p. 20). —Oiga, *m'hijita linda;* ya, déme lo que le pío (Romanángel, p. 12). —Mamita, *mamita linda,* ven (Durand, *Mi amigo,* p. 121). (RURAL): —Estudea, *m'hijito lindo,* pa que lleguís a ser lo que yo hay sío (C).

ECUADOR: Sabía conseguir favores de los cholos tratándoles de «*ñañito lindo*» (Icaza, *Media vida,* p. 14). —*Padre lindo,* San Jacinto

[9] For a thorough analysis of certain forms of address, cf. Frida Weber, "Fórmulas de tratamiento en la lengua de Buenos Aires," *RFH,* III (1941), 105–39. While the forms discussed are primarily Argentinian, references are made to usage in other countries. Cf. also A. Alonso, "Problemas. VII. Las abreviaturas de *señor, señora* en fórmulas de tratamiento," in *BDH,* I, 417–30. Cf. also Rosenblat, *Notas,* pp. 122–30.

(Gil Gilbert, *Nuestro pan*, p. 53); —*San Jacinto lindo*, míranos con ojos de misericordia (p. 54).

VENEZUELA: —*Mi amito*, don Fernando, *tan lindo*, haga que me dejen sin trabajar hoy (Uslar Pietri, p. 24).

EL SALVADOR: —*¡Mijo, mi lindo!* ¡Perdóname, cosita; taba como loco! (Salarrué, *Cuentos*, p. 86).

In Andalusia, *niño, -a* (equivalent to standard *señorito, -a*), is applied to an unmarried person of any age whatsoever, a practice attributable to the elastic southern imagination. This custom has survived, too, in much of Spanish America, especially the feminine form, which at times is extended to a married woman or a widow. Servants in particular are likely to address the unmarried children of the household as *niño* or *niña* (often stressed *niñó, niñá*), regardless of age. Sometimes (as in Ecuador, rural Colombia, etc.) *niño, -a*, is applied also to the master and mistress of the household as well as to anyone not of low social standing, regardless of age: "hombres y mujeres (remarks Mateus, p. 276), todos son *niños* y *niñas*, ninguno ha salido de la niñez; e infeliz del que se atreviere a decir *señor* o *señora*." The same applies to other regions, including Mexico, where the Spaniard, Sánchez Samoano, jocosely versified in 1892 (*Modismos*, p. 33): "No hay allí viejos ni viejas,/porque éstos son nombres rancios,/siempre son *niños* y *niñas*/aunque pasen de cien años."

In many countries (Mexico, Venezuela, Colombia, Peru, Ecuador, etc., but not in Argentina) *niño* was and is applied only to a (well-to-do) white child, *muchacho* being reserved for a Negro, Indian, or plebeian. For Mexico, Henríquez Ureña informs us: "*Joven* y *niño* se aplican a personas de clases acomodadas, mientras que para las de clases pobres se dice en Méjico *muchacho*. 'No es muchacho, que es *niño*,' hemos oído protestar a una mujer del pueblo en Méjico porque se le decía a su hijo en la calle: *quítate, muchacho*" (*BDH*, IV, 192, n. 8). In his recent Venezuelan novel, *Balumba* (1943), Briceño writes: "... estábamos divididos en clases: nosotros, los *muchachos;* Virgilio, el *niño*" (p. 13); "el menor de nosotros, que era yo, tenía diez y seis años, Virgilio tendría quince, pero la limpieza y cuidado de sus trajes y el olor a Agua Florida que siempre tenía en sus cabellos brillantes y peinados, nos hacía pensar que esto era propio de los *niños*. Nosotros seguíamos siendo *muchachos*. Cuando más, para la boca de los viejos, *zagaletones*" (p. 14). This was likewise true in the Antilles, where colored folk, whether Negro or mulatto, used *niño* in addressing their masters and, in general, any white person. It no longer holds for Cuba, despite the Academy dictionary, except in the case of very old Negroes (Suárez, p. 378; cf. also *BDH*, V, 220). (It may be said in passing that the same euphuistic tendency prescribes *moreno* for *negro*, *indígena* or *natural* for *indio*, and occasionally *pardo* for *mulato*.)

ARGENTINA: —¿Y?—preguntó la muchacha. —Vi a dir ahurita, no más, *niña*. —¿Y anoche, no fuiste? —Sí, *niña*. —¿Y la contestación? ... —¿Y él? —No lo vide, *niña* (Larreta, *Zogoibi*, p. 139). La sirvienta entró en el cuarto. ... —¿Qué pasa, *niña?* —Nada, Isabel (p. 155).

CHILE: En Chile es corriente decir también *la niña*, *las niñas* por toda mujer soltera que ha pasado de la adolescencia y no ha llegado a vieja; y aun las viejas solteras se tratan entre sí de *niña* (Román, IV, 17).

ECUADOR: —¡Rosalía!—llamé a la cocinera. ... —Mande, «*niñó*» (García Muñoz, *Estampas*, p. 222). (Mistress to Indian servant): —¡Consuelo! —¡Mandé, *niñá!* (Icaza, *Cholos*, p. 7); (Don Braulio, landowner, says to his son): —Come despacio. ... —Pero *niño*. ... Pareces un chancho. Sólo los longos ['Indian children'] comen así. Cualquiera diría que no eres un *niño decente* (p. 8); Un *niñito decente* come despacio. Un *niñito decente* no llora como longo (p. 9); —Consuelo. —Mandé, *niñó* [to don Braulio] (p. 10); —Güeno. —Bueno *niñá*, se dice, longo malcriado. —Güeno *niñá* (p. 53).

COLOMBIA (CASANARE): —¿La *niña* Griselda? —En el caño ... entró la *niña* Griselda (Rivera, p. 26); La *niña* Griselda se apresuró a traer una miel oscura ... para que endulzáramos la bebida. —Muchas gracias, *señora*. ... ¿Ese vestío lo cortó usté? [asks Griselda]. ... —No, *señora* [replies Alicia, who is from Bogotá (p. 28)]. ... Venga pa acá, *niña* Alicia [says Griselda (p. 29)]. (ANTIOQUIA): —No ve, mi *Niña*— plañe Cantalicia. ... ¿Y cómo le pareció, mi *Niña?* (Carrasquilla, *Hace tiempos*, I, 183); exclama mamá—¿Qué son todas las cosas que traés? —Pues ai irá viendo, *niñ'*Elisa. Cosas de misiá Doloritas (II, 245).

VENEZUELA: —La *niña* Anama ... está entre la vida y la muerte (Pocaterra, in *ACMV*, I, 163).

PANAMA: A viejas ochentonas, lelas y amojamadas, como dice Cuervo, las llama el pueblo *Niña* Fulana, *Niña* Zutana (Méndez Pereira, p. 23).

COSTA RICA: Cualquier vieja ochentona es por acá *niña* María o *niña* Juana (Gagini, p. 187).

NICARAGUA: Ya he oído censurar el uso de anteponer este título al nombre de las solteras: la *niña* Juana, la *niña* Leonor. Se le considera corruptela nicaragüense (Ayón, p. 219). Doña Ritana nunca se había casado ... tenía aquel aspecto de las que merecen llamarse doñas, y aun se llaman, sin serlo; y ella lo aceptaba con la excusa de que decirle a una *niña*, era un nicaragüenismo de mal gusto (Chamorro, *Entre dos filos*, p. 106). En la sierra, aun los mozos más respetuosos ... la llamaban «la Camila.» Y quienes ascendían en la gama del respeto, apenas si llegaban al «*niña* Camila,» cognomento con el que se designa también a las viejecitas (Robleto, p. 93). Se dice *niña* a las jóvenes y a las personas de edad que tienen alcurnia: *niña* Socorrito y *niña* Mariana (Castellón, p. 92).

HONDURAS: —La *niña* Maruca llegó seguramente hoy allí—decía el mayordomo (Carías Reyes, *La heredad*, p. 11); —Pues vea, *niña* Maruja (así la llamaban cordialmente desde que era pequeñita), novedades tenemos muchas (p. 12).

GUATEMALA: La *niña* Teresa López,/que frisa ya en los sesenta,/ frente a la cantina «El Tigre»/tiene una tienda (Arce, p. 99). La *niña* Meches ya pasa de los cuarenta años y aún no ha podido casarse. ... Se asegura que la *niña* Lola, viuda de López, murió de 85 años. ... El *niño* Chico no quiso casarse y murió de sesenta años. ... —Dile a la *niña* Julita que se vista pronto. ... Señora, el *niño* Paco no me hace caso. Oye, Adelina: ya es hora de que vayas al colegio por el *niño* Ramoncito (Sandoval, II, 125).

The vocative and narrative forms *ña* (sometimes *seña*, rarely *ñora*) and *ño* (sometimes *ñor* or *señó*) are still current in many rural sections of Spanish America, applied among the populace to older persons (from forty years of age on, says Sandoval [II, 154], for Guatemala) to avoid the familiarity of calling them by their first names. *Ña* and *ño* are used generally with the given name (*ña* Juana), occasionally with the family name (*ño* Pozo), and sometimes with nicknames and vituperative epithets, in this case corresponding to standard *so* (< señor): *ño ladrón* = standard *so ladrón* (*don ladrón* in the classics). The masculine form *ño* appears to be more restricted geographically than the feminine *ña*. The zones have not yet been definitely ascertained. In Spain *ña* is found in Asturias, according to Amado Alonso (*BDH*, I, 417), and *ño* is heard in Andalusia. *Ña* and *ño* are probably reductions of *señora* and *señor* used proclitically in vocative phrases (*señora* Juana), a position in which titles and forms of address are generally unstressed[10] (*señora* > *señoa* > *señuá* > *señá* > *ña*, and *señor* > *señó* > *ño*), though some have wished to derive *ña* from *doña*, or even from *niña*. Probably because of their low standing, both *ña* and *ño* are rapidly falling into desuetude, generally in favor of *señor, -a*. For *sise* (= *sí, señor*) and *nose* (= *no, señor*) in eastern Puerto Rico, cf. Navarro, p. 123.

In the same rural areas the form *misiá* (= *mi* + *siá* < *sea* < *seora* < *señora*) or *misia* (and *miseá*) is used in addressing or referring respectfully to ladies of a little higher social rank, generally to married women or widows. This form, originally of the highest standing, has long since been banished from most urban centers. For Colombia, Roberto Restrepo (p. 341) registers *mi sa* as popular in some regions, and in others (Antioquia and Caldas) this form "conserva cierto aire de distinción." *Su merced* is still heard in some rural regions in addressing a superior; in Colombia it is used in Bogotá as a term of endearment to children and close friends.

The title of *don, doña*, has fallen considerably from its original high estate. In the earliest centuries of the language it was reserved for royalty and high church dignitaries and later to those who rendered an important service to the state. In colonial times and even during the wars of independence the title *don* could be bought. Tobar (p. 203) reports the sale of *don* in the city of Lima in 1818 for 1,400 reales. Independence brought with it the abolition of titles, and any name could now flourish a *don* or *doña*. Its use spread through the middle and lower classes. In Ecuador, for instance—an extreme case—*doña* came to be applied to old Indian women (the young ones were and are called *huambras* or *longas*); so that, according to Tobar, *india* and *doña* have there become synonymous. In the list of Cuencan expressions (*morlaquismos* < Morlaquía = Cuenca) appended to his novel *Sumag Allpa* (1940), Mata defines *doñas* as "indias adultas casadas."

When *don* in turn fell into disrepute, the full forms *señor* and *señora* came to be preferred by the middle and upper classes, particularly in the cities. Naturally, economic and social conditions varying as they did among the republics, the hierarchy of these titles was not and is not uniform throughout Spanish America. An attempt to make minute geographical distinctions would here be impossible and futile. Suffice it to say that in limited regions, like Santo Domingo (*BDH*, I, 427), *don* continues to be used as in Spain, that is, in ad-

[10] Navarro Tomás, "Palabras sin acento," *RFE*, XII (1925), 353; *BDH*, II, 123.

dressing persons combining a certain age (at least thirty years) with an independent social position; in Mexico and much of Colombia and elsewhere *don* has been preserved in practically all classes; but usually it has, among the middle and upper classes, been replaced by *señor*.

We may say that in many rural regions the title is used before given names (sometimes family names) and alone as a mere vocative, especially in addressing a stranger. In this usage (¡Oiga, *don!*) it is sometimes felt to be slightly lacking in courtesy, a bit jocose or nonchalant. In the country *don* and *doña* are not restricted to any special social class. They are generally used by laborers, foremen, and the like, in addressing or referring to their master or mistress, boss, superiors, etc., or to a person who has distinguished himself within the same social rank (*Don Segundo Sombra*). In many rural regions *don* and *doña* correspond to urban *señor* and *señora*. In the country *doña* occasionally alternates with *misiá*. In the cities *doña*, while polite, is today often applied to the washerwoman, the storekeeper's wife, and others of that social category who have attained a certain age and a certain distinction within their class. In the cities, *don* (unlike *doña*) is today resuming some of its former significance, not as a token of nobility but merely as a social amenity. While *señor don* and *señora doña* are, in general, no longer used in Spanish America as they are in Spain and have yielded to simple *señor* and *señora*, a few Spanish-American newspapers insist on retaining *doña* in their social items, contrary to daily spoken usage.

ARGENTINA: —¡Qué *ña* Petrona, ésta! ¿Conque, al fin, la dejó mi compadre? (*Fray Mocho*, p. 17); Mire, compadre ... estoy recordando a *doña* Eloya, la puestera de la costa. ... La pobre me decía. ... «¡Qué hombre, *ña* Petrona, es su compadre!» (p. 18); —Cómo no, *doñ'* Amalia—dijo *ña* Martina indignada. ... —Callesé, *ña* Martina, es mejor—dijo *doñ'* Amalia (p. 131); *Misia* Robustiana, la señora de su jefe (p. 165). —¡Güen día, *don!* —Buen día, amigo (Lynch, *Los caranchos*, p. 32). —¡Caramba!—dijo el dueño del lobuno ... no la creíba tan aviada. ... —¡Qué quere, *don!* Me hi remediao con las empanadas y los chorizos (Wast, in *ACH*, p. 39). ¿Y cuánto tiempo,—habíale preguntado a su nuevo patrón,—estaremos en Güenos Aires, *don?* (González Arrili, p. 85). —Sería por algo, *don* ... por *algo-dón* ... y árnica (Filloy, p. 192).

URUGUAY: ¿Cómo le va, *doña?* ¿Qué hace, *ña* Martiniana? (Sánchez, *Barranca abajo*, II, 15); —¡El vecino *don* Zoilo Caravajal! —Sí, señor. Pero eso era antes, y perdone. Aura es el *viejo* Zoilo, como dicen todos ... cuando uno se güelve pobre, hasta el apelativo le borran (II, 16).

CHILE: —Ahora le toca a Ud., pues, *ño* Peiro. —Yastá, pues, compadre (Guzmán Maturana, p. 27); —*¡Ño Peiro:* pásele la guitarra a *on* [=don] Panchito! (p. 31). —Buenos días, *ña* Nicolasa. ¡Qué tempranito que le amaneció! —No tanto como a Ud., *don* Pancho (p. 82); Salió a recibirnos *misiá* Rosarito, muy pulcra en su traje campesino (p. 85). ¡Eh, *don!* le digo apenas pude sacar el habla ¡a quién se le ocurre ponerse a dormir así y con el sereno que empieza a caer! (Ernesto Montenegro, p. 26); —Mire, *don,* no me venga a mí haciéndose el gringo, porque a mí no me desprecea naiden (p. 158). —¿El Malo, *On* Chano, anda por aquí? —¿No lu' ha oyío, *su mercé?* (Latorre, *Hombres,* p. 23). —Si ya voy, *doña* (Latorre, *Zurzulita,* p. 34).

PERU: La *vieja* Melcha ... *doña* Melcha (Ciro Alegría, *La serpiente,* p. 140); —Nos daráste posadita, *don* Matish. ... —¡Dios se lo pague, *ñor!* (p. 148); donde la *eña* Mariana (p. 151); —Dios se lo pague, *ñores* (p. 161); *Doña* Mariana, acuclillada tras la puerta de su bohío (p. 168); —¿Ta el Cayo o *ña* Meche? —No, ellos murieron hace tiempo. ... Soy su hijo: el Lucas (p. 219). —*¡Misiá* Francisca! —¡Qui'ay! —Le vendo mi baúl y este Corazón de Jesús: una libra. Regateó la zambona [= mulata] largo rato (Diez-Canseco, *Estampas,* p. 24); *Misiá* Petita [owner of the *pulpería,* is a *zamba*]. (A customer says): —Otra mulita, *señora.* ... (Another says): —Ta mañana, *misiá* (p. 152); ¿Cómo te jué? —Pa servirlo, *ño* Ambrosio [= el viejo *don* Ambrosio] (p. 153). (Sixty years ago): Tan pronto como una distinguida señora viene a menos y baja de su rango, los grotescos *Dones* y *Doñas* que quedan descritos, se apresuran a apearle el tratamiento y a llamarla *ña* Fulana (Arona, p. 189).

ECUADOR: —¿Te acordás de la noche que *ña* Paula se moría? —No sea pendejo, *don* Leitón [= Tomás Leitón] (Aguilera Malta, p. 45). Se queja la *ña* Panchita/Que está bravo *ño* Tomás (Mera, p. 264). (Priest): —¿De dónde eres hijito? (Indian boy): —Onde *na* Alejita, pes (Icaza, *Cholos,* p. 59). (Priest): Y decíle a tu patrona: que es *mi señora* Alejita, que si podrá mañana reunirme unos cinco sucrecitos (p. 60); —¿Qué 's pes oís?—interrogó el cholo. —Se casó pes *ña* Alejita con *ño* Albertico (p. 150); pasó pensando en *ña* Blanquita (p. 151). (QUITO): —¿Qué 's de la longa Mariana? (Icaza, *En las calles,* p. 140); se lamentó *doña* Laura [wife of *don* Luis Antonio Urrestas, miembro de la Cámara de la Banca] (p. 185). Sarcástica-mente úsase [*doña, don*] entre nosotros: —«¿Quién ha roto ese plato? —¿Quién ha de ser sino la *doña* fulana, o el *don* fulano?» —Y estos *dones* no son sino unos infelices criados (Vázquez, p. 149). Los indios cogían los brazos de las *doñas* [= indias adultas casadas] por debajo del rebozo (Mata, *Sumag Allpa*, p. 13). —Usté m'ha cáido en gracia, *ñor* (La Cuadra, *Horno*, p. 58).

COLOMBIA (ANTIOQUIA): Usté es la *niña* Ricarda Marín, y me perdona la pregunta? —Sí. ... ¿Y usted es la criada de *misiá* Rosa? —Y suya, *niña*, y de esta *señora* (Carrasquilla, *Hace tiempos*, I, 193); La vieja calla un momento; el auditorio expresa su complacencia y yo suplico: —Cuente más, *ña* Melchorita (p. 214); —¿No cierto que es muy dichosa *ña* Melchorita?—dice *doña* Genoveva. —Muy dichosa, mi querida *señora* (p. 215); —Bueno, *ño* Matica (p. 294). Ahí tá *don* Barrera [family name] (Rivera, p. 37). (NORTH): ¡Adiós, *doña!* (Sundheim, p. 248). —Pero con una condición, mi *don*. —Diga a ver, mijo (Arias Trujillo, p. 119).

VENEZUELA: —Tú también, *ña* pazguata. La muchacha saltó hacia él (Pocaterra, in *ACMV*, I, 158). *Ño* Pernalete y *doña* Bárbara son uña y carne (Gallegos, *Doña Bárbara*, p. 149). —¡Si usted la viera, *doña!* (p. 181). —Son para la familia que viene de Caracas. ... *Misia* Águeda con las hijas y *misia* Carmelita con la niña Adelaida (Gallegos, *La trepadora*, p. 32; (author relates): En cuanto a *doña* Águeda ... gran señora, a la manera de los viejos tiempos (p. 43); (*Doña* Águeda speaks): —¡Hilario! ¿Cuándo viniste? —Acabo de llegar, *doña* (p. 47); (author relates): *Misia* Carmelita las hacía reír (p. 48). In Caracas *misia* is general: "*Misia* María, ¡a la orden, *misia!*" Servants to married women (*niña* or *señorita* to unmarried ladies), also respectfully in stores; people believe it derives from English *Mrs.* (Rosenblat).

COSTA RICA: —*Don* Bítor, sírbanos ai/entre los dos una media/de ron blanco ... ¿Y usté qué bebe, *ña* Juana? ... —¿Cómo *ñor* Serapio come? (Agüero, pp. 56–57). —Güenas noches, *ña*. ... —Muchas gracias, señora—exclama entonces el otro, que parece venido de ciudad. —*Ña* Rafela, le voy a presentar al *siñor* (Fabián Dobles, p. 198); mama se jué anoche pa casa de *ñor* Bermúdez (p. 377); —¡Se estaba muriendo, *ña!* ... —*Ñor* trajo el dautor (p. 378, etc.).

EL SALVADOR: —¡Pobre *ño* Guzmán! —¡Pobrecito *ño* Chomo! Ni uno solo supo decir: —¡Qué malvados! (Ambrogi, p. 108); La *señora* Quiteria aprobó el aserto. ... El *señor* Pedro y los suyos abandonaron por fin el río (p. 121); —¿Bas a la ciudá, Casimiro?—le preguntó una de las señoras. —Sí, *señora* Mercedes (p. 217).

GUATEMALA: *Ña* Ramona vino en busca de usted (Sandoval, II, 154); *Ño* Domingo fué el caporal de la finca durante su juventud. ... *Ñor* José está probablemente enfermo, porque no ha venido a sacar la basura (p. 155).

MEXICO (TABASCO): En el velorio en ca *don* Guadalupe, *seña* Paz, la mujer de *don* Mateo (José Luis Inurreta, *ap.* Gutiérrez Eskildsen, p. 81). Es general en Tabasco [but also elsewhere] decir: «¡Oiga *Don!*» «¿De dónde viene usted, *Don?*» «Venga, *Doña.*» «¿Qué quiere, *Doña?*» (Ramos Duarte, p. 214). Mire, *don*, a mí no me venga con calaveras de vaca, a espantarme (López y Fuentes, *¡Mi general!* p. 10); —Hasta la vuelta, *doña.* ... —Que Dios y la Virgen los lleve por buen camino, muchachos (p. 29). —¿Está *don* Chema, mi viejo amigo Chema? —*Don* Chema fué mi padre. ... Murió hace viente años. ... ¿Y *don* Nacho Arenas? —Murió. ... ¿Y *doña* Cuca López? —Murió (López y Fuentes, *Cuentos*, p. 127). (NUEVO LEÓN): —*Don* Ugenio [a storekeeper], un cinco de aceite ... pidió una viejecita encorvada. ... —¿Otra vez sus dolores, *doña* Petrita? —Otra vez, *don* Ugenio, pos qué quere usté (García Roel, p. 109).

NEW MEXICO: La cas'e *seña* Paula; La cas'e *ña* Paulita; ¿Ónde sta *'on* Juanito?; Dijo *ñor* Juan que ya venía (Aurelio Espinosa, *Studies*, II, § 33).

CUBA: Bamoh a bailal la *comay* Mamerta y yo como en loh buenoh tiempoh de nosotroh. La *comay* Mamerta era una vieja delgada (Ciro Espinosa, p. 150).

SANTO DOMINGO: (An old Negro bootblack speaks to a white youth): —¡Qué suerte, *don!* ... ¿Y no ha peleado nunca con nadie? (Requena, *Los enemigos*, p. 84). ¡Ey, *don!* (Bosch, *Dos pesos*, p. 69).

In Quechua the particle *y* (sometimes written *i*), attached to nouns ending in a vowel, expresses possession in the first person in the nominative and vocative cases: *tata* = *padre*, *tatay* = *mi padre* or *padre mío*. Probably as a borrowing, the same particle is used in Aymara as the vocative case ending for persons (Middendorf, § 216); it often expresses endearment.

BOLIVIA: —Buenas noches, *senorai* (Díaz Villamil, *La Rosita*, p. 93); —*Señoray*, hágame el favor de prestarme una brasita (*Plebe*, p. 192). —¿Cómo estás, *huahuay?* (Rodrigo, p. 9); —Aquí están, *hijitay*

(p. 12); —Aquí está, *huahuatay* (p. 13); —Sí, sí, *tatay* (p. 45); —*¿Niñitay?* —¿Qué quieres? (p. 61). —*Mamay*, el lunes iré por la semilla de papa (Unzueta, p. 32); —*¡Señoray*, doña Filo! (p. 90).

ARGENTINA (NORTHWEST): —*¡Mamaytay* querida! *¡Tatay* de mi corazón! (Heredia, p. 111).

SLANG INTERJECTIONS

The vituperative epithet *hijo de puta* or *hideputa* (lit. 'son of a prostitute') is no longer used in polite society as it occasionally was in Cervantes' day (*Don Quijote*, II, 31), but more generally by the populace, both to blame and to praise. Defined in the Academy dictionary as "expresión injuriosa y de desprecio," it is still current in vulgar speech. In Spanish America it assumes several euphemistic forms which vary from region to region. The full locution *hijo de la* (or *una*) (*gran*) *puta* (or *perra*) is exceedingly low and comparatively rare. The current reduced or altered and less offensive forms, generally rustic, are *hijuna, ahijuna* or *jijuna, hijue, juna* or *junagran, joeperra, jué pucha* (especially in Argentina), *hijuna pucha, jijo, hijo di un jujú* (New Mexico, where are also the inoffensive *hijo de nel, hija de nea* [Aurelio Espinosa, *Studies*, II, § 101*b*], and others given in the examples below. Apparently restricted to Mexico and part of Guatemala is *hijo* (or *jijo*) *de la chingada*, which because of its crudity is seldom found in print, though it is heard in its full form in very vulgar speech. Writers generally abbreviate to *hijo* (or *jijo*) *de la* (or *de un*) ... , the blank to be filled in by the reader; or they substitute *hijo de la tal* (*por cual*), *hijo de la gran siete, hijo de la gran flauta, hijo de la tiznada*, etc. The aforementioned phrases are often employed as interjections, and their force has sometimes become weakened to a *¡caramba!* or *¡caray!* equivalent to our 'damn it,' 'gosh,' 'gee whiz,' 'the devil with,' etc. Though they generally express wrath or a threat, they occasionally indicate pleasant surprise or joy.

The word *puta* itself is very common in vulgar and familiar speech among men as an interjection of surprise, admiration, alarm, disgust, and even joy, equivalent to standard *¡caramba! ¡caray! ¡canastos!* etc. It covers about the same gamut as does the innocuous and typically feminine *¡ay!* In many regions the expression *echar puteadas* (or *putas*), as well as the verb *putear*, means 'to use the interjection *¡puta!* frequently,' and by extension 'to swear.' The word itself has taken on many euphemistic forms, most of which occur generally in Argentina, Uruguay, Chile, Bolivia, Peru, Ecuador, and sporadically elsewhere. Some of these altered forms have completely lost their offensiveness, especially in rural areas, and are sometimes used by women: "simple e inofensiva exclamación que no hiere los oídos ni el amor propio, aunque mantenga, implícito, todo su significado original" (Inchauspe, *Voces*, p. 218); in New Mexico *¡pucha!* means 'my goodness!' (Kercheville, p. 26). The most frequent euphemisms are *ta*, *pucha(s)*, *cha(s)*, *puchita(s)*, *apuchas*, *pucha(s) con*, *puchas* (or *chas*) *digo* (in Chile *diego* or *Diego*, probably < *digo*), *puya*, *punta*, etc. It will be remembered that the form *hi de pucha* is found in the *Farsas* (1514) of Lucas Fernández of Salamanca (1867 ed., p. 147) and in Tirso de Molina (*la villana de Vallecas*, II, 5; *La gallega Mari-Hernández*, I, 10). For final *-s*, cf. *BDH*, II, 212.

Argentina: —*¡La gran puta*, cómo llueve! (Filloy, p. 11); salió *echando putas* como un energúmeno (p. 39); Cuando se empantanó la camioneta, yéndose a la zanja, apretó los dientes, férreamente. Y tragó saliva ... a ser otro, hubiese *puteado* (p. 154); Atajó ... con unas cuantas *puteadas* la persistencia del atropello (p. 212). Si la yerba llegara a quemarse, todos serían inflexibles y duros. El capataz gritaría, *putearía* el mayordomo y el administrador o el patrón lo echarían en seguida (Varela, p. 125). —*¡Cha* que sos animal!—grita, llevándose las manos a la cabeza (Lynch, *Palo verde*, p. 59). —*¡La pucha!*—dije al rubio, ¡qué golpazo! (Güiraldes, *Don Segundo*, p. 190). Pantalión ... la miraba: *¡Jué pucha!* ¡Cómo le parecía bien! (Lynch, *Romance*, p. 43); Doña Cruz se alzó entonces como leche hervida. —*¡Pucha*—dijo—*con* los desajeraos y malos lenguas! (p. 76); *¡Jué pucha con* el hombre hereje! ... Pantalión ... dijo muy contento: —*¡A la pucha!* ... Eso quiere decir que hay jugada ¿no? (p. 82). ¿Y por qué me insulta? *¡Joeperra!* (Larreta, *El linyera*, p. 62). ¡Chancleta! ... *¡Aijuna!* ¡No está! (Manuel Romero, p. 15); —*Pucha digo*, ¡cómo somos desgraciadas las mujeres! (p. 13). *¡Cha digo!* = ¡Pucha digo! (Saubidet, p. 117). (Northwest): —Todavía mi burrita sirve para hacer un favor. —*¡Pchá digo!*: si corría más ligero que mi caballo (César Carrizo, p. 181). Estaba una vieja un día/jugando con una rosa,/daba un suspiro y decía:/—*¡Ahijuna!* ... Quién juera moza (Draghi Lucero, *Cancionero popular cuyano* [1938], p. 139). *¡Hijo de la gran flauta!* (Rosenblat); *¡hijo 'el ... páis con gorra 'e vasco!* (*BDH*, II, 189).

Uruguay: —¡Epa, no se mueva o le tiramos! —*¡Junagran!* ... se le escapó un juramento (Montiel, *Alma nuestra*, p. 60); Cirilo no pudo contener la indignación y con el rebenque amenazador, apuntando hacia la estancia, con un sollozo de rabia, gritó: —¡No tienen ley pa nada! ... *¡hijos de una gran puta!* (p. 154). —*¡Pucha, con* la india fieraza!—comentaba el capataz (Pérez Petit, p. 75); (in praise):—*¡Jué pucha con* la moza linda!—decía un jovencito, comiéndosela con los ojos (p. 87); Aquello era demasiado para la esposa de don Carmelo Antúnez, la hombruna doña Ramona Solís. ... —¿Qué dijiste? *¡Aijuna,* si me ha contestao el muy sabandija! (p. 102); Eran los cuerpos exánimes de Margarito y el indio, en medio de unos charcos negruzcos. ... —*¡Juna gran!* ... barbotó Juan de Dios (p. 175). —*¡La pucha* que hace frío! ¡Brr! (Florencio Sánchez, p. 234); Una helada *de la gran siete* (p. 139). *¡Hijo de la gran flauta!* (Reyles, *El gaucho,* p. 217).

Paraguay: *¡La pucha! ¡Pucha digo! ¡La gran flauta! ¡la gran siete! ¡A la pinta! ¡A la madona!* (Morínigo).

Chile: *¡Puchas* qu'es fregao el viejo! (Romanángel, p. 20); —¿Cómo te va, *hij' una grandísima perra?*—me ijo cuando me vió. —Mecón que viene atropellaor—le ije (p. 23); —*¡Apuchas diego* la chicha güena, on Juan! (p. 27); *¡Apuchas* que lloraba la viua! (p. 40); *¡Chas diego* que hacía penetro [= frío] como a eso e las tres e la mañana! (p. 49); —*Chitas diego* (p. 80); *¡Chas* la payasá! (p. 118). —Juan de Dios ... acércate. ... —¡No quiero! —Anda. ... *Hijuna* ... que es tu abuela. —¡No quiero! —*¡Hijuna!* —¡Rosario! ¡Mira lo que hablas ... más decencia! (*Se persigna apresuradamente*). —Hablo como me da la gana, con mi lenguaje mío. —¡Bien lo decía yo, Dios mío! No lo podrá educar la pobre. ... ¡Rosario! eres demasiado «arrotada» (Sepúlveda, *Hijuna,* p. 34). —*¡Puchas* que hace calor! ... *¡Chitas!* yo que no quería dormir (Juan Modesto Castro, p. 190). —Por la *chitas,* compaire (*Tallas chilenas,* p. 147). Lo voy a *putear* bien *puteado* [= lo voy a insultar bien insultado] (C). Así me icía mi maire,/ Así me volvió a icir:/ El día que yo me muera/ *¡—ta!* que vay a sufrir (C).

Bolivia: Entonces el Pampino exclamó con displicencia: —*¡Pucha 'igo!* Si te salen pilas [= soldados paraguayos] al camino, les tocas bocina, pu, pa que se hagan a un lado (Céspedes, p. 190). —*¡Por la gran puta!* Indios maulas, les voy a enseñar aquí a contestar (Augusto Guzmán, p. 171).

Peru: —*¡La pucha, con* el niño tan porfiao! (Corrales, p. 233). —*¡Jijuna!* ¡Si eres hombre, sal p'ajuera! (Diez-Canseco, *Estampas,* p. 71); señalando a la moza con un guiño pícaro, otorgó un permiso:

—Mañana puedes dir tarde ... —*Jijuna* [expressing joy]. ... Y se abrazaron con una efusión de hermanos (p. 77); —¡Dos soles al jiro! —¡Pago, *jijuna!* —¡No vale mentar la madre! (p. 79).

Venezuela: (To a colt): —¡Ah, *hijo de puya* bien resabiao! (Gallegos, *Doña Bárbara*, p. 88). —¡Ah, *hijo e puya* este Cirilo! (Uslar Pietri, p. 84).

Colombia: —*¡Hijue* si será bien largo! (Arango Villegas, p. 141). *¡Hijuna pucha!* era exclamación frecuente de una viejecita de casa (Cuervo, § 672). *¡Hijueperra!* (Álvarez Garzón, p. 25); ¡Anda a la *punta* ... ! (p. 141). ¡Ah, *hiju 'e puerca!*, *hiju 'e mugre, hiju 'e míchica, hiju 'e p'arriba, hiju 'e la vida,* etc. (Flórez, p. 385).

Costa Rica: —*¡Hijo 'e la mama,* atrebío! (Agüero, p. 61).

Honduras: —¡Perro ... *hijo de tantas* ... ! (Carías, *Cuentos*, p. 66).

El Salvador: (Father on discovering the quack has betrayed his daughter): —*¡Aijuesesentamil!*—rugió Tules—¡Mianimo ir a volarle la cabeza! (Salarrué, *Cuentos*, p. 91). (To a dog): —¡Chucho *hijue ... puerca!* (Rivas Bonilla, p. 10); —¡Ve *quijue sesenta mil* ... ! (p. 20); (to rats): —¡Cabronas! ... *¡Hijas de noventa p* ... ! (p. 42).

Guatemala: *Hijo de la gran puta* = *hijo de la gran madre* = *hijo de la gran Bretaña* = *hijo de la que no tiene nombre* = *hijo de la tiznada,* etc. (Sandoval, I, 632). Es ya intolerable la costumbre que tienes de *putear* a casi todas las personas (II, 298).

Mexico: —¡Codorniz, *jijo de un* ... ! ¡Hora donde les dije!—rugió Demetrio (Azuela, *Los de abajo*, p. 21); —¡Ya me quemaron!—gritó Demetrio, y rechinó los dientes. *¡Hijos de ... !* (p. 23); —Por eso, pues, ¿quién *jijos de un* ... es usté?—interrogó Demetrio (p. 34). (Father on learning his daughter has gone astray): —¡Ah, *jija de la* ... ! (His wife replies): —¡Erria, tú ... ! ¡Para tu coche! ¡Ricuérdate nomás que soy su mama! (Rivas Larrauri, p. 178). —Yo te voy a quitar lo lebrón, *hijo de la tal* (Urquizo, p. 58); oímos muy claro los gritos de los revoltosos de ¡Viva Madero, pelones *hijos de la tal!* (p. 166); —*¡Hijos de la tiznada!*, ya me agujerearon mi sombrero; ora cuando llueva me voy a mojar (p. 237). Salió de la casa renegando: ¡Ay *hijo de la chingada!* ¡Ahorita arreglamos cuentas! (Galeana, p. 24). Y oye, *jijo de la gran siete,* ¿quién te enseñó a manejar ... ? —Tu *retiznada* madre—le contestó el cochero (Valle-Arizpe, p. 328); —Los doctores son unos perfectos *jijos de la gran siete* (p. 344).

BIBLIOGRAPHY

ACB = Saturnino Rodrigo. *Antología de cuentos bolivianos contemporáneos.* Buenos Aires: Sopena Argentina, 1942.

Acevedo Díaz = Acevedo Díaz, Eduardo. *Soledad* (1894).[1] Montevideo: C. García, 1941.

Acevedo Díaz (h.), Eduardo. *Argentina te llamas* (1934). 2d ed. Buenos Aires: El Ateneo, 1936.

———. *Cancha larga.* Buenos Aires: Sopena, 1939.

Acevedo Hernández, Antonio. *Por el atajo* (1920). Santiago, Chile: Nascimento, 1932.

———. *La canción rota* (1921). Santiago, Chile: Nascimento, 1933.

———. *De pura cepa.* Santiago, Chile: Nascimento, 1929.

———. *Árbol viejo* (1930). Santiago, Chile: Nascimento, 1934.

———. *Cardo negro.* Santiago, Chile: Nascimento, 1933.

———. *Pedro Urdemalas.* Santiago, Chile: Cultura, 1947.

Acevedo y Huelves, Bernardo, and Fernández y Fernández, Marcelino. *Vocabulario del bable occidente.* Madrid, 1932.

ACH = Manzor, Antonio R. *Antología del cuento hispanoamericano.* Santiago, Chile: Zig-zag, 1939.

ACMV = *Antología del cuento moderno venezolano* (1895–1935). Selección de Arturo Uslar Pietri y Julián Padrón. 2 vols. Caracas: Ministerio de Educación Nacional, 1940.

ACP = Bazán, Armando. *Antología del cuento peruano.* Santiago, Chile: Zig-zag, 1942.

ACR = *Antología de cuentistas rioplatenses de hoy.* Buenos Aires: Vértice, 1939.

Acuña, Carlos. *Mingaco.* Santiago, Chile, 1926.

———. *Huellas de un hombre que pasa.* Santiago, Chile, 1940.

Agüero, Arturo (Sinforoso Retana). *Romancero tico.* San José, Costa Rica: Trejos Hnos., 1940.

Aguilera Malta, Demetrio. *Don Goyo* (1933). 2d ed. Quito, Ecuador: Antorcha, 1938.

Aguilera Patiño, Luisita. *El panameño visto a través de su lenguaje.* Panama: Ferguson & Ferguson, 1947.

Alcalá Venceslada, Antonio. *Vocabulario andaluz.* Andújar, 1933.

Alcocer, Ignacio. *El español que se habla en México.* Tacubaya, D.F.: Instituto Panamericano de Geografía e Historia, 1936.

Aldao, Martín (Luis Vila y Chávez). *El caso de "La gloria de Don Ramiro."* 7th ed. Buenos Aires: A. Moen y Hno., 1913.

Alegría, Ciro. *La serpiente de oro* (1935). 2d ed. Santiago, Chile: Nascimento, 1936.

———. *Los perros hambrientos.* Santiago, Chile: Zig-zag, 1939.

———. *El mundo es ancho y ajeno.* Santiago, Chile: Ercilla, 1941.

Alegría, Fernando. *Leyenda de la ciudad perdida.* Santiago, Chile: Zig-zag, 1942.

———. *Lautaro, joven libertador de Arauco.* Santiago, Chile: Zig-zag, 1943.

Alfaro, R. J. *Diccionario de anglicismos.* Panama: Imprenta Nacional, 1950.

Alonso, Amado. "Problemas de dialectología hispanoamericana," *BDH*, I (1930).

———. *El problema de la lengua en América.* Madrid: Espasa-Calpe, 1935.

Alonso, Amado, and Henríquez Ureña, Pedro. *Gramática castellana, primer curso.* Buenos Aires: El Ateneo, 1938. 4th ed. Buenos Aires: Losada, 1944.

[1] Date in parentheses indicates first edition when it differs from that of edition consulted.

———. *Gramática castellana, segundo curso.* Buenos Aires: Losada, 1939. 4th ed. Buenos Aires: Losada, 1944.

ÁLVAR, MANUEL. *El habla del Campo de Jaca.* Salamanca: Consejo Superior de Investigaciones Científicas, 1948.

ALVARADO, LISANDRO. *Glosarios del bajo español en Venezuela.* Caracas, 1929.

ÁLVAREZ GARZÓN, JUAN. *Los Clavijos.* Bogotá: Cromos, 1943.

AMADO, MIGUEL. "El lenguaje en Panamá," *BAAL*, XIV (1945), 641–66.

AMBROGI, ARTURO. *El Jetón.* San Salvador: Diario la Prensa, 1936.

AMORÍM, ENRIQUE. *La carreta* (1932). 4th ed. Buenos Aires, 1937.

———. *El paisano Aguilar* (1934). 3d ed. Buenos Aires: Claridad, 1937.

ANDA, J. GUADALUPE DE. *Los bragados.* México: Compañía General Editora, 1942.

———. *Juan del Riel.* México: Compañía General Editora, 1943.

ANDRADE Y CORDERO, CÉSAR. *Barro de siglos.* Cuenca, Ecuador, 1932.

ÁNGULO CHAMORRO, G. A. *Carne de cuartel.* México, 1940.

ARANGO VILLEGAS, RAFAEL. *Bobadas mías.* Manizales, Colombia: Arturo Zapata, 1936.

ARCE Y VALLADARES, MANUEL JOSÉ. *Romances de la barriada.* Guatemala: Cultura, 1938.

ARÉVALO, TERESA. *Gente menuda.* Guatemala, 1940.

ARGUEDAS, ALCIDES. *Raza de bronce.* La Paz, Bolivia: González y Medina, 1919.

———. *Vida criolla: la novela de la ciudad.* Paris: Ollendorff, n.d.

ARIAS TRUJILLO, BERNARDO. *Risaralda* (1935). 2d ed. Bogotá and Medellín, 1942.

ARMELLADA, CESÁREO DE. "Apuntaciones sobre el hablar de Perijá," *Boletín de la Academia venezolana*, XV (1948), 189–200.

ARONA, JUAN DE (PEDRO PAZ SOLDÁN Y UNANUE). *Diccionario de peruanismos.* (Begun 1861.) Lima, 1883. "Biblioteca de Cultura Peruana," No. 10. Paris, 1938.

ARRÁIZ, ANTONIO. *Puros hombres.* Caracas, 1938.

ARRIAGA, EMILIANO DE. *Lexicón etimológico, naturalista y popular del bilbaíno neto.* Bilbao, 1896.

ASCASUBI, HILARIO. *Santos Vega* (1851), in *Poetas gauchescos*, ed. E. F. TISCORNIA. Buenos Aires: Losada, 1940.

AVELLANEDA, FÉLIX F. "Palabras y modismos usuales en Catamarca," in S. A. LAFONE, *Tesoro de catamarqueñismos*, pp. 265–375.

AYÓN, ALFONSO. *Filología al por menor.* León, Nicaragua, 1934.

AZÓCAR, RUBÉN. *Gente en la Isla.* Santiago, Chile: Zig-zag, 1938.

AZUELA, MARIANO. *Los de abajo* (1915). México: Botas, 1941.

———. *Los fracasados* (1908). 4th ed. México: Botas, 1939.

———. *Mala yerba* (1909). 3d ed. México: Botas, 1937.

———. *Los caciques* (1917). *Las moscas* (1918). México: La Razón, 1931.

———. *Las tribulaciones de una familia decente* (1918). 2d ed. México: Botas, 1938.

———. *Regina Landa.* México: Botas, 1939.

———. *Avanzada.* México: Botas, 1940.

———. *La Marchanta.* México: Seminario de Cultura Mexicana, 1944.

BAAL = *Boletín de la Academia argentina de letras.* Buenos Aires, 1933——.

BAFA = *Boletín de la Asociación folklórica argentina.* Buenos Aires.

BAPL = *Boletín de la Academia panameña de letras.* Panamá, 1926–35. Segunda época, 1944——.

BARÁIBAR Y ZUMÁRRAGA, FEDERICO. *Vocabulario de palabras usadas en Álava.* Madrid, 1903.

BARALT, RAFAEL MARÍA. *Diccionario de galicismos.* 2d ed. Madrid, 1890.

BARNOYA GÁLVEZ, FRANCISCO. *Han de estar y estarán.* Santiago, Chile: Zig-zag, 1938.

Baroja, Pío. *Zalacaín el aventurero.* New York: D. C. Heath & Co., 1926.

Barrantes Castro, Pedro. *Cumbrera del mundo.* Lima: Perú Actual, 1935.

Barreto, Mariano. *Idioma y letras.* 2 vols. León, Nicaragua. Vol. I: 1902; Vol. II: 1904.

Barrios, Eduardo. *El niño que enloqueció de amor* (1915). 6th ed. Santiago, Chile: Nascimento, 1939.

———. *Un perdido* (1917). 2 vols. Madrid, 1926.

———. *El hermano asno* (1922). 5th ed. Santiago, Chile: Nascimento, 1937.

Barros Grez, Daniel. *El huérfano.* 6 vols. Santiago, Chile, 1881.

Batres Jáuregui, Antonio. *Vicios de lenguaje: provincialismos de Guatemala.* Guatemala, 1892.

Bayo, Ciro. *Vocabulario criollo-español sud-americano.* Madrid, 1910. First published in *Revue Hispanique,* Vol. XLVI (1906), with the title "Vocabulario de provincialismos argentinos y bolivianos."

———. *Manual del lenguaje criollo de Centro y Sudamérica.* Madrid: R. C. Raggio, 1931.

BDH = *Biblioteca de dialectología hispanoamericana.* Buenos Aires: Instituto de Filología, 1930——.

Beinhauer, Werner. *Spanische Umgangssprache.* Berlin and Bonn, 1930.

Bellán, José Pedro. *El pecado de Alejandra Leonard.* Montevideo, 1926.

Bello, Andrés, and Cuervo, Rufino José. *Gramática de la lengua castellana destinada al uso de los americanos.* Paris: Roger & Chernoviz, 1921.

Benavente, Jacinto. *Señora ama* (1908), in *Teatro,* Vol. XVII. Madrid, 1909.

———. *De cerca* (1909). Madrid, 1917.

Benítez, José María. *Ciudad.* México: Porrúa, 1942.

Benvenutto = Benvenutto Murrieta, Pedro M. *El lenguaje peruano,* Vol. I. Lima, 1936.

———. *Quince plazuelas, una alameda y un callejón.* Lima, 1932.

Berro García, Adolfo. "Prontuario de voces del lenguaje campesino uruguayo," *BF,* Vol. I (1936–37).

BF = *Boletín de filología.* Montevideo, Uruguay, 1936——.

BICC = *Boletín del Instituto Caro y Cuervo.* Bogotá, Colombia, 1945——.

Blanco Fombona, Rufino. *El hombre de oro.* Madrid: América, n.d.

Blym, Hugo. *Puna.* Santiago, Chile: Ercilla, 1940.

Boj, Silverio. *Áspero intermedio.* Buenos Aires: Losada, 1941.

Bonilla Ruano, José María. *Gramática castellana,* Vol. II. 4th ed. Guatemala, 1940.

———. *Gramática castellana,* Vol. III: *Mosaico de voces y locuciones viciosas.* Guatemala, 1939.

Borao, Jerónimo. *Diccionario de voces aragonesas.* 2d ed. Zaragoza, 1908.

Bosch, Juan. *Camino real.* La Vega, R.D., 1933.

———. *La Mañosa.* Rev. ed. La Verónica, 1940.

———. *Dos pesos de agua.* Havana, 1941.

Bourciez, E. *Éléments de linguistique romane.* Paris, 1910.

Braue, Alice. *Beiträge zur Satzgestaltung der spanischen Umgangssprache.* "Hamburger Studien zu Volkstum und Kultur der Romanen," Vol. VII. Hamburg, 1931.

Briceño, Arturo. *Balumba.* Caracas: Elite, 1943.

Brunet, Marta. *Montaña adentro* (1923). 2d ed. Santiago, Chile: Nascimento, 1933.

———. *Bestia dañina.* Santiago, Chile: Nascimento, 1926.

Bueno, J. J. *Entretenimientos gramaticales.* 3d ed. Tuluá, Colombia, 1927.

Buitrago, Jaime. *Pescadores del Magdalena*. Bogotá: Minerva, 1938.
Bustamante, José Rafael. *Para matar el gusano*. Quito: Academia Ecuatoriana correspondiente de la Española, 1935.
Cajar Escala, José A. *El cabecilla*. Panama: Ferguson & Ferguson, 1943.
Calcaño, Julio. *El castellano en Venezuela*. Caracas, 1897.
Calderón. *Three Plays by Calderón*. Ed. G. T. Northup. Boston: D. C. Heath & Co., 1926.
Calero Orozco, Adolfo. *Sangre santa*. Managua: Atlántida, 1940.
Candioti, Alberto M. *Camino incierto*. Buenos Aires: Siglo Veinte, 1946.
Canellada, M. J. *El bable de Cabranes*. Anejo: *RFE*, 1944.
Cantarell Dart, J. *Defendamos nuestro hermoso idioma*. 2d ed. Buenos Aires: Jesús Menéndez, 1937.
Capdevila, Arturo. *Babel y el castellano*. Buenos Aires: Losada, 1940.
Carías Reyes, Marcos. *La heredad*. Tegucigalpa, Honduras, 1931.
———. *Cuentos de lobos*. Tegucigalpa, Honduras, 1941.
Cariola, Carlos. *Entre gallos y media noche, sainete criollo* (1919). 2d ed. Santiago, Chile: Hémette y Frías, 1920.
Carrasquilla, Tomás. *Hace tiempos: memorias de Eloy Gamboa*. 3 vols. Medellín, Colombia: Atlántida, 1935–36.
———. *Novelas*. Bogotá: Biblioteca Aldeana, 1935.
Carrizo, César. *Viento de la altipampa*. Buenos Aires: Macagno, Carrasco y Landa, 1941.
Carrizo, J. A. *Antiguos cantos populares argentinos* (*Catamarca*). Buenos Aires: Silla Hnos., 1926.
Casaccia, Gabriel. *El pozo* (*cuentos*). Buenos Aires: Ayacucho, 1947.
Casanova Vicuña, Mariano. *Diga 33*. "La escena," No. 43. Santiago, Chile: Cultura, 1937.
Casares, Julio. *Crítica profana* (1916). 2d ed. Madrid: Renacimiento, n.d.
———. *Crítica efímera*. Madrid: Calleja, 1918–19.
Cascante de Rojas, Claudia. *Castellano*. San José, Costa Rica: Universal, 1940.
Castellanos, Jesús. *De tierra adentro*. Havana, 1906.
Castellón, H. A. *Diccionario de nicaraguanismos*. Managua, 1939.
Castro, Américo. *La peculiaridad lingüística rioplatense y su sentido histórico*. Buenos Aires: Losada, 1941.
Castro, Juan Modesto. *Aguas estancadas*. Santiago, Chile, 1939.
Cavada, Francisco J. *Chiloé y los chilotes*. Santiago, Chile: Imprenta Universitaria, 1914.
CC = *Cuentos contemporáneos, recopilación, prólogo y notas por F. de Ibarzábal*. "Antologías cubanas," Vol. I. Havana: Trópico, 1937.
Cejador y Frauca, Julio. *La lengua de Cervantes*. 2 vols. Madrid, 1905–6.
Celestina = *Comedia de Calisto y Melibea* (*La Celestina*). Ed. Foulché-Delbosc. In Vol. XII of *Biblioteca hispánica*. Barcelona, 1902.
Centro, bimestre centroamericano. Managua, 1939–40.
Cerruto, Oscar. *Aluvión de fuego*. Santiago, Chile: Ercilla, 1935.
Certad, Aquiles. *Lo que le faltaba a Eva, comedia*, in *CLAEV*, No. 38, 1943.
Céspedes, Augusto. *Sangre de mestizos*. Santiago, Chile: Nascimento, 1936.
Cevallos, Pedro Fermín. *Breve catálogo de errores*. 6th ed. Quito, 1904.
Chamorro, Pedro Joaquín. *Entre dos filos*. Managua, Nicaragua, 1927.
———. *El último filibustero*. Managua, Nicaragua, 1933.
Chiarello, Florencio. *Casa de departamentos* (1939). "Argentores," Vol. VII, No. 176. Buenos Aires, 1940.

Cifuentes García, Luis. *Contribución al estudio de la sintaxis del castellano en Chile, MS.* Santiago, Chile, 1949.

Cione, Otto Miguel. *Lauracha.* 5th ed. Buenos Aires: Anaconda, 1933.

CLAEV = *Cuadernos literarios de la asociación de escritores venezolanos.* Caracas.

CLC = *IV concurso literario centroamericano, organizado por el Comité central de la feria nacional.* Guatemala, 1941.

Coello (h.), Augusto C. *La epopeya del campeño.* San Pedro Sula, Honduras, n.d.

Coen Anitúa, Arrigo. *El lenguaje que usted habla.* México: Vértice, 1948.

Cornejo, Justino. *Fuera del diccionario.* Quito: Ministerio de Gobierno, 1938.

Corominas, Juan. *Indianoromanica.* Reprinted from *RFH*, VI (1944), 1–35, 138–75, 209–54.

Corrales, Juan Apapucio (Clemente Palma). *Crónicas político-doméstico-taurinas.* Lima: Compañía de Impresiones y Publicidad, 1938.

Correas, Gonzalo. *Vocabulario de refranes y frases proverbiales.* 2d ed. Madrid: Real Academia Española, 1924.

Cortejón, Clemente. *Arte de componer en lengua castellana.* 4th ed. Madrid: V. Suárez, 1911.

Costa Álvarez, A. *El castellano en la Argentina.* La Plata, 1928.

Covarrubias Orozco, Sebastián de. *Tesoro de la lengua castellana o española.* Madrid, 1611.

Croce, Arturo. *Chimó y otros cuentos,* in *CLAEV*, No. 35, 1942.

Cuervo = Cuervo, Rufino José. *Apuntaciones críticas sobre el lenguaje bogotano.* 7th ed. Bogotá: El Gráfico, 1939. Earlier editions: 1st ed., Bogotá, 1867–72; 4th ed., Chartres, 1885; 5th ed., Paris, 1907; 6th ed., Paris, 1914.

Cuervo, Rufino José. *Diccionario de construcción y régimen de la lengua castellana,* Vol. I: *A–B* (1886); Vol. II: *C–D* (1893). Paris: Roger & Chernoviz.

———. "El castellano en América," *Bulletin Hispanique*, III (1901), 35–62.

———. *Disquisiciones sobre filología castellana.* Ed. Rafael Torres Quintero. Bogotá: Instituto Caro y Cuervo, 1950.

Dávalos, Juan Carlos. "Lexicología de Salta," *BAAL*, II (1934), 1–18.

Dávila Garibi, José Ignacio. *Del náhuatl al español.* Tacubaya, D.F., 1939.

Délano, Luis Enrique. *Viejos relatos.* Santiago, Chile: Zig-zag, 1940.

Del Campo, Estanislao. *Fausto* (1866), in *Poetas gauchescos*, ed. E. F. Tiscornia. Buenos Aires: Losada, 1940.

Del Campo, Juan (Juan Manuel Rodríguez). *Aventuras de Usebio Olmos.* 2d ed. Santiago, Chile: Centro, n.d.

Delgado, Rafael. *La calandria* (1891). 4th ed. México: La Razón, 1931.

d'Halmar, Augusto (Augusto Thomson). *La Lucero.* (Published as *Juana Lucero* in 1902.) Santiago, Chile: Ercilla, 1934.

———. *Pasión y muerte del cura Deusto* (1920). 2d ed. Santiago, Chile: Nascimento, 1938.

Díaz Rodríguez, Manuel. *Sangre patricia* (1902). Madrid, 1916(?).

Díaz-Solís, Gustavo. *Llueve sobre el mar (cuentos),* in *CLAEV*, No. 41, 1943.

Díaz Villamil, Antonio. *La Rosita* (1925). "Teatro Boliviano," Vol. IV. La Paz: Bibl. de la Sociedad de Autores, 1928.

———. *El traje del señor diputado.* La Paz, 1930.

———. *¡Cuando vuelva mi hijo!* (1926) and *El hoyo* (1941). "Teatro Boliviano." La Paz: "La Paz," 1942.

———. *Plebe, novela del arrabal paceño.* La Paz, 1943.

Diez-Canseco, José. *Duque* (1934). Santiago, Chile: Ercilla, 1937.

———. *Estampas mulatas.* Santiago, Chile: Zig-zag, 1938.

DIHIGO, JUAN M. *Léxico cubano*, Vol. I: *Letter A*. Havana: Academia de la Historia de Cuba, 1928. Vol. II: *Letter B*. Havana: Universidad de la Habana, 1946.
———. *El habla popular al través de la literatura cubana*. Havana, 1915.
DOBLES, FABIÁN. *Aguas turbias*. San José, Costa Rica: Trejos Hnos., 1943.
DOBLES SEGREDA, LUIS. *Por el amor de Dios*. 2d ed. San José, Costa Rica, 1928.
DRAGHI LUCERO, JUAN. *Las mil y una noches argentinas*. Mendoza-Cuyo, Argentina: Oeste, 1940.
DURAND, LUIS. *Mercedes Urízar*. Santiago, Chile: Nascimento, 1934.
———. *Mi amigo Pidén*. Santiago, Chile: Nascimento, 1939.
———. *Tierra de pellines*. Santiago, Chile: Nascimento, 1929.
———. *Campesinos*. Santiago, Chile: Nascimento, 1932.
ECHEVERRÍA, AQUILEO J. *Concherías*. 3d ed. San José, Costa Rica: María v. de Lines, 1927.
ECHEVERRÍA Y REYES, ANÍBAL. *Voces usadas en Chile*. Santiago, 1900.
EDWARDS BELLO, JOAQUÍN. *El roto* (1920). 4th ed. Santiago, Chile: Nascimento, 1927.
———. *Criollos en París*. 3d ed. Santiago, Chile: Nascimento, 1933.
———. *La chica del Crillón* (1935). 3d ed. Santiago, Chile: Ercilla, 1938.
ESPINO, LISANDRO. *Ensayo de crítica gramatical*. Panamá, 1925.
ESPÍNOLA (H.), FRANCISCO. *Raza ciega*. Buenos Aires and Montevideo: Sociedad Amigos del Libro Rioplatense, 1936.
ESPINOSA, AURELIO M. *Cuentos populares españoles*. 3 vols. "Stanford University Publications in Language and Literature," Vol. III, Nos. 1–3. 1923–26.
———. *Estudios sobre el español de Nuevo Méjico*, in *BHD*, Vols. I (1930), II (1946).
———. "Apuntaciones para un diccionario de nuevomejicanismos: algunas formas verbales raras y curiosas," *Estudios eruditos in memoriam de Adolfo Bonilla y San Martín*, II (Madrid, 1930), 615–25.
———. "Studies in New Mexican Spanish. II. Morphology," *Revue de Dialectologie Romane*, III (1911), 251–86; IV (1912), 241–56; V (1913), 142–72.
ESPINOSA, CIRO. *La tragedia del guajiro*. Havana, 1939.
ESTÉBANEZ CALDERÓN, SERAFÍN. *Escenas andaluzas*. Madrid, 1847.
EZQUER ZELAYA, ERNESTO E. *Poncho celeste—Vincha punzó*. Buenos Aires, 1940.
FABBIANI RUIZ, JOSÉ. *Mar de leva*. Caracas: Elite, 1941.
FALLAS, CARLOS L. *Gentes y gentecillas*. San José, Costa Rica, 1947.
Fausto; see DEL CAMPO, ESTANISLAO.
FEBRES CORDERO, JULIO. "El castellano en Venezuela," *Bitácora*, IV, 22–27. Caracas, June, 1943.
FENTANES, BENITO. *Espulgos de lenguaje*. Madrid, 1925.
———. *Tesoro del idioma castellano*. 2d ed. Madrid, 1927.
———. *Combatiendo barbarismos*. México: Botas, 1937.
FERNÁNDEZ, JORGE. *Agua*. Quito: Sindicato de Escritores y Artistas, 1936.
FERRETIS, JORGE. *Cuando engorda el Quijote*. México: México Nuevo, 1937.
———. *El sur quema*. México: Botas, 1937.
———. *San Automóvil*. México: Botas, 1938.
FIDEL SUÁREZ, MARCO. *Sueños de Luciano Pulgar* (1922——). 3d ed. Bogotá: Librería Voluntad, 1940–45.
FILLOY, JUAN. *Caterva*. Buenos Aires, 1937.
FLÓREZ, LUIS. "Reseña de *American-Spanish Syntax*," *BICC*, II (1946), 372–85.
FOGELQUIST, D. F. "The Bilingualism of Paraguay," *Hispania*, XXXIII (1950), 23–27.
Fogón de las tradiciones: material recopilado por "Don Pampa Viejo." 2d ed. Buenos Aires: Bell, 1940.

Folklore santandereano, Vol. I: *Coplas populares*. Bucaramanga, Colombia: Dirección de Educación Pública, 1924.
Forgione, José D. *Lo que no debe decirse* (1935). 2d ed. Buenos Aires: A. Kapelusz y Cía., n.d.
Fray Mocho = Álvarez, José S. *Cuentos de Fray Mocho* (1906). Buenos Aires: Tor, n.d.
Gagini, Carlos. *Diccionario de costarriqueñismos*. 2d ed. San José, Costa Rica, 1919. The first edition is: *Diccionario de barbarismos y provincialismos de Costa Rica*. 1892.
Galeana, Benita. *Benita, autobiografía*. México, 1940.
Gallegos, Rómulo. *La trepadora* (1925). 5th ed. Barcelona: Araluce, 1936.
———. *Doña Bárbara* (1929). 9th ed. Barcelona: Araluce, n.d.
———. *Cantaclaro* (1931). 2d ed. Barcelona: Araluce, 1934.
———. *Canaima*. Barcelona: Araluce, 1935.
———. *Pobre negro* (1937). Barcelona: Araluce, 1940.
Gamarra, Abelardo M. *Rasgos de pluma*. Lima, Peru, 1902.
———. *Algo del Perú*. Lima, Peru, 1905.
Gamboa, Federico. *Santa* (1903). 11th ed. México: Botas, 1938.
———. *Teatro* (1903–37). 3 vols. México: Botas, 1938.
Garay, Narciso. *Tradiciones y cantares de Panamá*. Panamá, 1930.
García, Antonio. *Colombia, S.A.* Manizales, Colombia: Gráficos, 1934.
García de Diego, Vicente. *Manual de dialectología española*. Madrid: Instituto de Cultura Hispánica, 1946.
García Jiménez, Juan. *Alma vernácula: poemas*. México, 1937.
García-Lomas y García-Lomas, G. Adriano. *Estudio del dialecto popular montañés*. San Sebastián: Nueva Editorial, 1922.
García Muñoz, Alfonso. *El médico que pretendió la gloria*. Quito, 1936.
———. *Estampas de mi ciudad, segunda serie*. Quito, 1937.
García Roel, Adriana. *El hombre de barro*. México: Porrúa Hnos., 1943.
García Soriano, Justo. *Vocabulario del dialecto murciano*. Madrid, 1932.
Garrigós, Florencio. *Gramaticales y filológicas de 'La Prensa.'* 2d ed. Buenos Aires: Mario Tato, 1945.
Garrote, Santiago Alonso. *El dialecto vulgar leonés hablado en Maragatería y Tierra de Astorga*. Astorga, 1909. 2d ed. Madrid: Instituto Antonio de Nebrija, 1947.
Garzón, Tobías. *Diccionario argentino*. Barcelona, 1910.
Gil Gilbert, Enrique. *Yunga* (1931–32). Santiago, Chile: Zig-zag, n.d.
———. *Nuestro pan*. Guayaquil: Vera & Cía., 1942.
Gili y Gaya, Samuel. *Curso superior de sintaxis española*. México: Minerva, 1943. 2d ed. Barcelona: Spes, S.A., 1948.
Godoy, Juan. *Angurrientos*. Santiago, Chile, 1940.
Gómez, Efe. *Mi gente*. Medellín: Imprenta Oficial, 1937.
Gómez Palacio, Martín. *El potro*. México: Botas, 1940.
González, Tulio. *El último arriero*. Medellín, n.d.
González Arrili, B. *Mangangá*. Buenos Aires: Argentina, 1927.
González Carrasco, Aurelio. *Diálogos de cazuela*. México: México Nuevo, 1939.
González Montalvo, Ramón. "Don Benja," *Diario la Prensa* (San Salvador), November 4, 1935.
———. "La cita," *Diario la Prensa*, December 7, 1935.
González Rucavado, C. *Escenas costarricenses*. 2d ed. San José, Costa Rica, 1913.
Gracián, Baltasar. *Tratados*. Ed. Alfonso Reyes. Madrid: Calleja, 1918.
———. *El criticón*. Ed. Romera-Navarro. Philadelphia: University of Pennsylvania Press, 1938–40.

GRANADA, DANIEL. *Vocabulario rioplatense razonado.* 2d ed. Montevideo, 1890.
GRECA, ALCIDES. *Viento norte.* 3d ed. Buenos Aires: Claridad, 1938.
GUERRERO, LEONCIO. *Pichamán.* Santiago, Chile, 1940.
GÜIRALDES, RICARDO. *Xaimaca* (1923). (*Obras,* Vol. V.) Madrid: Espasa-Calpe, 1931.
———. *Don Segundo Sombra* (1926). (*Obras,* Vol. VI.) Buenos Aires: Espasa-Calpe Argentina, 1937.
GUTIÉRREZ, A. *Gramática de la lengua castellana.* 2d ed. México, n.d.
GUTIÉRREZ, JOAQUÍN. *Manglar.* Santiago, Chile: Nascimento, 1947.
GUTIÉRREZ ESKILDSEN, R. M. *El habla popular y campesina de Tabasco.* México, 1941.
GUTIÉRREZ NÁJERA, MANUEL. *Cuentos frágiles.* México, 1883.
GUZMÁN, AUGUSTO. *Prisionero de guerra.* Santiago, Chile: Nascimento, 1937.
GUZMÁN, NICOMEDES. *La sangre y la esperanza.* Santiago, Chile: Orbe, 1943.
GUZMÁN MATURANA, MANUEL. *Don Pancho Garuya* (1933). 2d ed. Santiago, Chile: Minerva, 1935.
GUZMÁN RIORE, DARÍO. *Cuentos chapines.* Guatemala, 1932.
HANSSEN, FEDERICO. *Gramática histórica de la lengua castellana.* Halle, 1913.
HENRÍQUEZ UREÑA, PEDRO. "Observaciones sobre el español en América," *RFE,* VIII (1921), 357-90; XVII (1930), 277-84; XVIII (1931), 120-48.
———. *El español en Santo Domingo,* in *BDH,* Vol. V (1940).
HEREDIA, PEDRO. *Ucumar.* Buenos Aires: El Ateneo, 1944.
HERNÁNDEZ, JOSÉ. *Martín Fierro* (1872-79). Ed. TISCORNIA. *See* TISCORNIA.
HERNÁNDEZ CATÁ, A. *Sus mejores cuentos.* Santiago, Chile: Nascimento, 1936.
HERRERA, FLAVIO. *El tigre.* Guatemala, 1934.
HERRERA GARCÍA, A. *Vida y dolores de Juan Varela.* San José, Costa Rica, 1939.
HERRERO FUENTES, IGNACIO. "El castellano en Panamá," *Universidad: Revista de la Universidad Interamericana* (Panamá), XXII (1944), 81-101.
HERRERO MAYOR, AVELINO. *Presente y futuro de la lengua española en América.* Buenos Aires: Institución Cultural Española, 1943.
HIDALGO, BARTOLOMÉ. *Diálogos,* in *Poetas gauchescos,* ed. E. F. TISCORNIA. Buenos Aires: Losada, 1940.
Hispanoamericanos = JONES, W. K., and HANSEN, M. M. *Hispanoamericanos.* New York: Henry Holt & Co., 1941.
HUIDOBRO, EDUARDO DE. *¡Pobre lengua!* 3d ed. Santander, 1915.
ICAZA, JORGE. *Huasipungo* (1934). 5th ed. Quito, 1937.
———. *En las calles.* Quito, 1935.
———. *Cholos.* Quito, 1938.
———. *Media vida deslumbrados.* Quito, 1942.
ICAZBALCETA, JOAQUÍN GARCÍA. *Vocabulario de mexicanismos.* México, 1899.
INCHAUSPE, PEDRO. *Allá en el sur.* Buenos Aires, 1939.
———. *Voces y costumbres del campo argentino.* Buenos Aires: Santiago Rueda, 1942.
INCLÁN, LUIS G. *Astucia: el jefe de los hermanos de la hoja* (1865). 2 vols. México, 1908.
Inv. ling. = *Investigaciones lingüísticas.* 5 vols. México: Órgano del Instituto Mexicano de Investigaciones Lingüísticas, 1933-38.
JARAMILLO SIERRA, BERNARDO. *Pepe Sierra.* Medellín: Tip. Bedout, 1947.
JIMÉNEZ, R. EMILIO. *Del lenguaje dominicano.* "Academia dominicana de la lengua," No. 3. Ciudad Trujillo: Montalvo, 1941.
KENISTON = KENISTON, HAYWARD. *The syntax of Castilian prose: the sixteenth century.* Chicago: University of Chicago Press, 1937.

KENISTON, HAYWARD. *Spanish syntax list.* New York: Henry Holt & Co., 1937.
KERCHEVILLE, F. M. "A preliminary glossary of New Mexican Spanish," *University of New Mexico Bulletin,* V, No. 3 (1934), 1–69.
KUHN, ALWIN. *Der hocharagonesische Dialekt.* Leipzig, 1936.
LA CUADRA, JOSÉ DE. "Palo 'e balsa," *América,* Vol. X. Quito, 1935.
———. *Guásinton.* Quito, 1938.
———. *Horno.* 2d ed. Buenos Aires: Perseo, 1940.
———. *Los Sangurimas.* Madrid: Cenit, 1934.
LAFERRÈRE, GREGORIO DE. *¡Gettatore!* (1904). "La escena," Vol. III, No. 123. Buenos Aires, 1920.
———. *Locos de verano* (1905). "Argentores," Vol. II, No. 38. Buenos Aires, 1935.
———. *Las de Barranco* (1908). "Argentores," Vol. IV, No. 155. Buenos Aires, 1937.
LAFONE QUEVEDO, SAMUEL A. *Tesoro de catamarqueñismos, tercera edición, complementada con palabras y modismos usuales en Catamarca por Félix F. Avellaneda.* Buenos Aires: Coni, 1927.
LAMANO Y BENEITE, JOSÉ DE. *El dialecto vulgar salmantino.* Salamanca, 1915.
LARRETA, ENRIQUE. *La gloria de don Ramiro* (1908). New ed. Paris, n.d.
———. *Zogoibi* (1926). Buenos Aires: Espasa-Calpe, 1939.
———. *El linyera* (1932). Buenos Aires, 1937.
LAST-REASON. *A rienda suelta.* Buenos Aires: Gleizer, 1925.
LATORRE, MARIANO. *Zurzulita.* Santiago, Chile: Nascimento, 1920.
———. *Hombres y zorros.* Santiago: Ercilla, 1937.
LAVAL, RAMÓN A. *Contribución al folklore de Carahue* (Chile), Vol. I. Madrid: V. Suárez, 1916. Vol. II. Santiago, Chile: Imprenta Universitaria, 1920.
LCC = RAÚL SILVA CASTRO. *Los cuentistas chilenos.* Santiago: Zig-zag, n.d.
LEITÓN, ROBERTO. *Los eternos vagabundos.* Potosí, 1939.
LEMOS, GUSTAVO R. *Barbarismos fonéticos del Ecuador.* Guayaquil, 1922.
LEMUS Y RUBIO, PEDRO. *Aportaciones para la formación del vocabulario panocho o del dialecto de la Huerta de Murcia.* Murcia, 1933.
LENZ, RODOLFO. *Diccionario etimolójico de las voces chilenas derivadas de lenguas indíjenas americanas.* Santiago, Chile, 1904–10.
———. *La oración y sus partes.* 3d ed. Madrid, 1935. 1st ed., 1920; 2d ed., 1925.
LEÓN, AURELIO DE. *Barbarismos comunes en México.* Part I, México, 1936; Part II, México: Porrúa, 1937.
LEWIS = LEWIS, SAMUEL. *Anotaciones al "Tamborito" de Agustín Saz.* Panamá, 1932.
LEWIS, SAMUEL. "Observaciones al anterior estudio [de Sebastián Sucre J.]," *BAPL,* VII, No. 7 (1933), 55–71.
———. "Reparos a 'Modismos panameños' del Rev. Padre Celestino Mangado," *ibid.,* VIII, No. 8 (1935), 39–103.
Leyendas = *Leyendas de Costa Rica compiladas por Víctor Lizano H.* San José: Soley y Valverde, 1941.
LILLO, BALDOMERO. *Sub sole.* 2d ed. Santiago, Chile: Nascimento, 1931.
LIZARDI = FERNÁNDEZ DE LIZARDI, J. JOAQUÍN. *El pensador mexicano.* México: Universidad Nacional Autónoma, 1940.
LIZONDO BORDA, MANUEL. *Voces tucumanas derivadas del quichua.* Tucumán, 1927.
LÓPEZ ALBÚJAR, ENRIQUE. *Matalaché.* Piura, Peru, 1928.
———. *Nuevos cuentos andinos.* Santiago, Chile: Ercilla, 1937.
LÓPEZ Y FUENTES, GREGORIO. *Campamento* (1931). 2d ed. México: Botas, 1938.
———. *¡Mi general!* México: Botas, 1934.
———. *El indio* (1935). 2d ed. México: Botas, 1937.
———. *Arrieros.* México: Botas, 1937.

———. *Huasteca*. México: Botas, 1937.

LOVEIRA, CARLOS. *Los ciegos*. Havana, 1922.

LOZANO Y LOZANO, JUAN. "Un día de la vida," *El Tiempo* (Bogotá), March 12, 1944.

LULLO, ORESTES DI. "Algunas voces santiagueñas," *BAAL*, VI (1938), 145–204.

LUSSA, P. "Charlas de sobremesa," *Informador* (Guadalajara), July 31, 1941.

LYNCH, BENITO. *Los caranchos de la Florida* (1916). Buenos Aires: Austral, 1938.

———. *El romance de un gaucho* (1930). Buenos Aires: Anaconda, 1933.

———. *De los campos porteños* (1931). 3d ed. Buenos Aires: La Facultad, 1940.

———. *Palo verde y otras novelas cortas*. Buenos Aires: Austral, 1940.

LYRA, CARMEN (MARÍA ISABEL CARVAJAL). *Los cuentos de mi tía Panchita*. San José, Costa Rica, 1936.

LLANDERAS, N. DE LAS, and MALFATTI, A. *Cuando las papas queman, comedia asainetada*. "Argentores," Vol. II, No. 74. Buenos Aires, 1935.

———. *Giuanín, rey de la pizza, comedia asainetada*. "Nuestro Teatro," Vol. I, No. 15. Buenos Aires, 1936.

LLORENTE MALDONADO DE GUEVARA, ANTONIO. *Estudio sobre el habla de la Ribera*. Salamanca: Consejo Superior de Investigaciones Científicas, 1947.

MACHADO, JOSÉ E. *Cancionero popular venezolano*. Caracas, 1919.

MCHALE, C. F. *Diccionario razonado de modos de bien decir*. New York, 1930.

MACÍAS, JOSÉ MIGUEL. *Diccionario cubano*. Reprint. Coatepec, 1888. Earlier edition: Vera Cruz, 1885.

MCSPADDEN, GEORGE E. "Some semantic and philological facts of the Spanish spoken in Chilili, New Mexico," *University of New Mexico Bulletin*, V, No. 3 (1934), 71–102.

MADERO, LUIS OCTAVIO. "*Los alzados*" [1935] *y* "*Sindicato*" [1936]. México, 1937.

MAGDALENO, MAURICIO. *El resplandor*. México: Botas, 1937.

MAGÓN (MANUEL GONZÁLEZ ZELEDÓN). *Cuentos*. Ed. JOSÉ M. ARCE. San José, Costa Rica, 1947.

MALARET = MALARET, AUGUSTO. *Diccionario de americanismos*. 2d ed. San Juan, Puerto Rico, 1931. 1st ed. Mayagüez, 1925. Supplemented in *Boletín de la Academia Argentina de Letras*, Vols. VIII (1940), IX (1941), X (1942), and XI (1943). Supplement published separately with title *Diccionario de americanismos: suplemento*, Vol. I: *A–E*. Buenos Aires: Academia Argentina de Letras, 1942; Vol. II: *F–Z*. Buenos Aires: Academia Argentina de Letras, 1944. 3d ed. Buenos Aires: Emecé, 1946.

———. *Vocabulario de Puerto Rico*. San Juan, 1937. Earlier edition: *Diccionario de provincialismos de Puerto Rico*. San Juan, 1917.

———. "Geografía lingüística," *BAAL*, V (1937), 213–25.

———. *Semántica americana*. Cataño, Puerto Rico, 1943.

MALBRÁN, PEDRO A. *Los dos quesos de Balta Marín*. Santiago, Chile: Nascimento, 1920.

———. *El marido de la doctora*. "La escena," No. 61. Santiago: Cultura, n.d.

MALBRÁN, PEDRO A., and MARTÍNEZ, PEPE. *Las diez de última*. Santiago: Nascimento, 1923.

———. *En semana santa, sainete*. Santiago, 1928.

MALLEA, EDUARDO. *La ciudad junto al río inmóvil*. Buenos Aires: Anaconda, 1938.

———. *Fiesta en noviembre*. Buenos Aires: Club del Libro, 1938.

MALMBERG, BERTIL. "L'espagnol dans le nouveau monde: Problème de linguistique générale," *Studia linguistica*, I (1947), 79–116; II, 1–36.

MALUENDA, RAFAEL. *Escenas de la vida campesina*. Santiago, Chile, 1909.

———. *Los ciegos*. Santiago, Chile, 1913.

———. *Venidos a menos*. Santiago, Chile: "Los Diez," 1916.

MANGADO, CELESTINO. "Modismos panameños en el lenguaje," *BAPL*, VII, No. 7 (1933), 73–124. *See also* LEWIS, SAMUEL.

MANGELS, ANNA. *Sondererscheinungen des Spanischen in Amerika.* Dissertation. Hamburg, 1926.

MANSILLA, LUCIO V. *Una excursión a los indios ranqueles* (1870). Buenos Aires: La Cultura Popular, 1928.

———. *Entre-nos* (before 1890). "Grandes escritores argentinos," Vol. IX. Buenos Aires, 1928.

MARENGO, JUAN D. *La luz de los rincones.* Tucumán, 1937.

Martín Fierro. *See* HERNÁNDEZ, JOSÉ; TISCORNIA.

MARTÍNEZ CUITIÑO, VICENTE. *Atorrante o la venganza de la tierra* (1932). "Argentores," Vol. II, No. 39. Buenos Aires, 1934.

MARTÍNEZ GALINDO, ARTURO. *Sombra.* Tegucigalpa, 1940.

MARTÍNEZ PAYVA, CLAUDIO. *El rancho del hermano* (1926). "Argentores," Vol. III, No. 123. Buenos Aires, 1936.

MARTÍNEZ DE PINILLOS, CARLOS. *Método práctico para el vuelo ciego.* Lima, 1934.

MARTÍNEZ VIGIL, CARLOS. *Arcaísmos españoles usados en América.* Montevideo, 1939.

MARTÍNEZ ZUVIRÍA, GUSTAVO A. "Algunos vicios de lenguaje," *BAAL*, VI (1938), 383–88.

MATA, G. HUMBERTO. *Sanagüín.* Cuenca, Ecuador: Cenit 1942.

———. *Sumag Allpa.* Cuenca, Ecuador: Cenit, 1940.

MATEUS, ALEJANDRO. *Riqueza de la lengua castellana y provincialismos ecuatorianos* (1918). 2d ed. Quito: Ecuatoriana, 1933.

MECHÍN, T. P. (JOSÉ M. PERALTA). *Brochazos.* San Salvador, 1925.

———. *Candidato, comedia.* San Salvador, 1931.

———. *La muerte de la tórtola.* San Salvador, 1932.

MEDINA, J. T. *Chilenismos.* Santiago, 1928.

MEJÍA NIETO, ARTURO. *Relatos nativos.* Tegucigalpa, 1929.

———. *El solterón.* Buenos Aires, 1931.

MELÉNDEZ, LUIS. *Las mujeres están lejos.* Santiago, Chile: Antena, 1943.

MELÉNDEZ MUÑOZ, M. *Cuentos del cedro.* 2d ed. San Juan, Puerto Rico, 1937.

MEMBREÑO, ALBERTO. *Hondureñismos.* 3d ed. México, 1912. Earlier editions: Tegucigalpa, 1895; 2d ed., Tegucigalpa, 1897, entitled *Vocabulario de los provincialismos de Honduras.*

MENA BRITO, B. *Paludismo.* México: Botas, 1940.

MÉNDEZ BALLESTER, MANUEL. *Tiempo muerto, tragedia.* San Juan, Puerto Rico, 1940.

MÉNDEZ PEREIRA, OCTAVIO. "Ensayo de semántica general y aplicada al lenguaje panameño," *BAPL*, I, No. 2 (1927), 3–37.

MENDOZA, ANGÉLICA. *Cárcel de mujeres.* Buenos Aires: Claridad, n.d.

MENDOZA, JAIME. *Memorias de un estudiante.* Sucre, Bolivia, 1918.

———. *El lago enigmático.* Sucre, Bolivia: Charcas, 1936.

MENDOZA, V. T. *El romance español y el corrido mexicano.* México: Universidad Nacional Autónoma, 1939.

MENÉNDEZ, M. A. *Nayar.* México, 1941.

MENÉNDEZ PIDAL, RAMÓN. "El dialecto leonés," *Revista de Archivos, Bibliotecas y Museos, Tercera Época*, XIV (1906), 128–72, 294–311.

———. *Cantar de mío Cid*, Vol. I. Madrid, 1908.

———. *Manual de gramática histórica española.* 6th ed. Madrid, 1941; 8th ed., 1949.

MERA, JUAN LEÓN. *Antología ecuatoriana: cantares del pueblo ecuatoriano.* Quito: Academia Ecuatoriana, 1892.

Mery, Alberto. *Barrio matadero, comedia.* "La escena," No. 62. Santiago, Chile: Cultura, n.d.

Meyer-Lübke, W. *Grammaire des langues romanes*, Vol. III: *Syntaxe.* Paris: Welter, 1900.

Millares, Luis y Agustín. *Léxico de Gran Canaria.* Las Palmas, 1924.

Mir y Noguera, P. Juan. *Prontuario de hispanismo y barbarismo.* 2 vols. Madrid: Sáenz de Jubera Hnos., 1908.

Miranda, Marta Elba. *Aposento de brujos.* Santiago, Chile: Orbe, 1943.

Miranda Ruano, Francisco. *Las voces del terruño.* San Salvador, 1929.

Moglia, Raúl. "El lenguaje de Buenos Aires," *Nosotros*, LVI (1927), 249–56.

Monner Sans, Ricardo. *Notas al castellano en la Argentina.* 2d ed. Buenos Aires, 1924.

Montenegro, Carlos. *Hombres sin mujer.* México: Masa, 1938.

———. *Los héroes.* Havana: Caribe, 1941.

Montenegro, Ernesto. *Mi tío Ventura.* 2d ed. Santiago, Chile: Nascimento, 1938.

Monti, Daniel P. *Entre cielo y cuchillas.* Buenos Aires: Aurora, 1943.

Montiel Ballesteros, Adolfo. *Cuentos uruguayos.* Florencia, 1920.

———. *Alma nuestra.* Montevideo: Pegaso, 1922.

———. *La raza.* Buenos Aires: Nuestra América, 1925.

———. *Luz mala.* Buenos Aires: Nuestra América, 1927.

———. *Montevideo y su cerro.* Montevideo: C. García, 1928.

Moock, Armando. *Cuando venga el amor* (1920). Santiago, Chile: Nascimento, 1929.

———. *Un crimen en mi pueblo.* Santiago: Cultura, 1936.

Morales, P. Raimundo. *El buen decir*, Vol. I: *A–B;* Vol. II: *C, Ch, D.* Santiago, Chile, 1925, 1937.

———. "Apuntes sobre lenguaje," *Bol. Acad. Chilena*, IX (1947), 35–136.

Morínigo = Morínigo, Marcos A. Personal correspondence (1949).

———. *Hispanismos en el guaraní.* Buenos Aires: Instituto de Filología, 1931.

Moscoso Puello, F. E. *Cañas y bueyes.* Santo Domingo, R.D.: La Nación, n.d.

Mostajo, Francisco. "Algunas peculiaridades del lenguaje arequipeño," *Arequipa 1540–1940.* Lima: El Condor, 1940.

Muñoz R., José María. *Don Zacarías Encina.* Santiago, Chile: Nascimento, 1932.

Muñoz Seca, Pedro. *El roble de la Jarosa, comedia* (1915). 4th ed. Madrid, 1925.

———. *Todo para ti, comedia.* Madrid, 1931.

Navarro = Navarro, Tomás. *El español en Puerto Rico. Contribución a la geografía lingüística hispanoamericana.* Río Piedras: Universidad de Puerto Rico, 1948.

Navarro Tomás, T. "Impresiones sobre el estudio lingüístico de Puerto Rico," *Revista de Estudios Hispánicos*, II, No. 2 (1929), 127–47.

———. *Cuestionario lingüístico hispanoamericano.* Buenos Aires: Instituto de Filología, 1943; 2d ed., 1945.

Nichols, Madaline W. *Bibliographical guide to materials on American Spanish.* Committee on Latin American Studies of the American Council of Learned Societies. Cambridge: Harvard University Press, 1941. Additions by L. B. Kiddle, *Revista iberoamericana*, VII (1943), 221–40.

Noguera, María de. *Cuentos viejos.* San José, Costa Rica: Repertorio Americano, 1938.

Núñez, Sergio. *Tierra de lobos.* Quito, 1939.

Núñez Guzmán, J. T. *Infancia campesina.* México, 1937.

Obando, Luis de. *Corrección del lenguaje*. Bogotá: Biblioteca Aldeana, 1938.
Orozco. *See* Calero Orozco.
Ortiz, Adaberto. *Juyungo*. Buenos Aires: Americalee, 1943.
Ortúzar, Camilo. *Diccionario manual de locuciones viciosas y de correcciones de lenguaje*. 2d ed. Barcelona, 1902. 1st ed., Turin, 1893.
Osorio Lizarazo, J. A. *La cosecha*. Manizales, Colombia: A. Zapata, 1935.
———. *El hombre bajo la tierra*. Bogotá, 1944.
Pacheco, Carlos M. *La boca del riachuelo*. "El teatro argentino," Vol. XLIV Buenos Aires, 1921.
Padrón = Padrón, Alfredo F. "Giros sintácticos corrientes en el habla popular, culta y semiculta cubanas," *BF*, Vol. V, Nos. 37–39 (1948), 467–95.
———. "Los arcaísmos españoles," *BF*, Vol. III, No. 15 (1940).
Pareja Diez-Canseco, Alfredo. *El muelle*. Quito: Bolívar, 1933.
———. *La Beldaca*. Santiago, Chile: Ercilla, 1935.
———. *Baldomera*. Santiago, Chile: Ercilla, 1938.
———. *Hechos y hazañas de Don Balón de Baba*. Buenos Aires: Club del Libro, 1939.
Patín Maceo, Manuel A. "Americanismos en el lenguaje dominicano," *Anales de la Universidad de Santo Domingo* (Trujillo), Vols. IV (1940), V (1941), VI (1942), VII (1943).
———. *Dominicanismos*. "Academia dominicana de la lengua," No. 2. Ciudad Trujillo: Montalvo, 1940.
———. "Notas gramaticales," *Bol. acad. dominicana de la lengua*, Vol. VI (1946). Reprinted in *Revista de educación*, Vol. XVII (1946–47). Ciudad Trujillo.
Payno, Manuel. *El fistol del diablo* (1845). San Antonio, Texas, 1927.
Payró, Roberto. *El casamiento de Laucha* (1906). Buenos Aires: Mínimas, 1920.
Pereda, José María de. *Obras completas*. Madrid, 1894–1906. Vols. I–V, IX, XV, 3d ed.; VI–VIII, X–XIII, 2d ed.; XIV, XVI, XVII, 1st ed.
Pereira, Cuti. *El fantasma del puente viejo y otros relatos*. Buenos Aires: Huemul, 1941.
Pereira, E. C. *Gramática expositiva*. São Paulo, Rio de Janeiro, etc., 1941.
Pereyra, Diomedes de. *Caucho*. Santiago, Chile: Nascimento, 1938.
Pérez Guerrero, Alfredo. *Fonética y morfología*. Quito, 1933.
Pérez de Guzmán, Fernán. *Generaciones y semblanzas* (1450). Ed. Domínguez Bordona. "Clásicos castellanos," No. 61. Madrid, 1924.
Pérez Petit, Víctor. *Entre los pastos*. Montevideo, 1920.
Petit, Magdalena. *Los Pincheira*. Santiago, Chile: Zig-zag, 1939.
Petit de Murat, Ulises. *El balcón hacia la muerte*. Buenos Aires: Lautaro, 1943.
Pichardo, Esteban. *Diccionario provincial casi razonado de voces y frases cubanas*. 4th ed. Havana, 1875. Earlier editions: 1st ed., Matanzas, 1836; 2d ed., Havana, 1849; 3d ed., Havana, 1862.
Pico, Pedro E. *La verdad en los ojos*. "Argentores," Vol. I, No. 17. Buenos Aires, 1934.
Picón-Febres, Gonzalo. *Libro raro: voces, locuciones y otras cosas de uso frecuente en Venezuela*. 2d. ed. Curaçao, 1912.
Pino Saavedra, Y. *Crónica de un soldado de la guerra del Pacífico. Con un estudio dialectológico y notas históricas*. Santiago, Chile: Editorial Universitaria, S.A., 1950.
Pocaterra, José Rafael. *Vidas oscuras*. Madrid, 1916.
Posada R., Julio. *El machete*. Bogotá, 1929.
Prado, Pedro. *Un juez rural*. Santiago, Chile: Nascimento, 1924.
———. *Alsino* (1920). Santiago, Chile: Nascimento, 1928.

Publicaciones de la Academia guatemalteca (Guatemala), Vols. IV (1935), VII (1940).
PULGAR VIDAL, JAVIER. "Algunas observaciones sobre el lenguaje en Huánuco," *Revista de la Universidad Católica del Perú* (Lima), V (1937), 801–19.
QUESADA S., NAPOLEÓN. *Lecciones de gramática castellana.* 3d ed. San José, Costa Rica, 1935.
QUEVEDO, FRANCISCO DE. *El Buscón.* Ed. AMÉRICO CASTRO. "Clásicos castellanos," No. 5. Madrid, 1927.
QUEVEDO Y ZUBIETA, SALVADOR. *La camada.* México, 1912.
———. *México marimacho.* México: Botas, 1933.
———. *Las ensabanadas.* México: Botas, 1934.
QUIJANO HERNÁNDEZ, MANUEL. *En la montaña.* San Salvador, 1930.
QUINTANA, CARLOS ALBERTO. *Mal agüero.* Quezaltenango, Guatemala, 1937.
QUIROGA, CARLOS B. *4 á 2.* Buenos Aires, 1932.
QUIROGA, HORACIO. *Cuentos* (1904–34). 6 vols. "Biblioteca Rodó." Montevideo: C. García, 1937–40.
QUIRÓS, BLANCO. *Artículos escogidos.* San José, Costa Rica, 1904.
RAEL, J. R. "Associative interference in Spanish," *Hispanic Review,* VIII (1940), 346–49.
RAMÍREZ, MIGUEL ÁNGEL (EL NEGRO RAMÍREZ). *Tierra adentro.* San Salvador, 1937.
RAMOS, J. A. *Las impurezas de la realidad.* Barcelona, 1929.
RAMOS Y DUARTE, FELIZ. *Diccionario de mejicanismos* (1895). 2d ed. México: Herrero Hnos., 1898.
RAMSEY, M. M. *A text-book of modern Spanish.* 3d ed. New York: Henry Holt & Co., 1894.
RENDÓN, FRANCISCO DE. *Inocencia.* Medellín, Colombia, 1904.
REQUENA, ANDRÉS. *Los enemigos de la tierra* [*novela dominicana*]. 2d ed. Santiago, Chile: Ercilla, 1942.
———. *Camino de fuego.* Santiago, Chile: Ercilla, 1941.
RESTREPO, ANTONIO JOSÉ. *El cancionero de Antioquia.* 3d ed. Barcelona: Lux, 1930.
RESTREPO, ROBERTO. *Apuntaciones idiomáticas y correcciones de lenguaje.* Bogotá: Cromos, 1943.
RESTREPO JARAMILLO, JOSÉ. *20 cuentos.* Medellín, Colombia, 1939.
REVOLLO, PEDRO MARÍA. *Costeñismos colombianos.* Barranquilla, 1942.
REYLES, CARLOS. *El terruño* (1916). Madrid, 1927.
———. *El gaucho Florido.* Montevideo: Impresora Uruguaya, 1932.
RFE = *Revista de Filología Española.* Madrid, 1914——.
RFH = *Revista de Filología Hispánica.* Buenos Aires and New York, 1939——.
RIVAS BONILLA, ALBERTO. *Andanzas y malandanzas.* San Salvador, 1936.
RIVAS LARRAURI, CARLOS. *Del arrabal* (1931). México: Cicerón, 1937.
RIVERA, JOSÉ EUSTASIO. *La vorágine* (1924). Buenos Aires: Austral, 1941.
ROBLES, FERNANDO. *La virgen de los cristeros.* Buenos Aires: Claridad, 1932.
ROBLES CASTILLO, AURELIO. *¡Ay, Jalisco ... no te rajes!* México: Botas, 1938.
ROBLETO, HERNÁN. *Los estrangulados.* Madrid: Cenit, 1933.
RODRIGO, SATURNINO. *En la pendiente* (1926). "Teatro Boliviano," Vol. III. La Paz: Bibl. de la Sociedad de Autores, 1938.
RODRÍGUEZ, LUIS FELIPE. *La ciénaga* (1923). Havana: Trópico, 1937.
RODRÍGUEZ, YAMANDÚ. *Bichito de luz.* Buenos Aires: Anaconda, 1933.
———. *Cimarrones,* Buenos Aires: Anaconda, 1933.
RODRÍGUEZ, ZOROBABEL. *Diccionario de chilenismos.* Santiago, 1875.

Rodríguez Acasuso, Luis. *El barro humano* (1933). "Argentores," Vol. I, No. 11. Buenos Aires, 1934.

———. *La mujer olvidada.* "Argentores," Vol. I, No. 8. Buenos Aires, 1934.

Rodríguez Marín, Francisco. *El alma de Andalucía.* Madrid, 1929.

Rojas, Francisco de. *Teatro.* Ed. F. Ruiz Morcuende. "Clásicos castellanos," No. 25. Madrid, 1922.

Rojas, Manuel. *Hombres del sur.* Santiago, Chile: Nascimento, 1926.

———. *Travesía.* Santiago, Chile: Nascimento, 1934.

Rojas, Pepe. *La banda de Al Capone, sainete.* "La escena," No. 52. Santiago, Chile: Cultura. 1937.

Rojas, Pepe, and Fernández, Pepe. *La hoja de Parra.* "La escena," No. 49. Santiago, Chile: Cultura, 1937.

Rojas Gallardo, Luis. *Aventuras de Tristán Machuca, 2a serie.* Santiago, Chile: Cultura, 1935.

———. *Aventuras de Tristán Machuca, 3a serie.* Santiago, Chile: Cultura, n.d.

Román, Manuel Antonio. *Diccionario de chilenismos y de otras voces y locuciones viciosas.* 5 vols. Santiago, Chile, 1901–18.

Romanángel (Joaquín Moscoso G.). *Fidel Cornejo y Cía.* Santiago, Chile: Cultura, 1935.

Romero, Alberto. *La viuda del conventillo* (1930). 2d ed. Santiago, Chile, 1932.

———. *La mala estrella de Perucho González.* Santiago, Chile: Ercilla, 1935.

Romero, Emilio. *Balseros del Titicaca.* Lima, 1934.

Romero, Joaquín A. "Voces y giros usuales en el español de la Argentina," *Nosotros*, XXIII (1929), 398–99.

Romero, José Rubén. *La vida inútil de Pito Pérez.* 2d ed. México, 1938.

Romero, Manuel. *¡A trabajar, caballeros!* (1919). "El teatro argentino," Vol. II, No. 15. Buenos Aires, 1920.

Romero García, Manuel Vicente. *Peonía.* Madrid: América, 1920.

Rosenblat = Rosenblat, Ángel. Review of C. E. Kany, *American-Spanish Syntax*, in *Nueva Revista de Filología Hispánica*, IV (1950), 57–67. Personal correspondence (1949).

———. "Notas de morfología dialectal," *BDH*, II (1946), 105–316.

Rossi, Vicente. *Desagravio al lenguaje de Martín Fierro.* "Folletos lenguaraces," Nos. 14–22. Río de la Plata, 1933–37.

Rubín, Ramón. *Cuentos del medio rural mexicano*, Vol. I. Guadalajara, 1942.

Rubio, Darío. *La anarquía del lenguaje en la América española.* 2 vols. México, 1925.

———. *Refranes, proverbios y dichos y dicharachos mexicanos* (1937). 2d ed. 2 vols. México: A. P. Márquez, 1940.

Ruiz, Víctor. *Los que pagan* (1923). "Teatro Boliviano," Vol. V. La Paz: Bibl. de la Sociedad de Autores, 1928.

Sáenz (h.), Justo P. *Pasto Puna.* 2d ed. Buenos Aires, 1931.

Salarrué (Salvador Salazar Arrué). *Cuentos de barro.* San Salvador: La Montaña, 1933.

———. *El Cristo negro.* San Salvador: Biblioteca Nacional, 1936.

———. *Eso y más.* Cuscatlán, El Salvador, 1940.

Salas, Ángel. *Tres comedias.* La Paz: Crespi Hermanos, 1930.

Salazar García, Salomón. *Diccionario de provincialismos y barbarismos centroamericanos.* 2d ed. San Salvador, 1910. 1st ed.: *Vicios y correcciones de idioma español.* Sonsonate, 1907.

SALAZAR HERRERA, CARLOS M. *Cuentos*. San José, Costa Rica, 1936.
SALDÍAS, JOSÉ ANTONIO. *El pollo Almada*. "Argentores," Vol. II, No. 68. Buenos Aires, 1935.
SALESIANO = *Vocabulario de palabras-modismos y refranes ticos por un salesiano*. Cartago, Costa Rica, 1938.
SALOMÉ GIL (JOSÉ MILLA). *Cuadros de costumbres*. "Colección 'Juan Chapín,'" Vols. IV (Guatemala, 1935), X (1937).
———. *Un viaje al otro mundo*, "Colección 'Juan Chapín,'" Vols. VI, VII, VIII (1936).
SALVADOR, HUMBERTO. *Camarada* (1933). Buenos Aires: Claridad, n.d.
———. *Noviembre*. Quito: L. I. Fernández, 1939.
———. *Prometeo*. Quito, 1943.
SAMAYOA CHINCHILLA, CARLOS. *Cuatro suertes*. Guatemala, 1936.
SÁNCHEZ, FLORENCIO. *Teatro completo*. Ed. DARDO CÚNEO. Buenos Aires: Claridad, 1941. Earlier editions: 1st ed., 3 vols., Valencia and Buenos Aires, 1917–20; 2d ed., Barcelona: Cervantes, 1926; Buenos Aires: Sopena Argentina, 1939.
SÁNCHEZ DE BADAJOZ, DIEGO. *Recopilación en metro*. "Libros de Antaño," Vol. XI. Madrid, 1882.
SÁNCHEZ GARDEL, JULIO. *Los mirasoles* (1911). "Argentores," Vol. VI, No. 166. Buenos Aires, 1939.
SÁNCHEZ SEVILLA, P. "El habla de Cespedosa de Tormes (en el límite de Salamanca y Ávila)," *RFE*, XV (1928), 131–72, 244–82.
SÁNCHEZ SOMOANO, JOSÉ. *Modismos, locuciones y términos mexicanos*. Madrid, 1892.
SANDOVAL, LISANDRO. *Semántica guatemalense o diccionario de guatemaltequismos*. 2 vols. Guatemala, 1941–42.
SANTA CRUZ, ROSENDO. *Tierras de lumbre*. Guatemala, 1938.
SANTAMARÍA, FRANCISCO J. *El provincialismo tabasqueño*, Vol. I: *A, B, C*. México: Botas, 1921.
———. *Americanismo y barbarismo*. México, 1921.
———. *Glosa lexicográfica*. México, 1926.
———. *Diccionario general de americanismos*. 3 vols. México: Pedro Robredo, 1942.
SANTAMARÍA, FRANCISCO J., and DOMÍNGUEZ, RAFAEL. *Ensayos críticos de lenguaje*. México: Porrúa Hnos., 1940.
SANTIVÁN, FERNANDO. *La hechizada* (1916). 3d ed. Santiago, Chile: Nascimento, 1933.
SARMIENTO, DOMINGO FAUSTINO. *Facundo*. Ed. DELIA S. ETCHEVERRY. Buenos Aires: Estrada, 1940.
SAUBIDET, TITO. *Vocabulario y refranero criollo*. Buenos Aires: Guillermo Kraft Ltda., 1943; 3d ed., 1948.
SCHOCK, ALFREDO. *2.000 barbarismos que corrompen el buen decir*. 2d ed. Buenos Aires, 1945.
SEGOVIA, LISANDRO. *Diccionario de argentinismos, neologismos y barbarismos*. Buenos Aires, 1911.
SEIJAS, JUAN. *Diccionario de barbarismos cotidianos*. Buenos Aires, 1890.
SELVA, JUAN B. *El castellano en América*. La Plata, 1906.
———. *Guía del buen decir*. 2d ed. Buenos Aires, 1925. 1st ed. Madrid, 1916.
———. *Crecimiento del habla*. Buenos Aires, 1925.
SENET, RODOLFO. "El falseamiento del castellano en la Argentina y lo que significan en realidad las palabras del lunfardo," *BAAL*, VI (1938), 121–44.

Sepúlveda Leyton, Carlos. *Hijuna.* Linares, Chile: Ciencias y Artes, 1934.
———. *La fábrica.* Santiago: Ercilla, 1935.
———. *Camarada.* Santiago: Nascimento, 1938.
Silva, Víctor Domingo. *La pampa trágica.* Santiago, Chile: Zig-zag, 1938.
Solá, José Vicente. *Diccionario de regionalismos de Salta.* Buenos Aires: S. de Amorrortu e hijos, 1947.
Spaulding = Spaulding, Robert K. *Syntax of the Spanish verb.* New York: Henry Holt & Co., 1931.
———. *How Spanish grew.* Berkeley and Los Angeles: University of California Press, 1943.
Spitzer, Leo. *Aufsätze zur romanischen Syntax und Stilistik.* Halle, 1918.
———. "Sintaxis y estilística del español *que,*" *RFH,* IV (1942), 253–65.
Suárez, Constantino. *Vocabulario cubano.* Havana and Madrid, 1921.
Suárez, Víctor M. *El español que se habla en Yucatán.* Mérida: Díaz Massa, Talleres de Impresión, 1945.
Sucre J., Sebastián. "Provincialismos panameños," *BAPL,* VII, No. 7 (1933), 33–35. *See also* Lewis, Samuel.
Sundheim, Adolfo. *Vocabulario costeño o lexicografía de la región septentrional de la república de Colombia.* Paris: Librería Cervantes, 1922.
Tallas chilenas, suplemento Excelsior No. 11. 2d ed. Santiago: Ercilla, 1938.
Taracena, Alfonso. *Los abrasados.* México: Botas, 1937.
Tascón, Leonardo. *Diccionario de provincialismos y barbarismos del Valle del Cauca.* Bogotá: Santafé, 1935.
Teresa de Jesús, Santa. *Obras completas.* Ed. Luis Santullano. Madrid: Aguilar, n.d.
Tiscornia, Eleuterio F. *"Martín Fierro" comentado y anotado,* Part I: *Texto, notas y vocabulario.* Buenos Aires, 1925. Part II: *La lengua de "Martín Fierro,"* in *BDH,* Vol. III (1930).
Tobar, Carlos R. *Consultas al diccionario de la lengua.* 2d ed. Barcelona, 1907. Earlier ed. Quito, 1900.
Tobón Betancourt, J. *Colombianismos y otras voces de uso general.* Medellín: Tipografía Industrial, 1946.
Toro, Bernardo. *Minas, mulas y mujeres.* 2d ed. Medellín, Colombia, 1943.
Toro y Gisbert, Miguel de. "Voces andaluzas," *Revue Hispanique,* XLIX (1920), 313–645.
———. *L'évolution de la langue espagnole en Argentine.* Paris: Larousse, 1932.
Toro Ramallo, Luis. *Chaco.* Santiago, Chile: Nascimento, 1936.
Toruño, Juan Felipe. *El silencio.* San Salvador, 1935.
Torres Arjona, Rafael. *Correntada.* San Salvador: Arce, 1934–35.
Tovar y R., Enrique D. "Hacia el gran diccionario de la lengua española," *BAAL,* Vols. IX (1941), X (1942).
Trías du Pre, Emilio. *Forastero.* Montevideo: Biblioteca Rodó, 1941.
Unzueta, Mario. *Valle.* Cochabamba: La Época, 1945.
Urbaneja Achelpohl, Luis M. *En este país.* Buenos Aires, 1916.
Uribe Uribe, Rafael. *Diccionario abreviado de galicismos, provincialismos i correcciones del lenguaje.* Medellín, Colombia, 1887.
Urquizo, Francisco L. *Tropa vieja.* México, 1943.
Uslar Pietri, Arturo. *Las lanzas coloradas* (1931). Santiago, Chile: Zig-zag, 1940.
Valdés, Juan de. *Diálogo de la lengua.* Ed. José F. Montesinos. "Clásicos castellanos," No. 86. Madrid, 1928.
Valdés, Nacho (Ignacio de J.). *Cuentos panameños.* Panamá: Gráfico, 1928.
———. *Sangre criolla.* Panamá, 1943.

VALLE, ALFONSO. *Diccionario del habla nicaragüense.* Managua: La Nueva Prensa, 1948.

VALLE, JOSÉ. "El cristal con que se mira," *Nuestro Diario* (Guatemala), 1940–41.

VALLE-ARIZPE, Artemio. *El canillitas.* México: Polis, 1941.

VARELA, ALFREDO. *El río oscuro.* Buenos Aires: Lautaro, 1943.

VARGAS UGARTE, R. "Glosario de peruanismos," *Universidad Católica del Perú,* XIV (1946), 151–79.

VASCONCELOS, JOSÉ. *La tormenta.* México: Botas, 1937.

VÁSCONEZ HURTADO, GUSTAVO. *Camino de las landas.* Quito: Fernández, 1940.

VÁZQUEZ, HONORATO. *Reparos sobre nuestro lenguaje usual.* Quito: Ecuatoriana, 1940.

VIANA, JAVIER DE. *Gaucha* (1899). 4th ed. Montevideo, 1913.

———. *Leña seca* (1913). 6th ed. Montevideo: García, n.d.

———. *Abrojos.* Montevideo: García, 1919.

———. *Tardes del fogón.* Montevideo: García, 1925.

———. *Gurí y otras novelas.* Madrid, n.d.

VIDAL DE BATTINI, BERTA ELENA. *El habla rural de San Luis.* Parte I, in *BDH,* Vol. VII (1949).

VICUÑA CIFUENTES, JULIO. *Romances populares y vulgares recogidos de la tradición oral chilena.* "Biblioteca de escritores de Chile," Vol. II. Santiago, 1912.

VIGNATI, M. A. "El vocabulario ríoplatense de Francisco Javier Muñiz," *BAAL,* V (1937), 393–453.

WAGNER, M. L. "Amerikanisch-Spanisch und Vulgärlatein," *Zeitschrift für romanische Philologie,* XL (1920), 286–312, 385–404. Spanish trans. and notes by AMÉRICO CASTRO and P. HENRÍQUEZ UREÑA. Cuaderno I. Buenos Aires: Instituto de Filología, 1924.

WAST, HUGO (GUSTAVO A. MARTÍNEZ ZUVIRÍA). *Flor de durazno, drama.* Buenos Aires: Bayardo, n.d.

WEBER, FRIDA. "Fórmulas de tratamiento en la lengua de Buenos Aires," *RFH,* III, No. 2 (1941), 105–39.

WIJK, H. L. A. VAN. "Contribución al estudio del habla popular de Venezuela." Mimeographed thesis. Amsterdam, 1946.

WILSON, W. E. "*Él* and *ella* as pronouns of address," *Hispania,* XXIII (1940), 336–40.

WYLD OSPINA, CARLOS. *La tierra de las Nahuyacas.* Guatemala, 1933.

———. *La gringa* (1935). Guatemala, 1936.

YRURZÚN, BLANCA. *Changos.* Santiago del Estero, Argentina: Vertical, 1939.

ZAMORA VICENTE, ALONSO. *El habla de Mérida y sus cercanías.* Madrid: *RFE,* Anejo XXIX, 1943.

ZAÑARTU, SADY. *Llampo brujo.* Santiago, Chile: Nascimento, 1933.

ZUM FELDE, ALBERTO. *El problema de la cultura americana.* Buenos Aires: Losada, 1943.

ZÚÑIGA, LUIS ANDRÉS. *Fábulas.* 2d ed. Tegucigalpa, 1931.

INDEX

[Prepositional phrases are listed under the preposition, other locutions generally under the first word.]

PRINTED IN U.S.A.

Atlantic Ocean
Caribbean Sea
Pacific Ocean
MEXICO
MEXICO CITY
VERA CRUZ
YUCATAN
GUATEMALA
GUATEMALA CITY
HONDURAS
TEGUCIGALPA
EL SALVADOR
SAN SALVADOR
NICARAGUA
MANAGUA
COSTA RICA
SAN JOSE
PANAMA
COLON
PANAMA
HAVANA
CUBA
HAITI
SANTO DOMINGO
CIUDAD TRUJILLO
SAN JUAN
PUERTO RICO
BARRANQUILLA
LA GUAIRA
CARACAS
VENEZUELA
COLUMBIA
BOGOTA
BRAZIL
CARIBBEAN ZONE 1492-
MEXICAN ZONE 1519-
SCALE
0 100 200 300 400 500 MILES